*Applications of
a Social Learning Theory
of Personality*

Applications of a Social Learning Theory of Personality

JULIAN B. ROTTER
University of Connecticut

JUNE E. CHANCE
University of Missouri

E. JERRY PHARES
Kansas State University

HOLT, RINEHART AND WINSTON, INC.
New York   Chicago   San Francisco   Atlanta
Dallas   Montreal   Toronto   London   Sydney

Copyright © 1972 by Holt, Rinehart and Winston, Inc.
Library of Congress Catalog Card Number: 75–181018
ISBN: 0–03–083183–0
Printed in the United States of America
2 3 4 5   038   9 8 7 6 5 4 3 2 1

Preface

Man has produced many remarkable machines, some so intricate that only relatively few people with considerable training can fully understand their workings. However complicated his products, man himself is far more complex than anything he has built. To understand him, to predict his behavior, or to change him in a predictable way is a challenging task of immense magnitude. Confusion and discord develop when scientists approach the problem of understanding and prediction, each working in his own very narrow area and each developing his own abstractions. Broad theories are necessary to provide a common set of variables and an opportunity to integrate the work of different scientists.

In recent years more and more psychologists interested in human behavior are turning to theories which deal at a more molar level with the complex behavior of people in complex environments. While theories based on lower animals responding to relatively simple stimuli or stimuli complexes may have been valuable as a starting point for understanding

human behavior, they are too limited to provide much in the way of prediction or understanding of an organism which is constantly abstracting
his experience, uses language to classify new experiences and reclassify
old experience, weighs probabilities, and is motivated primarily by goals
that depend more on ideas than they do on reducing organic drives.

While theories of simple behavior of lower animals may lack many
important constructs needed to explain human behavior, they do have the
advantage of being testable. Operations for the measurement of variables
can be agreed upon and objective research to advance knowledge is possible. The field of personality has not lacked theories; the need, rather,
has been for theories of complex social behavior that are also operational,
allow for testing of hypotheses, and lead to objective research which will
advance knowledge and which can be applied to the practical problems
of human life.

The social learning theory described and illustrated in this book is an
attempt at a significant start in this direction. The theory was developed
by Rotter and his students and colleagues, and a full statement of it with
supporting research was published in 1954 in a book titled *Social Learning
and Clinical Psychology*. Since that time the theory has been expanded
and revised, but equally important it has led to a great many objective investigations. Early research reported in the 1954 volume dealt primarily
with basic hypotheses, but later research dealt increasingly with applications of the theory to many different areas of human behavior. In addition
to an up-to-date statement of the theory, this book includes a number
of recent experimental and theoretical articles selected to illustrate applications of this social learning theory of personality. It provides integrative
summaries of this research in the six areas of complex human learning,
personality development, personality theory and measurement, social psychology and the social sciences, psychopathology, and psychotherapy.

As a text in personality it will provide the advanced student with an
organized theoretical framework in which he may find not only a method
for describing individual differences but also a process theory to account
for how individual differences are acquired and stabilized. It will also help
him see how thoughts, ideas, wishes, goals, and states of the organism
relate to observable behavior. The book illustrates how basic theorizing
and basic research can move gradually toward useful application and that
the study of personality does not result merely in a set of curious and
interesting but isolated and often contradictory findings, nor is it a game
played by the psychologist for his own benefit.

By the inclusion of many detailed studies the student will be able to
discover how theory and research truly can be integrated. He will also

discover the value and importance of theory in the conceptualization of research and the practical applications of theory that give meaning to the entire enterprise.

We are deeply indebted to the many people and organizations who helped to make this book a reality. We are particularly grateful to the authors of the various reprinted papers and to their publishers for permitting us to reproduce them here. Individual acknowledgments appear on the first page of each paper. E. Jerry Phares derived some support during the period of his labors from National Science Foundation grants GS–1034 and GS–2406. Joseph Doster read an early draft of Part 1 and made many helpful comments.

For their unlimited patience with us and for their cheerful endurance in performing the many secretarial and technical tasks which the preparation of this manuscript entailed, we wish to thank our secretaries: Mary B. Davis, Kitty Ebbe, Vivian Idle, Rita Johnson, Sherri Schwartz, Louise Sturm, Pat Underwood, and Marilyn Whitaker.

Each of us is also grateful to our many past and present graduate students who have in so many ways, directly and indirectly, contributed to this volume.

Storrs, Connecticut	J. B. R.
Columbia, Missouri	J. E. C.
Manhattan, Kansas	E. J. P.
	January 1972

Contents

*Applications of
a Social Learning Theory
of Personality*

1 | An Introduction to Social Learning Theory

This chapter attempts to provide a brief, general introduction to a social learning theory of personality (SLT) and to the chapters that follow. This theory was developed over the past 25 years by Rotter, in collaboration with his students and other colleagues. In 1954, Rotter published a book, *Social Learning and Clinical Psychology*, which presented an explicit and detailed statement of the theory. The theory was developed as an attempt to account for human behavior in relatively complex social situations. Thus, it is a molar theory of personality which utilizes both an expectancy construct and an empirical law of effect. Although one can probably never trace all the specific antecedents in the development of any theoretical point of view, particular acknowledgment should be made to the influences of Alfred Adler, J. R. Kantor, and Kurt Lewin. At various points, influences of the writings of Tolman and his colleagues and those of Thorndike and the Hullian school are also apparent. In some ways SLT may be regarded as one attempt to integrate two diverse but significant trends in American psychology—the "S–R" or "reinforcement" theories on the one hand and the "cognitive" or "field" theories on the other.

SLT provides a tentative set of principles to account for complex human social behavior. As is the case with any theory, this one is expected ultimately to yield to a better, more comprehensive theory than has been available in the past. The student of personality is sometimes advised to choose among alternative theories on the basis of his personal preferences, since there is not sufficient objective data available in this complex area to justify unqualified acceptance of one and rejection of the others. Yet, some criteria for evaluating theories do exist, although they are often difficult to apply. One criterion is the heuristic value of the theory—what it has led to in the way of new knowledge and methods—but it is often hard to assess heurism when articles describing contributions are scattered in many different journals and books. This book is an attempt to bring together some of this material which has appeared since 1954. Out of this process of providing samples of the application of the point of view to a wide assortment of human problems, it is hoped that the reader will be provoked to think of still other applications to still other problems. It is also hoped that providing a succinct and up-to-date statement of the entire theory in conjunction with representative research will enable the reader to achieve a clearer understanding of both the theory and the research to which it has led.

A Construct Point of View. Most introductory texts of personality begin by defining personality. Often, several definitions are discussed, followed by the author's favorite. Indeed, Allport (1937) gives a wide variety of definitions which have been offered over the years. Such diversity of definitions attests to the fact that little agreement seems possible in selecting a specific and universal definition of personality. The logical conclusion from this diversity would appear to be that each scientist sees personality in a different light. Based upon his own experience and purposes, each theorist describes personality in his somewhat idiosyncratic fashion. For example, the psychoanalyst centers his description of personality around terms such as **id, ego, superego,** and so on. The Adlerian employs **masculine protest, striving for superiority,** and so on. The Rogerian talks about a **phenomenal self.** Thus, there is no entity called **personality;** there are simply many different views or constructions about the nature of man, each leading to a different definition of personality.

What then is the nature of these constructs? Whether we use global terms like **personality** or more specific ones such as **expectancies** or **egos,** the crucial thing to remember is that these terms arc not entities but are simply abstractions of reality made for some purpose. Take the term **attitude** as an example. Suppose we observe a person on several occasions, and each time he says or does something which can be construed as derogatory toward labor unions. He makes a number of hostile comments about George Meany, he voices strong support of right-to-work laws, and he takes every opportunity to write letters to the local paper in opposition to labor strikes. On the basis of a number of such observations, and in comparison with observations of other people who behave in a dissimilar fashion, an abstraction can be made. At least one common element in all these behaviors is distaste for or opposition toward unions. Thus, we are able to label such an abstraction as an **antiunion attitude.** Having made the abstraction, we can now entertain certain predictions about this person's behavior in future specified situations. In short, the concept of **attitude** is helpful in understanding and prediction. It is important to remember, however, that an attitude is not a thing. An antiunion attitude does not become an entity simply because we employ the term. One cannot see an attitude or hold it in one's hand. It is nothing more than a convenient abstraction serving useful and functional purposes. At some time in the future, **antiunion attitude** might be replaced by another construct with better predictive potential.

Such a characterization is not peculiar to attitudes. The formulation can be applied to superego, libido, reinforcement, phenomenal self, and so on. Indeed, entire theories may be discussed in a similar way. Social learning theory, psychoanalysis, personology, role theory, and so on, are all alike, inasmuch as each is a way of looking at reality; none is reality itself. The question is not whether **ego** is real and exists in the brain or in some other place but whether such a term is a useful way of abstracting reality. In many ways, conceptual systems are like tinted glasses. Each provides a view of the world which is slightly different from the other. Change your glasses and the world changes. Everybody has to look through the glasses of some conceptual system in order to view reality. It is difficult but important to remember that one is not viewing reality directly but only through the intervening conceptual system.

Recognizing the **truth,** or capture of the essence of reality, is impossible, we are then called to attempt to develop conceptual terms that are both reliable and utilitarian. Reliability here means that there must be a consensus among observers regarding their descriptions of an event. Reliability is essential if observers are to be able to communicate. If a given theory is composed of constructs which do not permit reliability in communication, then that theory is of very limited value. It may appear to be of great value so far as one person's understanding is concerned, yet if the individual cannot communicate his understanding, science does not progress. Likewise, there must be utility. By utility it is meant that descriptions of events in a given theoretical language lead to prediction of events.

While some people insist that their goal for a theory is understanding and not prediction, it is difficult to see how they can obtain objective or scientific understanding unless they are interested in prediction. Broadly interpreted, prediction is the only scientific method of determining the accuracy of understanding or the only ultimate way to test the truth value of a theory.

General Principles for a Social Learning Theory of Personality

The principles to be sketched in this section essentially state the "rules" by which the theory operates. They state a position on basic theoretical issues. These ground rules are the bases on which we proceed to study human behavior and to gain an understanding of the construct

personality. As noted above, it is important to understand that the constructs utilized by SLT are exactly that—constructs. If we ask, "What is intelligence really like?" there can be no answer. If, however, we ask questions regarding the best way of abstracting certain aspects of behavior so as to better predict success in college, for example, then the question permits an answer. As long as we ask questions regarding the "real" nature of man, there will be as many answers as there are people to ask the question.

The following paragraphs present the more important principles or postulates of SLT. These postulates and their corollaries are presented in greater detail elsewhere (Rotter, 1954).

The unit of investigation for the study of personality is the interaction of the individual and his meaningful environment.

This statement essentially provides the basis for a field theory approach to personality. Other approaches, as illustrated by Freud's (1938) instincts or mind entities, Kraepelin's (1913) disease entities, or Sheldon's (1942) constitutional types, seem to attempt to predict without systematic recourse to the environment or the situation. It is the position of SLT that most predictive instances require an adequate description of the situation before useful predictions can be made. To rely solely on internal determinants or states results in either highly general predictions or else inaccurate ones. The importance of a situational point of view is reflected throughout this book, and we shall have many occasions to illustrate it and comment upon it.

This approach to personality focuses on learned behavior. Since the theory deals with human social behavior, the learning emphasis should be apparent. We accept the notion that the major portion of human social behavior is learned or modifiable behavior. This view does not rule out the possibility that there may be other ways of describing human behavior. Likewise, there may be meaningful segments of human behavior that cannot be described from a learning point of view; particularly, the antecedents of early learned behavior may require other kinds of descriptions. However, it is our position that the most useful approach to take currently in dealing with human social behavior is a learning one.

As a corollary of the previous postulate, SLT utilizes an historical approach to the study of personality. That is, in order to adequately understand, explain, or in some instances, even describe personality, it is necessary to investigate antecedent events in the life of the individual. Obviously, the past does not cause the present. The past no longer exists except in its current residual effects. Nonetheless, it is our thesis that some recourse to the past is a technological necessity. Such recourse is necessary because our descriptive and/or diagnostic technology is not powerful enough currently to depend solely upon an ahistorical approach. Perhaps eventually we shall be able to take an individual, describe him as he is today, and understand him well enough to make valid predictions. Such, however, is not yet the case. Until our techniques improve, we must rely on the historical rather than the ahistorical approach to understand most complex behaviors. It should be recognized, however, that the degree of reconstruction of the past that is necessary must always be gauged in terms of one's predictive purposes. For example, one of the more cogent criticisms of traditional psychoanalysis as a technique of behavioral change is that it examines the past minutely rather than utilizing a sampling of past events to construct the present personality.

Personality constructs are not dependent for explanation upon constructs in any other field (including physiology, biology, or neurology). Scientific constructs for one mode of description should be consistent with constructs in any other field of science, but no hierarchy of dependency exists among them.

Behavior as described by personality constructs takes place in space and time. Although all such events may be described by psychological constructs, it is presumed that they may also be described by physical constructs, as they are in such fields as physics, chemistry, and neurology. Any conception that regards the events themselves, rather than the descriptions of the events, as different is rejected as dualistic.

In effect, the two preceding postulates reject notions of both reductionism and dualism. It is certainly true that descriptions of events are often correlated. For example, we may describe a mongoloid child in terms of chromosome anomalies, epicanthic folds, and so on. These are primarily physical descriptions. At the same time, we may discuss the child in terms of IQ points, frustration tolerance, affectional needs, and so on. These are essentially psychological constructs. A correlation between descriptive levels often exists. It does not follow, however, that it is appropriate to reduce psychological descriptions to a physical level of abstraction. As Cantor and Cromwell (1957) and Jessor (1958) point out, there are very basic difficulties with a reductionistic point of view. First, the implication often exists that by moving from molar levels to more molecular ones (from sociology to psychology or from psychology to biochemistry, for example) we get closer to truth or reality. As was noted earlier, however, no description of behavior is true. At best, one description is more useful **for a particular purpose** than for another. No theory or description is anything more than a construction of reality imposed by the scientist for predictive purposes. Second, it is often claimed that reduction to smaller units located within the organism necessarily improves prediction. Such a contention is not borne out. Each theory or description has a range of convenience. Although one might consult a neurologist concerning an abnormal reflex, one typically would not consult him to predict the outcome of a presidential election. The level of description employed is a function of the questions that need to be answered.

Thus, the question is not whether there are biochemical or neurological explanations for much of the behavior that we ordinarily describe from a psychological point of view. The antecedent conditions of all human behavior are logically capable of construction from many points of view—psychological, physiological, or what have you. Again, the real question is that of utility.

The second of the two immediately preceding postulates deals with **dualism.** That is, any conception that regards the physiological events as causing the psychological events is regarded as dualistic. Such terms as **physiological, psychological, biochemical,** and so on, refer to descriptive levels, not to reality. Therefore, to say that something biochemical causes something psychological is to say that one description causes another. Many people tend uncritically to agree with such statements. However, when these statements are translated into a concrete example, such agreement often evaporates. For example, suppose we observe a patient with bleeding ulcers. Such an event is certainly amenable to a physiological description (there is nothing like blood to start one thinking in physiological terms). If we consult a physician and ask him to explain such an event, he may, after lengthy investigation (usually a process of elimination), decide that our patient's ulcers are **caused** by psychological problems. Indeed, he may be more specific and assert that unfulfilled dependency needs are the root of the problem. Somehow, such an explanation has the ring of truth. But what the physician is saying is that one event described in physiological terms is caused by another event described in psychological terms. How can one description cause another? What has occurred, of course, is that the physician is unable to trace the physiological causal sequence back far enough. He does, however, notice the correlated unfulfilled dependency needs. These, unfortunately, cannot be described in physiological terms and so a dualistic explanation easily presents itself. In fact, the whole of psychosomatics is perhaps one of the best available illustrations of the dualistic approach. This is not meant to imply that many patients, described in a dualistic fashion, are not better off practically than they would be if not so described. However, it is our view that dualism leads to fuzzy theoretical thinking and, in the long run, leads to less progress than would be the case otherwise.

Not all behavior of an organism may be usefully described with personality constructs. Behavior that may usefully be described by personality constructs appears in organisms of a particular level or stage of complexity and a particular level or stage of development.

This postulate simply recognizes the obvious fact that each construction system has a particular range of convenience. Not all events can be usefully described in personality terms. Just as some events show little amenability toward description in chemical terms, so too are some events recalcitrant in terms of psychological conceptualization. Indeed, at this time, it is uncertain at what species level or at what point in the development of the human individual psychological constructs begin usefully to apply. These are undoubtedly empirical questions. Physiological or other constructs may be useful to describe some of the conditions present when personality characteristics are first acquired.

Likewise, physiological or other constructs may be used by psychologists for any practical purpose. This is especially true when stable correlations between physiological descriptions and psychological descriptions have been found and when, practically, it is difficult to make both kinds of observations. However, as Kantor (1947) pointed out, predicting from physiological constructs to psychological ones is of limited value. Indeed, physiological descriptions used by themselves are more often valuable in indicating what the individual **cannot** do; but rarely are they useful in predicting what he **will** do.

An individual may interact with himself in the sense of using learned meanings (or symbols) that describe in physiological terms or terms characteristic of other modes of description. The person may learn to describe himself as hungry or sexually aroused, for example. Such reactions may usefully be described in psychological terms. These reactions, even though using physiological language, may correlate very poorly with actual organic states as described by the physiologist. This disparity is illustrated in recent work on emotions (Schachter and Singer, 1962), where two individuals, reacting to exactly the same chemical stimulation, nonetheless reported widely varying descriptions of their emotional states depending upon the environmental cues present.

A person's experiences (or his interactions with his meaningful environment) influence each other. Otherwise stated, personality has unity.

Typically, the concept of **unity** has had at least two meanings. In the first, **unity** is defined essentially in terms of a core personality. That is, each individual is thought of as possessing a core unity which largely determines his behavior. Just as all roads lead to Rome, so too does all behavior lead from this central core. This is a reductionistic view of motivation wherein all behavior is explained in the light of, for example, one's "striving for masculinity," or his "oral fixation."

A second meaning of the term **unity** is the one intended here. That is, unity is defined in terms of stability and interdependence. As the individual becomes more experienced, personality becomes increasingly more stable. He tends to select new experiences and interpretations of reality on the basis of previous experiences and conceptualizations. This selectivity leads to increasing generality and stability of behavior. Similar views are accepted to varying degrees by theories ranging from psychoanalysis to behaviorism. The danger in such a view is that the notion of stability and generality can be given such total emphasis in a theory that possible impact of new experiences, even after development of behavior is well along, and the role of situational factors in determining behavior are completely ignored.

SLT also attempts to discard the term **cause** in favor of a view which holds that adequate description in terms of relevant past and present conditions is a more useful approach to explanation. Too often **cause** implies singularity. There is the implication of a final or basic cause that proves to be highly elusive. For example, if one asks the question, "Why did you appear for your lecture today?" the answer becomes very difficult. There are many different causes, each quite logical. Thus, I may have appeared because I was scheduled to lecture. A more basic reason, it might be argued, is my sense of responsibility or my love of teaching. A still more basic reason might lie in the fact that my parents brought me up to respond in a responsible way. Still more basic is the fact that my parents created me. One could go on and on until some conceptualization of God or perhaps swirling gases is reached. The point is obvious. When we search for "basic" causes, we very quickly become enmeshed in an infinite regress.

What actually is wanted is a specification of antecedent conditions adequate for prediction. How far back to go in terms of these antecedent conditions is a function of the degree of predictive accuracy desired and the use to be made of the information. The **single-cause** approach to explanation should give way to one that recognizes that there can be many different explanations for a single piece of behavior. We look for the variables that are relevant at any cross section of time for our predictive purposes.

Behavior as described by personality constructs has a directional aspect. It may be said to be goal-directed. The directional aspect of behavior is inferred from the effect of reinforcing conditions.

For most psychologists, the preceding principle is basically a familiar one. In essence, it states that human behavior is motivated. Whether one accepts a Freudian position (psychic determinism) or a Rogerian position (enhancement of the phenomenal self), some motivational doctrine seems at least implicit. In some theories (Kelly, 1955), a motivational position is denied. In others (Cattell, 1957), it is somewhat muted. Nonetheless, a motivational principle does appear to be widely regarded as useful in understanding the organization of human behavior.

It is the directional nature of behavior, accounting for selective response to cues and for choice behavior, which is the motivational focus of SLT. The individual seeks to maximize his positive reinforcements in any situation. **Directionality** does not imply teleology, nor does **maximization of rewards** imply that the individual is incapable of planning or thinking in such a way that he makes choices of lesser rewards in order to obtain greater rewards later.

An aspect of the preceding principle which should be emphasized is that it is based on an **empirical law of effect.** Historically, a great deal of theoretical difficulty has been encountered when reinforcement has been defined in drive-reduction terms. It is relatively easy to define a reinforcement as anything that reduces a need when one is dealing with relatively simple organisms or behaviors. However, when one is dealing with human social behavior the problem becomes complicated. For example, how is one to show that a person who is very high in need achievement has experienced drive or need reduction through receiving an A in a college course? In short, the reinforcement of an enduring psychological need does not appear to reduce the individual's need, even temporarily. Therefore, in order to operationalize complex interpersonal behavior, SLT utilizes an empirical law of effect. That is, any stimulus complex has reinforcing properties to the extent that it influences movement toward or away from a goal.

Many people object to an empirical law of effect because it appears circular. That is, there is no definition of a reinforcer independent of behavior. One cannot know whether something is reinforcing until the behavior has occurred. Practically, this is true if one is dealing with an individual from a strange culture. To a degree it may also be true in other, more familiar circumstances inasmuch as most of us are, in some instances, motivated by somewhat idiosyncratic goals. In some psychopathological cases, such idiosyncrasies pose particular problems. Individuals may, on occasion, show behavior that seems very resistant to explanation largely because the goals involved are highly removed from those ordinary men expect. (Indeed, perhaps the sensitivity of many clinicians can be partly ascribed to the fact that they are very astute in ferreting out these extraordinary goals.) Were it true that reinforcements or potential reinforcements could **only** be identified after they had occurred, then the concept would truly be circular. However, it is practically possible to identify specific events which have a known effect either for groups or individuals. In such instances, **predictions,** not just **postdictions,** can be successful. Pragmatically, so long as we can describe and objectively identify potential reinforcers in the majority of situations, there is no serious problem of circularity. Meehl (1950) has discussed this issue in great detail; the current emphasis on operant approaches also testifies to the efficacy of this view.

Drive reduction as an alternative view of reinforcement ceases to be useful in the study of complex social behavior. Needs, such as striving for recognition, love, social acceptance, and dominance, are not cyclical, so that hours of deprivation cannot be used as the operational measure for drive state. Nor can it be demonstrated that following reinforcement the social need is reduced or some presumed "primary" drive is reduced.

This SLT view of reinforcement is also consistent with modern studies of direct brain stimulation (Grossman, 1967; Olds & Olds, 1965), which indicate different brain centers for positive and negative reinforcement and also different patterns of response to such stimulation. In other words, it seems well established, neurophysiologically, that positive and negative reinforcements are two different processes, depending, at least originally, on built-in characteristics of the organism. Further, they do not require the innervation of noncentral nerve centers involved in drive reduction.

In discussing motivation, it is appropriate at this point to indicate that when we focus on the environmental conditions that determine the direction of behavior, we speak of **goals** or reinforcements. On the other hand, when we focus upon the person determining the direction, then we speak of **needs**. Both **needs** and **goals** are inferred from the same referents— the interaction of the person with his meaningful environment. The distinction between **goals** and **needs** is a semantic convenience.

Several additional points should be made concerning the nature of needs. First, the needs of a person as described by personality constructs are learned or acquired. Early goals or needs, and perhaps some later ones, may be regarded as arising from association of new experiences with reinforcement of reflex or unlearned behavior. Most later goals or needs are acquired as a means of satisfying earlier, learned goals. Learned behavior is goal-directed, and new goals derive their importance for the individual from their associations with earlier goals.

Second, SLT hypothesizes that early, acquired goals in humans appear as the result of satisfactions and frustrations that are, for the most part, controlled by other people. Initially, these people are the family or family surrogates. Recognition of the importance of others in the determination of goal acquisition leads to the conception of a **social** learning theory of personality. Initial psychological needs are inborn and are primarily satisfied by parents or parent surrogates. Mediation of our needs by others undoubtedly underlies the importance we humans place on such things as love and affection, recognition, status, and dependency.

Third, in order for any behavior to occur regularly in a given situation(s), it must have become available to the person using it by leading to some reinforcement(s) during previous learning experiences. Availability of behavior may have been based on direct previous reinforcement or it may come about through observation and imitation (Bandura & Walters, 1963).

Fourth, a person's behaviors, needs, and goals are not independent but exist within functionally related systems. The nature of these relations also is determined by previous experience. Although this point will be discussed in greater detail subsequently, it is important to point out here that many behaviors can lead to the same goal and that many subgoals derive their reinforcing properties because they lead, in turn, to the same more comprehensive goal. Thus, a group of behaviors all culminating in the same effect will develop a greater degree of intergroup similarity than will a group of randomly selected behaviors. Similarly, the values of a group of reinforcers that have been associated with the same past satisfaction will have greater intergroup similarity than a random group of reinforcers. These points argue that prediction need not involve just specific behavior-reinforcement sequences but may involve groups of functionally related behaviors or reinforcements as well.

The occurrence of a behavior of a person is determined not only by the nature or importance of goals or reinforcements but also by the person's anticipation or expectancy that these goals will occur. Such expectations are determined by previous experience and can be quantified.

This principle attempts to handle the question of how the individual, in a given situation, behaves in terms of potential reinforcers. The assumption is that a concept dealing with anticipation of reinforcement is important in accounting for behavior directed at specific goals. In short, one needs a concept other than simple value of reinforcement to account for human behavior.

Inclusion of an **expectancy** construct seems to be a growing trend in psychological theory. Theorists such as Brunswik (1951) and Postman (1951) have been influenced by an expectancy point of view. The influence of Tolman's (1934) work appears evident in these as well as more recent theoretical attempts (Atkinson, 1964). The seminal views of Lewin (1951) in this area are also apparent. Mowrer shifted from a habit to an **expectancy** formulation in 1960, and recently Pribram (1967) has described an expectancy theory of the orienting response which is central to his theory of emotions. The usefulness of an expectancy construct is particularly evident in prediction of human behavior, and, even when dealing with lower animals, there is increasing reliance on "anticipatory responses" in understanding complex behavior sequences.

In the preceding pages, some of the basic assumptions or ground rules of a social learning theory of personality have been outlined briefly. Succeeding pages will present a more detailed account of how the concepts of the theory are defined, measured, and utilized in the predictive process.

BASIC CONCEPTS

In SLT, four basic concepts are utilized in the prediction of behavior. These concepts are **behavior potential, expectancy, reinforcement value,** and the **psychological situation.** In addition, somewhat broader concepts are utilized for problems involving more general behavioral predictions, that is, those dealing with behavior over a period of time and those including many specific situations. These broader conceptualizations will be discussed later. This section is primarily concerned with definition and measurement of basic concepts relevant to more specific situations or to testing experimental hypotheses in laboratory settings.

Behavior Potential

Behavior potential may be defined as the potentiality of any behavior's occurring in any given situation or situations as calculated in relation to any single reinforcement or set of reinforcements.

Behavior potential is a relative concept. That is, one calculates the potentiality of any behavior's occurring in relation to the other alternatives open to the individual. Thus, it is possible to say only that in a specific situation the potentiality for occurrence of behavior x is greater than that for behavior z.

The SLT concept of behavior is quite broad. Indeed, behavior may be that which is directly observed but also that which is indirect or implicit. This notion includes a broad spectrum of possibilities—swearing, running, crying, fighting, smiling, choosing, and so on, are all included. These are all observable behaviors, but implicit behaviors that can only be measured indirectly, such as rationalizing, repressing, considering alternatives, planning, and reclassifying, would also be included. The objective study of cognitive activity is a difficult but important aspect of social learning theory. Principles governing the occurrence of such cognitive activities are not considered different from those that might apply to any observable behavior.

Expectancy

Expectancy may be defined as the probability held by the individual that a particular reinforcement will occur as a function of a specific behavior on his part in a specific situation or situations. Expectancy is systematically independent of the value or importance of the reinforcement.

While simple cognitions also may be regarded as having some of the characteristics of expectancies, throughout this book the term **expectancy** will be used to refer to the expectancy for behavior-reinforcement sequences (Rotter, 1960; **5–1***). Historically, expectancy has often been described as either an objective or subjective concept. Lewin (1951), for example, stressed the subjective nature of expectancy. Brunswik (1951), however, emphasized objective probability—a probability determined primarily by objectively describable past events.

In SLT the concept of expectancy is defined as a subjective probability, but this definition does not imply inaccessibility to objective measurement. People's probability statements, and other behaviors relating to the probability of occurrence of an event, often differ systematically from their actuarial experience with the event in the past. A variety of other factors operate in specific instances to influence one's probability

---

* Boldface numbers refer to papers included in this volume; in this case, the first paper in Part 5.

estimates. Such factors may include the nature or the categorization of a situation, patterning and sequential considerations, uniqueness of events, generalization, and the perception of causality.

Reinforcement Value

The reinforcement value of any one of a group of potential external reinforcements may be ideally defined as the degree of the person's preference for that reinforcement to occur if the possibilities of occurrence of all alternatives were equal.

Again, **reinforcement value** is a relative term. Measurement of reinforcement value occurs in a choice situation. That is, reinforcement value refers to a preference, and preference indicates that one favors something over something else. Such preferences show consistency and reliability within our culture and also, generally speaking, can be shown to be systematically independent of expectancy. These and other considerations will be discussed in greater detail later.

The Psychological Situation

Behavior does not occur in a vacuum. A person is continuously reacting to aspects of his external and internal environment. Since he reacts selectively to many kinds of stimulation, internal and external simultaneously, in a way consistent with his unique experience and because the different aspects of his environment mutually affect each other, we choose to speak of the psychological situation rather than the stimulus. Methods of determining generality or determining the dimensions of similarity among situations have been described by Rotter (1955).

Several writers have pointed out the difficulty of identifying situations independently of behavior. That is, how can one describe a situation, as one might a physical stimulus, independently of the particular S's response? However, the problem is not really so different from that of describing stimuli along dimensions of color, although it is perhaps vastly more complicated in social situations. In the case of color stimuli, ultimately the criterion is a response made by an observer, sometimes aided by an intermediate instrument. The response is one that is at the level of sensory discrimination and thus leads to high observer agreement. In the case of social situations, the level of discrimination is common sense based on an understanding of a culture rather than a reading from an instrument. As such, reliability of discrimination may be limited but still be sufficiently high to make practical predictions possible. Specific situations can be identified as school situations, employment situations, girl friend situations, and so on. For the purpose of generality, various kinds of psychological constructs can be devised to arrive at broader classes of situations having similar meaning to S. The utility of such classes would have to be empirically determined, depending on the S's response. The objective referents for these situations, which provide the basis for prediction, however, can be independent of the specific S. That is, they can be reliably identified by cultural, common sense terms.

Basic Formulas

The preceding variables and their relations may be conveniently stated in the formulas that follow. It should be remembered, however, that these formulas do not at this time imply any precise mathematical relations. Indeed, although the relation between expectancy and reinforcement value is probably a multiplicative one, there is little systematic data at this point that would allow one to evolve any precise mathematical statement.

The basic formula is stated thus:

$$BP_{x,s_1,R_a} = f(E_{x,R_a s_1} \& RV_{a,s_1}) \tag{1}$$

Formula (1) says, The potential for behavior x to occur, in situation 1 in relation to reinforcement a, is a function of the expectancy of the occurrence of reinforcement a, following behavior x in situation 1, and the value of reinforcement a in situation 1.

Formula (1) is obviously limited, inasmuch as it deals only with the potential for a given behavior to occur in relation to a single reinforcement. As noted earlier, description at the level of personality constructs usually demands a broader, more generalized concept of behavior, reflected in the following formula:

$$BP_{(x-n),s_{(1-n)},R_{(a-n)}} = f[E_{(x-n),s_{(1-n)},R_{(a-n)}} \& RV_{(a-n),s_{(1-n)}}] \tag{2}$$

Formula (2) says, The potentiality of functionally related behaviors x to n to occur, in specified situations 1 to n in relation to potential reinforcements a to n, is a function of the expectancies of these behaviors leading to these reinforcements in these situations and the values of these reinforcements in these situations. To enhance communication by reducing verbal complexity, three terms—**need potential, freedom of movement,** and **need value**—have been introduced. A formula incorporating these latter terms is:

$$NP = f(FM \& NV) \tag{3}$$

Thus, need potential is a function of freedom of movement and need value. In broader predictive or clinical situations, formula (3) would more likely be used, while formula (2) would be more appropriate in testing more specific, experimental hypotheses.

The fourth variable, **situation,** is left implicit in formula (3). SLT is highly committed to the importance of the psychological situation. It is emphasized that behavior varies as the situation does. But obviously, there is also transituational generality in behavior. If there were not, there would be no point in discussing **personality** as a construct or as a field of study. However, along with generality there is also situational specificity. While it may be true that person A is generally more aggressive than person B, nonetheless, there can arise many occasions on which person B behaves more aggressively than does person A. Predictions based solely on internal characteristics of the individual are not sufficient to account for the complexities of human behavior.

BEHAVIOR POTENTIAL

We have already indicated that our definition of **behavior** is a broad-gauged one. Included would be all human responses having an effect on the environment. Any response to a meaningful stimulus that can be **measured** either directly or indirectly would qualify. Behavior usually labeled as cognitive or implicit would also be included. Such behavior is not observed directly—it must be inferred from the presence of other behaviors. For example, the behavior of looking for alternative solutions studied by Schroder and Rotter (1952) is a case in point. Looking for alternative solutions to problems was inferred to be present when the test for its occurrence—increase in time taken by a subject for solution of a previously solved task and decrease in time for the solution of a new task requiring an alternative solution—took place. Likewise, rehearsal of thoughts about failure and its consequences may be measured by its effects on performance of a difficult task where concentrated attention is needed for problem solution.

Where behaviors are directly observable, measurement of behavior potential would involve determining either presence or absence or frequency of occurrence of the behavior. In any given situation, it is presumed that the behavior with the highest potential is the one that actually occurs. Measurement of behavior potential can be accomplished directly in terms of the frequency with which the behavior in question occurs over a series of situations.

The important problem in describing behavior, presumably implicit in nature, is to be able to demonstrate empirically that the observable behavior used as a referent for the implicit behavior varies in the manner expected from the theory. While logically consistent to stay within the realm of psychological descriptions whenever possible, sometimes for practical purposes it may be more expedient to describe a behavior from a physiological (or some other) frame of reference. The crucial thing here is the establishment of communicability and reliability of constructs, particularly when our purpose is to account for or to predict the acquired response of a person to his meaningful environment.

A comment on the question of the determination of units of behavior is also appropriate at this point. If we say that a person is behaving aggressively, we may mean simply that he is swearing at someone. On the other hand, we may also mean that he is scowling, making menacing gestures, growing livid, walking toward the object of his wrath, and uttering threatening words. In other words, we may discuss behavior in the relatively molecular terms of single acts or of entire sequences and patterns of acts. No simple or single meaningful way of establishing units for behavior exists. What constitutes a unit of behavior must, for the present, be determined by the purposes and predictive goals of the observer.

If **behavior potential** is a function of both **expectancy** and **reinforcement value**, it follows that in predicting **behavior potential** either **expectancy** or **reinforcement value** must be held constant while varying the other one. For example, if expectancies for any of five different behaviors are the same, we could predict which behavior will occur (have the highest behavior potential) by determining the different values of the reinforcements anticipated for each of the five behaviors. Reinforcement value would yield, in this instance, a direct prediction of behavior potential. If, in contrast, the reinforcements anticipated for all five behaviors were of equal value, we could predict behavior potential by measuring expectancies. While such procedures are quite satisfactory in highly controlled laboratory situations, in real-life situations their use becomes clumsy and difficult.

In addition, lack of a systematically worked-out mathematical formula denoting the relation between expectancy and reinforcement value presents further difficulties. Some relations between expectancy and reinforcement value will be discussed in a later section; however, the best evidence available now suggests a multiplicative relationship. Meanwhile, it is readily demonstrable that behavior potential is higher when expectancy and reinforcement value are both high, or when one is high and the other is moderate, than when both are low. Lack of a precise mathematical formula does not preclude stating and testing of hypotheses regarding behavior. Such hypotheses must, however, be stated in "more or less" terms for groups of Ss undergoing different experimental treatment or having different prior histories.

Although a multivariate theory such as this one does present problems, it possesses distinct advantages over theories relying upon a single variable to predict behavior. Neither reinforcement value, nor expectancy, nor the psychological situation taken alone seems as powerful in predicting behavior as when the three are considered in combination.

With emphasis placed as it is on social behavior, it should be apparent that the behavior studied is constantly undergoing some kind of change—increments and decrements in behavior potential. Behavior potential is not a static concept. As the individual encounters new experiences, his expectancies and reinforcement values are changed. As a result, behavior potential is altered.

REINFORCEMENT AND REINFORCEMENT VALUE

Earlier it was stated that SLT utilizes an empirical law of effect. That is, any event can be defined as a reinforcement when it can be shown that the event changes the potentiality for occurrence of a given behavior. Such a definition of reinforcement is not circular inasmuch as once initial observations that an event reliably alters a behavior potential are made, future predictions can be made without difficulty. Such a definition makes the concept of reinforcement operational and permits relatively simple measurement.

SLT also distinguishes between **internal reinforcements** and **external reinforcements.** Ideally defined, an internal reinforcement is the person's experience, or perception, that an event has occurred which has some value for him. This value may be either positive or negative. Positiveness or negativeness of value is determined by resultant effects upon the frequency of observable behavior. **External reinforcement** refers to occurrences of events or outcomes known to have predictable reinforcement value for a group or culture to which the person belongs. Of course, the relation between **internal** and **external** reinforcements is not always one to one. Some events may have reinforcing qualities for the individual and not for his group. The reverse situation is also found. Lack of perfect correlation between group and individual values suggests that we should be prepared to make predictions from group values where feasible, but also to check our guesses against data from the history of the individual.

Origin of Psychological Needs. Earlier it was stated that a person's behaviors are functionally related in terms of directionality of behavior. In short, functional relations among various behaviors and goals may be described in terms of **need** or the common directionality of response. More specifically, a **need** comprises **need potential,** which refers to the potentiality of occurrence of a group of functionally related behaviors in specified situations directed toward a group of functionally related reinforcements. Strength of **need potential** depends upon the variables of **freedom of movement** (a group of functionally related expectancies) and **need value** (preference for a group of functionally related reinforcements).

SLT hypothesizes that psychological needs arise initially out of physiological or other unlearned reinforcement. That is, early psychological needs are learned from the consequences of such events as hunger, thirst, contact comfort needs, changes in sensory stimulation, or other "built-in" reinforcements. Indeed, originally the strength of such psychological needs is a function of the strength of the unlearned reinforcements with which they are associated. However, as the child develops and attains language and cognitions, the strength of his needs can be predicted better from the relations of his needs to other psychological goals than from their relations to primary drives. The presence of appropriate cues in the environment rapidly becomes more important than internal states for predicting the directionality of acquired behavior, once initial learning has taken place. That is, most human social behavior appears much more a function of environmental cues than of cyclical internal states. Such may not be the case at subhuman levels or even with humans in early infancy. In the case of psychological needs, we are dealing with potential behaviors requiring only the appropriate cues to elicit them. Parenthetically, it may be possible to view the tasks of socialization and education largely as attempts to change potentials for behaviors, already present, by leading the individual to associate those behaviors with certain cues in the environment.

In short, SLT takes the position that a sufficient basis for behavioral prediction lies in the statement that behavior directed toward the attainment of a learned goal, or external reinforcement, may be predicted through knowledge of the organism's situation and knowledge of his past learning experience (expectancies and reinforcement values). Occasional physiological descriptions may be useful to account for the antecedents of very early learning and some instances of later learning under specialized conditions.

At this point, it is useful to introduce briefly a discussion of the determinants of the value of reinforcements generally. The notion is rejected that psychological goals depend for their value upon primary drive reduction, except historically. Instead, it is argued that psychological goals, needs, or reinforcements acquired during the individual's life depend upon other psychological reinforcements for their value. The value of any given reinforcement depends upon its association or pairing with other reinforcements. The value of a reinforcement is determined by the value of reinforcements with which it has been associated and by the expectancy that its occurrence leads to the subsequent occurrence of the associated or related reinforcements. A generalized formula from which the value of a reinforcement may be predicted is:

$$RV_{a,s_1} = f[E_{Ra \rightarrow R(b-n),s_1} \, \& \, RV_{(b-n),s_1}] \tag{4}$$

Formula (4) says, The value of reinforcement a in situation 1 is a function of expectancies that this reinforcement will lead to the other reinforcements b to n in situation 1 and of the values of these other reinforcements b to n in situation 1. Reinforcements may be expected to change value in different situations and under differing conditions to some extent. This formula provides a basis for determining these values given a variety of conditions. However, it also should be recognized that often reinforcement values have considerable stability across both situations and time.

Once the value of reinforcement a has been firmly established through its relation with reinforcement b, it is not necessarily true that subsequent failure of reinforcement b to occur with reinforcement a will lower the value of the latter. There are specific conditions under which lowering the value of *a* will be more likely. Extinction is more likely under conditions of massed trials, where the original learning was not partially reinforced or when the relation between the two goals has been verbalized by the person. To a great extent, however, a reinforcement will maintain its value until new associations or pairings with other reinforcements of different values (more positive or more negative) occur. Since most goals acquire their value under spaced rather than massed conditions of training, under partial rather than 100 percent reinforcement, and since the relations are frequently not verbalized, most reinforcements maintain their value except as they change on the basis of new pairings with other reinforcements.

Reinforcements may also become functionally related to other reinforcements, and be changed in value, on the basis of cognitive activities. Either by means of symbolic manipulations or by attending to the behavior of another person and its consequences for him, reinforcement values are altered. By cognitive means, man is not only able to learn extremely complex methods of solving immediate problems but also to recreate the past and to create through imagination events that have not actually occurred. Imaginative rehearsal of events can affect reinforcement value. For example, in a choice situation when the individual has to select only one of two possible alternative reinforcements, the one he does not choose does not occur. However, in the process of deciding and imaginatively rehearsing its occurrence, its reinforcement value may change through pairings with other events that also take place in thought or imagination. Usually such changes may be small and subtle, but they must certainly exist, and in some instances they may be very great indeed.

Similarly, when we attempt by an action to obtain a reinforcement and fail to do so, not only is our expectancy reduced for obtaining it later under similar circumstances but the reinforcement itself may become associated with the unpleasantness of failure and diminish in value. In contrast, in other circumstances because of imaginative rehearsal of additional reinforcements obtainable through later success, the value of the "lost" reinforcement could actually increase. The central point here is that both expectancies and reinforcement values may change as a result of thinking. Description and prediction of the many cognitive processes subsumed under the term **thinking** is a great challenge.

Thus far, discussion of the value of reinforcements has involved only single reinforcements. It is also possible to estimate the value of a given reinforcement by reference to its membership in a group of functionally related reinforcements. That is, knowing the value of a certain cluster of reinforcements, the value of others which are functionally related to the group can be predicted.

The basis for these functional relations among reinforcements is postulated to occur as the result of three processes: **primary stimulus generaliza-**

tion; an extended version of **mediated stimulus generalization;** and a special case of the latter, **generalization of expectancy changes.**

Primary stimulus generalization accounts for functional relations among goals or behaviors largely on a physical basis. For example, the responses to all four-legged animals, stuffed or moving, may be similar until differentiation occurs on the basis of learned differences. In the case of **mediated stimulus generalization,** behaviors leading to the same reinforcement acquire a functional equivalence. For example, if the child cries, pouts, frowns, or frets and the parent reacts to each behavior in a similar fashion, namely, gives the child his own way, then all four of these behaviors will develop a functional equivalence in the sense that a strong reinforcement (either positive or negative) of one of them will affect the potential occurrence of all of them.

In the special case of **generalization of expectancy changes,** the following situation obtains. Reinforcements are interrelated in such a way that occurrence of one of them affects the expectancy for the occurrence of the rest of them. For example, if the child is refused a candy bar, he is less likely to ask for another kind of sweet. Negative reinforcement of one request has affected (generalized to) the expectancy that a similar one will be honored in the same context. In contrast, his expectancy for getting a glass of milk might remain unaltered. Such a generalization gradient needs to be determined empirically, although it is likely that the gradient would follow a dimension of functional similarity of reinforcement. Of course, the expectancies linking reinforcement with reinforcement (see formula 4) also generalize, so that the values of specific reinforcements will also change as a result of such generalization.

Three studies illustrate quite clearly the generalization of expectancies. V. J. Crandall (1951) found that induced failure on a physical-skills task influenced TAT stories told after the failure. The greatest effect appeared in stories involving physical-skill activities; the next greatest, in stories involving academic accomplishment; and the least effect appeared in stories concerning relations with opposite sex peers. Jessor (1954) subsequently demonstrated that failure on an arithmetic task reduced stated expectancies regarding performances on a vocabulary task, a pursuit rotor, and a social-skills task, in that order. The generalization gradient obtained in both these studies corresponded to the gradient expected culturally on the basis of similarity of reinforcement. In neither study, however, was the element of stimulus similarity fully controlled. A later study by Chance (1959; 2–1) controlled for this factor and, again, supported the hypothesis that generalization of expectancies may be predicted along a dimension of functional or need relatedness, defined by a past history of similar reinforcements for two or more behaviors. A study in a similar vein (Dean, 1960) demonstrated that when the physical similarity of two tasks was held constant, the correlation between expectancy statements on the two tasks was significantly higher when the definitions of the tasks were similar than when the definitions were different.

The preceding analysis and research indicate the feasibility of approaching functional relations among reinforcements through concepts like psychological needs. On both logical and empirical grounds, it is possible to consider a person's behavior in terms of broad, generalized categories (he is **aggressive,** or **dependent,** and so on). Ideally, such categories should reflect functional relations which are established empirically and applied only in relation to specified cultures or subcultures.

It must be borne in mind, however, that the broader one makes functional classes, the lower the level of predictive utility one obtains. A class can represent a very narrow band of reinforcements and yield fairly high levels of prediction but also have very limited generality. Efficiency becomes a question. At the other extreme, one can deal with very broad classes, convenient to use, but limited predictively by their very breadth. An extreme example of the latter approach is represented by those essentially reductionistic systems which attempt to explain almost all significant behavior by use of a single, supreme need or class of reinforcements. Dean (1953) found that the more inclusive, or more general, the category utilized for predicting a specific behavior, the lower the prediction between any set of two or more independent referents within that category. It is as a result of the processes of generalization that classes of behaviors, expectancies, and reinforcements take on functional properties. That is, the strength of one member of the class can be predicted from sampling other members of the class. Functional classes then become the basis for delineation of content variables of personality. Some of these content variables will be discussed later in this chapter.

Measurement of Reinforcement Value. Reinforcement value was defined earlier as the degree of preference for any one of a group of reinforcements to occur, if the probabilities of all occurring were equal. Measurement of reinforcement, then, becomes a relative matter, and values of reinforcements can be determined only in relation to values of other reinforcements.

In general, two basic procedures have been used to measure reinforcement value. The first involves ranking. This procedure is illustrated in a study by Phares and Rotter (1956) in which 18 reinforcements (for example, "Be praised by the teacher for writing a good book report"; "Win a wrestling match with a friend"; and so on) were arranged in a randomly ordered list. This list was administered to groups of seventh- and eighth-grade boys. Ranking was preceded by the following instructions: "Imagine that you could do, become, or have all the things in the sentences. . . ." These instructions are designed to control expectancy during the measurement of reinforcement value. If such instructions are not used, a given S might well give a particular reinforcement a low rank, not because he dislikes it but because he has a very low expectancy that the reinforcement will actually occur.

A second technique for measuring reinforcement value is the behavioral choice method. Here, S actually chooses one reinforcement over another. Again, expectancy must be controlled. This technique is employed in a study by Lotsof (1956; 2–5). Other methods of measuring reinforcement value include rating procedures, hypothetical forced choices, and projective and semiprojective techniques.

Determinants of Reinforcement Value. Acquired reinforcements derive their value from associations with other reinforcements. It often happens that a currently valued reinforcement is no longer associated with the reinforcements from which its initial value was derived. This situation, however, does not imply that a reinforcement's current value is based on nothing but intrinsic considerations. The implication is that while a reinforcement may be functionally autonomous from its past, its **current value** is based upon relations or associations that have developed with **other current reinforcements.** That is, the original associations may have diminished or disappeared, but new associations have developed that enable the reinforcement to maintain or even to increase its value. Such relations need not be verbalized by S. He may have little insight into the fact that his attaining one reinforcement has value because he expects that it will lead to another reinforcement of value. Nonetheless, the relation can be inferred from his behaviors.

Several studies have tested the efficacy of this formulation of value determinants. Dunlap (1953) held expectancy constant while varying subsequent reinforcements following upon the attainment of a reinforcement of value. Ss were elementary school children and reinforcements were toys of various kinds. In essence, Dunlap found, as predicted, that Ss changed their preferences for toys according to whether play with the toys led to subsequent positive or negative reinforcement. In a complementary study, Hunt (1955) held constant value of the subsequent reinforcement but varied expectancy for its occurrence. His results indicated that changes in choice for certain toys varies as a function of expectancy that attainment of these toys will lead to subsequent reinforcement. Although Hunt's study supports the general formulation given above, an uncontrolled factor that might have influenced his results was the frequency with which later reinforcements had been associated with original reinforcements. Therefore, in a subsequent study, Schroder (1956) systematically studied this factor and found that frequency of subsequent reinforcement clearly could be ruled out as the determinant of reinforcement value, in favor of expectancy for future reinforcement.

Another study supporting the role of expectancies for future reinforcement in determination of reinforcement values is the study by Phares and Rotter (1956), cited earlier. They found that the ranked value of a reinforcement changes, depending upon the situation in which preference statements are obtained. That is, preference statements change as expectations that such statements will be reinforced change from one situation to another.

The role of delay of reinforcement in determination of reinforcement value is another important factor. It also can be accounted for in the formulation of value as a result of expected subsequent reinforcement. A study by Mahrer (1956; 2–6) and a series of systematic studies carried out by Mischel (1961b; 5–10; Mischel & Staub, 1965; 2–3) illustrate this point. Studies of the effects of delay have been performed over a variety of situations ranging from fairly restrictive laboratory conditions to cross-cultural settings. In sum, these studies suggest that delayed reinforcements are very often considered to be less valuable than immediate ones. Young children tend to prefer an immediate reinforcement over a delayed one, even though the latter may have greater value. Similarly, certain groups such as various psychopathic, criminal or juvenile delinquent, and neurotic types may show analogous preferences. Various disadvantaged subcultures, as well as more primitive groups, may behave similarly. All of these results indicate that time, in and of itself, is not the crucial variable. That is, the child, primitive adult, or delinquent may choose the immediate gratification, not because it is more valuable but rather because he has a relatively low expectancy that the promised larger reinforcement will actually occur at a later date. In effect, he has learned not to trust the future but to rely on the present. Naturally, there also may be specific conditions under which an immediate reinforcement will be more valuable than the same or greater reinforcement later. For example, if someone is offered a sandwich now and he is very hungry, he will very likely accept it in preference to a steak offered three days hence.

The implications of these statements regarding delay of reinforcement are of particular importance in the practice of clinical psychology. For example, many deviant behaviors may be construed as situations in which a patient chooses immediate gratification of lower reinforcement value (avoidance of an unpleasant situation) as compared to choosing a later, more valuable gratification which could occur were the patient to give up so-called symptoms.

The fact that a reinforcement derives its value from attached expectancies for future reinforcements places great importance on the power of language in human choice behavior. Expectancies for important future reinforcements frequently develop by means of verbal representation of them in thought or imagination. This formulation also suggests how important trust of others may be in determining our behavior. This is because so often our expectancies for future reinforcement depend upon the promises or statements of others.

A word should be said at this point about the relation between expectancy and reinforcement value. SLT postulates that these variables are **systematically** independent. That is, there is no necessary relation between expectancy and reinforcement value, although under specific conditions, they can be shown to be related empirically, because S has acquired a relation from his previous experiences. Under specific conditions, either expectancy or reinforcement value can serve as a cue for the other. For example, given a large potential reinforcement—for example, a new car in a dollar raffle—most people might have a lower expectancy of winning than if the reward were a bicycle. In another example, given a true 50-50 probability situation, a trend may appear in some tasks for a higher expectancy for positive than negative outcomes to be verbalized as a result of wishful thinking. It is not that relations between expectancy and reinforcement value do not occur, but rather that they depend on previous learning **in that situation,** and the relations can be negative, positive, or zero. Data pertinent to this question will be reviewed in Part 2.

EXPECTANCY

Expectancy has been defined as a subjective probability or contingency held by the individual that any specific reinforcement or group of reinforcements will occur in any given situation or situations. The subjective qualification is necessary because expectancies are determined not only by (1) probability calculated on the basis of one's past history of reinforcement (including special problems like recency, patterning of reinforcements, and the perceived nature of the causal relation between behavior and reinforcement) but also by (2) the generalization of expectancies from other related behavior-reinforcement sequences. In effect, what **subjectivity** means is that expectancies cannot be calculated on the basis of a relatively simple actuarial formula which takes into account only the S's objective history of reinforcement with a specific reinforcement. What must also be considered are his generalizations from related past experiences. His generalization of expectancies may, or may not, match those an observer might infer to be present. Nonetheless, they occur and therefore must be considered when calculating his expectancy.

Stated in more formal terms, we have:

$$E_{s1} = f(E'_{s1} \& GE) \tag{5}$$

Formula (5) says, Expectancy (E_{s1}) is a function of probability of occurrence based on past experience in situations perceived by S as the same (E'_{s1}) and his generalization of expectancies for the same or similar reinforcements to occur in other situations for the same or functionally related behaviors (GE).

In general, when the individual finds himself in some new or novel situation, generalized expectancies (GE) will weigh more heavily in the determination of his expectancy than will specific expectancy (E'). For example, a person's expectancy for winning a 100-yard dash on his first try will be largely determined by his past experience, generalized from other athletic situations. However, upon subsequent tries in the 100-yard dash, his expectancy of winning will be determined more and more by his specific experiences in those dash situations. Again, stated formally, we have: an expectancy (E_{s1}) as a function of the expectancy for a given reinforcement to occur resulting from previous experience in the same situation (E'_{s1}) and as a function of expectancies generalized from other situations (GE) divided by some function of the number of experiences in the specific situation (N_{s1}).

$$E_{s1} = f(E'_{s1} \& \frac{GE}{N_{s1}}) \tag{6}$$

The necessity for a generalization term is perhaps best demonstrated by the plethora of expectancy studies that utilize a level-of-aspiration paradigm. Such studies show clearly that marked and consistent individual differences occur among Ss in their expectancy statements. That is, even though 20 Ss may each experience identical reinforcement patterns during an experiment, they do not react by stating identical expectancies in response to identical reinforcement.

Recall from the previous discussion that behavior potential and reinforcement value are measured relative to other behavior potentials and reinforcement values, respectively. Expectancies, in contrast, may be measured on an absolute scale and obtained values are comparable across different situations. When reinforcement values are measured in controlled choice situations by a ranking procedure, the total value of all ranks for a given S will be the same as that for any other S. However, in the case of expectancies, one S may have low expectancies for all possible reinforcements while another may have high expectancies.

Measurement of Expectancy. There are two basic methods of measuring expectancy. The first is what might be called the behavioral choice method and is analogous to the method described earlier for measuring reinforcement value. This is a simple but relatively crude technique wherein one observes the behavioral choice of the S when the reinforcement value of every alternative is controlled. Under such circumstances, choice of alternative *a* over alternative *b* must, by definition, indicate a higher expectancy of achieving reinforcement by means of alternative *a*.

The second general set of methods of measurement involves verbal techniques, and a variety of these approaches have been utilized. For example, many studies have utilized a technique that asks the S to state a probability of a particular outcome on a scale (sometimes zero to 10; at other times, zero to 100). This procedure is illustrated in studies by Phares (1964a), Schwarz (1966; 2-2), and many others.

Another verbal technique also widely used involves the utilization of some task on which the S can receive any in a series of graded scores. The S is then asked what score he most expects to receive. The assumption is that the reported score is the one he feels most confident of receiving. This technique has been used, for example, by Chance (1959; 2–1), Jessor (1954), and Rychlak (1958).

A third verbal technique involves betting. Betting techniques evolved because, at times, Ss stated inordinately high or low expectancies out of a need, seemingly, either to impress the experimenter with their confidence or else to protect themselves against the possibility of failure. It was felt that betting would place a premium on accuracy and thus prove to be a superior technique. Use of this method is illustrated in a study by Ford (1963). Note, however, that using a betting method introduces new problems into the measurement of expectancy. For example, one needs to worry about such factors as the amount of money accumulated influencing the size of S's bet. Also, it has been the experience of several investigators that using very small amounts of money (probably regarded as trivial by most Ss) in betting studies is not much of an improvement over methods simply requiring a verbal statement regarding probability. As is often the case, when one utilizes a different method of measurement, he exchanges one set of problems for another.

In this connection, the issue can be raised whether a verbal statement or bet really signifies what it purports to. How do we know that when S states an expectancy of 7 (on an 11-point scale) he really has an expectancy of 7? Maybe it is really 5 or 10! The answer is that we **do not know.** Nor, by the same token, do we know that when a patient says he loved his mother, he really did love her. How do we know that when the needle deflects on a GSR apparatus that this event really signifies anxiety? Again, we do not know. In short, no one has a royal road to the measurement of reality. Operational techniques consistent with the theory are devised and tried out. When they demonstrate themselves empirically in the sense that they lead to acceptable levels of prediction, they are "good" measures. When uncontrolled variables (such as underestimating expectancies in order to protect against failure or other factors) consistently seem to cause problems, other measurement techniques are devised.

An early attempt to assess and compare several different operations for the measurement of expectancy among college students was carried out by Rotter, Fitzgerald, and Joyce (1954). In this study, four groups of Ss were given an identical prearranged sequence of scores on a symbol-substitution task. Following this training, the four groups were each provided with different instructions.

Group I Ss were asked to state the score they expected to make on the next trial, and emphasis was placed on accuracy. Following their statement, they were asked to rate, on a 10-point scale, their probability of making that score.

Group II Ss were instructed to rate, on a 10-point scale, their **absolute** probability of making each of six different possible scores on the next trial (Figure 1 shows these possible scores on the abscissa).

Group III Ss were asked to rate, on a 10-point scale, their probability of making a score of **at least** 20 or more on the next trial and, in the same manner, for the remaining five scores shown in Figure 1.

Group IV used the betting technique. These Ss were given 60 cents in six piles of 10 pennies each and were asked to bet up to 10 cents on making a score of **at least** 20 or more on the next trial and, in the same manner, for the remaining scores.

The basic results of this study are presented in Figure 1. Note that the betting method always yielded higher mean scores. At least among Ss in this study and for the reinforcement utilized, the betting method leads to higher expectancy scores; in contrast, the verbal technique yields scores

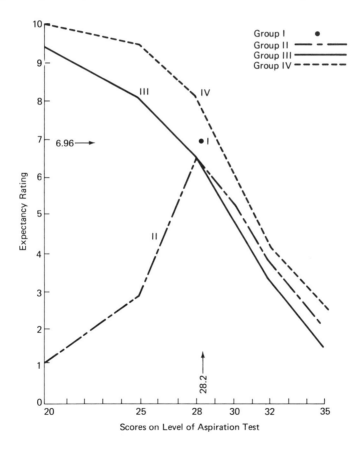

FIGURE 1. Mean expectancy scores for four groups with different instructions for reporting expectations. From Rotter, Fitzgerald, and Joyce, 1954, by permission.

closer to actuarial expectancy. However, the curves for groups III and IV correlated .99. Generally, all four methods tend to measure the same thing. The mean of statements of a single expected score coincides with the same score given the highest probability of occurring on an absolute basis. However, Ss asked to estimate their scores on the basis of absolute probability apparently overestimated the probability for any specific score, since the total for all scores exceeded 100 percent. When Ss were asked to state probabilities of obtaining at least a given score, the probabilities stated tended to be similar to those stated by other Ss asked to give the most expected score where comparison was possible.

Changes in Expectancy. Since behavior is a function of both expectancy and reinforcement value, changes in behavior can be brought about by changes in either of these variables. However, in the case of human adults particularly, it is often difficult to change reinforcement values. Although theoretically one can, by pairing one reinforcement with another of either greater or lesser value, change that reinforcement's value, it is often actually difficult to do so in practice, especially when dealing with major, broadly ramified need values. Thus, for practical purposes, it is usually easier to change expectancies in order to bring about behavioral changes. At any rate, the importance of finding effective means of altering behavior can hardly be overestimated. From many points of view, effective modification is the major task of psychology. The salience of understanding the bases of expectancy changes readily becomes apparent.

Social learning theory has hypothesized that there are two general variables that operate to affect the size of expectancy changes. The first might be described as the **surprise value of an occurrence.** With both positive and negative reinforcements, an unexpected occurrence has a greater effect than an expected one. A student who has consistently received low grades and then receives an A may change markedly his expectancy regarding his intellectual potential. Such unusual events must result in recategorization of the situation by the individual. In other words, the occurrence of the A grade must be of such a nature as to permit recategorization; otherwise, the person might simply regard its occurrence as random or specific to one situation only.

There is ample evidence in psychology to suggest that differences in persons' perceptions of situations are relative to their previous condition or experience. Reformulated in expectancy terms, the following statement is appropriate: the size of increment of expectancy following occurrence of a reinforcement is a function of the formula $1 - E$, where 1 represents the actual occurrence (stated as an expectancy of 1.0) and E represents the previously held expectancy (stated as some decimal value). The increment in expectancy is a function of the difference between the actual occurrence and the previously held expectancy. (In the case of a decrement from a failure of a reinforcement to occur, zero would be substituted for 1 in the formula).

The second general variable affecting the size of expectancy changes is the number of previous experiences the subject has had in the situation. Stated otherwise, the degree to which we base our expectancies on our most recent experience is a function of how much earlier experience we have had that is not consistent with the most recent experience. With a lot of experience in a given situation, a recent, inconsistent experience will have little effect on our expectancies (unless cues present suggest that the situation itself has changed). Formally stated, this principle is, The increment of a specific expectancy ($\Delta E'$), following the occurrence of any given reinforcement, diminishes as the subject has more experience in that specific situation. The two preceding principles may be combined into a formula:

$$\Delta E' = f(\frac{O - E}{N}) \tag{7}$$

N represents some function of the frequency or number of previous experiences in a given situation; O, the occurrence of the reinforcement stated as a decimal (which in cases of a specific reinforcement would be either unity or zero); and E', the expectancy previously held by S for the occurrence of the reinforcement. Studies by Good (1952) and Castaneda (1951, 1952) provide empirical support for the utility of such a conceptualization. An extension of this formulation into the area of frustration has been provided by Ford (1963).

A variety of studies within an SLT framework have attempted to explore specific conditions affecting expectancy changes. Some of these studies were cited earlier in connection with the discussion of generalization phenomena. A sample of others might include studies dealing with the relation between commitment and expectancy changes. For example, Mischel (1958a; 5–6) found a negative relation between degree of commitment and amount of expectancy change following negative reinforcement. Watt (1965), in an extension of Mischel's work, also found the hypothesized inverse relation between the degree of previous commitment and the amount of decrement in expectancy after failure. In addition, he noted that constraints of previous commitment on changes downward after failure were not obtained following a week's delay. Contrary to prediction, however, highly committed Ss raised their expectancies more after success than did less committed Ss.

A series of studies by Phares (1961, 1964a, 1964b, 1966) and Schwarz (1966; 2–2) investigated the role of delay during a sequence of trials and its effect on expectancy statements. In general, these studies suggest that a substantial delay period results in expectancy changes in the direction of the S's earlier held expectancies in the same situation and in the direction of expectancies generalized from other related situations. Patterning and frequency of reinforcement and their effects on generalized expectancies have been studied by Rychlak (1958). Rychlak and Eacker

(1962) have also investigated the effects of anxiety, delay, and reinforcement on generalized expectancies.

Several studies have explored the role of the skill-chance dimension of situations in influencing expectancy changes. Obviously, expectancies for future occurrence of behavior-reinforcement sequences are dependent upon whether S perceives the relation to be necessary (or causal) or chance, random, or determined by events beyond his control. Several studies exploring this dimension of **internal** versus **external control of reinforcement** and its considerable significance in learning and personality are included in later chapters.

BROADER CONCEPTIONS

The preceding discussion of SLT concepts has been essentially molecular in nature. That is, concepts were relevant to fairly specific units of behavior. We have been concerned, for example, with the potential for a given behavior to occur in relation to a single specific reinforcement. Expectancies were dealt with in terms of the probability of a single reinforcement occurring. Such an approach is particularly useful in laboratory investigations of a highly controlled nature and for experimental tests of theoretical principles.

However, as we move toward broader application of the theory outside the laboratory, remaining at a molecular level of analysis would clearly limit the utility of the theory. For the most part, the clinician is not concerned with a single unit of behavior. The clinician usually is interested in broader, functional classes of behavior, expectancies, or needs. He is less concerned with predicting a piece of very specific behavior, like his patient's swearing at John Smith, and more oriented toward predicting a class of behavior called **aggression**. He is less concerned with the patient's preference for candy bars over pennies than he is with broader needs for eating as compared with needs for status.

Therefore, the sections that follow deal with broader or more general concepts of needs, more broadly described stable behavior patterns, and functional classes of expectancies. The role of the psychological situation will also be discussed from a social learning point of view.

NEED POTENTIAL

The concept **need potential** is the broader analogue of behavior potential. The difference is that need potential refers to groups of functionally related behaviors rather than single behaviors. Functional relatedness of behaviors exists when several behaviors all lead to, or are directed toward, obtaining the same or similar reinforcements. The process of generalization occurring among functionally related behaviors allows for better than chance prediction from one specific referent of the category to another. (Similarity of reinforcement is not the only basis for functional relatedness of behaviors.) Need potential, then, describes the mean potentiality of a group of functionally related behaviors, directed at obtaining the same or a set of similar reinforcements, occurring in any segment of the individual's life.

The kinds of behaviors that can be grouped into functional categories may range from very molecular physical or objectively defined acts to implicit behaviors such as identifying with authority figures. Such categories may be progressively more inclusive depending upon one's predictive goal and the level of predictive accuracy required. For example, **need potential for recognition is more inclusive than need potential for recognition in psychology.**

In practice, estimates of need potential are made utilizing some sampling procedure. Perhaps, observations are made of how S behaves in selected or specified situations. Normally, the determination of the relation between behaviors and reinforcements is made on a cultural basis. That is, on a cultural basis we know that **studying** is related to a group of reinforcements called **academic recognition.** At this point a brief discussion of some need concepts used in social learning theory will be helpful in understanding the sections to follow.

It is crucial to the development of a theory of personality that a descriptive language be established which deals with the content of personality. One difficulty with many learning theories is their almost exclusive emphasis on the processes of acquisition of behavior and of performance and their almost total neglect of the content of personality. In contrast, many personality theories suffer from the reverse situation, emphasizing content (needs, traits, and so on) while neglecting process.

In developing content terms, SLT began by attempting to profit from the experience of clinicians, psychotherapists, and students of the culture generally. Development of a reliable, communicable, and valid language of description is an ever-evolving process. Furthermore, it is an empirical process, wherein the final test is predictive utility of the terms and not armchair rumination.

Based on the foregoing considerations, six need descriptions were developed at a fairly broad level of abstraction. From these relatively broad categories, more specific abstractions can be developed. Some of these can be included almost entirely within one of the broad categories, while some others might be related as well to one category as to another. The six broad categories arrived at and their definitions are the following:

Recognition-Status: Need to be considered competent or good in a professional, social, occupational, or play activity. Need to gain social or vocational position—that is, to be more skilled or better than others.

Protection-Dependency: Need to have another person or group of people prevent frustration or punishment, or to provide for the satisfaction of other needs.

Dominance: Need to direct or to control the actions of other people, including members of family and friends. To have any action taken be that which he suggests.

Independence: Need to make own decisions, to rely on oneself, together with the need to develop skills for obtaining satisfactions directly without the mediation of other people.

Love and Affection: Need for acceptance and indication of liking by other individuals. In contrast to recognition-status, *not* concerned with social or professional positions, but seeks persons' warm regard.

Physical Comfort: Learned need for physical satisfaction that has become associated with gaining security.

All of these categories were presumed to be at about the same general level of inclusiveness.

The general term **need** used in this context refers to the entire complex of **need potential, freedom of movement,** and **need value.** The term refers to a set of constructs describing directionality of behavior, **not** to a state of deprivation or arousal in the organism. Used in this way the concept **need** is neither the equivalent of **need value** (or preference for certain kinds of goals) only nor the equivalent of **need potential** only.

To return to the discussion of need potential, it should be apparent that relying exclusively on cultural definitions of terms can lead to problems in individual prediction. For example, even though many people may study in order to achieve academic reinforcements, it may be true that a few people study in order to attain affectional responses from their girl friends. Therefore, the latter kind of individual would not be demonstrating a high need potential for academic recognition, but rather, for love and affection from opposite sex peers.

Measurement of Need Potential. To measure need potential is to indicate the frequency of occurrence of certain behaviors. Perhaps one of the most striking examples of the confusion of concepts in attempts to assess personality is failure to differentiate among behaviors, preferences, and expectancies. This problem has been dealt with in considerable detail by Rotter (1960b; **4-1**). For example, to say an individual places a high value on love and affection goals is **not** to say also that he behaves in such a way as to achieve need satisfaction in this area. Thus, although **need value** may be high, **expectancy** for the successful utilization of behaviors leading to such goals may be low, and therefore, **need potential** is low. Many psychological tests, for example, are composed of a confusing amalgam of items, some of which deal with frequency of behavior, others with preference for certain goals, and still others with expectancy. A total score summing these three classes of items can be very misleading. By the same token, how could one predict behavior from psychological tests were the test items to deal solely with need value? Behavior occurs not just on the basis of strength of preferences but also on the basis of expectancy that such behavior will lead to the goals in question. A study by Lesser (1957) clearly illustrates the utility of separating the concepts of **behavior, needs,** and **expectancies.** Lesser found little relation between aggressive needs and aggressive behavior among schoolchildren; evidently TAT responses did not predict overt behavior. However, when information regarding maternal control responses toward the child's aggression (responses SLT would regard as referents for the child's expectancy for punishment for overt aggression) was added to the need for aggression scores derived from the TAT, then significant predictions of overt behavior were possible.

A variety of measures of need potential are possible. These might include direct observation of S over a period of time, paper and pencil or verbal choice techniques, rankings, paired comparisons, forced-choice questionnaires, and so on. However, in utilizing paper and pencil techniques or verbal questionnaires, the emphasis must be on what the subject does and not on what he would like to do or expects to do.

Projective tests have, in the past, not been particularly useful in assessing need potential. Their best application would seem to be more in the direction of assessing **need values** and **freedom of movement.** Carefully applied sociometric techniques offer promise in measurement of **need potential.** Indeed, in some ways this method simply asks others to report on their observations of S and is thus very much akin to other observational techniques. Sociometric methods allow behavior to be assessed in natural settings and are carried out by people who know S well enough to make meaningful ratings. This technique was utilized by Fitzgerald (1958; 4–3) to measure dependency behavior and by Phares (1959) to assess leaving-the-field behavior. Of course, crude predictions of need potential may be arrived at also by combining measures of freedom of movement and need value (Piper, Wogan, & Getter; 7–5).

NEED VALUE

Need value is defined as **mean preference value of a set of functionally related reinforcements.** Where **reinforcement value** indicates preference for **one** reinforcement over others, **need value** indicates preference for one **set** of functionally related reinforcements over another set (always assuming that expectancy for occurrence is held constant). Recall that functionality of reinforcements comes about either through stimulus generalization or through an extension of the principle of mediated stimulus generalization. Occurrence of functionality among reinforcements has been demonstrated empirically on a substitution basis, as in a study by

A. Lotsof (1953), as well as in terms of generalization of expectancies among functionally related behaviors, as in the previously noted studies of Crandall, Jessor, and Chance. Demonstration of functionality by substitution involves a situation where behavior toward a goal is blocked, and it is then noted which behavior is adopted as a substitute.

Earlier, when need potential was discussed, it was emphasized that descriptions of need categories based on functionally related behaviors must ultimately be arrived at on an empirical basis. Likewise, given a workable culture-based definition, one is cautioned about generalizing beyond the confines of one's own culture. Similarly, one must be cognizant of individual development of idiosyncratic need structures which may not follow those of the larger culture.

Measurement of Need Value. Interviews, objective tests, and projective tests have all been used to measure need value. It is also possible to use observations of behavior in situations where expectancies can be controlled.

One of the more systematic attempts to measure need value was made by Liverant (1958). Inasmuch as the SLT operational definition of need value implicitly suggests a choice or ranking technique for measurement, Liverant presented statements in a forced-choice arrangement and controlled Ss' expectancies through instructions. An inventory, called the **Goal Preference Inventory,** resulted from this procedure and is designed to measure Ss' relative need values for recognition **versus** love and affection. Item analysis, factor analysis, split-half and test-retest reliability, as well as correlations with the **Edwards Personal Preference Schedule** and use of criterion group methods, generally support the adequacy of the inventory as a valid and reliable indicator of relative need strength in the areas sampled.

Need value has been measured often by projective methods—most often with some version of the TAT. Rotter (1954) provides a general outline for construction of reliable judgmental procedures. Such procedures are illustrated in Fitzgerald's (1958; 4-3) study. A somewhat different approach to measuring need value from interview data is presented by Tyler, Tyler, and Rafferty (1962).

FREEDOM OF MOVEMENT

Freedom of movement is defined as mean expectancy of obtaining positive satisfactions as a result of a set of related behaviors directed toward obtaining a group of functionally related reinforcements. Thus, when an individual has a high expectancy of attaining reinforcements that define a given need area for him, he is said to have high freedom of movement in that need area. In short, he feels that his behavioral techniques will be successful for his goals. When freedom of movement is low, particularly in relation to a need area of high value, the individual may anticipate punishment or failure. Thus, the concept of **freedom of movement** bears a relation to the concept of **anxiety** as described by other theories. This correspondence will be discussed in more detail later.

Measurement of Freedom of Movement. Like its analogue **expectancy**, **freedom of movement** may be measured on either an absolute or on a relative basis. Furthermore, when it is possible to equate reinforcement values, freedom of movement can also be measured by assuming that the individual will choose the goal-directed behavior for which he has the highest set of expectancies. Direct methods of measurement include verbal statements of expectancy, behavioral techniques, such as betting on outcomes, and, possibly, decision times. Indirect methods of assessment often rely upon measures of avoidant behaviors or defensiveness. It seems reasonable to assume that to the extent an individual behaves defensively or in an irreal fashion in relation to certain goals, he possesses low freedom of movement in that need area. Low expectancy for success (or high expectancy for punishment) in a highly valued need area is correlated with defensiveness; thus, the latter can serve as a referent for the former. Naturally, the definition of what is **irreal, defensive,** or **avoidant** must derive from a study of the culture in which the individual operates. Such behaviors, although in some instances leading to immediate gratifications, do lead ultimately to negative reinforcements from society. It follows logically from this analysis that the person utilizing defensive behaviors is aware, at some level, of the potential for negative reinforcement involved. Put another way, if the person's defensive behaviors are characteristically followed by ultimate negative reinforcement, he uses the defensive behaviors because he expects greater punishment to result from his positive efforts than he does from negative or defensive efforts.

Possible origins of low freedom of movement are diverse. For example, the individual may simply not possess knowledge necessary to attain desired goals. An extreme illustration is the retardate, whose goals may be those of society's, but whose expectancy for goal attainment is low because he has neither the behavioral repertory nor the ability to acquire the appropriate behaviors (Cromwell, 1967; 6–5). In other instances, the individual may have learned to value certain goals which others regard as undesirable. As a result, he comes to anticipate punishment in that area. In still other instances, the individual may develop low freedom of movement based on faulty interpretations of the past. For example, he may have, as a child, experienced severe criticism from his family. Generalizing erroneously from this experience to the present, he may anticipate failure or punishment from all others he encounters.

Rotter (1942, 1943, 1954) has described a variety of level-of-aspiration patterns derived from controlled observation of goal setting. These patterns frequently identify avoidant techniques, suggesting low freedom of movement.

A variety of other studies use projective techniques like the TAT and develop systematic scoring methods to assess avoidance. Such studies include those of V. J. Crandall (1955a) and Fitzgerald (1958; 4–3). When **freedom of movement is low while need value is high,** we have a situation of **conflict.** To escape punishment and failure in an area of great importance to him, the individual adopts various avoidant behaviors. He may also try to reach his goals in **irreal** or **symbolic** ways, such as fantasy, which do not run the risk of incurring failure or punishment. Most behavior regarded as psychopathological is avoidant or irreal behavior. These issues are discussed in greater detail by Phares (6–1).

In summary, defensive behaviors provide an indirect measure of freedom of movement because such behaviors suggest the degree to which the individual expects negative reinforcement in a given need area. It is crucial in using this method that it first be established that the individual places a high value on the need in question. Otherwise, what seems avoidant may turn out to be an uncomplicated lack of interest.

MINIMAL GOAL LEVEL

Related to the concept of **low freedom of movement** is another SLT concept—**minimal goal level.** Specifically defined, **minimal goal level** refers to the **lowest goal in a continuum of potential reinforcements for some life situation which will be perceived by the person as satisfactory to him.** This definition suggests that reinforcements may be ordered from highly positive to highly negative. The point along this dimension at which reinforcements change from positive to negative in value for the person is his minimal goal level. Internalized minimal goals are responsible for the often observed instance where a person attains many goals that appear highly desirable to others and yet he, nonetheless, experiences a sense of failure or low freedom of movement. From his point of view, he is failing. When someone has extremely high minimal goals, whether in achievement, dominance, or love and affection, and is not obtaining reinforcements at or above this level, then by definition he has low freedom of movement.

The same analysis, in reverse, supplies the reason that a person may be contented, even though observers perceive his level of goal achievement to be exceedingly low. To the extent that problems in living often derive from a too high minimal goal level (or, more infrequently, from a very low minimal goal level), psychotherapy may concentrate on changing minimal goals by changing the value of reinforcements. As discussed in the preceding section on reinforcement values, value changes are accomplished by pairing the reinforcements in question with others of either a higher or lower value. For example, the individual is led to develop the expectancy that a previously negatively valued reinforcement—such as a grade of B—can lead to the positive reinforcements of praise and acceptance. The importance of changing minimal goals is discussed in more detail by Rotter (7–6).

While minimal goals are relatively stable, the values of all reinforcements are relative to others possible in a given situation (Crandall, Good, & Crandall, 1964; 3–5). For example, defensive and avoidant behaviors are acquired and maintained because they are positively reinforced by the avoidance of a strong negative reinforcement. At the same time, other behaviors leading to anticipated negative reinforcement may be negatively reinforced because anticipation itself can be negatively reinforcing. In situations of anticipation of strong negative reinforcement, minimal goals may shift markedly and avoidance (or partial avoidance) may be perceived as a positively reinforcing outcome. Similarly, in situations where strong positive reinforcements seem possible, a level of reinforcement that would be regarded as positive otherwise may be perceived as negative on that occasion.

THE SITUATION

Implicit in all the preceding discussions has been the idea that the **psychological situation** is an extremely important determinant of behavior. This view is in sharp contrast to those positions that adopt a "core" approach to personality and assert that once the basic elements of personality are identified, reliable prediction follows. Core views are inherent in both psychoanalytic theories of dynamics and in trait and typological descriptive schemes. In short, many theories are so preoccupied with identifying highly stable aspects of personality that they fail to make systematic use of the psychological situation in the prediction of behavior. The SLT approach contends that such a posture severely limits prediction by permitting only global statements about future behavior which are limited to a very low level of accuracy in prediction.

From the SLT view, each situation is composed of cues serving to arouse in the individual certain expectancies for reinforcement of specific behaviors. For example, even though an individual may be described as possessing an extremely strong predisposition to aggressive behavior, he will not behave aggressively in a given situation if the latter contains cues suggesting to him that aggressive behavior is very likely to result in strong punishment. Meanings that cues acquire for the individual are based on prior learning history and can be determined in advance in order to help us predictively. Again, some of these meanings can be assumed on a cultural basis, but the possibilities raised by idiosyncratic life experiences must be recognized also.

Recognition that behavior is not determined solely by personal characteristics but also by situational considerations specifies the necessity for descriptive categories for different situations. Psychology can be accurately said to have made less progress in devising classifications for situations than in almost any other area. As a preliminary effort in this direction, Rotter (1955) described several methods for determining similarity among situations. As in the case of psychological needs, the number and kinds of situational categories developed would be a function of the purpose of classification and the level accuracy of prediction required. Fairly generalized predictions would require less subtle distinctions among situations than would more precise predictions.

At least four methods of categorizing situations are based on need concepts. The first method involves sampling expectancies. That is, within a given culture, Ss could estimate their expectations for potential occurrence of certain reinforcements in specific situations. Situations could then be classified as similar to the extent that they aroused similar expectancies for reinforcement. A second method requires that we sample, through observations, actual reinforcements that occur in specific situations. Thus, two situations in which it is observed that a high frequency of love and affection rewards occur would be classified as similar. The third technique utilizes behaviors. If we have already classified behaviors in terms of the goal toward which they are usually oriented, then situations which produce similar behaviors could be classified together. The fourth method utilizes generalization. For example, we might pretest some behavior (or expectancy or reinforcement) in several situations; then, increase or decrease this behavior potential in one situation and test in the other situations for a generalization of the increase or decrease. The greater the generalization between two situations, the greater their similarity. In the following sections concerning generalized expectancies and short-term effects of reinforcement, additional ways of classifying situations will be discussed.

The individual's expectancy that a given behavior will be followed by a given reinforcement is dependent upon how he characterizes the situation. It is also the case that values of reinforcements will vary depending upon the situation in which they occur. Thus, the individual may expect to be rewarded for a behavior in one situation and not in another. Likewise, the degree of value attached to the reward may be high in one situation and relatively low in another.

These two points have been demonstrated empirically. A study by Henry and Rotter (1956) obtained behavioral differences as a function of varying instructions preceding the administration of the Rorschach. One group of Ss received standard instructions while another was told that the Rorschach was widely used in mental hospitals. The latter group behaved differently from the former because they expected different outcomes for their behavior. Phares and Rotter (1956) demonstrated that reinforcements change in value depending upon how the psychological situation is categorized by the individual. Using junior high school Ss, they found that the ranking (or value) of academic reinforcements decreased when carried out in an athletic situation, but increased when executed in an academic situation. The reward value of events is influenced by the total context in which they occur. The situation is akin to that of a little boy who loves to be kissed by his mother when he is in the home, but dreads it when he is out playing with his friends. This is because he anticipates they will make fun of him.

In summary, SLT emphasizes the crucial importance of situational determinants of behavior. Recall the situational subscripts in SLT formulas. These subscripts are explicit recognition that accurate prediction requires that measurement of all SLT variables be carried out with reference to the situation or classes of situations.

GENERALIZED EXPECTANCIES: PROBLEM-SOLVING SKILLS

Man is a categorizing animal. He continuously forms concepts, changes concepts, and discovers new dimensions of similarity. While similarity of reinforcements is an extremely important basis for his conceptualizations, there are also other dimensions along which he perceives similarity. Within SLT any part of the environment to which the individual responds, or its totality, is referred to as a situational determinant. When an individual perceives that a number of people are alike because they are of the same sex, color, occupation, or age, he develops expectations about these people. Experience with one of them generalizes to others of the same class. When generalization takes place, we have the basis for believing that functional relations exist. That is, prediction of one referent from another referent of the same class can be made at a better than chance level. Generalized expectancies about people, and the behaviors and reinforcements connected with them, are part of the basis for what has been traditionally called **social attitudes** in psychology. In a later paper in this volume, Rotter (1967a; **5–1**) describes in detail a social learning theory analysis of social attitudes and social action-taking behavior.

Situations, both social and nonsocial, may also be perceived as similar in that they present similar problems. For example, all of us are faced continuously with the problem of deciding whether what happens to us is contingent on our own behavior and can be controlled by our own actions, or whether it depends upon luck, the intervention of powerful others, or influences we cannot understand. We develop a generalized expectancy across situations which may differ in needs satisfied or reinforcements expected, but which are similar with respect to perception of control that we can exercise to change or maintain these situations. As with social attitudes, when generalization occurs from one situation to another, individual differences may develop in how the situations themselves are perceived or categorized. In such a case, generalized expectancies may deal with properties of situational stimuli. That is, the basis for similarity does not lie, in this instance, in the nature of reinforcements but in the nature of the situation. Behaviors relevant to these situationally mediated expectancies are also functionally related because of similarity of the problems to be solved.

When a behavior directed toward a goal is blocked, or fails to achieve the goal, the failure itself may be regarded as a property of a new situation involving a problem to be solved. A generalized expectancy that problems can be solved by a technique of looking for alternatives may also be developed regardless of the specific need or reinforcement involved. The degree to which a generalized problem-solving expectancy is developed may be an important source of individual differences in behavior.

Another common human experience is that of being provided with information from other people—either promises of reinforcements to come or merely statements of presumed fact. Implicit in all these situations is the problem of whether to believe or not to believe the other person. A generalized expectancy of **trust** or **distrust** can be an important determinant of behavior.

The mature human can probably perceive an extremely large number of dimensions of similarities in problem characteristics in complex social situations. Some dimensions, however, are broader than others and some, undoubtedly, are far more relevant for particular kinds of psychological predictions than others. In recent years, many SLT investigations have concerned some of these dimensions. Two of these are the dimension of **internal versus external control of reinforcement** and the dimension of **interpersonal trust.** Several papers in this volume deal with these generalized expectancies.

While inclusion of content dimensions makes the prediction of behavior more complex, it must be recognized that man is, in fact, a complex organism. A concept of generalized expectancies, as proposed here, requires some change in our previous formulation of expectancy. If we hypothesize that generalized expectancies derived from categorization of the problem will influence whether the individual anticipates that a particular behavior will lead to a particular reinforcement, then in addition to his generalized expectancy for the success of his behavior (GE) in obtaining that reinforcement, we have to make additional corrections to assess more accurately his expectancy about the particular character of the situation. For example, in a task where S believes that reinforcement (success) is controlled by the experimenter, a sequence of reinforcements such as $+ - - + - + + +$ might yield a low expectancy for success on the next trial. Where S believes reinforcement is determined by his own skill, the same pattern of reinforcements should yield a relatively high expectancy for success on the next trial.

Formula (8) schematizes this expansion. A subscript r is used to denote expectancies generalized from other similar attempts to obtain a given reinforcement, and the subscript ps denotes relevant generalized expectancies for classes of problem-solving situations cutting across specific need categories. As with other generalized expectancies for success in achieving a class of reinforcements, the more specific experience the individual has in that situation, the less influence generalized expectancies have; the more novel a situation, the greater is the influence wielded by generalized expectancies. As in preceding formulas, a hypothesis about the direction of influence of the variables is made, but no attempt to specify exact mathematical relations has been made. Predictions of increments and decrements in expectancy would have to be modified in many cases when particular generalized expectancies relevant to the situation being studied are present.

$$E_{s_1} = f(E' \ \& \ GE_r \ \& \ GE_{ps_1} \ \& \ GE_{ps_2} \cdots GE_{ps_n}) \over f(N_{s_1})$$
(8)

POSITIVE AND NEGATIVE REINFORCEMENTS AS SITUATIONAL CUES

Reinforcements, whether words, acts, or tangible objects, are also parts of the psychological situation, as are cues closely associated with occurrence of reinforcements. Content categories based on perceived similarities of reinforcement (needs), perceived similarities of social cues (social attitudes), and perceived similarities of the nature of the problems to be solved (generalized expectancies) have been discussed. There may also be similarities in situations based on the sign (whether positive or negative) or intensity of reinforcements, or combinations of these along with the circumstances in which they occur.

Occurrence of a negative reinforcement, or its anticipation, as already indicated, may lead to defensive or avoidant behaviors; and such behaviors can be understood as having a potential for a particular class of reinforcements. It may be characteristic of some people, however, that they respond with aggression, repression, withdrawal, projection, depression, and so on, somewhat independently of the kind (need category) of reinforcement. These responses may be a function of the sign or strength of the reinforcement rather than its particular form. In other words, we can talk not only about a behavior potential to repress competitive failures but a behavior potential to repress all strong negative reinforcements. How functional or general such potentials are across need areas is an empirical matter. Mild failure in an achievement-related task may increase the potential for some individuals to narrow their attention, increase concentration, and so on.

However, mild failure might not have the same effect should it occur in initiating a social relationship.

It is clear that strong reinforcements—positive or negative—or the anticipation that such a reinforcement will take place shortly is accompanied by changes in autonomic nervous system activity. Such autonomic changes can serve as cues and, along with other situational cues, can affect learned behavior (Schachter, 1966; Lazarus, 1968). Clearly, individuals differ in the kind of bodily changes that follow from the same reinforcement (Lacey, 1959), and some individuals are more aware of these bodily changes than others (Lazarus, 1969). Emotions have been a troublesome area for psychologists—partly, again, because of failure to separate behaviors from expectancies and bodily changes from the learned psychological patterns of response. Both have either strong reinforcement or its anticipation as a common antecedent. However, while strong reinforcement may be a common antecedent to both autonomic changes and learned behavioral responses, these two need not be highly correlated. Understanding and orderly description of this area is a current challenge to social learning theorists. Meantime, it may be hypothesized that these psychological responses called emotional behavior can also be regarded as similar to other learned behaviors where functional categories are related to the sign, strength, and nature of the reinforcements.

Anxiety (or certain behavioral referents for anxiety), aggression, repression, cautiousness, and rigidity are some of the characteristics that have been thought of in this way by many investigators. However, it has always been difficult to demonstrate the generality of these behaviors across different situations, at least in "normal" populations. Such behavioral characteristics appear to be more general when observing some "pathological" people and less general in the "normal" population. Behavior elicited by strong positive reinforcements like elation or behavior associated with mild positive reinforcement like relaxation have been investigated and considered much less than the behaviors associated with negative reinforcement, but they are equally important for a comprehensive account of human behavior.

PART 1: SUMMARY

This chapter describes a molar learning theory of complex behavior with special reference to behavior in which the reinforcements depend on the behavior of other people. The purpose of the theory is prediction of behavior and the internal or cognitive processes related to behavior. While the same principles may also be important in early acquisition of more simple behaviors, the theory is not primarily concerned with more molecular principles which explain why one thing in a complex situation is associated with another, nor how very simple responses are built up into complex patterns of response. It is not that such principles are unimportant; they simply are not the focus of this theory. Once the basic patterns of behavior have been developed, the problem is to determine when one is chosen over another in a specific situation. This is the focus of this theory.

In addition to the principles governing the processes of choice behavior, social learning theory attempts to describe various ways in which generality of behavior may be described. In other words, bases for a content theory of individual differences are developed. The most important of these bases is the similarity of reinforcements. Other categories of content are based upon the similarity of social objects (social attitudes) and similarities in the type of problem to be solved in a particular situation (generalized expectancies). A fourth category of behaviors may be based upon similarities in the sign and strength of reinforcements. Finally, the need for functional categories of situations characterized in common sense social terms is described. Such categories are prerequisite to prediction of behavior in a manner that attends to both its generality and its situational specificity.

It is the bare structure of the theory that is described here. More extensive explication and justifications for the theoretical position are presented in earlier publications. The goal of SLT is not to provide the "facts" of personality but, rather, to provide a vehicle for the conceptualization of the facts. The strength of the theory lies in its value as a method of analysis of psychological problems in personality and related areas. The remaining chapters in this book illustrate how the theory has been effective in the analysis of problems in six general areas: complex human learning, personality development, personality measurement, social psychology and the social sciences, psychopathology, and psychotherapy. The empirical and theoretical papers in each chapter have been selected from a large number of alternatives for their illustrative value.

2 | *Applications to Learning Theory*

INTRODUCTION

This section surveys the implications of SLT for the general area of learning. Seven papers have been reprinted which not only illustrate some substantive contributions of SLT to learning but also describe a variety of SLT methodological approaches to the study of learning phenomena. Although the selection of the papers to be reprinted was somewhat arbitrary, each typifies SLT contributions.

The study by Chance (1959; 2–1) illustrates how expectancies for success generalize along paths of need relatedness. Thus, the reinforcement of a specific behavior can easily have effects on other behaviors, and we can begin to see how the concept of generalization of expectancies enhances our understanding of the effects of reinforcement.

Schwarz (1966; 2–2) attacks the problem of delays during the learning process and shows that such delays result in a shift in expectancies toward the level of expectancies held in the beginning of the learning series. Again, we have evidence that reinforcement effects are altered by the influence of expectancies.

The studies by Mahrer (1956; 2–6) and Mischel and Staub (1965; 2–3) explicate the role of expectancies in determining preferences for immediate gratification as compared to delayed reinforcement.

Relations between expectancy and reinforcement value have long been of interest to psychologists generally and to decision theorists in particular. Studies by Worell (1956; 2–4) and Mischel and Masters (1966; 2–7) address themselves to problems in this area, while Lotsof (1956; 2–5) discusses decision time as it relates to reinforcement value.

In the summary at the end of this section, these studies are discussed along with many other SLT investigations which appear to add to our understanding of the learning process.

Generalization of Expectancies among Functionally Related Behaviors[1]

JUNE E. CHANCE

Some concept of generalization of response is an important part of most psychological theories which make use of learning as a basic process of behavioral change. This paper deals with generalization in an individual's expectations that given behaviors will lead to reinforcement. Expectations about the effectiveness of certain behaviors in obtaining reinforcement change as the individual has direct experience with the behaviors as means of obtaining desired goals, but they also change as a function of generalization from changes in expectancies for related behaviors. All personality theories, whether of a predictive or descriptive sort, presuppose that behaviors of a given individual are related or organized. Different bases or dimensions of organization are assumed by different authors. This study tests the hypothesis that generalization of expectancies occurs to the extent that behaviors are functionally related.

Functional relationships among behaviors within an individual's repertoire occur as the result of experience that the behaviors are reinforced in the same way; degree of functional relatedness varies with degrees of similarity of reinforcements obtained and/or the proportion of occurrences of the behaviors reinforced in the same manner. When a particular environmental event alters the individual's expectancy about the outcome of a given behavior, expectancies for other behaviors are simultaneously altered to the degree that these other behaviors have a history of reinforcement similar to that of the first behavior. For example, if a child is refused candy, it is likely that his expectancy of obtaining an ice cream cone from the same source is also diminished, whereas his expectancy of persuading a playmate to play a favorite game may remain relatively unaffected. Change in expectancies mediated along a learned dimension of similarity of reinforcements of goals is seen as one of the important bases of many complex behavioral phenomena with which personality theorists and clinicians must deal.

The experimental hypotheses and the conceptual framework on which they are based are derived from Rotter's social learning theory (Rotter, 1954). Social learning theory selects as its focus of interest the interaction of the individual with his meaningful environment. This interaction involves

[1] This article is based upon a portion of a dissertation submitted in partial fulfillment of the requirements for the degree of Doctor of Philosophy in the Department of Psychology at The Ohio State University. The author wishes to thank Dr. Julian B. Rotter, her advisor, and Drs. George A. Kelly and Delos D. Wickens for their guidance and encouragement during this study. A summary of this paper was read at the 1953 meeting of the Midwestern Psychological Association in Chicago, Illinois.

the individual's use of instrumental behaviors to attain potential satisfactions or to avoid potential frustrations which he perceives in the environment. In order to predict the occurrence of a particular behavior in a given situation, it is necessary to know what expectancy the individual holds that this particular behavior will lead to a given reinforcement and how much the given reinforcement or goal is valued by the individual relative to other goals available to him in that situation.

The social learning definition of expectancy as the subjectively held probability that a certain reinforcement or goal may be obtained by means of a given behavior is similar to definitions given by Tolman and Brunswik (1935), Brunswik (1943), and Lewin, Dembo, Festinger, and Sears (1944). Several previous studies within the social learning framework have studied changes in expectancy as a result of direct experience by means both of verbal estimates and observation of betting behavior in a "gambling" situation (Castaneda, 1951; Rotter, Fitzgerald, & Joyce, 1954).

The present study is most closely related to two previous studies of generalization of expectancies. The earlier study by Crandall (1951) demonstrated that induced failure on a physical skills task influenced TAT stories told after the failure experience. The greatest effect was found in stories involving physical skills activities, the next greatest in stories involving academic accomplishment, and the least effect in stories involving relationships with opposite sex peers. However, differences in the amount of change between the three need-areas sampled were not statistically significant. Jessor (1954), in a later study, demonstrated that induced failure on an arithmetic task reduced the individual's stated expectancies regarding performances on a vocabulary task, a pursuit rotor, and a social skills task. In both of these studies the generalization gradient obtained corresponded to the gradient which would have been predicted on the basis of similarity of reinforcement or the degree of functional relatedness among the behaviors. However, in neither study could the possibility be eliminated that the same gradients might also have been obtained on the basis of stimulus similarity. The present investigation is, in a sense, an attack on the same problem but with an effort to keep factors of stimulus similarity as constant as possible. The same stimulus or task materials were used with all Ss but the instructions regarding the goals or reinforcements toward which adequate response to these tasks were supposed to lead were varied.

Although every individual has a unique history of past reinforcements and therefore a unique organization of functionally related behaviors, for research purposes one may exploit certain similarities in the social learning of groups of people sharing similar backgrounds. For example, abstractions like recognition, love and affection, dominance, physical comfort, dependency, and independence have been shown by Rockwell (1951) to be useful ways of describing the functional relationships among behaviors of college students. In the present study similarity of reinforcement or functional relatedness was manipulated symbolically by means of the verbal labels applied to the experimental tasks. Labels were chosen which seemed likely to sample areas of relatedness in the college student's behavior.

This study was also designed to test the hypothesis that extent of disparity between expected and obtained outcome would influence extent of generalization. This hypothesis is suggested by the social learning proposition that extent of change in expectancy following the occurrence of a reinforcement is a function of the distance between the previously held expectancy and the actual occurrence. If this expectancy–occurrence disparity influences extent of changes mediated by direct experience, it should also influence extent of changes mediated by generalization.

The experimental hypotheses investigated were: (a) after success on one task Ss will predict a higher level of performance on a second task to the extent that both tasks are perceived as leading to the same goal or reinforcement; (b) predictions of performance level for the second, or generalization, task will increase significantly more when the disparity between initial expectancy for the first task and the "success" score received is larger.

METHOD

Ss were 167 students of both sexes enrolled in introductory psychology courses. The purpose of the experiment was announced as the refinement and validation of two new personality tests. All procedures were carried out during a period of one week near the beginning of the term to insure that Ss would be a naïve as possible about psychological tests. Ss met in small groups consisting of 6 to 10 people. Twenty sessions were conducted; each was numbered and on the basis of a table of random numbers each session was assigned to one of four experimental treatments. Each experimental group was divided into two subgroups on the basis of even- and odd-numbered seats in .the room.

Ss for each session reported to a small classroom where they were seated around a large table. Ss were then given test booklets, containing detailed instructions about two "tests" which they were to take. Instructions consisted of four parts: (a) descripton of the physical stimulus characteristics of the test and the way in which responses were to be made; (b) a brief statement of what the tests were supposed to measure; (c) a statement of the possible range of scores (0 to 100) and fictitious average scores; and (d) spaces in which S was asked to write his estimates of the scores he thought he was most likely to make on each of the two tests. Importance of making accurate estimates was stressed. The first, third, and fourth parts of the instructions remained constant for all groups; the second part, which stated what the tests were supposed to measure, varied from group to group.

Four major groups of Ss were used. Each group received a different variant of the statement about what the tests were supposed to measure. Group HH was told that both tests measured heterosexual adjustment and potentiality for happy marriage. Group LL was told that both tests measured leadership potential, i.e., ability to initiate, organize, and direct group activities. Group LH was told that the ink blot test measured leadership potential and that the word association test measured heterosexual adjustment. Group HL was told that the ink blot test measured heterosexual adjustment and the word association test measured leadership potential. Half of each of these groups received scores 7 points above their expectancy statements (low success) and half received scores 14 points above their expectancy statements (high success). The four major groups are relevant to testing the first hypothesis; the low and high success subgroups were included to test the second hypothesis.

The first "test" consisted of a series of 10 ink blots constructed by *E*. The blots were displayed in front of the room and *Ss* were instructed to check for each blot any two of ten items from a checklist which the blot most resembled. The second "test" was a word association list containing 25 items to which *Ss* were instructed to write the first word they thought of after hearing the word read aloud by the *E*.

Procedure

When a group was assembled in the room the following short introduction was given by *E:* "You are going to be given two personality tests as a part of a research program which we are carrying on in this department. Both tests will be described for you before you take them. At present, both these tests are new and are just being tried out. We have previously tried them out with more than a thousand students very much like you at another large university.

"We are also interested in the ways in which people estimate their probable scores *before* they have taken a test. In order to give you some idea of what you should be able to make on these tests, we will give you some of the results of students who have taken them before."

Then the first set of test booklets containing descriptions of both tests and answer sheets for the ink blot test were passed out. *E* read each test description and set of instructions aloud while *Ss* followed in their booklets. At the end of the description of the word association test, *Ss* were asked to write their estimate of their probable score on that test. Then the description of the ink blot test was read and *Ss* were asked to estimate their scores for that test. (Both tests were described fully and each *S* recorded estimates of his probable scores on both before either was administered.)

At this point *E* answered any questions which directly concerned what the *Ss* were to do in responding to each test. If questions arose about construction of the tests or scoring, *E* asked that they be postponed until the end of the session.

Ss were then instructed to turn to the answer sheets and each blot in the series was displayed in turn long enough for every *S* to make two choices from the appropriate list. When the ink blot test was completed, the booklets were collected and *E* said: "Since this test is set up on a multiple choice basis it is possible to score it rather quickly by means of a key. I'm going to score your tests now so that you may have your scores before you leave. While I'm doing that, I have another test I would like you to take. It is called an incomplete sentences test. It has nothing to do with the test that you have just taken or with the test that you will take when I finish the scoring. To be quite honest, it is not really a part of this experiment at all, but it is some extra data we are trying to collect for another study. We thought you might not mind doing it while you were waiting." The incomplete sentences blanks were then distributed. This task was introduced to make it difficult for Ss to attend too closely to E during the supposed scoring of the initial experimental task.

E then turned to the "scoring" procedure, which consisted of flipping quickly through the booklets, noting the score which the S stated he was most likely to make on the ink blot test. To this estimate E added 7 points for Ss seated in even numbered seats, 14 points for Ss seated in the odd numbered seats. A series of check-marks was made on each S's answer sheet before the predetermined score was recorded at the top. E occasionally referred to a rather formidable chart spread on the desk. E then copied each S's name and score on a separate card. No S, so far as E could tell, questioned the validity of the scoring procedure.

When all Ss had finished the sentences, these were collected and cards bearing scores were returned to Ss. No direct effort was made to prevent Ss from communicating with each other about scores; hence in some sessions a few comments were exchanged; however these did not seem to impair the face validity of the situation or rapport with the Ss. At this point many Ss asked again what the average score of students who had taken the ink blot test previously was. (The fictitious average used was 52.)

Booklets for the word association test were passed out and E reviewed the instructions for that test. Ss were asked to re-estimate what they now thought they might make on this test. They were told, "If you wish to change your first estimate, feel perfectly free to do so. Remember you are trying to estimate your most probable score as accurately as possible."

E then read the list of words aloud, repeating each word twice, and allowing roughly 10 seconds per response. Ss wrote their responses on an answer sheet provided. At the end of the session, these were collected and Ss were thanked for their cooperation and requested not to discuss the experiment with others. They were offered the reason that to talk about the tests would invalidate them for people taking them later. Although difficulties arising out of possible communication between groups had been anticipated, no such problem occurred. Throughout the entire week Ss seemed interested in performing both experimental tasks; no one seriously questioned any aspect of the experiment although Ss were invited at the end of each session to ask any question they liked, either in the group or afterward privately with E.

RESULTS

In order to test whether the "score" received on the ink blot task directly affected expectancy for that task, a small group of Ss (one session) within each of the four major experimental groups was asked to re-estimate their most probable score on the ink blots should they take

Table 1 Summary of Generalization Scores

| | TREATMENT GROUP[a] | | | | | |
	HH	LL	LH	HL	HH+LL	LH+HL
Low Success Sub-group	N = 21 M = .43 SD = 4.98	N = 21 M = 3.48 SD = 2.96	N = 20 M = 1.70 SD = 4.59	N = 20 M = .60 SD = 8.73	N = 42 M = 1.95 SD = 4.78	N = 40 M = 1.15 SD = 7.08
High Success Sub-group	N = 21 M = 5.62 SD = 6.26	N = 24 M = 5.21 SD = 5.72	N = 20 M = 2.05 SD = 4.47	N = 20 M = 1.67 SD = 4.21	N = 45 M = 5.40 SD = 4.04	N = 40 M = 1.86 SD = 4.73
Total	N = 42 M = 3.02 SD = 6.92	N = 45 M = 4.40 SD = 5.12	N = 40 M = 1.88 SD = 4.90	N = 40 M = 1.14 SD = 6.97	N = 87 M = 3.73 SD = 7.15	N = 80 M = 1.51 SD = 6.22

[a] HH is group told that both tests measured heterosexual adjustment.
LL is group told that both tests measured leadership potential.
LH is group told that ink blots measured leadership potential: word association, heterosexual adjustment.
HL is group told that ink blots measured heterosexual adjustment: word association, leadership potential.

them a second time. (These additional estimates were made after the second estimate for the word association task.) Inspection of the data indicated no tendency for differential changes to occur as a function of instructions concerning the tasks. Size of change in re-estimates was significantly related ($t=4.78$, $p < .001$, 28 df) to whether Ss received 7 or 14 points more than their stated expectancy for the ink blots. The respective means of these two groups were 10.29 and 14.88.

Since the measure of generalization in expectancy used was the change in estimate of probable performance (second estimate minus first estimate) for the word association task after receiving a score on the ink blot task, it was necessary first to be assured that the groups did not differ in their initial estimates for the word association task. An analysis of variance indicated no significant differences among the groups in their initial estimates.

The distributions of differences between the first and second estimates made for the word association task were either normal or else positively skewed to a small degree. The means and standard deviations of this generalization score and the N's for all groups are presented in Table 1.

Mean changes in expectancy statements for the word association task, when tested against the hypothesis of no change significantly different from zero, indicate that some change in expectancy or generalization took place in both experimental groups (HH and LL) and in one of the control groups (LH). Values of t are presented in Table 2. The tendency of some of the control Ss to show generalization may be attributed to such factors as both tasks being administered in the same situation, by the same E, and their both having been initially described as personality tests.

Values in the lower half of Table 2 indicate that while significant shifts in expectancies occurred in Group LL (told that both tests measured

Table 2   Significance of Mean Changes from Zero in Generalized Expectancies

Group	df	t	Group	df	t
HH	41	2.80**	Low LL	20	5.27***
LL	44	5.71***	Low LH	19	1.61
LH	39	2.41*	Low HL	19	.30
HL	39	1.02	High HH	20	4.01***
HH plus LL	86	4.84***	High LL	23	13.02***
LH plus HL	79	2.16*	High LH	19	1.99
Low HH	20	.39	High HL	19	1.73

  * $p < .05$
 ** $p < .01$
*** $p < .001$

leadership potential) under conditions of both low and high success, in Group HH (told both tests measured heterosexual adjustment) significant shifts occurred only under the high success condition. Perhaps Ss in Group LL had fewer real experiences against which to "invalidate" the score received on the ink blots than did Group HH and were therefore more influenced by the score received.

Two variants of the goal same/goal different instructions had been used in order to control the possibility that changes in expectancy might occur as a function of the specific need variable employed and/or the content of the task. Tests of the mean differences between experimental groups HH and LL and between the means of control Groups LH and HL yielded insignificant values of t (see Table 3). Experimental and control groups may, therefore, be combined in order to test the first hypothesis that generalization of expectancy will occur to a greater extent when both the original and generalization tasks are seen as leading to similar goals than when they are seen as leading to different goals. Despite the tendency of both experimental and control Ss to show some generalization, when the means of the combined experimental groups and combined control groups are compared the first hypothesis is confirmed ($t = 2.13, .05 > p > .02$).

Each of the four major groups had been further divided into two subgroups: a low success group, receiving 7 points more than their estimated score, and a high success group, receiving 14 points more than their estimated score. Table 3 also presents the values of t which result when the data are analyzed by these subgroups and when subgroups are recombined to test the second hypothesis of the study: that generalization will be significantly greater when the disparity between original estimated score and the "success score" received is larger. This hypothesis is con-

Table 3 *Significance of Mean Differences in Generalized Expectancy Changes*

COMPARISON BETWEEN GROUPS	df	t
HH and LL	85	1.04
LH and HL	78	.54
(HH+LL) and (LH+HL)	165	2.13*
Low HH and High HH	40	2.90**
Low LL and High LL	43	1.33
Low LH and High LH	38	.32
Low HL and High HL	38	.49
(Low HH+LL) and (High HH+LL)	85	11.39***
(Low LH+HL) and (High LH+HL)	78	.52
(Low HH+LL) and (Low LH+HL)	80	.59
(High HH+LL) and (High LH+HL)	83	3.68***

* p < .05
** p < .01
*** p < .001

firmed under conditions of need-relatedness ($t = 11.39$, $p < .001$). In the control groups amount of disparity between estimate and "score" does not make a significant difference in amount of generalization ($t = .52$). These results suggest not only that generalization of expectancies occur to a greater extent when behaviors are functionally related than when they are not, but also that degree of such generalization is systematically related to the size of the disparity between the expectancy and the actual event.

DISCUSSION

The findings of this study support the hypothesis that generalization of expectancies may be predicted along a dimension of functional or need relatedness, defined by the past history of similar reinforcements for two or more behaviors; they corroborate finds of earlier studies by Crandall (1951) and Jessor (1954). Certain aspects of the procedure used limit broad applications of the results, i.e., the use of verbal labels as a means of manipulating the degree of need-relatedness, the definition of needs in a cultural way rather than in terms of the individual S's history of rein-forcement, etc. The findings do suggest, however, that a better-controlled study of the dimension of need-relatedness among behaviors could be fruitful. For example, a study might be designed so that need-relatedness in varying degrees could be induced by a series of training trials for Ss before the test for generalization in change of expectancies.

The results of this study are also in accord with those of earlier investigations of generality of level of aspiration phenomena (Lewin, Dembo, Festinger, and Sears, 1944). Degree of positive correlation be-tween estimates made by the same S for different tasks varies with such conditions as whether tasks are administered in the same or in separate sessions (Frank, 1935a; Gould, 1939), the scale or units in which the performance scores are reported to subjects, the shape of the curve per-formance scores follow, and the degree of similarity of motivation of Ss toward the task (Heathers, 1942). In summary it might be said that level of aspiration is general or generalizes to the extent that the subject per-ceives the two tasks to be similar or two parts of a larger unit of behavior. The present study could be seen as investigating still a further parameter of the situation which affects generality of estimate, i.e., the application of verbal labels to the tasks. The study as interpreted within the social learning framework goes a step further by assuming that the effectiveness of verbal labels in producing generality is related to the individual's his-tory of reinforcement.

SUMMARY

The present study attempted to test two hypotheses regarding gen-eralization of expectancies derived from Rotter's social learning theory of personality. It was hypothesized that expectancies would generalize to a greater extent in situations where Ss saw two behaviors as leading to the same goal as contrasted with situations in which the two behaviors were seen as leading to different goals. A second hypothesis stated that generalization would be greater as the difference between the expected and obtained score was greater.

The design used was based on the level of aspiration paradigm. The special purpose of the study was to produce a situation in which the stimulus similarities between tasks could be held constant while the condition of functional relatedness could be varied. Two pseudo-projective techniques were used. Ss were 167 undergraduate students, divided into four groups who received varying structuring regarding what the "tests" were supposed to measure. Two groups were told that both tests measured the same thing; two, that the tests measured different things. Ss estimated their probable scores on both tests before taking either. One test was administered and Ss received "scores" based upon addition of either 7 or 14 points to their stated expectancy for that test. They re-estimated their probable score for the second test before taking it. The measure of generalization used was the difference between the first and second estimate for the second test.

Both experimental hypotheses were confirmed. It was concluded that similarity of reinforcement or goal is a significant dimension mediating generalization of expectancies from one situation to another. Extent of generalization was also related to the size of the disparity between the initial expectancy statement and the "score" obtained.

2-2 | Influences upon Expectancy During Delay[1]

J. CONRAD SCHWARZ

The purpose of the study was to identify variables which are predictive of individual differences in changes in the expectancy (E)
for reinforcement during a long delay in a sequence of reinforced
trials. A motor skill task was used to deliver predetermined sequences of success and failure. Groups of male college students
received one of the 4 combinations of 2 orders of success and 2
durations of delay. Before every trial a verbal statement of E for
success was elicited. Two hypotheses were tested: that a long
delay results in a shift of E (a) in the direction of E's held earlier
in the same situation, and (b) in the direction of E's generalized
from other related situations. The results supported both hypotheses.

Several studies (Phares, 1961, 1964; Humphrey, Miller, and Ellson, 1940)
have shown that delay in a reinforcement sequence significantly alters
the course of expectancy change from that which occurs with the same
sequence having no delay. The purpose of this study was to identify the
variables which are predictive of individual differences in changes in the
expectancy for reinforcement during a long delay in a sequence of reinforced trials.

The theoretical framework of this investigation is Rotter's (1954)
Social Learning Theory. There, expectancy is defined as the subjectively
held probability that a given reinforcing event will occur in a specific
situation contingent upon a particular behavior. Rotter considers expectancy (E) to be a function of two conceptually separate types of experience:
the reinforcements previously experienced in the same situation; and the
reinforcements which were experienced in other situations for functionally
related behaviors. The first type of experience produces a situationally
specific expectancy designated as E', and the second, an expectancy
referred to as *generalized expectancy* (GE). While GE is the sole determiner of the E in a novel situation, with each successive behavior-

[1] This article is based on a dissertation submitted in 1963 to the Graduate School
of The Ohio State University in partial fulfillment of the requirements for the degree
of Doctor of Philosophy. The project was supervised by Julian B. Rotter, now at the
University of Connecticut. His assistance is gratefully acknowledged. Sincere appreciation is also extended to E. Jerry Phares, Kansas State University, for his interest and
encouragement in the early phases of the study. Donald Mosher, Ohio State University,
Pietro Badia, Bowling Green State University, and Sanford Dean, Syracuse University,
made helpful suggestions concerning the preparation of this manuscript.

From *Journal of Experimental Research in Personality*, 1966, 1, 211–220. Copyright
1966 by Academic Press, Inc., and reprinted by permission of the author and the
publisher.

reinforcement pairing in the situation, E is determined more and more by E' until E' eventually becomes the major determiner of E in what has now become a familiar situation. Empirical support for these formulations is found in studies by Castaneda (1952), Dean (1953), and Good (1952).

Three studies by Phares (1961, 1964a) all led to the conclusion that the interposition of a 24-hour delay in a series of otherwise massed trials, consisting of a mixture of successes and failures, resulted in a decrease in the expectancy for reinforcement (i.e., success) subsequent to the delay. An additional nonfeedback warmup trial after delay did not attenuate the lowering effects of the delay. The tasks employed by Phares have been diverse: a symbol substitution task, Porteus mazes, and a very life-like social interaction task. Humphreys et al. (1940) found that the introduction of a delay in a series of massed trials produced an increase in the expectancy for reinforcement. They presented Ss with 24 "acquisition" trials in which a red light invariably followed a green light, and, in the continuing massed series, presented 24 "extinction" trials. Following a 4-minute post-extinction interval there was a 70 percent increase in the proportion of the Ss who again expected the red light to follow the green.

In Phares' studies the order of successes and failures produced low initial expectancies for reinforcement followed by an increase in expectancy prior to delay. In the study by Humphreys et al. the change in expectancy prior to delay was in the reverse direction: "acquisition" produced high initial expectancies for reinforcement (red light) followed by declining expectancies during "extinction" prior to delay. These data are consonant with the existence of an inverse relationship between the direction of expectancy change during a long delay and the predelay direction of expectancy change.

The findings above can be accounted for by assuming that the length of the interval between trials affects the strength of the influence of recent trials upon the E for the next trial. When trials are closely spaced the most recent trials strongly affect the current E; whereas, with a long delay between trials, earlier experience within the situation has relatively greater weight in determining E. It will be recalled that experience in the situation affects E through its affect on E'. Therefore, it is hypothesized, if the reinforcement sequence is such that the E' produced early in the sequence is divergent from the E' following later experience and trials have been closely spaced, the subsequent introduction of a long delay will cause a displacement of the post delay measurement of E in the direction of the earlier E'. The same reinforcement series preceding a short delay, in place of the long delay, will have an effect upon E which is consistent with the previous effects of similarly reinforced trials, i.e., produce no unusual change in the post-delay measurement of E.

Alternatively, Phares (1964a) reasoned that a long delay gave the S an opportunity to ruminate about a variety of experiences in other situations bearing some relation to the experimental task, and it was these ruminations which tended to lower E from the high predelay levels created by the reinforcement sequences employed in his studies. Put in the concepts of social learning theory, it is experience in other situations related to the experimental situation which creates the GE for the experimental situation. Consistent with Phares' explanation a second hypothesis may be stated in terms of general applicability: Generalized expectancy, which has a declining influence on E over a series of massed trials, will have an increased influence upon measurements of E obtained after an interpolated long delay. This influence will be reflected in a displacement of the post-delay measure of E in the direction of the original measure of GE, providing that the predelay E is in fact divergent from the original GE. The interpolation of a short delay (30 seconds) will be insufficient to renew the influence of GE upon E.

METHOD

Subjects

The Ss were 136 male college students enrolled in two lower level psychology courses at Ohio State University.

Apparatus

The behavioral task employed was the Vertical Aspiration Board (VAB), a task used previously in a study of changes in expectancy (See Rotter, Liverant, and Crowne, 1961, p. 165, for a photograph and description). Briefly the apparatus consists of a platform which is raised vertically along a graduated scale by pulling a cord. A steel ball is placed upon the platform, and the S is instructed to raise the platform slowly as high as possible before the ball rolls off. The ball is held on the platform by an electromagnet which can be switched on and off without the S's knowledge by a silent knee switch situated beneath the table top. By appropriately deactivating the magnet any score can be delivered to the S and yet be perceived to be the result of S's own effort.

Measurements

Immediately before each trial a statement of the S's expectancy for success was obtained using an eleven-point scale. Generalized expectancy for success on the VAB was measured by the S's first stated expectancy for success preceding the first trial on the novel task.

Procedure

Each of four groups experienced one of the combinations of two conditions of delay and two conditions of reinforcement. Whether a S volunteered for a one- or two-credit experiment determined his inclusion in either the short-delay or the long-delay groups. Within delay conditions Ss were assigned randomly to the two reinforcement conditions. Complete data were obtained for 25 and 22 Ss in the two short-delay groups and for 43 and 46 Ss in the two long-delay groups.

The initial part of the experiment was identical for Ss in all four groups. Subjects appeared individually for the experiment. The mechanics of the VAB were explained in terms which would lead Ss to believe that achievement depended entirely upon their skill at raising the platform smoothly. The task was characterized as being "rather difficult," and the total score was said to be predictive of ultimate proficiency in sports and muscular skills.

The following paragraph of instruction includes the only sentence which was different from any of the groups. For the short-delay groups it read as follows: "Since subjects do fluctuate from trial to trial in the scores they achieve, you will be given a series of 20 trials. All of the trials will be combined to get your overall score." For long-delay Ss, after the phrase ". . . a series of 20 trials," the following phrases were added: "eight today, eight tomorrow, and four on the following day."

Before obtaining the first E statement Ss were told that, since the average student usually achieved scores of 60 or 70, reaching the 80 mark or above on the VAB constituted a "successful" trial. Instructions like those of Phares (1961) were used to elicit the statements of E for success on each upcoming trial. In general, they described the use of the eleven-point expectancy scale and cautioned the S to be realistic in his choice of E statements.

Reinforcement Conditions Subjects randomly assigned to the two reinforcement conditions received the same total number, but different orders, of successes and failures (cf. Fig. 1, plus indicates success, minus indicates failure.) Each condition consisted of two blocks of eight trials, one beginning with success and ending with failure, the other beginning with failure and ending with success. Sequence A had the failure-success block in the first position and the success-failure

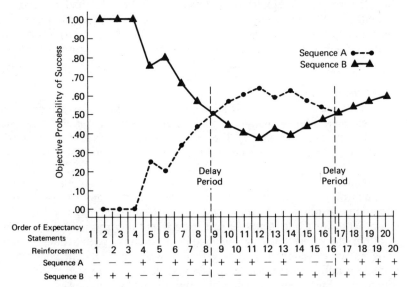

FIGURE 1. The objective probability of success at the time of each expectancy statement under two orders of reinforcement.

block in the second position. The order was reversed for Sequence B. Each block of eight trials contained the same scores, four of which were below the success level. The experimental task was concluded with four successes for each *S*. Figure 1 shows the curves of objective probabilities of success for the two reinforcement sequences employed.

Delay Conditions After the eighth and sixteenth trials, the long-delay groups experienced a 24-hour intermission. At the same points in the sequence the short-delay groups had a 30-second rest period, during which they remained standing before the apparatus. This rest period was introduced to mitigate the possible effects of fatigue upon expectancy for success in the short-delay groups.

After returning from each 24-hour delay period, the long delay *Ss* were given a nonfeedback warm-up. Each was asked to raise the platform without the ball up to the 100 mark. The warm-up was given to reduce any systematic lowering of expectancy which might result from a cold feeling or the absence of the muscle tone previously established by the activity. The expectancy statement was elicited after the warm-up and before the first reinforced trial after the intermission.

RESULTS

The mean E levels for long- and short-delay groups under reinforcement sequences A and B are plotted by trials in Fig. 2. It can be seen that both reinforcement sequences were effective in producing sequences of E which were characterized by a substantial difference between the E level held prior to the delay and that held earlier within the same block of eight trials. This condition was a prerequisite for testing the first hypothesis. Only when a difference exists between the magnitude of early and later E' levels would a change in their relative influences upon E be reflected in an alteration of the E level from pre- to post-delay

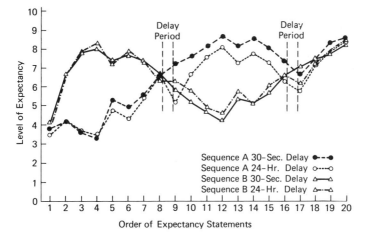

FIGURE 2. Mean levels of expectancy for short-delay (30 seconds) and long-delay (24 hours) groups under two orders of reinforcement.

measurement in the direction of earlier E' levels. Massed E statements after the first two or three trials are assumed to reflect primarily E', with the effects of GE now largely dissipated.

Experience within the Situation

From the first general hypothesis it is predicted that the long delay (relative to the short delay) will have a greater elevating effect upon E for success following a massed series of trials with reinforcements in the order of initial success–later failure, and that the longer delay will have a greater lowering effect following a series of trials with reinforcements in the order of initial failure–later success. A simple test of the difference between pre- and post-delay E levels is not adequate, since this difference reflects the effects of the trial which followed the last E statement before delay as well as the effects of delay itself. The relative effects of a short versus a long delay were tested by a comparison between delay conditions of the differences between pre- and postdelay E scores under identical conditions of reinforcement. Two *Delay Difference* scores were computed for each S: DD_1, the difference between E_8 and E_9, and DD_2, the difference between E_{16} and E_{17}. The means and standard deviations of DD scores for all groups are presented in Table 1.

Table 1 Means and Standard Deviations of Delay Difference Scores and Comparisons of the Delay Difference Scores between Short- and Long-Delay Groups

Sequence and position of Delay	N	M	SD	Variance Ratio F	Mann-Whitney U	z
Sequence A, DD_1 (Failure-success)						
Short Delay	25	+.56	.80	3.48***	119	5.47****
Long Delay	43	−1.53	1.50			
Sequence B, DD_2 (Failure-success)						
Short Delay	22	+.50	.72	3.47***	256.5	3.33****
Long Delay	46	−.48	1.35			
Sequence B, DD_1 (Success-failure)						
Short Delay	22	−.91	1.00	2.70**	353	2.01*
Long Delay	46	+.02	1.64			
Sequence A, DD_2 (Success-failure)						
Short Delay	25	−.76	.99	3.14***	478	.79
Long Delay	43	−.53	1.76			

   * P .05.
  ** P .02.
 *** P .002.
**** P .001.

A marked difference in the variance of DD scores was observed between the short-delay and the long-delay groups. Variance ratios for comparable DD scores of the two delay conditions are presented in Table 1 together with their associated p values for a two-tailed test. In each case, the variance of the long-delay group is significantly greater than that of the comparable short-delay group. Thus, long delay is different from short-delay in that it has more varied effects upon Ss within the same reinforcement condition.

To test for differences between the short- and long-delay groups in the magnitude of DD scores, the Mann-Whitney U-test was applied. All of the differences were in the predicted direction and three of the four were significant beyond the .05 level (see Table 1). Following a failure-success sequence, the relative effect of the longer delay was a net decrease in expectancy of -2.09 points at the first delay and of $-.98$ points at the second delay. Following a success-failure sequence, the relative effect of the longer delay was a net increase in expectancy of $+.93$ at the first delay and of $+.23$ at the second delay. The negative effects of a long delay following a failure-success sequence and the positive effects of a long delay following a success-failure sequence are indicative of an increased influence of late E' and/or a decreased influence of late E' upon E following long delay, thus supporting the first general hypothesis.

It follows from the first hypothesis that even within the same objective conditions of reinforcement, the greater the rise in an individual's E' from its earlier level to the predelay level, the greater will be the drop in E after a long delay, as a result of the change during delay in the proportionate influence of earlier and later E' upon post-delay E. To test this proposition two recent change (RC) scores were derived for each S. They reflected the magnitude of the change in E from the level reported after the first three trials of each eight-trial block to the level reported just prior to delay. Thus RC_1 was obtained by subtracting E_4 from E_8, and RC_2 by subtracting E_{12} from E_{16}.

For each block of eight trials RC scores were correlated with the respective DD scores. The latter reflected the magnitude of E change resulting from delay. Table 2 presents the means and standard deviations of RC scores and the product-moment correlation coefficients between RC_1 and DD_1 and between RC_2 and DD_2 for short- and long-delay groups under each reinforcement condition. All p values are for a two-tailed test of the significance of the difference of the coefficient from zero. For the short delay groups, in no case was the correlation between RC and DD statistically significant. In every case for the long delay groups the correlation between RC and DD was significant beyond the .01 level. Each of the correlations for the long delay groups was negative as predicted, thus supporting the first hypothesis.

Generalized Expectancy

The second general hypothesis states that GE will have a renewed influence as a determinant of E following a long delay which is preceded by a series of massed trials. It is assumed that GE, the pre-experimental expectancy, is reflected by E_1 which was obtained prior to the first trial.

Table 2   Means and Standard Deviations of Recent Change Scores and Correlations between Recent Change and Delay Difference Scores

Group	N	RC_1 M	SD	RC_2 M	SD	RC_1 AND DD_1 r	RC_2 AND DD_2 r
Short Delay							
Seq. A	25	+3.28	1.61	−1.28	1.71	.00	−.13
Seq. B	22	−1.27	1.21	+2.41	1.30	−.06	+.17
Long Delay							
Seq. A	43	+3.21	1.64	−1.75	1.62	−.46*	−.64**
Seq. B	46	−1.98	1.54	+2.09	1.53	−.39*	−.60**

* P .01.
** P .001.

Subsequent E statements are increasingly influenced by the outcome of experimental trials and relatively less by the original GE. But if, as predicted, a long delay produces a renewed influence of GE upon E, the greater the disparity between the original GE level (measured by E_1) and the level of the predelay E (E_8 or E_{16}), the stronger should be the tendency of the current E (E_9 or E_{17}) to be displaced in the direction of E_1 following a long delay.

To test this hypothesis the DD scores were again used as a measure of the change in E during delay. The disparities between E_1 and the predelay levels, E_8 and E_{16} of each S are referred to as the *Distant Change* scores (DC_1 and DC_2, respectively). Negative correlations were predicted between DC scores and DD scores for long-delay groups and no correlation for short-delay groups.

Table 3 presents the mean and standard deviation of DC scores and the product-moment correlation between DC and DD scores for all groups at each delay. In every case for the long-delay groups the correlation was negative and significant beyond the .01 level. For the short-delay groups in no case was the correlation significant, and in two instances the relationship was positive rather than negative. These results support the second general hypothesis.

Multivariate Prediction of Delay Change

Since the magnitude of E change resulting from recent experience (RC) as well as that representing a deviation from the initial GE (DC) were both found to be related to E change during a long delay, as measured by delay difference (DD) scores, the question arose as to whether each made an independent contribution to the prediction of DD scores. First order partial correlation coefficients were computed for recent change (RC) and DD scores, with distant change (DC) held constant, and

Table 3   Means and Standard Deviations of Distant Change Scores and Correlations between Distant Change and Delay Difference Scores

Group	N	DC_1 M	DC_1 SD	DC_2 M	DC_2 SD	DC_1 AND DD_1 r	DC_2 AND DD_2 r
Short Delay							
Seq. A	25	2.80	1.86	3.64	2.59	+.24	−.31
Seq. B	22	2.55	2.17	2.45	1.72	−.22	+.07
Long Delay							
Seq. A	43	3.23	2.24	2.84	2.35	−.59***	−.51***
Seq. B	46	2.39	2.08	2.78	1.97	−.44**	−.34*

* .02.
** .01.
*** .001.

for DC and DD with RC held constant. These computations were repeated for the sets of scores pertaining to the first and second delay of both Long-Delay Groups A and B (See Table 4).

When a long delay followed a success-failure sequence, both recent change and distant change related independently of one another to delay difference scores. This suggests that both earlier E levels within the situation and GE are factors which influence E during delay. The results were less consistent for the situation in which delay followed a failure-success sequence. Expectancy changes during the first delay (DD_1) following a failure-success sequence were related to distant change, independently of recent change, but recent change scores were not related to DD_1 scores independently of distant change scores. The situation was exactly reversed for the second delay following a failure-success sequence. There, it was recent change which was related independently of distant change to E change during delay, while distant change had no independent relationship to DD_2 scores. It cannot be concluded from these findings that early E levels and GE did not both influence E change during delay after a failure-success sequence. It may simply be that their influences were congruent.

The height of the predelay Es (E_8 and E_{16}) were found to be negatively correlated with E change during a long delay and positively correlated with recent change and distant change. Since the height of predelay E is dependent upon all preceding E changes, the observed relationship of predelay E to DD scores may have reflected simply the influence of these preceding E changes. But there was also the possibility that the height of the E just prior to delay had some influence, in its own right, upon the changes that occurred during the delay. For this reason, second order partial correlations were computed between predelay E and DD scores with RC and DC scores held constant. These coefficients are also presented in Table 4. None of the second order partial correlations between predelay E and DD scores were significant at the .05 level, which permits the conclusion that predelay E level alone cannot account for E changes during a long delay.

Multiple correlation coefficients were computed using RC and DC as predictors of the dependent variable, DD. The additional variance in DD scores which was accounted for by the simultaneous consideration of RC and DC was not appreciably greater than that which could be accounted for by considering DC alone, in the case of the first delay, and RC alone, in the case of the second delay. Neither did the addition of a third predictor variable, the predelay E, yield a multiple correlation coefficient which was appreciably larger than the simple correlation of either RC or DC with DD (see Table 4).

DISCUSSION

The results of this study show that a delay of 24 hrs. may have positive or negative effects upon expectancies, depending upon the preceding pattern of reinforcements and, perhaps more directly, upon the individual's idiosyncratic pattern of previous expectancy change. The inverse relationship between expectancy change prior to delay and the change during delay suggests that earlier expectancies specific to the situation have, as a consequence of the long delay, a relative increase in their importance as determiners of the current expectancy. Thus the person whose current expectancy was markedly altered by the immediately preceding trials moved his expectancy in the direction of former E' levels following a long delay. This study together with the studies by Humphreys *et al.* (1940) and Phares (1964a) constitute a significant group of findings, all indicating an inverse relationship between pre-delay pattern of expectancy change and expectancy change during delay, i.e., a tendency of expectancies to move, during delay, toward former levels. A study by Phares (1964b) published after the completion of this investigation further corroborates this conclusion, since there, also, expectancies were found to increase or decrease following delay in an inverse relation to the pre-delay pattern of expectancy change.

Knowledge of the external reinforcement pattern experienced by an individual is less predictive of his expectancy change during delay than knowledge of the pattern of change in his stated expectancies. Since the individual course of predelay expectancy change is influenced by variables unique to each S in addition to external reinforcements,. the experimenter must assess these individual variables prior to the experiment in order to achieve a precise advance prediction of delay change. The problem of identifying those people who exhibit unusual reactions to reinforcement sequences has been dealt with in studies by V. C. Crandall (1961), Rotter (1945), and Rychlak and Eaker (1962), but has no definitive solution at this time.

Generalized expectancy, as measured by E_1, apparently exerted an

Table 4 *Product-Moment, Partial, and Multiple Correlations Using Recent Change, Distant Change, and Predelay Expectancy Scores as Predictors of Delay Difference Scores*

Group and Position of Delay	Product Moment Correlation	First Order Partial Correlation	Second Order Partial Correlation	Multiple Correlation
Long Delay A 1st Delay Failure-success N = 43	$r_{01} = -.46^{**}$ $r_{02} = -.59^{**}$ $r_{03} = -.56^{**}$	$r_{01.2} = -.08$ $r_{02.1} = -.43^{**}$	$r_{01.23} = .00$ $r_{02.13} = -.30$ $r_{03.12} = -.22$	$R_{0.12} = .60^{**}$ $R_{0.123} = .62^{**}$
Long Delay B 1st Delay Success-failure N = 46	$r_{01} = -.39^{**}$ $r_{02} = -.44^{**}$ $r_{03} = -.42^{**}$	$r_{01.2} = -.29$ $r_{02.1} = -.36^*$	$r_{01.23} = -.20$ $r_{02.13} = -.30^*$ $r_{03.12} = -.03$	$R_{0.12} = .51^{**}$ $R_{0.123} = .51^{**}$
Long Delay A 2nd Delay Success-failure N = 43	$r_{01} = -.64^{**}$ $r_{02} = -.51^{**}$ $r_{03} = -.53^{**}$	$r_{01.2} = -.55^{**}$ $r_{02.1} = -.36^*$	$r_{01.23} = -.50^{**}$ $r_{02.13} = -.28$ $r_{03.12} = -.02$	$R_{0.12} = .69^{**}$ $R_{0.123} = .69^{**}$
Long Delay B 2nd Delay Failure-success N = 46	$r_{01} = -.60^{**}$ $r_{01} = -.34^*$ $r_{03} = -.38^{**}$	$r_{01.2} = .54^{**}$ $r_{02.1} = -.13$	$r_{01.23} = -.54^{**}$ $r_{02.13} = -.04$ $r_{03.12} = -.28$	$R_{0.12} = .61^{**}$ $R_{0.123} = .65^{**}$

Note. Variable 0 = Delay Difference Score. Variable 1 = Recent Change Score. Variable 2 = Distant Change Score. Variable 3 = Predelay E Score.
  * p .05.
  ** p .01.

influence upon expectancies during the 24-hour delay which tended to pull them in the direction of the original GE level. This finding supports the second general hypothesis. It may be noted that the absolute value of a S's initial expectancy reflects not only his expectancy as generalized from other related situations, but also notions communicated by the experimenter concerning the relative difficulty of the task. Thus, the relationship observed here between the net change from E_1 and the change in expectancy during delay may be construed as a renewed awareness of task-related communications following a delay rather than, or in addition to, a renewed influence of GE.

Joint Influence of GE and Earlier Expectancy Level

Neither the influence of GE nor that of prior specific expectancy level could be measured directly, since they act simultaneously upon expectancy during a delay. However, the analysis by means of partial correlations supports the contention that each of these variables has an independent influence upon expectancy during a 24-hour delay. Following a success-failure sequence, therefore, one might find a S with a low initial expectancy actually exhibiting a rise in expectancy during delay, simply because the positive influence associated with success expectancies held early in the sequence was stronger than the negative influence associated with the initial expectancy level. Herein may lie the explanation for the failure to find a significant difference between the magnitude of the second delay difference (DD_2) scores for short- and long-delay groups following the success-failure sequence despite the difference in variance between the two groups.

There is a gross similarity between the changes in expectancy which were observed to occur during a long delay that followed a pattern of declining expectancies and what has been labeled "spontaneous recovery" in classical and instrumental conditioning. Humphreys et al. made this observation in 1940. The current explanations of spontaneous recovery (Kimble, 1961, p. 284) do not serve well as explanations of the expectancy changes observed following 24-hour delay in this study; however, the hypotheses of this study and the behavior prediction model of Social Learning Theory (Rotter, 1954) could account for the phenomenon of spontaneous recovery in instrumental conditioning.

The findings of this study may have important implications for sequences of experience in which all trials are widely spaced. Using a sequence of reinforcement which yielded an increasingly objective probability of success, Phares (1961) observed expectancies to rise more slowly when each pair of trials was separated by a 24-hour delay than when trials were massed. Would there be a difference in expectancy change between spaced and massed conditions of experience if the reinforcement sequence yielded a decreasing objective probability of success? In the present study a long delay following a massed success-failure sequence tended to elevate expectancies, moving them in the direction of earlier levels contrary to the most recent reinforcement. Extrapolating, a condition of frequent long delay, i.e., a spaced condition, would probably produce a slower rate of expectancy decline than a massed condition under a reinforcement sequence yielding a decreasing objective probability of success. If this latter hypothesis were supported, one would have the basis for a broad generalization; namely, that expectancy change, either positive or negative, proceeds more slowly under conditions of spaced than of massed experience.

The very factors in this study which have been shown to influence expectancy change during delay, may alternatively be conceived of as factors making for consistency and stability in the personality. During a long delay these factors appear to nullify to some extent the effects of recent experience.

2-3 Effects of Expectancy on Working and Waiting for Larger Rewards[1]

WALTER MISCHEL and ERVIN STAUB

This study investigated the effects of situational and generalized expectancies for success on choices of immediate, less valuable, noncontingent rewards as opposed to more valuable contingent rewards. Measures of generalized expectancy for success were administered to 8th-grade boys who later worked on a series of problems and obtained either success, failure, or no information for performance. Thereafter, each S chose between less valuable, noncontingent rewards and more valuable rewards whose attainment was contingent on successful solutions of problems varying in their similarity-dissimilarity to the original problems and/or an additional delay period. As predicted, contingent rewards were chosen more after success than failure and Ss discriminated between specific contingencies. The effects of situational success and failure tended to minimize the effects of generalized expectancies. Moreover, in the no-information condition children with high generalized

[1] This study was supported by Research Grant M-06830 from the National Institutes of Health, United States Public Health Service. Grateful acknowledgement is made to the administrative officials and teachers of the Palo Alto Unified School System who cooperated in this study.

From *Journal of Personality and Social Psychology*, 1965, 5, 625–633. Copyright by the American Psychological Association and reprinted by permission of the authors and the publisher.

expectancies for success chose more contingent rewards than those with low expectancies and behaved like subjects in the success condition. Children with low generalized expectancies who received no information about their performance behaved like those with similarly low generalized expectancies who had obtained failure. Following failure, generalized expectancies for success affected willingness to wait for larger rewards even when their attainment was independent of performance.

Although there has been extensive speculation about the antecedents of delay of gratification (e.g., Freud, 1959), and widespread recognition of the importance of this aspect of self-control, experimental investigations in this area have been relatively scarce (e.g., Block & Martin, 1955; Livson & Mussen, 1957; Mahrer, 1956). This study is part of a program investigating the antecedents of choices in which immediate gratification is deferred for the sake of larger, more valued but nonimmediate outcomes. The paradigm confronts subjects with choices between immediately available, less valued rewards and delayed, more valued rewards. The antecedents and correlates of such choices were found to be associated with other indices traditionally subsumed under the "ego-strength" construct (e.g., Mischel, 1961a, 1961b, 1961c; Mischel & Gilligan, 1964). The task now is to further isolate the variables governing this behavior.

The conceptualization of this choice behavior is based on a social learning theory (especially Rotter, 1954) in which each choice is a function of the expectancy that it will lead to particular reinforcement in a given situation and of the value of the reinforcement. The expectancy that the delayed reward will be forthcoming is a main determinant of the choice to defer immediate gratification for the sake of a larger delayed reward. Support for this comes from studies by Mahrer (1956) and by H. Mischel (1963), which showed that performances for delayed rewards are affected by the individual's experimentally manipulated promise-keeping history, and the length of the delay interval (Mischel & Metzner, 1962).

Previous work studied choice conflicts between smaller, immediately available rewards as opposed to larger rewards which could not be attained without a delay period, but in most life situations the contingencies for attaining larger rewards involve more than simple waiting. The present investigation deals with contingent choices when the smaller reward is immediately available but the larger reward is contingent on instrumental activity, both with and without additional delay. It was reasoned that when attainment of the more valuable reward is contingent on satisfactory performance on a task, the individual's expectancy for success will be a main determinant of his choice. Moreover, when attainment of the more valuable reward is contingent on both successful performance and an additional delay period, the individual's expectancy for success, as well as his expectancy that the reward will be obtained in spite of the delay period, both enter as choice determinants.

Consider the components of expectancy itself. According to social learning theory, expectancy is a function of specific situational expectancies and of generalized expectancies prior to the specific situation, based on the individual's previous reinforcement history in similar situations (Rotter, 1954). Most studies on the generalization of expectancies conducted within social learning theory focus on how verbal expectancy *statements* are affected by success and failure on related tasks (e.g., Jessor, 1954; Mischel, 1958a).[2] The present experiment examined the interaction of generalized and situational expectancies and their effects on subsequent choice behavior.

A measure of generalized expectancy for success was administered to eighth-grade boys. Three weeks later, these subjects worked on problems and obtained one of three kinds of information about their performance. In one treatment subjects obtained success, in a second failure, and in a third no information. Following this, the children chose between less valuable, noncontingent, immediately available rewards and more valuable but contingent rewards. There were five variations in the contingencies for the more valuable rewards and each subject chose under all variations. Namely, the contingency was: (*a*) successful performance on a task similar to one of the treatment tasks, (*b*) same as *a* but with an additional delay period, (*c*) successful performance on a task dissimilar to one of the treatment tasks, (*d*) same as *c* but with an additional delay period, (*e*) only a delay period.

It was anticipated that subjects would discriminate between choice conditions as a function of the particular contingencies on which reward attainment depends. Contingent rewards should be chosen most when the probability for attaining them is greatest. Therefore, when the contingency for attaining more valuable rewards includes successful performance (work) as well as a delay period, they will be chosen less than when there is only one contingency (either working or waiting).

Second, rewards contingent on success on a task similar to one on which the person previously succeeded will be chosen more frequently than those requiring success on a task similar to one on which he previously failed.

This study also explored the extent to which obtained success and failure on tasks affect choice preferences when attainment of the larger reward is contingent on success on tasks dissimilar to the treatment tasks and when it is *not* contingent on the subject's own performance. The extent of such generalization is an empirical question, and no directional hypotheses were formulated. The question here was: does success or failure on tasks affect, or generalize to, choice preferences for larger rewards dependent on contingencies dissimilar to those on which success or failure was obtained, and on contingencies independent of the individual's own performance (i.e., delay only)? Further, if such generalization effects occur, are they related to generalized expectancies?

Finally, it was reasoned that when situational expectancies are minimal

---

[2] There have been important exceptions (e.g., Feather, 1959b, 1961) but these were conducted in a motive-expectancy-value model (e.g., Feather, 1963b) and not in social learning theory.

the effects of generalized expectancies will be strong and the converse. Thus, when the person succeeds or fails on tasks similar to those involved in the contingency for attaining the more valuable reward, specific situational expectancy is large and generalized expectancy should have little effect on choice. However, in the absence of information directly relevant to the contingencies on which the more valued reward depends, generalized expectancies for success should affect choices, with more contingent large rewards chosen by subjects with high generalized expectancies for success.

METHOD

Subjects
The data came from 89 eighth-grade boys from the physical education class of a public school in the Palo Alto, California, area.

Overall Procedure
A measure of generalized expectancies for success was administered to all subjects. Three weeks later these subjects worked on problems and obtained either success, failure, or no information. After these treatments, the children chose between immediately available, noncontingent smaller rewards or contingent larger rewards, with five kinds of requirements for attaining the larger reward.

Measurement of Generalized Expectancies for Success
This assessment was conducted in large groups in two consecutive hours by the same male experimenter. The subjects were told that a series of problems had been administered to many junior high school students. They were asked to estimate, as accurately as possible, by writing the appropriate numbers: "how many students at your grade level out of one hundred in your school" and "how many students at your grade level out of one hundred all over the country" would "have better results than you" on two different problems, described as requiring, respectively, "verbal reasoning" and "general information."

Assignment to Treatments and Design
Assignment of subjects to treatment groups was independent of generalized expectancy scores. To avoid possible differences between classrooms, all subjects were drawn by prior arrangement from a large physical education class divided randomly into six subgroups, with 13–25 children in each. The experimental procedures were administered to each subgroup in small classrooms in random sequence. Two subgroups received no information and within four subgroups half the subjects received the failure and half the success manipulations, with an odd-even seating procedure used to select which subjects obtained failure and which success. An approximately equal number of subjects were exposed to each treatment.

Note that the six subgroups served only as testing units and do not correspond with the cells of the design. After completion of all experimental procedures (described below), but before scoring the dependent data, subjects in each treatment were subdivided into those with high and low generalized expectancies. The four expectancy statements obtained from each subject were summed and the mean for each subject was computed. The median of this distribution of mean expectancy scores was 79.5 and subjects were dichotomized into those with "high" as opposed to "low" generalized expectancies on the basis of their position above or below the median. This provided the six groups of the design shown in Table 1: success, failure, and no information with high and low generalized expectancy groups in each treatment, and a range of 13–17 subjects in each group. To equalize the number of subjects in each group, 11 subjects were randomly eliminated, reducing each cell to the size of the smallest ($N = 13$ per cell). The total mean for all subjects with "high" generalized expectancies for success was 88.46 ($N = 39$) and for those with "low" generalized expectancies it was 45.21 ($N = 39$). The adequacy of the sampling procedures was supported by the fact that the mean generalized expectancy scores of subjects classified as high did not differ significantly between treatments. Likewise, the mean generalized expectancy scores of subjects classified as low were not significantly different between treatments. The overall design thus contained five sets of dependent measures (described below) for six groups.

Experimental Treatments

The experimental session was conducted by a new male experimenter described as coming from a different university and working on another project, so as to minimize the connection with the first session. All subjects were told that they would be tested on several abilities in order to compare their performance with other boys at their grade level. They were urged to do as well as possible and given four sets of problems. Three problems were adaptations from the Digit Span, Similarities, and Coding subtests of the Wechsler Intelligence Scale for Children. The fourth was called a "Verbal Reasoning" test and consisted of groups of words which had to be rearranged to relate meaningfully to neighboring words.

Subjects in the no-information condition were given only the above instructions and then performed the tasks without obtaining information about their performance. Subjects in the success or failure groups received false results after their performance on each problem.

In order to make the manipulated scores seem more plausible, subjects were told that sometimes boys who usually do well in many school subjects do not do as well on these tests and similarly that boys who may not be doing so well on some of their school work may perform well on these special ability tests. To increase the ambiguity of the scoring procedure and the plausibility of the false information, the time allowed for each test was too short to permit completion.

At the completion of each problem, worksheets were collected and in the success and failure groups the "score" was returned to the subject on a slip of paper with a letter grade and a percentile score. In the success group children received a "B" on the first problem and an "A" on each of the remaining three, with percentile scores ranging from 80 on the first problem to 90 on the last. The percentiles indicated their standing relative to other students at their grade level. In the failure group, subjects received a "D" on the first problem and an "F" on each of the remaining three problems with percentile scores indicating that their performance was below 80–90% of the students at their grade level. Communication about grades was not permitted.

Dependent Measures

After completing the problems, subjects in all groups were told that the experimenter wanted to

> find out how children and adults of different ages choose when they are offered choices between different objects. This does not have anything to do with abilities, but please consider carefully each choice you make so that you will really choose what you prefer.

All subjects were given a series of 25 choices, each between an immediately obtainable smaller or less valuable reward as opposed to a larger or more valuable reward. The more valued rewards could be obtained only under one of five conditions (Table 1). There were five choices in each condition and each subject chose under all conditions.

In four conditions attainment of the larger reward was contingent upon successful performance on a task. In two of these the task was described with the same general label as one of the tasks (verbal reasoning) on which success, failure, or no information had been obtained earlier. These are the *"contingent similar"* conditions (1 and 2 in Table 1), and in one of them (2) attainment of the larger reward was also dependent upon a waiting period ("contingent similar delay" condition). In the next two conditions the larger reward was contingent upon successful performance on a task described with a new label (general information) that had not been included in the series on which subjects had performed earlier. These are the *"contingent dissimilar"* conditions (3 and 4 in Table 1). Again, in one of these (4) the larger reward was also dependent upon a waiting period. Thus in Conditions 1–4 attainment of larger rewards was contingent upon successful performance on tasks similar and dissimilar to the initial tasks, with and without an additional delay period. In the fifth condition, the more valuable reward was not contingent upon any task performance and depended only on willingness to wait ("noncontingent delay"). The same set of five choice pairs was used in each of these five conditions, resulting in a total of 25 choices.

In each of the five conditions, subjects were presented with the following five objects as smaller, immediate rewards: $1.00; two *Mad* magazines; small bag of peanuts; one hit tune record; plastic checker set. These were paired, respectively, against the following five corresponding larger rewards: $1.50; three *Mad* magazines; large can of

Table 1 Experimental Design and Mean Choices of Large Rewards by All Groups in All Choice Conditions

TREATMENT AND GENERAL EXPECTANCY	CHOICE CONDITIONS (CONTINGENCIES)				
	LARGE REWARDS CONTINGENT ON TASK				LARGE REWARDS NONCONTINGENT ON TASK
	Similar to A		Dissimilar to A		
	Without delay (1)	Plus delay (2)	Without delay (3)	Plus delay (4)	Delay only (5)
Success on A					
High	3.39	2.69	2.92	2.92	4.08
Low	3.27	3.00	3.69	2.92	3.38
Failure on A					
High	2.31	1.54	3.00	3.08	4.08
Low	2.08	1.38	2.77	2.23	2.46
No information on A					
High	3.77	2.85	3.54	2.85	3.54
Low	2.08	1.54	2.15	2.15	3.23

Note. "A" refers to treatment tasks.

mixed nuts; three hit tune records; wooden checker set. The delay conditions always involved a delay of 3 weeks before the larger reward could be obtained. For example, the contingent similar delay condition refers to solving a problem requiring verbal reasoning plus waiting 3 weeks in order to obtain the larger reward, whereas the noncontingent delay condition merely required 3 weeks of waiting before the larger reward could be obtained.

The 25 choices were presented in the same random sequence, in the group administration procedure described previously (Mischel & Gilligan, 1964). Children were provided individual booklets containing on each page a brief description of a given set of paired objects and the associated contingency. After the experimenter had displayed both rewards and explained the contingency, the children were instructed to record their choice, and to turn the page in preparation for the next set of items. The subjects were also advised to choose carefully and realistically because in one of the choices they would actually receive the item they selected, either on the same day or after the prescribed contingency, depending upon their recorded preference. After the choices, subjects worked on one more problem on which they obtained high grades. This was exclusively for "therapeutic" purposes and was included because the explanation of the procedure and the purpose of the experiment was postponed until all data were collected. All children were instructed not to talk about the experiment.

RESULTS

Overall Analysis
As a first step, an overall analysis of variance was performed for the effects of generalized expectancy, treatments, and choice conditions on choices in all conditions (Lindquist, 1953, Type III). The results (Table 2) show a significant effect of generalized expectancy ($p < .05$) and significant effect of choice conditions ($p < .001$). Although none of the two-way interactions reached significance, the triple interaction was significant ($p < .05$). The effect of treatments ($F = 2.82$, $df = 2/72$) tended to approach but did not reach acceptable significance (an F of 3.13 is required for $p < .05$).

A selected comparison between the combined task contingent choice conditions (1–4) and the noncontingent choice condition (5) showed that larger rewards were chosen less frequently when they were dependent on successful task performance than when they required only waiting ($t = 23.94$, $df = 77$, $p < .001$). A selected comparison between task contingent conditions without delay (1 and 3 combined) and task contingent conditions plus delay (2 and 4 combined) showed that the addition of a delay period reduced the number of large reward choices ($t = 14.54$, $df = 77$, $p < .001$).

Effects of Success and Failure
A main aim was to investigate the effects of success and failure on an initial task upon subsequent choices in which the larger reward is contingent upon successful performance on a *similar* task. This required comparison of the success and failure groups in the contingent similar task conditions (1 and 2 combined). Further, a comparison was made of the

*Table 2 Overall Analysis of Variance of Large Reward
Choices in All Groups and All Choice Conditions*

Source	df	MS	F
Between subjects	77		
General expectancy (B)	1	29.36	4.68*
Treatment (C)	2	17.70	2.82
B × C	2	10.35	1.65
Error (b)	72	6.28	
Within subjects	312		
Choice condition (A)	4	17.39	13.69**
A × B	4	1.10	.87
A × C	8	1.88	1.48
A × B × C	8	2.71	2.13*
Error (w)	288	1.27	
Total	389		

*$p < .05$.
**$p < .001$.

number of large reward choices of the success and failure groups in the contingent *dissimilar* task conditions (3 and 4 combined). The question here was: Did success and failure treatments affect choice preferences when the larger reward was contingent on the successful performance of tasks dissimilar to those on which success or failure was initially obtained? An analysis of variance (Lindquist, 1953, Type III) was performed to examine the effect of success and failure treatments, generalized expectancy, and task similarity-dissimilarity on the number of task contingent large reward choices (Conditions 1–4). The results, summarized in Table 3, show significant effects of success and failure treatments ($p < .05$). The effects of similar versus dissimilar contingent choice conditions, the interaction between choice conditions and treatments, and the three-way interaction were all significant. The effect of generalized expectancy was not significant.

The effects of success and failure treatments were consistent with the hypothesis. Following success as compared to failure, all subjects (irrespective of generalized expectancy) chose significantly more large reward when the contingencies were similar ($t = 3.52$, $df = 50$, $p < .001$), but not when they were dissimilar ($t < 1$). Hence the significant double interaction in Table 3.

This double interaction (Treatment $\times$ Choice Condition) was even stronger for subjects with low than with high generalized expectancies. Hence there was a significant triple interaction (Table 3). Separate comparisons for subjects with high and low generalized expectancy in similar and dissimilar contingent conditions following success and failure are in Table 4. Both subjects with high and low generalized expectancy chose more larger rewards on similar contingent choices following success than failure. Although this mean difference was highly significant for low gen-

Table 3   Analysis of Variance of Large Contingent Reward Choices (Conditions 1–4) for the Success and Failure Groups

Source	df	MS	F
Between subjects	51		
General expectancy (B)	1	.50	
Treatment (C)	1	66.24	6.33*
B $\times$ C	1	9.22	
Error (b)	48	10.47	
Within subjects	52		
Choice condition (A)	1	25.01	7.15*
A $\times$ B	1	.40	
A $\times$ C	1	21.24	6.07*
A $\times$ B $\times$ C	1	27.79	7.79**
Error (w)	48	3.50	
Total	103		

* $p < .05$.
** $p < .01$.

eralized expectancy subjects ($t = 3.40$, $p < .01$), it just reaches acceptable significance for those with high generalized expectancy ($t = 1.84$, $p < .05$, one-tailed test).[3] Comparison of the success and failure groups on *dissimilar* contingencies showed no differences ($t < 1$) in the choices of children with high generalized expectancy but for those with low generalized expectancy there was a nonsignificant trend ($t = 1.63$, $df = 24$, $p < .15$, two-tailed test) for more large reward choices following success.

Comparisons of Contingent Choices by Subjects with High and Low Generalized Expectancies in Success and Failure versus No-Information Treatment

Table 4 compares the mean choices of subjects with high and low generalized expectancy separately in the success, failure, and no-information groups on similar and dissimilar contingent choice conditions. The results for success versus failure already have been presented. Comparing subjects with low generalized expectancy in the success and the no-information groups showed that after success they chose more contingent rewards on similar contingencies ($p < .01$) and likewise on dissimilar contingencies, although the latter difference approaches but falls short of acceptable significance with a two-tailed test ($t = 1.96$, $df = 24$, $p < .10$). In contrast, these comparisons did not reach or approach significance for subjects with high generalized expectancy (both t values < 1).

Comparing subjects with high generalized expectancies for success in the failure and no-information groups showed that after failure they chose fewer contingent rewards on similar but not on dissimilar contingencies. For subjects with low generalized expectancies for success, choices were not significantly different following failure and no information.

In sum, in the absence of information about performance, subjects with high generalized expectancies behaved like those who obtained success, whereas subjects with low generalized expectancies behaved like those with similarly low expectancies who obtained failure. For subjects with high generalized expectancies, failure (compared to no information) significantly reduced large reward choices only on similar contingencies. For those with low generalized expectancies, success (compared to no information) significantly increased large reward choices on similar contingencies with a strong trend also on dissimilar contingencies.

Effects of Generalized Expectancy

Recall that a significant effect of generalized expectancy was found in the initial overall analysis of variance (Table 2). The three-way interaction in the overall analysis of variance indicated, however, that generalized expectancies did not affect all experimental groups equally in all choice conditions and the analysis of variance for success and failure groups only on task contingent choices showed no significant effects of generalized expectancies although there were interactions.

[3] All t tests in this paper are two-tailed except for tests of the explicitly predicted differences on contingent similar choices following success as opposed to failure which are one-tailed.

Table 4 Comparison of Pairs of Means for All Treatments: Large Reward Choices in Contingent Similar and Dissimilar Conditions by Subjects with High and Low Generalized Expectancies

TREATMENT COMPARISONS

GENERAL EXPECTANCY	SUCCESS (I) VERSUS FAILURE (II)		SUCCESS (I) VERSUS NO INFORMATION (III)		FAILURE (II) VERSUS NO INFORMATION (III)	
	Contingent similar	Contingent dissimilar	Contingent similar	Contingent dissimilar	Contingent similar	Contingent dissimilar
High						
t	1.84*	<1	<1	<1	2.36*	<1
Direction	I > II				III > II	
Low						
t	3.40***	1.63	2.69**	1.96	<1	<1
Direction	I > II	I > II	I > III	I > III		

Note. t tests comparing success with failure on contingent similar are one-tailed (explicitly hypothesized differences); all other t tests are two-tailed; $df = 24$ for each test.

* $p < .05$.
** $p < .02$.
*** $p < .01$.

It was anticipated that in the no-information group subjects with high as opposed to low generalized expectancies would choose more task contingent large rewards (Conditions 1–4 in Table 1). This prediction was supported ($t = 2.45$, $df = 24$, $p < .03$). Comparable t tests in the success and failure groups did not reach significance ($t < 1$).

Noncontingent (Delay Only) Choices

The effect of generalized expectancies and treatments was also examined when the larger reward required delay but was not contingent on performance (Condition 5 in Table 1). It was not predicted that generalized expectancies for success would affect choices in this condition but the data indicated differences as a function of generalized expectancies (see Table 1). Analysis of variance for all treatment groups on choices in this condition showed a significant effect of generalized expectancies ($F = 8.72$, $df = 1/72$, $p < .01$). Treatment effect and interactions were not significant ($F < 2$). Subjects with high generalized expectancies for success waited for larger rewards more than those with low expectancies in all treatments (see means in Table 1 for Choice Condition 5). However, t tests showed that this mean difference was significant in the failure group ($t = 2.60$, $df = 24$, $p < .02$) while it did not approach significance in the success group ($t = .92$, $df = 24$, ns) and was negligible in the no-information group ($t = .48$). That is, following failure, subjects with high generalized expectancies for success chose to wait for larger rewards which were independent of performance more than those with low generalized expectancies. Following success and no information, generalized expectancies did not affect choices in this condition.

DISCUSSION

The highly significant effects of choice conditions clearly demonstrated the importance of the specific contingencies for attainment of larger or more valued rewards as determinants of waiting and working for them. Larger rewards whose attainment required only waiting were chosen more frequently than those that required successful work. Moreover, when larger rewards were contingent on waiting as well as successful work they were chosen less frequently than when they required only successful work. The findings show that accurate predictions about this aspect of self-control require detailed analysis of the specific contingencies for attainment of the more valuable outcome. The results suggest that behaviors frequently used as indices of "ego strength" and treated as if they were referents for relatively stable, general, and situation-free traits may largely be determined by situational contingencies.

Multiple contingencies (successful work plus additional delay) presumably reduced the subjective probability for attaining contingent rewards. It is also possible that the combined contingencies altered the reward value of the contingent larger rewards, by making their attainment more aversive rather than less probable. The present study was not designed to differentiate between these possibilities and illustrates only that individuals discriminate between contingencies in these choices, with additional risk contingencies decreasing willingness to work and wait for larger rewards. Likewise, the fact that "delay only" resulted in the greatest number of large reward choices should not lead to generalizations beyond the sample and tasks used. In some circumstances or cultures it is likely that contingencies involving successful work (even with a high risk of failure) would be more preferred than those requiring only a waiting period. This seems especially plausible when trust in the "promise-maker" is minimal or when waiting is a highly noxious activity (Mischel, 1958b). Obviously there are great individual differences with respect to this. Note, for example, that following both success and failure, children with low generalized expectancy for success chose slightly (not significantly) more larger rewards when the contingency required success on a task dissimilar to the initial task but without additional delay than when it required delay only (Table 1).

The results demonstrate that generalized expectancies for success, presumably based on previous reinforcement in similar earlier situations, are determinants of choices when there is no information in the situation relevant to success probability. In the absence of such information, subjects with low generalized expectancies behave like those with similarly low expectancies who actually obtained failure, whereas subjects with high generalized expectancies behave like those who succeeded.

However, when specific expectancies about outcomes within the situation are relatively clear, as in the success and failure treatments, they tend to minimize the effects of generalized expectancy, particularly when the contingencies are highly similar to those on which situational success or failure was obtained. There are major individual differences in the extent to which subjects discriminate between similar and dissimilar contingencies and specific contingencies interact both with treatment and with generalized expectancy. Treatment effects on dissimilar contingencies were minimal in this study, with trends only for subjects who had low generalized expectancies. This is consistent with the discussed data on specific contingencies and subjects' discriminations between contingencies, as well as the interactions with generalized expectancy.

It is also of interest that subjects' direct estimates of generalized expectancy for success, rather than indirect inferences about motivational states, provided useful measures which predicted delay of gratification behavior. The usefulness of such direct self-estimates from subjects supports earlier findings about the utility of self-predictions in a very different assessment context (Mischel, 1965).

Generalized expectancies produced an unpredicted significant effect in the noncontingent (delay only) choice condition. In this condition subjects with high generalized expectancy for success waited for larger rewards more than those with low expectancies. This difference was significant after the failure treatment but not after success or no information. It seems plausible that generalized expectancy, as measured in this study, was also correlated with expectancies that the promised reward will be forthcoming, even when this is independent of the person's own performance and contingent primarily on the promise-maker. However, since there were no significant differences between subjects with high and low generalized expectancies in willingness to wait for larger reward in the no-information and success groups, and since the difference was significant only in the failure group, it appears more reasonable that "confirmed failure" for subjects with low generalized expectancies decreased their discriminations about specific contingencies and generalized to choice situations in which attainment of a larger reward was independent of their own performance.

Extrapolating to life situations, in the absence of new information about outcomes relevant to the contingencies on which rewards depend, individuals with low generalized expectancies for success behave as if they cannot fulfill the contingency. That is, they behave like individuals who already failed on tasks similar to those on which reward is contingent. Following actual failure on tasks similar to those on which reward is contingent, they are less willing to wait for larger rewards than subjects with high generalized expectancies for success, even when the reward is not contingent on their own work and requires only waiting. However, when given information indicating that they can probably fulfill the relevant contingencies (success treatment) their willingness to work and wait for larger rewards increases and indeed they behave like subjects with high generalized expectancies for success. The implications for increasing an individual's willingness to work and wait for larger rewards are clear: increase the probability that he can fulfill the necessary specific contingencies. While this is hardly surprising, it needs to be taken seriously in therapeutic programs designed to enhance ego strength and suggests that specific training to increase the expectancy for success with respect to working and waiting for more valued outcomes is a potent means of strengthening this aspect of self-control.

2-4 The Effect of Goal Value Upon Expectancy[1]

LEONARD WORELL

Behavioral expectancies do not always appear to be governed by "realistic" factors in a situation, but seem also to be a function of wishes, fears, and doubts. Observers disagree, however, about the manner in which differentially valued goals affect expectancies. Some believe, for example, that expectancies are lowered, in the face of highly valued goals, as evident in the student before an important examination, while others maintain that they are raised, as in gambling situations. The present study attempts to examine some of the conditions under which expectancies may or may not be related to different levels of goal value.

This research was conceived within the framework of a social learning theory of personality developed by Rotter (1954). Within this system predictions of behavior are mediated by two major constructs, expectancy and reinforcement value. Expectancy is defined as "the subjective probability held by the individual that a particular reinforcement will occur as a function of, or in relation to, a specific behavior in a given situation or situations [1954, p. 112]." Expectancies are viewed as being determined by experience in particular situations and in related situations. Thus, a student taking a history course may have expectancies that studying will lead to a certain grade, based upon experiences in this history course, other history courses, other academic courses in general, and so on. The second construct, reinforcement value, is defined as "the degree of preference for any reinforcement to occur if the possibilities of their occurring were all equal [1954, p. 112]." This value may be either positive or negative. The terms goal value and reinforcement value are used interchangeably hereafter.

From a social learning point of view, there is no *necessary* relationship between expectancy and goal value. Under certain conditions a specific relationship may be anticipated, while under others the nature of the relationship is obscure. The purpose of this study is twofold, to pursue an empirical phenomenon of general interest and to contribute to the predictive power of Rotter's theory.

In examining the relationship of goal value to expectancy, previous investigators have consistently used mean expectancy scores derived from a

[1] Adapted from a dissertation submitted in partial fulfillment of the requirements for the degree of Doctor of Philosophy in the Department of Psychology, The Ohio State University. The writer wishes to express his appreciation to Professors Julian B. Rotter, Delos D. Wickens, Lauren G. Wispe and Robert J. Wherry for their helpful suggestions and advice. The writer is indebted to Russell Slater, director of the Child Study Division, and to the principals and teachers of the participating schools in the Columbus Public School System for their cooperation in making subjects available.

From *Journal of Abnormal and Social Psychology*, 1956, 53, 48–53. Copyright 1956 by the American Psychological Association and reprinted by permission of the author and the publisher.

series of trials. For this type of situation the nature of the relationship between the constructs cannot be logically deduced from Rotter's theory. From the standpoint of other systematic points of view and general observations, conflicting conceptions emerge. Thus, in Lewin's formulations (1944), as the difficulty level of a situation increases the value of success increases, while the subjective probability of success attainment decreases. The analysis of individuals confronted with high value situations seems to bear this out, for low expectancies are generally elicited. The suggestion follows that confidence in attaining goals decreases as they become more important, possibly because the acquisition of high goals in the past has involved considerable effort and competence. On the other hand, it seems equally reasonable to suppose that expectancies increase in highly valued situations. Our society might be seen as providing a particularly striking example, in that both striving for high goals and displaying confidence in one's ability to achieve them are held as the ideal. In view of these alternatives, the exact nature of the relationship between goal value and expectancy over a series of experiences in the same situation must be a matter for empirical determination.

On the basis of Rotter's theory, at least two conditions should lead to the absence of any observable relationship between the constructs. One of these hinges on an assumption of social learning theory that expectancies are a function of experiences in both a particular situation and in related situations. Expectancies in a relatively novel situation should thus be determined by experiences from related situations. Such related experiences may include the occurrence (or nonoccurrence) of past reinforcements and, possibly, the values of these reinforcements. With additional experience in a situation, expectancies should increasingly be determined by the actual occurrence of reinforcements in that situation (Dean, 1953; Good, 1952). Although the nature of the influence of different goal values upon expectancies cannot be specified in a novel situation, after experience with that situation expectancies should therefore be determined *only* by the occurrence and *not* by the value of the reinforcements.

The second condition in which differential goal values should produce little or no effect upon expectancies deals with the introduction of a penalty for inaccuracy in stating expectancies. Relatively widespread use has been made of penalties in level-of-aspiration experiments. According to social learning theory, a penalty may be viewed as a reinforcement value associated with accuracy. This additional reinforcement value (often interpreted as a negative reinforcement by the S) should counteract the tendency to make cautious or wishful expectancy statements engendered by high or low goal values. If the severity of the penalty is identical for different goal value conditions, therefore, expectancies should be uniform in relation to these goal values. In addition, expectancies should be more realistic or performance-oriented than in nonpenalty conditions.

In summary, three aspects of the relationship between goal values and expectancies are under investigation. The question is first asked whether (a) differential goal values affect expectancies over a series of experiences in the same situation. The remaining two aspects involve attempts to support extensions of Rotter's social learning theory. Thus, (b) the relationship, if any, observed in a is hypothesized to be a function of the amount of experience in the situation. Relatively novel situations may elicit a relationship between expectancies and differential goal values, but experience in these situations should produce uniform expectancy statements. Finally, (c) it is hypothesized that the introduction of a reinforcement value for accuracy leads to more realistic expectancies, on the one hand, and expectancies that are unaffected by the value of an event, on the other.

METHOD

Selection of Tasks

A number of requirements had to be met in the selection of tasks. First, the tasks had to be relatively novel, so that expectancies would not be established pre-experimentally. Second, they had to permit E to control performance, in order that the reinforcements would be uniform for all Ss under value conditions. Finally, they needed face validity for the goal area involved, i.e., athletic skills. From a pilot study, three tasks were chosen, each one representing a different goal-value level. These were (a) the Rotter level-of-aspiration board (1942) modified by a cover placed over the numbers so that S was unable to see his performance; (b) a rotary pursuit test (score measured by amount of time that the stylus is kept on revolving disc); and (c) a set of six blocks for a tapping test. The results of the pilot study indicated that the tasks were perceived as having differential goal values. Through a ranking procedure, it was found that the level-of-aspiration board and the rotary pursuit task were more highly valued than the tapping task. These initial preferences were coupled with instructions (see below) that assigned more or less value to each task.

Subjects

A total of 102 boys, ranging in age from nine to eleven, was selected from the fifth and sixth grades of the local public school system. Eight Ss who were unable to comply with the instructions were discarded.

Administration of Tasks

Each S was seen individually. He was seated at a table on which the three tasks were arrayed. The S was given a description of each task in terms of its relative merit in providing information about a person's athletic abilities. Three levels of goal value were employed, designated as high, medium, and low. For the high reinforcement-value task (level-of-aspiration board), S was told that this was the most important task, that it provided the most information about skills required in all sports, e.g., coordination, timing, and balance, and that this task was of greatest concern to E. The medium value task (rotary pursuit) was said to be not quite as useful and to provide less information about a person's abilities. Finally, the low value task (tapping) was described as much inferior to the others and of almost no interest to E. When tapping was followed by one of the other tasks, S was also instructed to "get this one over quickly, so that we can get on to the others."

A level-of-aspiration procedure was used in obtaining expectancies. The S was informed of the range of possible scores (0 to 50) and was asked to provide an estimate of his subsequent performance for each trial. This was followed over the series of six trials. Tasks were rotated, so that Ss performed differentially valued tasks in varying orders. A score of either 26, 27, or 28 was given S on each task immediately after his first performance. Following this, a predetermined series of scores was supplied which provided the same mean increase in performance over the six trials for each of the three tasks.

Seventy-one Ss performed the tasks without a penalty for inaccuracy of estimates. Another 23 Ss performed the same tasks with a penalty being established for inaccuracy by instructing S that he would lose twice the number of points that his expectancy fell below his actual performance, and that he would obtain exactly what he expected if his actual score were at or above his expectancy estimate. Each S was given detailed examples and was not permitted to begin the tasks until he could calculate his score on an example without assistance.

RESULTS

Analysis of data was based on the stated expectancies to the three tasks of high, medium, and low goal value. A D score was employed, the difference between the expected score and the preceding performance. Tests of the hypotheses, therefore, are focused on the differences between mean D scores (Table 1) for each of the reinforcement-value conditions.

Effects of Goal Value Bartlett's test of homogeneity of variance was applied before performing an analysis of variance and the assumption of homogeneity was supported. The analysis of variance indicated that the difference attributable to reinforcement-value conditions is highly significant ($p < .001$). Two-tailed t tests for correlated means were used in comparing mean D scores. Two of the three comparisons are significant (Table 2); the mean D score at the high value is significantly lower than either the medium or low values.

Effects of Experience As six trials were used, differences between expectancies might be anticipated at the first trial, while none should appear at the sixth trial. Analyses of variance indicated that the reinforcement-value conditions continued to provide significant sources of variance at both trials ($p < .001$ at Trial 1, $p < .05$ at Trial 6). When mean D scores are compared at Trial 1 (Table 2), the differences between the high and medium values and the high and low values are highly significant. At the sixth trial, a significant difference is found only between the high and low value conditions.

Effects of Penalty Table 1 contains the mean D scores for groups with and without a penalty associated to expectancy statements. Inspection of this table confirms the hypothesis that a penalty leads to more realistic expectancies. "Realistic" is defined in terms of the mean D scores'

Table 1 Mean D Scores and Standard Deviations for All Groups

GOAL VALUE	NONPENALTY GROUP						PENALTY GROUP	
	Six Trials		1st Trial		6th Trial		Six Trials	
	M	SD	M	SD	M	SD	M	SD
High	5.5	16.2	.9	4.6	.3	2.8	−3.7	14.6
Medium	11.6	17.1	3.8	4.9	.7	2.7	−.5	15.7
Low	10.6	14.6	3.0	4.5	1.0	3.0	2.8	14.6

Table 2 Mean Differences at Each Combination of Reinforcement Value

GROUP	N	REINFORCEMENT VALUE CONDITIONS								
		High and Medium			High and Low			Medium and Low		
		$\overline{D}$	t	p	$\overline{D}$	t	p	$\overline{D}$	t	p
Nonpenalty	71	6.1	3.82	<.001	5.1	3.53	<.001	1.0	.54	NS
1st Trial	71	2.9	4.10	<.001	2.1	2.91	<.01	.8	1.27	NS
6th Trial	71	.4	1.32	.20	.7	2.33	<.05	.3	.28	NS
Penalty	23	3.2	1.14	NS	6.5	3.01	<.01	3.3	1.92	.10

proximity to zero, or stated in another way, the extent that expectancy statements approach previous performance. The differences between penalty and nonpenalty groups are significant in all cases, falling at less than the .02, .01, and .05 levels at the high, medium, and low values respectively.

Our interest here, however, lies also in the differences between mean D scores at the three value conditions of the penalty group alone. As before, the analysis of variance continued to show that a significant source of variance may be attributed to the reinforcement-value conditions ($p < .05$). In applying two-tailed t tests for correlated means (Table 2) to the differences between mean D scores, the only significant difference is found between high and low conditions, although the difference between medium and low conditions approaches significance. When the differences between means in the penalty group are examined more closely, it appears that the effect of a uniform penalty at all value conditions is to produce more pronounced separations between high, medium, and low goal values.

DISCUSSION

The most general statement that may be drawn from the results is that the value of a goal has an effect upon the level of stated expectancy. It was found that (a) the presence of high goal values leads to significantly lower expectancy estimates over a series of experiences in the same situation than do either medium or low value conditions; (b) the amount of experience, though appearing to dilute somewhat the effects of goal values upon expectancy, does not eliminate the tendency for high goals to be associated with lower expectancies in the six trials of the experiment; and (c) with the inclusion of a penalty (reinforcement value) for inaccuracy, contrary to what was anticipated, expectancies continued to be lower in relation to highly valued goals. A penalty did, however, lead to more realistic or performance-oriented expectancy estimates.

The influence of reinforcement value upon expectancy was not demonstrated at all levels of goal value. That expectancies were relatively lower for high values suggests that the frequently quoted expression "the good things are always hard to get" may well be applied here and that individuals appear to perceive high goals as difficult in the Lewinian sense. The failure to obtain significant differences between medium and low value conditions, however, requires explanation. A possible factor may have been the relative absence of perceived separation between the experimental goal-value conditions. The division between the three goal values was made in accordance with an expected theoretical and experimental gradient. It is not known, however, how distinct the goals were or how important the distinction seemed to the Ss. A completely satisfactory method for measuring precise distances between goal values has yet to be developed.

Goal values appeared to exert their strongest influence upon expectancies in relatively novel situations. This finding suggests that different initial expectancies are held in relation to varying goal levels *from previous related situations*. People seem to differentiate relatively novel situations not only in accordance with the possible occurrence (or nonoccurrence) of reinforcements, but also with regard to the *values* of the reinforcements. The behavior of the Ss in this study suggests that individuals may ordinarily respond in terms of two steps along this continuum, e.g., high and low value. The presence of a penalty seemed to be a condition leading to more subtle discriminations between values.

Reference has already been made to the fact that the effects of goal value on expectancy did not disappear with experience. There was, however, a tendency for the influence of goal values to be diminished. This observation derives further support from a comparison of the mean changes that are found at each *combination* of reinforcement value between Trials 1 and 6. When the *t* test[2] is applied to these mean changes, the differences between trials for the high and medium ($t = 2.8$, $p < .005$) and the high and low ($t = 1.9$, $p < .03$) are highly significant, while that for the medium and low values approaches significance ($t = 1.6$, $p = .06$). This finding is interpreted to mean that differences between expectancies have been reduced at the sixth trial and that a more adequate test of the effects of experience would be made by extending the number of trials beyond six.

In securing a particular relationship between goal value and expectancy,

---

[2] Since these were anticipated outcomes of our hypothesis regarding effects of experience, one-tailed tests of the distribution of *t* were employed.

this study may seem merely to have added another conflicting result to an array of studies already in disagreement (Bayton, 1943; Frank, 1935b; Holt, 1945; Irwin, 1942; Marks, 1951). Representative of one kind of previous approach to the problem is a study by Marks (1951), which sought to determine the desirability of outcome on the stated expectations of children in certain choice situations. Using what may be referred to as a quasi-gambling technique, she found that the value of an event exerted a strong effect upon stated expectations. Contrasted with this, Holt (1945), employing what may be called a competitive level-of-aspiration technique, demonstrated no effect of "ego-involvement" on the stated expectancies of his college Ss. The present study adds to the picture of inconsistency.

A possible resolution may be achieved by differentiating the kinds of situations studied. At least two broad divisions of situations may be distinguished: *achievement* and *nonachievement*. In the former, performance is dependent upon ability or skill, and thus reflects upon an individual's competence. In the latter, which may include gambling, some play and simple choice situations, no ability or skill is prominently involved, and an individual's competence is not challenged. One might anticipate differing results of the effects of goal value upon expectancy under these two conditions, since the achievement situation introduces additional goal values.

This distinction appears to assist in resolving disparities in the results of studies such as that of Marks and the present one. Her results strongly indicated that *increased* value led to *increased* expectations. According to the present analysis, her study would fall within the non-achievement category, since children were expressing what they *wanted* to happen; no ability or skill was implied. In this sense, her Ss were faced with a form of gambling, and culturally, one may find a greater tendency to take risks in these situations. In this investigation, performance was related to ability, so that an additional goal value was introduced. Expectancies held in relation to previous *achievement* situations would therefore be most relevant. The results of this experiment demonstrated that expectancies *decreased* with *increasing* value in relatively novel situations. Whether this proposal has any merit aside from providing *post hoc* explanation will be determined by future experimentation.

The findings were somewhat equivocal with respect to the penalty for inaccuracy of expectancy statements. Though expectancies were more accurate, they did not appear to be removed from the effects of goal values. Before conclusions can be drawn, it would seem necessary to investigate the problem of penalties more thoroughly. Different severities of penalties and the effectiveness of instructions in communicating penalties could well bear further examination.

SUMMARY

In Rotter's social learning theory of personality, predictions of behavior are made through the operation of two central constructions, expectancy and reinforcement value. The present study was designed to investigate the effect of different goal (reinforcement) values upon expectancy.

Three levels of goal values were employed in a study of fifth- and sixth-grade boys. Expectancies developed from related situations were controlled by having each S perform each of three relatively novel tasks. In addition, the performance of S was controlled by giving prearranged sequences of scores. Thus, with both performance and experience from related situations controlled, the only factor varied was the value of each task.

The most consistent finding was that the value of an event has some effect upon stated expectancy. Further results of the study may be summarized as follows:

1. Expectancies observed over a series of experiences in the same situation were found to be significantly lower in highly valued situations as compared to situations of lower value.

2. Though the influence of different goal values upon expectancies appears to become more uniform with experience, expectancies continued to be significantly lower in high value conditions. The necessity of investigating more extensive amounts of experience than those considered here was suggested and discussed.

3. The association of a goal value for accuracy (penalty) to expectancy statements leads to more realistic expectancies, that is, expectancies tend to approach previous performance more closely. The penalty, however, did not appear to eliminate the effect of different goal values upon expectancy. Expectancies were found to be relatively lower to high goal values, as they had been in situations without a penalty.

Finally, in an attempt to provide a resolution of the seemingly contradictory results of previous studies in this area, the potential utility of a distinction between achievement and nonachievement situations was discussed.

2-5 Reinforcement Value as Related to Decision Time

ERWIN J. LOTSOF[1]

A. INTRODUCTION AND PROBLEM

Resolution of conflict and decision making appear to be ubiquitous phenomena and permeate almost all behavior. Decision making has been treated by Festinger (1943) and Cartwright (1943) with regard to psychophysiological phenomena, by Lewin (1935, 1938), Barker (1942) and by Brown (1942) and Miller (1944) from a behavioristic position. Systematic treatment of the factors entering into decision making might aid in the prediction and control of human behavior.

This study is related to Barker's (1942) but differs from it with regard to the methodology employed. Barker's Ss, 19 boys ages 9–11, were required to decide which one of two liquids they would drink in a "real" and "hypothetical" situation. Nine S's received the "real" situation first and after a 10-minute period were given the "hypothetical" situation; 10 S's received the reverse sequence. Prior to the actual experiment, each S ranked 7 liquids in order of preference. In the choice situations each liquid was paired with every other liquid. The present study differs from Barker's study in that it attempted to control the differences in the alternatives. This was accomplished by pretesting on a large group prior to the actual experiment. It was necessary to do this by virtue of the theory in which the problem was done. This study also utilized two separate groups for the "real" and "hypothetical" situations so that comparisons could be made between the groups. A larger sample was employed in this study as compared to Barker's, so that variability of performance might be reduced.

The problem has been formulated within Rotter's social learning theory of personality (1954) and attempts to demonstrate the usefulness of decision time[2] as a measure of reinforcement value. Rotter's approach utilizes the constructs of expectancy and reinforcement value for the prediction of behavior. Within the theory the potentiality of any behavior (B.P.) occurring is a function of (a) the expectancy (E) that the particular behavior will lead to a given reinforcement in a given situation and (b) the value of the given reinforcement (R.V.); B.P. = f (E & R.V.). Reinforcement value is inferred by the extent to which an S will select one object rather than another when expectancies for both are equal. Expectancy is the probability held by the individual that a behavior will lead to a given reinforcement and

---

[1] This paper is based upon a portion of a dissertation submitted to The Ohio State University in partial fulfillment of the requirements for the Ph.D. degree. The author wishes to express his appreciation to Dr. J. B. Rotter for his aid in this investigation.

[2] Decision time is defined as the time required to select one of two objects.

From *Journal of Psychology*, 1956, **41**, 427–435. Copyright 1956 by the Journal Press and reprinted by permission of the author and the publisher.

is measured for specific experiences for that behavior in that situation. Since behavioral potential is a function of both expectancy and reinforcement, it would follow that if expectancy were held constant, behavior potential should be a function of reinforcement value. In this study expectancy was held constant since the reinforcement always occurred.

The study is methodological in that it attempts to ascertain the usefulness of decision time as a basis for measuring reinforcement value. In day-to-day experiences it has been observed that individuals frequently have to choose between one of two tasks; the tasks may sometimes be pleasant and sometimes unpleasant, and the time taken to decide varies quite considerably. There is another kind of choice situation which is often overlooked; this is the choice between doing something and doing nothing. Just as doing something has a reinforcement value so refraining from action has reinforcement value. Where doing nothing becomes more punishing with the passage of time than doing something, the decision or making the choice is reached rather rapidly. If the time taken to decide between two alternatives varied with the degree of "pleasantness" and "unpleasantness," it would be possible to use decision time as a measure of reinforcement value. Thus, it was hypothesized that the more punishing a pair of alternatives, with the differences between a given pair eliminated, the longer the decision time. It was also hypothesized that the greater the difference in reinforcement value between two alternatives the shorter the decision time.

The experiment was also designed to compare differences in decision time between choices followed by real reinforcement and choices followed by hypothetical reinforcement. When the S was given the reinforcement he chose, it was defined as *real*. When he was merely asked to state a choice verbally and to do nothing else, the reinforcement was defined as *hypothetical*. It was hypothesized that a reinforcement act in the hypothetical situation is not as strong as a reinforcement act in the real situation. Thus, for example, for a given choice situation two negative real choices would be more negative than two negative hypothetical choices and hence would require a longer decision time. In the negative hypothetical situations the individual has a choice between doing nothing and doing something which, in this case, is selecting one of the liquids. It would appear that doing nothing becomes more punishing than doing something more quickly since in the negative hypothetical situation there is no real negative reinforcement to follow. Thus the negative hypothetical situation should take less time than the real.

Similarly it is hypothesized that the reinforcement value of the positive hypothetical situation is lower than the real situation. Thus, two positive real situations would be higher in reinforcement value than two positive hypothetical situations; consequently, there would be a shorter decision time when choices are made between the two real situations. In the positive hypothetical situation, the individual has a choice between doing nothing and doing something. Because doing nothing takes on negative consequences, he has to do something; but, since no actual positive reinforcement follows, the hypothetical positive choice takes more time than the real positive choice.

The study made it possible to determine the differences and similarities between behaviors followed by hypothetical or real reinforcement. In general, it might be expected that the principles derived from the real reinforcement acts can also be derived from the hypothetical reinforcement acts. If so, the more easily obtained hypothetical decisions might be useful in future experimental work.

B. METHOD

1. Test Objects

The names of 14 liquids were presented to 31 Ss who were instructed to rank order them from most to least preferred. The resulting scale values were computed on the basis of mean ranks. The following pairs of liquids were selected for the experiments since both members of each pair had approximately equal means and standard deviations on the scale, pineapple and tomato juice, flat root beer and flat cola, a .02 per cent quinine solution and a 5 per cent acetic acid solution (vinegar).

2. Materials

Liquids used in this experiment tend to fall into three categories which vary from some degree of positiveness to negativeness. The quinine and vinegar solutions can rather easily be categorized as "strong negative." Flat root beer and pepsi-cola might be categorized as "weak negative." Many of the Ss' comments seemed to indicate that while these liquids did not taste good they were not as unpleasant as the quinine solution. A problem arises in categorizing the pineapple and tomato juices. These liquids were at room temperature when presented to Ss and thus differed from the usual way in which they are served. While no S ever expressed marked disapproval, there were no indications that any S preferred to have his juices served at room temperature. As one S said, "These are good but not too good." Thus it is felt that perhaps the tomato-pineapple juice pair should be referred to as "weak positive" rather than "positive."

3. Subjects

Two groups of 33 Ss each were used, each S tested individually. The *real* group contained 17 males and 16 females; the *hypothetical* group contained 18 males and 15 females. All Ss were selected on a random basis from an alphabetical file containing all students taking the first course in elementary general psychology.

4. Procedure

One group was asked to choose and then to drink the selected liquid; the other group was asked merely to state verbal preferences. Each S, regardless of the group he was assigned to, tasted all six liquids which were presented in a random order and then he was asked to make choices between pairs of liquids. After testing each liquid, the S rinsed his mouth several times to avoid any after effects. Each liquid was presented in combination with every other liquid. The pairs of liquids were presented on cards. If the S was in the *hypothetical* group he was told: "I would like you to tell me which of the two liquids on this card you would prefer, if you had to drink one of them." In the *real* group, the S was told that after he selected the liquids he would have to drink approximately five cubic centimeters of it. A stop watch was used to measure decision time to tenths of a second.

C. RESULTS

Table 1 gives the rank order means and standard deviations of the liquids used in the choice situations. The difference in means between pineapple juice and tomato juice is 0.68, between flat pepsi-cola and flat root beer is 0.16, and between quinine and vinegar is 0.77. To determine whether decision time is a function of the inequality between the liquids placed in pairs, Tables 1 and 3 may be compared. Note that the most equal pair did not yield the longest decision time; nor did the pair with the greatest difference yield the shortest decision time. (Data in Table 1 are compared with 3 rather than 2 because both sets of choices were obtained in the hypothetical situation.) Thus the differences in decision time cannot be accounted for solely in terms of differences between the two members of the pair.

The manner in which this experiment was carried out permits us to compare decision times for real and hypothetical situations of varying degrees of acceptability where alternatives were of differential value as reinforcements. Intra-comparisons and inter-comparisons of the groups used were made. These comparisons should answer questions as to whether it makes a difference if a reinforcement act is given realistically or symbolically and whether decision time is systematically related to the value of the reinforcement involved. The *t* test was used to compare the decision times of the groups.

For the *real* choices, the relationship of decision time to acceptability (reinforcement value) of the pair of alternatives when the within pair differences are controlled is given in Table 2. The decision times are all in

Table 1   Rank Order of Liquids Hypothetically Selected for Use in the Experiment
$$(N = 31)$$

LIQUIDS	M	SD
Pineapple Juice	3.19	2.09
Tomato Juice	3.87	2.32
Flat Pepsi-Cola	8.03	2.02
Flat Root Beer	8.19	2.33
Quinine Solution	12.52	1.52
Vinegar Solution	13.29	1.08

Table 2 Decision Time for "Real" Choices between Liquids:
Comparison of the Two Weak Positives, Two Weak Negatives,
and Two Strong Negative Choices (in Seconds)

	M	SD	SEm
1. Pineapple Juice—Tomato Juice	1.88	.55	.09
2. Flat Pepsi-Cola—Flat Root Beer	2.64	.82	.14
3. Vinegar Solution—Quinine Solution	3.86	1.37	.24
Comparing 1 and 2. P < .01			
Comparing 1 and 3. P < .01			
Comparing 2 and 3. P < .01			

the predicted direction. It takes less time to choose between two weak positive reinforcement acts than between two weak negative ones, and it takes less time to choose between two weak negative reinforcement acts than between two more negative ones. Differences in decision time for each of the three comparisons are significant at the .01 level of confidence.

For the *hypothetical* choices, the relationship of decision time to acceptability of the pair of alternatives when within pair differences are controlled is presented in Table 3. Decision times are all in the predicted direction and significant at the .01 level of confidence. The results are similar to those obtained with the *real* choices.

It was hypothesized that the greater the differences in reinforcement value between two alternative reinforcement acts the shorter the decision time. The difference between any one liquid of a pair and a liquid of an adjacent pair was given a step value of one. The difference between liquids in the extreme pairs was given a step value of two. When the liquids are within the same pair the step value is zero. The means in Table 4 were derived by averaging all possible comparisons for a given step value.

For the *real* situation, it can be seen in Table 4 that as the step value increases the decision time decreases; that is, an inverse relationship exists between them. In the *hypothetical* situation, differences between one and two-step, and between zero and two-step values are statistically sig-

Table 3 Decision Time for "Hypothetical" Choices between Liquids
(in Seconds): Comparison of the Two Weak Positives,
Two Weak Negatives, and Two Negative Choices

	M	SD	SEm
1. Pineapple Juice—Tomato Juice	1.75	.45	.08
2. Flat Pepsi-Cola—Flat Root Beer	2.35	.58	.10
3. Vinegar Solution—Quinine Solution	3.09	.97	.17
Comparing 1 and 2. P < .01			
Comparing 1 and 3. P < .01			
Comparing 2 and 3. P < .01			

Table 4   Significance of Differences between Choices Measured in Step Value (in Seconds)

		M	N = 33 SD	SEm
	Real Situation			
0. Zero step value		2.79	.83	.59
1. One step value		1.85	.13	.05
2. Two-step value		1.50	.12	.07
Comparing 0 to 1.	$P < .01$			
Comparing 0 to 2.	$P < .01$			
Comparing 1 to 2.	$P < .01$			
	Hypothetical Situation			
0. Zero step value		2.39	.56	.40
1. One step value		1.82	.10	.04
2. Two-step value		1.47	.09	.05
Comparing 0 to 1.	$P < .20$			
Comparing 0 to 2.	$P < .01$			
Comparing 1 to 2.	$P < .01$			

0. Liquids in same category.   3 possible combinations
1. Liquids in adjacent categories.   8 possible combinations
2. Liquids in extreme categories.   4 possible combinations

nificant. Although the zero-one step value difference is not significant, it is in the predicted direction.

The conclusion appears warranted that it takes less time to decide between two reinforcements at opposite ends of a continuum than between two reinforcements which are close together on the same continuum. Decision time varies inversely with the degree of discrepancy between the value of two reinforcements.

Data in Table 5 indicate the relationship which exists between decision time and strength of a reinforcement when choices are presented *hypothetically* and *realistically*. When choices between two negatives are compared $P < .05$ and when the two weak negatives are compared $.05 > P < .10$. The differences between the two weak positives are not statistically signifi-

Table 5   Comparison of Decision Times in Real and Hypothetical Situations (in Seconds)

	REAL M	HYPOTHETICAL M	
Quinine—Vinegar	3.86	3.09	$P < .05$
Flat Pepsi-Cola—Flat Root Beer	2.64	2.35	$.05 \searrow P < .10$
Tomato Juice—Pineapple Juice	1.88	1.73	$P < .20$

cant. There were no differences between concrete and verbal behaviors, when the reinforcement acts could be characterized as weak positive, but there appear to be differences between concrete and verbal behaviors when choices had a negative value. The negative real reinforcement appears more punishing than the same negative reinforcement act presented symbolically.

D. DISCUSSION

These results tend to indicate that decision time might profitably be used to measure reinforcement value. Statistically significant differences were obtained in all tests except when the weak positives in the hypothetical and real situations were compared. With the weak positives the decision time for the hypothetical was less than for the real situation. That is to say, the real weak positive was a more punishing reinforcement act than the hypothetical weak positive. This finding raises an interesting question. Were the real weak positive choices actually less positive than the hypothetical choices? It should be recalled that the juices which the subject drank were at room temperature. Perhaps when these juices are warm they do not taste as pleasant as when they are cool. With the real weak positive choices we could have the following phenomenon taking place. When the S is told that he is going to taste some juices he has an expectancy and a minimal goal[3] as to how these juices should be; i.e., juice should be cold. In the real situation the S drinking the juice probably finds it below his minimal goal, while the S in the hypothetical situation does not experience this phenomenon. Thus, in the real positive situation, the Ss may have been receiving negative reinforcement acts which were more punishing than the hypothetical situations, consequently giving rise to longer decision times. In the hypothetical situation the Ss were not receiving the negative reinforcement acts. It might be conjectured that in this experiment the real choice was more punishing than the hypothetical for the weak positives.

Decision making has many implications for the clinical psychologist. One of the salient characteristics of maladjusted individuals is their rather marked inability to decide when faced with alternative behaviors as goals. A possible study which could be carried out might compare decision behaviors sampling various life situations before and after psychological therapy to determine to what extent the patient has "improved."

E. SUMMARY

This experiment was formulated within Rotter's social learning theory and the concept of reinforcement value was investigated. One group of Ss was asked to state verbal choices as to which one of a pair of liquids they would select if they had to drink one; another group of Ss was asked to

---

[3] The minimal goal is that point on a continuum where the occurrence of the act will increase the expectancy of the response but the next step down on the continuum will decrease the expectancy of the success. Reinforcement acts at the level of the minimal goal or higher would be positive, lower would be negative.

state choices and then consume the liquid chosen. The time required to make the choice was obtained for the *real* and *hypothetical* groups. (*a*) Analysis of the data indicated that decision time varied inversely with the degree of discrepancy between the reinforcement values of the two acts. (*b*) Where pairs of negative reinforcement values of approximately equal strength are compared, decision time varies directly with the strength of the reinforcements. (*c*) Decision time for verbal preferences in this experiment appeared to be determined by the same principles as for choices between real objects. (*d*) There was a trend toward significance between verbal and actual choices which was consistent with the predictions made regarding their relative reinforcement values.

2-6	*The Role of Expectancy in Delayed Reinforcement*[1]
	ALVIN R. MAHRER

To a large extent, human behavior is characterized by apparent choices between immediate and delayed rewards and punishments. Reviews of animal learning studies (Hilgard & Marquis, 1940; Hull, 1943; Melton, 1950) offer two findings: (*a*) immediate rewards are preferred over delayed rewards, and (*b*) the effectiveness of a reward or a punishment diminishes with increasing delay. These conclusions are supported by the comparatively little research on delayed rewards in human behavior. These studies dealt with performance on verbal mazes (Saltzman, 1951), classroom learning (Brenner, 1934; Nagge, 1942), solution of conflict situations (Brown, 1942; Dollard & Miller, 1950; Miller, 1944; Miller & Dollard, 1941), and selection of object preferences (Irwin, Armitt, & Simon, 1943; Irwin, Orchinik, & Weiss, 1950).

The findings of delayed reward research have provided the basis for extensive clinical applications. Mowrer and Ullmann (1945), for example, considered the delay of rewards and punishments to be a critical factor in the development of neurotic and criminal behavior. Shaw has incorporated the idea of delayed reward into some proposed postulates of psy-

[1] This paper is based on a dissertation submitted in partial fulfillment of the requirements for the Ph.D. degree in Psychology at the Ohio State University. The author is especially grateful to Dr. Julian Rotter

From *Journal of Experimental Psychology*, 1956, **52**, 101–105. Copyright 1956 by the American Psychological Association and reprinted by permission of the author and the publisher.

chotherapy. He said: "The problems dealt with in psychotherapy are in the nature of behavior which has immediately rewarding consequences [1948, p. 426]."

The proposed theoretical explanations of the two conclusions to delayed reward research have focused on the value of the reward.

They state, in effect, that a delay of a reward results in a decline of the value of that reward. With a decreased value, learning will be less effective and immediate rewards will be chosen over delayed rewards.

The present investigation was carried out within the framework of Rotter's social learning theory (Rotter, 1954). This theory distinguishes between the *value* of a reward of reinforcement, and the *expectancy for occurrence* of the reinforcement. The definition for each of these two terms follows: "The reinforcement value of any external reinforcement may be ideally defined as the degree of preference for any reinforcement to occur if the possibilities of their occurring were all equal. . . . Expectancy may be defined as the probability held by the individual that a particular external reinforcement will occur as a function of a specific behavior on his part in a specific situation or situations [Rotter, 1954, p. 107]."

In contrast to previous explanations, which focused on an hypothesized decline in the value of a delayed reward, the purpose of the present investigation is to introduce *expectancy* as a factor in delayed reinforcement situations. Since there are several meanings of "delayed reinforcement" and "delayed reinforcement situations," it should be emphasized that this study is concerned with human behavior in a situation involving an apparent choice between immediate and delayed reinforcements.

The present study hypothesized that in the course of previous experiences with delayed reinforcements, an individual will develop some level of probability (expectancy) that delayed reinforcements will occur. The level of the probability is presumed to be an important factor in the preference strength for the immediate or delayed reinforcement. Rotter (1954) suggested that a decrease in the expectancy of occurrence of delayed reinforcements will result in a decrease in the strength of the preference for these reinforcements. The first purpose of this study was to develop varying levels of expectancy of occurrence of delayed reinforcements, in order to determine whether or not corresponding changes in the strength of the preference for delayed reinforcements, as compared with immediate reinforcements, would occur.

Th second purpose was to investigate the extent to which training by one E generalized to a second E. It was hypothesized that social agents, perceived as instrumental to the occurrence or nonoccurrence of the delayed reinforcements, served as one of the important cues for the level of the expectancy. Different social agents would then be presumed to serve as cues for different levels of expectancy.

Hypotheses

When E_A offers the reinforcements there will be a regular decline in the choice of delayed reinforcements for high, moderate, and low expectancy groups respectively. Also, the high and low expectancy groups will have a respectively higher and lower choice of delayed reinforcements than will their respective control groups. In order to test the generalization of the effects of training, these hypotheses also apply to the situation where E_B offers the reinforcements. It is expected that there will be significant differences between E_A's subgroups and those of E_B.

METHOD

Subjects

Forty-five Ss were used in a preliminary research. There were 137 experimental and 97 control Ss. These Ss were matched, as far as feasible, in variables which appeared to be correlated with both the values of the reinforcements and the expectancy for occurrence of delayed reinforcements. These variables were: sex, age, grade, and socio-economic status. All Ss were males, 7 to 9, in Grades 2 and 3 of public schools located in a lower socioeconomic area of Columbus, Ohio.

Preliminary Study

A preliminary study was used to select two reinforcements which so differed in reinforcement value that approximately one-half of a group would choose the reinforcement of lower value when it was to be given to them immediately, and one-half of the group would choose the reinforcement of higher value when it was to be given to them a day later. With this pair of reinforcements, measurements could be made over a wide range of increases or decreases in the choice of reinforcements.

To select this pair, a measurement of the reinforcement value of a group of 11 toys was obtained by a rank-preference method. By progressively eliminating combinations of toys, a pair emerged in which half the group chose the immediate reinforcement of lesser value, and half chose the delayed reinforcement of higher value. The immediate reinforcement was a small metal airplane, and the delayed reinforcement was a small, plastic "flying saucer." As a reliability check on the reinforcement values of these two toys, 25 additional Ss chose the flying saucer (delayed choice) in preference to the airplane.

Experimental Groups

Three experimental groups were trained at three different schools, to prevent any effects of communication. To develop three levels of expectancy for the occurrence of delayed reinforcements, a series of five training trials was used. Following a preliminary activity, each S was told that he would receive a small balloon on the following day. This procedure was followed for five consecutive days, so that there was a total of four possible reinforcements. To develop the high, moderate, and low expectancy for delayed reinforcements, four, two, and none of the promised reinforcements were received, respectively.

Three days following the training trials, each *S* was offered his choice of an immediate or delayed reinforcement. In doing this, each experimental group was divided into two subgroups. One of these subgroups was given the choice by E_A, who was the *E* during the training trials; the other subgroup was given the choice by E_B, who had no prior contact with the groups. To maximize the differences between E_A and E_B, (*a*) the *E*s differed in age and sex; (*b*) three days intervened between training and the choice situation; (*c*) no mention of the choice situation was made during the training; and (*d*) in the choice situation the two *E*s saw their *S*s simultaneously in different rooms so that communication between groups was prevented.

Instructions

Each *S* was seen individually. On the first training day, for all *S*s, the *E* said:

"I am from a company that makes things for boys, and I am going to some of the schools. . . . Would you help me with these pictures? . . . These are coloring pictures. I want to know which is the best coloring picture . . . this one . . . or this one. Which is the best picture to color? . . . Thanks for helping me. . . . Do you like balloons? Would you like me to bring you a balloon tomorrow? . . . All right, I will bring you a balloon tomorrow."

On the next training day, if *S* was to receive the promised reinforcement, *E* said:

"I promised you a balloon today, and here it is. . . . Would you help me with these two other pictures today? . . . Which is the best coloring picture?"

The previous instructions were followed, again promising a balloon the next day.

If *S* was not to receive the promised reinforcement, *E* said, "I am sorry, but I just don't have any balloons today. . . ." He then continued with the above instructions.

On the test day, the instructions given by E_A, who had trained all the experimental groups, were as follows:

"I told you that I was from a company that makes things for children. . . . Do you like toys? . . . Here are two toys. Do you know what they are? I am going to *give* you *one* of these toys. Would you like that? If you want this one (e.g., the airplane) you can have it *right now*. If you want *this* one (the flying saucer), it is the only one I brought, so you can have it *tomorrow*. And I will see your class tomorrow to see that each boy got what he chose. . . . Do you understand? . . . All right, which one will you choose?"

If necessary, these instructions were repeated.

The instructions given by E_B required an introduction, since this was the first contact with her subgroup: "Hello, my name is Mrs.——. What is your name? . . . I am here to see some of the children in your school. . . . Do you like toys? . . . " From this point on the instructions used by both *E*s were identical.

Control Groups

Control groups were used in order to control for possible differences in the expectancies for occurrence of delayed reinforcements prior to the training sequence. These groups were given the final choice of immediate or delayed reinforcements without any training sequence. One control group was used at each of the three schools, and each was given the choice of reinforcements by E_A. In order to investigate the generalization or specificity of the expectancy for delayed reinforcements, a fourth control group was used at an additional school. This group was given the choice of immediate or delayed reinforcements by E_B. To minimize and control any effects of communication, the control groups were seen two weeks prior to the beginning of training of the experimental groups at each school.

RESULTS

Three control groups were given the choice of reinforcements by E_A. The chi-square values for comparisons among these groups were .205, .084, and .031. Since none of these values was statistically significant, these three groups were pooled, enabling chi-square tests to be made between experimental groups and the pooled control groups, and also among the experimental groups directly.

The basic data are given in Table 1 and in Fig. 1. A P value of .05 was taken as statistically significant. The high expectancy group had a significantly greater choice of delayed reinforcements than did either the moderate expectancy group ($.02 > P > .01$) or the low expectancy group

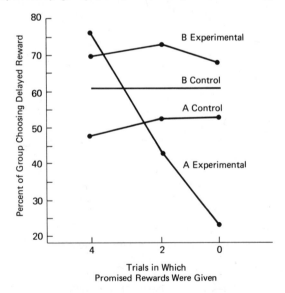

FIGURE 1. Choice of immediate and delayed reinforcements by experimental and control Ss.

Table 1   Choices of Immediate and Delayed Reinforcement

| | EXPECTANCY | | | | | | | | | POOLED | |
| NUMBER Ss CHOOSING REINFORCEMENT | HIGH | | | MODERATE | | | LOW | | | | |
	E_A	E_B	Control A	E_A	E_B	Control A	E_A	E_B	Control A	CONTROL A	CONTROL B
Immediate	6	6	12	15	5	12	18	7	10	34	10
Delayed	19	14	11	11	15	13	6	15	12	36	16
Total	25	20	23	26	20	25	24	22	22	70	26

$(P < .001)$ when E_A offered the reinforcements. The moderate expectancy group had an insignificantly greater choice of delayed reinforcements than did the low expectancy group $(.30 > P > .20)$ when offered the reinforcements.

The high and low expectancy groups had a respectively greater $(.05 > P > .02)$ and lower $(.02 > P > .01)$ choice of delayed reinforcements than did their respective control groups, when E_A offered the reinforcements. There were no significant differences in the choice of delayed reinforcements by the high, moderate, and low expectancy groups when E_B offered the reinforcements $(.80 > P > .50)$. There were no significant differences in the choice of delayed reinforcements by the high expectancy group and by its control group $(.70 > P > .50)$ and by the low expectancy group and by its control group $(.70 > P > .50)$, when E_B offered the reinforcements.

The low and moderate expectancy subgroups offered the choice by E_A, had a significantly lower choice of reinforcements than the respective subgroups, offered the choice by E_B $(P < .01; .05 > P > .02)$. There were no significant differences between the respective high expectancy subgroups $(P = .30)$. There were no significant differences between the pooled control groups, offered the choice by E_A, and the control group, offered the choice by E_B.

DISCUSSION

The results of this study suggest that a preference strength for a delayed reinforcement may be a direct function of the expectancy for delayed reinforcement. The apparent preference for immediate reinforcements, and the apparent decline in the effectiveness of a delayed reinforcement may, to a large extent, be a function of a lowered *expectancy*.

At least three implications may be drawn from these results. First, the effectiveness of a delayed reward or punishment may be increased, not necessarily by shortening the delay, but rather by increasing the expectancy that delayed reinforcements will occur. Second, depending on the nature of the training, an increased delay may function as a cue for a higher, lower, or the same expectancy for the occurrence of delayed rewards. Third, the preference strength for delayed reinforcements may be increased or decreased by increasing or decreasing expectancy while the value of the reinforcement remains constant.

Generalization of Expectancy

The results indicated that the effects of training with E_A failed to generalize to E_B. Instead, there were uniform reactions to E_B independent of the kind of training with E_A. Furthermore, there were uniform reactions to E_B whether or not the Ss had undergone prior training at all. Since the training was effective in raising or lowering the expectancies of the experimental groups, the lack of generalization may indicate that expectancies relating to E_B were already highly developed, so that training with E_A would fail to exert any appreciable influence on the expectancies relating to E_B.

According to this interpretation, behavior in a delayed reinforcement situation depends on the cues for various levels of expectancy for the occurrence of delayed reinforcements. Specifically, the results suggest that the two Es served as cues for different levels of expectancy. The implication is that delayed reinforcement behavior in general depends not only on the value of the reinforcements, but also on the expectancy for the occurrence of delayed reinforcements *as related to the social agent involved.* The effectiveness of a delayed reinforcement presumably will vary depending on the social agent who serves as the cue for the expectancy level.

SUMMARY

This study introduces Rotter's expectancy construct as an important factor in delayed reinforcement situations. The hypotheses were: (*a*) other factors being equal, the preference strength for a delayed reward will be low, moderate, or high as the expectancy for the occurrence of the delayed rewards is respectively low, moderate, or high; (*b*) social agents (i.e., Es) will serve as cues for different levels of expectancy.

The Ss were 294 second- and third-grade males, 7 to 9 yr. old. To select an immediate and delayed reward, a sequential analysis was made of the toy preferences of 70 Ss. E_A then trained three experimental groups to develop high, moderate, and low expectancies for the occurrence of delayed rewards. Three days later, one-half of the experimental group was given a choice of an immediate or delayed reward by E_A, and one-half by E_B, with whom they had had no previous contact.

The results show:

1. Expectancy for delayed reinforcements may be developed or modified by a set of experiences in which delayed or future reinforcements either occur or do not occur.

2. In the development or modification of the expectancy for delayed reinforcement, if other factors are equal, the behavior potential for selecting delayed reinforcements will increase or decrease with a relative increase or decrease in the expectancy for those delayed reinforcements to occur.

3. In the psychological situation, one of the important cues for the level of the expectancy for delayed reinforcements is the social agent perceived to be related to the occurrence or non-occurrence of the delayed reinforcement. The results suggest that different social agents may serve as cues for different levels of expectancy of delayed reinforcement and, therefore, different behavior potentials for choosing delayed reinforcements over immediate ones.

2-7 | Effects of Probability of Reward Attainment on Responses to Frustration[1]

WALTER MISCHEL and JOHN C. MASTERS

How do expectancies for ultimately obtaining a blocked or delayed reward in a frustration situation affect the value of the reward? Children viewed a film which was interrupted near the climax on the pretext of a damaged fuse. The probability that the film could be resumed was either 1, .5, or 0. Measures of the film's value were administered before and after the interruption. Thereafter, the fuse was "fixed" and all Ss saw the remainder of the film, with final value ratings obtained at the end. The hypothesis that the nonavailability of a reward increases its value was supported. Ss who were given a 0 probability for seeing the remainder of the film increased their evaluation of it more than those in the other groups, and this increase was maintained even after the entire film was shown.

Frustration may be defined as an imposed delay of reward and is typically operationalized by interrupting or blocking the organism's progress towards a valued goal. Various determinants of the ensuing responses have been investigated, with the speed and pressure of plunger-pushing frequently used as measures of the intensity of responses to frustration in human studies (e.g., Ford, 1963; Haner & Brown, 1955). There is considerable evidence from these studies, as well as from animal investigations, that the expectancy of goal attainment, *before* the imposed delay of reward, affects the amplitude of responses to frustration monotonically (Amsel, 1958; Ferster, 1958). That is, when subjects with a high expectancy of goal attainment are frustrated they respond more vigorously than those with lesser expectancies for reward.

Surprisingly, a quite different aspect of expectancy in the frustration situation has been relatively ignored. Namely, *after* the onset of frustration, how does the subject's expectancy for ultimately obtaining the blocked reward affect his responses? Especially when the objective probability for eventual goal attainment is ambiguous, subjective probabilities for obtaining the delayed goal may range from the definite anticipation of goal attainment to the expectation that the reward is lost irrevocably. It seems likely that such expectancies are potent determinants

[1] This study was supported by Research Grant M-06830 from the National Institutes of Health, United States Public Health Service. Grateful acknowledgment is due to the administrators and teachers of the Whisman School District who generously cooperated in this research.

of responses to frustration and the systematic manipulation of these expectancies is the focus of the present study. Change in the evaluation of the blocked reward is the reaction to frustration of main interest in this study.

In this experiment children were subjected to a frustration, in the form of an externally produced delay-of-reward. The experimental treatments involved variations in the probability that the frustration would be terminated and the blocked reward attained. More specifically, elementary school children viewed an exciting motion picture film which was interrupted near the climax on the pretext of a damaged electrical fuse. The experimentally presented probability that the fuse could be repaired and the film resumed was either 1, .5, or 0. A control group viewed the film without interruption. Response measures of the perceived value of the film, and the children's delay of reward behavior with other goal objects, were administered before and after the imposed delay period. Thereafter the fuse was "fixed" and the remainder of the movie was shown to all subjects, with another rating of its value and attractiveness obtained at the end.

There is some suggestive indirect evidence that the nonavailability of a reward increases its attractiveness or value (e.g., Aronson & Carlsmith, 1963). However, the relationship between expectancy or subjective probability and reward value or utility remains unclear. For example, Lewin, Dembo, Festinger, and Sears (1944) and Atkinson (1957) assume an inverse relationship between subjective probability and reward value, whereas Rotter (1954), Edwards (1954), and others argue for the independence of these constructs.

In a cogent discussion of this issue, Feather (1959a) has reasoned that, at least in our culture, persons learn to place greater value on the attainment of goal objects which are difficult to get because of the relatively consistent occurrence of sizeable rewards for the successful achievement of difficult goals and deprecation or punishment for failure to attain easy goals. Moreover, achievement of the difficult is probably more typically and highly rewarded when it was due to the person's own efforts or skill, rather than to chance factors beyond his control, and likewise failure to achieve the easy is chastised more when it was due to the person's lack of skill than when it was a chance occurrence. In view of this, Feather hypothesized that an inverse relationship between attainment attractiveness (goal value) and success probability would be more apparent in "ego-related" than in chance-related situations, and in achievement-oriented as opposed to relaxed conditions. Feather's (1959b) empirical results supported an inverse relationship between attainment attractiveness and success probability and indeed suggested that the independence assumption may be an oversimplification even for chance-related situations under achievement-oriented conditions. Similarly, Atkinson (1957) suggests that

the incentive values of winning qua winning, and losing qua losing, presumably developed in the achievement activities early in life, generalize to the gambling situation in which winning is really *not* contingent upon one's own skill and competence [pp. 370–371].

In the present experiment, it was reasoned that the learned inverse association between reward value and attainment probability in achievement-related situations generalizes to non-achievement-related frustration conditions in which goal attainment is not in the subject's control and is not contingent on his behavior. If in our culture persons acquire the generalized expectation that unlikely or unavailable positive outcomes are more valuable than likely or assured positive outcomes, then the value ascribed to an unattainable reward should be greater than that attributed to a reward that either may be attainable or whose attainment is assured. Accordingly, it was predicted that the perceived value of the delayed reward (film) would be greater when it is ultimately unattainable ($P = 0$) than when its attainment is assured ($P = 1$). Moreover, it was anticipated that certainty of reward attainment minimizes the effects of the imposed delay or frustration and therefore no differences were expected between the $P = 1$ treatment and the control group. Likewise, it was anticipated that the perceived value of the reward would be greater in the $P = 0$ condition than in the $P = .5$ group and that subjects in the latter would value the reward more than those in the $P = 1$ treatment or the control group. A posttest was included to determine whether differences between treatments in the perceived value of the delayed reward are maintained even after the frustration is terminated and the delayed reward is obtained.

It also seems plausible that when the perceived frustration is greater subjects will more frequently self-administer other available immediate rewards. Therefore, when the delayed reward is permanently unattainable, immediate self-reward (in the form of increased preference for immediate smaller as opposed to delayed larger rewards) should be greater than when it is ultimately attainable ($P = 0 > P = 1$). This was not hypothesized on the basis of any "compensatory mechanisms," but on the assumption that individuals in our culture learn that immediate self-reward is more acceptable following strong frustration than following minimal frustration.

METHOD

Subjects
The subjects were 56 boys and 24 girls, all sixth-grade students at two public schools in Mountain View, California.

Design and Procedure
Preexperimental Assessment of Delay-of-Reward Responses   In a preexperimental session the children were administered in their classroom groups a series of 14 paired rewards, in each of which they were asked to select either a small reward that could be obtained immediately, or a more valued item contingent on a delay period ranging from

1 to 4 weeks. The group administration (Mischel & Gilligan, 1964) proceeded in the following manner. Children were provided individual booklets containing on each page a brief description of a given set of paired objects and the associated time interval. After the experimenter had displayed both rewards and explained the temporal contingency, the children were instructed to record their choice and to turn the page in preparation for the next set of items. The subjects were also advised to choose carefully and realistically because in one of the choices they would actually receive the item they selected, either on the same day or after the prescribed delay period, depending upon their recorded preference. This promise was indeed kept.

Half of the sets of paired rewards involved small amounts of money (e.g., $.25 today, or $.35 in 1 week), while the remaining items included edibles (e.g., small bag of salted peanuts today, or a can of mixed nuts in 2 weeks), children's magazines, and various play materials (e.g., small rubber ball today, or a large rubber ball in 2 weeks).

Assignment to Treatments The total pool of subjects was divided into quartiles on the basis of the distribution of delay-of-reward responses. An equal number of children from each quartile was randomly assigned to each of the three experimental groups and the control group, thus producing groups similar in their initial willingness to defer immediate rewards for the sake of delayed, larger gratifications. The same proportion of boys and girls was assigned to each group.

At each of the two schools each of the four experimental conditions was administered once, with an approximately equal number of children from each school in each condition. Two new experimenters, unconnected with the preexperimental session, were used and each administered one half the treatments in one school and the other half in the second school. The temporal sequence of treatments at the two schools was balanced, the sequence in the second school being the reverse of the one in the first school.

Experimental Treatments Approximately 4 weeks after the assessment of delay-of-reward responses, the experimental sessions were conducted in a research trailer stationed at the school. From 8 to 12 subjects participated in each session. The experimenter was introduced as coming from "Deluxe Movie Studios" to prescreen an "exciting space movie" and to obtain the children's opinions about it. The film was a 20-minute documentary on space exploration. The children were told that they would fill out "audience estimate and opinion sheets" several times to determine their "feelings at different points." These sheets contained the value ratings described below. The experimenter explained that he was also interested in children's expectations about how attractive the film would be and therefore they would be asked to rate it before it actually commenced. This rationale was used to obtain a base level of attractiveness ratings in all groups to serve as a comparison point for any subsequent changes in the rated value of the film.

In the experimental groups the movie began as soon as the first value ratings were completed and collected. After 5 minutes, at a pre-determined climactic point in the film (just as the space ship was being launched) the projector failed. A confederate, posing as the "district electrician," entered and explained that the power failure was due to his overloading the circuits with electrical tools. This rationale was used to avoid connecting the cause of frustration with either the experimenter and his procedure or with the subjects' own behavior. The experimental treatments consisted of the following variations in the probability of resuming the interrupted film, announced by the confederate:

$[P = 1]$: I'm positive I can fix it—I've had things like this happen in the past, and I've always managed to fix them.

$[P = .5]$: I've had things like this happen before—sometimes I was able to fix them, sometimes I wasn't. I never know for sure . . . there's probably about a 50–50 chance.

$[P = 0]$: It takes a special fuse for this circuit, and there are none around here . . . I can't possibly fix it . . . there's no chance.

To increase credibility, the experimenter asked if the confederate was sure of his evaluation and the confederate reiterated his initial statement confidently in paraphrased form and left. The experimenter expressed his regret at the interruption but reminded the subjects that repeated "audience estimate" sheets were needed and circulated the second set of value ratings.

In the control group the movie was not interrupted and both sets of ratings were obtained before the movie began. The second set of ratings was administered approximately 5 minutes after the first set, and during the intervening period the experimenter prepared the film and projector. The rationale given to the children for readministering the ratings was in terms of the need for repeated measurements of their feelings at different times.

Following these second value ratings the children in all groups were administered a measure of immediate or delayed self-reward (described below).

Approximately 10 minutes after his first entry, and after the second ratings of the film and the delay-of-reward measures were completed, the electrician returned to all experimental groups, announcing that he had been able to fix the fuse and the movie would continue. The remainder of the film was shown and, when it ended, ratings of the movie were obtained for the third and final time. Table 1 summarizes the design and measures for all conditions.

Assessment of Reward Value. A four-item measure of reward or goal value was administered in printed booklets, the subject checking his responses to each item on a 7-point intensity scale. The items were:

(a) Let's pretend that you are the manager of a movie theatre. Instead of charging a set price for letting people see the movies you have, you do things differently—when you have a movie that you think is very good, you charge a lot for them to get in; when you think a movie

Table 1 Summary of the Experimental Design

Experimental Groups	Phase 1: First Measure of Film Value[a]	Experimental Treatments	Phase 2: Second Measure of Film Value and Re-administration of Delay Measure[b]	Film Completed	Phase 3: Third Measure of Film Value
I (N = 20)	Same	Film interrupted; P = 1 for resumption	Same	Same	Same
II (N = 20)	Same	Film interrupted; P = .5 for resumption	Same	Same	Same
III (N = 20)	Same	Film interrupted; P = 0 for resumption	Same	Same	Same
IV (N = 20)	Same	No interruption; film not yet begun	Same	Same	Same

[a] Following this, film begins in all groups except IV.
[b] Following this, film begins in Group IV.

is bad, you don't charge very much at all. Now let's pretend that the movie I have today is at your theatre—check about how much you would charge for tickets [0 to $1.00].

(b) Let's pretend that you have a month's allowance of $1.00 to spend on movies. Suppose the movie I have with me today is showing at a theatre you usually go to. Remember, you have $1.00 to pay for movies for a whole month, and if you go to see a show, part of your money will be gone. Now, let's also pretend that they *don't* have the regular prices at the theatre for this movie, but they have special ones —and you don't know exactly how much they are. How much would you pay [0 to $1.00], out of your dollar, to see the movie I have here today if it were at that theatre?

(c) We all go to see movies. Let's compare the movie I have here with some of the movies you have seen in regular theatres. Check above the words [from "much better" to "much worse"] that tell how well *you* feel this movie compares [or will compare] with others.

(d) We are interested in how good you think the movie is going to be [or is]. You are to put a check mark above the words [from "really good" to "awful"] which say how good *you* feel the movie is [or will be].

The above measures were given in the same random sequence to all subjects, with a different sequence used in each of the three administrations.

Assessment of Changes in Delay Behavior Immediately following the second set of ratings the children were administered a new series of 14 paired choices between immediately available smaller rewards and delayed larger rewards. The rewarding objects differed from those employed in the preexperimental sessions, but the money items were the same since pretesting revealed that subjects were unable to recall the exact amounts and temporal intervals involved. The experimenter indicated at the outset that these choices were unconnected with his own project and were being administered for a Stanford researcher during the available period in order to save time.[2]

RESULTS

Prior to the experimental manipulations the groups did not differ appreciably in their initial evaluation of the film. The first (Phase 1) mean value ratings of the movie in the control, $P = 1$, $P = .5$ and $P = 0$ groups, respectively, were 16.85, 16.90, 16.75, and 16.55. Figure 1 shows the mean value rating of the film at each of the experimental phases for each group.

---

[2] At the end of each experimental session the children were informed of the importance of not communicating with others about the experiment because it would "spoil things for us and take the fun out of it for the other children." All subjects agreed to this and were given the rewards they had been promised, either at this time or after the specified delay period, depending on the choice they had made. Informal postexperimental interviews indicated that there had been no communication about the particulars of the experiment.

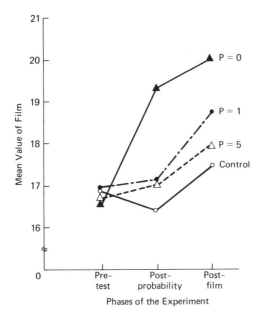

FIGURE 1. Mean value of film at each phase of the experiment.

To assess the effect of the independent variable, change scores were computed for the difference between each pair of value ratings in each group. Analysis of variance of the mean change in value ratings immediately after interruption of the film (difference between Phase 2 and Phase 1 ratings) revealed a significant effect ($F = 5.91$, $df = 3/76$, $p < .005$). Table 2 summarizes the results of t tests for differences between groups in mean value change. It is evident (Row 1 of Table 2) that subjects who

Table 2   Between-Group Comparisons of Mean Changes in Value of Film

MEAN CHANGE BETWEEN	$P = 0$ VERSUS CONTROL t	$P = 0$ VERSUS $P = 1$ t	$P = 0$ VERSUS $P = .5$ t	$P = .5$ VERSUS $P = 1$ t	$P = .5$ VERSUS CONTROL t	$P = 1$ VERSUS CONTROL t
1. Phase 1 and 2 (Preprobability to post-probability)	3.88**	3.12**	2.94**	.18	.94	.76
2. Phase 1 and 3 (Preprobability to postfilm)	2.69*	1.70	2.20*	.49	.49	.98

* $p < .05$.
** $p < .01$.

were told they would definitely not see the remainder of the film $(P = 0)$ increased their evaluation of it significantly more than those in all other conditions.[3] None of the other groups $(P = 1$, $P = .5$, control) differed from each other.

Moreover, as Figure 1 indicates, the increased evaluations of the film in the $P = 0$ condition was maintained even after the interruption was terminated and the movie completed. Analysis of variance of changes in value ratings from Phase 2 to Phase 3 indicated no significant differences between groups $(F < 1)$. However, analysis of variance of change from the first preexperimental value measure to the terminal rating after completion of the film indicated significant treatment effects $(F = 2.74$, $df = 3/76$, $p < .05)$. The between-group comparisons of these change scores (Table 2) show that subjects in the $P = 0$ condition tended to maintain their overevaluation of the movie even after they viewed the entire film, although the difference between the overall increment in the $P = 0$ group and the $P = 1$ condition falls short of acceptable significance.

The data clearly showed an increase in the evaluation of an unattainable goal but there was no evidence for a linear inverse relationship between the probability of attaining a goal and the value attributed to it. Value changes in the $P = .5$ condition were not significantly different from those in the $P = 1$ or control groups. Indeed, the mean terminal value rating was slightly (not significantly) higher in the $P = 1$ treatment than in the $P = .5$ condition.

The effects of treatments on changes in delay-of-reward behavior were examined by comparing the number of preexperimental and postexperimental immediate reward choices made in each condition. The control, $P = 1$, and $P = 0$ groups showed mean increases in immediate reward choices of 1.1, 1.5, and 1.3, respectively, whereas in the $P = .5$ condition there was a fractional decrease $(-.3)$. Analysis of variance of these data yielded no significant effect $(F < 1)$.

DISCUSSION

The results show that the value of a blocked or delayed reward can be affected by the expectancy for its ultimate attainment. When the probability for seeing the interrupted film was stated as 0, its rated value increased signficantly more than when it was 1 or .5. When resumption of the film was presented as a certainty, children evaluated the film no differently than those who saw it without interruption.

Although the value of the film increased most when its completion seemed nonattainable, and this change was maintained even after the film was completed, significant increases did not occur when an intermediate probability $(P = .5)$ was given. Subjects given an intermediate

---

[3] As a partial check on the internal consistency of the four items measuring the value of the film, the effects of the independent variable were examined separately for the first two items combined and the last two items combined. Since the results revealed highly similar trends the final analyses were based on all four items combined.

probability did not differ from those in the $P = 1$ and control conditions. An extension of the present study, using a large number of probability levels, would clarify whether the obtained effect of probability on value is restricted to unattainable outcomes ($P = 0$) or holds for highly unlikely outcomes (e.g., $P = .10$).

Since subjective probability does not necessarily match experimentally presented probability statements, it would also be interesting to assess the subject's expectancies for attaining the delayed reward and to examine the relationship between subjective probability and reward value in the present situation. For example, in the $P = .5$ treatment, most children may have had subjective expectancies for seeing the film which exceeded .5 considerably. Such effects may account for the lack of difference obtained between the $P = 1$ and $P = .5$ manipulations.

The present results indicate that in our culture unattainable positive outcomes may be more valued than those which are attainable and that the unavailability of a positive outcome enhances its perceived desirability. Moreover, the findings support the view that the higher value attributed to unlikely outcomes in achievement-related situations generalizes very broadly even to non-achievement-related situations in which the probability for goal attainment is clearly independent of difficulty level and in which goal attainment is entirely outside the subject's own control. These results have direct implications for understanding responses to frustration. If the nonattainability of a reward increases its desirability, persons who, on the basis of their previous histories, expect that delayed or blocked rewards are lost irrevocably will respond quite differently from those who anticipate their ultimate attainment. The individual who has learned that blocked goals tend to be unattainable may remain on the unhappy treadmill, expecting that what he wants cannot be obtained and overevaluating and wanting what he cannot have. Certainly this is not an unfamiliar clinical phenomenon. In contrast, the person who has learned that frustrated goals ultimately tend to become available may respond to delay of reward with equanimity.

The treatments did not significantly affect self-reward behavior in the form of changes in willingness to defer immediate rewards for the sake of larger but delayed outcomes. Unexpectedly, there was a slight, non-significant trend towards increased *delay* behavior in the $P = .5$ condition, whereas in all other treatments subjects tended to increasingly choose immediate rewards. It may be speculated that when the ultimate attainment of the blocked reward is uncertain children try to be especially "good," deferring immediate gratification in the irrational hope that their "good" behavior will increase the probability of obtaining the blocked goal. This is sheer speculation but may be interesting to pursue.

The present experiment was designed to minimize the occurrence of cognitive dissonance at the onset of frustration and therefore the frustration was deliberately unconnected with the subject's own behavior and not contingent on his own decisions. In contrast, when a temporary or permanent delay of reward is a consequence of the subject's own behavior, dissonance theory (Festinger, 1957) might generate predictions opposite to those of the present study. In a recent study by Carlsmith (1962), subjects were exposed to the possibility of electric shock with variations in the probability that they would actually receive the shock. The probability was ostensibly determined by the subject's performance on a fictitious personality test. Carlsmith's prediction of an increase in the rated "pleasantness" of the shock as a function of the probability of receiving it was supported and is consistent with dissonance theory. Comparisons between the present study and the Carlsmith experiment are precarious because they differ in several critical ways; for example, the latter was not a frustration paradigm, involved aversive rather than positive outcomes, and presented probabilities ostensibly determined by the subject's own performance.

In a very recent study by Turner and Wright (1965) children rated the attractiveness of toys before and after a number of experimental manipulations. In one condition they were informed that they could "never" play with one of the toys they had just rated and in another that they could play with it "later." The rated value of the toy decreased in the "never" condition and increased in the "later" condition. These findings appear inconsistent with the present results but again there are numerous problems that prevent clear comparisons. For example, in the Turner and Wright study the children may have interpreted the "never" condition as the punishing consequence of their own rating behavior. Perhaps even more important, in both the Carlsmith (1962) and the Turner and Wright (1965) studies, the postmanipulation ratings were obtained after brief temporal delays (15 minutes and 5 minutes, respectively) whereas in the present experiment the reevaluation occurred almost immediately after the announced probabilities. It may be that such temporal effects are critical determinants of the relationship between expectancy and value. The initial response to an unattainable positive goal may be to overevaluate it (as in this study) but after being faced with its unattainability for some time justification processes commence and the value of the reward becomes minimized. It would be interesting to test for a positive relationship between probability of goal attainment and reward value under dissonance-producing conditions (in which the frustration is the consequence of the subject's own behavior) using an extension of the present experimental design, and including a temporal variation in the amount of time elapsing between the onset of frustration and the measurement of reward value.

PART 2: SUMMARY

What are the implications of the preceding research, as well as other SLT research, for the acquisition and performance of behavior? Stated another way, how can the concepts of SLT be utilized to better understand the learning process?

Generalization of Expectancies

Perhaps one of the most important contributions of SLT to the learning process is the manner in which expectancies change and generalize. This is of crucial importance for SLT and also seems to have broad implications for an understanding of learning generally. This is true for at least three reasons. First, on the basis of both theoretical assumption and common sense observation, the value of a reinforcement is not the sole determinant of behavior. The expectancy that a given behavior will lead to a valued reinforcement is equally important. Second, an experience of positive or negative reinforcement does not universally affect every behavior in the individual's repertory. By the same token, it does not solely affect the specific behavior that produced the reinforcement. In short, the occurrence of such a reinforcement tends to have selective effects on the individual's behavioral repertoire. Third, the occurrence of a reinforcement following a given behavior may have little if any effect in raising the potential for the future utilization of that or any other behavior. To summarize, the effect of the occurrence of a reinforcement subsequent to a given behavior must be related to the manner in which it affects the expectancy for that behavior and other behaviors to lead to reinforcement again.

The paper by Chance (1959; 2–1) illustrates the role of generalization of expectancies. Previous work by Crandall (1951) showed that expectancies generated by failure on a physical-skills task influenced subsequent TAT stories. Generalization was most pronounced for physical-skills stories, least pronounced in stories dealing with interpersonal relations, and of moderate effect on stories relating to academic achievement. Similar results were obtained by Jessor (1954) but using different tasks. Building on these studies, but controlling for physical similarity of tasks, Chance was able to demonstrate that expectancy for success generalizes along lines of need relatedness. Dean (1960) reported similar results. In his experiment the design maximized generality and controlled physical similarity and performance, with the result that generalization of expectancies varied as a function of the need similarity of the situations. Taken together these four studies suggest that through the mediating effects of the generalization of expectancies, reinforcement of one behavior will affect other behaviors to the extent that such behaviors are functionally related (lead to similar goals).

Schroder and Rotter (1954), in an interesting departure from the previous studies, also confirmed the hypothesis that a change in behavior in one situation will generalize more to a second situation the more the latter situation contains cues that have been historically associated with the same reinforcement as the cues in the first situation. Of interest, however, is that they (1) used rats as Ss; (2) studied extinction as the behavior; and (3) controlled both response and stimulus similarity.

Particularly important is the use of a behavioral response rather than a verbal statement of an expectancy change. This point will be mentioned later, but it does demonstrate, for the moment, that such results are not restricted to verbalizations. Of course, the problem of generalizing these results to a human population is obvious.

Another study that moved away from measures of expectancy statements or goal levels was that of V. J. Crandall (1955a). He found that (1) frustration of behaviors in a given pathway resulted in decreased expectancies for success in that pathway; (2) the frustration generalized so that there was a decrease in expectancies for success in other pathways *related* to the same need as the pathway frustrated; (3) no generalization obtained in nonrelated needs. His measure of expectancy for success was judges' ratings of thematic stories.

All of these findings are of great importance for the learning process, since they suggest that the success or failure of a specific behavior may have effects on many other behaviors that are seen by the individual as leading to the same goal.

Another line of research relates to the issue of generalization of expectancy changes. A study by Mischel (1958a) investigated the effects of commitment on expectancy changes. Using several techniques to vary the degree of commitment involved in Ss' expectancy statements, Mischel's general results indicate that following failure, the greater the degree to which one has publicly committed himself to an expectancy, the more resistance there is toward the lowering of that expectancy. Watt (1965) also reported an inverse relation between extent of prior commitment and lowering of expectancies following failure. Such results did not obtain, however, when there was a one-week delay between expectancy statements. Presumably, this occurred because the constraints of commitment tend to dissipate with the passage of time. Contrary to prediction, highly committed Ss raised their expectancies more after success than less committed Ss.

Another aspect of the generalization phenomenon has to do with the distinction between specific expectancies (E') and generalized expectancies (GE) discussed in Part 1. The occurrence of a behavior is mediated by reinforcement value and expectancy. However, the latter is determined by two different kinds of experiences—E' and GE. E' involves one's history of reinforcement in x situations for functionally related behaviors. The importance of this distinction for the learning process resides in the fact that as experience in a specific situation accumulates, the likelihood of a given behavior occurring becomes increasingly a function of one's reinforcement experience in that situation. Conversely, when one has little experience in a specific situation, the probability of a given behavior occurring is largely a function of one's reinforcement history in other situations for functionally related behaviors. Stated otherwise, predictions about a behavior early in a learning sequence must give greater attention to the individual's reinforcement history in previous situations that elicited behaviors oriented toward similar goals.

Data on this point generally are supportive of the above analysis, although there are some exceptions. An early study by Dean (1953) showed that Ss receiving high scores on a first task tended initially to state expectancies on a subsequent task which were higher than their performance warranted. Succeeding blocks of trials did not show this. Neff (1956) found that even after a long series of successes, Ss who had shown a high GE initially required more failure trials to extinguish their expectancy for success. This is not, of course, consistent with what was expected based on the E'-GE formulation. Schwarz (1969) provides results which suggest that the influence of GE and E' are not simply related to number of trials experienced in a situation but instead are influenced both by the quality of reinforcement (positive or negative) and the pattern of reinforcement.

Further evidence that a simple reinforcement principle is insufficient to account for the expectancy changes that help mediate behavioral change comes from a study by Rychlak (1958). He showed that when frequency and value of positive reinforcement are held constant, the number of past tasks performed serves increasingly to stabilize generalized expectancies. This suggests, for example, that an individual receiving one reinforcement on each of five different tasks will show a more stable generalized expectancy than an individual receiving five similar reinforcements, all on one task. In short, when the sheer amount of previous experience is controlled, *variety* of previous experience is an important determinant of expectancy changes and thus behavior. Additional work by Rychlak and Eacker (1962) also suggests that individuals reinforced out of line with their initial expectancy modify their generalized expectancies more readily following a series of negative rather than positive reinforcements.

These studies, along with others dealing with generalized expectancies, provide us with an important concept to handle the apparent discontinuity between learning situations. Even when the individual encounters relatively unique learning situations, his expectancies generalized from past situations that involved behaviors related to present goals in the situation enable us to make meaningful behavioral predictions.

Individual Differences in Generalization

Thus far, the emphasis has been on factors that affect the learning process through their influence on expectancy changes or the generalization of expectancies. A frequently neglected factor in many learning theories is that of individual differences. Although such content factors are dealt with in greater detail in Part 4, it seems appropriate at least to comment briefly about several that relate directly to the process of learning.

It is probably fair to say that the influence of sequences of external reinforcement on expectancies is severely altered by idiosyncratic tendencies or styles of expectancy changes. Several studies have investigated the problem of identifying unusual reactions to reinforcement. Rotter (1945) discussed several patterns of goal-setting or expectancy behaviors on level-of-aspiration tasks that seem to relate to specific personality characteristics. This work is described in detail elsewhere (Rotter, 1954).

Rychlak and Lerner (1965) have studied the generalization of expectancies as it relates to the content category of manifest anxiety. Defining anxiety in SLT terms as a low generalized expectancy for success, this study suggests that (1) Ss high in manifest anxiety are less stable as regards their generalized expectancy statements than are nonanxious Ss, and (2) manifestly anxious Ss generalize expectancies from more recent experience while nonanxious Ss are more likely to transcend the immediate situation and thus show more stability in generalized expectancy.

The entire body of data available from the internal-external control of reinforcement research (Rotter, 1966) is also relevant here. That is, individuals who tend to see reinforcement as contingent upon their own efforts (internals) are more prone to alter their behavior as a function of reinforcement than are externals who see reinforcement as being non-contingent on their efforts.

Some very preliminary results (Phares & Davis, 1966) also suggest the role of individual differences in generalization. Using Pettigrew's Category Width Scale (1958), they showed that following failure, broad categorizers demonstrated significantly greater generalization of expectancies from one task to the next than did narrow categorizers.

In sum, these studies suggest that in order to maximize prediction of behavior in learning situations, it is necessary to consider individual differences both in the tendency to generalize from past situations and in the style or quality of those generalizations.

Delay during a Trial Sequence
Another variable that exerts an influence upon behavior through its effects on expectancy is delay. The study by Rychlak and Eacker (1962) provided some tentative evidence that when individuals are required to delay several minutes following experience with a series of tasks, they will show less change in their generalized expectancies than when delay is not required. The paper by Schwarz (1966; 2-2) describes in considerable detail his work, along with much of that of Phares (1961, 1964a, 1964b, 1966), which deals with the influence of delay upon expectancy changes. These studies provide still another contribution of SLT in demonstrating that the effects of reinforcement are tempered by the role of expectancy changes. In this instance specifically, delays during the learning process tend to shift the effects of reinforcement in the direction of expectancies held earlier in the situation and also in the direction of expectancies

generalized from related situations. Also, as Schwarz (1966) points out, such factors probably contribute toward consistency and stability in personality. That is, the induction of behavioral changes is made more difficult by virtue of the fact that in many human learning situations the reinforcement experiences are strung out over time. Therefore, the effects of reinforcement can be gauged only by calculating the influence that delay periods exert on the expectancies that are developing during the acquisition or learning process.

Delay of Reinforcement

The paper by Mischel and Staub (1965; 2–3) summarizes several studies that again point to the role of expectancies generalized from past similar situations in affecting behavior beyond what might be anticipated based on the value of the reinforcement. Mischel (1966) deals extensively with the antecedents of self-imposed delay of reward and presents the results of a program of research in the delay of reinforcement.

Studies by both Mahrer (1956; 2–6) and Mischel (1966) provide support for the view that when preferences for delayed reinforcement exist, they do so because of the expectancy that the reinforcement will be forthcoming. Mischel and Staub (1965) extend this analysis by showing that when the delay involves instrumental activity that determines reinforcement, contingent rewards were chosen more often after success than failure. Moreover, success and failure experiences in the experimental situation tended to minimize the effects of generalized expectancies. Also, individuals in a noncontingent, delay-only condition tended to wait for larger rewards to a greater extent when they had high generalized expectancies than when they had low expectancies.

This latter study is important for several reasons. First, it introduces instrumental activity into the delay picture and thereby probably comes closer to what actually occurs in real life. Second, it includes measures of generalized and specific expectancies for success and demonstrates the relation between them and delay phenomena. Third, the study involves choice *behavior* and not merely the effects of certain conditions on expectancy *statements*. This point is very important, since many of the previous studies on generalization of expectancies involve expectancy statements but do not deal with explicit behavior. The delay studies summarized by Mischel (1966) show quite clearly that an SLT analysis involving expectancies does apply directly to behavior and is not restricted to studies that solely enumerate conditions which affect expectancy statements.

Learning in Skill and Chance Situations

The effect of positive or negative rewards has been generally considered by most to either strengthen or weaken a response. However, in terms of SLT, this will occur only if the individual perceives reinforcements as being contingent upon his own behavior. Put in terms of a specific situational condition, the basic argument is that learning under *skill* conditions is quite different from learning under *chance* conditions.

Previous studies by Phares (1957), James and Rotter (1958), and James (1957) have demonstrated that major differences in the growth and extinction of verbal expectancies occur when tasks are perceived as being controlled by chance versus being controlled by skill factors. That is, these differences obtain when one anticipates that reinforcement occurs as a function of something external to himself in contrast to his belief that reinforcement is a function of his own behavior. Obviously, tasks could differ along this dimension in degree as well as kind. These previous studies suggest that the differences in behavior in the two kinds of tasks are not merely a matter of degree but involve different principles of learning. This is shown particularly in the reversal of partial versus 100 percent reinforcement conditions in the chance versus skill groups, with the typical finding (Lewis, 1960) of superiority of resistance to extinction in the partially reinforced condition found only in the externally controlled or chance task. Such findings are of considerable importance both in learning theory and in the application of learning principles to a complex life situation.

However, the above findings were all based on the use of a single task or tasks in which the difference between chance control and internal control was established by differential instructions. Rotter, Liverant, and Crowne (1961) studied the differences in the growth and extinction of expectancies using two different tasks which they hypothesized would be regarded as skill- and chance-controlled tasks on the basis of the previous cultural experience of the subjects rather than by instructions. Their results strongly supported the hypothesis that under skill conditions positive and negative reinforcement leads to greater increments and decrements in verbalized expectancies. Second, their results suggested that the extinction of expectancies under continuous negative reinforcement will reverse under chance and skill conditions, so that 50 percent is more resistant to extinction than 100 percent reinforcement under chance conditions, and 100 percent reinforcement is more resistant to extinction than 50 percent reinforcement under skill conditions.

Using a behavioral criterion of quitting the experiment, Holden and Rotter (1962) showed that both chance and ambiguous conditions required significantly more trials to extinction than did skill conditions. These two studies are of great interest, since they demonstrate the generality of results from instructions to culturally defined tasks and from expectancy statements to behavioral responses.

Extending these results to a perceptual situation, Phares (1962) found that tachistoscopic threshold decrements were lowered significantly more when learning took place under conditions of personal control than under chance conditions.

In some additional studies, James (1957) successfully replicated the extinction data noted earlier, and Bennion (1961) and Blackman (1962) studied sequential factors which help determine whether reinforcement is perceived as skill or is chance determined.

In an interesting program of research at an animal level, Seligman, Maier, and Solomon (1969) have provided analyses and results highly similar to the above human work carried out with an SLT framework.

The foregoing research seems to demonstrate clearly that the effects of reinforcement are quite different depending upon whether the individual perceives such reinforcement as dependent upon his own efforts or upon factors beyond his control. This is another way of saying that the learning process differs depending upon whether skill or chance factors are operative. When one considers how much research in psychology is carried out under laboratory conditions which may lead S to suspect he is not really in control, then the question arises as to how much generality such research possesses.

The Relation between Expectancy and Reinforcement Value

For many years the relation between expectancy and reinforcement value has been of great interest. Such a relation, if any, has especially intrigued decision theorists and those learning theorists who analyze behavior as being a resultant of choices among alternatives. The issue has been approached both in terms of whether attractiveness of outcomes is influenced by probability of attainment and whether subjective probability is influenced by the nature of the outcome. Feather (1959a) has summarized several theoretical positions regarding the relation between the two variables. For example, Atkinson (1957) and Lewin et al. (1944) stress an inverse relation between subjective probability and reward value. Edwards (1954) and Rotter (1954) consider them to be independent. Indeed, in SLT these two variables are regarded as *systematically* independent. There is no necessary relation, although under specific conditions they can be shown to be related due to prior learning experiences.

The element of wishfulness or magical thinking (especially when children are used as Ss) is quite important here. The study by Crandall, Solomon, and Kellaway (1955) addressed itself to this variable. They attempted to control for "wishfulness" in Ss, a factor that may have helped produce the results of Marks (1951) and Irwin (1953), which indicated that desirable outcomes increase Ss' stated probabilities while undesirable outcomes depress them. Crandall et al. found that with an accuracy incentive, the value of an event affects expectancy statements only when objective probability is .50. Subsequently, the same authors (1958) showed both that the acquisition of expectancies for positive events is faster than for negative ones and that positive-event expectancies extinguish less rapidly than negative-event expectancies. Two studies by Jessor and Readio (1957) suggest (1) no evidence that value influences expectancy when children are the Ss, and (2) with college students, as the value of an event increases, so too does expectancy (especially at the .50 level of objective probability). Hess and Jessor (1960) also indicate that the rate of learning and asymptotic level of expectancies are independent of the value of the expected event.

The preceding studies, although somewhat equivocal, seem to suggest that as the value of an event increases, so does the expectancy for its occurrence. The generality of such a conclusion may be limited, particularly when no control for "wishfulness" is exerted. The study by Worell (1956; 2–4) is especially interesting here because he found reverse results. That is, a more valued event tended to decrease expectancies for its occurrence. To resolve this discrepancy in results, Worell suggests that we distinguish between achievement and nonachievement situations. Thus, when our competency is challenged (as in skill or achievement situations) defensive reactions may be evoked with a resultant lowering of expectancies. In chance or nonachievement situations there is no need for defensiveness and, indeed, wishfulness may even come to play a more prominent role. Such an analysis is of particular interest when we consider that the earlier research, suggesting that expectancy increases when reward value increases, was largely carried out in chance-gambling situations. In this vein, Phares (1965b) could find no support for the hypothesis that desirable outcomes tend to enhance stated probability of attaining the goal when both skill and chance situations were used.

Turning to the other side of the coin, Mischel and Masters' (1966; 2–7) paper investigates the effects of expectancy upon reward value in the context of frustration. Based on the notion that there is a *learned* inverse relation between expectancies and reinforcement value, these authors go even further and suggest, on the basis of Atkinson's (1957) and Feather's (1959a) analysis, that this relation generalizes to nonachievement situations. Their results support such a hypothesis. However, it is not clear exactly which need area is involved for their Ss, nor is it clear how far one can generalize their results to frustrating situations which involve such need areas as sex, dependency, or dominance.

The preceding brief review of relevant research suggests that the relation between expectancy and reinforcement value is exceedingly complex. We can only state again the SLT view that, although relations between expectancy and reinforcement value may develop on a learned basis, these relations may be positive, negative, or zero.

The tendency of investigators to pursue research in restricted classes of situations may be responsible for their view of the relation between the two variables. Thus, Atkinson's (1957) view regarding the inverse dependency of the two variables may stem from his exclusive emphasis on achievement situations. Many of us learn that "sure things" are not great accomplishments. In the achievement area, it is the improbable outcomes that truly attain high value. For a professional football team to win from a high school team would not be reinforcing. However, in other need areas, the highly probable may not detract from the value of a reinforcement. For example, a male five minutes away from an orgasm with a beautiful girl may well have a very high expectancy that the orgasm will occur. Yet it is not clear that this expectancy tends to detract from the value of the event. Similar examples might be drawn from such need areas as dependency or dominance. Therefore, although it is true that many reinforcements may, in part, derive their value from their rarity or the sense of pride which stems from their achievement, it may be just as true that others do not.

Conversely, it is probably true that highly valued events are often accompanied by high expectancies for their occurrence. However, in view of the research noted earlier, this often seems to be a function of wishful thinking. Gambling situations, with failure to achieve at one's expectancy level, may not always be negatively reinforcing.

It almost appears as if one position is that there is no relation between expectancy and reinforcement except under certain specific conditions, while the other position suggests that there is a relation except under certain specific conditions. If so, then the real problem becomes the identification of the situational variables that affect the relation (or lack of it) and its magnitude. From an SLT viewpoint, it would be anticipated that since both expectancy and reinforcement value are to some extent situationally determined, in specific situations the level of expectancy or the value of the reinforcement may in itself be a cue that determines the quantity of the other variable to some extent.

Research on Decision-Making

The relation between expectancy and reinforcement value is intimately involved with the whole area of decision theory. A series of studies, including that of Lotsof (1956; 2–5), illustrate some of the variables that affect decision time and also how decision time can be utilized as measures of SLT concepts.

By holding expectancy constant, Lotsof (1956) found that decision time varied inversely with degree of discrepancy between two reinforcing alternatives, and also that when pairs of negative reinforcement values are about equal, decision time varies directly with the strength of the reinforcements. The foregoing was true both for hypothetical and for real choices.

A second study by Lotsof (1958) held constant the value of reinforcement but varied expectancy and substantiated the hypothesis that the higher the expectancy for positive reinforcement, the shorter the decision time. Further, Lotsof (1959) notes that certainty of response can be utilized much as are decision time measures.

Rotter and Mulry (1965), in studying the construct validity of the internal-external control variable (Rotter, 1966), provided results which also have implications for decision theory. In line with Lotsof's (1956) results, they confirmed the hypothesis that internals would take longer to make a difficult discrimination in a skill situation while externals would take longer to make that discrimination in a chance situation. Both frequency and order of reinforcement were controlled. This study not only demonstrates the generality of Lotsof's findings that decision time can be used as a measure of reinforcement value but it also has implications for decision theory. By showing that external Ss do not decrease decision time in a chance situation (rather, they tend toward an increase), their results suggest a limitation of Feather's (1959a) results. Feather assumes reinforcement in a chance task results from the value of the reinforcement alone, but in skill tasks it is a combination of the value of the reinforcement and the value of success. Rotter and Mulry's results suggest that this analysis may apply only to internally oriented Ss.

Pursuing the role of individual differences, Liverant and Scodel (1960) found that internally oriented Ss tended to prefer intermediate probability bets or extremely safe bets over long shots and that they tended to bet more money on safe as against risky bets when compared to external Ss. These results, along with those of Rotter and Mulry, suggest the utility of theoretically derived measures of individual differences in order to maximize prediction in this area.

Lefcourt (1965) found results that parallel, in many respects, those of Liverant and Scodel. Blacks, in a gambling situation, behaved in an internally oriented fashion. That is, they chose less low probability bets, made less shifts in bets, and generally took fewer risks than whites. The implication may be that the perception of blacks that success in conventional tasks is controlled by forces outside themselves is reversed in games of chance.

Verbal Conditioning

Another example of the role social learning theory can play in understanding the level of performance of an acquired response is in the area of verbal conditioning. Generally, the research literature suggests that neither sheer exposure to reinforcement nor S's discovery of the reinforcing cue and its contingency to the critical response is sufficient to account for response change. If one focuses on the expectancies of the individual as a determinant of verbal conditioning, the role of internal versus external control of reinforcement (Rotter, 1966) becomes relevant. A series of studies (Crowne and Liverant, 1963; Odell, 1959; Strickland, 1962; Gore, 1962; Ritchie & Phares, 1969) suggests that externals tend to rely on others in social influence situations while internals are more likely to react negatively toward attempts to influence them, particularly in the case of disguised influence.

On the basis of such research, Getter (1966) hypothesized that those who perceive their reinforcements to be controlled by themselves (internals) resist attempts to condition their verbal behavior, while those who feel others control reinforcement (externals) are more likely to yield to experimenter influence. Getter found support for this hypothesis and, of especial interest, was able to identify a large number of "latent conditioners." These were Ss who showed no evidence of conditioning during the training trials, but during extinction, in the absence of reinforcement, showed a significant rise in the previously reinforced verbal response. These Ss were significantly more internal than either Ss who did not show such latent conditioning among nonconditioners or who conditioned during the training trials.

The foregoing is a particularly good example of how a personality variable derived from SLT can be employed to understand the variability in rate of emission of a phenomenon ordinarily considered the predominant domain of the laboratory, experimental psychologist. It once again affirms the notion that such learning situations are composed of cues that arouse expectancies for response-reinforcement sequences. To predict the response adequately, we must understand the expectancies and reinforcement values operative even in such relatively molecular laboratory situations.

Persistence Behavior

Persistence behavior has long been variously ascribed to internal trait states or motivational variables (Feather, 1962). Two recent studies from a social learning theory framework have investigated persistence as a function of expectancy variables. Lefcourt and Ladwig (1965) showed that black reformatory inmates who believed the task involved personal skills of musicians (skills that they possessed) persisted longer than either of two control groups (Ss who either knew nothing about music or were intermediate in their experience). The results were taken to show the role of expectancy in persistence behavior.

Battle (1965), in a study with junior high school students, found that persistence on an academic task was positively related to expectancy for success. Neither minimal goal level nor attainment value were significant predictors. However, minimal goal "certainty" scores and discrepancy between expectancy and minimal goal (both derived expectancy measures) also related to persistence.

Looking Behavior

Certainly in humans, the learning process is, to a great extent, a function of paying attention to the proper cues. When attention is focused in the right direction, learning is presumed to be better. Efran and Broughton (1966) used SLT to formulate the hypothesis that "looking behavior" in Ss would be directed toward whichever peer they expected to be more approving. Results indicated that visual interaction was strongly influenced by differences in expectancy for approval. A subsequent study (Efran, 1968) also showed that the reinforcement value or importance of persons, as well as the likelihood of their giving approval, determines visual focus in some situations.

These studies, then, demonstrate that visual focus is significantly affected by both reinforcement value and expectancy in social interaction situations. This is particularly important when one considers that an enormous amount of human learning takes place in such situations.

The Situation

The importance of situational cues in affecting the learning process can hardly be overemphasized. It is clear that situational cues greatly influence expectancies for behavior-reinforcement sequences. Since this role is discussed both in Part 1 and in Part 4, it will not be described again in detail.

A study by Schroder and Rotter (1952) clearly shows how the behavior potential of looking for alternative solutions can be raised by increasing, through training, the expectancy that such behavior will be rewarded. Moss (1961) showed how the situation becomes an important determinant of cautious behavior—especially when personality differences are also considered. The point regarding the interaction of personality and situation is discussed by Rotter (1960a), particularly as it affects the testing situation. A general discussion of the importance of the situation is also provided by Rotter (1955). Studies by Phares and Rotter (1956) and Henry and Rotter (1956) show the influence of situationally determined expectancies in the alteration of reinforcement values, which, in turn, affect behavior. Any study of learning can be similarly analyzed to show the relation between cues and expectancy for behavior-reinforcement sequences.

Concluding Remarks

In discussing the role of this theory in the learning process we have tried to deal with some of the more important conditions that relate to the learning process. This is, indeed, the role of a process theory as compared to content theories which operate at the level of individual differences (Rotter, 1967c).

Of course, one should distinguish between those definitions of learning that emphasize the acquisition of behavior and those that emphasize performance. Within SLT, the emphasis is clearly on performance; that is, determination of the factors that contribute to the performance of one behavior in the individual's repertoire rather than another.

It is clear that much human learning takes place at an observational level (Bandura & Walters, 1963; Mischel, 1968) and does not require any direct reinforcement. Likewise, the role of classical conditioning and the importance of stimulus contiguity are apparent. This social learning theory has not been oriented toward a detailed accounting of the acquisition of highly specific bits of human behavior. It is recognized that through such avenues as observational learning and classical conditioning even the most backward human being builds up an enormously varied and complex hierarchy or repertory of potential behaviors. Given such a repertory, with the application of SLT, we can begin to understand and predict which behavior will occur in a given situation and which conditions may lead to a modification in behavior potentials.

Thus, it may be fair to say that with humans and their vast repertory of responses, a question of crucial importance concerns why the individual does what he does rather than something else. Nearly everyone knows how to behave aggressively or dependently, and so on. Why, then, does one behavior occur in distinction to another? Indeed, even in those cases where a specific behavior is not in the individual's repertory, he generally knows what steps to take to learn the behavior. The prime issue then becomes an analysis of appropriate expectancies and reinforcement values. It is, of course, important to distinguish between those instances in which the individual fails to perform because the behavior is not available and those in which the failure involves inadequate levels of reinforcement value and expectancy. In general, it is possible to make this distinction by systematically increasing the levels of these two variables and noting the effect on behavior. If the behavior still does not occur, the probable conclusion is that the behavior has not been acquired.

Finally, the importance of the inclusion of an expectancy construct should again be mentioned. Much of the preceding work can be construed as showing how expectancies affect or moderate the role of reinforcement in human behavior. In a sense, one of the major contributions of SLT may be the effective and systematic inclusion of both reinforcement and expectancy within the same theory. The trend toward the inclusion of expectancy-cognitive variables has been growing in recent years. That is, beginning with the recognition of the value of habit strength and anticipatory goal reaction in the S–R, Hullian framework and also with Mowrer's (1960) and Pribram's (1967) work, we have increasing evidence of the utility of an expectancy formulation.

3 | Applications to Personality Development

INTRODUCTION

Is it possible to construct a theory so that a single set of theoretical constructions can be useful with different methods and contexts of behavioral observation, and so that a relation observed in one context can be "transferred" and used to pose questions in another context? Rotter's Social Learning Theory (SLT) was originally developed with such an aim; albeit, Rotter's earlier concerns directed his attention toward questions about deviant personality processes and clinical change which could eventually be answered in an experimental context. However, the resulting theory has usefulness for describing personality change whenever it occurs. The constructs and their interrelations, which are useful in describing behavior change in psychotherapy or in a learning experiment, are equally useful in describing socialization and personality development.

The reprinted selections in this section are a sample from a sizable literature utilizing SLT in research concerning problems of personality development. The papers included cover a range of psychological method in the field of development—from observations of relatively unconstrained child behavior through studies based on test scores and interview data to investigations more nearly approximating traditional experimental method. As can be seen in the summary at the end of this section, the content of questions that can be asked about personality development within this theoretical framework is also varied. It may, therefore, surprise the reader that the papers presented in Part 3 display a noticeable selectivity toward those concerned with achievement striving. Two reasons lie behind these choices. First, a good many papers that might have been included in this section appear in other sections of the book. Though those papers deal with problems of personality development, they are also directly pertinent to other topics. The summary at the end of this section will bring together these studies, along with many others not included in this volume, and will attempt to convey an over-all perspective about the body of research in personality development.

Papers reprinted here represent many of the questions and problems that are more or less classic in the domain of developmental research. Accounts of the history of developmental psychology often refer to early baby "biographies" as the first method produced in the field. Usually, however, the next sentence deplores the method as overly prone to bias and so "rich" in data as to defy adequate management. Nevertheless, many developmental investigators are still struck with a compelling sense that watching and recording child behavior must be a valid thing to do— if we can correct the faults of the method and find a way of producing order in the data. Rafferty, Tyler, and Tyler (3–1) attempt to apply SLT for exactly that purpose, devising a system for observing the behavior of nursery school children.

Crandall, Dewey, Katkovsky, and Preston (3–2) address themselves to the practical question of what variables of parental attitude and practice predict school achievement performance. Battle (3–3) demonstrates effectiveness of variables like "expectancies," "values," and "standards" for meaningfully describing children's attitudes toward their school achievement and also for providing a high level of prediction of future academic performance. Chance (3–4) examines the predictive value of children's generalized expectancies for personal control of reinforcing academic consequences, as well as maternal antecedents of these expectancies.

Crandall, Good, and Crandall (3–5) pose the interesting question, "When is it that an outcome of behavior is reinforcing for the human child?" Employing both direct manipulation of adult reaction to performance on an experimental task and assessment of the child's generalized expectancy of success—brought with him into the experimental situation— they are able to predict nicely when the child will behave as though "succeeding" or "failing" is occurring. Pisano (3–6) manipulates expectancies in an experimental procedure, involving modeling of rationalizing behavior and observations of consequences to a model. This manipulation, in conjunction with subjects' assessed predispositions to possess, or to lack, more positive and constructive behaviors for coping with failure, demonstrates the interaction of effects of model exposure and subject predisposition in changing expectancies.

3-1 Personality Assessment from Free Play Observations[1]

JANET E. RAFFERTY, BONNIE B. TYLER, and F. B. TYLER

Observation of behavior in "natural" situations has been one of the most enduring methods for studying behavior of preschool children. However, certain methodological problems have tended to reduce the value of this approach. It is the purpose of this paper to specify criteria for maximal utility of observational measures and to demonstrate the use of these criteria in the development of an observation measure for personality assessment of preschool children.

A review points up the important considerations in the development of an observational measure, as well as providing a capsule history of the emergence of psychology as a science. As emphasis on the need for objectivity and quantification increased, the early diary type of observation method (Darwin, 1877; Shinn, 1900) was rejected as naive, unsystematic, biased, and nonquantified and was largely replaced by time sampling or category recording (Arrington, 1943; Bott, 1933; Goodenough, 1928; Loomis, 1931; Parten, 1932). While the latter emphasis led to systematization, objectivity, and quantification, it in turn has been criticized for several reasons: "(1) it provides no checks on recording individual instances of behavior, (2) it is inflexible and omits descriptive detail thus divorcing acts from their context and perhaps violating their meaning, (3) it permits fewer opportunities for the later working of the data than do diary-type, anecdotal notes [Gellert, 1955; p. 182]," and (4) ". . . concern with reliability led to progressive modifications of the categories . . . until inter-rater agreement was at a maximum . . . (but) as a result the categories . . . became more and more removed from any theoretical basis and their predictive efficiency was minimal [Heyns & Lippitt, 1954; p. 371]."

Because of the limitations of the older methods of category recording, there has been a shift in emphasis in recent research. Two trends are apparent. First, an attempt has been made to develop a method which would combine the advantages of the early diary methods (flexibility and potential for qualitative analyses) with the advantages of category recording (systematization, objectivity, and quantification). This trend has been reflected in the increased utilization of refined diary type methods such as running records, impression records, and anecdotal records (Stone & Church, 1957).

[1] This investigation was supported by a research grant, M-1137, from the National Institute of Mental Health, Public Health Service, and by research funds from Southern Illinois University.

Secondly, an increasing emphasis has been placed on theoretical, inferential approaches. Thus, newer observational systems more frequently require the observer to make inferences from behavior concerning motives and feelings and more often are theoretically oriented so that considerations of underlying theory, rather than reliability *qua* reliability, are more crucial in determining what is to be observed (Heyns & Lippitt, 1954).

From a consideration of the methodological problems extant in observational measures, the authors have abstracted the following criteria as focal to the development of maximally useful observational measures: (a) theoretical orientation, (b) systematization, (c) quantification, (d) reliability, (e) economy, and (f) use of minimally overlapping categories. In this research these criteria served as a guide for the development of an observational measure for personality assessment of preschool children in their usual nursery activities. A discussion of the way in which these goals were accomplished is presented in the following sections.

PROCEDURE

Subjects

The Ss were children, ages 2–6 to 5–0, enrolled in a cooperative preschool located on a college campus. Data were collected for a total of 34 children: first sample $N = 18$, second sample $N = 16$.

Criterion of Theoretical Orientation

The importance of the theoretical orientation lies in the fact that it provides coherence and coordination of the total research program. In this research the theoretical assumptions were as follows: (a) all behavior is motivated; (b) such motivations may be categorized, i.e., those behaviors which lead to the same or similar goals may be subsumed within one category; (c) prediction of behavior is more efficiently made using a two variable, rather than a single variable system, i.e., utilization of both a strength of motivation variable and a probability of reward variable; and (d) the situation or environmental context is fundamental to prediction. While some or all of these assumptions are held in common with many current theories (Dollard & Miller, 1950; Feather, 1959a; Lewin, 1954; Mowrer & Kluckhohn, 1944; Rotter, 1954; Tolman, 1955), Rotter's social learning theory of personality (Rotter, 1954) was most influential in this research.

The motivational categories used in this study were as follows: recognition-status (concern with skill or competence in social, intellectual, or play activity), love and affection (concern with acceptance, warmth, liking or being liked by others), dominance (concern with direction or control of others), protection-dependence (concern with having others prevent frustration, make decisions), and independence (concern with self-mediated satisfactions including reliance on oneself). Within each of these need categories, behavior was analyzed as to its need value (importance to the individual) and as to the individual's level of expectancy (subjective probability for success).

Criterion of Systematization

In an effort to overcome three potential sources of bias in the collection of observational data (time bias, observer bias, and situational bias), the following procedures were followed: For each sample two observers collected data for the first three months of school. Daily six children were observed (three by each observer) for four five-minute periods. In this way each child was observed at least once a week. The observation mean was 261 minutes for the first sample and 306 minutes for the second sample. Observations were made both indoors and outdoors and were distributed over the various nursery school periods, e.g., party time, free play, and story time. Indoor observations were made from an observation booth through a one-way vision mirror.

Criteria of Quantification

Typically there appear to be two decisions the researcher using observational methods must make. One of these concerns whether scoring shall be done concurrent with or subsequent to observations, and the second is whether the scoring will be derived from a category system, rating scale, or based on over-all impression. For this research, immediate scoring of behavior was rejected because such an approach would not permit rating of behavior by an individual who had not made the observations and thus would not allow for an uncontaminated estimate of reliability. Consequently, the decision was made to use running records. All observations were made in a shorthand system and were descriptive and inclusive, so that, insofar as possible, all behaviors and interactions of the child were recorded with no attempt to select or to attend to particular behaviors.

A scoring-by-example manual was developed for rating the observations. Such a method seemed preferable to scoring based on impression because it would provide: (a) potentially greater reliability since ratings are based on many verifiable referents, rather than on global clinical impressions, (b) a comparable basis for rating each set of child observations, and (c) operational definitions of the concepts. While a category system may offer many of the same advantages, that approach was rejected because the only quantification it allows is frequency counts.

The scoring manual was constructed with five need sections, each of which has two subcategories, need value and expectancy. For each subcategory, behavioral descriptions are given with specific examples for each. These descriptions and examples are ordered along a seven-point scale and make it possible to assign each ratable behavior a need value and expectancy score in a need category, e.g., a behavior might be scored recognition-status, need value 6, expectancy 2.

Within the scoring system the environmental context or situation has been viewed as essential to assessing the meaning of a particular response, i.e., the score assigned a behavior is contingent upon the situation in which that behavior occurs. Consequently, situations have been classified as to reinforcement "loading" on the basis of (a) general cultural expectations for children of preschool age (e.g., we expect them to seek help with some articles of clothing, as boots, coats, etc.) and (b) cues for reinforcement provided by the initiator of the activity and/or by the structure of different nursery school periods (story time, party time, etc.). The classifications of situations and their relation to the scoring are given below.

A *maximally loaded situation* is defined as one in which the majority of overt cues are highly related to a single need. Because of the preponderance of cues that "insure" reinforcement in such situations, behavior which occurs within the structure of the situation is assumed to have no more than average value and is assigned a score of 3 or 4. For example, the situation is maximally loaded for recognition-status when the teacher asks, "Who knows the story about the three bears?" The behavior is assigned a score of 4 in recognition-status when the S responds, "I do."

A *medially loaded situation* is defined as one in which the overt cues might be related to more than one need, but are maximized for none. Because the cues are fewer and less highly related to any specific need, behavior occurring in such a situation is considered to have more importance and is assigned a score of 5. For example, the situation is medially loaded for love and affection when two children are in close proximity. The behavior is assigned a score of 5 in love and affection if the subject smiles and pats the child next to him.

A *minimally loaded situation* is defined as one in which there seems to be a lack of overt cues for the specific need in question. Because there are few cues for reinforcement, the behavior occurring in such a situation is assumed to have great importance to the individual and is assigned a high score. For example, the situation is minimally loaded for love and affection when other children are distant from S. The behavior is assigned a score of 6 or 7 if the subject walks across the playground to the other child, puts his arm around him, and pats him gently.

Finally, a low score is obtained only by rejection of a maximally loaded situation. For the subject to reject reinforcement which is "assured" suggests that such reinforcement has a low value to him. For example, the situation is maximally loaded for love and affection when a child puts his arms around S and pats him gently. The behavior is assigned a score of 1 if S kicks, hits, or bites the initiator. It should be noted that in the example given, the S would also receive a high score for dominance, since the situation fits the designation of a minimally loaded situation for dominance, as well as being maximally loaded for love and affection.

RESULTS

Criterion of Reliability

Interrater reliability of the manuals has been assessed by computing Pearson *r*s for mean child scores based on independent ratings of the two observers and an independent judge. In both samples the two observers rated all children on the total number of observations, whereas the independent rater scored observations of 10 randomly selected children from each sample on two-thirds of the total number of observations. In each case rs were computed for the subcategories, need value and expectancy, for the needs: recognition-status, love and affection, dominance, protection-dependence, and independence.

Interrater Reliability between Observers Data concerning reliability between observers are reported in Table 1, columns 5 and 10. In general, it would appear that the manual provided a reliable measuring instrument for qualified observers, although the correlations for love and affection and the two independence variables are somewhat lower than is the case for the other variables. It should be noted that the reliabilities for the first sample, whose protocols were used in constructing the scoring manual, were not materially different from those of the second sample.

Interrater Reliabilities for Three Raters In an effort to assess the communicability of the scoring system, correlations were computed among the ratings of the two observers and an independent rater. From Table 2 it may be seen that for judges I and II (the observers) the range of correlations was from .00 to .93, the median r was .72, 21 correlations were significant at the .05 level or above, and 9 were nonsignificant. For judges I and III the range of rs was from .05 to .87, the median r was .49, 13 correlations were significant at the .05 level or above, and 17 were nonsignificant. The range of correlations for judges II and III was .11 to .95, the median r was .63, 20 correlations were significant at the .05 level or above, and 10 were nonsignificant.

When these data are compared with those obtained from two observers rating all the data on all subjects (Table 1), it can be seen that for three raters there was a wider range of correlations and the median rs were somewhat lower. While these findings are based on data from fewer children and on fewer data for each child, amount of data is probably the more significant variable. This conclusion seems warranted because of the fact that: (a) median rs based on ratings of two-thirds of the data for 10 children (Table 2) are comparable to median rs based on ratings of two-thirds of the data for samples of 18 and 16 children (Table 1, columns 4 and 9); and (b) when correlations based on ratings of two-thirds of the data for 10 children were corrected for length using the Spearman-Brown formula, they yielded median rs (Table 2) which are comparable to those obtained when all data are rated for all children (Table 1, columns 5 and 10).

In view of the comparability of findings for judges I and II (the observers) and judges II and III, it should be noted that there does not seem to be an observer bias. However, there is some indication of possible individual bias between raters I and III, since the number of significant correlations and the median rs were considerable lower between these two raters.

Criterion of Economy
Although numerous studies have used 100- and 150-minute totals of observational time, the range has varied widely from less than one hour to

Table 1 Correlations for Need Value and Expectancy Ratings Using Variable Amounts of Data

| | AMOUNT OF OBSERVATIONAL DATA | | | | | | | | | |
| | Sample No. 1 (N = 18) | | | | | Sample No. 2 (N = 16) | | | | |
CATEGORY	1st ⅓	2nd ⅓	3rd ⅓	⅔	Total	1st ⅓	2nd ⅓	3rd ⅓	⅔	Total
Recognition-Status										
Need value	.67**	.58*	.65**	.74***	.86**	.58*	.57*	.86**	.53*	.76**
Expectancy	.67**	.47*	.66**	.74***	.77***	.63**	.77**	.69**	.71**	.75**
Love and Affection										
Need value	.16	−.04	.78***	.08	.29	.69**	.57*	.62**	.73**	.77**
Expectancy	.75**	.80**	.81***	.91***	.90***	.67**	.58*	.90**	.77**	.78**
Dominance										
Need value	.52*	.82**	.77***	.91***	.93***	.76**	.81**	.87**	.88**	.95**
Expectancy	.49*	.60**	.78***	.71***	.79***	.87**	.62*	.30	.85**	.72**
Protection-Dependence										
Need value	.10	.48*	.75***	.60***	.70***	.75**	.41	.46	.53*	.76**
Expectancy	.41	.69**	.77***	.58*	.69***	.19	.70**	−.19	.65**	.75**
Independence										
Need value	.04	.24	.81**	.31	.69***	.61*	.75**	.65**	.79**	.83**
Expectancy	.45	.64**	.35	.60***	.62**	.53*	.72**	.21	.81**	.60*
Median r	.46	.59	.77	.65	.74	.65	.66	.64	.75	.76
Range of r	.04–.75	−.04–.82	.35–.81	.31–.91	.29–.93	.19–.87	.41–.77	−.19–.90	.53–.88	.60–.95

$*\ p \leq .05.$
$**\ p \leq .01.$

Table 2   Correlations among Ratings of Observers (I and II) and the Independent Rater (III)

		PEARSON r			S-B PROPHECY		
		Sample 1 N = 10	Sample 2 N = 10	Comb. N = 20	Sample 1 N = 10	Sample 2 N = 10	Comb. N = 20
I-II:							
R-S	NV	.79**	.92**	.82**	.85**	.94**	.87**
	EXP	.93**	.87**	.75**	.95**	.91**	.82**
L&A	NV	.10	.41	.49*	.14	.51	.59**
	EXP	.89**	.80**	.82**	.92**	.85**	.87**
Dom	NV	.90**	.85**	.70**	.93**	.90**	.77**
	EXP	.63*	.80**	.84**	.72*	.86**	.89**
P-D	NV	.68*	.71**	.63**	.76*	.79**	.72**
	EXP	.57	.72**	.76**	.66*	.79**	.82**
Ind	NV	.46	.00	.16	.56	.00	.23
	EXP	.08	.12	.19	.11	.16	.27
I-III:							
R-S	NV	.37	.68*	.56*	.46	.76*	.65**
	EXP	.86**	.73**	.37	.90**	.80**	.47*
L&A	NV	.14	.34	.27	.20	.44	.35
	EXP	.87**	.80**	.80**	.91**	.86**	.86**
Dom	NV	.66*	.72**	.57**	.74*	.80**	.66**
	EXP	.11	.78**	.49*	.16	.84**	.59**
P-D	NV	.57	.44	.48*	.66*	.54	.58**
	EXP	.31	.37	.42	.40	.46	.52*
Ind	NV	.52	.07	.05	.61	.11	.08
	EXP	.34	.10	.21	.44	.14	.29
II-III:							
R-S	NV	.27	.71*	.79**	.35	.79**	.85**
	EXP	.90**	.84**	.64**	.93**	.89**	.72**
L&A	NV	.53	.49	.61**	.63*	.59	.70**
	EXP	.93**	.95**	.85**	.95**	.96**	.89**
Dom	NV	.50	.83**	.58**	.60	.88**	.68**
	EXP	.11	.86**	.62**	.16	.90**	.71**
P-D	NV	.86**	.46	.78**	.90**	.56	.84**
	EXP	.69*	.34	.60**	.77**	.44	.69**
Ind	NV	.64*	.42	.29	.73*	.54	.38
	EXP	.37	.71*	.50*	.46	.78**	.60**

* $p \le .05$.
** $p \le .01$.

several hours (Jersild & Meigs, 1939). While there has been general agreement that reliability is likely to increase with increased number of observational samples, with few exceptions there has been little systematic treatment of this question (Olson, 1930–31; Smith, 1931). Because economy was considered to be one of the important criteria of usefulness of an observational measure, an effort was made in this study to determine the minimal amount of data necessary to obtain stable ratings. Accordingly, the data from each subject were divided into thirds, each third consisting of equal amounts of observational data from each observer and covering about one month of observational time. Thus, for the first sample reliabilities were computed for each 87-minute time period, for 174 minutes, and for the total 261 minutes. For the second sample reliabilities were computed for each 102-minute unit, for 204 minutes, and for the total 306 minutes. These findings are reported in Table 1. The fact that reliabilities were greater for each successive third for the first sample (.46, .59, and .77), but were approximately the same for successive thirds in the second sample (.65, .66, and .64), probably reflects degree of experience with the scoring manual; i.e., as the raters became increasingly familiar with the manual, greater stability of ratings occurred. Noting columns 1, 4, and 5 of Table 1, it appears that with inexperienced judges stable measures require about 175 minutes of observational time, but that more satisfactory reliability correlations occurred with about 260 minutes of observation. In contrast, noting columns 6, 9, and 10, it appears that with experienced raters relatively stable measures were obtained with 100 minutes of observation, although more satisfactory correlations were obtained with 200 minutes of observation.

These findings were obtained with a rather complex rating system. It was also possible to assess amount of data required for a category system by computing reliabilities for assignment of referents to motivational categories, without regard to the score assigned within the category. In many respects this kind of analysis corresponds more closely to that frequently reported in the literature. These data, reported in Table 3, parallel those from the rating system, although the correlations were consistently higher for the category system; for one-third, two-thirds, and total data, the median rs are .82, .81, and .89 for the first sample and .91, .96, and .95 for the

Table 3   Correlations for Need Category Ratings Using Variable Amounts of Data

| | AMOUNT OF OBSERVATIONAL DATA | | | | | |
| | Sample 1 $(N = 18)$ | | | Sample 2 $(N = 16)$ | | |
	⅓	⅔	Total	⅓	⅔	Total
R-S	.95**	.92**	.95**	.97**	.97**	.96**
L&A	.78**	.76**	.86**	.81**	.89**	.90**
Dom	.93**	.95**	.95**	.93**	.97**	.95**
P-D	.82**	.81**	.89**	.72**	.72**	.80**
Ind	.74**	.73**	.87**	.91**	.96**	.96**
Median r	.82	.81	.89	.91	.96	.95

** $p \leq .01$.

second sample. As with the rating system, it appears that amount of experience in rating is an important variable although its effects are not as marked.

Summarizing, it appears that the amount of data necessary for stable ratings is a function of the complexity of the scoring system and the degree of experience of the raters. With inexperienced raters, high reliability coefficients were obtained for a category system using 87 minutes of observation, but for a complex rating system similar reliabilities were obtained only with 260 minutes of observation. Comparable reliabilities for experienced raters required proportionally less time.

Criterion of Minimally Overlapping Categories

In an attempt to avoid superfluous or contaminated variables, the independence of categories was assessed in two ways. One method was measurement of the degree of relationship between each need category and every other need category, both for need value and expectancy. From these correlations, which are reported in Table 4, it can be seen that none of the interrelationships is of sufficient magnitude to warrant assigning a single need value or expectancy score for an individual. It appears that there is virtually no cross-need generality for need value; median r is .04 and only two of the 30 rs are significant at the .05 level. For expectancy, while the median r is higher (.20) and eight of the 50 correlations are significant at or beyond the .05 level, it would appear that any cross-need generality is confined to recognition-status with love and affection, recognition-status with dominance, love and affection with dominance, and possibly love and affection with protection dependence.

The second test of independence of categories was made by correlating variables within need categories. From Table 5 it can be seen that need

Table 4   Intercorrelations of Need Variables

NEED SUBCATEGORIES	NEED VALUE			EXPECTANCY		
	Sample 1 $N=18$	Sample 2 $N=16$	Comb. $N=34$	Sample 1 $N=18$	Sample 2 $N=16$	Comb. $N=34$
R-S, L&A	−.26	.04	−.07	.50*	.23	.44**
R-S, Dom	.33	.13	.29	.53*	−.01	.44**
R-S, P-D	.31	.25	.28	.17	.47	.22
R-S, Ind	.25	.44	.25	−.09	.04	−.05
L&A, Dom	.06	−.17	−.02	.65**	.66**	.68**
L&A, P-D	.15	−.17	−.03	.43	.35	.45**
L&A, Ind	−.17	−.52*	−.36*	−.07	.27	−.02
Dom, P-D	.16	.17	.17	.03	.06	.05
Dom, Ind	−.03	−.01	−.03	.04	.38	.10
P-D, Ind	−.17	.04	−.08	−.10	.09	−.10

* $p \le .05$.
** $p \le .01$.

Table 5   Correlations between Scores of Need Value and Expectancy for Each of the Need Variables

	SAMPLE 1 $N = 18$	SAMPLE 2 $N = 16$	COMB. $N = 34$
R-S	.38	.29	.34*
L&A	.00	−.22	−.01
Dom	.66**	.87**	.71**
P-D	.62**	.73**	.61**
Ind	.71**	.75**	.73**

* $p \le .05$.
** $p \le .01$.

value and expectancy measures are positively and significantly inter-correlated, except for the love and affection variable.

Since other research has shown need value and expectancy measures to be relatively independent for adults (Tyler, Tyler, & Rafferty, 1959), the results obtained here may be a function of the fact that preschool children do not differentiate between importance of a particular goal and the probability of achieving it.

Another possible reason for the lack of independence of need value and expectancy measures found here may be related to the technique of measurement. Observations of behavior in situations where there is relative freedom of response may not provide information regarding the entire range of expectancy and need values of a person. If the behavior which occurs in a given situation is a function of need value and expectancy, the behavior most likely to occur in a "free" situation would be that in which both need value and expectancy are above a minimal level. In contrast, structured situations, such as interviews or experimental situations, would be more likely to elicit information throughout the entire need value and expectancy continua.

SUMMARY

The research reported here had as its goal the development of an observational measure for personality assessment of preschool children. Criteria for maximal utility of such a measure were specified, and the steps taken to meet these criteria were discussed. The theoretical assumptions of this research were outlined and were shown to relate to the development of a scoring-by-example manual. The scoring system was found to be adequately reliable both for the observers and for an independent rater. Analyses regarding economy demonstrated that amount of data required for stable ratings was a function of the complexity of the scoring system and the degree of experience of the raters. Data regarding the independence of measures suggested that there is little relationship among the need categories measured. However, moderate relationships between need value and expectancy variables within need categories were found, and possible reasons for their existence were discussed.

3-2 Parents' Attitudes and Behavior and Grade-School Children's Academic Achievements

*VAUGHN CRANDALL, RACHEL DEWEY,
WALTER KATKOVSKY, and ANNE PRESTON*

A. PROBLEM

Since the time of Binet's pioneering attempts to predict children's academic achievements from their performances on intelligence tests, psychologists and educators have been concerned with factors producing individual differences in young children's scholastic attainments. Early research addressed to this question was primarily devoted to the role which general intellectual abilities played in academic performances. More recently, educational and child-development researchers have concerned themselves with factors other than ability which might also contribute to performance differences. Personality variables such as achievement motivation and anxiety have been brought into the picture. The achievement need has been the center of recent concerted research efforts by a number of investigators: e.g., McClelland and his colleagues (Atkinson, 1958; McClelland, Atkinson, Clark, & Lowell, 1953). So, too, has anxiety been used as a predictor variable for intellectual and academic performances: e.g., McCandless and Castaneda (1956); Sarason, Davidson, Lighthall, Waite, and Ruebush (1960).

Research on determinants of such achievement performances has indicated that both ability and motivational variables are useful and necessary predictors. Another broad, and basic, question still remains: What are the *antecedents* of differences in children's intellectual achievement motivations and performances? In other words, what environmental factors in children's everyday experiences facilitate or impede the development of intellectual and academic competence? Many persons and situations influence a child's personality development. Parents, teachers, siblings, and peers all interact with a child in the course of his daily experiences, and each of these individuals can be an important social reinforcer of the child's behaviors. This is true whether the area of personality under consideration is the development of aggressive, dependent, affiliative, or achievement behaviors.

Concerning the development of achievement motivations and behaviors, it is apparent to the careful observer that most children have developed by the time they enter grade school, fairly consistent differences in the values they attach to intellectual and academic achievements, in their expectations of success in these activities, in the standards they use to judge their efforts, and in the methods and strategies they employ in their attempts to attain achievement goals. What factors produce these differences? This

From *The Journal of Genetic Psychology*, 1964, **104**, 53–56. Copyright 1964 by The Journal Press and reprinted by permission of the authors and the publisher.

is the general question to which this research is directed. The present article describes one study of a larger research project concerned with parents as identification models and reinforcers of young children's achievement behaviors.[1] The investigation explored relationships between parents' attitudes and behaviors and their early-grade-school-age children's academic performances.

B. METHODS

1. Sample

The sample was comprised of 120 Ss: 40 early-grade-school-age children, and their fathers and mothers. The child sample contained 20 boys and 20 girls equally distributed in the second, third and fourth grades at the time the children were administered academic-achievement tests. The socioeconomic status of the families was assessed by Hollingshead's Two Factor Index of Social Position (Hollingshead & Redlich, 1953). The proportions of families in Hollingshead's social classifications I through V were 10, 30, 29, 31, and zero respectively, indicating that all but the lowest social classification was reasonably represented. Slightly more than one-half of the fathers and one-fourth of the mothers were college graduates. Table 1 presents information regarding the intellectual levels and academic-achievement test performances of the children. The children's intellectual abilities were assessed with the Stanford-Binet Intelligence Test; their academic performances, with the California Achievement Test.[2] As indicated in Table 1, the children of the study were intellectually superior to national norms; all but two had IQs above 100, and approximately three-fourths of the children obtained scores more than one standard deviation above the national average. The mean IQ of the group was 124. Intellectual abilities within the sample, however, varied appreciably. The children's IQs ranged from 79 to 164, with a SD of 16. As might be expected from their intelligence-test scores, the children's performances on the standard academic-achievement tests were generally above grade level. Only two of the children were reading below grade level, and only five were not performing at or above their grade level in arithmetic.

2. Assessment of Parent Attitudes and Behaviors

The parents were interviewed individually at the Fels Research Institute for the Study of Human Development. To prevent communication between parents, each set of parents was interviewed concurrently but separately.[3] The interview sessions averaged from two-and-one-half

[1] This study was a part of the project "Parents as identification models and reinforcers of children's achievement development," partially supported by USPH Grant M-2238, awarded the first-listed author.

[2] The second author of this report administered the academic-achievement tests. Appreciation is expressed to Dr. Virginia Nelson, who gave the Stanford-Binet Intelligence Tests to the children.

[3] The fathers were interviewed by the third-listed author; the mothers, by the fourth author.

Table 1   Intelligence and Academic-Achievement-Test
Performances of the Children

	NUMBER OF CHILDREN
Stanford-Binet IQ	
Below 100	2
100–114	9
115–129	13
130–144	14
145 and over	2
Reading age vs. chronological age	
RA less than CA	2
RA 1–9 months beyond CA	7
RA 10–19 months beyond CA	19
RA 20–29 months beyond CA	5
RA 30–39 months beyond CA	4
RA 40–49 months beyond CA	2
Arithmetic age vs. chronological age	
AA less than CA	5
AA 1–9 months beyond CA	12
AA 10–19 months beyond CA	13
AA 20–29 months beyond CA	7
AA 30–39 months beyond CA	3

to three hours, and were electronically recorded for subsequent interview analyses. Two interviews were given each parent during the interview session. The first was concerned with the parent's attitudes and reported behaviors toward his child's everyday achievement efforts. This interview covered four achievement areas, only one of which—the intellectual achievement area—is relevant to the present study. The second interview covered several general (nonspecific to achievement) behaviors of the parents. These included parental affection, rejection and nurturance.[4] Copies of the parent interview schedules and rating scales may be obtained.[5]

3. First Interview

Interview I obtained information regarding the following parental attitudinal and behavioral variables:

a. The Parent's Attainment Value for His Child's Intellectual Performances This referred to the degree of importance or value the parent attached to his child's intellectual achievements. This rating assessed the intensity of the parent's desire that his child show interest and participate in intellectual activities; and the value the parent placed on his child's effort, persistence, and competence in these situations.

[4] A fourth general parental-behavior variable—dominance—was also assessed in Interview II for a study other than the present one, and is not discussed in this report.
[5] Virginia Crandall, Fels Research Institute.

b. The Parent's Evaluation of His Child's Intellectual Competence This variable was concerned with the level of competence the parent felt his child characteristically demonstrated in intellectual activities.

c. The Parent's Satisfaction-Dissatisfaction with His Child's Intellectual-Achievement Performances Ratings of this variable focused on the amount of satisfaction *vs.* dissatisfaction the parent expressed regarding his child's intellectual-achievement performances This rating was exclusively concerned with relevant parental feelings as these were expressed to the interviewer; the parent's reported overt reactions (praise, criticism, etc.) to his child's efforts were *not* a part of the rating.

d. The Parent's Minimal Standards for His Child's Intellectual-Achievement Performances Here the "personal yardstick" the parent used to judge his child's intellectual performances was considered. The major judgment for this rating entailed the determination of the minimal level of intellectual competence below which the child's performance produced parental dissatisfaction and above which the parent felt more satisfied than dissatisfied with his child's efforts.

e. Parental Instigation of Intellectual Activities This (like the remaining variables of Interview I) was concerned with reported parental behaviors rather than parental attitudes. Parental instigation referred to the frequency and intensity of the parent's attempts to increase his child's participation and competence in intellectual activities. The parent's reactions to his child's efforts *after* he had performed were not included here. To be a relevant behavioral referent for this variable, the parent's behavior must have preceded some activity on the part of his child. Examples of instigation included such events as the parent arranging for his child to receive special lessons or experiences in some intellectual pursuit, the parent making a special effort to convey to his child the importance of intellectual experiences, and the parent encouraging and/or demanding that his child participate in intellectual-achievement activities.

f. The Parent's Participation with His Child in Intellectual-Achievement Activities This variable pertained to the extent that the parent actively engaged in intellectual-achievement pursuits with his child. Both the frequency of parental participation and the amount of personal involvement while so engaged constituted rating referents for this variable.

g. Positive Parental Reactions Here the frequency and intensity of the parent's positive reactions to his child's intellectual-achievement behaviors were assessed. These included the degree to which the parent responded favorably to his child's interest and participation in intellectual-achievement activities, as well as the parent's positive reactions to the effort and the competence his child exhibited in these pursuits. Positive parental reactions might take the form of direct verbal approval or other less-direct symbols of approbation, such as granting special privileges or giving rewards (e.g., money, gifts, etc.) for intellectual achievements.

h. Negative Parental Reactions This variable was concerned with the frequency and intensity of disapproval and criticism which the parent expressed to his child for any lack of interest, participation, effort and/or competence in intellectual-achievement activities.

4. Second Interview

Interview II sampled the parents' reported behaviors with their children which were nonspecific to the children's intellectual-achievement performances, but were aspects of parent-child interaction which might possibly influence (either directly or indirectly) children's intellectual-achievement efforts. The variables rated were:

a. Parental Affection This variable pertained to the amount of overt affection and acceptance which the parent reported expressing toward his child.

b. Parental Rejection Here the raters focused on the degree that the parent directly expressed dissatisfaction with, was critical of, or punitive about, his child's general personality attributes or characteristic behaviors.

c. Parental Nurturance The behavioral referents for this rating were those relevant to the frequency and quality of emotional support and instrumental help given the child by the parent.

5. Rating Procedures and Methods of Data Analysis

The criterion rater for Parent Interview I rated all interviews of the 80 parents from typescripts of the interviews. Reliability raters rated 40 randomly picked father and mother interviews. All identifying information (e.g., parent, child, and sibling names, etc.) was removed before the interview protocols were rated. Interview II was rated after the rater listened to the interview recordings.[6] It was felt that, while the data in Interview I was concerned with specific parental attitudes and behaviors which could be assessed from typescripts, Interview II data included important parental feelings and expressions which were less likely to be represented accurately in typed protocols. For example, in Interview II, two fathers (or mothers) might say that their children were "little hellions" in certain situations; yet one parent might mean (and convey) that he thoroughly disapproved of this behavior, while a second parent might make the same statement, but indicate (through his intonation) that he actually approved of these behaviors on the part of his child.

The children's academic-achievement-test scores used in the study were achievement-ratio scores; the reading-achievement score for each child was his reading age divided by his chronological age, and his arithmetic score was obtained by dividing his arithmetic age by his chronological age.

---

[6] The criterion rater for Parent Interview I was the senior author. The reliability raters for this interview were the third author, for the mother interviews; and the fourth author, for the father interviews. The criterion rater of Parent Interview II was Virginia Crandall. The reliability ratings (made from 40 randomly selected father and mother interviews) were done by the fourth author and the third author, respectively.

Statistical analyses employed in the study were exclusively non-parametric tests. The rank-difference correlation was used for all measures of association, and Wilcoxin's Unpaired Replicates Test was employed for all assessments of differences (Siegel, 1956).

C. RESULTS AND DISCUSSION

1. Interrater Reliabilities
The interrater reliability coefficients for Parent Interview I are presented in Table 2. The magnitude of rater concordance for these variables, with one noticeable exception (the mothers' reported negative reactions), ranged from moderately acceptable to highly acceptable agreement. Interrater reliabilities of the mother interviews of Parent Interview II were, for the variables of affection, rejection, and nurturance respectively, .87, .61 and .68. Correlations of interrater agreement for the same variables in the father interviews were .76, .85 and .78.

2. The Child Variables
Relations between the children's IQs and their scholastic-achievement-test performances were assessed. Intelligence-test scores correlated .57 and .59 with reading and arithmetic-achievement-test scores respectively for the girls, and .66 and .50 for the boys. These correlations are similar in magnitude to associations found in previous studies of children's intelligence and their performances on standard academic-achievement tests. These data indicate, as have the results of previous investigations, that general intelligence is one major factor in children's academic achievements. However, the fact that less than one-third of the variance was held in common by these sets of variables (i.e., intelligence- and achievement-test performance) suggests that other factors may also be influential. Parents' attitudes and behaviors influencing children's intellectual-achievement motivations and behaviors may account for some of this variance.

3. Relations between General Parental Behaviors and Children's Academic-Achievement-Test Performances
Associations between general parental behaviors (i.e., affection, rejection, and nurturance) and the children's reading- and arithmetic-test performances were evaluated separately by sex of parent and sex of child. Of the 24 correlations run, only three were significant beyond the .05 level of confidence according to Old's Tables (Siegel, 1956). This is only slightly better than might be anticipated by chance. That the significant correlations obtained were probably not chance occurrences, however, is suggested by the fact that all significant associations pertained only to the mothers and their daughters. Girls who were competent readers had both less affectionate and less nurturant mothers than did the girls who demonstrated less proficiency in that academic area; correlations between the girls' reading-achievement-test scores and their mothers' affection and nurturance were −.38 and −.43, respectively. In addition, girls who performed better on the

Table 2   *Interrater Reliabilities for Parent Interview I (Parent Attitudes and Reported Behaviors toward the Children's Intellectual-Achievement Efforts)*

PARENT VARIABLE	RE. MOTHERS	RE. FATHERS
Attainment value	.50	.80
Evaluation of competence	.78	.94
Satisfaction-dissatisfaction	.85	.96
Achievement standards	.63	.57
Instigation	.63	.76
Participation	.70	.84
Positive reactions	.86	.80
Negative reactions	.22	.79

arithmetic-achievement test had mothers who were also relatively low on nurturance; the Rho obtained was −.45.

Why should low maternal nurturance and affection seem to foster academic competence in the girls? Several possibilities are likely. First, the affectionate and nurturant mothers, by rewarding their daughters' affection-seeking and dependent behaviors, may have "taught" these girls to expect such overtures to be more effective means of attaining personal security than behaviors requiring independent initiative and achievement striving. In contrast, girls who did not receive as much maternal affection and support might have turned to other potential sources of satisfaction and security, such as achievement *per se*. Second, previous research has demonstrated that maternal nurturance fosters children's dependence and impedes the development of independence and achievement behaviors (Crandall, 1960; Winterbottom, 1958). Restrictions of learning experiences in independence and achievement in the more highly nurtured girls of the present study may have produced: (*a*) fewer possibilities for developing independent problem-solving techniques to handle achievement situations, and (*b*) less confidence (and more anxiety) regarding abilities to do so. One final explanation for the negative relations obtained between maternal nurturance and affection and the girls' academic achievements pertains to young girls' attempted identification with, and emulation of, their mothers. All parents act as learning models for, as well as direct reinforcers of, their children's behaviors. The mother who readily proffers love and help to her child may derive personal satisfaction from such maternal behaviors, and may serve as a model to her daughter to this effect. On the other hand, the mother who withholds affection or rejects her child's help-seeking and emotional support-seeking may be less involved with the maternal role and be more achievement-oriented. Consequently, her daughter is, to the degree she uses her mother as an identification model, more likely to emulate her mother's achievement behaviors, values and motivations, and to attempt to become competent in academic achievement situations.

4. *Relations between Parents' Specific Attitudes and Behaviors toward Children's Intellectual Achievement Efforts and Children's Performances on Standard Achievement Tests*

Data relevant to this portion of the study are summarized in Tables 3 and 4. The first four parent variables listed in these tables are attitudinal variables; the last four are behavioral variables. Each will be discussed in turn.

a. Attitudinal Variables The *attainment values* the parents placed on their children's intellectual competence were essentially unrelated to their children's academic-achievement-test performances. In fact, the only significant correlation of the eight pertaining to this variable was an unanticipated negative one: fathers who expressed strong desires that their daughters be intellectually competent had daughters who performed less

Table 3   Parents' Attitudes and Actions and Children's Reading Achievement*

PARENT VARIABLE	MOTHERS RE.		FATHERS RE.	
	Girls	Boys	Girls	Boys
Attainment value	.14	.35	**−.38**	.03
Evaluations	**.44**	**.48**	.28	.21
Satisfaction-dissatisfaction	**.51**	**.48**	.38	.23
Standards	**.48**	.18	.15	.26
Instigation	**−.52**	.18	**−.43**	−.07
Participation	−.10	.06	−.28	−.25
Positive reactions	−.11	.09	**.42**	−.17
Negative reactions	−.27	−.18	**−.45**	.06

* **Boldface** correlations are significant at or beyond the .05 level of confidence (one-tailed test).

Table 4   Parents' Attitudes and Actions and Children's Arithmetic Achievement*

PARENT VARIABLE	MOTHERS RE.		FATHERS RE.	
	Girls	Boys	Girls	Boys
Attainment value	.17	.23	−.26	−.05
Evaluations	.23	.35	.20	.04
Satisfaction-dissatisfaction	**.76**	.28	.19	.07
Standards	**.50**	.00	−.12	.34
Instigation	**−.42**	.05	**−.38**	−.31
Participation	.13	.05	−.09	**−.55**
Positive reactions	.14	.01	**.41**	−.19
Negative reactions	**−.33**	−.24	**−.44**	−.14

* **Boldface** correlations are significant at or beyond the .05 level of confidence (one-tailed test).

adequately on the reading-achievement test than did daughters of fathers who were less concerned with their daughters' intellectual activities and abilities.

The mothers' *evaluations* of their children's general intellectual competence were associated with their children's academic performances, but the evaluations of the fathers were not. Both the boys' and girls' reading-test performances were positively and significantly related to their mothers' assessments of their general intellectual competence. The children's arithmetic-test performances were positively correlated with the mothers' evaluations, though falling just short of statistical significance. In contrast, none of the fathers' evaluations of their children was related to these children's scholastic-achievement, test-taking behaviors. This finding—that the mothers' evaluation of their children's general intellectual performances were similar to their children's academic performances, while the fathers' evaluations were not—may have been due to the fact that mothers are usually home to receive the after-school reports from their children regarding their academic successes and failures, while most fathers are not. In addition, it is a common observation that mothers far outnumber fathers in school situations where concrete information is provided regarding their children's academic performances, (e.g., PTA meetings and parent-teacher conferences). Finally, it may be that fathers more frequently based their judgments of their children's general intellectual competence on their intellectual performances observed in the home (e.g., efforts on puzzles, quiz games, etc.) than did the mothers.

Consistent with the findings on evaluations was the fact that the mothers' *satisfactions and dissatisfactions* with their children's general intellectual-achievement efforts were also more often positively associated with the children's achievement-test performances than were those of the fathers: three of the four significant correlations obtained pertained to the mothers' expressed satisfaction with the adequacy of their children's intellectual-achievement performances.

Parental *standards* for the children's general intellectual performances were unrelated to the children's demonstrated competence on the academic-achievement tests with two exceptions. Both of these pertained to the standards the mothers held for their daughters. Mothers who set high standards for their daughters' intellectual-achievement efforts, in contrast with mothers whose standards were less demanding, had daughters who were more proficient on both the reading- and arithmetic-achievement tests. These correlations, as well as a number of those found in the tables which follow, illustrate an inevitable problem inherent in most parent-child research. When significant correlations are obtained between parent and child behaviors when might it be legitimate to assume the former caused the latter, and when might the opposite be true? The positive association of the mothers' achievement standards for their daughters and these girls' academic-test performances may have been a function of the following: (a) high maternal achievement standards induced the girls to strive for, and become proficient in, the academic areas under consideration, while low maternal standards produced the opposite effect; or (b) the mothers adjusted their intellectual-achievement standards for their daughters according to the girls' demonstrated academic proficiencies; or (c) the correlations obtained may be a function of both (a) and (b).

b. *Behavioral Variables* The remaining correlations listed in Tables 3 and 4 focus on reported parental behaviors rather than parental attitudes. The degree of the parents' *instigation* of their children toward intellectual-achievement pursuits was predictive of the children's achievement-test performances only for the girls. Girls who performed especially well on the tests had mothers and fathers who were *less* prone to encourage and push them toward intellectual activities than were parents of the less academically proficient girls. Regarding the parents' *participation* with the children in intellectual activities, these parental behaviors bore little relation to the competence the children demonstrated on the academic-achievement tests. In only one instance—i.e., the fathers' participation and their sons' performances on the arithmetic-achievement test—was the correlation significant; fathers of boys who were especially competent in this area spent less time with their sons in intellectual activities than did the fathers of the less competent boys. There was, thus, no evidence in the present study that the amount of parental participation with children in intellectual activities *per se* had any positive impact on the children's academic achievements. The negative correlations obtained between parental instigation and participation and the children's achievement-test performances suggest, though cannot prove, that these parental behaviors might be reactions to the children's efforts rather than antecedent and causal factors in these performances. It is possible, for example, that many parents of grade-school-age children—when the children's academic efforts are competent ones—feel little need to encourage such endeavors or to spend additional time with the children in these pursuits. Conversely, parents of a child who performs relatively poorly in academic situations may become concerned with his ineptitude, and increase their instigational efforts and participation with him in intellectual-achievement activities.

The two final antecedent variables of this study pertained to *parental reactions* to the children's intellectual-achievement behaviors as these predicted the children's academic-achievement-test performances. These variables, historically, have been the major focus of attention of researchers concerned with parent behaviors as determinants of children's personality development. In the current investigation, an attempt was made to assess the reactions of the parents to their children's intellectual-achievement efforts, and to relate these reactions to the levels of performance which the children evidenced on standard academic-achievement tests. The only finding indicating an influence of these parental behaviors on the children's performance—if a causal relationship is assumed—was a cross-sex one; both positive and negative reactions of the fathers to their daughters' intellectual efforts predicted their daughters' academic proficiency. The mothers' reactions, in contrast, were essentially unrelated to their daughters' performances, while neither the fathers' nor the mothers' reported praise or criticism was predictive of their sons' achievement-test scores. In short, the only evidence that the parents' direct rewards and punishments may have influenced their children's academic performances occurred exclusively between fathers and their daughters. Girls who performed especially well on the reading-achievement test had fathers who more often praised and rewarded, and less often criticized and punished, their general intellectual-achievement behaviors. A similar relation obtained for the girls' arithmetic performances.

D. *SIGNIFICANT FINDINGS*

When the total pattern of significant correlations found in the current study is evaluated, the most striking finding is that the parents' attitudes and behaviors (both general and specific) were associated with their daughters' performances on the scholastic-achievement tests much more frequently than with those of their sons. Of the 18 significant correlations obtained between the Parent Interviews I and II data and the children's demonstrated academic competence, only three pertained to the boys. Why should these differences obtain? One possibility for this finding is that grade-school-age boys may differ from girls in their susceptibility to adult influence. Two unpublished sets of data by the authors of this report support this idea. First, ratings of free-play behavior of another sample of children in the same age range as the current child sample revealed that the amount of the children's achievement efforts and the amount of their approval-seeking from adults were positively and significantly related for the girls (Rho = .46), but unrelated (Rho = .03) for the boys. In other words, the girls' achievement strivings were directly related to their apparent desire for approval from adults, while the boys' achievement behaviors were more autonomously determined. It appeared that the boys had less need to use adults' reactions to define the competence of their efforts than did the girls, possibly because the boys may have developed more-internalized achievement standards. Additional evidence suggesting that young boys' achievement performances may be less contingent on the reactions of others than are those of girls' was obtained on the sample of Ss employed in the current study. As a part of a different (as yet unpublished) investigation, the children were administered a specially constructed Children's Intellectual Achievement Responsibility Questionnaire. This questionnaire was designed to measure the extent a child attributes his intellectual-achievement successes and failures to his own instrumental behaviors rather than as a product of the behaviors and reactions of other persons. The boys' belief in self-responsibility correlated positively with their performances on the academic-achievement tests used in the current study, while these variables were not significantly related for the girls. The specific correlations between the boys' belief in self-responsibility and their reading- and arithmetic-achievement-test performances were .49 and .36 respectively. For the girls, these correlations were −.16 and −.23. In summary, to the degree that boys' achievement striving has been found to be unrelated to their approval-seeking from adults, and, to the degree that their academic proficiencies were associated with their belief in self-responsibility, their achievement behaviors appeared to be more independent and autonomous of adult reactions than those of the girls. Because of this, parental attitudes and behaviors may have less impact on, and therefore be less predictive of, the academic performances of boys of this age than of girls. The findings of the current study are congruent with this possibility. It should be strongly emphasized, however, that this reasoning rests on several assumptions, as well as limited research data, and must await more definitive tests in future investigations.

E. SUMMARY

This study investigated relations between parents' attitudes and behaviors toward their children's general intellectual-achievement efforts, and their children's performances on standard academic-achievement tests. The sample was comprised of 40 early-grade-school-age children and their fathers and mothers. The children were administered standard intelligence and scholastic-achievement tests. The parents were individually interviewed regarding their general parental behaviors (affection, rejection, nurturance), as well as their specific attitudes and reactions to their children's everyday intellectual-achievement efforts.

The following results were obtained:

1. Correlations between the children's IQ scores and their performances on the scholastic-achievement tests were of the same general magnitude found in most past research on children's intelligence and academic performances.

2. General parental behaviors which significantly predicted the children's academic-test performances pertained solely to mothers and their daughters; mothers of academically competent girls were less affectionate and less nurturant toward their daughters than were the mothers of the girls who were less proficient.

3. Certain specific attitudes and behaviors of the parents toward their children's intellectual-achievement behaviors were predictive of the children's academic-test performances; others were not. First, neither the mothers' nor fathers' expressed values for the children's intellectual experiences were positively associated with the children's observed performances. Second, both the mothers' evaluations of, and satisfactions with, their children's general intellectual competence were positively related to these children's actual academic performances, while those of the fathers were not. Third, parental instigation and participation, when correlations were significant, were negatively associated with the children's academic performances. Fourth, the positive and negative reactions of the parents to the children's intellectual-achievement efforts were predictive of the children's academic-achievement-test performances for father-daughter combinations only; the more proficient girls had fathers who more often praised, and less often criticized, their everyday intellectual-achievement attempts than did the less academically competent girls.

4. Many more significant relations obtained between the parents' attitudes and behaviors and their daughters' academic proficiency than occurred between these parental attitudes and behaviors and the boys' performances.

3-3 Motivational Determinants of Academic Competence[1]

ESTHER S. BATTLE

Academic performance in mathematics and English was predicted for junior high school students. The main independent variables, assessed separately for each of the 2 courses, were the student's minimal standard, his certainty of reaching this standard, the grade he expected to attain, and the value to him of doing well. The effect of IQ and sex differences, social desirability, and a discrepancy between minimal standard and grade expected was also examined. Each of the main predictors related positively to school performance. The relationship between grades expected and minimal standards was shown to have either a facilitating or an interfering effect, depending on the grade expected. All motivational variables except the relative value of excelling in English contributed to prediction over and above IQ. Grade expected was a more powerful predictor than IQ. There were no sex differences in attitudes to math, though they occurred in English. Motivational variables were equally predictive of performance for both sexes. Attitudes and performance were independent of social desirability.

It has been well established that IQ test scores and other ability variables play an important part in the prediction of academic success. Less is known about the relative contribution of various motivational factors which help to differentiate competent from incompetent performance. The largest concentrated attempt in this direction has come from McClelland (1953) and his colleagues (e.g., Atkinson, 1958; Veroff, Atkinson, Feld, & Gurin, 1960), who rely on TAT measures of achievement themes in fantasy as a means of predicting achievement behavior. More closely related to the present study is an investigation by Crandall, Katkovsky, and Preston (1962) who found that TAT *n* Achievement themes did not predict achievement test performance for young school children. In contrast, self-report estimates of a child's expectation of success, his minimal standards of performance, and the importance he attached to intellectual competence were found to be predictive of these same types of achievement behavior. In a subsequent study, Crandall, Dewey, Katkovsky, and Preston (1964) explored possible antecedents of grade-school children's academic achievement by relating

[1] This study was part of a larger project on children's achievement development, financed by United States Public Health Service Grant MH-02238, Virginia Crandall, principal investigator, and by National Institutes of Health Grant SRF-00222. Her critical assistance and advice were greatly appreciated by the author.

these same achievement attitudes held by parents for their children to the child's actual performance.

The present study represents a related attempt to increase prediction of the academic performance of junior high school students, over and above that which may be accounted for by intelligence test performance alone. Rotter's (1954) social learning theory, with some modification, provides the theoretical context for this study. Six motivational determinants of differential academic achievement behavior were examined in the two subject-matter areas of mathematics and English.

1. Relative Attainment Value   This construct refers to the importance an individual places on being competent in a given academic activity, compared with his desire to be proficient in other school subjects. This variable is akin to the more general constructs of "valence" (Lewin, 1935) and "need value" (Rotter, 1954) which refer to the relative value of attaining reinforcements in one need system rather than another. Used in its present context, one would anticipate that children who value the attainment of success in mathematics, for example, more highly than that in any other academic field would choose to spend more time on schoolwork which involves mathematics than in other subject-matter areas. Other things being equal, these children should eventually perform more competency than those who attach low value to the attainment of mathematics success.

2. Absolute Attainment Value   This construct was an addition of the present study, although Crandall, Katkovsky, and Preston (1960, 1962) have dealt with a similar concept. The version used in this study examines the possibility that some children may place little or great importance uniformly on the attainment of competence in a number of school subjects. For these students, the results from a ranking procedure, such as the relative attainment value measure, would be spurious. Greater prediction should be achieved by comparing the performance of children who value competence in mathematics or English per se, regardless of their attitudes toward other subjects, with children who assign little importance to the mastery of that academic subject matter.

3. Minimal Goal Level   This refers to a child's standards—the minimum degree of excellence which he demands of his own performance. Rotter (1954) calls the lowest goal in the continuum of potential reinforcements which will be perceived as satisfaction the "minimal goal level." For example, the child with a minimal goal of B will feel satisfied with that grade or better, but dissatisfied when he receives a C, while another may be satisfied with any grade above an F. It will be recalled that Crandall et al. (1962) also considered the motivating properties of a child's standards. Considering this variable singly, one would expect more competent performance from children who are satisfied only when they achieve high grades than from students who feel satisfied with less adequate performance.

4. Minimal Goal Certainty   Not only should the height of a child's minimal goal affect his performance, but the subjectively held probability of reaching this minimal goal, that is, the child's minimal goal certainty, should also be a factor. The individual's feeling of competence in the activity will determine how certain he feels that he will attain at least minimal satisfaction. Indeed, in a previous study (Battle, 1965), it has been shown that, for the child whose standards exceed the grade he expects to achieve, the closer his minimal standards are to the level of performance he expects to achieve, the higher is his minimal goal certainty. It would be expected that children who feel very certain that they will be able to attain at least minimal satisfaction will be more likely to be positively motivated toward academic effort than those who are uncertain that they will experience any feeling of accomplishment.

5. *Expectancy for Success* Expectancy is defined as the level of probability held by the individual that a particular reinforcement (in this case, successful academic performance) will occur as a function of a specific behavior on his part (here effort) in a given situation. Todd, Terrell, and Frank (1962) found that students with a greater expectancy for academic success were more likely to be normal achievers than underachievers. In the previous study (Battle, 1965) it was shown that children who perceive themselves as highly capable in a given activity were more persistent at an academic task than those who had a low assessment of their abilities. Thus, the degree to which a child expects to succeed also appears to be a relevant variable in the prediction of achievement behavior. The level of performance which the child feels he can expect to achieve (e.g., the grades he expects to get in school) will help to determine his certainty that he will attain at least minimal, and perhaps maximal, satisfaction.

6. *Combined Motivational Variables* A combination of these theoretical variables may increase the prediction of academic performance. For example, it has been shown (Battle, 1965) that children whose minimal goals exceed the level of performance they expected to be able to achieve did not persist at an academic task. That is, children who will be satisfied only if they do very well on a task, but do not expect to be able to perform well, are foredoomed to feelings of failure and discouragement and readily give up. In contrast, for children who have a high expectation of success and who have set minimal goals for themselves which are within their reach, achievement performance is undertaken with the feeling that success is highly probable, and the individual is freed to pursue this end. Discrepancies of this sort may prove to have predictive utility in addition to that of any variable singly or in simple additive relationships with other variables.

If the achievement attitudes described above are shown, in fact, to be of use in predicting school performance, it then becomes important to determine whether individuals tend to hold the same attitude from one course to another, or whether these attitudes are specific to particular school subjects. A related question refers to the similarities or differences in *performance* in English and mathematics. Individual differences in attitudes and behavior between children should also be studied. The most probable interindividual difference is between boys and girls in the amount of importance attributed to competence in mathematics versus English. Even if there were no sex differences in this respect, there might be a differential preference for the two subjects between boys and girls. To examine such possibilities, the interaction of sex with attitudes toward these and other subject-matter areas was studied. Abbreviated measures were obtained to assess the child's favorite school subject and the one in which he felt he was best.

IQ. Because IQ scores have already been demonstrated to predict differential academic competence, it was clear that motivational variables found to relate significantly to performance would have to increase the prediction of achievement behavior beyond that accounted for by IQ. In some cases (Crandall et al., 1964) IQ test scores have been shown to hold only one-third of the variance in common with reading and arithmetic achievement test scores. The purpose of this study is to identify some of the other factors which may relate to variability of performance.

Social Desirability Scores The possibility was examined that some children might give attitude statements which were primarily designed to obtain the approval of the examiner. If the child were to recognize that the culture approved the aspiring student, and if it were important to him to obtain such approval, he might be more likely to state higher standards and attainment values than he actually holds. A social desirability measure was included in this study as a control, to assess whether this was a major source of response distortion.

METHOD

Subjects
Over 500 seventh-, eighth-, and ninth-grade children were tested from a community in southwestern Ohio with a population of approximately 28,000.[2]

Procedure
Two subject-matter areas were studied in a beginning attempt to examine the generality of academic achievement attitudes and behavior. The choice of English and mathematics was based on the fact that both courses are required throughout elementary and junior high school and that because of the consistent stress on these two subjects attitudes would be well crystallized. In addition, the question of sex-typed attitudes toward math and English would be amenable to study.

Female examiners, clearly identified with the Fels Research Institute, presented the children in separate classroom groups with a one-page questionnaire.[3] The student was asked to indicate his minimal goal and minimal goal certainty levels for mathematics and English. These were inserted among a number of filler items.

[2] The author wishes to thank the teachers and students of the Fairborn Junior High School for their cooperation in the data collection, and Robert Martin, principal, and Jaenice Middleswart, secretary, for arranging the schedule.

[3] The author appreciates the help of Virginia Crandall, Suzanne Good, Elinor Waters, Shelley Wing, Beverly Collins, and Janet Robbins with this phase of the study.

The *minimal goal level* question stated:

Circle the grade below which shows the lowest grade that you could get in mathematics (English) and still be satisfied.
    A A−   B+ B B−   C+ C C−   D+ D D−   F.

Immediately below this item, the *minimal goal certainty* question asked:

How *certain* are you that you could get at least the grade you circled above?
        1   2   3   4   5   6   7   8   9   10
            Uncertain   Certain.

On the same questionnaire, the child was asked to name the two school subjects in which he thought he was "best."

In an effort to obtain independent measurements, the two additional questionnaires were administered a week later by examiners who were new to the children. The first questionnaire contained the statements from which the *expectancy* and *attainment value* scores were obtained.

The instructions for *expectancy* stated:

Circle the grade below which shows the grade you *really expect* to get in mathematics (English) on your next report card for this grading period.
    A A−   B+ B B−   C+ C C−   D+ D D−   F.

The *absolute attainment value* statement said:

Circle the number below which shows how important it is to *you* to do well in mathematics.
        1   2   3   4   5   6   7   8   9   10
        Not very important   Very important.

On the same questionnaire, the student was asked to indicate his *relative attainment value:*

Write on the lines below, the names of the following school subjects to show how important it is *to you* to be good in each of them: Social Studies (History or Geography); Mathematics; Art; Science; English; Physical Education. List them from the most important to the least important.

A statement of the child's subject preference was obtained by asking him to state his "favorite" academic subject.

The second questionnaire was a 25-item form of the Children's Social Desirability scale (*CSD* scale—Crandall, Crandall, & Katkovsky, 1965). This true-false questionnaire is constructed so that a child must characterize himself in a highly improbable way if he is to appear socially desirable. An example is: "I never get angry."

The IQ measure was the Henmon-Nelson Test of Mental Ability and had been administered to the students when they were in the sixth grade. The mean IQ was 109.2; the standard deviation, 12.4; and the range of scores, 76–145.

Statistical Analysis

McCall T scores were assigned for all variables because the scores on most variables did not constitute normal distributions. Measures of association, unless otherwise noted, are product-moment correlations. The p values reported resulted from two-tailed tests of significance. All analyses are based on those of the 500 subjects for whom there were data.

RESULTS AND DISCUSSION

There is evidence that grades in both math and English are closely related to school performance in general. Grade in math and grade in English were each correlated with the average of grades in all subjects. These correlations, run separately for the two sexes, range from .86 to .90 ($p < .001$) and suggest that generalizations from the present sample of performance to other forms of academic achievement may be made.

Since performance in math and English is fairly comparable ($r = .72$, $p < .001$, for boys; $r = .70$, $p < .001$, for girls), correlations were computed between attitudes, relative to the two subjects, to determine whether separate analyses by subject area were justified. These are presented in Table 1, in an intercorrelation matrix of the motivational variables. (The correlation of the relative attainment value score in English with that in mathematics is not presented since the two variables are not independent; that is, choice of mathematics as the most important subject precludes a first-place rating for English.) The correlation of each variable across subject-matter areas is italicized; for example, the expectancy statement for mathematics correlates with English expectancy with an $r = .51$.

From Table 1, it is clear that the amount of variance shared by the two sets of attitudes (i.e., toward math and English) ranges only from 24 to 39%. Thus, it appeared that there was enough specificity of attitudes to warrant analysis within each subject area.

Motivational Variables

The primary purpose of this study is to determine whether knowledge of a student's expectations, standards, and attainment values increases the ability to predict his achievement performance. Considering grades in math and English separately, the correlation between scores on these motivational measures and school grade achieved may be seen in Table 2.

The data in Table 2 indicate that all of these achievement attitudes and values, with the exception of relative attainment value for English for the sexes separately, do relate significantly to the academic grades received by the student. These relationships will be discussed in turn.

The large variance shared by expectancy and grades suggests that students have a clear idea of the grades which they expect to receive and that they are able to state this estimate accurately when asked. The relationship also suggests that academic performance may be mediated by

Table 1 *Intercorrelations of the Motivational Variables*

VARIABLE	2	3	4	5	6	7	8	9	10
1. Math expectancy	.65***	.48***	.41***	.23***	**.51*****	.45***	.28***	.22***	.03
2. Math minimal goal		.32***	.36***	.25***	.43***	**.62*****	.19	.19	.07
3. Math minimal goal certainty			.29***	.17	.20***	.17	**.49*****	.14	.03
4. Math attainment value absolute				.37***	.23***	.27***	.24***	**.47*****	.03
5. Math attainment value relative					.01	.03	.02	.03	
6. English expectancy						.73***	.43***	.45***	.22***
7. English minimal goal							.28***	.40***	.08
8. English minimal goal certainty								.30***	.06
9. English attainment value absolute									.46***
10. English attainment value relative									

Note.—N = 250–500. **Boldface** indicates correlation of each variable across subject-matter areas.
*** p < .001 (2-tailed).

Table 2   Correlation of Achievement Attitudes with Grade Attained by Subject Matter and Sex

	MALE		FEMALE		TOTAL	
	N	r	N	r	N	r
Mathematics						
Expectancy + grade	245	.74***	213	.78***	458	.76***
Minimal goal + grade	253	.56***	220	.66***	473	.60***
Minimal goal certainty + grade	253	.42***	220	.52***	473	.46***
Attainment value (absolute) + grade	247	.31***	213	.34***	460	.31***
Attainment value (relative) + grade	241	.23***	211	.24***	452	.20***
English						
Expectancy + grade	243	.81***	208	.85***	451	.84***
Minimal goal + grade	252	.67***	220	.70***	472	.68***
Minimal goal certainty + grade	251	.32***	219	.39***	470	.36***
Attainment value (absolute) + grade	246	.28***	211	.42***	457	.37***
Attainment value (relative) + grade	241	.03	210	.09	451	.13**

** $p < .01$ (2-tailed).
*** $p < .001$ (2-tailed).

the grades one expects to get, perhaps by determining the amount of persistence in the face of difficulty, the amount of effort expended, etc. The question then occurred whether some of the variance not held in common by expectancy scores and grades might come from more inaccurate expectancy statements on the part of students who were doing poorly in school. Grades achieved in math were split at the mean, and the correlation of expectancy with grade was examined for those students whose performance was above average as well as for those who were below average (see Table 3). As might be expected, students who were doing well in mathematics gave more accurate expectancy statements than those whose performance was poor. Many of the children who were having difficulty with this subject matter gave estimates which exceeded the grade they actually attained. Their statements may have more nearly represented grades they wished to get, rather than those which they actually expected. In contrast to this, the correlation of expectancy with grade was approximately the same for the two groups of students in English. This may reflect the fact that there is greater pressure on students to excel in mathematics than in English, so that the student who is having trouble in math resorts to wishful statements rather than admitting his inadequacies.

In general, it was shown that the higher the minimal goal level set by

Table 3   Correlation of Achievement Attitudes with Grade Attained
by Subject Matter for Students with Above- and
Below-Average Grades

	GRADES ABOVE AVERAGE (r)	GRADES BELOW AVERAGE (r)	BOTH (r)
Expectancy and math grade	.68***	.38***	.76***
Expectancy and English grade	.59***	.65***	.84***
Minimal goal and math grade	.56***	.18***	.60***
Minimal goal and English grade	.53***	.38***	.68***
Minimal goal certainty and math grade	.19**	.32***	.46***
Minimal goal certainty and English grade	.05*	.26***	.36***

* $p < .10$.
** $p < .01$.
*** $p < .001$.

the student, the higher the grade he actually achieves. However, analysis of the data revealed again that it was primarily the students with high grades who were accounting for this direct relationship (see Table 3).

The weaker relationship between minimal goal level and grade for the poorer student was not unexpected. It was suggested on the basis of the previous study discussed above (Battle, 1965) that, in some cases, a combination of minimal goal level and expectancy would be more predictive of performance. The child who holds high goals and has little expectation of reaching them would presumably become discouraged and stop trying because his standards were unobtainably higher. Other children would obtain poor grades because their standards would be too low, and they would stop working before they attained a high level of proficiency. In other words, among poor performers, one would not expect standards to bear a monotonic relationship to grades. This possibility was examined with an analysis of variance procedure for unequal n's (Winer, 1962). Children were divided into four groups: those with high and low minimal goal levels and high and low expectancies; the dependent variable was math-grade performance. A significant F ratio was found for the independent effects of expectancy $F = 92.44, p < .01$) and minimal goal ($F = 15.65, p < .01$) as well as for the interaction ($F = 8.26, p < .01$). Subsequent t tests were computed. The differential effect of the minimal goal level was clearly shown for children with high expectancies. Holding a high minimal goal level appeared to facilitate performance if the level of expectancy was also high, while having low standards seemed to impede performance, probably because the child was too easily satisfied.

The situation is quite the opposite if the student does not expect to perform competently (i.e., has a low expectancy). Holding a high minimal goal then seems to be a debilitating factor, for this student performs no more competently than the child who holds low expectations and low minimal goals ($t = 1.35$, $p > .05$). One should not conclude, however, that for children with low expectations of success, it was only the level of expectancy which determined performance and that their minimal goals were irrelevant.

The function of minimal goal certainty demonstrates the importance of the child's minimal goal level itself. It has been demonstrated (Battle, 1965) that minimal goal certainty is positively related to persistence at an academic task. Children who held much higher goals for themselves than the grade they expected to achieve (i.e., low minimal goal certainty) were shown to be least persistent. Holding such unobtainable minimal standards should result in low certainty of satisfaction. If this reasoning is correct, one would predict that the student who *continues* to hold high minimal standards, despite his low expectations, would have low minimal goal certainty and below-average performance.

The correlations of minimal goal certainty with grades may be examined in Table 2 for total groups and for boys and girls separately. Thus, for children in general, high minimal standards of performance appear to facilitate performance unless expectations of success are low, in which case high standards are "unrealistic," produce low minimal goal certainty, and serve a debilitating function. Reference to Table 3 will show that when the minimal goal certainty level was related to performance for children who had *low* math grades, the relationship proved to be somewhat stronger than was the same association for those who obtained above-average math grades. In English also, minimal goal certainty related more strongly to grades for below-average performers than for the better students. These results suggest that the height of the minimal goal *relative to the level of expectancy* has a more pronounced effect on the performance of the below-average student. The more certain he is of obtaining at least minimal satisfaction, the more capable he performs relative to other below-average children. If he holds unobtainably high minimal goals, he has low minimal goal certainty and, as has been shown, performs even more poorly among his below-average peers than does his more certain counterpart.

As for the two measures of importance: In mathematics, there was a tendency for absolute attainment value to account for more of the variance shared with grade performance ($r = .31$, $p < .001$) than did the relative attainment value score ($r = .20$, $p < .001$). The former correlation is significantly greater than the latter at the .06 level. In the field of English, the absolute attainment value statement also proved to relate more significantly to school grades ($r = .37$, $p < .001$) than did the relative attainment value ($r = .13$, $p < .01$). Again the absolute attainment value correlation is significantly stronger ($p < .001$) than the relative attainment value relationship. These findings provide some support for the hypothesis that within an academic field the comparison which accounts for more of the variance is between the child who values achievement in that subject and the child who disavows its importance. Information concerning the relative importance attributed by the same child to one academic subject rather than another is somewhat less predictive.

In summary, these straightforward relationships provide support for the original hypothesis that differential academic performance may be predicted from the child's expectations, minimal goals, attainment value, and minimal goal certainty statements. In each case the relationship was positive: the higher the scale score, the more competent the performance in math and in English. For the first three motivational variables, these findings were more applicable to the child who performed well in school. However, for children who were receiving poor grades the certainty they had of achieving at least minimal satisfaction was an additional relevant source of information for the prediction of their academic performance.

IQ and the Motivational Variables

It was important to investigate the extent to which the motivational measures operated independently of intelligence test scores and contributed additional prediction of academic performance.

A "least squares" analysis of variance procedure (Winer, 1962) was completed within subject-matter area, for each motivational variable and IQ. Scores were divided at the mean for each measure and for IQ. Math grades and then English grades were used as the dependent variables. Table 4 presents the results of these analyses, giving the F ratios and significance levels for each analysis.

From Table 4 it is clear that all of the motivational variables, except the English relative attainment value, have independent effects on the

Table 4 F Tests for the Effect of Motivational Variables and IQ on Academic Grades[a]

	MOTIVATIONAL VARIABLE F	IQ SCORE F	INTER-ACTION F
Mathematics			
Expectancy	159.81**	55.76**	15.06**
Minimal goal	83.57**	70.02**	8.23**
Minimal goal certainty	26.70**	77.71**	5.38*
Absolute attainment value	11.95**	81.82**	3.13
Relative attainment value	19.87**	92.91**	4.40*
English			
Expectancy	224.03**	47.96**	.11
Minimal goal	165.45**	61.53**	.32
Minimal goal certainty	11.06**	10.82**	.00
Absolute attainment value	24.11**	104.18**	.07
Relative attainment value	3.51	134.11**	.18

[a] $df = 1/300$ in each case.
* $p < .05$.
** $p < .01$.

Table 5   Means and Standard Deviations of McCalled Math Grades
for Students Divided on Mathematics Attitudinal
Variables and Level of Intelligence

				IQ		
		High			Low	
	N	X̄	SD	N	X̄	SD
Expectancy high	95	59.89	6.31	45	50.22	8.71
Expectancy low	65	46.80	7.73	112	43.47	5.63
Minimal goal high	94	58.92	8.08	55	49.07	7.58
Minimal goal low	68	48.71	7.74	108	43.79	6.49
Minimal goal, high certainty	89	57.70	8.14	56	47.24	7.11
Minimal goal, low certainty	73	50.89	9.49	107	44.71	7.27
Attainment high, value, relative	102	56.75	8.08	94	46.29	7.29
Attainment low, value, relative	56	50.43	10.37	61	44.00	7.19

variance of grade performance, over and above that which is accounted for by the IQ score.[4]

The interaction of the attitudinal variables with IQ and their effect on the grade attained in mathematics was examined by computing t tests on the data in Table 5. A simple additive effect was demonstrated, so that children scoring high on the motivational and IQ measures performed significantly better than those with low scores on both measures.[5]

In addition, considering the children of high and low ability level separately, it was found that for children with high IQs each motivational variable interacted with IQ to produce a performance difference significant at the .05 level or better. The same was true for children with low IQs with the exception of the relative attainment value measure, in which case it was found that only for children of high IQ did the level of the relative attainment value score relate systematically to the grade attained.

With this exception, it may be said that for students with both above- and below-average IQs, math performance was better if motivational scores were high than if they were low. For the student with below-average IQ, the relative attainment value had a less powerful effect than the IQ level. Performance was superior when IQ was in his favor.

An additional finding worth noting was that students who were above average IQ, but had low levels of expectancy, performed *significantly more poorly* than those who had a high expectancy and were of below-

[4] Each motivational variable was also shown to be significantly related to grades when IQ was partialed out. These partial correlations were all significant at the .01 level or better.

[5] All t tests were significant at the .05 level or better.

average IQ ($t = 2.12$, $p < .05$). This would seem to indicate that one's expectancy of success is a more powerful determinant of performance than is ability when the two factors are in opposition.

While the reason for this finding remains to be investigated, this social learning theory would suggest that the expectancy estimate is derived from reinforcements the child has received as the result of his own past performance. Only one of the determinants of that performance has been his ability level. Other motivational and situational factors will have influenced his performance and the resultant feedback he has received. Thus, when a child is asked to estimate his own future performance from his past performance, his estimate will take into account not only the ability which has gone into his performance, but also other determinants of it. He is essentially predicting from response to response, and it is not surprising that his is a more accurate prediction than is an attempt to predict the response from only one (IQ score) of its determinants. Also, prediction from the level of expectancy holds the situational variable more constant than does the IQ score. The child's expectancy statement is given relative to his reinforcement in a given classroom for a given school subject; performance on an intelligence test is less specific to any single subject in a particular academic setting.

Sex Differences

The question of sex differences in the amount of preference for, and importance attributed to, math and to English was explored. For mathematics, the only sex difference was that the mean relative attainment value was shown to be significantly higher for boys than for girls ($t = 4.43$, $p < .001$). There were no significant differences between the sexes in the frequency with which math was listed as the favorite subject, nor in the absolute attainment value of mathematics. These results would tend to contradict the common cultural assumption that boys have a higher overall preference for mathematics than do girls.

There were more traditional, clear-cut sex differences in attitudes toward English. While boys stated that they *expected* to perform significantly better than girls in English ($t = 7.62$, $p < .001$), they stated their noninvolvement in the subject in several ways. They chose English as their favorite subject significantly less often than girls ($x^2 = 14.58$, $p < .01$), they listed English as their best subject less frequently than girls ($x^2 = 27.41$, $p < .001$), and their mean absolute attainment value for English was lower than the girls' ($t = 4.48$, $p < .001$). They also stated significantly lower minimal goal levels for English ($t = 5.07$, $p < .001$) than did girls, and were significantly less certain that they would reach even their minimal standards ($t = 4.48$, $p < .001$). The data would indicate that achievement attitudes toward mathematics are homogeneous for the two sexes, while clear sex typing occurs for English. It is important to note, however, (Table 2) that the correlation of each achievement attitude with grade attained is roughly comparable for the two sexes.

Considering all children, in no case was social desirability found to bear a significant relationship to either motivational or performance variables. The only significant findings were for girls, in that those who were high on the social desirability scale tended to choose English as their "best" subject more often than low CSD scorers $(r_{pt\ bis} = .21, p < .01)$. Girls with high CSD scores also listed English as their "favorite" subject significantly more often than girls with low CSD scores $(r_{pt\ bis} = .16, p < .05)$.

| 3-4 | *Academic Correlates and Maternal Antecedents of Children's Belief in External or Internal Control of Reinforcements*[1] |

JUNE CHANCE

The purpose of this study was to test the predictiveness for school achievement performance of children's attitudes toward their own role in determining the reinforcing outcomes of school achievement efforts. Within these same data it was also possible to examine maternal variables related to both differences in children's attitudes and child differences in achievement performances. A number of earlier studies had demonstrated the ability of the generalized expectancy for internal-external control of reinforcement to predict school grades and achievement test scores (Crandall, Katkovsky, & Crandall, 1965; Crandall, Katkovsky, & Preston, 1962; McGhee & Crandall, 1968). Coleman and his associates (Coleman *et al.*, 1966) also found in a large-scale study of U.S. schoolchildren that belief in personal control of academic rewards was a strikingly predictive variable in relation to academic achievement.

Generalized expectancy for internal-external control of reinforcements has a special appeal as a predictor of achievement performance. As suggested by Cromwell (1967b, 6–5), and earlier by Lewin, the experiences of succeeding or failing—as opposed to the experiences of pleasure or pain— seem predicated on the belief that one's own efforts and/or characteristics

[1] The research reported here is a part of a larger project conducted by the author under a research grant from the National Institute of Mental Health, United States Public Health Service (MH-5268). This paper has been specifically prepared for this volume; however, certain portions of data reported here were previously included in two papers given at the Society for Research in Child Development Meetings, March, 1965, Minneapolis, Minnesota. These papers were titled, "Internal control of reinforcements and the school learning process" and "Independence training and children's achievement."

are related to goal attainment. Rotter (1966, 4–7) has summarized a variety of studies indicating that individual differences in generalized expectancies for internal versus external control of reinforcement are related to individual differences in learning performances. When belief is strong that one can exert personal control over goal attainment, then experience should modify future behavior in a fashion consistent with the history of reinforcement. When a contrasting attitude of external control prevails, reinforcing outcomes may fail to alter behavior in a consistent way. For instance, a child receiving a good grade on a test may regard the good grade as a function of an especially easy test, a favor of the teacher, luck, and so on, rather than his own activities and efforts. The influence of the grade on his future behavior (amount of study for future tests, aspiration level, and so on) will differ with degree of internality or externality of his attitude.

Katkovsky, Crandall, and Good (1967) explored possible childrearing antecedents of differences in this attitude, in which stable individual differences are apparent by the time children are in the third grade. They found that parental behaviors which would be described as "warm, praising, protective, and supportive" were associated with greater internality of child attitude toward achievement activities. Davis and Phares (1969) examined internal-external control expectancies of college students and their characterizations of their parents' attitudes toward them. These investigators found that internal students—more than external students—saw their parents as less rejecting and hostile, more positively involved, and more consistent in their attitudes toward them, their offspring.

The picture emerges that the parent who fosters generalized expectations for internal control of reinforcements is a loving, supportive, nonpunitive, and possibly protective parent. However, if it is hypothesized that internal control expectancy is, in part, a result of successful experience in coping with tasks and problems, then warm and supportive parental attitudes alone may not be a sufficient condition for its development. It may be desirable, in addition, to know about parental attitudes toward early mastery and self-reliance experiences and their interactions with other parental attitudes.

Whether one elects the hypothesis that early independence training provides opportunities for the child to strive to achieve and to be rewarded for striving (thereby organizing the directions in his behavior ever more strongly toward achievement goals), or whether one elects the McClelland hypothesis that *earliness per se* sets up a condition for the child in which striving and satisfaction occur under strong affective arousal (leading to the development of a *motive* whose effects are pervasive and lasting), the development of independence and of achievement striving have become closely associated in the socialization literature. However, summaries of many investigations resulting from this association do not lead to unequivocal conclusions (Crandall, 1963; Crandall & Battle, 1970). Some investigators find correlates suggesting that development of independence enhances achievement motivation and behaviors; others find correlates suggesting that maintenance—or even cultivation—of childhood dependence is associated with more frequent and intense achievement striving.

While alternative logical resolutions of this contradictory picture are possible, empirical investigation employing a multivariate approach might also offer clarification. For instance, Chance (1961) suggested that effects of maternal independence expectations (and whatever kinds of behavior they imply on mother's part) might be differential, depending upon the over-all context of mother-child interaction in which they occur.

The present study explores the usefulness of such a multivariate examination of the interrelations of child attitudes—generalized expectancy about control of reinforcement outcomes in the classroom, needs for achievement and affiliation, and self-reported anxiety—to child school performance on the one hand and to mothers' expressed attitudes toward independence and toward more general issues of childrearing and family roles on the other. While a large number of specific questions could be asked in order to simplify this presentation, a few general questions will be emphasized.

First, questions will be raised regarding the predictiveness of the generalized expectancy for control of academic achievement reinforcements. How well does the Intellectual Achievement Responsibility (IAR) measure predict achievement performance? Is its predictiveness general, or is it specific to certain kinds of performances? How well do other child variables like intelligence, needs for achievement and affiliation, and self-reported anxiety predict these achievement performances? Do the interrelations of IAR and the other child variables shed any further light on the origins of child differences in attitudes about their control of academic rewards?

Second, what are the maternal correlates of more internal attitudes about school achievement, stronger need for achievement or affiliation, or greater anxiety? Will examination of combinations or interactions of maternal attitudes in relation to child outcomes help to resolve some of the conflicting conclusions which might be drawn from previous literature regarding the socialization of achievement behavior?

A third set of questions arose, in part, from some findings presented later in this paper. The source of these questions is the apparent contradiction between some outcomes in the boys' data and those in the girls' data. Answers to these questions are presented in the form of speculative hypotheses which go beyond the simple problem of resolving boy/girl differences and which might have future value in explaining *how* socialization variables influence achievement motivation and behaviors.

METHOD

Subjects and Setting

*S*s were 59 boys and 55 girls attending the Laboratory School of the University of Missouri at Columbia and their mothers. All families included in the study would be characterized as belonging to classes 1, 2, or 3 of Lloyd Warner's classification scheme (Warner, Meeker, &

Eels, 1949). About 60 percent of fathers were employed in some professional or administrative capacity by the university. The remainder were primarily owners and managers of local businesses, independent professionals, and prosperous farmers.

All children came from intact homes and had no marked physical or personality problems. Most of them would have been characterized as being several years more advanced in their standard achievement test scores than would have been predicted from their grade placement. The children of the sample were very bright; the average IQ for boys was 125; and for girls, 126. No child included in the sample had a measured IQ of less than 100. Mothers varied in estimated age from 26 to 45 years; their median education was the bachelor's degree. The median education of fathers was some graduate work completed.

The school provides classes from kindergarten through senior high school. Each grade has one classroom and a class consists of 25 to 30 children. There was, for the duration of this study (1961–1966), relatively low turnover in both children and teaching personnel, providing a very stable setting in which to do a study.

Collection and Preparation of Data

Scores on the California Achievement Test (Forms X or W) were compiled for all children who had been enrolled in the school at the end of third grade and for whom mother interview data were available. Among these 114 children, approximately 85 percent had been in continuous attendance in the school since first grade. Results of a Stanford-Binet (Form L-M) administered within 18 months of the collection of the school achievement data at the end of third grade were available for each child. Since achievement scores at the completion of third grade were actually taken from several different intact classes, raw scores were converted into standard scores within each particular third-grade class, making combinations of data possible.

Measures of need achievement and need affiliation were obtained from an incomplete stories technique, individually administered to each S. The child was given seven short instructions to: "Tell me a story about . . . ." The instructions to boys were:

Tell me a story about a boy who is just leaving his house.
    . . . a boy in school.
    . . . a mother and her son—they look worried.
    . . . a father and son talking about something important.
    . . . two men standing by a machine—one is older.
    . . . brothers and sisters playing—one is a little ahead.
    . . . a child putting together a puzzle—his mother is watching.

For girl Ss story stems were modified to say "girl" or "daughter" when appropriate. The "house" stem was always given first as the introduction to the task and was not scored. Presentation order of the remaining six stems varied randomly from child to child. Scores were based upon responses to these six. The examiner was permitted to ask S these questions if S's initial response did not cover the following points: "What happened in the story? What happened before? What is he/she thinking about? How does he/she feel? How will the story come out?"

Stories were scored as belonging in one of two categories: clearly containing achievement imagery or containing unclear or unrelated imagery. For a story to be scored as containing achievement imagery it had to involve at least one of the following: competition with a standard of excellence, unique accomplishment, or long-term involvement. The story did not need to picture successful goal attainment.

When scoring for need affiliation was undertaken on the same stories at a later time, a parallel system was employed. A story was judged to contain affiliation imagery if one or more characters were concerned with establishing, maintaining, or restoring a positive affective relation with another person. Inclusion of either direct expression of or very strongly implied feelings on the part of the characters was necessary before affiliation could be scored. All stories were scored by two judges, working independently, and agreement was high—95 percent for need achievement and 87 percent for need affiliation.

Both distributions of need measures yielded positively skewed distributions, which were normalized by means of a common log transformation. These normalized scores, however, still showed systematic differences related to the age of S at the time of testing. While most children had been tested during the year they attended third or fourth grade, some of the group had been tested as late as in the fifth or sixth grades. The normalized scores were, therefore, converted into standard scores within the age group to which the child belonged at the time he was tested.

Responses to the Crandall Children's Achievement Responsibility Questionnaire (IAR) were obtained in individual interviews with children in grades 3, 4, and 5. The questionnaire was administered to groups of sixth and seventh graders. A child's score is the number of times an internal alternative is chosen over an external alternative. The Children's Manifest Anxiety Scale (CMAS) was also administered individually to the younger children and in groups to older children.

Data were obtained from mothers in individual interviews of a highly structured sort. Among the total group of mothers contacted during a four-year period, slightly fewer than 1 in 15 rejected the interview. The mothers' interview included the Parent Attitude Research Instrument (Schaefer and Bell, 1958) and an adapted and extended version of Winterbottom's Independence Training Attitude Questionnaire (1958). The latter asked mother at what age she would expect her child (or children) to be able to be depended upon to do the thing in question. Sample items are: "To try to do hard things without asking for help; to select his own clothes to wear to school; to hold brief conversations with grown-up friends who visit the family; to show pride in his ability to do things well." Twenty new items had been added to Winterbottom's original 20. An item analysis revealed that 31 of the 40 items were predictive of total score; responses to these were used to obtain each mother's score (MAIT). The PARI was initially scored for its 23 component subscales; these scores were then combined into three factor scores, following the findings of Zuckerman, *et al.* (1958), representing Maternal Control (I), Hostility-Rejection (II), and Democratic Attitudes (III).

Raw scores obtained from the mothers' attitude data also demonstrated differences related to the ages of their children. Consequently, mother data were grouped according to the age of their child in the study at the time of the interview, and raw scores were again converted into standard scores. Analyses of relations among variables employed the Pearson product-moment correlation coefficient and partial correlation.

SOME FINDINGS AND HYPOTHESES

First, what is the degree of predictiveness for achievement performance of the IAR variable in relation to variables of need achievement, need affiliation, and the Children's Manifest Anxiety Scale? Relations shown in Table 1 indicate that the greater the belief on the part of the child (boy or girl) that he, himself, controls his reinforcement outcomes in the area of intellectual achievement, the better he performs on both a generalized achievement measure (IQ) and on specific school achievement tests. (Partial correlations performed with these relations suggest that IAR scores and achievement test results remain related, even when the effect of general intelligence is held constant.) Insofar as reading, arithmetic, and spelling represent distinct kinds of achievement at third-grade level, the correlations obtained do not suggest that IAR is more predictive of one kind of achievement than another.

The predictiveness of the need measures for achievement performance is more equivocable. While both stronger need achievement and stronger need affiliation are associated to some extent with higher IQs and higher achievement test scores among boys, the only trend in the girls' data suggests that stronger need achievement may be associated with poorer, rather than better, school performance.[2] Higher levels of self-reported anxiety (CMAS), like more external IAR scores, show a small (not statistically significant) tendency to be associated with poorer school achievement among all children. (However, although CMAS and IAR scores are related, partial correlation indicates that IAR prediction of school performance is unaffected by holding CMAS scores constant.)

Two other relations reported in Table 1 deserve some attention and

---

[2] Despite over-all fuzziness of relations between need variables and achievement measures presented in Table 1, examination of the relations of need measures to ipsative achievement scores is provocative (Chance, 1968). An ipsative score quantifies within-child differences in achievement performance. Boys obtaining lower scores in need-achievement, as compared to higher scores in that need, perform relatively more poorly in arithmetic and in spelling than they do in reading. Need-achievement scores show no relation to girls' patterns of achieving, but higher need-affiliation scores, as compared with lower, among girls are associated with relatively better performance in reading than in arithmetic or in spelling. The IAR measure is also unrelated to ipsative differences in achievement patterns.

will be discussed later in light of data concerning mothers' attitudes. First, more internal attitudes about control of reinforcement are associated with fewer achievement-related stories told by both boys and girls; and second, there is an intimation in the patterns of correlation between need measures and anxiety scores that development of a need pattern atypical for the sex of the child may be associated with greater anxiety. Note in relation to the latter point that in the present data boys as a group had significantly higher need-achievement scores than did girls, and girls had significantly higher need-affiliation scores than did boys (Chance, 1968). Also note in Table 1 that the two need scores are independent and not inversely related to each other.

Data shown in Table 2 describes the interrelations of maternal variables. The variables of maternal attitudes measured are generally less independent within the boys' than within the girls' data. These relations are useful in interpreting correlations presented in Table 3. Table 3 presents the relations of the IAR measure to variables of maternal attitudes and education, along with the relations of the other measures of child personality and achievement to these maternal variables.

Table 1   *Intercorrelations among Children's Personality Measures and Their Achievement Performances*

	IAR	NEED ACHIEVEMENT	NEED AFFILIATION	ANXIETY
IQ	+.34** (+.33)*	+.26* (−.13)	+.35** (−.08)	−.08 (−.06)
Reading	+.50** (+.45)**	+.01 (−.22)	+.34** (+.09)	−.24 (−.22)
Arithmetic	+.46** (+.51)**	+.27* (−.27)*	+.15 (+.05)	−.26 (−.30)*
Spelling	+.56** (+.38)**	+.22 (−.25)	+.41** (−.11)	−.24 (−.03)
Need affiliation	+.25 (+.15)	+.19 (+.11)	— —	+.22 (−.24)
Need achievement	−.28* (−.44)**	— —	— —	+.07 (+.23)
IAR	— —	— —	— —	−.37** (−.28)*

Note.—In Tables 1, 2, and 3, the boys' ($N = 59$) correlations are shown in each instance first and the girls' ($N = 55$) correlations are shown in parentheses below them; all tests of significance of correlations are two-tailed.
   * $p < .05$.
   ** $p < .01$.

Table 2 Intercorrelations among Measures of Maternal Variables

	PARI I	PARI II	PARI III	MATERNAL EDUCATION
MAIT	+.45**	+.02	−.27*	−.20
(Independence Training)	(+.14)	(+.08)	(−.12)	(+.08)
PARI I	—	+.26*	−.30**	−.38**
(Maternal Control)	—	(+.22)	(−.12)	(−.57)**
PARI II	—	—	+.04	+.06
(Hostility-Rejection)	—	—	(+.05)	(−.20)
PARI III	—	—	—	+.03
(Democratic Attitudes)	—	—	—	(−.06)

Table 3 Intercorrelations of Maternal Variables and Children's Personality and Achievement Measures

	INDE-PENDENCE TRAINING (MAIT)	CONTROL (PARI I)	REJEC-TION (PARI II)	DEMOC-RACY (PARI III)	MATERNAL EDUCATION
Intellectual Achievement Responsibility	−.47**	−.48**	−.06	+.06	−.45**
	(−.20)	(+.10)	(+.10)	(−.03)	(−.13)
Need Achievement	−.43**	+.09	−.30*	+.06	−.16
	(+.28)*	(+.04)	(−.05)	(+.01)	(−.05)
Need Affiliation	−.21	−.21	−.09	+.39**	+.15
	(−.05)	(−.08)	(−.09)	(−.42)**	(+.11)
Anxiety	+.36**	+.30*	.00	−.08	−.05
	(+.34)**	(+.35)**	(+.08)	(.00)	(+.09)
IQ	−.30*	−.29*	−.24	+.24	+.36**
	(−.09)	(−.26)	(+.10)	(.00)	(+.20)
Reading	−.09	−.45**	+.04	+.08	+.43**
	(+.08)	(−.41)**	(.00)	(−.10)	(+.27)*
Arithmetic	−.29*	−.50**	+.02	+.16	+.41**
	(+.03)	(−.35)**	(−.05)	(−.12)	(+.14)
Spelling	−.31*	−.56**	−.08	+.10	+.36**
	(+.02)	(−.35)**	(−.06)	(+.05)	(+.24)

Stronger belief on the part of boys that they control the reinforcing outcomes of intellectual achievement efforts is associated with mothers who maintain earlier independence expectations (MAIT), express less concern about controlling the child's behavior (PARI I), and possess more education. (While maternal education is associated with both boys' internal control scores and their achievement test scores, partial correlations, holding maternal education constant, do *not* indicate that the relations shown in Table 1 between IAR and achievement scores are dependent upon concurrent differences in maternal education. Although mothers' attitudes about independence and about control are related in the boys' data, further use of partial correlation suggests that each maternal attitude has some independent association with sons' IAR scores.)

Like the IAR variable, stronger need achievement among boys appears to be related to earlier maternal independence expectations, but in contrast to IAR, need achievement appears unrelated to maternal attitudes about controlling the child's behavior. However, recall in Table 2 that among this sample of boys' mothers, MAIT and PARI I are associated in such a way that early-independence expectations and permissiveness tend to occur together, and later-independence expectations and greater concern for control occur together. A possibly obscuring effect of this association between MAIT and PARI I can be taken into account by calculating the relation between need achievement and each maternal attitude, holding the effect of the other maternal attitude constant. The value of the partial r between need achievement and MAIT, holding PARI I constant, is $-.43$. In contrast, partial r for need achievement and PARI I, holding MAIT constant, becomes $+.35$. (The original zero order r between need achievement and PARI I was $+.09$.) In other words, when the relation between MAIT and PARI I is held constant, it now appears that both need achievement and IAR are associated with earlier maternal independence expectations. In contrast, stronger need achievement is associated with relatively greater maternal concern about controlling the boys' behavior, while higher IAR is associated with more permissive mothers' attitudes.[3] The negative association noted earlier between frequency of achievement stories told and degree of internality may be, in part, a function of the context in which mothers' independence expectations manifest themselves. The use of achievement themes by children in this study may be more readily interpretable as an index of conflict about achievement-goal pursuits than as a simple index of preference for achievement goals over other goals (Fitzgerald, 1958, 4–3). This author (Chance, 1965) had also suggested in an earlier paper that some individual differences in IAR might represent defensiveness or negative and

---

[3] Although it is proposed here that mothers of boys manifesting higher need achievement are relatively more concerned about control than other mothers in the population of the study, bear in mind that the nature of this population was such that almost *no* mothers expressed extremely controlling or negative attitudes toward their children. The modal attitude of all mothers on PARI I was biased in the permissive direction.

avoidant behavior. The child wanting to attain achievement goals, but lacking confidence that he is able to do so, might attribute control of his school performance to outside factors to guard himself against painful disappointment.

The girls' data show no relations between either IAR or need achievement and any maternal variable except MAIT. The relation of MAIT to girls' IAR scores, while not significant statistically, is, however, in the same direction as that obtained in the boys' data. Table 3 also reports that later maternal expectations for independence—rather than earlier— are associated with higher need achievement among girls. This finding is similar to a finding regarding females from another very small study reported by McClelland (1953).

Greater self-reported anxiety (CMAS) on the part of all children is also associated with both greater maternal emphasis on controlling the child's behavior (PARI I) and with later independence expectations (MAIT). These correlates parallel those related to children's IAR scores and are also consistent with negative trends reported in Table 1 between CMAS scores and school performance.

As noted earlier, some trends shown in Table 1 suggest that anxiety may be greater among children whose need pattern is not typical of that expected for a child of that sex—that is, a relatively achievement-striving girl or a relatively affiliative boy. This observation, coupled with the observation that this sort of anxiety is correlated with later independence expectations of mothers, leads to a question about the function of early maternal independence expectations. Do earlier expectations induce greater compliance in the child to the role that his, or her, mother wants the child to develop into? Rosen (1964) suggested that early-independence expectations may make the child more malleable to his mother's values. His data indicated that earlier-trained boys had values more similar to maternal values. Rosen hypothesized that earlier training produced this effect because it aroused anxiety which compliance with maternal values could reduce.

The present data suggest a more refined hypothesis which may clarify what earlier-independence expectations on the part of mother imply about her relation to her child and her effects on his behavior. This hypothesis could also help to explain the finding that later, rather than earlier, expectations appear to be associated with stronger need-achievement development in the female case.

First, it is proposed that the result of earlier maternal independence expectations is to induce greater child compliance to the role *expected of him* by his mother (in contrast to compliance with her personal values). In our society for a boy, this role is likely to be one emphasizing striving, mastery, problem-solving, competition, and autonomy; for a girl, more likely the emphasis will be on sensitivity, responsibility, and dependence on others.

While the effect of early-independence expectations may be to induce compliance to mothers' training goals, the actual outcome of socialization also will be influenced by the particular mother's organization of goals.

To the extent that mothers are relatively conventional in their expectations for their children, one might expect that the boy-girl differences indicated above should be observable. What of the instances where mothers' expectations about child and later adult roles are less conventional? Some relations shown in Table 3 are pertinent. The second and third factor scores from the PARI generally failed to show many relations to other variables; however, greater maternal rejection of her own role (PARI II) was related to less strong need achievement among boys, and more strongly democratic attitudes (PARI III) were positively related to need affiliation among boys and negatively related to the same need in girls. If rejection of the wife-mother role and expressed inclination to want to reduce role differences between adults and children are taken as indicators of a relative lack of conventional expectations on mothers' part, then these mothers could be seen as socializing a less conventional child personality.

In addition, the present data don't indicate much that would lend substance to an "anxiety reduction *via* compliance to mother's demands" explanation of how the effect of earliness of independence explanations occurs. Rather, the data support the hypothesis that it is the later-trained youngster who is more likely to report that he is susceptible to anxiety arousal.

What alternative explanation can be offered to the effects of mothers' attitudes about early mastery and self-reliance being mediated by "earliness," either as a suitable condition for strong affective arousal (McClelland, 1958) or for anxiety arousal (Rosen, 1964)? The nature of the questions asked on the MAIT questionnaire and the responses which mothers made to them point to one alternative explanation. Those items of the MAIT which are most internally consistent, and ultimately best related to the other correlated variables, tend to involve fairly complex accomplishments—"trying hard," "participating," "choosing," "deciding"— rather than specific accomplishments of a more tangible sort. It is also characteristic of these discriminating items that they display much inter-mother variation in the age responses they elicit (Chance, 1961; 1968). These items are ambiguous from the standpoint that they require the observer to set some criterion at which she will judge that the activity is accomplished, and this criterion will vary from observer to observer. It seems likely that when mothers are asked to state ages at which they expect or want their child to perform certain activities, the mothers in their responses are stating something about the criteria they employ for evaluating and rewarding the child's behavior. It is hypothesized that mothers who "favor earlier independence," as opposed to "later," are less stringent in their requirements for the quality of the child's performance. In other words, these mothers are likely to reward more incomplete responses on the part of the child and to reward effort to some degree independently of the quality of performance. Crandall, Katkovsky, and Preston (1960a) noted, in a study in which parents were asked to state their referents for achievement behavior on the part of their children, that parents included *interest* in potential achievement situations and *participation* in such, as well as the notion of *competence* in those situations.

It is hypothesized that the effect on the child of the mother's greater leniency regarding what level of accomplishment is rewardable induces in the child an "appetite" for and an expectancy of further rewards from her. This expectancy impels the child to become increasingly sensitive toward, and aspiring to, the role the mother projects for him. In other words, early-independence expectations, and their accompanying inferred differences in maternal-reward standards, do not necessarily produce effects specific to need achievement—or any other need or expectancy. Rather, they produce greater compliance on the part of the child to his mother's conception of what this child should be and is to become. To the extent that mothers' expectations for child roles is conventional, it is predictable that mothers will differentially reinforce achievement striving in boys and affiliative activity in girls. The child of the mother stating early-independence expectations need not be seen as complying with his mother's patterns as a result of anxiety and defense. Rather, he can be seen as being optimistic about his prospects of being able to attain positive reinforcements from her by his efforts.

The mother who is more stringent about evaluating the child's level of accomplishment perhaps induces her child to devaluate his own efforts and to regard them as mostly ineffective in controlling his world. At the same time, she may also fail to develop as strong a value for her child as a source of reward as does a mother who is liberal with rewards. The more stringent mother perhaps leaves the child's socialization more open to other sources of influence.

Having speculated on the way in which maternal attitudes (and inferred behaviors) operate to increase generalized expectancy for internal control of academic reinforcements, one further summary speculation on the nature of what IAR measures and the basis of its predictiveness for school achievement in the early elementary grades is in order. From an overview of the data, the picture emerges of the child with strong generalized expectancy for internal control of academic reinforcers as one who achieves well and is in the process of being rather comfortably and effectively socialized toward his or her adult social role. Motive to do well in the early grades of school seems to derive from effects of a close, positive mother-child relation (an appetite for maternal approval and a high expectancy of attaining it), rather than from either a specific motivation to achieve or even specific expectancies regarding achievement possibilities.

3-5 Reinforcement Effects of Adult Reactions and Nonreactions on Children's Achievement Expectations: A Replication Study[1,2]

VIRGINIA CRANDALL, SUZANNE GOOD, and
VAUGHN J. CRANDALL

This study was a replication and extension of an investigation concerning possible reinforcing effects of adult nonreactions (silence) on children's expectations of success in achievement situations. Also, differential sensitivity to adult verbal reactions was predicted from the generalized expectancy for success that children brought to the testing session. Results substantiated those of the earlier experiment. E nonreaction produced changes in children's expectations of success opposite to those produced by preceding positive or negative verbal reactions. It was demonstrated that such changes could not be accounted for by extinction. Findings also indicated that high expectancy children changed their expectancies more as the result of negative adult reactions, while low expectancy children responded more to positive adult reactions.

Although psychological researchers have recently devoted much time and effort to the investigation of the differential influences of verbal reinforcements on attitudes and behaviors, little attention has been given to the possible reinforcing effects of silence. It is apparent in normal social intercourse that children often behave as though such silent nonreactions from others had active reinforcing properties, at least under certain conditions. For instance, when a mother who is typically voluble in her praise of her child's efforts fails to give such praise, the child may try to improve his performance. Presumably he has interpreted the unexpected lack of maternal praise as implicit criticism. Conversely, silence following customary criticism seems to take on positive qualities. An example of this is the statement of the music pupil who observed, "Well, I guess I must have played better today; the teacher didn't 'gripe' at everything I played the way she usually does." The music teacher's nonreaction

[1] This study was partially supported by USPH Grant M-2283, Vaughn J. Crandall, Senior Investigator.

[2] The authors wish to express their appreciation to the administration and faculty of Ferguson Junior High School, Greene County, Ohio (especially to Mr. Robert Peters, Principal, and Mr. John Drury, Guidance Director), and to Mr. Clayton Wiseman, Greene County School Psychologist, for their cooperation in securing subjects for this study.

was apparently a positive experience for this pupil. When a child has become accustomed to negative reactions from a given adult, unexpected silence from that adult may be interpreted as implicit approval; the silence of a usually praising adult may be thought of as criticism. The treatment hypothesis of this study pertains to this possibility and is as follows: "Children who are given positive adult reactions to their achievement efforts in an experimental situation will interpret subsequent nonreactions from that adult as negative reinforcement, while children who have previously received negative E reactions will perceive her subsequent nonreactions as positive reinforcement."

This "contrast" hypothesis was tested in a previous study (Crandall, 1963). After positive E reactions and after negative E reactions, silence produced changes in the children's expectations of success which were opposite to those caused by the E's preceding verbal reactions. The children's expectancies returned to points similar to those from which they had started at the beginning of that experiment. However, it was felt subsequently that the changes obtained from nonreaction could perhaps be due to either the active, learning contrasting process which had been hypothesized or simply to the passive extinction of the previous reinforcement effects. The present investigation replicated the experimental procedure of the former study, using another examiner and a new sample of children. The design was also extended to include two additional groups of control Ss in order to examine extinction per se as compared with the possible active reinforcing effects of nonreaction.

In addition to assessing the treatment effects discussed above, the present study attempted to predict differences in the amount of impact these same treatments might have on different children. The children were divided into two groups on the basis of their Generalized Expectancies of Success (G Ex). As presently used, the definition of this concept is consistent with that suggested by Rotter in his social learning theory of personality. He defined Generalized Expectancy as, ". . . the generalization of the expectancies for the same or similar reinforcements to occur in other [new] situations for the same or functionally related behaviors [Rotter, 1954; p. 166]." Or, stated in its present more limited context, G Ex pertains to the relative amount of success (or failure) which the child expects to have on a new achievement task, presumably based on his experiences in past achievement situations which he perceives as similar. When, in past achievement situations, he has often been told that he is right, that he has succeeded, that his actions are approved of, etc., he will presumably generalize a high expectancy for success to future achievement situations. The obverse would be true for children with past histories of predominantly negative reinforcement; i.e., they should evolve low expectancies for success in new situations. (Data supporting this suggested link between the presently assessed personality variable, G Ex, and the Ss' probable past histories of reinforcement will be discussed in the Results section.) It seemed reasonable to suppose that being told he is wrong will have maximum impact upon a child with a high expectancy of success because he is not accustomed to such negative reactions. The same negative statement should have less impact on a child who has a low G Ex of success because he has more frequently received such reactions.

Previous research findings—while limited to experimentally induced reinforcement effects—would seem to point to the conclusion above. Jessor (1954) found, in a study of satiation under social reinforcement, that the same adult reaction given repeatedly over a period of time to the same child begins to lose its reinforcing strength. It might be anticipated, then, that children with high G Ex of success would be less sensitive to positive adult reactions because they have experienced such reactions time and again. Positive reactions from others would gradually lose some of their reinforcing strength for such successful children as compared, at least, with unsuccessful children (low G Ex) to whom positive reactions are a relative novelty. It has also been found (Austrin, 1950) that a series of positive verbal reinforcements gradually raised Ss' expectations of success; but, when a negative reinforcement was introduced after the positive series, this single "unexpected" reinforcement caused, by itself, a significant drop in expectancy. If such findings can be extrapolated to the child's general life situation, it might be anticipated that the negative adult reactions of the present experiment would have an especially strong impact on a child who has come to the testing session with a history of mostly positive reinforcements and, therefore, a high G Ex of success. The individual difference hypothesis of this study, then, is as follows: "A child who enters an achievement situation with a high G Ex of success will decrease his expectations of success more as the result of the negative adult reaction treatment than will a child who enters with a low G Ex. Conversely, low G Ex children will show a greater rise in their success expectations as the result of positive adult reactions than will high G Ex children."

METHOD

Subjects and Design

One hundred forty-four eighth grade boys were assigned to four treatment groups following the scheme shown in Table 1. Ss were first divided on the height of their Generalized Expectancy of Success (G Ex), resulting in two groups of 72 Ss each: (a) high G Ex Ss (whose G Ex estimates fell above the 29.9 median score of all boys tested), and (b) low G Ex Ss (whose G Ex estimates fell below the median). Then, individuals were matched across treatments on the basis of their G Ex scores, with a maximum range of five score points for each set of individuals.

Of the 72 Ss falling within the high G Ex group, half of the boys from each matched set (36 Ss) received an initial series of *positive* verbal reactions from the E, while the other 36 received an initial series of *negative* verbal reactions. The same two treatments were applied to two similar groups of 36 boys each within the low G Ex group. A further division of Ss was made for the presentation of the second

Table 1   Allocation of Subjects to Experimental and Control Conditions

GENERALIZED EXPECTANCY SCORE	FIRST CONDITION	SECOND CONDITION
1. High G. Ex. (N = 72)	1. E administered positive reaction (N = 36)	1. E administered nonreaction (N = 18) 2. E removed (N = 18)
	2. E administered negative reaction (N = 36)	1. E administered nonreaction (N = 18) 2. E removed (N = 18)
2. Low G. Ex. (N = 72)	1. E administered positive reaction (N = 36)	1. E administered nonreaction (N = 18) 2. E removed (N = 18)
	2. E administered negative reaction (N = 36)	1. E administered nonreaction (N = 18) 2. E removed (N = 18)

treatment condition. Of all *Ss* who had received the initial *positive* reaction treatment, 18 of the high G Ex group and 18 of the low G Ex group were administered a second series of trials by the *E* in which no verbal reactions were given. The remaining 18 individuals in each Ex group acted as control *Ss* and administered their own second series of trials with the *E* removed from the experiment proper. Similarly, of all *Ss* who had received the initial *negative* reaction treatment, 18 of the high G Ex *Ss* and 18 of the low G Ex *Ss* received the *E*-administered nonreaction second series. The remaining *Ss* performed under the control condition (*E* removed).

Procedure
Essentially, each *S* gave an initial expectancy estimate, was administered a 12-trial series with nine positive or nine negative reactions from *E*, then gave a second expectancy estimate. Each *S* then had a second 12-trial series using the same stimuli, either administered by *E* but with no reactions from her or else self-administered with *E* removed. Then, at the end, the *S* gave a third and final expectancy estimate.

The task used was the same angle-matching task used in the original study and was specifically constructed to be both novel and ambiguous. These characteristics made it possible for the *E* to react in the manner required by the experimental design because the S could not tell, from the task materials alone, whether he was right or wrong. The S's evaluation of his own performance was dependent solely on the social reinforcements given by the adult. This task also made it possible to use the same number and sequence of verbal reactions and nonreactions in the positive and negative treatments.

The instructions given to each S were identical to those presented in the original experiment except as otherwise noted below. Expectancy-of-Success estimates were also obtained in the same manner as in the original study. The first estimate (Ex_1) was secured just before the S started on the experimental task and comprised the operational measurement of Generalized Expectancy in this study.

Upon completion of the first series of positive or negative reaction trials, each S was requested to give a second expectancy estimate (Ex_2). The difference between this second estimate and the S's original estimate (Ex_1) was used as an index of the reinforcing direction and strength of the E's verbal reactions.

At this point the experimental design used in the original study was altered for this experiment. Only half of the Ss who had received the initial positive reactions, and half of those who had experienced negative reactions, were assigned to the experimental groups. These groups, as in the first study, were administered a repetition of the angle-matching series except that the E now gave no verbal reactions to their responses (the "examiner nonreaction" condition).

The remaining children were used in control groups. These Ss were given a score sheet on which to write their own answers, and were instructed as follows: "Now I'd like you to do the test again. I have some work over there that I have to finish (E points to a table in another part of the room), so will you please go through the cards by yourself just like we did the first time. Write the letter of the figure each card matches here on this paper. Look at each card just once and try to take about the same amount of time as we did before. Put your name on the paper; and, when you have finished, please put your paper face down in that box over there (E indicates box)." E then turned her attention away from the S and busied herself at her work table. When these Ss had completed their second series, they placed their answer sheets face down in a box removed from the E's view, so that the E had no opportunity to evaluate or react to their performance during this second series of trials (the "examiner-removed" control condition). At the conclusion of the second trial series, all Ss (both experimental and control) were required to give a third expectancy estimate (Ex_3).

The results of the former study demonstrated that the nonreaction series empirically produced expectancy changes which were opposite to the direction of the reinforcements previously given. However, it was not possible to determine whether these expectancy changes during the nonreaction condition resulted from the Ss' attributing active reinforcing properties to the E's silence or whether the changes were simply the dissipation of original reinforcement effects, as in a usual extinction series. (Although the term "extinction" is classically applied to the diminution of overt acts, it may be that a cognitive response such as Expectancy also extinguishes.) In order to test this alternative, the present study introduced the control situation in which the examiner was removed during the second trial series. The removal of the reinforcing agent thus eliminated the possibility of social reinforcement. If extinction were sufficient to account for the previously obtained results, a comparison of the second-trial series responses of the experimental group (*E* administered nonreaction) and the control group (*E* removed) would indicate no significant difference. However, if significant differences between these groups *were* found, with the *E*-present condition producing the greater expectancy changes, then this adult nonreaction could be presumed to possess active reinforcement properties. Thus, in the current study it was hypothesized that second-series changes in expectancy would be significantly greater for the experimental groups than for the control groups.

Statistical Analyses

In order to test both hypotheses: (a) that children's expectancy estimates would show directional changes depending on the experimental treatments they were given and (b) that the amount of these changes would depend on the height of the *S*'s original G Ex, change scores between each *S*'s successive expectancy estimates were used as the measures of the dependent variable. That is, the difference between each *S*'s first expectancy estimate (Ex_1) and his second (Ex_2) was computed, indicating changes in the children's expectancies resulting from either positive *E* verbal reactions or from negative *E* verbal reactions. In the like manner, change scores between the second (Ex_2) and third (Ex_3) expectancy estimates were computed and used as a measure of the Ss' responses to the *E*-administered nonreaction or of their change under the self-administered control condition.

In testing for homogeneity, one of the variance ratio tests was significant (the first change scores for high and low subgroups under negative treatment yielded an *F* of 3.36, $df = 2$ and 35, significant beyond the .01 level). Therefore, parametric tests were not applicable and nonparametric Wilcoxon tests of difference were employed. Wilcoxon's matched-pairs signed-rank test (Siegel, 1956) was used to assess treatment effects since Ss had been matched on G Ex across treatments. Wilcoxon's unpaired replicates test (Wilcoxon, 1949) was used to assess individual differences in reactions of high vs. low G Ex Ss to specific treatments. One-tailed levels of significance are reported throughout, since both theory and the obtained results of the earlier study seemed to warrant unidirectional predictions.

RESULTS AND DISCUSSION

Changes in Expectancy Resulting from Experimental Treatments
Differential treatment effects may be observed in Figure 1. The figure is based on the median scores of the various groups, in order that the

reader may evaluate the increases and decreases in expectancy under the several treatment and control conditions.

Before the results of specific tests of the hypotheses are presented, it may be of interest to note that, for the 72 Ss who experienced *positive* reactions from the E, there was a highly significant rise from their Ex₁ to their Ex₂ estimates. The Wilcoxon matched-pairs signed-rank test of this difference yielded a sum of ranks of least frequent sign (T) of 568 (p = .0001). As for the 72 Ss in the *negative* treatment, their expectancy changes were even more dramatic. In this instance the T value was zero (i.e., without exception, every S dropped his score), p = .0000001 for N of 72. These data indicate that both treatments were highly effective in raising and lowering the children's expectations of success in the anticipated directions. The E's positive and negative verbal reactions were thus demonstrated to be reinforcing and, for the remainder of this discussion, will be referred to as "reinforcements."

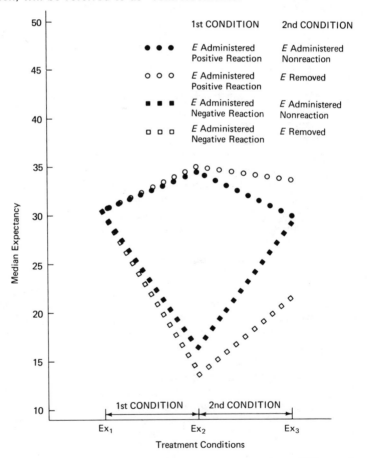

FIGURE 1. Median changes in expectancy estimates under experimental conditions.

It should also be noted that under the positive, as well as under the negative, treatment there were no significant differences between the magnitude of the *first* change scores of the children who were subsequently assigned to the experimental groups as compared with those who became members of the control groups.

In reference to the treatment hypothesis concerning the "contrast" effect of adult nonreaction, changes which occurred during the second series of trials for the experimental Ss are relevant. Figure I indicates that Ss who experienced E-present nonreaction dropped their expectations of success if they had had prior positive reinforcement and raised their expectancy estimates if they had received prior negative reinforcement. The drop between Ex_2 and Ex_3 for the 36 prior-positive Ss yielded a T of 95 ($p = .0005$). The rise between Ex_2 and Ex_3 for the 36 prior-negative Ss yielded a T of zero (i.e., without exception, every S raised his score), $p = .000001$. As in the former study, the E's nonreactions were associated with changes in the Ss' expectations opposite to those resulting from her preceding verbal reinforcements.

It should be pointed out that the second expectancy changes of the control groups were *also* significant ($p = .05$ after previous positive reinforcement and .001 after previous negative reinforcement). These changes, occurring in the same direction as those of children experiencing E-present nonreaction (see Figure 1), can be mainly accounted for by the process of extinction.

However, and most important for the test of the treatment hypothesis, the Ex_2 to Ex_3 changes in the two experimental groups were significantly *greater* than those of their controls. The Wilcoxon matched-pairs signed-rank test comparing the magnitude of all the experimental Ss' second change scores ($N = 72$; 36 initial positive and 36 initial negative) with that of all the control Ss (also 36 prior positive plus 36 prior negative) resulted in a T of 615 ($p = .001$). Experimental vs. control differences following prior positive reinforcement were also evaluated separately from those following prior negative reinforcement. In the nonreaction condition following prior positive reaction, the difference yielded a T of 180, $p = .058$. After the negative treatment the T value was 135.5, $p = .002$. The Ex changes were greater for the experimental Ss as may be seen in Figure 1.[3] Thus, the treatment hypothesis is substantiated. The process in the child seems to be one of *assigning an opposite informational interpretation* to the adult's silence, rather than simply forgetting or inhibiting responses learned to earlier reinforcements. It is suggested that such a contrasting process may take place in various reinforcer-child inter-

[3] Reference to the procedure section will reveal certain additional alterations in administration of the second "test" for the control groups necessitated by the removal of E. No such situational change occurred in administration for the experimental Ss. The alteration of the administration of the second series to the control subjects may have increased the magnitude of their second change scores. Since the degree of this influence was unknown, caution demanded that the entire change for these groups be attributed to extinction. Thus, the present design probably produced a conservative estimate of the difference between nonreaction and pure extinction effects.

actions—at home with parents, in school with teachers, etc.—wherever the child has learned to anticipate verbal reinforcements of a given sign from an adult.

The results of this aspect of the study may have implications apropos of certain common psychological research paradigms. In many learning studies, for example, social reinforcements are used to define right or wrong responses during acquisition periods. Subsequently, the E refrains from giving such reinforcements when the phenomenon of extinction is under consideration. The implicit assumption in such research is that experimenter nonreaction during such times has no reinforcement properties—that such a situation is a *neutral* condition. However, the results of this study indicate that caution should be employed in making such an assumption. The data presented here indicate that, when an E is present but not reacting to the S's performance, this situation cannot necessarily be considered neutral, but may have a consistent reinforcing effect that is opposite in direction to whichever reinforcement the E employed during the original acquisition series.

Changes in Expectancy as a Function of Differences in
Generalized Expectancy of Success

Before considering the influence of the children's Generalized Expectancies of Success on their expectancy changes, it seems advisable to examine the relation of Generalized Expectancy to indices of the child's probable history of reinforcement in everyday achievement experiences. Relevant information in school records was used for this purpose. Positive and significant (*rho*) correlations were found (two-tailed *p*s reported) between (a) these Ss' report card grades and their G Ex at the beginning of the experiment (.32, $p = .001$); (b) their percentile ranks on standardized achievement tests (Iowa Tests of Basic Skills) and their G Ex (.26, $p = .01$); (c) their IQs (California Mental Maturity) and their G Ex (.21, $p = .02$); and (d) their school "ability group" placement and their G Ex (.26, $p = .01$). While none of these correlations can be used as conclusive evidence that the children with high G Ex had a history of mostly positive social reinforcement in achievement situations, these data do suggest that this was probably the case. At least the children with high G Ex had encountered numerous intellectual and scholastic success experiences from which it would seem reasonable to presume that positive social reinforcements had accrued to them. The converse could be presumed for low G Ex Ss. Moreover, direct support of this theoretical relationship was found in the earlier study from which the present study grew. In that study a questionnaire was given to the children to determine the frequency with which they perceived their parents as responding positively or negatively to their behavior. The product-moment correlation between children's reports of parental "positiveness" and the height of their G Ex was .26 ($p = .02$ for the N of 90 Ss used in this earlier study). These diverse data, thus, suggest that the presently assessed personality variable, Generalized Expectancy of Success, is at least a partial derivative of children's past histories of reinforcement in their everyday achievement endeavors.

The individual difference hypothesis of the current study proposed that children who expect to be unsuccessful in achievement situations (low G Ex) should respond more to an adult's *positive* verbal reactions than do children who expect to be successful (high G Ex). Change-score differences in the first experimental condition indicate that children with low initial expectations of success raised their Ex scores significantly more ($T = 1032$, $p = .005$) than the high G Ex Ss as the result of adult positive reactions. Conversely, the hypothesis also proposed that children who expect to be successful in achievement situations (high G Ex) should respond more to an adult's *negative* verbal reactions. Data from the negatively-reinforced group also confirm this part of the hypothesis. Children with greater expectations of success (high G Ex) dropped their expectancies more drastically than did the low G Ex Ss ($T = 998.5$, $p = .0005$). These two sets of results are consistent with those of the original study. Both investigations suggest that children are more sensitive to adults' reactions which are not congruent with those they have come to expect in their daily life experiences (the "noncongruent" hypothesis).

However, the present experimental design was such that "ceiling" and "floor" effects could have been operative in the change scores used as the dependent measure in this study. If a child's original Ex estimate was high and he wanted to raise his expectancy of success following positive reinforcement, his change score was necessarily limited because he could indicate no more than the fiftieth stick figure for his second estimate. A similar limitation existed for the low G Ex child who started at the lower part of the range and wanted to drop his estimate following negative reinforcement. An examination of the change score variances of the high and low Ex groups in each of the two verbal reaction treatments disclosed that there was no significant difference between the two G Ex groups as the result of positive reinforcement, indicating that a ceiling effect for high G Ex Ss was unlikely. In the negative treatment condition, on the other hand, there was a significant difference between the variances of the two G Ex groups (F max / F min $= 3.36$, $p = .01$). The lesser variance did, in fact, derive from the data of the low G Ex group and suggests that a floor effect may have been operative. In the light of this possibility, a more conservative data analysis of the individual differences under the negative treatment was undertaken. It was decided to omit those low Ex Ss whose original Ex estimates were so low that floor effects in their change scores could have occurred. In order to do this, it was reasoned that floor effects would be essentially inoperative for high G Ex Ss in the negative condition and the median amount of their change scores was calculated (mdn $= 17.83$). An additional point was added to this median since level of aspiration studies have often found that Ss are reluctant to place themselves at the very lowest point of any expectancy scale. Then a Mann-Whitney U test of differences was run omitting those Ss whose Ex_1 estimates were so low that they did not have room to indicate a 19-point drop in their expectancies after negative reinforcement. This resulted in the exclusion of five of the 36 low G Ex Ss. The test yielded a U of 308 ($z = 3.14$, $p = .001$). Thus, a significant difference is evident even with this more conservative procedure. The results still indicate that negative adult reactions are more strongly negatively reinforcing for high G Ex Ss than for low G Ex Ss. Thus, the noncongruent hypothesis remains substantiated.[4, 5]

Additional Data

No specific hypotheses were made concerning the comparative impact of positive reactions vs. negative reactions on the children's expectations of success. However, the data lend themselves to such an examination since the reinforcement schedules of the positive and negative groups during the first condition of this experiment were made exactly comparable as to sequence and ratio of reinforced to nonreaction trials. Thus, the reinforcement strength of the positive vs. the negative verbal reactions could be examined. The Wilcoxon matched-pairs signed-rank test revealed that the negative treatment used here was much more effective in reducing expectations of success than the positive treatment was in raising them ($T = 113.5$, $p = .00001$). This result is consistent with that obtained in the previously mentioned earlier experiment. Whether such demonstrated superiority of reinforcement strength may be accounted for by the inherent "negativeness" of the reaction or by some other attribute of the verbal reaction "that's wrong" is an unanswered question. For example, "right" might empirically produce smaller changes in behavior, not because it is positive in sign, but because it is used so frequently in normal social intercourse in our culture to indicate encouragement or support that it has lost some of its original reinforcement strength. That is, perhaps "right" can no longer be accepted as a dependable index of correctness or competence of performance. There are probably other reasons for the differing reinforcement effects of a given positive or negative reaction such as the temporal sequence in which it appears, the importance to the individual of the need system involved, etc. Therefore the present writers do not mean to imply that the data of this and the previous study are presented as evidence of the superiority of "negative" vs. "positive" reinforcements, in any theoretical sense. We wish simply to report that both studies have found empirically (for whatever reason) that an adult's statement "that's wrong" is more effective in changing children's expectancy-of-success estimates than the statement "that's right." In this respect, other investigators (Buchwald, 1959a; 1959b; Buss, Braden, Orgel, & Buss, 1956; Ferguson & Buss, 1959; Meyer

---

[4] The authors' recent concern for floor and ceiling effects prompted an additional analysis of the individual difference data published in the original study. Similar conservative statistical treatment of these data yields significant differences which continue to support the noncongruent hypothesis.

[5] Individual differences in reinforcement sensitivity to *second*-series nonreaction were also tested, and no significant differences were demonstrated. It may be that the contrast effect experienced by the Ss during this second series was so strong as to mask any evidence of individual differences in sensitivity to the inferred reinforcing properties of nonreaction.

& Seidman, 1960, 1961) have also reported that reinforcement combinations pairing "wrong" with "nothing" were more effective in discrimination learning and concept formation problems than were combinations of "right" with "nothing."

In addition, when the effect of adult nonreactions following negative reinforcement was compared with the influence of nonreactions following positive reinforcements in the current study, the former were also found to be significantly stronger in reinforcement effectiveness ($T = 46$, $p =$ .00002 for the 36 pairs of Ss in the experimental groups). This result is again similar to that found in the earlier study. Whether the greater reinforcement strength of nonreaction following negative reaction is due to the greater strength or to the negative sign of the prior verbal reinforcements, or both, is again difficult to determine. However, the fact that identical nonreaction series acquired *differing amounts* of reinforcement effectiveness (as well as differing reinforcement directions) depending on what reinforcements preceded them is taken as additional support for the hypothesis that nonreaction has active reinforcing qualities.

| **3-6** | *Modeling of Defensive Behavior As a Function of Freedom of Movement* |

SAMUEL F. PISANO[1]

Some concept of defensive behavior remains a central feature accounting for psychopathology in most social learning systems. Within Rotter's Social Learning Theory (SLT), it is subsumed under the construct freedom of movement (FM). FM refers to a series of related expectancies that need satisfaction will occur and is defined by Rotter as: *"The mean expectancy of obtaining positive satisfaction is a result of a set of related behaviors directed toward the accomplishment of a group of functionally related reinforcements"* [*1954, p. 194*]. In other words, within SLT, FM refers to a generalized expectancy for success and satisfaction, either within a particular need or across need areas. A person's FM is low if he

[1] The author is indebted to Drs. Donald L. Mosher and Thomas O. Karst for their advice and helpful criticism of this study.

This paper is published for the first time in this volume. We are grateful for the author's permission to use it.

has a high expectancy for failure and, conversely, FM is high when a high expectancy for success prevails. While high freedom of movement (HFM) leads smoothly toward goal-directed activity, low freedom of movement (LFM) eventuates, according to Rotter, in the familiar defensive operations described in abnormal texts.

The present study tests these formulations of FM and attempts to demonstrate that the nature of this nonconstructive behavior—unspecified within Rotter's system—can be profoundly shaped through simple imitation. The study draws upon leads provided by Bandura, who has shown most fully that much social behavior can be molded through exposure to, and imitation of, a model (Bandura & Walters, 1963). Broadly stated, it asks the questions: Can nonconstructive reactions be elicited differentially from HFM versus LFM subjects by exposure to a defensive model? and, Can the form of such defensive behavior be shaped through imitation of that model?

METHOD

One hundred and twenty first- and second-grade boys, nominated by their teachers as resembling brief generalized descriptions of LFM and HFM patterns,[2] were exposed to a filmed model who failed at a task. The model—a clean-cut but green basic-trainee soldier—was shown attempting to qualify on a pistol range in order to win a medal for marksmanship in the U.S. Army. The film chronicles his failure. During the scene, the soldier—tentatively at first and then with mounting conviction—consistently enacts the defense of rationalization (for example, "Aw, my finger slipped"; or, "I'm much better with a different gun").

While the children watched the film, three response-consequent conditions were provided differentially by *E* in the form of aside comments as follows: *positive* (sympathy—for example, "It's too bad that keeps happening."); *neutral* (no comment); and *negative* (interpretation—for example, "The worse he does, the more he seems to blame the gun"). Following exposure to the model and the concurrent response-consequent condition, children were placed in a miniature version of the soldier's task—attempting to qualify on an electronically controlled gun game. Brightly emblazoned ribbons, paralleling the classes of medals the soldier was attempting to win, were displayed as prizes. However, both experimental and control *S*s received failing scores; controls did not view the imitation film.

To ensure verbalization during the gun game, five separate queries ("What's happening?") were made of each *S* during the game. All verbalizations were recorded.

Two dependent measures were employed—word-for-word imitative defensiveness and total elicited defensiveness. (Total defensive-

---

[2] An example of the HFM description employed read: "In the classroom he sets goals within his reach and manages to complete them successfully."

ness includes both imitative plus all other nonimitative verbalizations receiving high independent interjudge agreement as to their defensive intent; for example, "I never could shoot 'cause I got heart trouble"; or, "My eyes keep changing"). Predictions were similar for these two classes of behavior. It was hypothesized that the model would serve to elicit increased generalized defensiveness and to shape specific defensive behaviors along imitative lines. On the basis of Rotter's position that LFM represents a dispositional variable for engaging in nonconstructive behavior, it was expected, further, that LFM Ss would show more modeling effects than HFM Ss.

Two patterns of LFM from among the nine basic patterns identified by Rotter (1954; pp. 319–321) were employed in the present study. The first group (LFM$_A$) shows failure-avoidant behavior predominantly, while the second group (LFM$_F$) characteristically retreats into fantasy achievement—braggadocio and big talk—in the face of failure.[3] Inasmuch as both measures of imitation are verbal in nature, and thus, more congruent with the verbal stylistic pattern of the fantasy achievement Ss (LFM$_F$), it was assumed that this group would show more effects of model exposure than their failure-avoidant (LFM$_A$) counterparts. Therefore, the following increasing order of both total and imitative defensiveness was anticipated for the three groups: HFM, lowest; LFM$_A$, moderate level; and LFM$_F$, highest.

Finally, it was expected that the response-consequent conditions would facilitate differentially the appearance of imitative behavior in the following order: *positive* (or sympathy), most; *neutral* (or no comments), moderate; and *negative* (or interpretation), least.

FINDINGS

Broadly, the results of this study demonstrate the important effects of a model on both the elicitation and shaping of defensive behavior. They are consistent, therefore, with the considerable body of evidence that models have powerful influences on a wide range of social behavior—aggression (Bandura & Huston, 1961); moral judgments (Bandura & McDonald, 1963); delay of gratification (Bandura & Mischel, 1965); and now defensive behavior.

Examination of group differences (LFM versus HFM), however, reveals that only the LFM boys show the expected disinhibitory and imitative modeling effects. HFM boys were neither induced into increased imitative defensiveness nor increased total defensiveness as a result of model exposure. (See Figures 1 and 2.)

With respect to the relative susceptibility of the three personality groups to modeling effects, it was predicted that HFM Ss would show

[3] Illustrative of the descriptional patterns used in the selection of LFM Ss were (a) LFM$_A$: "This student is hesitant to speak up in the classroom . . . and to try new tasks." (b) LFM$_F$: "This student would like to be noticed but in the absence of success resorts to big talk and bragging."

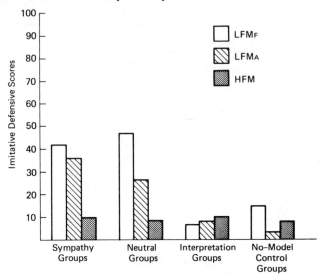

FIGURE 1. Imitative defensive scores for the FM groups under four experimental conditions.

the least amount of both total and imitative defensiveness; LFM_A Ss (avoidant pattern), a moderate level; and LFM_F (fantasy-achievement pattern), the highest level. With total defensiveness as the dependent measure, predictions are confirmed. LFM_A and LFM_F children reveal moderate and high levels of verbal defensiveness, respectively, and differ significantly from each other. With imitative defensiveness as the dependent measure,

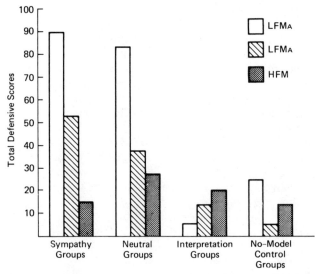

FIGURE 2. Total defensive scores for the FM groups under four experimental conditions.

the differences between the two LFM groups fade out and they appear to operate more alike, a finding that invites explanation. It seems likely that this difference is a result of two factors: (1) the generally more cautious nature of LFM_A Ss and (2) their more dominant stylistic pattern of relying upon avoidant defenses. On the first point, Mosher (1965b) has noted that within SLT, effects of models can be conceptualized in terms of their potential for altering expectancies. For example, models not punished for socially disapproved behavior provide cues which apparently change the observer's expectancy that such behavior will be punished, resulting, thereby, in imitation of that behavior. Within this framework, it seems likely that the generally more cautious nature of LFM_A Ss allows them to imitate only that socially disapproved behavior for which guidelines concerning expected consequences have clearly been established, but prevents their generalizing these expectancies to other responses even within the šame class. Thus, they show as much imitative defensiveness as the other LFM group, but significantly less total defensiveness. Second, verbal responses and not avoidant behavior constituted the variable—total defensiveness. Had avoidant behavior additionally been measured—a style more consistent with the LFM_A group—the outcome might have been as expected.

Finally, the predicted effects of the three response-consequent conditions (sympathy *versus* neutrality *versus* interpretation) received partial support. For all model-exposed groups, interpretation clearly served as a powerful suppressing agent upon both over-all and imitative defensiveness—a finding that parallels previous reports concerning inhibiting effects of negative response consequences upon deviant response elicitation (Walters, Leat, & Mezei, 1963; Bandura, 1965). However, sympathy failed to demonstrate facilitative effects different from neutrality in the elicitation of either general or imitative defensiveness. This finding may reflect something of the importance of the context in which sympathy is offered, being valued chiefly within the setting of an established relation. When it comes from a stranger-experimenter, it may not provide much solace in the face of an important failure.

In summary, the import of this study lies in several areas. It provides strong support for Rotter's contention that freedom of movement serves as a dispositional variable for engaging in constructive *versus* nonadaptive behavior. It points up, generally, the importance of considering personality variables in conceptualization and extension of future work on modeling effects. The study provides us, in addition, with a promising laboratory analogue for opening an important class of behavior—defensive behavior—to rigorous empirical inquiry. Questions concerning other defensive styles, the patterning of defensive behavior, the alteration of defensive styles, and even the possible acquisition of defense through imitation—all seem possible extensions.

PART 3: SUMMARY

The purpose of this section is twofold: (1) it sketches briefly the scope of many social learning papers which are not among the papers reprinted in this volume; and (2) it provides some suggestions about how this theoretical approach may have special relevance or utility for questions about the development of personality.

In common with other theories dealing with personality development, Social Learning Theory (SLT) is concerned with complex behaviors occurring over some span of time. Also in common with other theories, SLT assumes that such behavior is integrated and that its productive study requires delineation of that integration. However, unlike many developmental theories (for example, Freud or Piaget) which emphasize a maturational basis of change, SLT emphasizes behavioral changes that are a function of individual experience and variations in psychological situations. Maturationally oriented theories of personality development, although usually recognizing the importance of experience, are typically vague about the manner in which the experiences affect behavior. In contrast, all too frequently learning theories examine the processes of learning without more than a faint intimation that there is an individual person (either maturationally or experientially) who does that learning. In recent years several theorists—Bandura and Walters, Miller and Dollard, Sears and his associates, along with Rotter—have attempted to construct theories that would amalgamate the scientific advantages of laboratory-tested theory with the insights of more clinical or person-oriented methods into the needs and cognitions of learners.

However, these other social learning theories attempt to combine constructs about the processes of learning, derived primarily from American experimental psychology, with constructs about the contents of behavior, derived either directly or indirectly from psychoanalytic approaches to personality development—for example, anxiety, dependency, aggression. Rotter's SLT, in contrast, attempts to employ constructs developed within a unitary viewpoint which are capable of describing both processes of behavioral change and the content of that which is changed.

SLT emphasizes three sets of variables—expectancy of reinforcements, value of the reinforcement, and effects of the psychological situation on both expectancy and value. Definitions and the basic structure of SLT are presented in Part 1 of this volume. This section discusses these variables as they are relevant in both description and prediction of personality development.

STUDIES OF SOCIALIZATION

Rotter employs a number of assumptions about behavior having implications for the study of socialization. The theory assumes that behavior is goal-directed and that common directions in behavior can be observed, described reliably, and used predictively. These goals, directions, and so on, are fixed neither by biology nor by a primacy of the order in which they occurred in the individual's experience. The goals of importance in predicting human social interaction are best described by referring to responses which S expects and wants to be made toward him by other persons. This conception of S's expectations need not imply that S is clearly aware of his anticipations nor necessarily that his anticipations are accurate. It does imply that his anticipations are manifest in his behavior and that a properly situated observer will potentially be able to define directions of S's goal striving and to observe S's experience of their consequences. An observer possessing these data should be able to predict either persistence or cessation of given behaviors or changes in goal direction and choice over time.

Within this point of view, the process of socialization involves both acquisition of behaviors and development of expectancies and values attached to the outcomes of their performance. The process of personality development can be understood by looking at behavior and its relation to the person's psychological situation rather than by making accounts that seek to reduce explanation to either historical origins of behavior on the one hand or to biological descriptions of human functioning on the other. This view also demands that questions about socialization be asked not solely in terms of what is done to or for the child but also in terms of what the parents' (or others') expectations and goals are in relation to the child. While few writers concerned with personality development have failed to recognize the reciprocity of socialization, it is quite rare to find a theory in which the child's and parents' behavior can be described within the same framework.

Two different research programs have shown the feasibility of deriving consistent, communicable, and useful descriptions of behaviors of parents and their children. The work of Tyler and his associates has demonstrated that goal directions in behavior can be described within the same system for parents and child, so long as it is recognized that the particular referents employed for descriptions will differ with age, sex, status, and the situation of S when observed. Two papers growing out of this work are included in the present volume (3–1; 4–3). The paper by Rafferty, Tyler, and Tyler (1960, 3–1) represents one facet of this work—the applicability of the SLT approach to the time-honored methods of observing free play in children.

The program of Crandall and Crandall and their associates has investigated broadly aspects of children's achievement behavior; however, of special interest here is their development of a set of constructs to describe achievement values and expectancies of both parents and children, and to do so in a manner that recognizes the specificity of these concepts to particular psychological situations (Crandall, Katkovsky, & Preston, 1960a). The early work of these investigators demonstrated both the necessity and the utility of a more specific conceptual structure to be applied to the processes of observation and comparison in socialization studies (Crandall, Orleans, Preston, & Rabson, 1958; Crandall & Preston, 1961; and Crandall, Preston, & Rabson, 1960). The latter paper focuses upon the effects of the mother on her young child, showing that behaviors that mothers specifically rewarded in interactions with children produced more accurate predictions of children's nursery behaviors than did assessments of mothers' general attitudes. However, such findings still leave the question *how* mother selects what behaviors to reinforce and how she "teaches" the child to make these particular behaviors.

Subsequent papers, one of which is reprinted in this volume (Crandall, Dewey, Katkovsky, & Preston, 1964, 3–2), as well as Katkovsky, Preston, and Crandall (1964a, 1964b), applied their conceptual scheme for studying achievement to mothers and fathers as well as to children. These investigators find similarity between the values and standards that parents hold for themselves and the values and standards by which they evaluate their children's achievement behavior; this similarity is reflected in their responses to the child's achievement behavior and is related to the child's achievement behavior in school. At the same time, their findings also clearly indicate that many other factors having to do with parental perceptions of the child himself (sex, age, level of real competence in school or sports, and so on) also influence the parents' responses toward him. Socialization of achievement behavior is not a one-way process, but is truly an interaction.

Moss (1967) has studied interactions between primaparous mothers and their infants at three weeks and three months of the child's age. His data suggest that, even from the early days of life, the relation between mother and child is best characterized as an interaction. The mother, by her prompt, contingent responses to the infant's signals, acquires for him reinforcing value; however, the infant's response to the mother's attention also influences the subsequent pattern of her responses to him. Differences among children in their activity level, irritability, soothability, and so on, can shape the character of mothering behavior and the eventual strength of the mother-child attachment. Moss's effort, based on the SLT point of view, is in contrast to earlier studies of mothering which tend both to treat maternal behavior at a much broader level of generality and also to imply a high level of maternal-response stability and consistency which overlooks the possible effects of the child's responses on the mother's behavior.

ANTECEDENTS OF ATTITUDES ABOUT CONTROL OF REINFORCEMENT

While the socialization studies in the preceding section were generally selected to show the fruitfulness of applying the SLT viewpoint to socialization studies, the studies in this section and the next will be more particularly focused upon understanding the conditions that precede and enhance the development of certain classes of generalized expectancies.

Several investigators have examined the effects of socialization practices on development of generalized expectancies for reinforcement control in children. Lewis and Goldberg (1969) propose that prompt and contingent responses on the part of mothers to infants' signals facilitate development within the infant of a generalized expectancy that his responses are capable of influencing his environment. In other words, mother's responding to the child's signals not only provides him with stimulation and a source of direct reinforcement for his behavior but also sets up conditions under which a generalized expectancy of being able to exert control upon one's environment can begin to develop. These investigators hypothesize that this generalized expectation, in turn, facilitates a more active approach by the infant to all sources of environmental stimulation and thereby enhances early cognitive development. Assuming that decrement in time spent looking at a repeated stimulus was a measure of infants' cognitive development, they found predicted relations with mothers' responsiveness (amount, contingency, and latency of response) observed while mothers and infants waited in a standard situation.

Katkovsky, Crandall, and Good (1967) examined childrearing correlates of generalized expectancy for control of reinforcement among older children, measured by the Crandall Intellectual Achievement Responsibility Questionnaire (IAR—Crandall, Katkovsky, & Crandall, 1965). These studies found that parents' behaviors described as positive, warm, supportive, permissive, and praising toward the child were associated with greater belief on the child's part that the quality of his own efforts determined both his academic successes and his academic failures.

Chance (3–4) also investigated maternal childrearing antecedents of children's achievement behavior and their attitudes toward it. She found that maternal early expectations for child independence and mastery, when they occurred in conjunction with generally positive and permissive attitudes toward the child's behavior, were associated with a stronger generalized expectancy on the child's part that his own efforts and characteristics determined reinforcements obtained in school. Her data also suggested that more internal generalized expectancies about control occurred in children who were also less anxious and who more closely approximated a need organization consistent with cultural sex-role expectations.

Chance sees the predictiveness of mother's independence-training attitude for these outcomes as suggesting importance not of earliness of training *per se*, but rather suggesting the importance of the quality of response that mother requires before she is likely to reward the child. Mother's liberalness or stinginess with rewards for the child's achievement *efforts* may mediate both the degree to which she becomes a highly valued source of rewards and the child's attitudes about the degree to which he is instrumental in obtaining his own rewards. Earlier, Crandall, Katkovsky, and Preston (1960a) had noted that when parents defined achievement behavior by supplying instances from their child's behavior, their definitions included the child's manifestation of *interest* in potential achievement situations and the fact of *participation*, in addition to the idea of *competence*.

Davis and Phares (1969), using a more generalized measure of internal-external attitudes (I-E) with college-age Ss and their parents, found the same sort of associations between more positive parental attitudes and greater internality expressed by their offspring. In addition, they found that consistent, as opposed to inconsistent, parental discipline seems to be associated with stronger student internality.

All these studies suggest that perceived personal control of reinforcements is facilitated by an early parent-child relation which can be characterized in terms of relatively greater parental concern for enhancing the child's potential for behavior than for controlling his potential for misbehavior. The child's attitude is associated with parental standards for "deciding" when to give or when to withhold rewards which are adjusted to some extent to realistic, and probably lenient, pictures of the child's capability, and with interpersonal relations in which the child can find predictability and stability of others' behaviors in relation to himself.

Still other studies have addressed themselves to demographic correlates of I-E differences. Battle and Rotter (1963) and Zytkoskee, Strickland, and Watson (1971) examined I-E attitudes in older children in relation to social class and to race. They find that lower-class children are generally more external in attitude than middle-class children, and that lower-class status and being black may interact to produce rather extreme external attitudes. These findings imply that differences in socialization practices related to both income level and ethnicity may be involved; they also suggest that differences in I-E attitudes may be related to differences in interpersonal trust, discussed in Part 4. Note, however, that Zytkoskee *et al.* did not obtain evidence of any direct relation between I-E differences and trust when choice of delayed over immediate outcomes on the part of their Ss was the dependent variable.

In an earlier study, Crandall, Katkovsky, and Crandall (1965) had not found their measure of internality of attitudes related to socioeconomic status; however, their measure (IAR) focuses more specifically on attitudes toward school performance while the Battle-Rotter Children's Picture Test and the Bialer-Cromwell Locus of Control Scale (Bialer, 1961) employed by Zytkoskee *et al.* sample a wider variety of situations. Also, perhaps, the Crandall *et al.* study, because it did not include a sample from a large metropolitan area, did not obtain a large representation of Ss of really lower-lower–class status.

Other variables, like birth order (Crandall, Katkovsky, & Crandall, 1965) and psychiatric diagnosis of schizophrenia (Cromwell, Rosenthal, Shakow, & Zahn, 1961), have been shown to relate to I-E attitudes in a manner suggesting differential socialization outcomes.

INTERPERSONAL TRUST AND DELAY

Another generalized expectancy whose developmental antecedents have been of interest is *interpersonal trust*. If behavior choices are determined by expectancy of desired outcomes, and many desired outcomes involve either responses that others make toward us or events in which activities of others must mediate the outcome for us, then *trust* becomes basic to prediction of behavior. In contrast to the construct of I-E control of reinforcement which represents expectations held about the efficacy of the individual's own behavior in relation to the world, interpersonal trust represents generalized expectancy about the behavior of others toward the person. Behavior choices across situations will vary depending upon the individual's expectation that a variety of social others will react in the expected or promised manner.

Unlike Ericson's concept of *basic trust*, this generalized expectancy is not regarded as the development of any single period of the individual's lifetime nor as the result of any unitary source of influence, such as the quality of mothering. Rather, its level is, at any given time, the outcome of a wide variety of antecedents and it is subject to modification with the person's changing life situation. As a generalized expectancy, it may also be temporarily modified or put into abeyance when characteristics of behavioral situations invoke more particular expectancies about the intentions and dependability of the social other.

Rotter (1967b, 4–7) has described the development and some of the demographic correlates of an interpersonal trust scale appropriate to use with college students. He found small but stable differences in trust scores among Ss who varied in socioeconomic origin and in religious affiliation. Katz and Rotter (1969) investigated the similarity of responses made by college students and by their parents to this scale. They found similarity between trust scores of fathers and their sons, but not between fathers and their daughters. Also, they found only a weak trend for mothers' scores to be related to scores of either sons or daughters. Since the interpersonal trust scale focuses on social relations and roles found largely outside the home, the stronger similarity of sons' attitudes to fathers' than to mothers' seems reasonable. Up to the period of late adolescence, the father is the more likely of the parents to represent and to interpret the world outside the family for the child, and perhaps the son, in preparation for his future masculine role, is more likely than the daughter to be attuned to his father's interpretation.

Closely related to the concept of interpersonal trust is the study of choice of delayed, larger rewards over smaller, immediate ones. Although such choices are complexly related to many variables (Mischel, 1966) associated with both expectancy and reinforcement values, Ss' expectancies that rewards promised by others will materialize later should clearly affect choices. Mahrer (1956, 2–6) has demonstrated a relation between children's choices of delayed rewards and their experimenter-induced expectancy that indeed they would receive the delayed reward if it were chosen. Other early studies by Mischel (1958b, 1961a, 1961b, 1961c, 1966) map relations between choice of delayed rewards and a variety of personal and cultural indexes; all these studies suggest that the more favorable a child's experiences—either direct or vicarious—with promises kept and postponements rewarded, the more likely he is to make delayed choices.

It should be noted here (Bialer, 1961; Mischel & Metzner, 1962) that effects of the child's experiences on his capacity to delay are also in some part a function of his level of cognitive development. For example, can he conceptualize *time* in a meaningful way? Are smaller and larger rewards seen as reliably different? From a broader view, these developmental data may suggest that an expectancy-choice formulation has its most relevant applications past that point at which cognitive development is sufficient to insure elementary comprehension of such conceptions as *time, quantity,* and so on.

Rotter (1967b) proposes that the concept of *trust* employed in the development of the interpersonal trust scale is related to Merton's concept of *normlessness* as a facet of the broader sociopersonal syndrome of *alienation.* Jessor (1964), and Jessor, Graves, Hanson, and Jessor (1968), in a comprehensive study of the parameters of deviant drinking behavior in a tri-ethnic community, examined the role of personality structure in determining occurrence of deviant behavior. Utilizing SLT-derived descriptions of personality and viewing them in a structure analogous to Merton's theory of *anomie* (1957) and the Cloward-Ohlin (1960) extension of Sutherland's theory of differential association (1947), they propose that, as disparity between an individual's needs and his expectancy of attaining satisfaction increases, so increases the pressure to engage in illegitimate means to attain the missing satisfaction. The "push" of personal disjunction is either balanced or enhanced by several aspects of both the personal belief structure (including alienation) and the personal control structure (including tendencies toward immediate gratification, short time-perspective, and so on).

Regarding socialization as the process at the interface between culture and personality, Jessor *et al.*—in one phase of their study—examined responses of their high school-aged sample in the light of their mothers' interview responses regarding socialization events occurring during the preadolescent and early adolescent years. These authors concluded that family characteristics conducive to nondeviant behavior—and to non-alienated attitudes—on the part of adolescent children reflected favorable family atmosphere, as well as a more favorable location of the family in the sociocultural system of the community. The more benign family atmosphere included presence of a nonalienated mother, in combination with warm affection, rational limits and discipline, and absence of deviant models for behavior. Generally, these findings are congruent with those of Katz and Rotter (1969) regarding correlates of interpersonal trust and Mischel's (1966) findings concerning the antecedent conditions associated with choice of delayed rewards in younger children.

The preceding formulation could be expanded beyond an account of social disenchantment, failures of self-regulation of reinforcement-seeking behavior, and deviance in the societal sense to include also some account of hypothesized developmental antecedents of psychopathological behavior. The severely disturbed person (for example, a schizophrenic) can be said to have very low expectancies that his interpersonal needs will be met, coupled with strong desire for those same satisfactions. This excessive disjunction, coupled with an unfavorable history of development which has given rise to a deep distrust toward others and a relative inability to adjust behavior to long-range, rather than short-range, interpersonal goals, could indeed provide the setting conditions for psychopathological behavior. Lefcourt and Steffy (1966) have employed a similar formulation to account for many findings emerging from the Duke schizophrenia research project (Rodnick, 1963). They propose that differences in family structure (mother or father dominant) and its effect on the development of generalized expectancies in the child can account for observed differences in schizophrenic behavior. With this formulation, they are able to predict differential cooperation of "process" and "reactive" schizophrenics in response to male and female examiners.

Studies reviewed in the preceding sections have largely emphasized socialization (parent-child interaction) or investigation of antecedent psychosocial conditions influencing personality development. These studies have utilized the vantage point of the theoretical outlook of SLT and have organized their data gathering and made their predictions in terms of the constructs of the theory. The next sections will focus on studies directed toward prediction and understanding of child behavior per se in terms of social-learning formulations.

EFFECTS OF EXPECTANCIES

Of the three basic SLT predictive variables—*expectancy, reinforcement value,* and *psychological situation*—expectancy has received the larger share of researchers' attention. As indicated earlier in this paper, SLT has a special pertinence for the study of personality development in the middle childhood years and beyond. Employing the view that much important behavior is a function, on the one hand, of our perceptions of opportunities for social reinforcers, and, on the other, of our perceptions of our behavioral resources for obtaining them, then SLT becomes a particularly sharp analytic tool.

Expectancy (and its related concepts) has proved singularly valuable in prediction of various aspects of childhood behavior. A number of studies have demonstrated that expectancy statements made regarding academic performance predict actual performance. Battle (1966, 3–3) found strong relations between junior high school students' grades in mathematics and English and their stated expectancies for those subjects. Crandall and McGhee (1968) reviewed data from five of their studies in which expectancy statements were related to teacher grades assigned and/or outcomes obtained on standard achievement measures. In each set of data, significant correlations (+.26 to +.64) were obtained. In an extremely large study of samples of U.S. schoolchildren, Coleman and his associates (Coleman *et al.*, 1966) showed that among white children an expectancy variable is the most predictive of achievement test scores among all those variables studied (attitudes, family variables, and teacher and school variables). Expectancy is also the second most predictive variable among nonwhite children, where it is exceeded only by measures of how much the child believes his academic outcomes are determined by factors which are under his own control.

Uhlinger and Stephens (1960) found that among extremely able college students higher achievement performance was related to higher stated achievement expectancies; in contrast, they found no differences between high- and low-achieving Ss in measured achievement needs. Crandall, Katkovsky, and Preston (1962), in a study of children in the first three grades of school, also found no relation between a need-achievement measure based on TAT stories and amount of intellectual striving manifest in free-play activities or achievement test performance. In contrast, intellectual-success expectancy statements obtained from boys (but not girls) were related to these dependent measures.

The question can be raised why expectancy statements predict achievement behaviors as well as they do. (In most of the instances cited above, correlations obtained were quite similar to correlations between IQ measures and performance likely to be obtained on similar samples.) One element in the predictive efficiency of expectancy statements is obviously the fact that under some circumstances an expectancy statement is a report of the individual's previous reinforcement history. The report is especially likely to be predictive under circumstances in which the person has been able satisfactorily to meet standards defining success—either societal ones imposed upon him or ones he imposes upon himself, his minimal goal level (MGL). The report is also likely to be accurate to the extent that past experience suggests that possible outcomes are the result of either his own efforts or abilities. Predictive accuracy will also differ, depending upon the age of the S, amount of pertinent experience, and the degree of similarity between the task for which expectancy is stated and the criteria to be predicted (Battle, 1966, 3–3; Crandall & McGhee, 1968).

However, expectancy statements—accurate and otherwise—also predict because they yield information about S's approach and persistence behaviors regarding the goal for which the expectancy is stated. Battle (1965) found that expectancy for mathematics grades predicted the persistence shown by adolescents attempting to solve a difficult mathematical puzzle. Tyler (1958), in an experiment using college Ss, has shown that manipulated anticipation of eventual success—rather than eventual failure—in employing logic to solve a difficult pattern-learning problem was associated with greater success in obtaining logical solutions. Feather (1963a) showed that college Ss with initially high expectations of success on a difficult perceptual reasoning problem persist longer in attempting to solve it than those with low expectations.

Other studies have demonstrated the predictive efficiency of the generalized expectancy for internal control of reinforcements in relation to academic performance. Chance (1965, 1968, 3–4), Crandall, Katkovsky, and Crandall (1965), Crandall, Katkovsky, and Preston (1962), and McGhee and Crandall (1968) have all obtained results suggesting that belief in internal control of reinforcing outcomes is associated with generally better performance in school. These data also suggest that such a generalized expectancy about academic achievement is well developed in children by third grade, although it continues to increase slightly with age thereafter. Though related to intelligence test scores, IAR scores are by no means identical with them. The Crandall work with the IAR scale suggests that there may be different developmental patterns for claiming responsibility for failure as opposed to claiming credit for success; also, these patterns may differ for girls and boys.

Cromwell and his students (1967a, 6–5) have investigated—using a different measure of the construct (Bialer, 1961)—the effect of locus of control ascribed to reinforcing outcomes on various dependent variables, for example, delay of gratification and choice to resume a task previously failed over a task previously succeeded upon. All measures—delay of gratification, repetition choice, and locus of control—were found to be interrelated and, in turn, related to both mental age and chronological age (Bialer, 1961). Crandall and Rabson (1960) earlier had demonstrated age and sex differences in repetition choice. Mischel and Staub (1965, 2–3) demonstrated that voluntary choice of delay of reward in the interest of obtaining larger rewards later is a function of expectancy—specific or generalized—of success in performing the intervening instrumental activity supposedly required to obtain the reward.

Cromwell proposes a theory of developmental shift in motivation from early childhood, when most behavior is governed by hedonistic considerations, to middle childhood, when behavior increasingly reflects needs to achieve success or to avoid failure (6–5). Self-perceptions of succeeding or failing, according to Cromwell's definition, are possible only insofar as the subject can perceive goal attainment or loss as contingent upon his own behavior.

EFFECTS OF REINFORCEMENT

Studies cited in the earlier portion of this summary pointed to the influence of parental behavior on the kinds of goals that children pursue and on preferences shown by them for some goals over others. Social learning theory proposes that *reinforcement value* is a function of the individual's expectancy that a particular goal pursued implies an increased expectancy of obtaining still other goals. This definition is in contrast to definitions of similar constructs in other theories. SLT does *not* see reinforcement value to be a direct function of some intrinsic characteristics of the object, nor are values fixed. They change with experience. Hunt (1955) tested this proposition directly in a study showing that children's preferences for selected toys could be increased after play with those toys (as contrasted with others) led to praise and rewarding attention from the experimenter. Apart from its theoretical import, Hunt's study also provides a very straightforward demonstration of the mechanism by which children are induced either to maintain or to change preferences for various activities as a function of their interactions with adults and with peers. The SLT principle concerning determination of *reinforcement value* provides a useful description of the process by which changes in individuals' goals can occur as a function of developmental or situational shifts.

Effectiveness of reinforcing events is a function of the context of expectancy—situational and personal—in which they occur. The Crandall, Good, and Crandall study (1964, 3–5), as well as an earlier study by Crandall (1963), nicely demonstrated that the impact of an experimenter's nonreaction to a child's performance depended upon the expectancy the child had previously developed in the experimental situation. Children previously "successful" saw nonreaction as negative, and children who had been "not successful" reacted as though nonreaction were positive. This same study (3–5) also showed the influence of the child's generalized expectancy for succeeding on his response to nonreaction.

Cromwell (1963, 1967a, 6–5) examined in a variety of studies the effect of generalized expectancy for success on performance and on the impact of reinforcements on behavior. He has reasoned that the mentally retarded person has a life history likely to lead to lower generalized expectancies for success than do normals. These lower generalized ex-

pectancies are hypothesized to lead to the retardate's responding to reinforcing events somewhat differently than does a normal. Expecting failure,
the retardate is likely to be less responsive to failure than to success.
Intellectually normal Ss typically redoubled their efforts after a failure
trial; retardates were far less likely to do so. Also, successful experience in
tasks where increased effort per se could improve performance improved
retardate performance more markedly than it did the performance of
normals.

In addition to the influence of generalized expectancies for success
or failure on perception of reinforcing outcomes, individuals define standards for themselves concerning extent of goal attainment which influence
their evaluations of particular amounts or kinds of rewards. Minimal goal
level (MGL) is defined as the lowest value of a reinforcement that can
occur with which the individual will still feel pleased or gratified. (More
objectively, MGL would be the lowest strength of reinforcement that
would lead to an increased probability of a behavior.) Battle's study
(1965) demonstrated that disparities between MGL and expectancy
(MGL > E) are likely to lead in a hard task to earlier quitting or leaving
the field than when MGL and E are more nearly equal. In another study
(3–3), the same investigator examined the relation of MGL for mathematics and English grades to actual grades obtained. She found that higher
MGLs might either facilitate or interfere with performance, depending
upon whether "above average" or "below average" grades were expected.
Uhlinger and Stephens (1960) also found among college students that the
degree to which expectancy for academic achievement exceeded MGLs
for academic achievement was positively and significantly associated with
excellence of grades obtained.

OBSERVATIONAL LEARNING AND IMITATION

A number of SLT-based studies have employed a modeling paradigm
to study change in behavior. SLT does not emphasize the distinction
between response acquisition and performance emphasized by Bandura
and Walters (1963). Within the social learning view, behavior is not
acquired just once, but rather can be said to be acquired as many times
as it enters into a new relation with an expectancy for given outcome in
a given situation. Since *reinforcement* is defined in terms of the actor's perception of movement toward a goal, there is no paradox in proposing that
expectancy and reinforcement value may change when no direct con-
summatory effect has been experienced. The advantage of the SLT
approach in the area of observational learning is that the theory permits
conceptualization and prediction of imitative behaviors with the same set
of constructs useful for other classes of behavior.

Observational learning, or effects of observing a model, may influence expectancy, reinforcement value, self-reward standards (MGLs), and categorization of situations. Mischel and his associates (1966) have performed a variety of investigations having to do with the effects of modeling on acquisition of various self-control behaviors. Bandura and Mischel (1965) investigated the effects of models on children's delayed-choice behavior. Models displayed choices—immediate or delayed—and made remarks about their choice behavior in the presence of children. This procedure was effective in influencing the direction of the child's choices, even four weeks later. Mischel and Liebert (1966) found that both model behavior of self-reward standards and the consistency, or inconsistency, of those reward standards with those the model applied to the child affected the reward standards the child applied to himself; they also affected those he imposed on another child. Effects of model characteristics (rewardingness and future control over the child) were varied by Mischel and Grusec (1966) to study their effect on rehearsal and transmission of both neutral and aversive model behaviors. Their results suggest that model characteristics are influential in altering both expectancies and reward values for rehearsing and transmitting behaviors.

Henker and Rotter (1968) examined the effects of model characteristics—competence and interpersonal role toward the child—on imitation in a play situation and in a psychomotor task. Their findings suggest that model behaviors are important clues used by the child to evaluate the nature of a situation and to forecast the likely outcomes of various behaviors in it. A paper by Pisano (3-6), using modeling of defensive statements in a frustration situation, highlights the effectiveness of reinforcing consequences to the model in manipulating children's expectancies which elicit and shape defensive behavior. Two other aspects of Pisano's study are of particular interest here. First, he demonstrated that boys low in freedom of movement are influenced by their observations, while those high in freedom of movement are not. The S's predisposition interacts with situational parameters to determine how much and which aspects of observed behaviors will have impact on him. Second, this study employs two measures of defensive behavior—that which is directly imitated and that which is within the same category of behavior but not "identical" with the behavior observed in the model. That observation should increase occurrence of behaviors in a similar as well as in an identical category suggests that expectancy changes produced in this manner generalize as do expectancy changes produced by direct experience.

CONCLUSION

This discussion has considered the versatility of the SLT approach to problems of personality development from both the conceptual and the methodological standpoint. The reader has seen how development of behaviors as diverse as achieving, persisting, accepting responsibility for oneself, trusting others, choosing to work for larger delayed *versus* smaller immediate rewards, learning by observation of behavior and of outcomes to others, and so on, can be handled within the same theoretical framework. The use of the theory has been coupled with investigative methods ranging from traditional experimentation to controlled observation and correlations. In the field of personality development where experiments are the ideal, but investigators must often employ other methods, the theory provides both a structure for organizing observations and a source of hypotheses for explaining the mechanisms that mediate the observed relations. Recognition of the potential contributions to behavior of both situational variables and the individual predispositions of our human subject has increased the yield of information from the use of experimental methods with problems of personality development.

4 | Applications to Personality Theory and Personality Measurement

INTRODUCTION

A basic tenet of social learning theory is that test-taking behavior is subject to the same variables as any other behavior. The same kinds of processes, the same motivations, and the same principles of learning apply to responding to a test as they do to responding in other situations. Consequently, the methodology of measurement is closely allied to the personality theory itself. Contributions of social-learning theory to personality theory and to the methodology of personality measurement have been combined into one section. The problem of selection has been particularly difficult here, since so many articles are available. For example, the published research on internal-external control as a generalized expectancy numbers over two hundred articles at the time of this writing. Studies of situational effects on test-taking behavior are also quite numerous. The articles reprinted in this chapter have been selected as representative of the research derived from social-learning theory in these two broad areas. They are, however, only a small portion of the available studies.

The first article is a general theoretical one by Rotter (4-1) on the implications of social learning theory for test-taking behavior. It is followed by Moss's study (4-2) of cautious behavior illustrating the value of the interaction design in studying personality.

These articles are followed by a group of papers that describe in detail techniques for the measurement of psychological needs. Included here are Fitzgerald's (4-3) comparison of projective-test interview and sociometric approaches to dependent behavior, Crowne and Marlowe's (4-4) description of a scale for the measurement of social-approach need, and Efran and Broughton's (4-5) study of social-approval need and visual behavior.

Part of the contribution of social-learning theory to personality theory is the concept of generalized expectancies for problem-solving as a basis for individual differences affecting broad areas of behavior. The last three articles describe such generalized expectancies and methods of measuring them. They include Rotter's (4-6) monograph on generalized expectancies for internal versus external control of reinforcement, Rotter's (4-7) development of a scale for the measurement of interpersonal trust, and Mosher's (4-8) study of guilt conceived of as a generalized expectancy and its relation to the inhibition of unacceptable behavior.

The summary does not follow the outline of the reprinted papers, but rather deals with five crucial and persistent problems that face theory builders in the field of personality. It assesses the contributions of social learning theory toward the solution of these problems, drawing on the papers presented in this section as well as in other sections of this book and on other sources that could not be included here, and provides a table of operations which have been developed to measure SLT individual-differences variables.

4-1 Some Implications of a Social Learning Theory for the Prediction of Goal Directed Behavior from Testing Procedures[1]

JULIAN B. ROTTER

Many sophisticated observers are aware that a wide gap exists between personality theory and the techniques or procedures used to measure personality variables. The low level of prediction of such testing procedures may well be a function of the failure to apply the theories themselves to the methods of measurement. Particularly, it is a failure to apply an analysis of the determinants of behavior in general to the specific test taking behavior of the subjects (Ss).

The gap itself may be described as having three aspects. The first of these relates to the question of the constructs used in the theory and the constructs which the tests were developed to measure. In many instances rather than devising tests which measure specific theoretical constructs which are carefully defined and for which the test behavior can be understood as a logical referent, the descriptive constructs used to classify test response do not logically relate to the new theoretical constructs but are bent or twisted to measure the new variables. That is, test constructs which were used to classify test responses developed earlier are "translated" to be measures of the new variables. Examples of this are use of Rorschach variables such as color, movement, and shading which arose from imagery-type theory, to measure such constructs as "ego strength," "rigidity," and "tolerance for ambiguity." The Rorschach was not developed to assess such variables and in translating or twisting older methods of Rorschach scoring to measure these variables it is quite likely that a loss of prediction results.

A second aspect of this gap between personality theory and methods of measurement of personality lies in the testing procedure itself. For example, where the theory may emphasize the significance of differences in behavior in the presence of authority figures vs. peers or males vs. females, the formal test procedure assumes no such variables are important. That is, no difference in interpretation of test results follows from the fact that the examiner may have a different social stimulus value in one case than in another or under one set of conditions rather than another. In such an instance although the theory itself recognizes (and experimental data such as Gibby, Miller, & Walker, 1953, and Lord, 1950, support) the importance of the effect on behavior of the nature of the social stimulus, the test procedure itself does not take it into account. An example would be in the application of Murray's theory (1952) which sees behavior as

[1] I am indebted to Shephard Liverant for his helpful comments and suggestions about this paper.

a function of internal *needs* and environmental *presses.* Tests have been developed using this theory (Thematic Apperception Test, as clinically used; Edwards Personal Preference Schedule) which presume to measure the strength of various needs but fail to account for the test behavior as a function of the testing situation itself (an environmental press) as one of the variables determining the test behavior. Other characteristics of this discrepancy between theory and test taking procedure will be discussed more fully later.

A third aspect of the gap lies in the area of inference from test behavior. The issue here is that there is an absence of logic or contradiction in the assumed relationship between what the S does, or test behavior, and what is inferred from such behavior. Peak (1953) and Butler (1954) among others have discussed this problem earlier. Jessor and Hammond (1957) have noted such a gap in the inferences made from the Taylor Anxiety Scale. Another example could be drawn from the Edwards Personal Preference Schedule (Edwards, 1953) in which Ss are asked to state their preferences for different kinds of goals but there is no theoretical basis provided to allow one to make predictions about *nontest behavior* from such preferences. Of course, it can be assumed that the preferences have some one-to-one relationship with some criterion behavior, but it is unlikely that even the test authors would make such a theoretical commitment. In other words, it is not clear exactly what can be predicted or should be predicted from the test responses. Individuals using such tests, however, can defend themselves by stating that prediction is after all an empirical matter and one has to find out what can or should be predicted. It is likely, however, that the construction of tests which are systematically or theoretically pure, in that they are devised to measure variables or to make specific predictions, with the method of measurement and inference consistent with the theory will ultimately provide much better predictions of behavior as well as a test of the utility of the theory itself.

The purpose of this paper is to explicate some of the implications of a social learning theory of personality for the measurement of personality variables. The particular point of emphasis is the measurement of goal directed behavior conceptualized in social learning terms as *need potential.* Secondarily, the paper aims at illustrating the nature of the relationship between testing procedures and inference about behavior more generally.

In social learning theory (Rotter, 1954) the basic formula for the prediction of goal directed behavior is as given below:

$$BP_{x,s_1,R_a} = f(E_{x,R_a,s_1} \& RV_{a,s_1}) \tag{1}$$

The formula may be read as follows: The potential for behavior x to occur in Situation 1 in relation to Reinforcement a is a function of the expectancy of the occurrence of Reinforcement a following Behavior x in Situation 1 and the value of Reinforcement a, in Situation 1. Such a formula, however, is extremely limited in application for it deals only with the potential for a given behavior to occur in relationship to a single specific reinforcement. The prediction of responses from personality tests requires a more generalized concept of behavior and the formula for these broader concepts is given below:

$$BP_{(x-n),s_{(1-n)},R_{(a-n)}} = f(E_{(x-n),s_{(1-n)},R_{(a-n)}} \ \& \ RV_{(a-n),s_{(1-n)}}) \qquad [2]$$

This may be read: The potentiality of the functionally related Behaviors x to n to occur in the specified Situations 1 to n in relation to potential Reinforcements a to n is a function of the expectancies of these behaviors leading to these reinforcements in these situations and the values of these reinforcements in these situations. For purposes of simplicity of communication, the three basic terms in this formula have been typically referred to as need potential, freedom of movement, and need value as in the third formula below:

$$NP = f(FM \ \& \ NV) \qquad [3]$$

In this formula the fourth concept, that of the psychological situation, is implicit. The variables referred to above and operations for measurement have been defined and further explicated in a previous publication (Rotter, 1954).

In order to illustrate the social learning theory implications for measurement of personality and for the measurement of goal directed behavior, it seems expedient to consider three basic approaches to this problem based on the number of determinants used theoretically to predict such goal directed behavior and the problems, limitations, and advantages of each approach.

STRENGTH OF NEED AS A BASIS FOR PREDICTING BEHAVIOR

Although many esoteric systems of prediction utilize essentially the strength of need, drive, or instinct approach, this method can be described as the simplest or least complicated approach. Basically a series of constructs are formulated more often on an a priori basis than empirically, or at least on a presumed clinical rather than experimental basis. These descriptive terms may refer to instincts, drives, needs, factors, entities, or vectors of the mind (i.e., the Minnesota Multiphasic Personality Inventory, Edwards Personal Preference Schedule, Rorschach, Humm-Wadsworth, etc.). They all have in common that there is more than one basic characteristic, that these two or more characteristics are in some way measurable along a continuum and presumably the individual's behavior can be predicted from the characteristics which are "stronger" and the characteristics which are "weaker."

Sometimes the personality disposition can be predicted from the strength of other constructs according to either simple or complex statements of relationship formally postulated, hypothesized, or informally asserted. These relationships can become quite complex as in psychoanalysis or quite esoteric as in Szondi's explanation that motivated behavior is a result of the interaction of dominant and recessive genes. Because the methods of measurement in some instances cannot be direct, as in the assessment of unconscious drives in psychoanalysis, an impression of great complexity is given but regarded entirely from the point of view of the prediction of behavior, the system may still have a simple character. The potential for a given kind of behavior is still directly predictable from the strength of the drive, instincts, needs, or energies postulated.

There is another form of this model in which the various drives, dispositions, or needs are considered to interact. For example, the individual may be conceived of as being controlled by his intellect and his emotions, but his behavior must be understood in light of the interaction of these two forces with a third variable, the will as in the Rorschach Test (1942). Again, this makes complex the calculation of strength or weakness but does not change the over-all method of making predictions. Whether dealing with will, intellect and emotions or ego, superego and id, the effect of interaction is only to increase or decrease the tendency of one of the needs to function or to strengthen or weaken one of them or perhaps to produce a fourth or fifth additional need. The basic method of prediction stays the same although the calculation of strength or weakness in such a model becomes more difficult.

The obvious problem, of course, for such rudimentary method of prediction is how to predict anything at all. If a system included five instincts or needs and these are ordered on some metric system from high to low, does one assume that the person will always act in the fashion to be predicted from his strongest or highest need? If an S is more oral than anal, does he always act in an oral fashion? Actually the most logical assumption in regard to any specific instance is that he will always act the same way. One might presume on a statistical basis, as it is sometimes done, if the individual is at the 70th percentile on Need A and at the 30th percentile on Need B, 70% of the time he would act in one fashion and 30% of the time in the other over some undefined period of time. However, the only sensible statistical or logical prediction in any specific instance, if no other variables are concerned, is that he would act in accordance with the higher need. This might still give fairly good prediction if only 2 variables are involved, but if 20 variables are involved and many of them are very close in value or "strength," then the amount of error begins to increase. In fact, it becomes a problem to predict even slightly above chance and, indeed, except for some limited and highly controlled experimental situations, this is the problem in psychology now. A recent illustration of this failure is reported in a carefully controlled study by Little and Shneidman (1959) who failed to find much relationship between interpretations of psychological tests (Rorschach, MAPS, TAT, and MMPI) and anamnestic data. Loevinger (1959) summarizing the predictiveness of individual tests in the recent *Annual Review of Psychology* states, "To date the only tests which meet standards for individual prediction are those of general ability" (p. 305). Previous reviewers have made similar statements.

Another problem which arises in the prediction of behavior with this simple model is that it soon becomes apparent that the strength of a wish, need, or drive to achieve some goal such as being taken care of, obtaining love, or injuring someone is not a good predictor of the occurrence of behavior directed towards the achieving of that goal. To some extent this problem can be dealt with by the notion of interaction of needs, but usually in order to account for the discrepancy between need or wish and behavior, constructs of the same order do not provide sufficient explanatory basis. It is actually necessary to postulate some other kinds of internal constructs to account for the discrepancy between what might be called wish, desire, need, or instinct and observable behavior.

In the measurement of these need strengths all varieties of tests and devices have been used. To some extent, the personality questionnaire is utilized a little more by people adopting such a predictive scheme as that described above, but also projective tests, observation, interviewing, and many other techniques of personality measurement have been used in this fashion. Test construction methodologies may currently be more sophisticated in that they control for social desirability of items, motivation, faking, lying, and inability to understand directions. Recent tests may also rely on purification of factors, cross-validation, or item analysis. However, with all these "modern improvements" in test design one is still left with a series of figures which are of doubtful utility for the actual prediction of behavior at a level satisfactory for either practical application or for the clarification of theoretical issues.

THE ADDITION OF AN EXPECTANCY CONSTRUCT IN THE PREDICTION OF GOAL DIRECTED BEHAVIOR

The absence of additional variables explicitly defining the relationship of need and behavior appears to be not so much a matter of simple theoretical structure as it is merely the absence of any real explicit theory about human behavior. The development of a predictive model which recognizes the discrepancy between need and behavior and tries to systematically take it into account represents a second level of sophistication.

At an earlier date perhaps psychoanalysis dealt with this problem most effectively in introducing concepts such as repression, sublimation, suppression, defense, reaction formation, etc., to account for the discrepancy between observed behavior and the presumed internal drive, need, or instinctual urge.

At this level of theorizing some systematic variable is added to the internal motivational state in order to predict behavior. Perhaps another way of saying this is that in addition to some measure of preference or value of a specific goal another systematic concept must be introduced, not only in a hit-or-miss fashion but perhaps directly into our assessment procedure. The psychoanalytic solution has been criticized because many specific concepts are introduced to account for a discrepancy between drives, urges, or needs and observable behavior, but these concepts are not readily measurable. In addition, one does not know when one explanation, i.e., reaction formation, is the explanatory concept or another such as sublimation or simple repression.

In social learning theory (Rotter, 1954) it is presumed that the relationship between goal preference (reinforcement value) and behavior can be determined only by introducing the concept of the individual's expectancy, on the basis of past history, that the given behavior will actually lead to a satisfying outcome rather than to punishment, failure, or, more generally, to negative reinforcement. Since the early formulations of Tolman (1932), expectancy theories have become more and more widely relied upon both in human learning and personality theories. It is possible to conceptualize more specific constructs such as repression and reaction formation as only special cases of an expectancy for severe punishment and that a more general relationship holds which includes perhaps all of these and also expectancies for punishment or failure of which the individual is quite aware For example, an individual may wish very much to be a good dancer and to dance with members of the opposite sex. He makes no attempts, however, to dance at a party or a dance because he can tell you "but I look like a fool when I go out on the dance floor." We need, in other words, to introduce no specific construct involving the "unconscious" to explain the discrepancy between his wish and his behavior. The S may or may not be aware of expectancies which influence his behavior. Whether or not he is aware of them may affect the degree to which these expectancies change with new experience as well as other variables. The degree of awareness may be an important additional variable; however, the level of expectancy itself is the broader variable which bears a direct relationship to the potential occurrence of a specified behavior.

The question arises, then, of how one takes into account such factors in an actual testing situation. It could be said that no one is really so naive as to believe that the strength of an internal motivational condition or need is a direct predictor of behavior. Somehow or other, whether or not the individual had learned a given behavior or expected it to work is also an important aspect of prediction. However, more often than not this aspect of prediction has been treated as a source of error, something to be eliminated if possible, both in testing or in the validation of a test instrument. As a matter of fact, many currently used instruments attempting to assess the strength of motives, drives, or needs are usually confounded. Although they may be quite sophisticated in methodology, the test items or the test variables usually refer in part to what the individual did, i.e., overt behavior ("I frequently lose my temper"), in part to what he wished ("I would like to have more friends"), and in part to what he expected to be the outcome of his own behavior ("I feel that other people do not appreciate my good intentions"). To some extent these impure items probably add to prediction by providing more than one kind of referent for behavior, but the nonsystematic way in which they are used also limits prediction.

In trying to predict goal directed behavior from tests, two possibilities are open. One of these is to attempt to predict behavior from other behavior which presumably is functionally or predictively related to the test behavior. What this involves is analyzing test situations as behavioral samples under a given set of test conditions. For example, to assess dependent behavior one could use direct observation techniques, perhaps in problem solving situations, in which the S is scored for help-seeking behavior (cf. Naylor, 1955). In questionnaires the items should refer to what the S does, not to what he expects, wishes, or feels. The use of behavior samples for predictions or the regarding of all kinds of tests including projective tests essentially as samples of behavior to be analyzed in terms of what the S does under these conditions has been described elsewhere (Rotter, 1954). Like the work sample test in industry it undoubtedly provides the best prediction to a limited specific behavioral criterion since it requires the fewest intermediate constructs and the fewest assumptions regarding the action of other variables.

However, there are many problems, both theoretical and clinical, when it is important to break down this behavioral measure into its major determinants of reinforcement value and expectancy for the occurrence of the reinforcement. For example, in psychotherapy an understanding of how some behavior or group of behaviors may be most readily changed requires analysis into at least these two components. Even when strictly concerned with predictions of behavior in a broad band of life situations, rather than change, analysis into separate determinants may provide greater prediction than a work sample or behavioral technique. In this second alternative it is important either to control or systematically vary the other variable or measure both. For example, Liverant (1958) has measured some needs by presenting pairs of items involving goal preference matched for social desirability, and Jessor and Mandell (Mandell, 1959) are developing a similar test to measure expectancy for success in satisfying the same needs.

In using projective material such as the TAT, Crandall (1951) has demonstrated that expectancy for need satisfaction, for which the term freedom of movement is used in social learning theory, can be reliably measured by selecting particular kinds of referents. The work of Mussen and Naylor (1954), Kagan (1956), and Lesser (1957) gives strong evidence that the relationship between theme counts of aggression on the TAT and overt aggressive behavior depends to a large extent on whether or not that overt behavior is socially acceptable in the Ss' own homes or social climates. The relationship between theme count and overt aggressive behavior appears to hold only when the Ss do not have a high expectancy that aggressive behavior will be punished. Atkinson and Reitman (1956) report that in a number of studies of need achievement, it has become clear that prediction of behavior is enhanced if, in addition to taking a measure of need achievement based upon achievement theme counts in TAT-like material, an additional measure of expectancy for success is also taken into account.

In dealing with this type of testing material the recently published study of Fitzgerald (1958) provides a more systematic analysis. Using a highly reliable sociometric technique of nomination of fraternity brothers as his behavioral criteria and dealing with the need dependency, Fitzgerald found no relationship between theme counts and overt behavior. Presumably, dependent behavior is not socially acceptable among male college students. He had, however, independent interview ratings of need value, that is preference or desire for dependency satisfactions and of freedom of movement, or expectancy that behavior directed toward achieving dependency would be satisfied.

He found that by using these measures he did obtain a significant correlation between theme counts and the *discrepancy* between need value and freedom of movement. More specifically, what he called a conflict score or score indicating the degree to which the individual preferred dependency or desired dependency satisfactions but expected that he could not achieve them correlated with theme counts for dependency.[2] On the other hand, an Incomplete Sentences Blank measure of dependency which utilized behavioral referents as well as reinforcement value and expectancy referents did show a low but significant relationship of the number of completions dealing with dependency with both the sociometric and interview measures of need potential or actual dependent behavior. Although an actual analysis was not made, it seems very likely that the reason for the correlation in the case of the ISB and not the TAT is that at least some of the ISB completions were descriptions of actual behavior. Possibly a purer measure of behavior would have shown a greater relationship to the sociometric and interview rating assessment of actual dependent behavior in life situations.

Should we build two instruments or at least two sets of testing operations to separately assess need value and freedom of movement, or should we attempt to use behavioral measures in order to make our predictions about behavior, we would still be faced with the problem of predicting in a specific situation. Given measures of six behavioral potentials, however arrived at, the problem remains that of knowing which of these is likely to be the behavior preferred in some specific situation. One is again forced to predict that the behavior with the highest potential always occurs and one is limited again in prediction to a very low level of accuracy. In the laboratory situation where we can reduce the possible alternatives to two, significant, although not predictive results, are possible. In the life situation where the alternatives are very frequently of a large order, the question arises of whether or not any useful prediction is possible. This leads us to a third level of sophistication, one in which the psychological situation is one of the variables on which prediction is based.

THE PSYCHOLOGICAL SITUATION AS A THIRD DETERMINANT OF GOAL DIRECTED BEHAVIOR

Few would deny that the psychological situation will affect the potential of occurrence of any behavior or class of behaviors. However, the fact that behavior will vary from situation to situation is most often treated as a source of error, something to be avoided. If possible, one should construct tests or find personality variables which rise somehow above the situation.

---

[2] Whether or not the relationship between theme count and high reinforcement value and low expectancy is general is not yet known. It appears at this time to depend possibly on whether or not the test material and testing situation is conducive to the free expression of fantasy.

It is probably no exaggeration to say that thousands of hours of wasted work have been done by psychologists in the vain goal of finding either tests or variables which would, somehow or other, predict regardless of the situation in which the test is given or regardless of the situation in which the predicted behavior is expected to occur.

There are three separate problems here which will be discussed as one basic problem. The first problem is to understand the effect of the testing situation on test results. For example, Sarason (1950) has provided an excellent discussion of some of the influential situational variables in intelligence testing. The second problem is to understand the nature of the criterion situation which affects the criterion measures. The third and ultimately most important problem is to devise our tests with full consideration of the nature of the test situation in order to predict behavior in other situations for which the test was constructed. In other words, we need to devise tests not to predict personality or needs or behavior in the abstract but in specified situations or classes of situations if we want high prediction. *We need to know and take into account the dimensions of situation similarity in devising test procedures.*

Cronbach (1956) has criticized the failure to regard differentially the criterion situations in which tests are applied. In regard to the test situation we have only attempted to standardize the test procedure but usually have ignored the importance of the social context in which the test is given. Perhaps the most important thesis of this paper is that the psychological situation needs to be understood and systematically considered in our predictive formula, not treated as a source of error or something that can be ignored because part of the total situation is standardized.

Recently there have been a number of studies which demonstrate that almost all tests are subject to faking, to instructional variation, to examiner influences, to testing conditions, etc., regardless of the type of test (Borislow, 1958; Green, 1951; Gross, 1959; Mussen & Scodel, 1955; Rotter, 1955). The general inference drawn from these studies is that the tests are poor. Actually the implication of such findings is that we are making inefficient use of our tests. If the test situation for many personality tests is one in which social conformity or acceptability is easily achieved and no other satisfactions are given up in achieving acceptability, then for some purposes this motive should be controlled. However, the test situation can also be utilized to measure the importance of social conformity for the individual. *What we call faking is only our recognition of the fact that the S is taking the test with a different purpose or goal than the one the examiner wants him to have.* For some purposes it might be important to understand what kind of goals he exhibits in this kind of situation. More often than not we simply try to control what we should be studying. For example, in giving intelligence tests it might be better to study systematically the effect on performance of encouragement and discouragement rather than to attempt some mythical neutral attitude which is presumably the same for every examiner. Knowledge of the effects of situational variations would be of particular value in understanding the frequently diverse and contradictory results of apparently similar research investigations. For example, Henry and Rotter (1956) found that large, predicted differences were obtained between two comparable groups on the Rorschach test if one group was reminded before the regular instructions that the test had been used frequently to study psychopathology. An obvious implication of this study is that investigators using this same test in the college laboratory and in the clinical setting may well produce diverse results.

Another example of how the situation can be used in testing is provided by the patient who is being assessed for possible benefit from psychotherapy. If the clinic or hospital can provide both male and female therapists and also therapists who rely on support and direction as well as therapists who remain distant and passive, then the testing procedures can be varied so that those situational influences are present. The testing could provide information to indicate what kind of therapy and what kind of therapist is likely to provide *this* patient with the most efficient conditions for relearning. For more conventional purposes of clinical testing, it is still more important to know under what conditions the patient behaves in a paranoid fashion and under what conditions he does not, than it is to know how many percentiles of paranoia he has.

Not only can the test situation itself be analyzed as a behavioral sample but situational referents can be incorporated into the content of items by systematic sampling. For example, questionnaire items can deal with the *conditions* under which the S feels tense, nervous, happy, has headaches, etc. as Mandler and Sarason (1952) have done for some intellectual test taking situations. Similarly, projective methods, particularly TAT-type tests, can systematically vary the situation through the selection of test stimuli as has been done by Crandall (1951) and McClelland, Atkinson, Clark, and Lowell (1953). More recently Murstein (1959) has suggested a conceptual model for stimulus variation with thematic techniques.

The many studies indicating marked effects of testing conditions suggest that it is of great importance in the publication of any test that descriptions of the differences in test results that are likely to be associated with different kinds of testing situations be provided. No test can be adequately understood unless the data regarding its standardization or use includes systematic descriptions of the differences in test results which are a function of different kinds of testing conditions and different kinds of purposes in taking the test for similar samples of Ss. Only when we know whether an S is likely to produce different test results when he is taking the test to demonstrate how imaginative he is as compared to taking it to prove that he needs help will we be adequately able to understand the meaning of test results and to predict future behavior from them.

There have been personality theorists who have made much of the importance of the individual's life space. Kantor (1924) was one of the first to emphasize that the basic datum of psychology is the interaction of an individual and his meaningful environment. For Kantor, people do not have internal characteristics in the same sense as for other theorists; rather they have a reactional biography of interactions with the environment. Lewin (1951) has also emphasized the importance of the life space or psychological situation in the determination of human behavior. Brunswik (1947) has repeatedly called for analyses of and sampling of psychological situations for predictive purposes. Helson (1948) has applied his theory of Adaptation Level to social psychology stating that the effect of the total field can be quantified by careful ordering of the field of exposed stimuli. Recent concern with the importance and need for systematic study of situation variation has been expressed by Allport (1958) and Cronbach (1957).

In a more limited and less systematic way, psychoanalysis has suggested, in a few areas, that certain kinds of goal directed behavior depended upon the psychological situation. This is done in making distinctions between the individual's potential response to authority figures vs. nonauthority figures and males vs. females. Beyond this, little systematic analysis of differences in life situations has been made by the traditional analyst. Murray's (1952) formulation of the nature of personality stresses that behavior is a function of the interaction of an individual with a psychological situation which he felt could be categorized as "press." At a more specific level Atkinson and Raphelson (1956) have shown the value of including situational variables in studying achievement behavior. This general point of view has also been represented in sociology by Thomas (1951) and Coutu (1949).

In social learning theory, it has been hypothesized that the situation operates primarily by providing cues for the S which are related to the magnitude of his expectancies for reinforcement for different behaviors. The effect on the value of the reinforcement itself operates through expectancies for associated or subsequent reinforcements which may differ from situation to situation. It has also been hypothesized that situations may be usefully categorized in terms of the predominant reinforcements as culturally determined for any large or small culture group. There are many other possible ways of categorizing situations depending upon the predictive purposes involved.[3] Methods of determining generality or determining the dimensions of similarity among situations have been described in an earlier paper (Rotter, 1955).

Two illustrative studies of an increasing number of experimental analyses of behavior which vary both internal characteristics and the psy-

---

[3] Several writers have pointed out the difficulty of identifying situations independently of behavior. That is, how can one describe a situation as one would a physical stimulus independently of the S's response? The problem is not different from that of describing stimuli along dimensions of color although perhaps vastly complicated in social or other complex situations. In the case of color stimuli ultimately the criteria is a response of the scientist or observer, sometimes a response to an intermediate instrument, and one that is at the level of sensory discrimination and so leads to high observer agreement. In the case of the social situation, the level of discrimination is common sense based on an understanding of the culture rather than the reading of an instrument. As such, reliability may be limited but still be sufficiently high to considerably increase prediction. In this way specific situations could be identified as school situations, employment situations, girl friend situations, etc. For the purpose of generality various kinds of psychological constructs could be devised to arrive at classes of situations which have similar meaning to the S. The utility of such classes would have to be empirically determined depending on the S's response. The objective referents for these situations, which provide the basis for prediction, however, can be independent of the specific S. That is, they can be reliably identified by cultural, common sense terms.

chological situation systematically in the same study are described below. These studies follow the basic paradigm that the presumed relevant individual (personality) and situational (experimental manipulations) variables can be observed simultaneously and their interaction studied.

ILLUSTRATIVE STUDIES VARYING BOTH THE SITUATION AND INTERNAL CHARACTERISTICS

A recent doctoral dissertation by James (1957) illuminates very clearly the potential of greater prediction when both the situation and the internal characteristic are varied in the same study. The behavior being studied by James involved a variety of learning variables, including acquisition, changes or shifts, extinction, generalization, and recovery of verbalized expectancies for gratification. Two general hypotheses were involved in this study growing out of previous work by Lasko (1952), Phares (1957), Neff (1956), and James and Rotter (1958). Hunt and Schroder (1958) have also dealt with what appears to be a related variable. The first of these hypotheses might be stated as a situational one. That is, that the nature of a learning process differs depending upon whether or not the situation is one in which the reinforcements that occur are a direct outcome of some internal characteristic of the individual such as skill, a physical characteristic, or whatever, versus a situation where the reinforcements are essentially controlled by someone else or by chance or by conditions or powers beyond the S's control. Perhaps a good example of the latter would be a dice game or the winning of a door prize or having soup spilled on one because a waiter tripped, etc. James utilized line and angle matching tasks reinforcing each S positively on his guesses in six of the eight training trials. He specifically hypothesized when the situation is structured in such a way that the S expects the occurrence of reinforcements to be beyond his control or partly beyond his control, increments and decrements in expectancy for gratification as a result of experience are smaller, the number of unusual shifts, that is, shifts up after failure or down after success, are greater, extinction is faster, and there is less generalization from one task to another and greater recovery following extinction.

The measurement of individual differences in this study followed from the previous work of Phares which suggested that individuals can be differentiated in the degree to which they see the world and the things that happen to them as controlled by others or as determined by chance or unpredictable forces. The second hypothesis, then, was that all the differences which would occur as a result of the situational conditions would also be true of individuals within all groups as a function of their general attitude towards "control of reinforcement."

In order to predict the individual differences in attitude, James enlarged and revised the questionnaire first devised by Phares. This was given to all Ss at the end of each experiment. The results are most striking. All of the predicted outcomes hypothesized above resulting from the differences in instructions or situations were obtained and all were statistically significant with the exception of recovery following extinction, which showed a strong trend in the predicted direction. Similarly, within each group the individuals high as compared to low on the questionnaire differed significantly in exactly the same way as did the groups themselves as a result of the different instructions or situations presented. Although individual prediction was not the concern of this investigation, it is quite clear that a simple formula could be devised which could predict all of the learning variables involved in this study with a fair degree of accuracy. Certainly it is clear that a greater degree of accuracy is possible when both the situational and individual variables are taken into account. Perhaps far more important, this study indicates that various experimental paradigms in studying human learning are likely to produce different kinds of results. Whether or not a given learning task is one in which the S feels that success is dependent upon the experimenter's manipulation (for example, when he is expecting to predict a random sequence of red or green lights) or is the result of his own skill provides a crucial difference in the nature of the learning process itself.

The study of James, however, does not provide a satisfied feeling that it illustrates all of the problems of prediction involving both the individual's characteristics and the situation from which the prediction is made. It gives an almost too simple picture of the interaction of these two variables. Another recent dissertation by Moss (1958) suggests that this relationship can be more complex, and illustrates more clearly the effect of the testing situation on more commonly used types of assessment procedures.

Moss studied a general behavioral characteristic which he called cautiousness. Essentially this was defined as the avoidance of risk, the selection of the safest alternative in a situation where failure or negative reinforcement was possible. He varied the situation by reacting differently to three groups following the administration of a questionnaire which he described as a measure of social acceptability. One group was shown false norms at the conclusion of the questionnaire that indicated that they were in the ninetieth percentile of social acceptability for a college group. Another group of Ss was shown that they were at the tenth percentile, and a third group was given no information about the results of this supposed test of social acceptability. He hypothesized that cautious behavior would increase with negative reinforcement. Immediately following this procedure, the Ss were given two projective type tests and behavior on these tests was analyzed as to degree of cautiousness.

Prior to the giving of the "social acceptability" questionnaire the Ss had been tested on the level of aspiration board. Behavior on the level of aspiration board (Rotter, 1942) was categorized into cautious or noncautious patterns.[4] The general tendency to seek safe alternatives in the

[4] Cautious and noncautious behavior was characterized according to the patterns described by Rotter (1954, pp. 318–324). Patterns 1 and 3 were considered as noncautious and 2, 4, 7, and 8 as cautious patterns. The latter group are characterized by a variety of techniques presumably aimed at avoiding failure to reach explicit goals. Patterns 1 and 3 are characterized by higher expectancies than performance but within "normal" bounds and consequently a higher number of failures to reach one's estimates.

obtaining of satisfactions then was measured in a situation in which the S himself has some control over failure or success.

One kind of behavior studied was that of sorting figures taken from the MAPS test. The S was presented the figures and asked to sort them into two piles any way he wished. The procedure was repeated a second time asking for a different kind of sort, and a third time. The sorts themselves were characterized as being safe or cautious in that they dealt with highly objective characteristics of these figures, or less safe in that they dealt with characteristics which were more abstract or had to be read into many of the figures. For example, sorts based on personality characteristics were considered as noncautious as opposed to safer or more cautious sorts such as those into groups of men and women, children and adults, Negroes and whites, etc.

A second kind of behavior studied was the S's response to a series of four TAT pictures. In this case the S's stories were treated as Weisskopf (1950) has treated them with her measure of transcendence. A cautious or safe interpretation was one sticking close to the characteristics of the picture and one in which the theme itself was a common one.

Moss found some differences among his groups in the direction he had hypothesized, that is, that the threatened group, the group that was told that it was at the tenth percentile, showed greater cautiousness than the other two groups. The differences between groups, however, although consistently in the direction he predicted, only approached significance and were not large. However, when Moss divided his Ss within groups into cautious and noncautious on the basis of their level of aspiration patterns, he found some highly significant differences. The cautious Ss showed no significant differences among the three conditions. However, the noncautious Ss showed significant differences between conditions. That is, noncautious Ss in one condition responded differentially from noncautious Ss in another condition. These differences were primarily due to greater noncautious behavior in the no-information group. Differences in test behavior between cautious and noncautious Ss were also highly significant on both tests within the no-information group but not in the other groups.

In spite of the complexity of this study, a few findings seem relatively clear from an analysis of group means as well as significance of differences. Ss who were cautious on the level of aspiration test, which is a somewhat free situation, were also cautious in the other test conditions. Of course, this does not mean that they were cautious in situations which were not perceived by them as evaluation situations. On the other hand, Ss who were noncautious on the level of aspiration test appeared to maintain this greater risk taking behavior under test situations where no information about results was given. However, when they were negatively reinforced, they became more cautious and they also did not appear to be different from cautious Ss under conditions where they were quite successful. Perhaps this is related to the presumed conservatism which follows from success. There was no consistent prediction from the level of aspiration situation to the two "projective tests" which could be made without considering the situation. In at least two of the situations the cautious Ss were not significantly different from the noncautious Ss. On the other hand, the psychological situation or the three different situations seemed to have no effect on the cautious Ss. Only in the interaction of the noncautious Ss with the situational variables was prediction possible from the level of aspiration test.

A similar type of result to that of Moss was recently reported by Lesser (1959). Lesser found that intercorrelations among various measures of aggression were significantly higher under experimental conditions of low anxiety than under conditions of high anxiety about aggression.

James' results suggest a rather simple relationship between dispositional and situational variables, but it is clear from the study of Moss and other studies that a simple additive or multiplicative relationship will not always describe the nature of the interaction. An important implication of this principle is that there is a general lack of efficiency in research studies in which only one'set of variables, that is only dispositional or situational, are systematically varied, since the conclusions of the two sets of studies cannot be put together in a simple fashion. Unless both kinds of variables are systematically varied *within the same investigation*, both an understanding of the determinants of behavior and the prediction of it may suffer.

A striking example of the importance of studying the effects of dispositional and situational influences simultaneously is provided by Helson, Blake, Mouton, and Olmstead (1956). In applying Adaptation Level theory to a study of attitude change they found important interactional effects when situations were varied in external influence pressure and individuals were distributed on a measure of ascendancy-submissiveness.

It is true that many of the above propositions are obvious. Most psychologists recognize that there is a difference between overt behavior directed toward certain goals and the desires that individuals have to obtain these goals. Similarly, most psychologists know that the psychological situation is a determinant of the occurrence of a given behavior. The thesis here, however, is not merely that this is the case but that all of these variables must be ordered and studied systematically, in order to make predictions.

SUMMARY

The major contention of this paper has been that the prediction of goal directed behavior of human subjects from test procedures has been and will continue to be at an extremely low hit-or-miss level because of inadequate conceptualization of the problem. Findings are frequently not replicatable because of the failure to systematically differentiate behavior, reinforcement value, and expectancy as internal variables and to recognize that these variables are affected by the psychological situation.

The psychological situation of the patient in the clinic is so different from that of the elementary psychology student taking a test as part of an experiment that it is possible that the kinds of predictions which can be made in one situation would hardly hold in the other. The evidence that faking is possible and that different norms obtain when subjects are job applicants, employees, or volunteers does not necessarily mean that a test is no good. Nor is prediction essentially hopeless because it can be demonstrated that two experimenters, whether the same sex or opposite, or slight changes in the wording of instruction, will differentially affect test or experimental results. All of these things indicate only that the psychological situation, perhaps acting primarily through the expectancies they arouse by the cues present, considerably affect behavior. It is necessary that we do not consider such influence as error to be ignored, as difficulty to be avoided or as the problem of some other profession to investigate. Rather it is necessary to study these influences and consider them regularly and systematically in a predictive schema. That is, for some purposes, factors such as social desirability of items, examiner's behavior, and the subject's goals in the test situation should be controlled, and in other cases they should be allowed to vary. In all cases, however, they must be systematically considered.

Implicit in this entire paper is the belief that a satisfactory theory of goal directed behavior is a primary prerequisite for developing adequate tests. Knowledge of statistics and test construction procedures can be valuable but they cannot supplant an adequate theory of behavior which is applied to the test taking behavior itself.

To arrive at a fully systematic model for relating these general or high order constructs and to coordinate them in turn to lower level sets of content variables, devised for different purposes, will be a long and arduous but rewarding task.

4-2 | The Influence of Personality and Situational Cautiousness on Conceptual Behavior[1]

HOWARD A. MOSS

A number of psychologists have stressed the importance of considering situational and personality factors as codeterminants of behavior. Newcomb (1943) dealt with the interaction of situational and personality factors in his classic study of attitude change among college students. As

[1] Adapted from a dissertation submitted to the graduate school of the Ohio State University in partial fulfillment of the requirements for the Doctor of Philosophy degree.

The author wishes to express his appreciation to Julian B. Rotter, committee chairman, for his invaluable assistance in the preparation of this report.

From *Journal of Abnormal and Social Psychology*, 1961, **63**, 629–635. Copyright 1961 by the American Psychological Association and reprinted by permission of the author and the publisher.

early as 1935 Lewin stated "the actual behavior of the child depends in every case both upon his individual characteristics and upon the momentary structure of the existing situation" (p. 71). In a recent review of the literature, Masling (1960) discusses the decreased predictive power of studies that fail to consider the combined influence of situational and personality factors.

The complex effects of personality and situational variables require more than the simple acknowledgment that they both contribute to behavior. Not all subjects are equally responsive to different situational cues. A situational variable may influence only the behavior of subjects who exhibit a particular personality characteristic. By pooling subjects, without regard for personality differences, the influence of the situation may be masked or greatly attenuated. On the other hand, the variance associated with the personality variable may be neutralized by strong situational cues. That is, different personality tendencies may be observable only under certain conditions. The optimum approach for assessing psychological processes should be based on the study of these two types of variables both as separate and combined determinants of behavior; as Rotter (1960b) contends, it is necessary to study the interaction of situational and personality variables if we are to increase the power of our predictions and provide a basis for replicability.

This investigation deals with the way responses are modified by the subject's expectancy of success or failure on the experimental tasks. Persons who fear that they will be perceived in a negative light frequently exercise certain controls over their test behavior. These controls are defensive since they protect the person from revealing aspects of himself that might result in failure and/or disapproval. Defensive reactions should be greater when an individual has a generalized low expectancy for success or in a situation that specifically engenders low expectancies.

The term *cautiousness* is used to describe the class of defensive behaviors dealt with in this investigation. Cautiousness is regarded as "the tendency to behave in a manner designed to avoid potential failure or disapproval experiences, and this goal is achieved often at the expense of other satisfactions." That is, the cautious person is more concerned with avoiding failure than with obtaining success. In order for cautiousness to be observed there must be a basis for judging certain response alternatives as entailing less risk and less potential satisfaction than other alternatives. The level of aspiration paradigm provides a task situation that meets these criteria. The subject can behave in a cautious way by stating low goals, even when these expressed low goals place restrictions on his maximum possible score. That is, the subject is told that his score can be no higher than his expectancy statement. On the other hand, unrealistically high expectancy statements are discouraged by penalizing the subject for failing to score as high as he predicted he would.

The use of the level of aspiration as a measure of cautiousness has been discussed frequently in the psychological literature. Lewin, Dembo, Festinger, and Sears (1944) conclude that fear of failure is a major determinant of level of aspiration behavior. Persons who have a strong need to avoid failure behave cautiously by stating low goals. Frank (1935b) states that cautiousness is a generalized personality trait that influences level of aspiration behavior. He did not obtain any independent measure of caution but inferred the trait from the level of aspiration behavior. Gould (1939) concludes from her results that goal setting behavior often serves a person as a protection of the ego in which the stated estimates are designed to shield him from failure.

Cautiousness is also reflected by the conceptual approach used in responses to visual stimuli. The verbal labels used to conceptualize a visual stimulus may vary considerably. For instance, responses to TAT pictures can be descriptive or, conversely, highly inferential. The descriptive statements are objective and their accuracy cannot be easily challenged. In addition, descriptive responses are nonprojective and provide the subject with a way of evading disclosure of internally held beliefs, conflicts, or needs. Descriptive responses are therefore assumed to represent a cautious approach since there is minimal risk of criticism and/or personal exposure. Inferential responses can be idiosyncratic, personalized, and imaginative. These responses are more open to evaluation of either a critical or favorable nature and would generally reflect a noncautious approach.

The hypotheses tested by this investigation are as follows:

1. Cautiousness, when induced by an experimental situation of failure, leads to increased descriptiveness in verbal responses to TAT pictures and conceptual sorts (MAPS figures).

2. The degree to which the failure situation leads to increased descriptiveness is determined by the subject's personality disposition. That is, personality and situational factors interact in the prediction of descriptive response.

3. Cautiousness, as a general personality characteristic (determined from level of aspiration behavior), is associated with greater descriptiveness in verbal responses to the personality test materials. The relationship should be most pronounced when assessed under neutral conditions (Control group).

METHOD

Subjects
The sample consisted of 109 students enrolled in the introductory psychology classes at the Ohio State University: 61 females and 48 males from 17 to 30 years of age.

Procedure
The subjects were randomly assigned to three experimental groups and each subject was seen individually for two separate sessions.

Session 1 Prior to the experimental conditions all subjects performed on the Rotter (1942) Level of Aspiration Board, to provide a behavioral measure of characteristic cautiousness.[2] The subjects were seated at the end of a table on which the Level of Aspiration Board was placed and the standard instructions were administered.[3] Each subject had 20 trials on this task, and a difference score (D score) was obtained between subject's actual performance score and his subsequent expectancy statement for each trial.

Rotter (1945) has described nine patterns characterizing level of aspiration behavior, regarded as "points of concentration which can be used as flexible standards for understanding individual cases," and based on a combination of three factors: his D score, the frequency of shifts, and the occurrence of unusual shifts (up after failure and down after success):

1. *Low positive D score pattern.* This is generally considered the most realistic response. Estimates are usually higher than past performances with an average number of shifts and unusual shifts absent.

2. *Low negative or very slightly positive D score patterns.* This pattern is similar to Number 1, but with a lower D score.

3. *Medium high D scores.* This pattern is characterized by frequent usual shifts (up after success and down after failure) and high D scores.

4. *Achievement followers.* These subjects' estimates are constantly changed to equal or closely approximate the previous performance.

5. *The step pattern.* Here the subject never lowers his estimate.

6. *Very high, positive D score patterns.* In this pattern the subject behaves unrealistically by stating high goals regardless of characteristically lower performance levels.

7. *High negative D score patterns.* This is characterized by frequent shifts down after success and negative D scores.

8. *Rigid pattern.* This pattern is defined by an absence of shifts.

9. *The confused or breakdown pattern.* Here there are a high number of shifts in addition to frequent unusual shifts, i.e., shifts upward after failure and downward after success. D scores can be any size.

The subjects within each of the three experimental groups were classified as either cautious or noncautious from their level of aspiration pattern. Research findings indicate that the pooling of similar patterns provides greater generality and predictability than classifications based solely on the use of the specific patterns (Neems & Scodel, 1956). In this study, Patterns 1 and 3 were classified as noncautious and 2, 4, 7, and 8 as cautious. Ten subjects who obtained nonclassifiable patterns (5, 6, and 9) were omitted from the part of the analysis pertaining to personality differences. The interrater agreement for scoring the nine patterns was 85 percent; for the pooled cautious and noncautious patterns it was 97.5 percent.

Session 2 All subjects were administered a brief specially con-

---

[2] A questionnaire was constructed as a second measure of characteristic cautiousness. This questionnaire proved to be a less effective predictor than the Level of Aspiration Board and was not included in the paper.

[3] Taken from unpublished manual prepared by J. B. Rotter.

structed paper-and-pencil form that they were told was a "test of social acceptability," consisting of 25 statements concerning social attitudes. The subjects were instructed to rate themselves on a five-point scale for each of these 25 statements. For Groups 1 and 2, the experimenter pretended to score the test in the presence of the subject and compared these results with false norms he had in front of him. The subjects in Group 1 were told that they scored in the "lower 10 percentile" (Failure group, $N = 36$),[4] and the subjects in Group 2 were told that they scored in the "upper 10 percentile" (Success group, $N = 36$). This procedure was omitted for Group 3 (Control group, $N = 37$). After experiencing the experimental condition all subjects were asked to take two more tests which they were told were also measures of "social acceptability." These two tests were to "make up a story" for Pictures 2, 4, 17GF, and 20 of the TAT and to sort into two groups, according to the subject's own idea, 22 cut-out human figures taken from the MAPS test (Shneidman, 1952). The sorting procedure was repeated three times for the complete group of figures. The TAT and MAPS responses were used to assess cautious conceptual behavior.

TAT Each TAT story was scored for conceptual level on a four-point scale. The most descriptive stories obtained a score of 1 and the most inferential ones obtained a score of 4. Intermediate stories on the descriptive-inferential dimension and popular themes, as determined from normative studies (Eron, 1950; Rosenzweig & Fleming, 1949) were given scores of 2 and 3. The interrater reliabilities, based on product-moment correlations, for Pictures 2, 4, 17GF, and 20, respectively, were 1.00+, .67, 1.00+, and .95.[5]

MAPS Conceptual Sorting Task The 22 figures in the MAPS test— including representations of males, females, figures with features, those where the features had been omitted, figures in costume, figures in everyday clothes, others in protective and gesticulating poses, and ones assuming a relatively static stance, etc.—suggested a variety of conceptual dimension. The subject had the opportunity to sort according to clearly physical qualities of the stimuli or on a more highly inferential basis. Each of the three MAPS sorts was scored according to the same 1-4 point scale of descriptiveness to inferentiality used in the scoring of the TAT stories. The interrater reliability for this score was 1.00+.[6]

Ohio State Psychological Examination (OSPE) scores were obtained from the university records for all the subjects for whom such scores were recorded. The OSPE scores provided an estimate of intellectual

---

[4] At the conclusion of the experiment the Failure subjects were given information that negated the earlier failure experience.

[5] These coefficients were corrected, because a limited number of broad categories were used in rating these variables, by a procedure described by Peters and Van Voorhis (1940). Lack of precision in the correction results in some correlations of 1.00+. These correlations do indicate reliabilities in the high .90s.

[6] See Footnote 5.

Table 1   Descriptive Statistics with Respect to the MAPS Sorts
and TAT Conceptual Scores

| | | SORTS | | TAT | |
	N	M	SD	M	SD
Failure group					
Total	31	6.45	2.49	9.03	3.96
Cautious	14	6.50	2.56	9.07	4.28
Noncautious	17	6.41	2.43	9.00	3.68
Success group					
Total	32	7.00	2.44	9.38	3.40
Cautious	14	6.79	2.01	9.21	2.98
Noncautious	18	7.17	2.71	9.50	3.69
Control group					
Total	36	7.50	2.62	9.47	2.88
Cautious	15	6.13	2.00	8.33	2.55
Noncautious	21	8.48	2.58	10.29	2.83

ability and were correlated with the scores obtained on the experimental measures.

RESULTS

The three groups (Failure, Success, and Control) were each dichotomized into cautious and noncautious subgroups on the basis of the subject's level of aspiration performance. The N, mean, and standard deviation for each group and subgroup are presented in Table 1. High scores on the sorts and TAT indicate inferential behavior and low scores reflect descriptiveness. The Mann-Whitney U test was used for comparing groups as to the degree of descriptive behavior on the MAPS sorts and TAT. The U values were converted into z scores[7] so that all group comparisons are expressed as z score values.

Table 2 presents data pertaining to the first hypothesis. While the Failure group was more descriptive than the Success or Control groups for all comparisons, as hypothesized, these differences were not statistically significant. Thus, the hypothesis pertaining to the influence of conditions was not supported.

The second hypothesis stated that the Failure condition would have its greatest effect in increasing descriptive responses when the subject's

[7] Siegel (1956) states that as the N in either group increases in size, the sampling distribution of U approaches the normal distribution. Therefore, a formula is provided for converting the obtained U into a z score when the N in either group exceeds 20. This conversion is also recommended as a correction when the same rank occurs for scores involving both groups. Since all of the observations meet either one or both of these conditions, all of the U's are converted into z scores.

Table 2   *Differences between Experimental Groups on Descriptiveness (expressed as z score values)*

CONDITION	SORTS	TAT
Failure vs. Success	.91 F[a]	.31 F
Failure vs. Control	1.45 F	.87 F
Success vs. Control	.68 S	.61 S

Note.—z score of 1.96 needed for .05 level.
[a] The letter F, S, or C indicates whether Failure, Success, or Control group was higher on descriptiveness.

Table 3   *Differences between Experimental Groups (Cautious and Noncautious subgroups analyzed separately) on Descriptiveness (expressed as z score values)*

CONDITION	NONCAUTIOUS SUBJECTS		CAUTIOUS SUBJECTS	
	Sorts	TAT	Sorts	TAT
Failure vs. Success	.76 F[a]	1.56 F	.49 F	.39 F
Failure vs. Control	2.41*** F	1.27 F	.59 C	.07 C
Success vs. Control	1.50 S	.88 S	1.10 C	.86 C

[a] The letter F, S, or C indicates whether Failure, Success, or Control group was higher on descriptiveness.
*** $p < .02$; two-tailed test.

personality disposition was taken into consideration. This was tested by comparing the influence of the conditions for the cautious and the non-cautious subjects separately. The findings pertaining to this hypothesis are reported in Table 3. As can be seen, the Failure condition promoted increased descriptive responses for noncautious but not for cautious subjects. However, the only statistically significant comparison was between the Failure and Control conditions for the MAPS sorts ($z = 2.41$, $p < .02$; two-tailed). The cautious subjects did not respond differentially to Failure as compared with Control and Success conditions. The increase in descriptiveness under the Failure condition, noted in Table 2, appears, thus, to have been contributed by the noncautious subjects.

The mean scores presented in Table 1 provide a basis for summarizing and better understanding the foregoing results. The cautious subgroup in each of the three experimental conditions were quite similar in descriptiveness. They had attained preexperimentally, a plateau on desciptiveness and were not appreciably influenced by the conditions. The noncautious subjects were most inferential in the Control condition and became more descriptive in the experimental conditions, particularly in the Failure condition. Therefore, the cautious subjects remained stable on descriptiveness across conditions, whereas, the noncautious subjects exhibited a degree of descriptiveness comparable to the cautious subjects only in the Failure condition.

Accordng to the final hypothesis, the cautious subjects should be more descriptive in their responses to the sorts and TAT than noncautious subjects, and the difference should be most pronounced for a neutral situation (Control condition). Table 4 shows the comparisons between the cautious and noncautious subgroups for descriptiveness on the sorts and TAT within each condition. The z score was again used to evaluate the significance of the difference for these comparisons.

The cautious and noncautious subgroups did not differ in descriptive behavior for the Failure and Success condition. However, for the Control condition, the cautious subjects were significantly more descriptive than the noncautious subjects on both the sorts ($z = 2.84$, $p < .01$; two-tailed) and TAT ($z = 2.07$, $p < .05$; two-tailed). The effects of the personality variable appear to have been obscured by the strong situational forces operating for the Failure and Success conditions. When these situational forces were minimized (Control condition) the influence of the personality variable became quite evident. While the cautious subjects were not more descriptive in all conditions as predicted, the fact that they demonstrated greater descriptiveness in the neutral situation indicated a basic relation-

Table 4   Differences between Cautious and Noncautious Subgroups on Descriptiveness
(expressed as z score values)

CONDITION	SORTS	TAT
Failure (Cautious vs. Noncautious)	.01 NC[a]	.06 NC
Success (Cautious vs. Noncautious)	.27 C	.10 C
Control (Cautious vs. Noncautious)	2.84 **** C	2.07** C

[a] NC or C indicates whether the noncautious or cautious subgroup was higher on descriptiveness.
    ** $p < .05$; two-tailed test.
    **** $p < .01$; two-tailed test.

Table 5   Product-Moment Correlations between Experimental Measures and OSPE Scores

CONDITION	SORTS	TAT
Failure group ($N = 28$)	−.02	−.10
Success group ($N = 30$)	.32*	−.02
Control group ($N = 28$)	.02	−.52****

    * $p < .10$; two-tailed test.
    **** $p < .01$; two-tailed test.

ship between descriptiveness and cautiousness. That is, descriptiveness on the sorts and TAT was associated with characteristic cautiousness and this relationship held only for the Control condition.

Scores on the OSPE were available for the majority of the subjects. Correlations with the conceptual scores on the TAT and MAPS sorting task for each of the situational conditions are presented in Table 5.

The MAPS conceptual score and OSPE were correlated for the subjects in the Success condition ($r = .32$, $p < .10$; two-tailed). These MAPS responses were confounded with an experimental condition; this correlation is, therefore, difficult to interpret. On the other hand, the TAT conceptual score and OSPE were negatively related for the Control condition ($r = -.52$, $p < .01$; two-tailed). That is, the brighter subjects gave more descriptive TAT responses.

The two significant correlations reported in Table 5 increase the complexity of the experimental findings. These relationships do not appear to detract from the stated hypotheses, but rather, suggest that additional dimensions also contributed to the conceptual behavior.

The TAT and MAPS conceptual scores were positively correlated ($r = .30$, $p < .01$; two-tailed). Cautiousness on the Level of Aspiration and OSPE scores were unrelated ($r_{bis} = .16$, not significant).

DISCUSSION

When all subjects were pooled there was no relation between descriptiveness and the situation. However, when personality differences were considered, the situation became a significant determinant of descriptive behavior, only noncautious subjects being influenced by experimental conditions. Failure induced descriptiveness in the noncautious subjects, but did not increase descriptive responses among the cautious subjects, who had a pre-experimental set to respond to all conditions as if failure were imminent. This finding highlights the importance of systematically investigating individual differences in susceptibility to situational cues. By so doing, one is able to increase the power of predictive hypotheses. This position is underscored by some findings obtained by Marlowe and Crowne (1961), who observed that persons differ in their need to subscribe to socially desirable behaviors and that differences in this need predict sensitivity to situational cues.

The second major finding was that personality differences predicted descriptive behavior only for a neutral situation. That is, cautious subjects were more descriptive than noncautious subjects for the Control condition, but not under Failure or Success, which apparently masked the variance otherwise associated with the personality variable. This finding bears on the need to consider both situational and personality variables. Certain situational conditions can easily obscure personality differences leading investigators to conclude erroneously that no differences exist.

Fear of failure is a function of both situational and personality factors. Subjects defended against it by being more descriptive on the conceptual tasks. On both the MAPS and TAT, tests frequently used to assess content variables, the personality and situational variables were both associated with descriptiveness. Yet the possible occurrence of many substantive responses is contingent on the conceptual level used by the subject. If a subject is highly descriptive, the range of potential responses is reduced. Furthermore, pronounced descriptiveness precludes the occurrence of many personalized responses which, by definition, are inferential. These findings emphasize the importance of considering the presence of general defensive patterns, such as cautiousness, in interpreting psychological test results.

No specific predictions were made concerning the Success group, which turned out to be intermediate between the Failure and Control groups on descriptive behavior. The positive reinforcement given the Success group might have been expected to decrease Cautious behavior. However, such was not the case. An alternative explanation, in line with the obtained findings, is that the positive reinforcement on the social attitudes test actually evoked cautiousness on the subsequent, functionally related tasks. That is, the provision of a reinforcement for one task (positive or negative) may structure other tasks in that situation as potential success or failure experiences. The reinforcement, regardless of its direction, increases involvement for the related tasks. Support for this position is suggested by Lazarus, Baker, Broverman, and Mayer (1957), who state that "psychological stress involves the thwarting of a motive state" and that "a motive state has to be present in order for stress to occur." Furthermore, in keeping with the results of this study, they found that "stressor conditions" served to make subjects low in achievement motivation more literal on a task where they were required to listen to and reproduce tape recorded paragraphs.

In addition to showing the interplay between situational and personality variables, the study provides evidence for the moderate generality of cautiousness over a variety of situations. Cautiousness on the Level of Aspiration task predicted descriptiveness on the sorts ($r_{bis} = .56$, $p < .01$) and on the TAT ($r_{bis} = .42$, $p < .05$) for the Control condition. Descriptiveness on the sorts and TAT were positively correlated for the total sample. Furthermore, cautiousness induced by the Failure situation predicted descriptive behavior.

SUMMARY

This investigation dealt with the influence of situational and characteristic cautiousness as codeterminants of conceptual behavior. A Failure condition produced situational cautiousness and the level of aspiration measured characteristic cautiousness. Cautious conceptual responses consisted of descriptive responses to TAT cards and a figure-sorting task.

The major findings were as follows:

1. The Failure condition contributed a significantly greater amount of descriptive responses than the Control condition only for subjects judged to be noncautious prior to the experimental conditions. When all subjects were pooled this relationship largely disappeared.

2. The personality variable predicted descriptive behavior only for a neutral situation. That is, cautious subjects were significantly more descriptive than noncautious subjects on the sorts and TAT for the Control condition, but not for the Failure or Success conditions.

4-3	*Some Relationships among Projective Test, Interview, and Sociometric Measures of Dependent Behavior*[1]

BERNARD J. FITZGERALD

The need for experimental evaluation of projective test data as used for describing and evaluating behavior has frequently been pointed out (Lindzey, 1952; Soskin, 1954). Some authors disparage such experimental evaluation, suggesting that perhaps clinically useful evidence is distorted or lost in the process of quantification (Hanfmann, 1952; Korner, 1950). However, it would seem that systematic investigation of projective test data is essential, particularly in view of the failure of many studies to predict successfully from projective test responses to overt behavior, even on the basis of clinical evaluation of the data.

The present study was developed using descriptive constructs from Rotter's social learning theory (Rotter, 1954). From the point of view of social learning theory, any given situation has within it possibilities for the satisfaction of many different needs. Which of these needs an individual will strive to satisfy will depend upon two factors, the *value* that the satisfaction of a given need has for him and his *expectancy* that his behavior will lead to that satisfaction. The value which the satisfaction of a given need has for the individual is termed Need Value. In the measurement of Need Value, emphasis is upon what need satisfactions the individual *prefers*. An individual's expectations that particular behaviors will lead to the desired need satisfaction is termed Freedom of Movement.

[1] This paper is based on a doctoral dissertation done at the Ohio State University. The author acknowledges with gratitude the advice and guidance given him by J. B. Rotter, under whose direction this study was carried out. The writer also is grateful to Gordon Rader for his helpful criticism of this manuscript.

Emphasis is upon what the individual *expects* to happen. Freedom of Movement is high if the individual expects his behaviors to lead to need satisfaction. An individual's Freedom of Movement is low if he expects failure or punishment for such behaviors. One method of measuring Freedom of Movement depends upon identifying the frequency with which the individual, when seeking any particular need satisfaction, resorts to symbolic, rather than direct, overt behavior to obtain that satisfaction; the more he resorts to symbolic behavior, the lower his Freedom of Movement.

In terms of this study, it was hypothesized that if projective test responses represent, in part, symbolic ways of obtaining gratification, then frequency of response should be highest when Freedom of Movement is low and Need Value high. This hypothesis assumes that a projective test provides a situation in which symbolic gratification is possible; therefore, the individual tends to give responses involving satisfactions that have a high value for him but for which he has a low expectancy of realization. Such a situation, where Need Value is higher than Freedom of Movement, is considered in this study to be a situation of important conflict.

The purpose of this study was to provide data related to the interpretation of needs as reflected in the content of projective test responses. Dependency, the need investigated, may be defined as the need to have other individuals prevent frustration or punishment and provide for the satisfaction of other needs. The projective tests used were the Murray TAT and the Rotter Incomplete Sentences Blank (ISB). The measures of overt behavior were a sociometric technique and an interview. The measures of Need Value and Freedom of Movement for Dependency were also derived from the interview.

The hypotheses of this study are as follows:

1. Frequency of n Dependency responses in a projective test is positively related to sociometric and interview indices of Dependent behavior; and

2. Frequency of n Dependency responses in a projective test is positively related to the importance of conflict in n Dependency.

METHOD

Eighty Ss, 20 from each of four social fraternities, participated in the study. All Ss had been members of their respective fraternities for at least six months and students at the Ohio State University for at least one year. A pilot study was devoted to the development of the interview, the sociometric measure, and judges' manuals for scoring interview and projective test responses.

The criteria of overt behavior were a sociometric index and an interview measure of Dependent behavior. A nominating technique was used as the sociometric measure. Two descriptions were provided the Ss in order to make their nominations. One of these descriptions was worded to describe certain behaviors considered most and another

worded to describe behaviors least representative of Dependent behavior. Care was taken not to label the descriptions as representative
of any particular kind of behavior, e.g., Dependent. Ss were asked to
select from the members of the group those who, in general, best fit one
or the other of the two descriptions. The nominations were made
alternately, i.e., the one S who behaved most Dependently, the one S
who behaved most non-Dependently, and so on. In this manner, then
all Ss made three nominations for each description.[2]

A structural clinical interview was developed to elicit from these
same Ss historical data relevant to their Dependent behavior and data
relevant to their Need Value and Freedom of Movement for Dependency
satisfaction. The interview was divided into eleven areas: school, home,
advisor, major academic subject, roommate, friends, girl friends, health,
personal problems, and religion. A manual for scoring the interview variables of Dependent behavior, Need Value, and Freedom of Movement for
Dependency satisfaction was developed. Included in the manual were
the definition of Dependency and a set of general principles derived
from the definition, as well as examples from interview protocols
obtained in the pilot study. Examples were derived from these interviews to correspond to the points 1, 4, 7, and 10 on a ten-point rating
scale. The in-between points were included to allow finer discriminations than were possible from the selected referents in the manuals.
The values attached to the examples in each of the manuals were
arrived at by the experimenter's first assigning crude values consistent
with the context from which the examples were taken. Two independent raters also assigned values to these examples, and the scale values
were adjusted to maximize agreement among the three raters. Finally,
these refined scales were discussed with the interview judges. Changes
were made in the scales where necessary for complete agreement
among the judges, and the examples were then assigned final values.

Judges' scoring manuals were similarly developed for the TAT
(Cards 3BM, 4, 6BM, 7BM, 8BM, 10, 12M, 13MF, 15, 17BM, 18BM, 20)
and the ISB. From the TAT stories obtained in the pilot study, a manual
was prepared to aid in the determination of the presence or absence
of a Dependency plot for any given story. In the development of the
manual, each pilot protocol was carefully read, and any story which
could be considered to have a Dependency plot was noted. Two projective test judges and the experimenter discussed those stories which
were "borderline" or difficult to judge for n Dependency. Following discussion of each borderline story, the three judges agreed on each story
as representative of either Dependency or non-Dependency. These
stories, as well as stories clearly representative of n Dependency, were
included in the final form of the manual. Dependency plots were identified in relation to both the Hero and the Other Figures. Suggestions

---

[2] The method of nominating only the extremes of a group has been found to be at
least as reliable as rating an entire group and to provide a distribution of ratings similar
to that obtained when each member of a group is to be rated by every other member.

were included in the manual to promote agreement among the judges in the determination of the Hero figure. From ISB responses obtained in the pilot study, as well as from a large pool of items gathered previously by others, a manual for scoring ISB responses for n Dependency was developed in a similar fashion. In making their ratings, the judges were asked to use the manuals by comparing the TAT or ISB item to be rated with examples included in the manuals. Approximately 30 hours were spent in training the judges in the use of the manuals.

Procedure

The Ss were first seen at their respective fraternity houses, where the sociometric and projective measures were obtained. Following the group's completion of the sociometric ratings, the TAT cards were projected on a screen. Ss were allowed six minutes, the TAT card remaining in view, to write each story. Finally, the ISB was administered. Each S was interviewed individually within a two-week period following the group testing. All interviews were recorded on the Gray Audograph, and the judges made their ratings of the interviews from these recordings. The experimenter and two interview judges, working independently, rated the interviews. The experimenter and two different judges, working independently, rated the projective test responses. The protocols and interviews were coded so that the identity of the individual Ss was not known to the judges. All TAT and ISB responses for any given card or item were rated before continuing to the next item, and all responses were rated by at least two judges.

Estimates of the interrater reliabilities for the interview variables, the TAT, and ISB were obtained by correlating (Pearson r) the ratings obtained from each judge with those of each of the other two judges. The interview variables were each rated on a ten-point scale. For the TAT and the ISB, each S was given a score by counting the number of stories or items rated as Dependent. The average interrator correlations for the interview were as follows: Dependent behavior, .54; Need Value, .45; Freedom of Movement, .56. The average interrater correlations were for the TAT (Hero), .75; TAT (Other), .11; and the ISB, .78. Because of the unreliable TAT Other Figure ratings, this index was dropped from consideration. The sociometric ratings yielded corrected split-half reliability of .83.

RESULTS

A test of the first hypothesis concerning the relationship between projective test responses and overt Dependent behavior was made by correlating (Pearson r) the interview and the sociometric ratings of Dependent behavior with the frequency-of-response ratings on the TAT and on the ISB. It appears from Table 1 that there is no evidence of a relationship between frequency of response in n Dependency on the TAT and either the interview or the sociometric measures of Dependent behavior. The

ISB, in terms of frequency of response in n Dependency, yields indices which are related to both at low but significant magnitudes.

The second hypothesis concerning the relationship of frequency of response in n Dependency to importance of conflict in n Dependency, as determined from the interview, was evaluated by the chi-square test. In order to make this test, Ss were divided into two groups for each projective test respectively, i.e., those Ss with a high number (four or more on the TAT; seven or more on the ISB) vs. those with a low number (three or less on the TAT; six or less on the ISB) of Dependency responses. The high and low groups for each test were compared on the basis of an importance-of-conflict score which was derived in the following manner: Ss with Freedom of Movement equal to or greater than Need Value were considered to have "No Important Conflict" in n Dependency and were compared with those Ss whose Freedom of Movement was less than Need Value. These latter Ss were considered to have an "Important Conflict" in n Dependency. The results of this comparison are reported in Table 2. It appears that those Ss who have a relatively higher Need Value

Table 1   Correlations between the Measures of Dependent Behavior and Frequency of Response Ratings on the Projective Tests
(N = 60)

	TAT	ISB
Interview	.07	.28*
Sociometric	.06	.25*

* $p = .05$.

Table 2   Chi Square of the Frequency of Dependency Responses on the Projective Measures Compared to Conflict in Need Dependency
(N = 60)

	TOTAL NUMBER OF DEPENDENCY RESPONSES			
	TAT		ISB	
CONFLICT	High D Group	Low D Group	High D Group	Low D Group
"Important Conflict" (Freedom of Movement less than Need Value)	88	27	183	79
"Not Important Conflict" (Freedom of Movement equal to or greater than Need Value)	16	18	65	37
	$\chi^2 = 12.24$; $p = .001$.		$\chi^2 = .99$; $p = .30$.	

than Freedom of Movement for Dependency satisfaction give significantly more responses in n Dependency on the TAT. The results for the ISB are not significant.

It seems evident also from Table 2 that the TAT tends to elicit dissimilar data, in terms of a frequency-of-response measure, from that elicited by the ISB. Comparisons of these two tests in terms of frequency of response in n Dependency as related to interview and sociometric measures of Dependent behavior (Table 1) support this conclusion. Further evidence that these two instruments tend to elicit dissimilar data is given by their low intercorrelation (.09).

On the other hand, the correlation between ratings of overt Dependent behavior from the interview and from sociometric measures was .59. Important to note here is the potential usefulness of the economic sociometric technique in relation to the laborious clinical interview as a quantified index of certain kinds of overt behavior.

CONCLUSIONS AND DISCUSSION

The following conclusions, all in terms of frequency of response in n Dependency, may be drawn from this study:

1. There is no evidence that TAT responses are related to interview or sociometric indices of Dependent behavior.

2. TAT responses are significantly related to an interview measure of importance of conflict in n Dependency.

The foregoing conclusions lend support to two assumptions listed by Lindzey in his review of the clinical use of the TAT. One assumption states, "The dispositions and conflicts that may be inferred from the story-teller's creations are *not always* reflected *directly* in overt behavior." Another holds that, "Themes that are recurrent in a series of stories are particularly apt to mirror the impulses and conflicts of the story-teller [Lindzey, 1952; p. 3]." The similarity of these assumptions to the hypotheses in this study is evident.

3. ISB responses tend to be related to interview and sociometric measures of overt, Dependent behavior.

4. ISB responses show no evidence of relationship to an interview measure of importance of conflict in n Dependency.

The third conclusion is similar to that of McClelland (1953), who, using a Sentence Completion Test to measure n Achievement, argued that this test provides results which are dissimilar to those provided by the TAT and which are more similar to conscious self-judgments. Blyth (1953) found also that the ISB differentiated between groups of veterans who behaved dependently or independently in terms of accepting or rejecting offers of psychotherapy.

It is evident that the TAT and the ISB, although both projective tests, provide dissimilar data in terms of frequency of response in a given need category, and that inferences from one test cannot be generalized to the other. More specifically, where inferences about overt behavior are to be made, a highly structured, behaviorally oriented projective test, such as the ISB, may be the more appropriate. The TAT does not appear to be particularly useful as a source of inferences about overt behavior. Where inferences about conflict in a given need area are to be made, a projective test that allows considerable freedom of response, such as the TAT, is probably appropriate. The ISB appears to be less appropriate as a source of inferences about conflict in a given need.

The unmodified TAT and the ISB were used in this study as they generally are employed in clinical psychological work. It is important to emphasize again that the measure used in relation to the projective test responses was a frequency-of-response measure. It is not intended to imply that such a measure of projective test responses is the only possible one or that such a measure is more valid or economical than other possible uses of such projective test responses. In fact, it is evident that a frequency-of-response measure makes no more than minimal use of the data provided by the TAT and the ISB. Nevertheless, with descriptive constructs from Rotter's social learning theory, which provided for an objective and communicable method, a predictive relationship was demonstrated between frequency of response in n Dependency on the TAT and an interview measure of importance of conflict in n Dependency.

SUMMARY

Data relevant to two hypotheses concerned with the evaluation of projective test responses were obtained in this study. The projective test measure was frequency of response in n Dependency on the TAT and on the ISB. A structured clinical interview and a sociometric technique were used as measures of overt Dependent behavior. The clinical interview also was structured to provide measures of Need Value and Freedom of Movement for n Dependency. Eighty Ss participated in the study. A pilot study with 20 of these Ss provided data for judges' scoring manuals for the interview and projective test situations. All Ss were tested in groups and interviewed individually.

Results of the study may be summarized as follows:

1. Frequency of response in n Dependency on the TAT yielded no evidence of relationship to the interview and sociometric measures of overt Dependent behavior.

2. Frequency of response in n Dependency on the ISB was related to interview and sociometric measures of overt Dependent behavior.

3. Importance of conflict in n Dependency, as derived from the interview, was related to frequency of response in n Dependency on the TAT. The results for the ISB were not significant.

4. Dissimilar data, in terms of frequency of response in n Dependency, were elicited by the TAT and the ISB.

5. A high degree of similarity was found between the sociometric and interview ratings of overt Dependent behavior. This suggests the usefulness of sociometric ratings in lieu of clinical interviews to obtain an approximate, quantifiable measure of certain kinds of overt behavior.

4-4

A New Scale of Social Desirability Independent of Psychopathology

DOUGLAS P. CROWNE and DAVID MARLOWE

It has long been recognized that personality test scores are influenced by non-test-relevant response determinants. Wiggins and Rumrill (1959) distinguish three approaches to this problem. Briefly, interest in the problem of response distortion has been concerned with attempts at statistical correction for "faking good" or "faking bad" (Meehl & Hathaway, 1946), the analysis of response sets (Cronbach, 1946, 1950), and ratings of the social desirability of personality test items (Edwards, 1957). A further distinction can be made, however, which results in a somewhat different division of approaches to the question of response distortion. Common to both the Meehl and Hathaway corrections for faking good and faking bad and Cronbach's notion of response sets is an interest in the *test behavior* of the subject(S). By social desirability, on the other hand, Edwards primarily means the "scale value for any personality statement such that the scale value indicates the position of the statement on the social desirability continuum . . ." (1957, p. 3). Social desirability, thus, has been used to refer to a characteristic of *test items*, i.e., their scale position on a social desirability scale.

Whether the test behavior of Ss or the social desirability properties of items are the focus of interest, however, it now seems clear that underlying both these approaches is the concept of statistical deviance. In the construction of the MMPI K scale, for example, items were selected which differentiated between clinically normal persons producing abnormal test profiles and clinically abnormal individuals with abnormal test profiles, and between clinically abnormal persons with normal test profiles and abnormal Ss whose test records were abnormal. Keyed responses to the K scale items tend to be statistically deviant in the parent populations. Similarly, the development of the Edwards Social Desirability Scale (SDS) illustrates this procedure. Items were drawn from various MMPI scales (F, L, K, and the Manifest Anxiety Scale [Taylor, 1953]) and submitted to judges who categorized them as either socially desirable or socially undesirable. Only items on which there was unanimous agreement among the 10 judges were included in the SDS. It seems clear that the items in Edwards SDS would, of necessity, have extreme social desirability scale positions or, in other words, be statistically deviant.

Some unfortunate consequences follow from the strict use of the statistical deviance model in the development of social desirability scales. With items drawn from the MMPI, it is apparent that in addition to their scalability for social desirability the items may also be characterized by

From *Journal of Consulting Psychology*, 1960, **24**, 349–354. Copyright 1960 by the American Psychological Association and reprinted by permission of the authors and the publisher.

their content which, in a general sense, has pathological implications. When a social desirability scale constructed according to this procedure is then applied to a college student population, the meaning of high social desirability scores is not at all clear. When Ss given the Edwards SDS deny, for example, that their sleep is fitful and disturbed (Item 6) or that they worry quite a bit over possible misfortunes (Item 35), it cannot be determined whether these responses are attributable to social desirability or to a genuine absence of such symptoms. The probability of occurrence of the symptoms represented in MMPI items (and incorporated in the SDS) in a college undergraduate population is undoubtedly low. Thus, the achievement of high SD scores may simply reflect the low frequency of pathological symptoms in this population and not the *needs* of Ss to present themselves in a favorable light. Of course, if one is only concerned with the properties of test items (their social desirability scalability), this is not a relevant issue. If, however, major importance is attached to the needs of Ss in psychometric situations and the influence of these needs on test responses, it is essential to be able to discriminate between the effects of item content and the needs of Ss to present themselves in a socially desirable (or undesirable) light.

In the present research, a social desirability scale was developed according to a different psychometric model, avoiding the ambiguities of the statistical deviance approach. Basic to this model is the sampling procedure employed in the selection of items from a defined universe. The population from which items were drawn is defined by behaviors which are culturally sanctioned and approved but which are improbable of occurrence. This will readily be recognized as the rationale underlying the Lie scale of the MMPI (Meehl & Hathaway, 1946). Items in the present scale, however, are probably less extreme than the Lie items.

METHOD

Development of Scale

A number of current personality inventories were consulted by the authors in order to devise a set of items for a new social desirability scale (M-C SDS). For inclusion in the scale, an item had to meet the criterion of cultural approval described above and was required to have minimal pathological or abnormal implications if responded to in either the socially desirable or undesirable directions. A set of 50 items meeting these criteria was submitted to 10 judges, both faculty members and graduate students in the Department of Psychology of Ohio State University, for social desirability ratings. The judges were instructed to score each item in the socially desirable direction from the point of view of college students, using true and false response categories. Unanimous agreement was obtained on 36 items and 90% agreement on 11 additional items. These 47 items constituted the preliminary form of the scale.

A major objective in the development of the M-C SDS was the elimination of pathology-relevant item content. To test this and for comparative purposes, both the M-C SDS and the Edwards 39-item SDS (Edwards, 1957) were submitted to 10 additional judges, again including both faculty members and graduate students in the psychology department, for ratings of the degree of maladjustment implied by socially undesirable responses to the items. A 5-point scale, ranging from extremely well-adjusted (1) to extremely maladjusted (5), was employed for this purpose. The mean rating for all the items in the M-C SDS was 2.8, slightly below the midpoint of the scale (implies neither good nor poor adjustment). The mean rating for the Edwards SDS items was 3.9, indicating that the judges considered socially undesirable responses on this scale to be definitely indicative of maladjustment. The t test of the significance of the difference between these means is 15.27, which is significant well beyond the .0001 level.

The preliminary scale was then administered to 76 students in two introductory psychology courses, and an item analysis completed. There were 33 items that discriminated at the .05 level or better between high and low total scores. Of the 33 items, 18 are keyed true and 15 false, making a response set interpretation of scores highly improbable. These 33 items constitute the final form of the M-C SDS and are listed in Table 1 with the socially desirable response scoring indicated.

Reliability

The internal consistency coefficient for the final form of the scale, using Kuder-Richardson formula 20, is .88. This was computed on 39 Ss, 10 males and 29 females, who were enrolled in an undergraduate abnormal psychology class at Ohio State University. The mean age of this sample was 24.4 years, with a range of 19 to 46 years. Thirty-one of these Ss took the scale on two occasions separated by a month interval. A test-retest correlation of .89 was obtained.

Table 1   The Marlowe–Crowne Social Desirability Scale

PERSONAL REACTION INVENTORY

Listed below are a number of statements concerning attitudes and traits. Read each item and decide whether the statement is *true* or *false* as it pertains to you personally.

1. Before voting I thoroughly investigate the qualifications of all the candidates.   (T)
2. I never hesitate to go out of my way to help someone in trouble. (T)
3. It is sometimes hard for me to go on with my work if I am not encouraged.   (F)
4. I have never intensely disliked anyone.   (T)
5. On occasion I have had doubts about my ability to succeed in life.   (F)

Table 1   Continued

PERSONAL REACTION INVENTORY

---

6. I sometimes feel resentful when I don't get my way.   (F)
7. I am always careful about my manner of dress.   (T)
8. My table manners at home are as good as when I eat out in a restaurant.   (T)
9. If I could get into a movie without paying and be sure I was not seen I would probably do it.   (F)
10. On a few occasions, I have given up doing something because I thought too little of my ability.   (F)
11. I like to gossip at times.   (F)
12. There have been times when I felt like rebelling against people in authority even though I knew they were right.   (F)
13. No matter who I'm talking to, I'm always a good listener.   (T)
14. I can remember "playing sick" to get out of something.   (F)
15. There have been occasions when I took advantage of someone. (F)
16. I'm always willing to admit it when I make a mistake.   (T)
17. I always try to practice what I preach.   (T)
18. I don't find it particularly difficult to get along with loud mouthed, obnoxious people.   (T)
19. I sometimes try to get even rather than forgive and forget.   (F)
20. When I don't know something I don't at all mind admitting it. (T)
21. I am always courteous, even to people who are disagreeable.   (T)
22. At times I have really insisted on having things my own way. (F)
23. There have been occasions when I felt like smashing things. (F)
24. I would never think of letting someone else be punished for my wrongdoings.   (T)
25. I never resent being asked to return a favor.   (T)
26. I have never been irked when people expressed ideas very different from my own.   (T)
27. I never make a long trip without checking the safety of my car. (T)
28. There have been times when I was quite jealous of the good fortune of others.   (F)
29. I have almost never felt the urge to tell someone off.   (T)
30. I am sometimes irritated by people who ask favors of me.   (F)
31. I have never felt that I was punished without cause.   (T)
32. I sometimes think when people have a misfortune they only got what they deserved.   (F)
33. I have never deliberately said something that hurt someone's feelings.   (T)

Relationship to Edwards SD Scale
The correlation between the M-C SDS and the Edwards SDS is .35, which is significant at the .01 level. The sample on which this correlation is based included, in addition to the 39 abnormal psychology students, 81 students in a course on exceptional children. The correlation shows a general tendency for scores on the two tests to be associated.

In Table 2, the means and standard deviations of both SDSs are reported. The distribution of M-C SDS scores rather closely approximates a normal distribution, while negative skewness, consistent with previous findings (Edwards, 1957), is found for the Edwards *SD* distribution. It is interesting to compare the Edwards SD mean found in the present research with that originally reported. The means of 28.6 and 27.1 for males and females reported by Edwards are considerably lower than the value found in this study.

Correlations with Other Scales
A considerable portion of the research on social desirability has involved the correlation of SDSs with MMPI variables. To compare the present scale with the Edwards SDS, Pearson product-moment correlations were computed between the two SDSs and the following MMPI and derived scales: *K*—Test-taking attitude; *L*—Lie; *F*—Validity and test-taking attitude; *Hs*—Hypochondriasis; *D*—Depression; *Hy*—Hysteria; *Pd*—Psychopathic Deviate; *Pa*—Paranoia; *Pt*—Psychasthenia; *Sc*—Schizophrenia; *Ma*—Manic; *Pr*—Prejudice (Gough, 1951); *St*—Status (Gough, 1948); *Es*—Ego Strength (Barron, 1953b); MAS—Manifest Anxiety (Taylor, 1953); *A*—Anxiety (Welsh, 1956); *R*—Repression (Welsh, 1956).

The 39 *S*s referred to above who served in the study were administered the M-C SDS, the 39-item Edwards SDS, and the MMPI in that order. The first two tests were given on the same day and the MMPI about a month later. Thirty-four *S*s completed all of the tests and 37 of them completed all but the derived MMPI scales.

Table 3 presents the correlations between the M-C SDS and the Edwards SDS and the 17 MMPI validity, clinical, and derived scales. It is at once apparent that uniformly higher correlations obtain between the Edwards SDS and the various MMPI scales than between the M-C SDS and these MMPI variables. A general trend, which is consistent with

Table 2   Means and Standard Deviations of the Social Desirability Scales

SCALE	N	MEAN	SD
M-C SDS	120	13.72	5.78
Edwards SDS	120	31.83	5.06
(From Edwards, 1957)	84	28.6 Males	6.5
	108	27.1 Females	6.5

Table 3   Correlations between the Social Desirability Scales and Various MMPI Scales for 37 Males and Females

MMPI Scales	M-C SDS	Edwards SDS
K	.40*	.65**
L	.54**	.22
F	−.36*	−.61**
Hs	−.30	−.62**
D	−.27	−.72**
Hy	.15	.09
Pd	−.41**	−.73**
Pa	.21	−.02
Pt	−.30	−.80**
Sc	−.40*	−.77**
Ma	−.24	−.42*
Pr[a]	−.27	−.58**
St[a]	.16	.14
Es	.17	.46**
MAS[b]	−.25	−.75**
A[b]	−.23	−.61**
R[b]	.28	.07

* Significant at the .05 level.
** Significant at the .01 level.
[a] $N = 36$.
[b] $N = 34$.

previous research, is found in the positive correlations between the SDSs and the validity scales of the MMPI, and negative correlations with most of the clinical scales. Four clinical scales correlate highest with both SDSs, with the single exception of *D* which correlated − .27 with the M-C SDS: *Sc, Pd, Pt,* and *Hs.* Two of these four, *Sc* and *Pt,* are considered to be among the most "pathological" of the clinical scales.

DISCUSSION

The most important feature of the findings of this study is found in the marked differences overall in the magnitude of the correlations between the two SDSs and the MMPI. Consistently higher correlations were found between the Edwards SDS and the MMPI scales than were obtained between the M-C SDS and the MMPI scales. The high Edwards SDS-MMPI correlations, in general, confirm findings previously reported by Edwards (1957) and Fordyce (1956). Correlations between the Edwards SDS and the *Pt, Sc,* and MAS scales, in fact, approach the asymptotic value of the reliabilities of the separate tests. With correlations this high, it is necessary to raise the question of whether the Edwards SDS and these MMPI scales are not, in effect, functionally unitary. It would appear to be difficult to hold the view that SD scores and MAS, *Pt,* and *Sc* scores can be interpreted differently. More in accord with the evidence would be to attribute the covariance of the Edwards SDS and these MMPI scales to item similarity and to the "pathological" content of both sets of items. This would lead to an interpretation of the Edwards scale as a measure of the willingness to admit to certain symptoms of a "neurotic" nature or as a measure of general "neuroticism." But this does not enable one to discriminate between high SD scorers who genuinely do not have the symptoms represented in the SDS items from those Ss who conceal (consciously or unconsciously) their symptoms and whose responses are motivated by social desirability. To the extent, then, that the Edwards SDS measures social desirability, it does so in the very restricted sense that high *SD* scores imply that it is bad or undesirable to have or admit to symptoms. Possibly, such attitudes have little generality and would not be related to other test behavior or social behavior. Sarason (1959) has also raised the question of the interpretation of Edwards SDS as an unconfounded measure of social desirability.

In the development of the M-C SDS, social desirability was defined more broadly to refer to the need of Ss to obtain approval by responding in a culturally appropriate and acceptable manner. This conception does not involve the acquiescence or denial by S of pathology. The significantly different maladjustment ratings obtained on the two SDSs support the hypothesis that the Edwards SDS involves the admission or denial of maladjustive symptoms and indicate that socially undesirable responses on the M-C SDS do not imply maladjustment.

The smaller correlations between the M-C SDS and the various MMPI scales would be predicted if one views social desirability as accounting for a fraction of the MMPI variance but not all or most of it. The problem of overlapping meanings is thereby avoided. Thus, it is submitted that the M-C SDS–MMPI correlations more accurately indicate the amount of MMPI scale variance which may be attributed to differences in the need to give socially desirable responses.

It may additionally be pointed out that the M-C SDS and the Edwards SDS differ considerably in the amount of content or item overlap with the various MMPI scales. The present scale contains one exact and four approximate replications of *L* items and one repetition of a *K* scale item. By contrast, the Edwards SDS, it will be recalled, was constructed from a heterogeneous pool of MMPI items and not inconsiderably overlaps with many MMPI validity and clinical scales. The two SDSs have no items in common.

Certain additional aspects of the present findings are worthy of note. Positive correlations are found for both SDSs with the *K* and *L* scales, on which high scores are generally interpreted to indicate "defensiveness" and the attempt by S to cast himself in a favorable light. The M-C SDS correlates much more highly with *L*, however, than does the Edwards SDS. The negative correlations with the *F* scale are accounted for by the interpretation of a high *F* score as an indication of "plus getting." Regarding the clinical and derived scales, in general those MMPI scales on which a high score indicates maladjustment are negatively correlated with the SDSs. In part, the exceptions to this may be explained in terms of the distinction between subtle and obvious scoring on some of the clinical scales. Item subtlety, meaning the relative absence of social desirability implications, would account for the negligible correlations between the Edwards SDS and the *Hy* and *Pa* scales, for example. The fairly substantial correlations between the Edwards SDS and the *Pr* and *Es* scales may again be a function of similarity in general item content. In the judgment of the present authors, about half of the items in the *Es* scale would be classed as "pathological," while roughly a third of the *Pr* items would be so considered.

The positive correlation between the M-C SDS and the *Pa* scale, however, is an interesting possible exception. While this *r* falls short of significance, it might suggest that high SDS scores (implying in the present definition of the construct a high need for the approval of others) tend to be associated with concern or suspicion about the motives of others. Correlations between the Edwards SDS and Welsh's *A* and *R* scales have not, to the writers' knowledge, been previously reported. The Edwards SDS correlated highly, as one would expect, with the *A* scale but not at all with *R* which has a rather heterogeneous item content in terms of pathology. The M-C SDS does better in this case with an *r* of .28. This is in the predicted direction since all of the items on the *R* scale are keyed false. The M-C SDS correlation with the *A* scale is of the same magnitude as the correlation with the MAS and is consistent with expectation. It would appear from the correlations of the SDSs with *A* and MAS that the latter are approximately equivalent measures.

SUMMARY

In this research, an alternative model to Edwards' conception of social desirability was proposed. Basic to the present construct of social desirability is the definition of a population of culturally acceptable and approved behaviors which are, at the same time, relatively unlikely to occur. Test items were drawn from this population in the development of a new social desirability scale, the Marlowe-Crowne Social Desirability Scale. This scale was correlated with 17 MMPI validity, clinical, and derived scales and the results compared with the correlations of the Edwards SDS with these MMPI variables. The very high correlations obtained with the Edwards scale cast doubt on the interpretation of this test as a measure of the influence of social desirability on test responses. The magnitude of the correlations of the new scale with the MMPI was considered to be more in accord with a definition of social desirability in terms of the need of subjects to respond in culturally sanctioned ways.

4-5 Effects of Expectancies for Social Approval on Visual Behavior

JAY S. EFRAN and ANDREW BROUGHTON

To investigate the relationship between expectation for social approval and visual behavior, 33 male college students were required to talk about themselves for 5 min. in front of 2 confederates. Prior to performing this task each S had been given an opportunity to engage in friendly conversation with 1 of his 2 partners but not with the other. The results strongly confirmed the major hypothesis, derived from Rotter's social learning theory, that Ss maintain more eye contact with individuals toward whom they have developed higher expectancies for social approval. In addition, scores on the Marlowe-Crowne Social Desirability scale were found to relate positively to the amount of time Ss spent looking at their partners.

The subjective importance of visual cues in maintaining social communication is illustrated by the compelling, if mundane, example of the automobile driver who finds it difficult to engage in conversation with the individual sitting on his right without taking his eyes off the road to glance at him. Findings recently reported by Exline and his co-workers (Exline, 1963; Exline, Gray, & Schuette, 1965; Exline, Thibaut, Brannon, & Gumpert, 1961; Exline & Winters, 1965a, 1965b) provide experimental evidence that individuals manifest different patterns of eye contact, and that these patterns can be related to a variety of situational and personality factors. The purpose of this study was to extend and clarify these findings by investigating the relationship between an individual's pattern of visual behavior in a triad and his expectation for the receipt of approval from the other members of his group.

The hypotheses tested in this study were derived from Rotter's (1954) social learning theory. Rotter's theory is an expectancy learning theory which postulates that "the probability of a behavior's occurrence is a function of both a preference for certain reinforcements (more broadly, needs) and a subjective probability (expectancy) that these reinforcements can be obtained in a given situation [Conn, 1965, pp. 14–15]." If this theory is to have relevance for the prediction of visual behavior, hypotheses relating these three major theoretical variables (reinforcement value, expectancy, and the psychological situation) to patterns of visual interaction must be specified and tested. The present study deals mainly with the effects of expectancy on visual behavior; the expectancy variable was manipulated while the general nature of the situation and

From *Journal of Personality and Social Psychology*, 1966, **4**, 103–107. Copyright 1966 by the American Psychological Association and reprinted by permission of the authors and the publisher.

the value of the relevant reinforcements were held constant. The task designed for this purpose required a subject to talk about himself in front of two peers. The peers were prohibited from talking to the subject during the task, thus forcing the subject to rely on visual cues for feedback concerning his performance. The situation selected for study thus emphasized the cue-seeking function of the subject's visual behavior.

The major hypothesis of the study can be stated as follows: If visual cues of approval or acceptance are of at least moderate importance to an individual in a given situation (i.e., need value for visual approval is moderate or high), and, if he perceives these cues as potentially available from two social agents, then he will engage in more eye contact with the agent toward whom he has developed higher expectancies for these reinforcements.

A second hypothesis concerns individual differences and follows from the assumption that an individual's reinforcement history creates generalized expectancies which affect his reactions to experimental manipulations. The hypothesis is that individuals with relatively low generalized expectancies for social approval will engage in more avoidant and/or maladaptive behavior—they will look less at the other group members, and will particularly avoid exchanging glances with the group member from which they expect less positive feedback.

METHOD

Subjects

The subjects were 41 male undergraduate students who were fulfilling a requirement of the introductory psychology course. The data from 8 of these subjects were discarded because of errors in stooge performance (3 subjects), prior knowledge about the experiment (1 subject), prior acquaintance with the confederates (1 subject), and suspiciousness concerning the procedures (3 subjects).

Confederates

Nine advanced undergraduates served as confederates.[1] Each of them played both of the stooge roles, and their positions at the conference table were systematically varied. Complexity of scheduling prohibited control over the pairings of stooges, but only two stooges worked together a considerable number of times (five). Two others worked together three times, while nine pairings occurred twice and seven pairings occurred once.

The roles of the stooges were designed to insure that subjects would develop different expectancies for approval from each of his two "partners." This manipulation of expectation was accomplished by engineering a friendly meeting between the subject and one of the stooges just prior to the task proper, and by not allowing the subject

[1] The authors wish to thank the following individuals for participating as confederates: Anthony Biglan, Ronald Cole, Daniel Hungerford, Donald Polzella, Bruce Sales, Donald K. Stein, Martin R. Stolar, Gaylord Thayer, and Robert Tindall.

time to make the acquaintance of the second stooge. This manipulation and the other elements of the procedure will be described in detail below.

Procedure

When the subject arrived for the experiment, he found one of the confederates already seated in the waiting room. This confederate (hereafter referred to as the "approving" stooge) engaged him in friendly conversation by using several standard statements.[2] This confederate also responded warmly to any conversation initiated by the subject. The second confederate (or "neutral" stooge) arrived approximately 4 minutes later. No time was allowed for this second confederate and the subject to meet or converse, for the experimenter immediately entered the waiting room and conducted the three to a room with a one-way mirror. They were asked to choose numbers from 1 to 10. To the subject, it appeared that the seats were assigned at the circular table as a function of the numbers they had chosen, but actually the subject was always placed in the middle position, opposite the one-way glass, and the stooges were seated in predetermined order to the left and right of the subject. In front of each place at the table was a closed looseleaf book marked either A, B, or C. The subject always received the book marked A. The instructions read to the group by the experimenter were as follows:

> We are interested in the impressions people form of each other when they meet in small groups and communicate about themselves. I will ask each of you to spend about five minutes telling the other members of your group something about yourself. There isn't any set topic—you can talk about your goals for the future, what you hope to be doing in five or ten years, your hobbies and interests, the kind of person you might like to marry, or any other things that might give a picture of the kind of person you are. The booklets in front of you, which I'd like you to leave closed until I tell you to open them, contain a brief form which I'll ask you to fill out after you have spoken. So that I don't get in your way, I'll go behind that one-way mirror, where I can monitor the time and give you instructions over our intercom. Incidentally, I'll ask "A" to go first, then "B," and then "C." Do you have any questions? Okay. While you are thinking over what you might like to say about yourself and your plans, I'll go next door. Then I'll let "A" know that we're ready, and you [looking at A] can begin at any time. I'll let you know when your five minutes are up.

The experimenter left the room and A was allowed to speak for 5 minutes. After A had finished his 5-minute presentation, he was asked (over the intercom) to open his looseleaf book and complete

---

[2] The statements used were: "Hi! Are you here for the experiment, too?" "I wonder what this is going to be about?" "I hope it won't be too bad," and "What are you majoring in?"

the questionnaire inside. As soon as he had completed this form, the experimenter returned to the room, announced that the experiment was over, conducted a brief interview with the subject, and then told him about the use of confederates.

During the 5-minute period in which the subject spoke, an observer behind the one-way mirror kept a continuous record of the subject's visual behavior by depressing telegraph keys which activated the pens of an Esterline-Angus multipen recorder. The observer closed one key to indicate when the subject appeared to be looking at Stooge B and closed another key when he appeared to be looking at Stooge C. Data concerning the reliability of this method of recording visual behavior have been presented by Exline (1963), who reports 90% agreement between an individual's record of being looked at and an observer's record of the same events. He also reports a correlation of .98 between the recordings of two independent observers.

Following procedures used by Exline et al. (1965), the stooges were instructed to look at the subject throughout his presentation (although they attempted to avoid maintaining an unchanging fixed stare). The approving stooge was allowed to smile in response to the subject's remarks if it seemed appropriate; the neutral stooge was allowed to look interested in the presentation, but not to smile or nod.

Personality Measures

To test the hypothesis that individual differences in generalized expectancies for social approval are related to visual behavior, two inventories were utilized. Both were administered earlier in the semester during a group testing session. Subjects were unaware of any connection between these questionnaires and the experiment proper. The first inventory was a revised form of the Minnesota Inventory of Social Behavior (MISB; Williamson & Darley, 1937).[3] This questionnaire requires subjects to react on a 5-point scale to statements like, "I am nervous and ill-at-ease with most people." Individuals who receive high scores on this scale can be characterized as admitting a lack of confidence in relationships with other people. Thus, a subject's score on the MISB is hypothesized to correlate negatively with the time he spends looking at the other group members, and positively with the exclusiveness with which he focuses on the approving stooge.

Scores on the Marlowe-Crowne Social Desirability (M-C *SD*; Crowne & Marlowe, 1960) scale were utilized as a second, and somewhat more disguised, measure. It consists of a series of statements which embody cultural mores, characterizing truthfully a small, if existent, proportion of the population. The extent to which an individual checks these statements in the socially desirable direction yields a measure of his tendency to depict himself "in improbably favorable terms [Crowne & Marlowe, 1965, p. 39]." Subjects who receive high

---

[3] Copies of the revised form of the MISB and the postsession questionnaire are available upon request from the senior author.

scores on this scale have been characterized as "approval dependent"; recent research demonstrates that they engage in "avoidant, self-protective behavior in anticipation of social rejection and threat to self-esteem [Crowne & Marlowe, 1964, p. 165; see also Conn, 1965]." In accordance with the second hypothesis, M-C *SD* scale scores are hypothesized to correlate negatively with the time spent looking at others, and positively with the degree of visual focus on the approving stooge.

RESULTS

Effectiveness of the Expectancy Manipulation

A test of the major hypothesis required that subjects develop differential expectations for approval from their two partners. The responses of subjects to a postsession questionnaire provided evidence that the manipulation designed to establish these differential expectations was successful. In answer to the forced-choice question "If you had to take a guess at this point, which subject (B or C) would you say likes you better?" all subjects chose the stooge who played the approving role. Another forced-choice item posed the question somewhat differently: "If you were to talk with just one person, instead of two, would you have felt more comfortable talking with subject B or with subject C?" Again, all subjects indicated a preference for the approving stooge. A more refined index of the same preference was obtained by asking subjects to indicate on two 25-point rating scales how confident they were that each of their partners liked them. The mean difference between ratings of the approving and neutral stooges was 5.12 ($SD = 3.71$), which was significant ($t = 7.80$, $p < .001$).

Visual Behavior Measures

The analysis of visual behavior was based on recordings made by the observer during the first 4 minutes of each subject's 5-minute presentation. (The last minute of these presentations was not analyzed because some subjects ran out of things to say before the full time period had elapsed.) Two measures of visual behavior were derived from these records: the percentage of presentation time spent looking at the stooges, and the percentage of this "looking time" which was directed toward the approving stooge. The means and standard deviations for these measures appear in Table 1. The two measures appear to be independent ($r = -.08$). Table 1 reveals that the subjects in this study spent 15.6% of their time looking at their partners. Exline and Winters (1965a) have reported an almost identical figure (16%) for male college students engaged in a similar task —telling stories to Thematic Apperception Test cards in front of two examiners. Higher figures have been reported for female students and for other kinds of situations (Exline, 1963; Exline et al., 1965; Exline et al., 1961; Exline & Winters, 1965a, 1965b).

Table 1   Means, Standard Deviations, and Intercorrelations for Visual Behavior and Personality Measures
$$(N = 33)$$

| | | | CORRELATION | | |
MEASURE	M	SD	LT	AT	MISB
Visual behavior					
Time spent looking at partners (LT)[a]	15.6	12.5			
Degree of focus on the approving stooge (AT)[b]	71.2	24.0	−.08		
Personality scales					
MISB	54.1	10.1	.21	−.02	
M-C SD	14.3	5.2	.45*	−.04	−.22

[a] Expressed as a percentage of presentation time.
[b] The percentage of LT spent looking at the approving stooge.
* $p < .01$.

Expectancy for Approval and Visual Behavior

The major hypothesis—that expectations for social approval influence eye-contact pattern—was strongly confirmed. Twenty-seven of the 33 subjects spent more time looking at the approving stooge, with whom they had prior acquaintance and toward them they had developed higher expectations for approval. Rather than spending an equal amount of time looking at the two stooges (chance expectation), the subjects spent 71% of their looking time exchanging glances with the approving stooge ($t = 4.95$, $df = 31$, $p < .001$).

Personality Differences

Intercorrelations of visual behavior and personality measures are presented in Table 1. Only one is significant: scores on the M-C *SD* scale are positively related to the percentage of presentation time subjects spend looking at their partners ($r = .45$, $p < .01$). This finding, that subjects receiving higher scores on the M-C *SD* scale look *more* at their partners, is contrary to the hypothesized negative relationship between these variables. Further, the hypothesized relationship between M-C *SD* scores and the *degree* of focus on the approving stooge was not confirmed.

DISCUSSION

This study offers clear support for the hypothesis that expectations influence visual behavior. More specifically, it shows that when an individual who places importance on the receipt of visual cues of approval talks in front of two peers, he spends more time looking at the peer toward whom he has developed higher expectations for reward. The generality of this finding is enhanced by the fact that a variety of individuals with different personality characteristics were used as stooges. (It should be noted, however, that the results are relevant only to an individual's looking behavior *while speaking*.)

The observers in the present study noted that many subjects showed a strong visual preference for the approving stooge from the start of their presentation, and that this preference did not diminish appreciably during the 4-minute period. This observation was confirmed by a minute-by-minute analysis of the eye-contact data, which revealed no significant differences in the degree of focus on the approving stooge for any of the individual time periods. The implication of this finding is that the first component of the experimental manipulation (i.e., the pretask meeting between stooge and subject) was effective in inducing differential expectations. The second component of the manipulation (i.e., the nodding and smiling of the approving stooge) may have played a role in maintaining the expectation for approval, but it did not increase the level of focus on the approving stooge. This finding is consonant with Exline and Winters' (1965a) report that in an "interview" study the effect of social reinforcers, such as nods and smiles, was minimal.

The individual difference hypothesis was not supported by the data. Subjects with lower expectancies for social approval did not spend less time looking at their partners nor did they focus more exclusively on the approving stooge. In fact, contrary to the first part of the hypothesis, subjects with high M-C *SD* scale scores looked more at their peers. These subjects, who previous research characterizes as approval dependent and defensive, reacted in this situation by expending more than the average amount of time "soaking in" what visual cues of approval and reassurance were available. The failure to confirm the *second* portion of the hypothesis (that subjects with high M-C *SD* scale scores would more scrupulousy avoid looking at the neutral stooge) may have been due to the potency of the experimental manipulation which might have restricted the range of individual variation on this variable.

The revised MISB was used in this study because of its face validity for the measurement of lack of confidence in social situations; unlike the M-C *SD* scale there is no body of validating behavioral data for this instrument. The failure to find a relationship between scores on this scale and "looking time" (paralleling the relationship found with the M-C *SD* scale) may be due to erroneous assumptions concerning the meaning of the paper-and-pencil performances of the subjects. The lack of relationship between overt behavior and paper-and-pencil test content scores has been frequently noted in the literature and discussed by a number of authors (e.g., Crowne & Marlowe, 1965). It is also possible that the M-C *SD* scale identifies only a particular type of individual from among the larger group of individuals who lack confidence in social situations, and that this approval-dependent subgroup reacts by seeking more eye contact where approval cues are potentially available. Other reaction patterns (such as total visual avoidance) are possible, and the MISB may identify a more heterogeneous group of subjects who nevertheless share a willingness to admit lack of confidence in social situations.

Further work will be directed toward exploring the effects of expectations in other kinds of situations, and toward investigating the effects of the reinforcement value variable. Additionally, since expectation can be shown to relate to visual behavior, it may be possible to utilize measures of eye contact as an index of expectation in studies where expectancy is the unknown rather than the manipulated variable.

4-6	*Generalized Expectancies for Internal Versus External Control of Reinforcement*
	JULIAN B. ROTTER[1]

The effects of reward or reinforcement on preceding behavior depend in part on whether the person perceives the reward as contingent on his own behavior or independent of it. Acquisition and performance differ in situations perceived as determined by skill versus chance. Persons may also differ in generalized expectancies for internal versus external control of reinforcement. This report summarizes several experiments which define group differences in behavior when Ss perceive reinforcement as contingent on their behavior versus chance or experimenter control. The report also describes the development of tests of individual differences in a generalized belief in internal-external control and provides reliability, discriminant validity and normative data for 1 test, along with a description of the results of several studies of construct validity.

The role of reinforcement, reward, or gratification is universally recognized by students of human nature as a crucial one in the acquisition and performance of skills and knowledge. However, an event regarded by some

[1] Most of the work reported by the author was completed at the Ohio State University. The program of research was supported by a 4-year grant from the United States Air Force under Contract No. AF 49(638-741), monitored by the Air Force Office of Scientific Research, Office of Aerospace Research. Secretarial assistance for writing this report was provided by the University of Connecticut Research Foundation.

From *Psychological Monographs*, 1966, 80, No. 1 (Whole No. 609). Copyright 1966 by the American Psychological Association and reprinted by permission of the author and the publisher.

persons as a reward or reinforcement may be differently perceived and reacted to by others. One of the determinants of this reaction is the degree to which the individual perceives that the reward follows from, or is contingent upon, his own behavior or attributes versus the degree to which he feels the reward is controlled by forces outside of himself and may occur independently of his own actions. The effect of a reinforcement following some behavior on the part of a human subject, in other words, is not a simple stamping-in process but depends upon whether or not the person perceives a causal relationship between his own behavior and the reward. A perception of causal relationship need not be all or none but can vary in degree. When a reinforcement is perceived by the subject as following some action of his own but not being entirely contingent upon his action, then, in our culture, it is typically perceived as the result of luck, chance, fate, as under the control of powerful others, or as unpredictable because of the great complexity of the forces surrounding him. When the event is interpreted in this way by an individual, we have labeled this a belief in *external control*. If the person perceives that the event is contingent upon his own behavior or his own relatively permanent characteristics, we have termed this a belief in *internal control*.

It is hypothesized that this variable is of major significance in understanding the nature of learning processes in different kinds of learning situations and also that consistent individual differences exist among individuals in the degree to which they are likely to attribute personal control to reward in the same situation. This report is concerned with reviewing a number of studies which have been made to test both hypotheses; to present some heretofore unpublished experimental results; and to present in detail new data regarding the development, reliability, and validity of one measure of individual differences in a generalized belief for internal versus external control of reinforcement.

Theoretical Background

Social learning theory (Rotter; 1954, 1955, 1960b) provides the general theoretical background for this conception of the nature and effects of reinforcement. In social learning theory, a reinforcement acts to strengthen an *expectancy* that a particular behavior or event will be followed by that reinforcement in the future. Once an expectancy for such a behavior-reinforcement sequence is built up the failure of the reinforcement to occur will reduce or extinguish the expectancy. As an infant develops and acquires more experience he differentiates events which are causally related to preceding events and those which are not. It follows as a general hypothesis that when the reinforcement is seen as not contingent upon the subject's own behavior that its occurrence will not increase an expectancy as much as when it is seen as contingent. Conversely, its nonoccurrence will not reduce an expectancy so much as when it is seen as contingent. It seems likely that, depending upon the individual's history of reinforcement, individuals would differ in the degree to which they attributed reinforcements to their own actions.

Expectancies generalize from a specific situation to a series of situations which are perceived as related or similar. Consequently, a generalized expectancy for a class of related events has functional properties and makes up one of the important classes of variables in personality description. Harlow's (1949) concept of high-level learning skills seems similar to this notion that individuals differ in learned generalized expectancies involving relationships between a wide variety of behaviors and their possible outcomes. A generalized attitude, belief, or expectancy regarding the nature of the causal relationship between one's own behavior and its consequences might affect a variety of behavioral choices in a broad band of life situations. Such generalized expectancies in combination with specific expectancies act to determine choice behavior along with the value of potential reinforcements. These generalized expectancies will result in characteristic differences in behavior in a situation culturally categorized as chance determined versus skill determined, and they may act to produce individual differences within a specific condition.

Specific expectancies regarding the causal nature of behavior-outcome sequences in different situations would also affect behavior choice. From social learning theory one would anticipate that the more clearly and uniformly a situation is labeled as skill or luck determined, in a given culture, the lesser the role such a generalized expectancy would play in determining individual differences in behavior.

Related Conceptions

In learning theory it has been recognized that differences in subject behavior are related to task differences along a dimension of skill and chance. Goodnow and Postman (1955) and Goodnow and Pettigrew (1955), for example, present data to show that probabilistic learning theory is not applicable where the subject feels that the occurrence of the reinforcement is lawful. Wyckoff and Sidowsky (1955) similarly felt that their subjects' behavior changed when they no longer felt that the task was a "guessing" problem. Cohen (1960) has extensively studied differences in subjects' behavior or strategy in choice and skill games noting the tendency for the "gambler's fallacy" to appear in chance games . . . an effect opposite to the usual effect of reinforcement. A somewhat different approach to chance and skill task differences is assumed by Feather (1959a) who felt that motivation was lessened in chance tasks as compared to skill tasks. In general, however, a *theoretically based, systematic study* of chance and skill differences in acquisition and performance has not been made prior to the series of studies to be reported here.

The literature of personality theory does contain discussions of a number of variables which may have some relationship to the one of major concern in this paper. The significance of the belief in fate, chance, or luck has been discussed by various social scientists over a long period of time. Most of their concern, however, has been with differences among groups or societies rather than individuals. Typical of an early discussion of this kind is that of Veblen (1899), who felt that a belief in luck or chance represented a barbarian approach to life and was generally characteristic of an inefficient society. Although Veblen was not concerned with individual differences, his discussion implied that a belief in chance or luck as a solution to one's problems was characterized by less productivity and, consequently, bears some parallel to the hypothesis that a belief in external control of reinforcements is related to a general passivity. Veblen also stated, "In its simple form the belief in luck is this instinctive sense of an unscrutable, teleological propensity in objects and situations." In other words, Veblen states that the belief in luck is related to or similar to a general belief in fate.

More recently, Merton (1946) has discussed the belief in luck more or less as a defense behavior, as an attempt "to serve the psychological function of enabling people to preserve their self esteem in the face of failure." He states it "may also in some individuals act to curtail sustained endeavor," or, in other words, he too suggests a relationship between passivity and the belief in chance or luck.

The concept of alienation which has played an important role in sociological theory for many years does seem related at a group level to the variable of internal-external control. The alienated individual feels unable to control his own destiny. He is a small cog in a big machine and at the mercy of forces too strong or too vague to control. Marx, Weber, and Durkheim placed great importance on this concept, and more recently Merton (1949) has stressed its importance in the study of asocial behavior. Seeman (1959) has linked the concept of alienation as it refers to *powerlessness*, to internal-external control as a psychological variable. Some sociologists (Nettler, 1957; Srole, 1956) have developed a crude individual measure of alienation.

In psychology, White (1959) in discussing an alternative to drive reduction has noted how the work of many authors has converged on a belief that it is characteristic of all species to explore and to attempt to master the environment. He has labeled this concept *competence*. While White was not specifically interested in individual differences he has noted that such a motive or drive is not explained by primary drive and although perhaps not as strong as some primary drives it is moderate in strength and persistence. Angyal (1941) has also noted the significance of the organism's motivation towards *autonomy*, or the active mastery of the environment.

There are a number of other psychological variables which appear to bear some relationship to the concept under investigation. Some of these are undoubtedly related, but, for others, it is possible that the relationship is more apparent than real.

Perhaps one of the major conceptions which bears some relationship to the belief in internal versus external control of reinforcements is that of need for achievement. The work of McClelland, Atkinson, Clark, and Lowell (1953) and of Atkinson (1958) and their colleagues working primarily with adults, and Crandall (1963) with children, suggests that people who are high on the need for achievement, in all probability, have some belief in their own ability or skill to determine the outcome of their efforts. The relationship is probably not linear, however, since a person high on motivation for achievement might not be equally high on a belief in internal control of reinforcement, and there may be many with a low need for achievement who still believe that their own behavior determines the kinds of reinforcements they obtain.

Another variable which may bear some genuine relationship to the variable of internal versus external control of reinforcement is the concept of "field determined" versus "body oriented." The work of Witkin, Lewis, Hertzman, Machover, Meissner, and Wapner (1954) suggests that people can be ordered on a continuum, in some perception experiments, describing whether they derive most of their cues from the field or from internal sources. A study by Linton (1955) suggests that people who are "field oriented" or "field dependent" tend to be more conforming. However, unpublished data of the author indicate no relationship between an individual measure of internal-external control and the Gottschalk Figures Test, a measure frequently used as an operation for "field determined."

Perhaps less clear is the relationship of internal versus external control of reinforcement to the notion of "ego control." Although the concept of ego control is not always defined similarly, it seems to contain the ideas of confidence and ability to deal with reality. While it seems likely that the individuals at both extremes of the internal versus external control of reinforcement dimension are essentially unrealistic, it is not as likely that the people toward the middle of the distribution are less confident. We do have indications, however, that the people at either extreme of the reinforcement dimensions are likely to be maladjusted by most definitions, and, to the extent that ego control is another type of definition of maladjustment, it would bear some curvilinear relationship to the variable we are concerned with here.

Similar to the conception of Witkin et al. is that of Riesman (1954), who has attempted to describe an apparently comparable distinction. Riesman's conception is based on the degree to which people are controlled by internal goals, desires, etc. versus the degree to which they are controlled by external forces, in particular social forces or conformity forces. Although this variable may bear some relationship to the one under investigation, it should be made clear that the apparent relationship is not as logical as it appears. Riesman has been concerned with whether the individual is controlled from within or from without. We are concerned, however, not with this variable at all but only with the question of whether or not an individual believes that his own behavior, skills, or internal dispositions determine what reinforcements he receives. While the conformist (the opportunist, in particular) who is actively trying to learn and adjust to the rules of the society he lives in is at one end of Riesman's continuum, he is likely to be in the middle of the continuum with which we are concerned.

Finally, a word should be said about the general concept of causality. This psychological dimension is one which has been neglected for some time, although it is one of the strong interests of Piaget (1930), who studied how the notion of causality developed in children. Pepitone (1958) has recently discussed several aspects of the attribution of causality in social interactions. However, individual differences in how causality is assumed to relate events has not been a subject of investigation. It would seem that some relationship would exist between how the individual views the world from the point of view of internal versus external control of reinforcement and his other modes of perception of causal relationships.

STUDIES OF COMPLEX LEARNING

The notion that individuals build up generalized expectancies for internal-external control appears to have clear implications for problems of acquisition and performance. If a human can deal with future events with the use of verbal symbols and can perceive an event as following a preceding behavior of his own, then the strength of that connection will depend at least in part on whether or not he feels there is a causal or invariable relationship between his behavior and the event. Once a person has established a concept of randomness or chance the effects of reinforcement will vary depending upon what relationship he assigns to the behavior-reinforcement sequence.

A person who is looking for an unusual brand of tobacco and is finally able to find it will return to the same place where he was reinforced before when he needs tobacco again. However, an individual who needs money and finds a five dollar bill in the street is not likely to return to that spot to look for a five dollar bill when he needs money. A behavior of looking on the ground may be strengthened to some degree in the latter case. However, the individual is selective in what aspects of his behavior are repeated or strengthened and what aspects are not, depending upon his own perception of the nature or causality of the relationship between the reinforcement and the preceding behavior.

In its simplest form, our basic hypothesis is that if a person perceives a reinforcement as contingent upon his own behavior, then the occurrence of either a positive or negative reinforcement will strengthen or weaken potential for that behavior to recur in the same or similar situation. If he sees the reinforcement as being outside his own control or not contingent, that is depending upon chance, fate, powerful others, or unpredictable, then the preceding behavior is less likely to be strengthened or weakened. Not only will there be a difference of degree but also a difference, in some instances, in the nature of the function as the result of a series of trials. It is evident that if this analysis is correct then different kinds of learning paradigms or situations are going to produce different kinds of learning functions. A learning situation such as that in which the experimenter arbitrarily determines the right response for whether or not food is given, regardless of the behavior of the subject, will produce a different kind of learning than one where the subject believes his behavior determines whether or not the reinforcement will occur. In other words, learning under *skill* conditions is different from learning under *chance* conditions.

To test this hypothesis a series of studies was undertaken comparing verbal expectancies for future reinforcement under conditions of chance and skill learning. In this group of studies it has been necessary in order to compare skill and chance learning tasks directly to provide a similar sequence of reinforcement in both cases which was controlled by the experimenter without the subject's knowledge of such control. Two strategies are used. The first is to provide a relatively ambiguous task under two conditions, one in which the subject is *instructed* that it is skill determined. Obviously in these studies we are dealing with a continuum in which in one situation the task is likely to be perceived as relatively more skill determined. The second strategy is to present different tasks which are also surreptitiously controlled by the experimenter and which are defined as skill and chance essentially through previous cultural experience. For example, although they have certain problems of comparability, dice throwing is generally recognized as a chance task, while solving arithmetic problems and throwing darts are generally recognized as skill tasks.

The first of these studies was undertaken by Phares (1957). Phares used color matching as an ambiguous task and instructed half of the subjects that the task was so difficult as to be a matter of luck and the other half of his subjects that success was a matter of skill and that previous research had shown that some people were very good at the task. The subjects matched samples to finely graded standards. He used a second task of matching lines of slightly varying lengths to standards placed on cards at different angles. For both tasks a fixed order of partial reinforcement (right or wrong) was used and the measure of expectancy was the number of chips a subject would bet on his probability of being correct on the succeeding trial.

Phares found, as hypothesized, that the increments and decrements following success and failure, respectively, were significantly greater under skill instructions than under chance instructions. Reinforcements under skill conditions had a greater effect on raising or lowering expectancies for future reinforcements. He also found that subjects shifted or changed their expectancies more often under skill conditions. (Another measure of the same data described above.) Finally he showed a strong trend toward unusual shifts in expectancies, that is, up after failure or down after success (the gambler's fallacy) under chance conditions. The significance of this last finding was marginal ($p = .07$, two-tailed test).

This study was followed by one by James and Rotter (1958). In this study the emphasis was on the extinction of verbal expectancies. Under conditions of partial and 100% reinforcement an extrasensory perception (ESP) type of task was used with experimenter control, and the exact same sequence of 50% partial reinforcement was given to two groups of subjects (two other groups had 100% reinforcement) for 10 training trials. Two groups were told that guessing in the task had been shown by scientists to be entirely a matter of luck, and two groups were told that there was evidence that some people are considerably skilled at the task. While the groups did not differ significantly at the end of the training trials, the chance and skill groups did differ significantly in the number of trials to extinction. Extinction was defined as stating an expectancy of 1 or 0 on a scale of 10 for three consecutive trials.

The interesting thing about the results of this investigation was that the usual findings of superiority of partial over 100% reinforcement in trials to extinction was true only of the group with chance instructions, but under skill conditions the mean number of trials to extinction for 100% reinforcement was longer (22.9) than under 50% reinforcement (19.8). Trials to extinction under partial reinforcement were significantly longer for chance than for skill instructions, and trials to extinction for 100% reinforcement were significantly longer for skill than for chance instructions. The findings were interpreted to indicate that under chance conditions the extinction series was interpreted as a change in the situation, a disappearance of previous lucky hits in the 100% reinforcement condition but not in the 50% reinforcement conditions. For the subjects with skill instructions, the greater the previous reinforcement the longer it took the subject to accept the fact that he was not able to do the task successfully.

A further check on these studies was made by Rotter, Liverant, and Crowne (1961), who studied the growth and extinction of expectancies in chance-controlled and skilled tasks. This study involved using two tasks, one the ESP task referred to above and, the second, a motor task presumably involving steadiness which would typically be perceived as a skill task. Again in both tasks similar sequences of reinforcement were used. In this case instructions were identical, the difference in the cultural perception of the tasks being the experimental variable. This study utilized eight groups, four chance and four skill with 25%, 50%, 75%, and 100% reinforcement over eight training trials followed by an extinction series. This study confirmed the previous findings of both Phares and James and Rotter. During the training trials, subjects (except for 100% reinforcement groups) showed greater increments or decrements following success and failure respectively under skill conditions than under chance conditions. Major differences in extinction were obtained independently of the expectancy levels at the end of the training trial. In this study, extinction curves for the two groups cross over completely, so that all of the findings of the James and Rotter studies were replicated, but, in addition, 100% reinforcement took significantly longer to extinguish than 50% reinforcement in the skill task. Differences between the groups were smaller at the 25% and 75% reinforcement schedules than at 50% or 100%. The latter findings were interpreted as suggesting that at the 25% and the 75% levels the chance task was being rewarded or reinforced more often or less than could be accounted for by chance alone. The frequency of reinforcement itself may tend to make the task appear more like a skill task. In the case of 100% chance reinforcement, however, the abrupt change from continuous positive reinforcement to continuous negative reinforcement suggests a change in the nature of the situation.

The question could arise as to whether or not differences in extinction patterns would be the same with a behavior criterion other than verbalized expectancies. To test this, Holden and Rotter (1962) again used the ESP task instructing one group of subjects that it was a skill task and the other group that it was determined entirely by luck. Subjects were given two dollars in nickels and told they could bet a nickel on each trial on whether or not they would succeed until they wished to discontinue and keep the remaining money or until they ran out of nickels. Three groups all given

50% partial reinforcement were used, one with skill instructions, one with chance instructions, and one with ambiguous instructions. Results showed a clear difference, with the subjects given chance instructions and those who were not told it was either a chance or a skill task having significantly more trials to extinction (almost twice as many) than the skill group. Extinction was defined as voluntarily quitting the experiment.

An unpublished dissertation by Bennion (1961) using the same tasks as in the Rotter, Liverant, and Crowne study, rather than instructions to produce the skill and chance difference, examined a partial reinforcement sequence that was predominantly positive but in which reported scores differed in variability to two groups. Overall mean score and frequency of success and failure as defined by the experimenter were controlled. Bennion hypothesized that greater variability of scores either under chance or skill conditions would produce results similar to that of the difference between the chance and skill conditions. There would be greater responsiveness in changes in expectancy to success and failure under the less variable conditions. He found support for this hypothesis as well as replicating the difference in responsiveness under chance and skill conditions obtained by Phares and by Rotter, Liverant, and Crowne in previous studies.

In another unpublished dissertation, James (1957) studied some of the same variables and in addition the generalization of expectancies and the "spontaneous recovery" of expectancies. He used both a line-matching and an angle-matching task. Two groups, one with chance and one with skill instructions, were given 75% reinforcement for a sequence of eight trials and then were tested for generalizations of expectancies by having one trial on the new second task. Two other groups were given the same 75% reinforced eight training trials followed by a series of extinction trials, then given a 5-minute rest and given two additional trials on the same task. These latter groups were examined for "spontaneous recovery." James' findings again replicated the differences between chance and skill groups in the growth of acquisition of expectancies. He found, as hypothesized, significantly greater generalization of expectancies from one task to another under skill instructions than under chance instructions. He also found more "spontaneous recovery" under skill instructions, but the difference in this case only approached significance.

Bennion's study of the effect of variability in scores on a task can be interpreted as defining one of the conditions which make for the perception that the task is in fact skill or chance determined. Other conditions affecting such a perception were studied by Blackman (1962). Blackman used the well-replicated finding that under chance conditions extinction in a 50% reinforcement sequence is likely to be considerably longer than under skill conditions. In a counterbalanced design he used numerous sequences of presumably random appearing lights, controlling for the percentage of reinforcement. The task was one of attempting to predict whether a red or a green light would appear on the following trial. He varied the length of sequences in which the same light would appear consecutively, and he varied the degree of patterning from presumably purely random through an easy pattern to a complicated pattern. Extinction began when the red light ceased to go on, and the measure of extinction was based upon the elimination of subject predictions of red responses. He found, as he hypothesized, that the length of sequences significantly affected the number of red responses in extinction and the expectancies associated with them. The longest sequences extinguished more quickly. Similarly, the easy but not the complicated pattern, which was apparently not perceived, also resulted in quicker extinction. These results are interpreted to indicate that longer sequences and recognizable patterns suggest to the subject that there is not a random pattern but an experimenter-controlled one. Consequently, when extinction begins and the red light no longer appears the subject interprets the situation as one in which the experimenter has changed the sequence of lights. If, however, the subject interprets the original sequence as random, he will persist much longer before extinguishing on anticipation that the red light will appear again.

Implications from the studies of Rotter, Liverant, and Crowne (1961), Bennion (1961), and Blackman (1962) can be summarized. Subjects are more likely to see a sequence of reinforcement as *not* being chance controlled when the percentage of reinforcement significantly deviates from a 50–50 percentage in a right-wrong situation, when the sequence of reinforcements appears to have a pattern, when unusually long sequences of one of two alternative events occur, and when variability of performance is minimal in a task allowing for scoring along a continuum.

A somewhat different variable was investigated by Phares (1962), who studied perceptual thresholds for shock-associated stimuli in chance-controlled versus skill situations. Phares used a tachistoscopic exposure of nonsense syllables, some of the stimuli being accompanied by shock. The skill group was told that the shock could be escaped by pressing the correct button which could be learned. The chance group was instructed that they could press any of the sequence of buttons and this may or may not avoid the shock depending upon chance. The skill group was run first and then the chance groups. In this way the experimenter could control the number of shocks, so that he was able to match the chance group with the skill group in the total number of shocks obtained during the 10 training trials. Recognition thresholds for the syllables were taken before and after the training. He found, as hypothesized, that the recognition thresholds dropped significantly more in the skill-instructed than in the chance-instructed groups although they had had the same number of shocks on the same trials and for the same nonsense syllables. Phares concluded that subjects who feel they have control of the situation are likely to exhibit perceptual behavior that will better enable them to cope with potentially threatening situations than subjects who feel chance or other noncontrollable forces determine whether or not their behavior will be successful.

Investigations of differences in behavior in skill and chance situations provide relatively clear-cut findings. When a subject perceives the task as controlled by the experimenter, chance, or random conditions, past experience is relied upon less. Consequently, it may be said that he learns less, and under such conditions, he may indeed learn the wrong things and develop a pattern of behavior which Skinner has referred to as "superstitious." These studies strongly imply that the interpretation of investigations of acquisition and performance must be made in light of the position on the continuum of complete chance control to complete skill control at which the particular task falls. Differences in learning are not merely a matter of degree but also of nature or kind as indicated by the dramatic reversal of extinction curves as demonstrated by Rotter, Liverant, and Crowne (1961). Perhaps more important are the implications for the learning theory favored by psychologists in general. Such theory is often based upon experimental paradigms which involve experimenter control. That is, they use tasks where the experimenter decides in a more or less arbitrary fashion when he will reinforce or where he will reinforce but not ones where the subject feels that his own performance determines primarily whether or not he will be successful at the task. However, many, if not the majority of learning situations of humans in everyday life situations, are in fact perceived as skill controlled. The direct application of theories of learning based upon experimenter controlled tasks to such learning is in grave doubt.

Although there is no direct proof that "experimenter control" is equivalent to "chance control," it would seem logical that the subject perceiving no regularity or predictability to the reinforcement would regard it similarly. This conclusion is supported by the earlier mentioned Blackman (1962) experiment . . . a typical "experimenter control" paradigm . . . where he obtained longer extinction times when the training sequence of partially reinforced red and green lights lacked discernible patterns. It is also supported by the fact that tasks with chance instructions produce the same kind of differences between 100% and 50% partial reinforcement in extinction rates as do the typical experimenter control experiments.

INTERNAL VERSUS EXTERNAL CONTROL AS A PERSONALITY VARIABLE

Development of Measures of Internal-External Control

The first attempt to measure individual differences in a generalized expectancy or belief in external control as a psychological variable was begun by Phares (1957) in his study of chance and skill effects on expectancies for reinforcement. Phares developed a Likert-type scale with 13 items stated as external attitudes and 13 as internal attitudes. The scale was developed on a priori grounds, and he found some suggestive evidence with his first crude attempt at measuring individual differences that prediction of behavior within a task situation was possible. In particular, he found that the items stated in an external direction gave low predictions, approaching statistical significance, that individuals with external attitudes would behave in a similar fashion as did all subjects when placed in a chance situation versus a skill situation. That is, they tended to show more unusual shifts, smaller magnitude of increments and decrements, and a lower frequency of shifts of expectancy in any case than did subjects who scored low on these 13 items.

Phares' work was followed by James' (1957) dissertation, previously referred to. James revised Phares' test still using a Likert format and wrote 26 items plus filler items based on the items which appeared to be most successful in the Phares study. He similarly hypothesized that within each of his groups, regardless of chance or skill instructions, those individuals who scored toward the external end of the continuum would behave in each group in the same way as the difference between the chance group and the skill group for all subjects. James was able to find low but significant correlations between his test and behavior in the task situation. External subjects had smaller increments and decrements following success and failure, generalized less from one task to another, and recovered less following the period of extinction. They also tended to produce more unusual shifts (up after failure and down after success) in expectancy.

The James-Phares scale has been used in some research involving correlates of individual differences in a generalized expectancy for internal-external control. However, the late Shephard Liverant in association with J. B. Rotter and M. Seeman undertook to broaden the test; develop subscales for different areas such as achievement, affection, and general social and political attitudes; and control for social desirability by the construction of a new forced-choice questionnaire. The earliest version of this scale included a hundred forced-choice items, each one comparing an external belief with an internal belief. The scale was item analyzed and factor analyzed and reduced to a 60-item scale by Liverant on the basis of internal consistency criteria.

Item analysis of the 60-item scale indicated that the subscales were not generating separate predictions. Achievement items tended to correlate highly with social desirability, and some subscales correlated with other scales at approximately the same level as their internal consistency. On this basis, items to measure more specific subareas of internal-external control were abandoned.

Data were collected for a large group of subjects to provide item correlations with the Marlowe-Crowne Social Desirability Scale (Crowne & Marlowe, 1964). The overall correlation of the scale with the Social Desirability scale for different samples ranged from .35 to .40 which was deemed to be too high. Reduction and purification of the 60-item scale was undertaken by S. Liverant, J. B. Rotter, and D. Crowne. Validity data from two studies were used along with internal consistency data. Item validity for most of the items was available from a study of Seeman and Evans on tuberculosis patients who had evidenced greater self-effort towards recovery versus those who were more passive. Item validity for the prediction of individual differences in trials to extinction in the previously cited study of Rotter, Liverant, and Crowne (1961) was also available. In this final revision, wording of some items was changed to make the items appropriate for noncollege adults and upper level high school students.

By eliminating those items which either had a high correlation with the Marlowe-Crowne Social Desirability Scale, a proportional split so that one of the two alternatives was endorsed more than 85% of the time, nonsignificant relationship with other items, or a correlation approaching zero with both validation criteria, the scale was reduced to 23 items. The final version of the scale, the one on which most of the subsequent data to be reported are based, is a 29-item, forced-choice test including 6 filler items intended to make somewhat more ambiguous the purpose of the test. This measure will be referred to in the remainder of this article as the I-E scale.

The I-E scale is presented in Table 1. Instructions for administration are presented in Appendix A. Biserial item correlations with total score *with that item removed* are given for 200 males, 200 females, and the

Table 1   The I-E Scale with Correlations of Each Item with Total Score, Excluding that Item

	BISERIAL ITEM CORRELATIONS		
ITEM	*200 M*	*200 F*	*400 M + F*
1.a. Children get into trouble because their parents punish them too much. b. The trouble with most children now-adays is that their parents are too easy with them.		(Filler)	
2.a. Many of the unhappy things in people's lives are partly due to bad luck. b. People's misfortunes result from the mistakes they make.	.265	.250	.260
3.a. One of the major reasons why we have wars is because people don't take enough interest in politics. b. There will always be wars, no matter how hard people try to prevent them.	.214	.147	.182
4.a. In the long run people get the respect they deserve in this world. b. Unfortunately, an individual's worth often passes unrecognized no matter how hard he tries. as well for me as making a decision to take a definite course of action.	.238	.344	.289
10.a. In the case of the well prepared student there is rarely if ever such a thing as an unfair test. b. Many times exam questions tend to be so unrelated to course work that studying is really useless.	.227	.252	.238

Table 1   Continued

ITEM	BISERIAL ITEM CORRELATIONS		
	200 M	200 F	400 M + F
11.a. Becoming a success is a matter of hard work, luck has little or nothing to do with it.			
b. Getting a good job depends mainly on being in the right place at the right time.	.391	.215	.301
12.a. The average citizen can have an influence in government decisions.			
b. This world is run by the few people in power, and there is not much the little guy can do about it.	.313	.222	.265
5.a. The idea that teachers are unfair to students is nonsense.			
b. Most students don't realize the extent to which their grades are influenced by accidental happenings.	.230	.131	.179
6.a. Without the right breaks one cannot be an effective leader.	.345	.299	.319
b. Capable people who fail to become leaders have not taken advantage of their opportunities.			
7.a. No matter how hard you try some people just don't like you.	.200	.262	.229
b. People who can't get others to like them don't understand how to get along with others.			
8.a. Heredity plays the major role in determining one's personality.		(Filler)	
b. It is one's experiences in life which determine what they're like.			
9.a. I have often found that what is going to happen will happen.	.152	.172	.164
b. Trusting to fate has never turned out			
13.a. When I make plans, I am almost certain that I can make them work.			
b. It is not always wise to plan too far ahead because many things turn out to be a matter of good or bad fortune anyhow.	.252	.285	.271

Table 1 Continued

ITEM	BISERIAL ITEM CORRELATIONS		
	200 M	*200 F*	*400 M + F*
14.a. There are certain people who are just no good.		(Filler)	
b. There is some good in everybody.			
15.a. In my case getting what I want has little or nothing to do with luck.			
b. Many times we might just as well decide what to do by flipping a coin.	.369	.209	.288
16.a. Who gets to be the boss often depends on who was lucky enough to be in the right place first.	.295	.318	.307
b. Getting people to do the right thing depends upon ability, luck has little or nothing to do with it.			
17.a. As far as world affairs are concerned, most of us are the victims of forces we can neither understand, nor control.	.313	.407	.357
b. By taking an active part in political and social affairs the people can control world events.			
18.a. Most people don't realize the extent to which their lives are controlled by accidental happenings.	.258	.362	.310
b. There really is no such thing as "luck."			
19.a. One should always be willing to admit mistakes.		(Filler)	
b. It is usually best to cover up one's mistakes.			
20.a. It is hard to know whether or not a person really likes you.	.255	.307	.271
b. How many friends you have depends upon how nice a person you are.			
21.a. In the long run the bad things that happen to us are balanced by the good ones.	.108	.197	.152
b. Most misfortunes are the result of lack of ability, ignorance, laziness, or all three.			
22.a. With enough effort we can wipe out			

Table 1   Continued

ITEM	BISERIAL ITEM CORRELATIONS		
	200 M	200 F	400 M + F
political corruption.			
b. It is difficult for people to have much control over the things politicians do in office.	.226	.224	.227
23.a. Sometimes I can't understand how teachers arrive at the grades they give.	.275	.248	.255
b. There is a direct connection between how hard I study and the grades I get.			
24.a. A good leader expects people to decide for themselves what they should do.		(Filler)	
b. A good leader makes it clear to everybody what their jobs are.			
25.a. Many times I feel that I have little influence over the things that happen to me.	.521	.440	.480
b. It is impossible for me to believe that chance or luck plays an important role in my life.			
26.a. People are lonely because they don't try to be friendly.			
b. There's not much use in trying too hard to please people, if they like you, they like you.	.179	.227	.195
27.a. There is too much emphasis on athletics in high school.		(Filler)	
b. Team sports are an excellent way to build character.			
28.a. What happens to me is my own doing.			
b. Sometimes I feel that I don't have enough control over the direction my life is taking.	.331	.149	.238
29a. Most of the time I can't understand why politicians behave the way they do.	.004	.211	.109
b. In the long run the people are responsible for bad government on a national as well as on a local level.			

Note.—Score is number of underlined items.

combined group. It can be seen that these are moderate but consistent. The letter preceding the external choice in every item is italicized. The score is the total number of *external* choices.

A careful reading of the items will make it clear that the items deal exclusively with the subjects' *belief* about the nature of the world. That is, they are concerned with the subjects' expectations about how reinforcement is controlled. Consequently, the test is considered to be a measure of a generalized expectancy. Such a generalized expectancy may correlate with the value the subject places on internal control but none of the items is directly addressed to the *preference* for internal or external control.

Test data on the I-E scale have been obtained in a series of samples. Results are summarized in Table 2. Where no source is given, the data have been collected by the author and are being reported here for the first time.

Internal consistency estimates are relatively stable as shown in Table 2. While these estimates are only moderately high for a scale of this length, it should be remembered that the items are not arranged in a difficulty hierarchy, but rather are samples of attitudes in a wide variety of different situations. The test is an additive one and items are not comparable. Consequently, split-half or matched-half reliability tends to underestimate the internal consistency. Kuder-Richardson reliabilities are also somewhat limited since this is a forced-choice scale in which an attempt is made to balance alternatives so that probabilities of endorsement of either alternative do not include the more extreme splits.

Test-retest reliability for a 1-month period seems quite consistent in two quite different samples. The somewhat lower reliabilities for a 2-month period may be partly a function of the fact that the first test was given under group conditions and the second test was individually administered. In the studies of test-retest reliability, means for the second administration typically dropped about 1 point in the direction of less externality.

Correlations of the 60-item I-E scale with the Marlowe-Crowne Social Desirability Scale were obtained in a number of college student samples and typically ranged between −.35 and −.40. The attempt to reduce this correlation in the new scale was moderately successful. The correlations for the new scale range from −.07 to −.35. The greater range may reflect differences in testing conditions. A correlation of −.22 represents the median for the different samples of college students where males and females are combined.

The unusually high correlation between the Marlowe-Crowne Social Desirability Scale and the I-E scores for the prisoner population is probably best understood in terms of the testing conditions. These prisoners were tested shortly after entering the reformatory in the admission building during the same period of time when they were receiving other classification tests. They were told that the test was not being given for administrative but experimental purposes and that the test scores would not become part of their permanent records. It is doubtful, however, that many of them believed these instructions. This interpretation tends to be supported (see Table 3) by the fact that the mean score for these prisoners was significantly lower than for college students although one might naturally expect them to be more external than the college student population.

Both the Strickland (1962) sample and Ladwig's (1963) sample of male prisoners show negligible correlations with intelligence. Cardi's (1962) sample, however, suggests a somewhat different relationship for male and female and is consistent with earlier studies of the 60-item scale and the James-Phares scale. In any case, the correlations with intelligence are low.

Means and standard deviations of the I-E scores for a variety of popula-

Table 2   Internal-External Control Test Data: Reliability and Discriminant Validity

SAMPLE	TYPE	N	SEX	r	SOURCE
		Internal consistency			
Ohio State University	Split half	50	M	.65	
Elementary psychology students	Spearman-Brown	50	F	.79	
Sample 1		100	Combined	.73	
	Kuder-Richardson	50	M	.70	
		50	F	.76	
		100	Combined	.73	
Ohio State University	Kuder-Richardson	200	M	.70	
		200	F	.70	
Elementary psychology students		400	Combined	.70	
National stratified sample Purdue opinion poll 10th, 11th, and 12th grades	Kuder-Richardson	1000	Combined M & F approximately Equal Ns	.69	Franklin (1963)
		Test-retest reliability			
Ohio State University	1 month	30	M	.60	
Elementary psychology students	Group administration	30	F	.83	
		60	Combined	.72	
Prisoners Colorado Reformatory	1 month	28	M	.78	Jessor (1964)
Ohio State University	2 months	63	M	.49	
Elementary psychology students	1st group administration	54	F	.61	
	2nd individual administration	117	Combined	.55	

Table 2   Continued

SAMPLE	TYPE	N	SEX	r	SOURCE
Correlation with Marlowe-Crowne Social Desirability Scale					
Ohio State University		166	M	−.16	
Elementary psychology students		140	F	−.32	
		306	Combined	−.21	
Ohio State University		136	M	−.22	Schwarz (1963)
Elementary psychology students					
Ohio State University		180	F	−.12	Strickland (1962)
Elementary psychology students					
Ohio State University		103	M	−.17	Watt (1962)
Elementary psychology students		77	F	−.35	
		180	Combined	−.29	
Kansas State University		113	45M, 68F Combined	−.28	Ware (1964)[a]
Elementary psychology students					
Ohio Federal prisoners		80	M	−.41	Ladwig (1963)
Ages 18–26, 8th grade plus reading					
Correlation with intellectual measures					
Ohio State University	Ohio State				
Elementary psychology students	Psychological exam.	107	F	−.09	Strickland (1962)
Ohio State University	Ohio State				
Elementary psychology students	Psychological exam.	26	M	.03	Cardi (1962)
		46	F	−.22	
		72	Combined	−.11	
Ohio Federal prisoners	Revised beta IQ	80			
Ages 18–26, 8th grade plus reading			M	.01	Ladwig (1963)

[a] Personal communication.

tions are given in Table 3. As in Table 2, if no other source is given the data have been obtained by the author. Appendix B provides cumulative frequencies for 575 males and 605 females of the Ohio State sample. This sample reported in Table 3 and in the appendix includes tests obtained at different times of the year over a 2-year period in a variety of experiments. In all cases, however, the test was given in group administration in psychology classes and does not overlap other samples reported in Table 3.

Sex differences appear to be minimal except in the case of the University of Connecticut sample. In this sample the means tend to be somewhat higher generally than in Midwestern samples, but it is not clear whether this is in fact a sectional difference or results from other factors of selection or testing. One important difference between the University of Connecticut sample and the others was the large size of the University of Connecticut classes, with 303 subjects comprising a single class. The difference between male and female means for this sample was significant.

Although the college Negro population was obtained from psychology classes in an equivalent fashion to the other college samples, it does appear to be slightly more external than the Midwestern college sample but not more external than the University of Connecticut sample. However, significant differences between Negroes and whites in mean I-E scores were obtained by Lefcourt and Ladwig (1965) with comparable samples. They used 60 white and 60 Negro inmates from two correctional institutions who were not significantly different in social class, age, intelligence, or reason for incarceration. Negroes were significantly more external (Means, 8.97) than white offenders (Means, 7.87).

The very low scores for Peace Corps volunteers can be accounted for in two possible ways. The data do not allow determination for which variable was playing the greater role. As a select group we would expect

Table 3   Means and Standard Deviations of I-E Scores for Samples of Several Populations

Sample	Testing Conditions	N	Sex	Mean	SD	Source
Ohio State University Elementary psychology students (combined samples)	Group Experimental	575 605 1180	M F Combined	8.15 8.42 8.29	3.88 4.06 3.97	
Kansas State University Elementary psychology students	Group Experimental	45 68 113	M F Combined	7.71 7.75 7.73	3.84 3.79 3.82	Ware (1964)[a]

Table 3   Continued

Sample	Testing Conditions	N	Sex	Mean	SD	Source
University of Connecticut	Group	134	M	8.72	3.59	
Elementary psychology students	Experimental	169	F	9.62	4.07	
		303	Combined	9.22	3.88	
Florida State University	Group	116	Combined	9.05	3.66	Gore and Rotter
Negro students, psychology classes	Experimental		62M, 54F			(1963)
Peace Corps trainees (three	Group	122	M	6.06	3.51	
programs combined)	Assessment	33	F	5.48	2.78	
		155	Combined	5.94	3.36	
Prisoners, age 18–26	Individual					
8th grade plus reading	Experiment(?)	80	M	7.72	3.65	Ladwig (1963)
Columbus, Ohio	Small groups	41	M	8.46	3.89	Stack (1963)
12th grade, college applicants	(3–12) Experimental	32 73	F Combined	7.31 7.96	3.64 3.80	
National strati- fied sample, Purdue opin- ion poll	Various	1000	Combined M & F	8.50	3.74	Franklin (1963)
10th, 11th, and 12th grades			Approxi- mately equal Ns			
18-year-old sub- jects from Boston area	Individual	32 25 57	M F Combined	10.00 9.00 9.56	4.20 3.90 4.10	Crowne and Conn (1965)[a]

[a] Personal communication.

from a validity point of view that a group of Peace Corps volunteers would be highly internal overall, and, in fact, they were. However, the test was given in three different training groups as part of an assessment battery, and the subjects knew that scores on this as well as other tests would determine in part whether or not they would be judged to be acceptable for appointment as Peace Corps volunteers and sent overseas on assignment. It seems natural that they would interpret the internal response as more desirable under these circumstances. Whether in fact Peace Corps volunteers are more internal than unselected college students will have to be determined under comparable testing conditions.

While we would expect Peace Corps trainees to be more internal than unselected college students, we would also expect that young male prisoners, most of whom were incarcerated for car stealing, would be more external. This is clearly not the case. However, more internal mean scores can be accounted for on the basis of the high correlation with social desirability under the particular testing conditions (see previous discussion). There seems to be little doubt that scores on this test, as on all personality measures, can be significantly affected by the testing conditions.

The Franklin sample of high school students taken from the Purdue Opinion Poll differs on two important grounds from the samples of Crowne and Conn[2] and Stack (1963). One difference lies in the fact that the administration procedures are essentially unknown and vary from school to school for the Purdue Opinion Poll sample, but probably include many instances where the tests were administered by the pupils' own teachers or principals. Secondly, and more important, is the fact that the Purdue Opinion Poll is an anonymous poll in contrast to all our other samples in which the subject's name is recorded.

While the Stack sample appears to agree with the anonymous Franklin sample, they are not actually comparable. The Stack study was concerned with reactions to acceptance and rejection for college admission, and his sample was drawn from a group of subjects all of whom were applying for college. The Crowne and Conn sample was drawn from a follow-up of the subjects studied by Sears, Maccoby, and Levin (1957). They were all about 18 years of age, a few were freshmen in college, a few had dropped out of school, but most were seniors in high school.

In summary, it seems most logical that the somewhat higher external scores obtained by Crowne and Conn would be more characteristic of unselected high school students who are given a test under experimental conditions by an examiner who does not have other authority relationships to them. The difference between the Stack sample and the Crowne and Conn sample suggests that students in high school seeking to go to college are more internal than is an unselected high school population.

This interpretation is supported in fact by one of Franklin's (1963) findings that among his subjects those students who intended to go on to college were significantly more internal than those who did not so intend.

---

[2] Personal communication, 1965.

Additional Test Characteristics

Two factor analyses have been completed. The first, based on the same 400 cases for which the item correlations are given in Table 1, indicated that much of the variance was included in a general factor. Several additional factors involved only a few items, and only a small degree of variance for each factor could be isolated. These additional factors, however, were not sufficiently reliable to suggest any clear-cut subscales within the test. Franklin (1963) also factor analyzed his 1,000 cases of high school students and obtained essentially similar results. All of the items loaded significantly on the general factor which accounted for 53% of the total scale variance.

In considering discriminant validity, the question of the relationship of the scale to adjustment comes up. Theoretically, one would expect some relationship between internality and good adjustment in our culture but such a relationship might not hold for extreme internal scores. However, there is clearly an interaction between internality and experience of success. The internal subject with a history of failure must blame himself. In regard to the other end of the distribution, externality may act as an adequate defense against failure, but very high scores toward the external end may suggest, at least in our culture, a defensiveness related to significant maladjustment. Extreme scores which were also true scores would suggest a passivity in the face of environmental difficulties, which, at least for many subjects, would result in maladjustment in our society.

In substance, the relationship between I-E scores and adjustment would not be a linear or a clear one from a theoretical point of view. We might expect seriously maladjusted groups to have more variability on I-E scores and probably more frequently to have high scores in the direction of externality. Within a relatively homogeneous (normal) group such as unselected college students or high school students theoretical expectation would be for a low linear correlation.

Several samples of Ohio State elementary psychology students have been examined for the relationship between the I-E scale and the Rotter Incomplete Sentences Blank (Rotter & Rafferty, 1950). In general, linear correlations have not been significant, and, while some curvilinear correlations have been significant, they are not u-shaped distributions and cannot be explained simply. Ware (1964)[3] found a correlation of .24 between the I-E scale and the Taylor Manifest Anxiety scale for his 111 subjects (significant at the 5% level). Efran (1963) used a shortened form of the Taylor Manifest Anxiety scale and of the I-E scale and examined the relationship for 114 combined male and female tenth-, eleventh-, and twelfth-grade high school students. His obtained correlation was .00.

In summary, the test shows reasonable homogeneity or internal consistency, particularly when one takes into account that many of the items are sampling a broadly generalized characteristic over a number of specific or different situations. However, at least with the relatively homogeneous sample studied the test is limited in ability to discriminate individuals.

[3] Personal communication, 1964.

Other populations may provide a greater spread of scores but for college students in the middle 50% of the distribution the test is more suitable for investigations of group differences than for individual prediction. Whether or not a more refined measure of such a broad characteristic can be developed is an open question. Relationships with such test variables as adjustment, social desirability or need for approval, and intelligence are low for the samples studied and indicate good discriminant validity.

Multimethod Measurement

Campbell and Fiske (1959) have indicated the importance of multi-method measurement in the determination of construct validity of personality tests. Earlier studies with the 60-item scale of the forced-choice I–E test typically produced correlations between .55 and .60 with the earlier James-Phares Likert-type scale. The largest sample studied was that of Blackman (1962), who obtained a correlation of .56 for his 151 elementary psychology student subjects. Florence Johnson (1961) obtained a correlation of .58 for 120 subjects.

Two studies of nonquestionnaire approaches to the measurement of internal-external control have been made with the 23-item scale. Adams-Webber (1963) compared the forced-choice I–E scores with scores from a story-completion test. The story beginnings involved a central character who initiates an "immoral" course of action. Scoring was based upon whether the consequences of this act in the story completions appeared to follow from the individual's behavior or were caused by it or were more a function of external conditions or agents. Judges rated story endings from a crude manual. Adams-Webber analyzed his data by dividing his 103 subjects into groups based on the number of external endings for his three story completions. Analysis of variance indicated a highly significant difference among the groups ($p = <.001$). The "projective" test of tendency to see punishment for moral transgression as being externally imposed or as being the result of the immoral behavior was significantly related to I–E scale scores.

In a study of academic failure, Cardi (1962) developed a measure of internal-external control from a semistructured interview which ranged from 35 minutes to an hour. Judges' ratings following a manual were correlated with I–E scale scores obtained at an earlier time and independently of the interview. As in the Adams-Webber study the judges' ratings were satisfactorily reliable. She obtained a biserial correlation of .61 ($p = <.002$) for her 25 subjects between subjects rated high or low from the interview data and I–E scale scores. The variable being studied here is capable of reliable measurement by a variety of test methods.

Social-Class Differences in Internal-External Control

When the Warner scale based on father's occupation was used, studies of the Ohio State samples of elementary psychology students did not show significant social-class differences. However, the college student population utilized was highly homogeneous. Similarly, Gore and Rotter (1963) failed to find significant social-class differences in a somewhat lower social class but similarly homogeneous grouping at a southern Negro college. Studies with younger or noncollege age samples, however, have shown differentiation. Franklin (1963) recorded a significant relationship between higher socioeconomic class and internality based on his national stratified sample of 1,000 cases. Battle and Rotter (1963), using Negro and white sixth- and eighth-grade children and a projective type test, did find a significant social-class effect with race and intellectual level controlled. There was also a significant effect for race, but most of the variance was accounted for by an interaction in which the lower-class Negroes were considerably more external than the groups of middle-class Negroes or upper- or lower-class whites. This finding is similar to the Lefcourt and Ladwig (1965) study of Negro and white prisoners, most of whom were lower socioeconomic class.

Political Affiliation

One analysis of the relationship of the test to political identification has been made. This study included 114 Ohio State elementary psychology college students. No significant differences were found in the mean scores of 49 students who identified themselves as Republican, 20 who identified themselves as Democrats, and 45 who said they were independent or not identified with either major party. With the earlier 60-item scale Johnson (1961) found no significant differences in I–E scale scores between 73 college student supporters of Nixon and 47 supporters of Kennedy. However, such results may not be typical of another geographical area where there are sharper differences in political liberalness between the two major parties.

Children's Tests of Internal-External Control

Three measures of internal-external control for children have been devised. The first of these by Bialer (1961) was modified from the James-Phares scale. It is a 23-item questionnaire with yes-no responses. With younger children the items are read, and the child answers yes or no. A typical item is, "Do you really believe a kid can be whatever he wants to be?"

Crandall, Katkovsky, and Preston (1962) developed a scale (Intellectual Achievement Responsibility—IAR) for "self-responsibility" in achievement situations. The items dealt with whether or not the child felt that he, rather than other persons, usually caused the success and failures he experienced in intellectual achievement situations. The child chose between alternatives as in the following example: "Suppose you did better than usual in a subject at school. Would it probably happen (a) because you tried harder, or (b) because someone helped you?"

A third test for children, more projective in nature, was developed by Battle and Rotter (1963). This test presented the subject with six situations modeled on the Rosenzweig picture frustration approach. The child was told how he would fill in the balloon, as in comic strips, for an outline drawing: for example, where one child is saying, "How come you didn't get what you wanted for Christmas?". A reliable scoring manual for this test was developed. This projective measure correlated significantly (.42) with the Bialer questionnaire in a group of 40 white and Negro children. Data obtained from all three of these tests will be referred to in the following section.

PERSONAL CORRELATES OF A GENERALIZED EXPECTANCY FOR INTERNAL-EXTERNAL CONTROL: CONSTRUCT VALIDITY OF THE I-E MEASURES

Performance in Controlled Laboratory Tasks

The first investigations of individual differences in the I–E variable were made in connection with learning or performance tasks in which skill and chance instructions were given. Phares (1957) obtained prediction bordering on significance for 13 chance-oriented items for individual differences in the size of the increments or decrements following success and failure and in the frequency of unusual shifts within conditions: that is, those shifts in expectancy where the subject raises his expectancy after a failure or lowers it after a success.

James (1957), in the previously cited experiment, found low but significant prediction with revised scale and individual differences *within* each condition. In each case the behavior of externals differed from that of internals in the same way that the overall population differed under chance instructions as compared with skill instructions. James found that the size of increments and decrements in expectancies following reinforcement, the frequency of unusual shifts, the tendency to generalize from one task to another, and the number of trials to extinction were significantly related to his questionnaire of internal-external control.

Later studies using task differences rather than instructions and in some cases other types of tasks have not been as successful as James in predicting individual differences within conditions using either the James-Phares scale or the more recent I–E scale. More consistent prediction has been made of the frequency of unusual shifts during a controlled reinforcement sequence. Several investigations have found this difference to be significant or near significant and the trend is always in the same direction, namely, that externals tend to produce more unusual (or gambler's fallacy) shifts. Battle and Rotter (1963) also found that the Bialer scale significantly predicted the number of unusual shifts for sixth- and eight-grade Negro and white children.

Liverant and Scodel (1960) examined the preferences for bets in a dice-throwing situation using the earlier 60-item version of the I–E scale. They found that subjects scoring toward the internal end of the scale tended to prefer intermediate probability bets or extremely safe bets over the long shots and that they tended to wager more money on safe as against risky bets when compared to those subjects scoring at the external end of the continuum.

In general, individual prediction in competitive laboratory situations for college students has been only partially successful. Apparently, the rather narrow range of internal-external control attitudes in college students and the strong situational determination of the competitive laboratory tasks limits prediction. The behavior most susceptible to individual prediction is that which deals most directly with risk taking and expectancies of the real influence of luck as demonstrated by belief in the gambler's fallacy.

Attempts To Control the Environment

In the following sections for the sake of brevity subjects in the upper half of the distribution of scores on the I–E scale or other measures will be referred to as externals and those in the lower half as internals. It should be made clear that we are dealing here with only one variable affecting behavior and that we are *not* implying a typology of any kind. In fact, in some of the studies involving college populations those subjects being characterized as relatively more external may in fact be more internal on the average than the mean of the population at large.

Perhaps the most important kind of data to assess the construct validity of the internal-external control dimension involves the attempts of people to better their life conditions, that is, to control their environment in important life situations. It is in this sense that the I–E scale appears to measure a psychological equivalent of the sociological concept of alienation, in the sense of powerlessness. The first study of this type was undertaken by Seeman and Evans (1962), who employed a revision of the 60-item I–E scale not too different from the later-developed 23-item scale. They investigated the behavior of patients in a tuberculosis hospital, measuring how much they knew about their own condition, how much they questioned doctors and nurses about their own condition, and how satisfied they were with the amount of feedback they were getting about their medical status. They used 43 matched pairs of white male patients, each pair being matched for occupational status, education, and ward placement. As hypothesized, they found that the internals knew more about their own condition, questioned the doctors and nurses more (according to doctors' and nurses' independent ratings), and expressed less satisfaction at the amount of feedback or the information they were getting about their condition from the hospital personnel.

Seeman (1963a) followed this study with one of reformatory inmates, investigating memory for various kinds of information which they were exposed to in incidental fashion. He found a significant correlation, independent of intelligence, between internality-externality and the amount of information remembered about how the reformatory was run, parole, and long-range economic facts which might affect the persons after they left the reformatory.

Gore and Rotter (1963) obtained signed commitments from students at a southern Negro college regarding activities to be undertaken during vacation in behalf of the civil rights movement. Students who were willing to take part in a march on the state capitol or to join a freedom riders' group were clearly and significantly more internal than those who were only willing to attend a rally, were not interested in participating at all, or avoided even filling out the requested form. Since these were all-Negro students who must have had high involvement in the integration issue, the willingness of some to take part in active attempts to change, and others not to, must have been related to their own generalized expectancy that their behavior could, in fact, effect a change in the prejudice which surrounded them as well as other variables. While this study had strong face validity, in that the students who signed up for these activities expected to take part in them, no follow-ups were made as to whether or not they actually did take part. A study by Strickland (1965) investigated activists in a Negro civil rights movement in a different state in comparison to Negroes matched for education and socioeconomic status who did not take part in such issues. She again found a significant difference with the activists more internal on the I–E scale.

Phares (1965b) in a more stringent test of a generality of internal-external control attitudes selected two samples, one internal and one external, on the I–E scale but matched for the attitudes towards maintaining fraternities and sororities on campus. He instructed both groups to act as experimenters to change the attitudes of other students. He found, as hypothesized, that his internal subject-experimenters were significantly more successful in changing attitudes of others than the external subject-experimenters, who did not differ significantly in the amount of change achieved from a control group who were not subject to any influence condition.

In two separate studies the author has investigated the relationship between petition signing and internal-external control. In both instances, subjects were given the opportunity to sign petitions pro or con some issue such as Red China's being admitted to the United Nations or pro or con postseason football games, on the pretext that only by providing both alternatives could the petitions be passed out in classes. It was hypothesized that internality on the test would relate to signing the petitions in either direction versus nonsigning. In both cases, the I–E scale failed to predict who would be signers and who would not. Whether or not the signing of a petition under classroom conditions involves other variables which were not taken into account and masked any internal-external control variance was not clear. In any case, the test failed to predict petition signing under these conditions.

A recent investigation in this area involves a different cultural population. Seeman (1964)[4] studied workers in Sweden with a translated version of the I–E scale. Seeman's results seem to point clearly to the fact that membership in unions versus nonmembership, activity within the union, and general knowledge of political affairs were all significantly related to internality. Correlations were low but significant and held up when controlled for variables such as education, age, and income.

Perhaps related to this feeling that one can control the environment is also a feeling that one can control himself. Some studies of the relationship of internal-external control to smoking perhaps are relevant. Straits and Sechrest (1963) found that nonsmokers were significantly more

---

[4] Unpublished manuscript.

internal than smokers, and James, Woodruff, and Werner (1965) replicated that finding and in addition reported that following the Surgeon General's report, among male smokers, those who quit and did not return to smoking in a specified period of time were more internal than those who believed the report but did not quit smoking. The difference was not significant for females who apparently were motivated by other variables including, for example, the tendency to gain weight when not smoking.

This group of studies lends strong and relatively consistent support to the hypothesis that a generalized expectancy—that one can affect the environment through one's own behavior—is present in at least two different cultures, can be reliably measured, and is predictive of logical behavioral construct referents.

While significant correlations have been referred to throughout this section, it should be made clear that for the most part they are low and leave room for much in the way of specific attitudes in the particular areas of behavior that were investigated. Perhaps some explanation may be called for here for the fact that variance due to the specific situation was not accounted for by the two factor analyses of the test. In the factor analyses done by the author, several factors involving small but significant variance were isolated, each involving only two or three items with significant loadings. These factors, however, were highly specific and did not constitute broad enough subareas to appear useful to the author. It must also be remembered that most items involving achievement had to be dropped from the scale because of their apparently great susceptibility to social desirability influence.

Internal-External Control and Achievement Motivation

It would seem a logical extension of the notion of internal-external control that those at the internal end of the scale would show more overt striving for achievement than those who felt they had little control over their environment. However, there are two limitations on the potential strength of this relationship, particularly as it applies to college students or adults. One of these is that among college students and adults, particularly with males, there are more defensive externals or people who have arrived at an external view as a defense against failure but who were originally highly competitive. Many such people still maintain striving behavior in clearly structured competitive situations but defensively account for failures by expressed external attitudes. The other limitation is one of specificity in that internal-external control attitudes are obviously not generalized across the board, and in the highly structured academic achievement situation there is probably more specificity determining response than in other kinds of situations. With children who have less experience in the competitive academic situation, a higher relationship could be anticipated than with a select population of college students.

The Crandall et al. (1962) scale (IAR) developed for use with children is specific to the achievement area and Crandall et al. did find free play achievement behavior and achievement test scores in boys but not in girls related to test scores. Neither the Children's Manifest Anxiety scale nor the Thematic Apperception Test (TAT) achievement measure predicted either boys' or girls' achievement behavior.

Cellura[5] found a direct relationship between the SRA academic achievement test, with IQ partialled out, of lower socioeconomic status boys and the IAR scale. Crandall's subjects were predominantly middle class, and Cellura's were all in Hollingheads' fourth and fifth categories.

In Franklin's (1963) study of high school students involving the national stratified sample of 1,000 he hypothesized 17 relationships of the I–E scale to *reported* evidences of achievement motivation. These included such things as early attempts to investigate colleges, intention to go to college, amount of time spent doing homework, parents' interest in homework, etc. He found a significant relationship in the predicted direction in 15 of his 17 relationships.

A study by Efran (1963) produced an indirect but extremely interesting indication of the relationship between striving for achievement and internal-external control. Using a balanced-order controlled procedure he studied high school students' tendency to forget (repress) failures versus successes and found that the tendency to forget failures was significantly related to scores towards the internal end of the dimension. It is possible that the functional value of a defensive tendency towards externality is indicated by these findings. The results suggest that the external has less need to "repress" his failures since he has already accepted external factors as determining his success and failure to a greater extent than those subjects scoring as more internal on the I–E control scale.

A study by Rotter and Mulry (1965) also supports the stronger motivation of internals in achievement situations. In this study, 120 male and female unselected subjects were placed in an angle-matching situation of extreme difficulty. Half of the subjects were instructed that the task was so difficult as to be chance determined and half that it was difficult but that previous data had shown that some people were very good at it. All subjects were then given eight trials of which 75% were positively reinforced, followed by an extinction series of no correct answers until their verbalized expectancies reached 1 or 0 for two consecutive trials. Within the skill and chance groups, subjects were divided into internals and externals at the median. Decision time was measured for all subjects from the time they were given the sample for judging until they selected a standard. The subject was unaware that he was being timed. Analysis of variance produced a significant interaction. Internals took longer to decide on a matching standard under skill conditions than did externals but took a shorter time under chance conditions than did externals. Most of the difference was attributed to the internals who had very long decision times under skill conditions and very short times under chance conditions, these being significantly different. The externals took longer under chance conditions than under skill conditions but the difference was not significant. The result not only shows the greater involvement of internals under

---

[5] Unpublished manuscript, "Internality as a determinant of academic achievement in low SES adolescents," Syracuse University, 1963.

skill conditions but in general suggests that internals tend to value reinforcements for skill much more than chance, and if the opposite cannot
be said for the more external subjects of this study, it is at least clear
that there is no significant differentiation for them.

In summary, the expected relationship between the tendency to perceive what happens to a person as dependent upon his own actions and
greater motivation in achievement is generally supported although prediction was not consistent for boys and girls using the Crandall et al. scale
with children.

Internal-External Control and Resistance to Subtle Suggestion

One other area of construct validity has been investigated in some
depth. This involves the variables of independence, suggestibility, and
conformity as related to internal-external control. It seems that internals
would be more resistive to manipulation from the outside if, in fact, they
are aware of such manipulation. If they were aware, they would feel deprived of some of their control of the environment. Externals expecting
control from the outside would be less resistive. One special consideration
here, however, is in the area of conformity. If the internally oriented person perceives that it is to his advantage to conform he may do so consciously and willingly without yielding any of his control. It is only where
it might be clearly to his disadvantage that he would resist conformity
pressures.

An investigation of the latter hypothesis was carried out by Crowne
and Liverant (1963). They studied unselected college students, dividing
them at the median into internals and externals and observing them in
an Asch conformity situation. Under one set of conditions the usual Asch
instructions were used. In the second set of conditions, subjects were
given a certain amount of money and allowed to bet on each of their
judgments. Subjects could choose to bet or not to bet and could determine the amount they were willing to bet on each judgment. In the normal
Asch situation, there were no differences between internals and externals
in the amount of yielding. However, under betting conditions the internals
yielded significantly less than the externals. They also bet more on themselves when going against the majority than did externals on their independent trials. The internals had no significant differences between their
bets on conforming and independent trials, but the externals bet significantly less on independent trials than they did on trials on which they
yielded.

Other tests of the tendency to yield to external influence were
obtained from studies of Strickland (1962) and Getter (1962) relating
scores on the I-E scale to verbal conditioning. On the basis of a thorough
postexperimental interview, Strickland divided her subjects into those
who were aware of the reinforcement contingency and those who were
not. In addition, of those who were aware she divided those who conditioned from those who did not. While she found no overall relationship
between conditionability and I-E scale scores, she did find large and
significant differences between those subjects who were aware and did
not condition and those subjects who were aware and did condition. As

expected, the subjects who were aware and did not condition were considerably more internal than those who were aware and did condition.

The study by Getter involving a somewhat different technique produced a fairly large number of latent conditioners. That is, subjects who showed no significant evidence of conditioning during the training trials, but during extinction when no reinforcement was given, showed a significant rise in the reinforced response. Again, these subjects were significantly more internal than either subjects who did not show such latent conditioning among non-conditioners or who conditioned during the training trials.

Both of these studies suggest a kind of negativism to external manipulation on the part of internals. However, a study by Gore (1962) helps to clarify this issue. Gore used an experimenter influence paradigm in which she presented TAT cards to three groups of subjects, ostensibly to determine which cards produced longer stories. One condition involved overt influence in which she specified which card she thought was the best. The second condition involved subtle influence in which she presented the same card, saying to the subjects and smiling, "Now let's see what you do with *this* one." The third condition was a control condition of no influence. She also used unselected subjects dividing them at the median into internals and externals. Her results showed no significant differences between internals and externals under the overt suggestion condition and control condition, but under the subtle suggestion condition the internals produced significantly shorter stories than did externals and significantly shorter stories than did control subjects in the no suggestion condition. It is under the subtle suggestion conditions they reacted by telling shorter stories or were, in fact, negativistic. However, in the overt condition, there were no traces of this negativism. Apparently, when given the conscious choice the internal is not resistive. However, when he is aware that an attempt is being made to subtly manipulate him he does become resistive.

The four studies taken as a whole support one another. The individual who perceives that he does have control over what happens to him may conform or may go along with suggestions when he chooses to and when he is given a conscious alternative. However, if such suggestion or attempts at manipulation are not to his benefit or if he perceives them as subtle attempts to influence him without his awareness, he reacts resistively. The findings have considerable significance for the general area of persuasion and propaganda.

Antecedents of Internal-External Attitudes

Relatively little work has been done on antecedents for developing attitudes of internal versus external control. The consistent indication that lower socioeconomic level groups are more external allows for a number of alternative explanations. Graves (1961) predicted and found differences among Ute Indians, children of Spanish-American heritage, and whites in an isolated triethnic community. As he expected the Indians are most external, the Spanish-Americans in the middle, and the whites more internal. The implication is for direct cultural teaching of internal-external attitudes since, in fact, the Spanish-Americans were financially more deprived than the Indians although it is true that the Indians who were partially supported by the government had fewer occupational outlets. In support of this interpretation of the influence of direct teaching, Shirley Jessor (1964)[6] found a correlation of .38 between mothers' coded answers to interview questions of internal-external attitudes and responses of their high school children to a 23-item questionnaire similar to the 23-item scale described here. Her sample included 81 pairs drawn from the same cross-cultural sample.

In the previously cited study by Battle and Rotter (1963), the highly external group was the low-socioeconomic-level Negro group in contrast to middle-class Negroes or whites of either lower- or middle-class identification. Interestingly enough, within this group there was a significant relationship between intelligence and externality. This relationship was counter to the socioeconomic level findings. It was the more intelligent Negro children in the lower socioeconomic level who were the most external. The findings are based on a small N and may be regarded as only suggestive. However, what they imply is that the perception of limited material opportunities and of powerful external forces is one variable making for an external attitude. Similarly, Cellura (See Footnote 5) found that with both the Bialer scale and the Crandall et al. IAR scale the parents of the more external children had significantly lower education levels.

One investigation with college student subjects attempted to relate orthodoxy of religious beliefs to internal-external control (Rotter, Simmons, & Holden, 1961[7]) using the McLean scale which measures belief in the literalness of the Bible. No relationship was found. With other college student groups there were no significant differences between individuals of one religious faith versus another. Interviews with individual subjects in a college population at least suggest that religion may well have a role in the development of internal or external attitudes. However, it is the specific emphasis that is placed upon the role of external fatalistic determination by parents which is more likely to determine the attitude than the abstract doctrines of the sect. These studies bearing on the problem of antecedents of internal-external beliefs are indirect, and work needs to be done in this area of investigation. One obvious antecedent worthy of study would be the consistency of discipline and treatment by parents. Clearly it would be expected that unpredictable parents would encourage the development of attitudes of external control.

SUMMARY

The studies reported here represent an unusually consistent set of findings. For most findings there are replications sometimes in other laboratories, sometimes with other kinds of populations, and sometimes

[6] Personal communication, 1964.
[7] Unpublished manuscript, 1961.

with different methods of measurement and techniques of producing condition or situational effects. The broad findings are summarized below.

1. People in American culture have developed generalized expectancies in learning situations in regard to whether or not reinforcement, reward, or success in these situations is dependent upon their own behavior or is controlled by external forces, particularly luck, chance, or experimenter control, which are fairly consistent from individual to individual. If subjects perceive a situation as one in which luck or chance or experimenter control determines the reinforcements, then they are less likely to raise expectancies for future reinforcement as high following success, as if they perceived the reinforcement to be dependent upon skill or their own efforts. Similarly, they are less likely to lower expectancies as much after failure. They are less likely to generalize experiences of success and failure or expectancies of future reinforcement as much from one task to another similar task. The pattern of extinction is markedly different involving a reversal of the typical 100% versus 50% partial reinforcement findings. When perceived as skill determined, 100% reinforcement takes longer to extinguish than does 50% reinforcement. Finally, under conditions where they perceive the task as luck, chance, or experimenter controlled they are more likely to raise expectancies after a failure or to lower them after a success. In general, under skill conditions behavior of a subject follows what might be considered a more logical or commonsense model. It is particularly important that many of the learning paradigms utilized by psychologists are of the type where reward is experimenter controlled. These results suggest that generalizing "laws of learning" from such studies is a dangerous procedure. In substance, one main interpretation of these studies is that research in human learning should be understood or interpreted in light of the position on a continuum of internal to external control that the task and procedure will be perceived by the subjects.

2. Not only do subjects in general differentiate learning situations as internally or externally determined but individuals differ in a generalized expectancy in how they regard the same situation. Such generalized expectancies can be measured and are predictive of behavior in a variety of circumstances. These characteristic differences in viewing behavior-reinforcement contingencies can be measured in children and adults by different methods with reasonably high intercorrelations between different methods of measurement.

3. Data are presented on one scale for measuring individual differences in generalized expectancy for internal-external control which has been used in the largest number of studies of this variable. This is a forced-choice 29-item scale including 6 filler items. Item analysis and factor analysis show reasonably high internal consistency for an additive scale. Test-retest reliability is satisfactory, and the scale correlates satisfactorily with other methods of assessing the same variable such as questionnaire, Likert scale, interview assessments, and ratings from a story-completion technique. Discriminant validity is indicated by the low

relationships with such variables as intelligence, social desirability, and political liberalness. Differences in means of selected populations is generally a weak criterion of validity. Nevertheless, differences obtained for different types of populations are generally consistent with expectancies.

4. Most significant evidence of the construct validity of the I-E scale comes from predicted differences in behavior for individuals above and below the median of the scale or from correlations with behavioral criteria. A series of studies provides strong support for the hypotheses that the individual who has a strong belief that he can control his own destiny is likely to (a) be more alert to those aspects of the environment which provide useful information for his future behavior; (b) take steps to improve his environmental condition; (c) place greater value on skill or achievement reinforcements and be generally more concerned with his ability, particularly his failures; and (d) be resistive to subtle attempts to influence him.

Table B1   Distribution of I-E Scale Scores for 575 Males and 605 Female Ohio State Elementary Psychology Students

MALES[a]			FEMALES[b]		
I-E score	*f*	*Cum. %*	*I-E score*	*f*	*Cum. %*
			21	1	100.00
20	1	100.00	20	1	99.83
19	1	99.83	19	3	99.67
18	4	99.65	18	7	99.17
17	10	98.96	17	10	98.02
16	10	97.22	16	8	96.36
15	10	95.48	15	17	95.04
14	15	93.74	14	23	92.23
13	31	91.13	13	37	88.43
12	32	85.74	12	31	82.31
11	32	80.17	11	42	77.19
10	49	74.61	10	42	70.25
9	53	66.09	9	64	63.31
8	73	56.87	8	53	52.73
7	52	44.17	7	50	43.97
6	52	35.13	6	66	35.70
5	41	26.09	5	37	24.79
4	43	18.96	4	42	18.68
3	29	11.48	3	37	11.74
2	22	6.43	2	22	5.62
1	10	2.61	1	8	1.98
0	5	0.87	0	4	0.66

[a] $N = 575$; $Mean = 8.15$; $SD = 3.88$.
[b] $N = 605$; $Mean = 8.42$; $SD = 4.06$.

APPENDIX A

Instructions for the I-E Scale

This is a questionnaire to find out the way in which certain important events in our society affect different people. Each item consists of a pair of alternatives lettered a or b. Please select the one statement of each pair (*and only one*) which you more strongly *believe* to be the case as far as you're concerned. Be sure to select the one you actually *believe* to be more true rather than the one you think you should choose or the one you would like to be true. This is a measure of personal belief: obviously there are no right or wrong answers.

Your answers to the items on this inventory are to be recorded on a separate answer sheet which is loosely inserted in the booklet. REMOVE THIS ANSWER SHEET NOW. Print your name and any other information requested by the examiner on the answer sheet, then finish reading these directions. Do not open the booklet until you are told to do so.

Please answer these items *carefully* but do not spend too much time on any one item. Be sure to find an answer for *every* choice. Find the number of the item on the answer sheet and black-in the space under the number 1 or 2 which you choose as the statement more true.

In some instances you may discover that you believe both statements or neither one. In such cases, be sure to select the *one* you more strongly believe to be the case as far as you're concerned. Also try to respond to each item *independently* when making your choice; do not be influenced by your previous choices.

4-7 | *A New Scale for the Measurement of Interpersonal Trust*[1]

JULIAN B. ROTTER

One of the most salient factors in the effectiveness of our present complex social organization is the willingness of one or more individuals in a social unit to trust others. The efficiency, adjustment, and even survival of any social group depends upon the presence or absence of such trust.

[1] This investigation was supported by a grant from the National Institute of Mental Health (MH 11455).

Interpersonal trust is defined here as an expectancy held by an individual or a group that the word, promise, verbal or written statement of another individual or group can be relied upon. This definition clearly departs significantly from Erikson's (1953) broad use of the concept of *basic trust* which Erikson describes as a central ingredient in "the healthy personality."

Various writers have already indicated that a high expectancy that others can be relied upon is an important variable in the development of adequate family relationships and of healthy personalities in children. The failure to trust others, particularly representatives of society, such as parents, teachers, and powerful community leaders, has frequently been cited as an important determinant in delinquency (Redl & Wineman, 1951). Difficulties in race relationships and in minority group–majority group relationships have, likewise, been frequently related to expectancies of one group that the verbal statements of the other cannot be accepted. Many psychotherapists believe interpersonal trust is a major determinant in the success of psychotherapy. In fact, an expectancy that others can be believed must be an important variable in human learning in general. Much of the formal and informal learning that human beings acquire is based on the verbal and written statements of others, and what they learn must be significantly affected by the degree to which they believe their informants without independent evidence.

It seems evident that an adequate measure of individual differences in interpersonal trust would be of great value for research in the areas of social psychology, personality, and clinical psychology. Social scientists have investigated some of the conditions relating to interpersonal trust using game theory (Deutsch, 1958, 1960; Rapaport & Orwant, 1962; and Scodel, 1962). For the most part these investigations have shown that a typical reaction of two strangers in a two-person non-zero-sum game situation involving trust produces behavior usually indicative of competitive rather than cooperative attitudes. One might conclude that Americans at least are a highly suspicious and extremely competitive group who would give up many benefits rather than cooperate with someone else. The results of these studies, however, do not seem consistent with a common-sense analysis of our own society. From the family unit to big business, cooperation seems to mark the everyday behavior of individuals and organizations to a far greater degree than would be anticipated from the study of two-person game situations. Perhaps this is the result of special reactions to these laboratory situations which are highly competitive in nature and are specific to these situations, or at least have limited generality. The writer has previously published an analysis of some of the factors involving specificity of reaction to test and experimental laboratory situations which may be applicable here (Rotter, 1955, 1960b).

Studies involving the communication of information (Mellinger, 1956; Loomis, 1959; Kelley & Ring, 1961) have several characteristics in common with game approaches but present situations somewhat closer to the present study. These investigations indicate that people who trust others more are also more trustworthy, or cooperative. Similar findings were obtained by Deutsch (1960) using the "game" paradigm.

Other recent literature has dealt with trust indirectly. Discussions of Machiavellianism, i.e., the tendency to manipulate others to gain one's own ends (Christie & Merton, 1958), and anomie (Merton, 1949), suggest that, at least in part, distrust of others is dependent upon normlessness in the social organization.

The problem of trust in the present research is being viewed from the perspective of social learning theory (Rotter, 1954). From this orientation, choice behavior in specific situations depends upon the expectancy that a given behavior will lead to a particular outcome or reinforcement in that situation and the preference value of that reinforcement for the individual in that situation.

It is a natural implication of social learning theory that experiences of promised negative or positive reinforcements occurring would vary for different individuals and that, consequently, people would develop different expectancies that such reinforcements would occur when promised by other people. It is also natural to expect, to some degree, that such expectancies that promises of other social agents will be kept would generalize from one social agent to another. That is, individuals would differ in a *generalized expectancy* that the oral or written statements of other people can be relied upon. The development of such a generalized attitude may be learned directly from the behavior of parents, teachers, peers, etc., and also from verbal statements regarding others made by significant people or trusted sources of communication such as newspapers and television. It is ironic that we can learn to distrust large groups of people without personal experience validating such distrust, because people who are themselves trusted teach distrust.

Previous work on the choice of a smaller immediate reward versus a more highly valued, delayed reward by Mahrer (1956) and Mischel (1961b, 1961c) is related to the concept of trust as defined here. These studies strongly suggest that children who have experienced a higher proportion of promises kept by parents and authority figures in the past have a higher generalized expectancy for interpersonal trust from other authority figures.

CONSTRUCTION OF THE INTERPERSONAL TRUST SCALE

As a first step in the construction of the scale a number of items were written using a Likert format. An attempt was made to sample a wide variety of social objects so that a subject would be called upon to express his trust of parents, teachers, physicians, politicians, classmates, friends, etc. In other words, the scale was constructed as an *additive* scale in which a high score would show trust for a great variety of social objects. In addition to the specific items, a few items were stated in broader terms presumed to measure a more general optimism regarding the society. Finally, a number of filler items, intended to partially disguise the purpose of the scale, were written and included in the first experimental form.

The experimental form was group-administered to two large classes of students in an introductory psychology course. The sample comprised 248 male and 299 female subjects. Along with this scale the

Marlowe-Crowne Social Desirability Scale (Crowne and Marlowe, 1964) of "need for social approval" was administered.

Three criteria were used for inclusion of an item in the final scale: (a) the item had to have a significant correlation with the total of the other trust items with that item removed; (b) the item had to have a relatively low correlation with the Marlowe-Crowne Social Desirability Scale score; and (c) endorsement of the item showed reasonable spread over the five Likert categories of (1) strongly agree, (2) mildly agree, (3) agree and disagree equally, (4) mildly disagree and (5) strongly disagree. A final form of the scale was determined by dropping three items from the a priori scale.

In the experimental form of the test, half of the crucial items were written so that an "agree" response would indicate trust, and half so that a "disagree" response would indicate trust. In the final form of this scale the items selected were similarly balanced so that 12 indicated trust for agreeing and 13 distrust for agreeing. Filler items did not show significant relationships to the trust items but helped partially obscure the purpose of the test. The final form of the test included 25 items measuring trust and 15 filler items. Some sample items are presented below:

> In dealing with strangers one is better off to be cautious until they have provided evidence that they are trustworthy.
> Parents usually can be relied upon to keep their promises.
> Parents and teachers are likely to say what they believe themselves and not just what they think is good for the child to hear.
> Most elected public officials are really sincere in their campaign promises.

In addition to the Marlowe-Crowne Social Desirability Scale, the 547 subjects completed a personal information questionnaire which included information on age, socioeconomic level, father's occupation, father's and mother's religion and place of birth, and siblings, so that position in the family and family size could be determined. College Aptitude scores were also available on these subjects and were obtained directly from the students' admission records. At later dates several of the students were subjects in other studies involving the administration of the same trust scale. It was therefore possible to obtain test-retest reliabilities for long periods of time, where the testing conditions were different for the two administrations. An analysis of these data is presented below.

TEST CHARACTERISTICS

Internal Consistency and Test-Retest Reliability
Table 1 below provides means and standard deviations of the 248 male and 299 female college student subjects. Internal consistency based on split-half reliability, corrected by the Spearman-Brown formula, are also provided. While these consistencies are not high for objective type tests,

Table 1   Test Data for the Interpersonal Trust Scale

Group	N	Mean	SD
Males	248	73.01	10.23
Females	299	71.91	9.95
Total	547	72.41	10.90

SPLIT-HALF RELIABILITY

	N	r	p
Males	248	.77	<.001
Females	299	.75	<.001
Total	547	.76	<.001

ᵃ Corrected by the Spearman-Brown Prophecy Formula.

it should be remembered that these are *additive* scales sampling a variety of different social objects rather than a measure of intensity limited to a narrow area of behavior. Regarded in this light these internal consistencies are reasonably high. The difference in mean scores for males and females is not statistically significant and distributions of scores for both sexes are similar.

Two estimates of test-retest reliability are available. The first of these involves 24 subjects, 10 male and 14 female, who took the test originally in a large group-testing situation and repeated the test as part of a sociometric study to be described later. The average length of time between first and second tests was approximately seven months. The correlation was .56 ($p < .01$). The second measure of test-retest reliability was obtained on students who had also taken the test originally in a large group situation. Their second test was part of an experiment in which the trust scale was given in groups of from two to 13 with two other tests appearing equally often in first, second, and third positions in order of administration. There were 34 males and eight females in this group, and the approximate average time between tests was three months. The correlation was .68, ($p < .01$). Considering the important differences in administration procedures and the relatively long periods of time between tests, these test-retest coefficients indicate surprising stability of test scores.

For the 248 male subjects the correlation with the Marlowe-Crowne S-D Scale was .21; for the 299 females, .38. The overall correlation was .29. All correlations were statistically significant. These results suggest that trust is regarded as a socially desirable trait but that the total amount of variance in the trust scale accounted for by the social approval motive is relatively small. To determine the relationship, if any, with general ability, 100 male and 100 female subjects were selected at random and their trust scores correlated with the college entrance (SAT) scores. The correlation for the 100 females was −.16 and for the 100 males −.06.

At least for this sample of college students, ability has no significant in-fluence on trust scale scores.

Demographic Characteristics of High and Low Trust Individuals

From the personal information sheet filled out by all of the 547 stu-dents who took the Interpersonal Trust Scale, analyses of variance were computed for the variables of ordinal position, family size, religion, socio-economic status, age, and number of semesters in college. In addition, the subjects were grouped into two categories based on whether or not the reported religions for both parents were the same or different. Since male and female subjects were essentially similar throughout this analysis, data were combined for the sexes.

There were no significant differences in test scores for subjects of different ages or according to the number of semesters of college at-tended. However, the range for both of these variables was extremely narrow. The data of family size were dichotomized into three children or less, or more than three children. Students from larger families did not show significantly different trust scores from those with three or less children. Significant differences were obtained on all the other variables.

Table 2 presents mean scores for the various breakdowns of subjects for the variables of ordinal position, religion, religious differences, and socioeconomic status. A multiple-comparisons test for a single degree of freedom contrast (Myers, 1966) was made to determine differences among means. It should be noted that in many cases there are significant differences because of the large number of subjects in the sample, but actual mean differences are relatively small.

Inspection of the findings for birth order reveals one significant dif-ference, but the actual mean differences are sufficiently small to suggest no important psychological variability in this group. However, in a sepa-rate smaller sample, Geller (1966) also found youngest children to be the least trusting and significantly different from all other ordinal positions. While this finding cannot be interpreted without additional data, it is possi-ble that the youngest child has less interaction with his parents and has the least acceptance of the adult interpretation of the verities of our society.

The data on religion are more clear-cut. Students who fill out the blank by stating any religion tend to be more trusting than those who state they are agnostics, atheists, or who write "none." Since it is clear that such students are already expressing less faith in one currently accepted institution, it is not surprising that they show a generalized lower degree of trust in others.

Perhaps most interesting are the lower trust scores for subjects with religious differences between parents. In any case where the student indicated a religious difference for the two parents, including one parent being atheistic and the other not, the subject was put into the religious difference category. This group includes all subjects who listed different religions for the parents, regardless of the religion stated for the subject himself. Only nine of the 100 subjects so classified gave their own re-

Table 2   Demographic Data for the Interpersonal Trust Scale

VARIABLE AND GROUP	N	MEAN	SIGNIFICANT DIFFERENCES AMONG GROUPS ($p < .05$)
Ordinal position			
Only	52	73.08	
Oldest	195	72.21	
Middle	129	73.02	Youngest
Youngest	171	71.97	Middle

ANOV overall $F = 3.71, p < .05$

Religion			
Left blank	12	71.50	Jewish, none
Jewish	85	74.65	All groups except Miscellaneous
Protestant	197	73.31	Jewish, Catholic, none
Catholic	203	71.33	Jewish, Protestant, non, misc.
Miscellaneous	17	73.82	Catholic, none
None, agnostic, atheist	33	67.48	All groups

ANOV overall $F = 46.78, p < .001$

Religious Differences			
No information	13	72.38	
Parents same	434	73.13	
Parents different	100	69.29	Parents same and no information

ANOV overall $F = 75.06, p < .001$

SOCIOECONOMIC LEVEL	N	MEAN	SIGNIFICANT DIFFERENCES AMONG GROUPS ($p < .05$)
No information	25	73.48	V
Warner Group I	117	73.45	III, V
Warner Group II	150	72.70	V
Warner Group III	91	71.81	I
Warner Group IV	64	72.48	
Warner Group V	100	70.97	No information, I, II

ANOV overall $F = 8.63, p < .01$

ligion as "none," "atheist," or "agnostic," so that this group of subjects has only a minimum overlap with the students who were classified as non-religious in the previous analysis. It seems reasonable that a child subjected to two different kinds of adult interpretations in such an important area as religion would grow up to be more cynical of the verbal communications of authority figures.

Finally, the data on socioeconomic status more or less follow the expected progression for more trust at the highest economic level to less trust at the lowest economic level. For this analysis, subjects were classified according to Warner's system based upon father's occupation. The interpretation again seems to be consistent with the general notion that those students who had least reason to accept the status quo as defined and defended by the authorities in the social system tended to show the least trust of those authorities. It should be reiterated here, though, that the differences are again small and the overlap among groups is very great.

VALIDITY OF SCALE

In order to assess the validity of the Interpersonal Trust Scale it would be optimal to obtain one or more natural life criterion situations. The two-person non-zero-sum game seems like a face-valid procedure to investigate interpersonal trust. However, the results of these studies suggest that the situation is reacted to by many if not all subjects as a competitive game, often regardless of special instructions. For the reasons cited earlier it was decided to test the validity of the scale against observations of every-day behavior by a sociometric technique. Two fraternities ($N = 35$, $N = 38$) and two sororities ($N = 41$, $N = 42$) on the University of Connecticut campus were asked to cooperate in the study. Lump sum payments were provided to each of the four organizations if they could promise that all members would be available for a single evening and all would agree to take the sociometric rating of trust and two brief tests. However, members would only be used in the study if they had lived in the house for a period of at least six months prior to the date of testing. The data was collected by the author and, in each case, a research assistant of the same sex as the subjects.[2] In addition to asking the subjects to nominate members of the group who were the highest and lowest in interpersonal trust, subjects were also asked to nominate others high and low on dependency, gullibility, and trustworthiness. As control variables, scales were also included for humor, popularity, and friendship. Finally the subjects were asked to make a self-rating of trust on a four-point scale of (1) much more than the average college student, (2) more than the average college student, (3) less than the average college student and (4) much less than the average college student.

To avoid halo effect, elaborate instructions were given asking each subject to pay special attention to the different characteristics required for each sociometric description. Confidentiality was assured as well as the fact that we were not interested in individuals and that we would eliminate the use of names as soon as the data were obtained, substituting numbers for each individual. To avoid stereotyping, no labels were used for the socioeconomic scales, but rather descriptions of typical behaviors. In each group the order of presentation was first the trust scale, second the sociometric scales, and last the Marlowe-Crowne Social Desirability Scale. However, the Marlowe-Crowne S-D Scale was not given to the first group.

[2] Grateful acknowledgment is made to Ray Mulry and Linda Yuccas who assisted in this research.

One other difference occurred in the procedure for the first of the four groups. In this group, a sorority, each subject was asked to nominate the five highest and five lowest persons on each sociometric scale. These data were analyzed using four methods of scoring. In the first method the highest was weighted 5, the next highest 4, the next 3, and so on, and the negative nominations were similarly weighted −5, −4, −3, etc. The second was also a weighting method but using only the first three nominations for the negative and positive ends of each scale. The third method involved no weighting but gave a score of +1 for each mention, utilizing all five nominations. The last method gave a score of +1 only for the top three and the bottom three nominations. Intercorrelations of the four methods indicated no substantial differences among them. Since subjects met difficulty in finding five names for the top and bottom of each scale, subsequent groups were asked to nominate only the top three and bottom three. Each mention was then scored either ±1 to give an overall score on that scale.

Instructions for the sociometric rating of trust are given below as are the descriptions for the trust variable. The order of presentation was (1) dependency, (2) trust, (3) humor, (4) gullibility, (5) trustworthiness, (6) popularity, (7) friendship, and (8) self-rating of trust. During the administration of the sociometric scale a strong attempt to keep a serious atmosphere was more or less successful, success being greater in the sororities than in the fraternities.

Sociometric Instructions

On the following pages you will be asked to nominate some people in your group who fit various descriptions. Please do so as thoughtfully as possible, paying special attention to the *different characteristics* called for in each description. Again let me assure you the results are confidential and we have no interest in you as individuals. The data from these questionnaires will be placed on IBM cards identified only by numbers, not names.

In the next seven pages various kinds of people will be described. Place the name of the person who most closely fits the description after the (1), next most closely after the (2), and so on until you have listed the three people in the group who most closely fit the description. *List only the names of people who are here in the group now. Do not list any members who are not present.*

Do each page in order. Do not look at the page ahead until you have finished the one you are working on. You may wish as you go along to use some of the same names on different descriptions.

You may find the task difficult but we hope you will take it seriously and do the best you can. We feel we are doing important research and hope you will cooperate with us to the fullest.

Description of Trust Variable

This person expects others to be honest. She is not suspicious of other people's intentions, she expects others to be open and that they can be relied upon to do what they say they will do.

This person is cynical. She thinks other people are out to get as much as they can for themselves. She has little faith in human nature and in the promises or statements of other people.

The correlations to be reported below are combined for the four groups. They were obtained by calculating separate correlations for each group, transforming to z scores, finding the average z score, and then transforming to an r for the entire group. Before testing the validity of the trust scale against the sociometric scale it was necessary to determine whether or not the sociometric ratings were reliable. This was done by dividing each group into random, equivalent halves and obtaining the sociometric score on each variable for each person in the two subgroups. The resulting correlations shown in Table 3 indicate the degree to which the members of the group are likely to see each other in a similar way. It can be seen that the correlations are unusually high, suggesting not only good cooperation but also that the members of the groups were basing their ratings on a common core of observations.

The intercorrelations for the 10 variables are presented in Table 4. This includes the Trust Scale, the seven sociometric ratings, the self-rating of trust, and the Social Desirability Scale. It can be seen from Table 4 that the Interpersonal Trust Scale was significantly related to the sociometric trust score. Individual correlations in the four groups range from .23 to .55. The overall correlation of .37 is significantly higher than that for the control variables of humor, popularity, and friendship, indicating that the sociometric rating for trust was measuring an independent variable and was not merely the result of halo effect. Both the trust scale and the sociometric rating of trust correlated significantly with trustworthiness, providing strong support for the belief that people who trust others are regarded themselves as being dependable.

It is of considerable interest that no significant relationship was found between gullibility which was defined on the sociometric scale as "naïve and easily fooled in contrast to sophisticated, experienced, etc.," and trust as measured by the sociometric scale or the Interpersonal Trust Scale. While it is somewhat difficult conceptually to entirely separate gullibility from interpersonal trust, it is clear that in practice the individuals in our sample made such separation and saw the two traits as independent.

The other significant relationships with the trust scale were for the self-rating of trust and the negative relationship with dependency. The trusting individual is seen as less dependent on others (making decisions, seeking advice and help) than the individual rated as low in trust. But dependency is seen as a clearly negative trait correlating $-.46$ with popularity and $-.53$ with friendship. Some of this relationship may be negative halo since it is clear that there is a significant although quite low positive relationship between trust and friendship and popularity. The correlation between self-rating of trust and the sociometric rating of trust (.39) is also indicative of the cooperation and seriousness with which the subjects completed the sociometric task. It may be surprising to some

Table 3 *Split-half Reliabilities of Sociometric Scores, Combined Groups*
$$(N = 156)$$

Variable	r^a
Dependency	.88
Trust	.87
Humor	.93
Gullibility	.93
Trustworthiness	.89
Popularity	.95
Friendship	.82

[a] $r = .21$ for $p < .01$.

Table 4 *Combined Intercorrelations of Sociometric and Test Scores, Combined Groups*
$$(N = 156)$$

Variable	2	3	4	5	6	7	8	9	10[a]
1. Interpersonal Trust Scale	−.23	.37	.09	−.03	.31	.20	.19	.29	.13
2. Sociometric Dependency		−.07	−.36	.78	−.45	−.46	−.53	−.06	−.05
3. Sociometric Trust			.34	.13	.62	.43	.42	.39	.02
4. Sociometric Humor				−.33	.26	.61	.66	.14	−.08
5. Sociometric Gullibility					−.24	−.43	−.60	.01	.01
6. Sociometric Trustworthiness						.57	.50	. 24	.01
7. Sociometric Popularity							.83	.05	−.11
8. Sociometric Friendship								.09	−.15
9. Self-Rating of Trust									.31
10. Marlowe-Crowne S-D Scale[a]									

[a] $N = 114$ for all correlations involving the S-D Scale.
$r = .21$ for $p < .01$ ($N = 156$).
$r = .16$ for $p < .05$ ($N = 156$).
$r = .18$ for $p < .05$ ($N = 114$).

that the self-rating showed a relatively high relationship (.39) with the rating of trust made by others. It should be remembered, however, that the self-rating came at the end of the sociometric task and all of the subjects knew that they were being rated on the same trait by others, providing pressure on them toward honesty. Similarly, the relationship between the trust scale and the self-rating of trust (.29) might not have been so high if the knowledge that others had just rated them had not influenced the self-rating.

The insignificant correlation between the Trust Scale and the S-D Scale may appear surprising in light of the correlation of .29 found in the large sample. However, the S-D Scale was given in this case after a sociometric task in which each subject knew he was being rated by others on a number of variables. As a result mean scores for the S-D test were significantly depressed in the direction of greater honesty. The mean S-D score for the sociometric study was 12.4, for the earlier study it was 14.3.

While trust and trustworthiness showed a significant relationship, some evidence that they are also regarded somewhat differently can be found in the correlations of both variables, measured sociometrically, with popularity and friendship. Trustworthiness is clearly seen as the more desirable trait with a significantly higher relationship to popularity.

In summary, sociometric analysis reveals relatively good construct and discriminant validity for the Interpersonal Trust Scale as against observed behavior in groups who have had ample opportunity and a long time to observe each other. Trust as measured sociometrically was negatively related to dependency, not significantly related to gullibility, and positively related to humor, friendship, popularity, and especially trustworthiness.

SUMMARY

Interpersonal trust, defined as a generalized expectancy that the verbal statements of others can be relied upon, appears potentially to be a fruitful variable for investigation in several fields of psychology. A new, Likert-type scale was developed and refined on the basis of item analysis of internal consistency, relative independence of social desirability, and item spread. Overall internal consistency and test-retest reliability appear satisfactory. Demographic data were examined for 547 college students. Trust scale scores are related significantly to position in the family, socioeconomic level, religion, and religious differences between parents. A first assessment of construct and discriminant validity was attempted by a sociometric study of two fraternities and two sororities. Results indicate both good construct and discriminant validity for the Interpersonal Trust Scale.

4-8 Interaction of Fear and Guilt in Inhibiting Unacceptable Behavior[1]

DONALD L. MOSHER

80 male college students completed the Mosher Incomplete Sentences Test which was scored for sex guilt. The *S*s were assigned by alternation to a fear-reduction or fear-induction experimental condition which preceded a perceptual defense task. The results supported the prediction derived from social learning theory that the inhibitory behavior of *S*s who score low on a measure of sex guilt is more influenced by situational cues relevant to the probability of external punishment for sex-related behavior than is the inhibitory behavior of the high-sex-guilt group. The results suggested that the high-sex-guilt *S* is relatively insensitive to situational cues concerning the probability of external punishment.

A distinction can be made between two motives for the inhibition of morally unacceptable behavior. One motive is fear of external punishment for transgressing societal standards. A second motive is guilt, which has developed as a result of a past reinforcement history which favored the internalization of moral standards. The guilt-motivated person assumes the task of inhibiting behaviors which he defines as morally unacceptable to avoid experiencing intense feelings of guilt.

While distinctions between fear and guilt are commonly made, little attention has been paid to their interaction. There is no reason to assume that fear of punishment ceases to operate when the person develops internal standards which lead to the guilt-motivated inhibition of unacceptable behavior. Research studies of guilt often seek to control fear of punishment by attempting to allay the person's fear of detection or punishment. For example, MacKinnon (1938), in an early study, left the room and provided the subjects with an opportunity to cheat while observing whether the subject violated the prohibition through a one-way screen. This, in effect, is a means of reducing or eliminating the subjects' fear of being caught and punished, and the inhibition of cheating then becomes a function of the presence or absence of internalized guilt controls. While this research strategy can expand our knowledge of internal controls, ex-

[1] This paper is based on a doctoral dissertation presented in partial fulfillment of the PhD requirement at the Ohio State University. I wish to acknowledge my considerable indebtedness and to express my appreciation to the late Shepard Liverant who served as my adviser. Thanks are due Julian B. Rotter for his assistance and encouragement of my attempts to employ and extend Social Learning Theory in conceptualizing guilt.

perimental designs also need to examine the interaction between these two motives for inhibiting prohibited behavior. This paper will examine a theoretical conception of fear and guilt, present an hypothesis concerning their mode of interaction in inhibiting socially-morally unacceptable behavior, and provide empirical evidence concerning the nature of their interaction.

A Social Learning Theory Conceptualization of Fear and Guilt

Rotter's Social Learning Theory (SLT; Rotter, 1954) provides a vehicle for the theoretical conceptualization of fear and guilt. SLT utilizes three basic constructs, *Behavior Potential*, *Expectancy*, and *Reinforcement Value*, in a prediction formula which highlights the use of the situational variable. The basic formula is:

$$BP_{(x-n),\ s(l-n),\ R(a-n)} = f(E_{(x-n),\ s(l-n),\ R(a-n)}\ \&\ RV_{(a-n)})$$

This may be read as follows: The potentiality of the functionally related behaviors x to n to occur in the specific situation l to n in relation to potential reinforcement a to n is a function of the expectancies of these behaviors leading to these reinforcements in these situations and the values of these reinforcements [Rotter, 1954, p. 109].

In relating SLT to fear and guilt, the expectancy variable is seen as subsuming both. The expectancy construct may be viewed as being composed of an expectancy for external punishment (fear) and an expectancy for internal punishment (guilt). In situations involving the inhibition of unacceptable behavior, the expectancy for external punishment (E^e) is a function of situational cues related to the probability of the unacceptable behavior leading to negative reinforcement. The expectancy for internal negative punishment is assumed to be a generalized expectancy based on the individual's history of reinforcement, which is to a large degree independent of cues concerning the probability of external negative reinforcement in the immediate, current situation.

Guilt may be defined as a generalized punishment (i.e., negative reinforcement) for violating, anticipating the violation of, or failure to attain internalized standards of proper behavior. The standards of proper behavior are seen as encompassing both the internalized prohibitions ("should not's") and the internalized positively valued idea-goals ("ought to's") which are related to the individual's feelings of self-worth. The generalized expectancy for guilt (GE^G) is a function of the person's past history of reinforcement in regard to violating standards of proper behavior. The GE^G develops in a context of parent-child relationships in which the parents promise vague and delayed external punishment for improper or immoral behavior as they define it.[2] The GE^G is initially anticipatory of vague and delayed parental punishment but becomes anticipatory of self-critical or self-punishing behavior with the adoption of standards of proper behavior. The self-appropriation or internalization of standards of proper conduct is reinforced since it gains approval and avoids punishment. This internalization of the standards of proper behavior determines its relative independenece of situational cues. While situational cues would lead to the categorization of the situation as a "guilt" situation, the inhibitory potential of the GE^G is a function of behavior-internal reinforcement sequences which are relatively independent of E^e's based on behavior-external reinforcement sequences in the current situation. Situational cues affect the GE^G only by activating the expectancies for internal negative reinforcement which were established as a function of previous childhood experiences. The E^e is a direct function of situational cues related to the subjective probability that the unacceptable behavior will lead to external negative reinforcement. This type of conceptualization permits the retention of the important distinction between fear of external punishment and guilt.

In a fear-guilt situation, which would be defined on a consensual or cultural basis, conflict is engendered because the goal response may lead to both positive and negative reinforcement. Presumably, the behavioral response made in the situation is a function of the relative strengths of the expectancies and values of the conflicting reinforcements. In SLT, every situation is seen as a conflict situation as long as alternative responses or expectations for alternative outcomes following behavior are possible. Perhaps, the important distinction implicit in designating a situation as "conflictual" is that, in these situations, the behavior potentials are closer in "strength" than in other situations.

Combining Miller's (1959) model of conflict behavior with Rotter's SLT constructs may be useful. Rotter's basic formula can be construed as a combination of behavior potentials related to approach and avoidant behavior in a situation productive of fear of external punishment and guilt.

$$BP_{x^{AP}, \ sf-g, \ r_a} = f(E_{x, \ sf-g, \ r_a} \ \& \ RV_a)$$

$$BP_{x'^{AV}, \ sf-g, \ r_{a'}} = f(E_{x'^e, \ sf-g, \ r_{a'}} \ \& \ RV_{a'} \ \& \ GE^G)$$

The first formula may be read: The potential for approach behavior x to occur in a fear-guilt situation in relation to positive reinforcement a is a function of the expectancy that approach behavior x will lead to positive reinforcement a in the fear-guilt situation and the value of the positive reinforcement a. The second formula may be read: The potential for avoidance behavior x' to occur in a fear-guilt situation in relation to external negative reinforcement a' is a function of the expectancy that behavior x' will lead to external negative reinforcement a'; the value of external reinforcement a'; and the generalized expectancy for self-mediated punishment for violating, anticipating the violation of, or failure to attain internalized standards of proper behavior related to behavior x'. The behavior with the higher potential in the situation would occur.

---

[2] Mosher (1961) has discussed a social learning theory conception of the acquisition of E^e and GE^G which speculates about the child-rearing practices which foster the development of external and internal expectancies for punishment.

Hypothesis

The present study was designed to investigate aspects of the interaction of E^e and GE^G in inhibiting socially-morally unacceptable behavior. It is speculated that situational cues largely determine the strength of the E^e, while the GE^G is relatively independent of present situational cues since it is based on a history of behavior-reinforcement sequences which have become internalized or self-controlled. Hypothesis: It is predicted the subjects who have a relatively weak GE^G are more influenced by situational cues related to external negative reinforcement than are subjects with stronger GE^G. This does not mean that subjects with a strong GE^G will not be influenced by situational cues. However, the influence of situational cues regarding the probability of punishment is seen as affecting their E^e and not their GE^G. If subjects do not have an influential GE^G, their inhibiting behavior will be entirely a function of situational cues relevant to their E^e. If $BP_{x'AV} = f(E^e \& RV \& GE^G)$, and GE^G is not present then the potential for an avoidant or inhibitory behavior x' to occur in a fear situation in relation to an external negative reinforcement is a function of the expectancy that behavior x' will lead to the external negative reinforcement and the value of the external negative reinforcement.

METHOD

The subjects in this study were 80 male college students enrolled in an introductory psychology course who "volunteer" for research studies as part of their course requirement. The subjects were administered a sentence-completion measure of guilt in small groups. They were seen individually for the remainder of the experiment. All subjects participated in the task called the arousal condition. After completion of the arousal task the subjects were randomly assigned by alternation to the fear-reduction condition or fear-induction condition. Following one of these experimental manipulations, all subjects participated in the perceptual defense task.

Measure of Guilt

The subjects completed the 50-stem Mosher Incomplete Sentences Test (MIST). The MIST employs referents suggested by psychoanalytic theory as the operational basis for scoring sentence completions for guilt. Three subcategories of guilt (sex guilt, hostile guilt, and morality-conscience guilt) are distinguished, and 14 stems pertain to each subcategory. The MIST scoring manual for guilt (Mosher, 1961) contains a set of scoring principles suggested by psychoanalytic conception of guilt and extensive scoring examples of completions of males and females which enable completions to be scored along a five-point dimension of guilt. The guilt category includes such stems as "Masturbation . . . ," "If in the future I committed adultery . . . ," and "When I have sexual desire. . . ."[3] Theoretically, scores for the 14 sex-guilt stems could range from 0 to 56. The obtained range was from 18 to 48 with a mean of 32.43, a median of 33, and a standard deviation of 6.88. An interscorer reliability coefficient of $r = .92$ was obtained on a sample of 30 male MIST protocols scored for sex guilt by two independent raters. Mosher (1961) reports test-retest and split-half reliability coefficients of .77 and .72, respectively, for the sex-guilt category of the MIST. Mosher found that the sex-guilt stems were not significantly correlated with intelligence (as measured by the Ohio State Psychological Examination), the Edwards (1957) Social Desirability scale, or the Marlowe-Crowne (1960) Social Desirability scale.

Arousal Condition

All subjects participated in the condition. The subjects were shown six "pin-ups" of nude and seminude females and were asked to rate them on several characteristics. The following instructions were read to the subjects:

> Before we begin the main experiment, I'd like to take a few minutes to get your opinion about something else. Several men's magazines claim to have a large percentage of readers who are college students. We are interested in securing the reaction of male college students to see if it is as favorable as these magazines claim and to determine what are the characteristics of the magazine that have the most appeal. In particular, we are interested in the college male's reaction to the "pin-up" pictures these magazines feature. In general, we are interested in seeing if college males agree on which women are most attractive. I am going to show you six "pin-ups" taken from a popular men's magazine and ask you to rate them on several characteristics. I want you to look at the pictures one by one. After you have finished with one picture, you may go on to the next, but you may not return to look at an earlier picture. You will have to make your ratings from memory. Here is a pencil and paper that you may use to take notes if you so desire. Do you have any question about what you are supposed to do?

After the subjects had finished looking at the pin-ups, they were asked the following questions:

1. Which girl do you think has the prettiest face?
2. Which girl do you think has the best figure?
3. Which girl do you think is the most sexually desirable?
4. Which girl do you think would have the best personality?
5. Which girl do you think would make the best wife?

Their responses were recorded and the experimenter commented, "As you may have guessed, one of our purposes in asking these questions is to see what are the relationships among beauty, personality, and marital choice for the college male."

---

[3] Copies of the MIST and scoring manual for guilt are available from the author upon request.

Fear-Induction Condition

Forty subjects were randomly assigned by alternation to this condition. This condition was designed to provide situational cues leading to an expectancy for punishment for behavior related to sex. The following directions were read to the subjects:

> We are also interested in your opinion about the effects of looking at "pin-up" pictures. People have different opinions about such pictures, some opinions are favorable, some unfavorable. We are interested in how you feel about them. No matter what your personal opinion is, you may be sure that many other people would agree with you. I am going to read some opinions and statements taken from interviews with "experts" and other college students. After I read each statement, I want you to say "agree" or "disagree" depending on your own opinion about the statement. Time does not permit us to fully discuss any of these, and it may be hard for you to confine your answer to a simple "agree" or "disagree" only. After we have completed the main experiment we can discuss some of your answers in the remaining time if you so desire. Do you understand?

The following 10 statements were then read:

1. Looking at erotic pictures is sexually arousing.
2. Sex perverts often own large collections of erotic pictures.
3. I would be ashamed to show my mother erotic pictures.
4. Erotic pictures lead to increased masturbation.
5. To enjoy looking at erotic pictures is a sign of "loose" morals and a "morally" deprived background.
6. Many psychologists feel erotic pictures are sexually stimulating and may lead to sex crimes.
7. Erotic pictures are obscene and degrade those who enjoy them.
8. Erotic pictures should not be sold to young boys as they are damaging to suggestible individuals.
9. It is a sin to enjoy looking at erotic pictures.
10. Many prominent educators believe erotic pictures should not be sold on the newsstands.

Every time the subjects said "agree," the experimenter encouraged them by saying "mm-hmm" and nodding his head affirmatively. This behavior coupled with the condemnatory statements about pin-ups was intended to increase the subjects' fear of external punishment for unacceptable behavior related to sex.

Fear-Reduction Condition

Forty subjects were randomly assigned by alternation to this condition. This condition was designed to provide situational cues which would decrease any apprehension that behavior related to sex would be disapproved or punished. The subjects were read the same instructions used in the fear-induction condition. Then, the following 10 statements were read:

1. It is normal for college males to enjoy looking at "pin-up" pictures.
2. Court decisions are almost unanimous that "pin-ups" are not obscene; the judges must feel that such pictures are not damaging.
3. Kinsey, the famous investigator of sexual practices, believes excessive prudery, such as censoring "pin-ups," is often psychologically damaging.
4. "Pin-up" pictures have an artistic value which should not be thoughtlessly censored.
5. "Pin-up" pictures are common possessions of college males who enjoy looking at beautful women.
6. Most males look at "pin-ups," swear, and talk about sex; they should not be ashamed of these normal reactions.
7. Many psychologists believe "pin-ups" are a useful outlet for the expression of sexual needs.
8. "Pin-ups" should not be thoughtlessly classified as pornographic or obscene and banned from newsstands.
9. If "pin-ups" and sex were not regarded as evil by narrow-minded people, there would be less sexual problems and less divorce among married people.
10. I enjoy looking at "pin-ups" and feel this is a natural interest for college males to have.

Whenever the subjects said "agree," the experimenter would say "mm-hmm" and nod his head affirmatively. This behavior coupled with the positively toned statements about pin-ups was intended to decrease the subjects' fear of external punishment for socially condemned behavior related to sex.

Perceptual-Defense Condition

All subjects were presented the perceptual-defense condition. Perceptual-defense scores were used as a measure of the subjects' tendency to inhibit the expression of taboo sexual responses. The subjects were presented five taboo and five neutral words in a random order by the successive carbons method (Cowen & Beier, 1950) employing the usual instructions which encourage guessing. Twenty carbon copies of each word were typed in capital letters on an electric typewriter and placed in a booklet ordered from the least clear copy to the clearest copy. All of the words consisted of five letters. The taboo words were: whore, urine, bitch, penis, and raped. The neutral words were: ranch, scent, towel, spray, and cable.

The perceptual-defense task was selected as the dependent variable, since it involves a conflict between a behavior potential to report the word as soon as possible and a behavior potential to avoid taboo words. The choice of a perceptual-defense task was not dictated by a concern with the issue of unconscious perception which according to Eriksen (1958, 1960) seems unlikely. Rather, following Eriksen and Browne (1956), the differential responding to taboo and neutral words was construed as a manifestation of an anxiety-produced inhibition of response. The anxiety-produced inhibition of response was specifically hypothesized to be a function of an expectancy for external punishment in the situation and a generalized expectancy for self-mediated punishment for violation of internalized standards of proper behavior related to sex.

RESULTS

Restating the hypothesis in terms of the specific measure used to operationally define the constructs, it was predicted that the perceptual defense scores of subjects who are low on a measure of sex guilt are more influenced by the experimental conditions of fear-reduction or fear-induction than are the perceptual defense scores of subjects who score high on a measure of sex guilt. The fear-induction condition was expected to lead to a higher perceptual-defense score than the fear-reduction condition. Subjects who score high on sex guilt were expected to have higher perceptual-defense scores than subjects who score low on sex guilt.

A double classification analysis of variance was used to analyze the predicted interaction. One classification was based on the experimental conditions of fear-reduction or fear-induction. The other classification into two groups reflected a splitting of the distribution of sex-guilt scores at the median to obtain a high-sex-guilt group and a low-sex-guilt group. Table 1 contains the means and standard deviations of the neutral words, taboo words, and perceptual-defense scores for the four groups resulting from the double classification. The perceptual-defense score is a difference score computed by subtracting the number of pages required to recognize the five neutral words from the number of pages required to recognize the five taboo words.

Table 1   Means and Sigmas of the Experimental Groups for the Neutral Words, Taboo Words, and Perceptual Defense Scores

Experimental Group	N	Neutral Words		Taboo Words		Perceptual Defense Scores	
		M	SD	M	SD	M	SD
Fear reduction							
High sex guilt	18	43.61	11.08	48.33	8.40	4.72	4.19
Low sex guilt	22	44.04	5.56	46.86	7.29	2.82	4.86
Fear induction							
High sex guilt	20	44.10	7.83	48.75	7.01	4.65	5.10
Low sex guilt	20	43.20	7.16	50.90	7.09	7.70	6.63

The perceptual-defense scores served as the dependent variable in the analysis of variance presented in Table 2. Bartlett's test for homogeneity of variance was not significant.

The presence of the significant interaction between sex guilt and the fear conditions revealed in Table 2 and an examination of the means of the perceptual-defense scores reported in Table 1 indicate the hypothesis was supported. Subjects who score low on sex guilt were, indeed, significantly more influenced by the experimental manipulation of their expectancy for external punishment than were the high-guilt subjects.

Table 2   Analysis of Variance of Perceptual Defense Scores

Source	df	MS	F
Sex guilt (A)	1	4.20	.14
Fear conditions (B)	1	125.00	4.26*
A × B	1	124.72	4.25*
Within groups	76	29.38	

Note. A constant of 10 was added to all perceptual-defense scores to simplify computations.
* $p < .05$.

DISCUSSION

In this study it was predicted that subjects who are relatively uninfluenced by an internalized sense of guilt will be more dependent on external cues in determining the inhibition-expression of unacceptable behavior. This prediction was supported. The rationale for the prediction was based on a theoretical conception of inhibitory behavior potentials as a joint function of an expectancy for negative reinforcement (and the value of that negative reinforcement) and a generalized expectancy for self-mediated punishment for a violation of an internalized standard of proper behavior. If the subjects have a weak GE^G, then the E^e will be the effective contributor to the strength of the inhibitory potential. Situations which provide cues related to the probability of punishment will, thus, have a greater effect on subjects who are little guided or not guided by a GE^G.

However, aspects of the results are surprising. It was expected that subjects who are low on sex guilt and in the fear-reduction condition should have the lowest mean perceptual-defense scores, and this was the case. Also, it was expected that subjects who are high on sex guilt and in the fear-induction condition should have the highest mean perceptual-defense score, and this was not the case. Rather, the highest mean perceptual-defense score was obtained by the subjects in the low-sex-guilt, fear-induction group. The high-sex-guilt subjects, whose mean perceptual-defense scores are nearly identical, appear to have been uninfluenced by the experimental conditions designed to increase or decrease fear of external punishment. On the other hand, the subjects who were low on sex guilt show a marked discrepancy in performance on the perceptual-defense task as a function of the experimental conditions. One possible explanation of these findings might invoke a differential sensitivity to external cues related to punishment between persons with highly developed and poorly developed internalized standards governing unacceptable behavior. Perhaps, individuals who attend almost exclusively to external cues in governing their unacceptable behavior become more sensitive to situational cues related to the probability of external punishment or disapproval. If no external controls prohibit a desired but culturally unacceptable behavior, they do as they wish. If, on the other hand, they fear punishment from others, they may very effectively inhibit their behavior. Since their unacceptable behavior is governed almost exclusively by the probability of punishment, they become attuned to the cues which others provide about their attitudes toward the culturally unacceptable behavior. The so-called psychopath is sometimes described in a similar fashion. A person who has internalized standards which prohibit culturally unacceptable behaviors will inhibit their expression regardless of the chances of being punished by others. Is it possible that over a period of time he becomes somewhat insensitive to cues which are related to the probability of external punishment?

The stability of the perceptual defense scores for the high-sex-guilt group in the face of the experimental manipulations and modifiability of the same scores for the low-sex-guilt group is intriguing. It suggests the possibility, as pointed out above, of a differential sensitivity to situational cues on the part of subjects who are high or low on guilt which has not been suspected. More precisely, the finding that subjects who are low on guilt may be hypersensitive to cues related to external punishment is not altogether surprising, but the possibility that subjects who are high on a measure of guilt are hyposensitive to cues related to the probability of external punishment suggests a new avenue for future research.

PART 4: SUMMARY

Every new field of knowledge develops around a purpose or interest. As one or more scholars become interested in new problems and find that the variables or constructs of the established fields are not satisfactory or sufficient to deal with these problems, they begin to invent new constructs. The new problems and new concepts they become concerned with eventually become considered a field of study of their own. For the most part in American psychology, an interest in individual differences in personality followed an interest in individual differences which was restricted largely to intellectual functions. The variables or constructs that were used to describe individual differences and abilities, most of which came from faculty psychology, were not satisfactory to describe, understand, or account for individual differences in character, temperament, mental pathology, or other problems which were of interest to a growing number of psychologists. In the absence of a research methodology to deal with complex human behavior and consequently with little feedback, it soon became relatively common for each person interested in the field to develop his own constructs and ultimately for a large number of theories to arise—some global, some miniature, some systematic, and some helter-skelter.

With time we have become more sophisticated in our knowledge of theory construction and have gradually accumulated a research methodology to test hypotheses and, hopefully, to reduce ultimately our theories to few in number. While we may always have different theories, a stable and communicable body of knowledge will accumulate only when the different theories have in common a large number of constructs. Without such common constructs or variables, research done from one theoretical point of view would provide little or no information to theorists who rely on an entirely different set of constructs.

At least five persistent problems face the ambitious theory builder in the field of personality. We still have a long way to go before they are solved. The discussion of social learning work in this area will be concerned with these five problems and the contributions that have been made toward their eventual solution. We may state these as a series of questions. The first question is, "What are the variables and relations that describe an adequate process theory suitable to explain behavior in complex social interactions, making use of past experience and able to predict future behavior?" That is, a useful process theory must account for how personality characteristics develop and explicate the conditions under which they remain relatively stable or change.

The second question facing the personality theorist is, "What are the most important content variables necessary to adequately describe individual differences?" Out of the literally thousands of choices to describe individual differences, the personality theorist must choose those few that will account for the generality of behavior in the important situations of life in which he is most interested. Too many such constructs, which are highly overlapping, make for considerable inefficiency and for extreme difficulty in prediction. Too few such constructs result in failure in the ability to describe important individual differences or to allow for anything but the grossest prediction.

The third question the personality theorist must answer is, "How can the process theory and the content theory be integrated?" A process theory must explain how the characteristics in the content variables are acquired and developed and how they can be changed. It is not sufficient merely to state in some general terms that the characteristics are acquired through learning or that they develop through an instinctual unfolding, but if any utility is to be achieved in understanding one individual as different from another, then the process theory must be able to account for how a specific characteristic is acquired and how it is changed. The content theory, in other words, should be a logical outgrowth of the process theory.

If people could be counted on always to act in the same way, the development of personality theories would be a lot easier. It is clear that a great deal of specificity is present in human behavior. In the development of any theory, the question arises of how much specificity should be accounted for and how much generality. Do we wish to describe and predict only very broad trends in behavior or be able to predict all individual responses in all kinds of situations? In the past personality theories tended to be on the highly general side. Fine distinctions were ignored and descriptions dealt only with gross differences over long periods of time. Such theories do not allow for prediction in many important and interesting problems. On the other hand, theories that could account for all the specific responses would be extremely unwieldy. The problem facing the theorist is how to account for and describe both generality and specificity in both the process and content aspects of his theory.

Finally, we come to the fifth question, but certainly not the least important: "How is one to measure the constructs, both process and content, and consequently allow for the testing of hypotheses and the establishment of the utility of the theory?" The contributions of social learning theory to the resolution of these five problems will be discussed below.

The Process Theory

That the process theory described here is sufficiently complex to deal with a variety of problems is attested to by the contents of this book. Social learning theory has been used to analyze problems and to make predictions in laboratory and field studies as disparate as studies of delay of reinforcement, decision time, delinquency, aggression, guilt, electric shock therapy, social action, social influence, and cultural differences. It is indeed a complex theory, more complex than most, although the terminology is not particularly esoteric. It appears to have great flexibility in dealing with complex behavior. SLT approaches problems with four classes of variables (behaviors, expectancies, reinforcements, and situations) rather than with one or two, as is characteristic of most personality theories, including those that *seem* to be more complex because of the use of more esoteric or less measurable constructs.

The process theory itself is described in earlier sections, and much of the basic research testing the theory is reported in an earlier book (Rotter, 1954).

Formula 8 in Part 1, which includes generalized expectancies for problem-solving, undoubtedly complicates the problem of accurate prediction, but at the same time it provides a new and promising approach to a vast number of problems. The consistent and replicated findings described in the monograph on internal-external control (Rotter, 4–6) reflect this. The paper on attitude measurement in the next section (Rotter, 5–1) illustrates the intricacy and complexity of the problem of prediction when one considers the great variety of generalized expectancies that may be involved in a single choice situation. The strategy of theory development that we have followed was to start with the fewest and broadest classes of variables and add other variables as the necessity appeared and as it became clear that the existing constructs did not allow for efficient prediction. The strategy was to add new classes of variables only after it was clear how they could be measured and how they would fit systematically into the theory. The work reported here on internal-external control of reinforcement is only a small portion of the studies that illustrate how the addition of generalized expectancies for problem-solving allow for increased prediction in problems involving learning, perception, social action, psychopathology, cognitive development, achievement, moral behavior, and others.

The theory, in fact, is so intricate that mathematical prediction seems further away now than it did before the addition of generalized expectancies for problem-solving as a major class of constructs. It has become increasingly clear that the accuracy of prediction in any choice behavior of human beings depends not only upon the variables one uses to abstract but also on the adequacy of the selection within a group of variables of those that are most relevant for a particular problem.

The Content Theory

The content classes of social learning theory are derived from the process theory. When the members of a group generalize their experiences, and consequently build a more or less similar way of reacting to a class of events, there is a potential basis for abstracting a variable describing individual differences which will be functional in nature—functional, that is, in that the observation of one or more instances of behavior will allow for prediction of others in specified situations or under specified conditions. But the human is capable of perceiving similarity along a vast number of dimensions and at many levels of generality. One characteristic that may be unique to social learning theory is the emphasis on the process theory determining how one selects classes of content variables. The advantages are obvious, since the process theory immediately points to hypotheses regarding how the individual differences in the content variable were developed or maintained and are changed. Second, we have avoided the use of terms, no matter how widely used or how long their history, unless there is a genuine basis for assuming the generalization process, or functionality. Although we may often deal with the same behavioral characteristics of individuals as other approaches, for this reason we have avoided content categories in terms of psychopathological diseases, or disease entities, and broad but badly defined concepts such as anxiety and emotions.

In early research the content categories that were most emphasized were psychological needs. Needs are characterized by perceived similarity of the reinforcement and include as subclasses behaviors leading to the same or similar reinforcements (need potential), expectancies for the attainment of these similar reinforcements (freedom of movement), and the preference or desirability attached to these reinforcements (need value). In addition to the broad needs that may characterize everyone in a culture and include large numbers of reinforcements, the concept of needs includes any group of reinforcements that are perceived as similar. As pointed out in the article on social learning theory implications for testing (Rotter, 4–1), there are several advantages to this view of motivated or goal-directed behavior. For one, it does not emphasize only the objective behaviors or the implicit goal strengths or the cognitive perceptions of a situation but includes all three. Enhanced prediction results in considering all three as important and necessary aspects of goal-directed behavior.

Much of the research on social learning theory has dealt with relatively broad needs and some of the more specific needs which are clearly subclasses of one of the broader needs such as academic recognition or physical-skills recognition or love and affection from opposite-sex peers. There are many other concepts that cut across the broad needs described in Part 1. Crowne and Liverant (5–7) have dealt in this way with conformity. Crowne and Marlowe (1964) describe a series of impressive studies on social approval conceived of as a need, and Mosher (1965b) has approached the concept of aggression with a series of studies in which aggression likewise is conceived of as a goal-directed behavior to inflict pain on others. When aggression is regarded as a need, it then includes a series of related behaviors (need potential) and of expectancies (freedom of movement) that those behaviors will lead to a differentially valued set of reinforcements (need value) contingent upon the situation. Mosher (1965b) has carefully analyzed aggression in this way and is developing a program of research investigating the determinants of aggression from this point of view. Such a view contrasts with those that regard aggression either as an instinctual response to frustration or as part of an instinctual reservoir which is inherent in all humans. Altruistic behavior has been similarly analyzed and studied by Rettig (1956).

Just as perceived similarities of reinforcements will lead to generalization and the building up of stable modes of response, so will certain other aspects of the situation lead to similar generalizations and classes of stable behavior. One of these is the kind of problem presented in the situation, that is, the nature of the kinds of alternatives that are open for obtaining satisfactions (that is, the use of skill versus luck). After considerable experience, the individual builds up a generalized expectancy that this kind of situation or this kind of problem can be solved by the use of a variety of behaviors. While the behaviors utilized may differ considerably from one to another, what is common is the way different persons perceive the situation as presenting a particular kind of problem. So, for example, one individual sees skill as the basis of problem solution or satisfaction attainment while another feels that luck or chance will determine the outcome of his behavior. We have termed this a belief in internal versus external control of reinforcement.

Mosher (1968b; 4–8) and his students have completed a series of investigations studying guilt, conceptualized as a generalized expectancy for self-mediated punishment following moral transgression. Much of his work to date has been in studying the functionality of the concept and in assessing construct validity of a series of measures of guilt.

Another generalized expectancy, perhaps of great potential importance in understanding broad trends in our society, is interpersonal trust, a generalized expectancy that others can be believed. Moss (4–2) and Efran and Korn (1969) have worked with a generalized expectancy which might be called cautiousness or a belief that one must be careful and avoid risks, particularly in ambiguous situations. Such a concept certainly overlaps heavily the notions of success strivers versus failure avoiders in social psychological problems of conformity and in studies of achievement and risk-taking behavior (Feather, 1968; Birney, Burdick, & Teevan, 1969). What makes these content variables different from those of needs is that what is generalized from one situation to another is the similarity of the *problem of obtaining satisfaction* in different situations rather than the similarity in the nature of the ultimate reinforcement. Trust may be involved in situations in which the ultimate reinforcement might be love, achievement, or physical safety. It is not the nature of the reinforcement that leads to a common expectancy but rather that in all these situations whether some other person can be believed in his communications is the common or similar element.

Another class of content variables for the description of individual differences may be characterized as defense and enhancement behavior in which the common element of a series of events is the sign and strength of the reinforcement. Some individuals may characteristically generalize not only the nature of the reinforcement but perceive as similar different situations involving different reinforcements all of which are nevertheless strongly positive or strongly negative. In such situations there may develop techniques of enhancement or defense to maintain positive reinforcement or minimize negative reinforcement. For example, one person *may* react to all strong threats regardless of what goal is being blocked by withdrawal, another to the same strong, negative reinforcements with perceptual distortions. The area is not an easy one to investigate and has historically led to a variety of partially overlapping concepts such as emotions, anxiety, emotional behavior, affective responses, defensive behavior, and frustration. In many instances behavior that has been considered under these latter categories may be better thought of as instrumental behavior or goal-directed behavior, learned perhaps early in life, but nevertheless predictable on the basis of expectancies and reinforcement values. Nevertheless, there is indication that individuals will differ consistently in immediate responses to strong positive or negative reinforcement or the anticipation of either of these in the immediate situation. We have just begun to investigate these reactions as a separate content class for the study of individual differences. Studies of some short-term effects of negative reinforcement have been published by Ford (1963) and by Mischel and Masters (2–7). Ford's study suggests that overt aggression appears only when the subject feels that the frustration is unfair and not the result of his own lack of skill. Mischel and Masters' investigation supported the hypothesis that the arbitrary nonavailability of an expected reinforcement increased the value of the reinforcement.

In order to obtain a maximum predictive efficiency or if one prefers to understand the determinants of behavior, it is necessary to characterize not only generality in terms of individual characteristics but also the generality of situations. In fact, we have been talking about such generality or situational categorization implicitly throughout this section. If expectancies for reinforcement are determined by the situation, then it is clear that situations may be described as similar in that they are characteristically perceived as leading to one kind of reinforcement rather than another. In this sense we may talk about achievement situations or love and affection situations or social acceptance situations, and so on, or ambiguous situations or novel situations. In fact, in the literature this problem is sometimes dealt with by concepts such as arousal, instigation, press, threat, and so on.

People differ in the degree to which they perceive the world as controlled by their own efforts, skills, and characteristics versus by chance, luck, fate, or powerful others, and situations, too, will differ for the subculture as a whole in the degree to which they are perceived as being skill or chance controlled. In other words, generalized expectancies for problem-solving carry with them the potential classification of situations based on the nature of the problem to be solved, or the characteristics of the situation that determined how the individual is likely to obtain satisfaction. Similarly, strong positive or negative reinforcement or the anticipation of them also suggests a situational characteristic for the subculture as a whole, or an effective way of describing similarity in situations. Halpin and Winer (1952) have found great utility and enhanced predictiveness in studying leadership and the characteristics of desirable leaders when they discriminate among situations in the degree of outside threat to which the group is exposed. There are many other ways in which situations can be characterized as similar, depending, of course, on the problem being investigated. As we shall see in the next section, social attitudes provide another class of content variables in which the principle of generalization is applied to social objects as part of the situation.

What we have contributed to the study of content of personality is not a new taxonomy of traits nor a new taxonomy of situations nor a new typology of people but rather classes of content variables all of which are integrated with a process theory and consequently all of which can be studied with leads fo their development and change provided by the process theory. We have provided a method of analyzing problems but not a series of answers. The answers must come from empirical study and will undoubtedly be constantly revised with the acquisition of new knowledge. The problem of the investigator, whether his concern is to help a particular person clinically or to do an exploratory study or to test a theoretical hypothesis, is to *select* those variables to work with that seem the most promising on the basis of knowledge already accumulated from among the several classes of content variables. Once these are selected, the process theory provides the basis for hypotheses and directs attention to the kind of information, constructs, or empirical data that needs to be obtained in order to test these hypotheses.

Generality-Specificity

The problem of generality-specificity is related to the discussion on selection of relevant variables. At what levels of generality should the student, clinician, or applied social scientist work or think about his problem? It has been demonstrated that the more specific the categories one works with, the higher the degree of prediction one can generate from one situation to another. To predict whether or not an individual will study for a particular examination in a psychology class, a general measure of "achievement need" based on the values of content of stories he tells to a set of pictures could not possibly achieve the same level of prediction that is possible if we were to base prediction on a concept of need to obtain a high grade in psychology and measure how much he studied for the previous examination. *The broader the concepts we work with, the less predictability from one random referent to another.* The same thing is true if we are speaking of situation similarity or situational categories. Attempts to predict defensive behavior using a broad classification of "frustration situations" will produce much less accuracy in predicting from one randomly selected referent to another than if we use more specific categories such as "love rejection" or "arbitrary failure" as the basis for assuming a constancy of behavioral response. It must be clear that there is no single answer to the question of how specific our descriptive variables should be. A theoretical approach that is highly general in its description of individual differences will fail to make many important discriminations among individuals (Will he benefit more from a male than a female therapist? Will he show hostility to everyone or only to authority figures? Will it be all authority figures or only those who use overt dominance behaviors? and so on). On the other hand, if we wish to study interpersonal trust, do we need a measure of interpersonal trust of doctors, another one for interpersonal trust of lawyers, another one for interpersonal trust of high school teachers, and still another for interpersonal trust of college teachers? Obviously, this choice must be made on the basis of the scientist's purposes. *Not only must he choose the variables that are most relevant to study his problem but he must choose a level of generality that is most efficient for his purposes. What is necessary is that the theory provide potential classes of content variables and also the alternative of selecting specific variables at any level of generality, provided functional utility can be demonstrated.* The same rules that apply to the selection of any broad or highly general variable apply to the selection of much more specific variables. The principle of mediated stimulus generalization and the test for its occurrence can provide the basis for the selection of any variable at any level of specificity. The papers selected in this section illustrate not only the several classes of content variables that can be used to study a specific problem but also the range of generality-specificity.

Tyler, Tyler, and Rafferty (1961) demonstrated that prediction of children's motivations is possible from the assessment of parents' need values and freedom of movement. Parental motives for recognition status, love and affection, and dominance were assessed from free-response interviews. Children's motives for the same variables, as well as independence and protection-dependency, were judged from narrative descriptions of preschool activities. Adequate interrater reliability for both kinds of measures was established utilizing score-by-example manuals. Using much more specific variables, Phares and Rotter (1956) demonstrated that predictable situational differences exist between a school room used for academic teaching and a gymnasium and that these will significantly affect the response to a questionnaire asking for ratings of the value of a series of reinforcements.

The Measurement of Personality Variables

It is probably in the area of the methodology of personality measurement that social learning theory has made its best-known contributions. These contributions take two forms: (1) the development of a series of measures that have proved useful in hypothesis testing for a variety of problems; and (2) the clarification of several issues involving the nature of reliability, validity, the relation of test format to predictive efficiency, the effects of situational variables, and the role of social desirability or other so-called response styles.

Many of these issues are discussed in detail in Rotter's paper (4–1). Several points can be valuably repeated. From a social learning theory point of view, a test is an operation for a construct, and test-taking behavior is subject to the same influences as any other behavior. Consequently, every test response must be regarded as a behavior that involves an expectancy for one or more reinforcements. The expectancies are controlled in part by the situation. Not only can the examiner, the instructions, the physical place of testing, and the purpose for which the individual is there influence test results but knowing something about these variables can suggest the way in which they will influence test responses by raising or lowering expectancies for particular reinforcements in that situation. One cannot regard this merely as so much error to be tolerated or hopefully to be eliminated by making certain aspects of the situation standard. Rather, one must accept the more complicated but obvious truth *that the validity or the utility of a test can be established only for a particular population in a particular set of testing conditions.* To use a situation *systematically* means that we are ready to describe some important variables about the situation which will allow us to make predictions about situational generality or the class of situations about which we might make predictions. Mulry (1966) has shown that group means on an incomplete-sentences measure of adjustment (Rotter & Rafferty, 1950) differ significantly under two common conditions for administering a battery of tests. In one condition subjects must wait for the whole group to finish before going on to the next task. In the other condition each subject goes on to the next task as soon as he is finished with the incomplete sentences. Presumably, embarrassment in the former condition produces quicker, less revealing responses in some subjects and consequently lower maladjustment scores. A measure taken in the former condition could be expected to be predictive only in situations in which the criterion is a measure of adjustment involving an obvious response obtained under public conditions. Of course, not only is situational similarity important in understanding when tests may be appropriately used but the process of validation also requires an understanding of the dimensions of situational similarity before one can select reasonable criteria.

A tendency to respond to test items by providing a response one thinks will bring social approval from the examiner is not error to be controlled but information that will provide a basis for determining under what conditions the test scores will predict behavior. Conceiving of social approval as one of many reinforcements in the situation changes our conception of the variables to be measured. The variable to be measured may bear a strong relation to social approval as a motive, and attempts to exclude social approval or make its influence zero may, in fact, eliminate powerful referents needed to make an adequate test in the first place. Finally, if we do eliminate social approval from the items or from the test procedure, then it should be eliminated also from the situations about which we wish to predict. If people are likely to make a more trusting verbal response because social approval calls for them to be more trusting, then in some behavior criterion situation they also make a more trusting response because social approval requires that response in that situation.

Another contribution of social learning theory to understanding the principles involved in test construction lies in the concept of the *additive* test in contrast to the *power* test. While additive tests have been constructed, they frequently have been without any clear or explicit theoretical justification. Frequently, the purpose of a test is to provide cross-situational generality or to make predictions in a variety of different situations. The notion then of a population of referents for a construct leads naturally to sampling of referents in order to obtain a general measure. The construction of two tests on this principle are described in the articles included on the trust scale (Rotter, 4-7) and the I-E scale (Rotter, 4-6). Rather than working on a narrow or highly specific variable in which the items differ in degree or power, the attempt is to make the items of more or less equivalent power and to sample a broad variety of different kinds of situations. Such tests are useful for particular kinds of applications and also for measures of theoretical variables in order to test a series of hypotheses. Additive tests also have different characteristics than power tests. It may be expected that the intercorrelation among items, though positive, would be low, and consequently measures of internal consistency would also be relatively lower than power tests.

Another logical inference from social learning theory is that what can be predicted from a test becomes a hit-or-miss proposition if one does not construct the test to measure either behavior, expectancies, or reinforcement values rather than mixing them in unknown proportions. Goal preferences alone do not predict choice behavior efficiently. Expectancies alone do not predict choice behavior efficiently. However, we may wish to measure need values or reinforcement values to make some tests of theoretical hypotheses or to measure generalized expectancies such as trust or internal-external control, because such expectancies can lead to behavioral predictions in specific situations, when additional knowledge of that situation is taken into account. It does follow, however, from social learning theory that the best predictor of a class of behaviors is behavior. General measures of behavior should sample behavior. The theory does lead to an implication that those tests which are likely to give the highest prediction are essentially work-sample tests. But work-sample tests involve only one or a few limited situations, and while they may have predictive power for very similar situations, they may give lower prediction for dissimilar situations than would a very generalized test which has sampled many situations. The generalized test can predict perhaps at a lower level in some situations, but can predict significantly to more situations than can a very specific test. For example, a measure of trustworthiness based upon whether or not people returned extra change they were not entitled to in a supermarket might predict with reasonable accuracy whether or not they would be honest in leaving money for newspapers on a stand run on an "honor" basis. However, such a test might bear no relation to their trustworthiness in telling their own child about their sexual behavior prior to marriage. The point might be made by studying the intercorrelations of items in an additive scale. While certain similar items would show high correlations among them, the average of the correlations of any item with all the other items would typically be lower than the average correlation of the total score with all of the individual items, with that item excluded. Nevertheless, some unobtrusive behaviors (see Webb, Campbell, Schwartz, & Sechrest, 1966) may be useful as broad measures when the subject is not aware of what is being measured and is less likely to change the behavior in different situations, for example, the use of decision time (Rotter & Mulry, 1965; Mulry, 1966) or eye contact (Efran & Broughton, 4–5).

A subtle and interesting implication of social learning theory has to do with the utilization of projective tests (particularly those involving "novel" tasks and "unstructured" instructions) for personality measurement. It follows from the theory that when the situation is ambiguous and there are few cues to determine what behavior will be most satisfying, the subject will search for cues to provide additional information or respond to cues that might otherwise be ignored as not significant. One would expect, therefore, and the evidence seems to bear this out (Henry & Rotter, 1956; Rotter, 4–1; Masling, 1960), that such tests would be maximally subject to slight differences in instructions, examiner characteristics, influences of the physical place of testing, and so on. Such tests may, in fact, be more suitable for studying the effects of subtle cues or for studying person-situation interactions than for investigating traits or trans-situational ways of responding. In a study of impression formation using stories told from slides, Opochinsky (1965) did study the interaction effect of stimulus and individual variables of expectancy and value on the dominant content of the stories. Some other implications of SLT for an understanding of projective tests are described by Rotter (4–1).

Finally, the value of this theory in part lies in the fact that constructs are added only as they can be operationalized. In attacking a series of problems with relatively new concepts and new ideas of the nature of adequate theoretical operations, it has been necessary to develop a series of new measures, some developed for very specific purposes, others for much more general purposes. The list varies widely in the degree to which their predictability or validity has been explored and replicated. Table 1 lists the variables for which measurement has been attempted, with their major references.

Table 1   Measures of Some Social Learning Variables

NEEDS			
Need	*Variables*	*Method*	*Population*
1. Recognition Status			
a. Tyler, Tyler, & Rafferty, 1961; Rafferty, Tyler, & Tyler, 3–1; Tyler, 1960.	NP, NV, FM	Interview, behavioral	Adults, children
b. Jessor, Graves, Hanson, & Jessor, 1968.	NV, FM	Questionnaire	Adults (noncollege)
c. Liverant, 1958.	NV	Questionnaire	College students
d. Crandall, 1955.	FM	Projective	College students
2. Love and Affection			
a. Tyler, Tyler, & Rafferty, 1961; Rafferty, Tyler, & Tyler, 3–1; Tyler, 1960.	NP, NV, FM	Interview, behavioral	Adults, children
b. Jessor, Graves, Hanson, & Jessor, 1968.	NV, FM	Questionnaire, sociometric	Adolescents, adults (noncollege)
c. Liverant, 1958.	NV	Questionnaire	College students
d. Crandall, 1955.	FM	Projective	College students
e. Lotsof, 1953.	NV	Interview	College students
f. Rafferty, 1952.	NV	Interview, projective	College students
3. Dominance			
a. Tyler, Tyler, & Rafferty, 1961; Rafferty, Tyler, & Tyler, 3–1; Tyler, 1960.	NP, NV, FM	Interview, behavioral	Adults, children
4. Dependency			
a. Tyler, Tyler, & Rafferty, 1961; Rafferty, Tyler,	NP, NV, FM	Behavioral	Children

Table 1 Continued

NEEDS			
Need	*Variables*	*Method*	*Population*
& Tyler, **3–1**; Tyler, 1960.			
b. Fitzgerald, **4–3**.	NP, NV, FM FM-NV Conflict	Projective, interview, sociometric	College students
c. Naylor, 1955.	NP	Projective, behavioral	College students
d. Blyth, 1953.	NP	Semiprojective	Adults
e. Dunlap, 1951.	NP	Semiprojective	College students
f. Jessor, Graves, Hanson, & Jessor, 1968.	NV, FM	Questionnaire	Adults (noncollege)
g. Crandall, Orleans, Preston, & Rabson, 1958.	NP	Behavioral	Children
5. Independence			
a. Tyler, Tyler, & Rafferty, 1961; Rafferty, Tyler, & Tyler, **3–1**; Tyler, 1960.	NP, NV, FM	Behavioral	Children
b. Blyth, 1953.	NP	Semiprojective	Adults
c. Jessor, Graves, Hanson, & Jessor, 1968.	NV, FM	Questionnaire	Adults (noncollege)
6. Academic Recognition and Achievement			
a. Naylor, 1955.	NV, FM	Projective	College students
b. Jessor, Graves, Hanson, & Jessor, 1968.	NV, FM	Questionnaire, behavioral	Adolescents
c. Liverant, 1958.	NV	Questionnaire	College students
d. Crandall, 1955.	FM	Projective	College students
e. Lotsof, 1953.	NV	Interview	College students
f. Rafferty, 1952.	NV	Interview, projective	College students
g. Crandall, Orleans, Preston, & Rabson, 1958.	NP	Behavioral	Children
h. Crandall, Katkovsky, & Preston, 1962.	NV, FM	Questionnaire	Children

Table 1   Continued

NEEDS

Need	Variables	Method	Population
7. Social Approval			
a. Crowne & Marlowe, 1964.	NP	Questionnaire	College students
b. Efran & Broughton, 4–5.	NP	Behavioral	College students
c. Crandall, Crandall, & Katkovsky, 1965.	NP	Questionnaire	Children
8. Aggression			
a. Mosher, Mortimer, & Grebel, 1968.	NP	Behavioral	Adolescents
b. Adams, 1969.	FM	Questionnaire	Adolescents
9. Altruism			
a. Rettig, 1956.	NP	Questionnaire	College students

GENERALIZED EXPECTANCIES

Variable	Method	Population
1. Guilt		
a. James & Mosher, 1967.	Questionnaire	Adolescents
b. Mosher, 1966.	Projective, behavioral	College students
c. Okel & Mosher, 1968.	Questionnaires (two types)	College students
d. Mosher, 1968b.	Questionnaire, projective	College students
2. Internal-External Locus of Control		
a. James, 1957.	Questionnaire	College students
b. Rotter, 4–6.	Questionnaire	College students, adolescents, adults (noncollege)
c. Crandall, Katkovsky, & Crandall, 1965.	Questionnaire	Children
d. Jessor, Graves, Hanson, & Jessor, 1968.	Questionnaire, interview	Adults (noncollege), adolescents
e. Bialer, 1961.	Questionnaire	Children
f. Battle & Rotter, 5–9.	Semiprojective	Children
g. Rotter & Mulry, 1965.	Behavioral	College students

Table 1   Continued

	Needs	
Variable	*Method*	*Population*
h. Adams-Webber, 1969	Projective	College students
i. Cardi, 1962.	Interview	College students
3. Time Perspective		
a. Jessor, Graves, Hanson, & Jessor, 1968.	Interview	Adults (noncollege), adolescents
4. Delay of Gratification		
a. Jessor, Graves, Hanson, & Jessor, 1968.	Projective, behavioral	Adolescents
b. Mischel, 1958.	Behavioral, questionnaire	Children
5. Cautiousness		
a. Moss, 4–2.	Projective, behavioral	College students
b. Efran & Korn, 1969.	Sociometric, behavioral, questionnaire	College students
6. Interpersonal Trust		
a. Rotter, 4–7.	Questionnaire, sociometric	College students
b. Geller, 1966.	Behavioral	College students
c. Hochreich, 1966.	Semiprojective	Children

Applications to Social Psychology and the Social Sciences

INTRODUCTION

The papers in this section are organized into two groups. The first group contains papers dealing with contributions to social psychology, beginning with Rotter's (5–1) article on "Beliefs, Social Attitudes and Behavior." This analysis describes the basic hypotheses in this area, and the papers that follow can be regarded as tests of these hypotheses, or at least investigations derived from them. The study by Hamsher, Geller, and Rotter (5–2) illustrates the significance of personality variables in social attitudes. The following three papers, Phares's (5–3) study of social influence, and Gore and Rotter's (5–4) and Strickland's (5–5) studies of social action are illustrative of a large series of studies relating internal-external control to the potential of the individual to take part in activities that lead to bettering his environment.

Mischel's (5–6) paper on the effect of commitment on verbalized expectancies may also be regarded as an investigation derived from the analysis presented in the lead article, supporting the hypothesis that the need for public consistency is an important variable in the prediction of verbal behavior.

The last paper in the first group is Crowne and Liverant's (5–7) study of conformity under varying conditions of personal involvement. This investigation helps throw new light on individual differences in conforming behavior.

The second group of studies deals with contributions of social learning theory to sociology and anthropology. Seeman (5–8) describes the potential benefits for particular problems both to sociology and to social learning theory in theory development and research as a result of a partial integration of the two orientations. Battle and Rotter (5–9) and Lefcourt and Ladwig (5–11) describe certain differences between blacks and whites with particular emphasis on internal-external control. Mischel (5–10) employs the delay-of-gratification variable, conceptualized in expectancy for reinforcement terms, as a cross-cultural variable and is able to make certain predictions within cultures from it. The summary analyzes the relations among the social sciences, with special reference to the value of SLT in the other social sciences, and describes the utility of the other social sciences to the SLT theorist.

5-1

Beliefs, Social Attitudes and Behavior: A Social Learning Analysis

JULIAN B. ROTTER

One of the persistent problems in developing constructions regarding internal psychological processes is to be able to specify clearly the behavioral or observable consequences of such processes. Without clear designation of consequences, the constructions are limited in predictive utility and, perhaps of greater moment, it is not possible to test the adequacy of the constructions themselves. While this problem is somewhat less bothersome for students of concept formation and intellectual problem-solving, it is pernicious in the study of beliefs or attitudes. This follows from the fact that students of concept formation typically start with consequences, initially focusing on behavioral outcome. Social psychologists are aware that a simple behavior such as saying "true" or "false" to an attitude item questionnaire is a very complex event, subject to many different sources of variance. They have attempted to reduce the complexity of the problem, in many cases, by simply ignoring many of the sources of variance, or by trying to control them. Usually only a few sources are admitted into a systematic model which includes principles for the growth, maintenance, and change of the attitude or belief presumably being measured. Apparently the failure to account systematically for many variables results from the fact that approaches to attitude theory are typically *miniature* theories of attitude structure and change.

The purpose of this chapter is threefold: first, to describe from a social learning point of view the nature of beliefs; second, to show how such beliefs enter into the prediction of behavior in a model which includes systematically many other sources of variance in addition to the belief itself; and third, to illustrate in some detail the effects on behavior of one such determinant which has recently been investigated in some depth.

Unfortunately, this model will not serve to simplify the problem of prediction and will perhaps complicate it enormously. Since human beings are enormously complex animals, however, there seems to be no escape from complicated models if we are to achieve even a reasonable level of understanding or prediction. The hope is to include in a single model as many of the significant variables as possible and to indicate their systematic relationships to each other. In order to achieve this, I will attempt to describe some important determinants, first of the behavior of responding to an attitude question regarding the characteristics of Negroes, and, second, of the somewhat different kind of behavior, that of agreeing to take part in some direct social action to effect a social change favorable to Negroes. I hope, thereby, to show how beliefs, expressed attitudes, and

From R. Jessor and S. Feshback (eds.), *Cognition, Personality and Clinical Psychology* (San Francisco, Calif.: Jossey-Bass, Inc., 1967). Reprinted by permission of the author and the publisher.

overt social behavior are related and also how they are clearly different. I have stated or implied most of the formulations to follow in previous writings (1954; 1955; 1960b). They have not, however, been explicitly applied to the specific problems of concern in this paper.

Some justification is in order for the content of this chapter. While the paper does not deal with clinical psychological problems per se, it does apply a social learning approach to personality, that is, an individual-differences model with a strong emphasis on individual motives, to understanding the relationship between beliefs, verbal test behavior, and other behavioral choices. The chapter may help, therefore, to clarify some comparable problems in the prediction of behavioral choices of significance in clinical psychology, such as the prediction of nontest behavior from personality questionnaire responses and the relationship between a belief in one's own maladjustment and the decision to seek psychotherapy.

A SOCIAL LEARNING INTERPRETATION OF BELIEFS AND ATTITUDES

I equate a *simple expectancy* regarding a property of an object or series of objects or events with the terms *belief* or *simple cognition*. Simple cognitions, expectancies, or beliefs may appear phenomenally to have an all-or-none quality, but in fact they may vary in magnitude between zero and one, and they are subject to change. The child looking at the adult may believe that he is smiling or that he may be smiling. The four-legged creature is a dog or may be a dog; additional experience may teach him it is a cat. (Cats are likely to scratch him, dogs are not likely to scratch him, and so on.) In other words, simple expectancies, beliefs, or simple cognitions may be regarded as having the properties of subjective probabilities varying in magnitude from zero to one and constantly subject to change with new experience.

No necessary awareness, that is, ability to verbalize, is implied by the term "simple expectancy." In casting the concept of cognition into the language of an expectancy-reinforcement social-learning theory, I am implicitly hypothesizing that the laws governing the growth and change of expectancies as well as those governing the relationship of expectancies to observable behavior will also apply to simple cognitions.

The early experience of the child involves a great variety of stimuli which he eventually learns to discriminate. Since many of the stimuli affect him in similar ways, he also begins to abstract or to recognize similarity. The experienced similarity of objects or events is ultimately labeled, and the label represents to the individual an expectancy regarding the nature or properties of the objects or events involved. That is, he forms concepts. Concepts are attached to events and relate to or identify similar characteristics of these events. The recognition of similarity may precede the actual labeling process, but eventually labels are learned to describe the events, each label dealing only with selected aspects of a given event and each one being a description or shorthand method of abstracting some property or properties of the event. When a series of objects or events has been similarly labeled, new experiences with one of these will generalize to the others, so that gradually a collection of generalized expectancies is built up relating to a *class* of animate or inanimate objects or events.

The acquisition of verbal symbols or language enhances the process of generalization and allows for the formation of broad beliefs on the basis of verbal communication from others, without requiring the direct experience of the person involved. Thus, beliefs can be formed in regard to a class of objects or events without any direct experience with these objects or events. Similarly, beliefs can be formed as a result of observing the experiences of others.

Such a collection of generalized expectancies can be regarded as a set of beliefs, so that one can speak of beliefs regarding a series of objects like chairs, radiators, people, Negroes, and so on. If one were to explore all of the expectancies held by a particular person or a group regarding a group of events, he may find these more or less functional. That is, one specific belief may be predictable, at least to some degree, from another, or they may be completely independent. Two expectancies are functionally related if one changes as a result of a change in the strength of the other. When this happens in a group of people, then the two expectancies will be significantly correlated in that group. For example, the belief that dogs have four legs may, in a sample of individuals, be completely independent of the belief that dogs are dangerous because they bite. To use a more pointed example, if it were shown that beliefs regarding the inborn intellectual potential of Negroes were correlated with beliefs about the degree of amorality among Negroes, these two beliefs would be functionally related. However, if it were shown that beliefs about the average weight of Negroes were not correlated with either of the beliefs about intelligence or amorality, then the belief regarding the average weight of Negroes would not be part of a functionally related set of beliefs about Negroes. Functionality is likely to exist only for certain kinds of abstractions about events which are themselves related in the individual's or group's experience. A social attitude from this point of view would be a set of functionally related beliefs about a class of people or socially determined events.

Perhaps the most significant aspects of all events are how they affect the individual. For a child, dogs are warm and friendly; adults feed and protect him; radiators will hurt him; chairs are to sit on. As the child acquires more and more experience with objects of his environment, he not only develops expectancies about their simple physical properties, but about related behavior-reinforcement sequences. If you touch the radiator, it will hurt you. If you hit the dog, he will bite you. If you pet the dog, mother will smile. Initially, behavior-reinforcement expectancies develop from one's own experiences, but with the acquisition of more and more concepts and hierarchies of concepts, behavior-reinforcement expectancies will generalize from one set of events to another set of events which, although discriminable, have similar characteristics.

The simple cognitions regarding the properties of objects determine, in part, expectancies for behavior-reinforcement sequences by defining the gradients along which generalization takes place. As a consequence they determine, in part, what kinds of behaviors are likely to be tried out for novel objects and consequently what behavior-reinforcement sequences are likely to be experienced. In the prediction of stable behavior, it is the expectancies for behavior-reinforcement sequences, however, which play the major role. Behavior-reinforcement sequences in which expectancies for reinforcement are concerned solely with the characteristics of the object alone or with its potential as a source of reinforcement are only one determinant of a specific behavior choice in a given situation (don't sit on the radiator, you may get burned). In social situations particularly, a specific behavioral choice may involve a number of reinforcements which are relatively independent of the properties of the object but which are, in fact, dependent upon other social agents present in the situation (don't sit on the radiator, it's not polite).

In the social learning theory being described here, a general formula for prediction of goal-directed behavior is postulated. Reinforcement follows from an empirical law of effect, and no drive assumptions are made. The potential for a specific behavior directed toward a reinforcement to occur in a particular situation is a function of the expectancy of the occurrence of that reinforcement following the behavior in that situation and the value of the reinforcement in that situation.

The formula, however, is limited for predictive purposes. That is, it deals only with the relationship between the potential of a single behavior and the expectancy for a specific reinforcement while in fact there is always a variety of potential reinforcements that follow from any given behavior. So it is necessary, in order to make an actual prediction, to measure not only the expectancy for one reinforcement and the value of that reinforcement but to measure the expectancy for many reinforcements and the values of all of the reinforcements. For example, the decision to study for an examination not only involves a potential grade and its value but also involves the loss of other satisfactions and the potential reactions of parents, teachers, and schoolmates. Were we, in fact, to be able to measure most of the important variance involved in such a behavioral choice, we still would not know whether or not the individual would choose such a behavior until we knew the relative value of other behavioral choices in that situation.

Simple expectancies regarding the properties of objects and events which the person perceives as desirable or undesirable in their effects upon him—that is, properties which are positively or negatively reinforcing —are also beliefs. A set of such simple expectancies, beliefs, or cognitions determines in part the reinforcement value of the event, along with learned expectancies for reinforcement sequences (see Rotter, 1954, pp. 151–161).

For actual prediction in a specific situation, reinforcement value in our basic formula applies to a group of variables rather than to a single one, and similarly, expectancy in our generalized formula also represents several variables. When an individual recognizes and classifies an object or complex of objects in a situation as similar to others in his experience, his behavior will be based upon a generalization of expectancies developed in these similar situations. On the other hand, as he gains more and more experience with a specific situation, his behavior tends to be determined more and more by the experience in that particular situation. The expectancies for behavior-reinforcement sequences generated in a specific psychological situation can be thought of as being dependent upon specific expectancies developed in that situation, which we have labeled E', and generalized expectancies (G.E.). The relative importance of these is a function of the amount of experience in that specific situation.

The generalized expectancies may be of many kinds, and they can be more or less inclusive. For example, generalized expectancies for academic success in psychology may involve expectancies derived from all achievement situations or just from achievement situations most similar to those being studied. They may also include generalized expectancies which deal with different aspects of a particular behavioral choice. For example, one generalized expectancy in an academic problem-solving situation might have to do with the generalized expectancy for academic success and another with a generalized expectancy for the usefulness of a particular kind of problem-solving behavior (for example, looking for alternatives) applicable to a wide array of problems including the one being studied. The latter type of generalized expectancy is similar to the concept of learning set or higher-level learning skill. In applying the general formula for behavior potential, it is necessary to choose from among many possible generalized expectancies the one or ones which are most appropriate for the particular kind of prediction to be made.

It is these generalized expectancies which give stability to the individual's behavior across situations. What we may think of in personality theory as stable behavioral traits or characteristics *which allow prediction from one situation to another* are largely a function of generalized expectancies and of reinforcement values which are *relatively* less situationally determined. However, the importance of specific expectancies (E's) should not be overlooked, and the tendency to regard specific situational forces only as potential sources of error is a recurring mistake in predicting behavior and testing hypotheses, as recent analyses of the psychological testing situation amply demonstrate (Masling, 1960; Rotter, 1960b).

These brief descriptions of some aspects of social learning theory are concerned with process variables. The content variables of such a theory are empirically derived from examining functional relationships. For example, functionally related behaviors leading to the same or similar goals (for example, need potential for dependency) form a class of content categories. Functionally related beliefs about social objects and events form a class of social attitudes. The broad generalized expectancies similar to the higher-level learning skills mentioned above introduce another set of content categories which have only recently been subjected to intensive investigation. Psychological situations which are functionally related similarly provide another set of potential content terms (Rotter, 1955). I say potential content terms since little work has been done in the field of psychology to describe the relevant dimensions of situational similarity for specific purposes.

At the present time, common sense, cultural experience, and clinical study have to be combined with experimental data to provide working content terms. An enormous amount of research must be done before wholly adequate sets of content categories, related to the process variables, can be achieved.

BELIEFS AND EXPRESSED ATTITUDES

These theoretical conceptions perhaps can be best understood by an illustration applying them to a concrete behavioral prediction. I have chosen two such illustrations. The first is an attempt to analyze some of the major determinants of variance in what appears to be a relatively simple behavioral choice, that of answering "true" or "false" to an item of an attitude questionnaire. For the purposes of the illustration, we can assume that the statement is "Even if Negroes had the same education and opportunities as whites, they would still be less intelligent." A schematic representation of some of the major variables is presented in Figure 5-1.

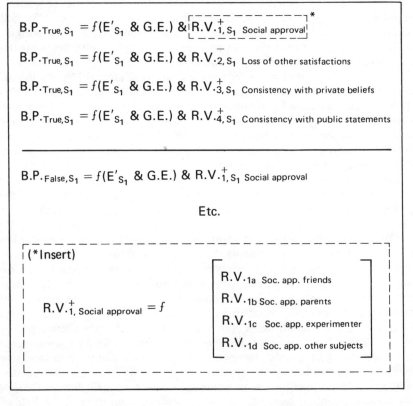

$$B.P._{True,\,S_1} = f(E'_{S_1} \text{ \& G.E.) \& } \overset{+}{R.V.}_{1,\,S_1} \text{ Social approval}^{*}$$

$$B.P._{True,\,S_1} = f(E'_{S_1} \text{ \& G.E.) \& } \overset{-}{R.V.}_{2,\,S_1} \text{ Loss of other satisfactions}$$

$$B.P._{True,\,S_1} = f(E'_{S_1} \text{ \& G.E.) \& } \overset{+}{R.V.}_{3,\,S_1} \text{ Consistency with private beliefs}$$

$$B.P._{True,\,S_1} = f(E'_{S_1} \text{ \& G.E.) \& } \overset{+}{R.V.}_{4,\,S_1} \text{ Consistency with public statements}$$

$$B.P._{False,\,S_1} = f(E'_{S_1} \text{ \& G.E.) \& } \overset{+}{R.V.}_{1,\,S_1} \text{ Social approval}$$

Etc.

(*Insert)

$$\overset{+}{R.V.}_{1,\, Social\ approval} = f$$

R.V.$_{1a}$ Soc. app. friends
R.V.$_{1b}$ Soc. app. parents
R.V.$_{1c}$ Soc. app. experimenter
R.V.$_{1d}$ Soc. app. other subjects

FIGURE 5–1. Some major sources of variance in the determination of the choice of a "true" response to a social attitude question.

Shown in Figure 5-1 are formulas for determining behavior potential for the choice "true" in relation to four different reinforcements or groups of reinforcements. These reinforcements are arranged in a hypothesized order of their importance, assuming that the subjects are college students and the experimenter is a regular teacher giving them the test during a classroom period. The behavior potentials are for these specific conditions, designated as s_1 in Figure 5-1.

It is not accidental that we have placed uppermost in this list the reinforcement of social approval as probably being most important in determining the subject's response, although in fact many researchers attempt to control or eliminate such variance as a source of error. With the first formula we are attempting to describe the extent to which the potential reinforcement of social approval enters into subject's responding "true" to the attitude question. If he expects that "true" is a more socially approved response, and if he places a great deal of value on social approval, then the behavior potential will be high. The subject may feel that in general a "true" response is the one that is more likely to be approved as being the more liberal and Christian belief, so he would have a high generalized expectancy. He may feel, however, that in this particular testing situation the experimenter's attitude suggests or a previous persuasive communication indicates that "true" will not be the rewarded response. This would reduce the subject's E'. Or the opposite may be the case; the subject's general expectancy could be that the "true" response is not acceptable to friends, relatives, and colleagues but is clearly the only response which will meet with the experimenter's approval. Both sources of variance need to be taken into account. In fact, Rosenberg (1965), in repeating the Cohen (Brehm & Cohen, 1962) study of dissonance, which showed an inverse relationship between attitude change and amount of monetary reward, did not obtain similar results. He concluded that the failure to replicate was due to his having changed experimenters for the measurement of attitude change, thereby reducing the expectancy that the desired change would be socially approved. The programs of research by Rosenthal (1963) and Orne (1962) have emphasized the great sensitivity of subjects to the expressed and unexpressed biases of the examiner.

The value the individual places upon a social-approval reinforcement is an equally important determinant of behavior. Some subjects may be far less concerned with social approval than with other needs or motives, and some much more so. In actuality, we have lumped together a whole series of reinforcements and labeled them social approval. I have projected some of these onto the bottom of the figure for illustrative purposes. The value placed upon social approval from friends, parents, the experimenter, and other subjects may all enter into the subject's choice of a "true" response, each with its own E' and G.E. Interestingly enough, these may vary considerably, and consequently different subjects will be differently affected by the attitudes of the experimenter and other subjects in typical experimental design. To be technically consistent, in social-learning theory, a group of functionally related reinforcements such as those illustrated is referred to as need value.

The importance of this general reinforcement or need value in the measurement of attitudes is perhaps best exemplified in the work on persuasibility or attitude change as the result of the personal characteristics of the persuader and his relationship to the subject. Hovland, Janis, and Kelley (1953) have noted strong effects of fear of social disapproval in changing expressed attitudes. Recently Crowne and Marlowe (1964) have been studying the approval motive and have evolved a measure which, although not pure, may be regarded primarily as a measure of need value for social approval. A series of studies has shown this scale to be capable of predicting individual differences in response to a persuasive communication or a subtle indication of experimenter attitudes (Crowne & Marlowe, 1964). In a study involving 41 subjects, Crowne and Conn (1964) found a correlation of .45 between the social-approval scores and the amount of change on an attitude-toward-conformity scale following a tape recorded persuasive communication regarding conformity. While I do not wish to review the literature in this area in greater detail, it seems clear that expressed attitudes are heavily affected by specific expectancies, generalized expectancies, and a variety of reinforcement values for social approval. If one attempts to eliminate the variance attributable to these variables in one situation and make predictions to another where they are not eliminated, *prediction will suffer remarkably.*

In the second formula in Figure 5-1, I have tried to group together a number of other important variables which will affect response, although they may be less significant in a test-taking situation than in other situations calling for expressed opinions. The public statement of a "true" response may involve generalized expectancies not only for gain or loss of social approval, but also for potential loss of employment, for payment as a subject, and in some instances, for physical harm. Perhaps more significant, in our typical experimental testing situations, is the E′ associated with the instructor who is also acting as the experimenter in giving the attitude questionnaires. Here the selection of the "wrong" response may involve an expected effect on grades, and where there is high reinforcement value attached to the belief being examined, such variables can play a heavy role, as in the examination of Negroes' attitudes by white school teachers and experimenters or vice versa. Even when the experimenter is not the instructor, for many subjects any test may be a cue for evaluation and lead to expectancies for some specific or vague fear of the consequences of giving the "wrong" response. Confidentiality of response plays a role here, and it would be hypothesized that different results would be obtained, at least in some testing conditions, when confidentiality is assured than when it is not. It is a matter of common sense that the relative role of many of these other reinforcements will depend to a large degree on the nature of the attitude being examined and the circumstances of testing.

Our third formula deals with the felt need for consistency between what one believes and what one says. It is here that the simple cognitions or generalized beliefs regarding the properties of the social objects involved may play their most direct role in that they determine what in fact would be the veridical response. That is, subjects who place a high value on truthfulness would tend to select the true response if it fitted more closely to their beliefs regarding the nature or properties of the social objects involved. While E' for what is true might be expected to play a lesser role in this formula, the notion that subjective truth will change as the result of situational determinants cannot be overlooked. An important implication here is that the need for consistency between private beliefs and expressed opinions is dependent upon *individual differences* in the value placed upon such consistency.

From this point of view, the many studies of cognitive dissonance are dealing essentially with an individual-difference phenomenon rather than a universal cognitive process. Indeed, many of the studies of cognitive dissonance, though they report a measurable effect, may not find the effect at all in the majority of their subjects. Whether or not overall effects are found in a particular experiment would depend largely on the sample and culture studied. For example, it seemed to me when I was growing up in Brooklyn that there were a large number of people of Jewish origin whose responses to postdecisional conflict were the opposite of those typically reported. If they had to choose between difficult alternatives, they always seemed to be convinced afterward that they had made the wrong choice, apparently increasing their dissonance. Perhaps other motives are involved here—perhaps these people wish to demonstrate to the world that the fates are conspiring against them or even to super-stitiously ward off bad luck by claiming they have already had their share. The point is that many people place little or no value upon maintaining consistency between private beliefs and expressed opinions. Increasing the discrepancy between these two will affect different individuals in different ways.

It might be noted here that in many instances one's true or internal beliefs will correlate with socially approved beliefs since what one be-lieves to be true may well be a reflection of what others believe to be true. In such instances, it may appear that consistency with internal beliefs is determining response to an attitude questionnaire to a greater degree than is actually the case since, to varying degrees, the more important motive may not be consistency but merely social approval.

Our fourth formula deals with the need to maintain consistency among public statements and has been dealt with sometimes as the effects of commitment. Mischel (1958a) and Watt (1965) have demonstrated strong effects of public commitment on resistance to changing expressed ex-pectancies for reinforcement in task situations, and Hobart and Hovland (1954) have demonstrated that public commitment leads to more resistance to attitude change. Again such variables depend for their total effect on individual differences. There are some situations in which change is more likely to be approved than disapproved, and E' would obviously play a differential role in different kinds of studies. Generalized ex-pectancies that a response of "true" would lead to public consistency reinforcement, of course, will depend upon the degree to which the subject in the past has presented a consistent series of public statements. Salman

(1965) found that subjects high on the need for social approval evidenced a much stronger effect of public commitment on attitude change than other subjects.

Such public consistency probably tends to be valued more by psychologists and highly educated people in general than by the public at large. The failure to maintain a consistent set of opinions is regarded in the classroom and in intellectual arguments as a weakness, but this is a value formed only in some people, and it will vary considerably in strength from person to person.

To the degree that the responses "true" and "false" are perceived by the subject as being truly opposite, it is likely that the values we would obtain in the formulas for the response "true" would bear a reciprocal relationship to those for the response "false." If, however, we were dealing with a series of alternative responses, it would be necessary to measure these variables for all the response alternatives in order to determine which alternative had the highest behavior potential.

Later I will draw some implications from this illustration. The specific reinforcements included are not exhaustive nor is terminology important. It seems likely to me that reinforcements related to reaction formation or displacement of aggression may play a significant role in determining the social attitudes of some persons. These motives can be treated similarly to those I have examined since I am implying no *necessary* awareness of the relationship between the behavioral choice and the reinforcement.

For the present, I would like only to indicate that the model reflects the hypothesis that there are a great many significant variables mediating any relationship between internalized cognitions regarding the nature of a social object and the response to an attitude test item. Beliefs play a significant role in determining these other variables, but they are beliefs about events other than those which are concerned only with the characteristics of the social object itself. Beliefs involving specific expectancies and generalized expectancies for a wide variety of reinforcements and beliefs about the nature of these reinforcements are basic determinants of response. Beliefs about the object itself play an important role in determining the response to an attitude questionnaire, but not such an important one that we can afford to ignore, consider as error, or try to regularly control these other sources of variance. If one were mainly interested in assessing true beliefs about the nature of the social object from such tests, either a large number of other variables would have to be controlled or they would have to be measured and their effects partialed out. It is, of course, in either case a difficult task, and for some purposes it may be more useful in making predictions to study differences in expressed attitudes under several systematically different conditions in order to draw inferences regarding behavior in other situations.

BELIEFS, ATTITUDES, AND SOCIAL ACTION

I would now like to make a similar analysis of some of the potential variance that must enter into the prediction of a social action. While this may lead us further from our simple cognitions about properties of social objects, it may suggest other profitable variables for studying social action.

For example, let us assume that an individual is approached with a request to take part in some civil disobedience, a disapproved march on the Capitol or a sit-in strike aimed at doing away with segregation in some locality.

In Figure 5-2, I have arranged potential determinants, again in a hypothesized order of importance. Again, I have placed social approval at the top of the list. Situationally determined expectancies here would involve the nature of the person doing the asking and the degree to which the individual feels the *specific* action contemplated would or would not meet with social approval from significant others. Differences between E' and generalized expectancies could also account for some people agreeing but somehow managing not to actually carry through with their commitment. The generalized expectancies would involve expectancies for the general class of actions for a variety of social agents and be relatively independent of specific circumstances. Reinforcement values might differ

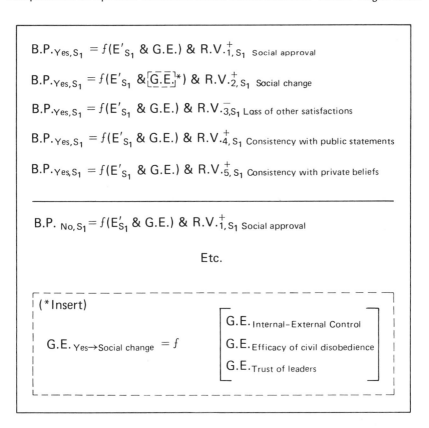

FIGURE 5–2. Some major sources of variance in the determination of the decision to take part in social action.

in sign for different social agents, and the overall strength of a need value for social approval would of course differ among individuals.

The overall strength for such a need value as social approval in our culture is reflected in the actions of millions of people during time of war. Although thousands of persons, and possibly millions, have no desire to endanger themselves, have no strong interests in the causes involved, and do not wish to interrupt the normal course of their lives, they nevertheless allow themselves to be drafted or, in fact, enlist largely because of the fear of social disapproval for any other action. Similarly, people will go into battle in spite of strong motives to the contrary partly because of the strong social disapproval involved in taking one of various other alternatives such as "goldbricking." Where feelings are intense, as in taking social action with regard to segregation in the South, expectancies for strong social disapproval can be very high and extremely important in determining behavioral choice.

In addition to different beliefs regarding the nature of Negroes or the injustice of present social conditions, people will still differ considerably in the degree to which they place value on effecting a social change. The extremeness of their belief in the injustice of present conditions may bear some relationship to the strength of value they would place on social change, but it is probably far from a perfect relationship. Situational factors may again play a role in the expectancy that the behavior involved will lead to social change. The individual involved might consider it the wrong place or the wrong time, or the leadership the wrong leaders. Generalized expectancies that this type of social action, that is, civil disobedience, will lead to social change may also play a significant cross-situational role.

I have chosen to illustrate some of the different generalized expectancies involved here in the same way as I illustrated in Figure 5-1 the different kinds of reinforcement values which might be included in a general reinforcement value or need value for social approval. These generalized expectancies are projected at the bottom of Figure 5-2. The first listed, internal versus external control, is a variable with which considerable research has been done over the past five years, and I would like to describe some of the data obtained dealing with this variable. In general, internal-external control refers to the degree to which the individual believes that what happens to him results from his own behavior versus the degree to which he believes that what happens to him is the result of luck, chance, fate, or forces beyond his control.

The second generalized expectancy is for civil disobedience of many kinds. The individual may have developed on the basis of previous experience, his own or that of others, an expectancy that such efforts do a great deal of good or none at all and, in fact, some professed liberals claim that such behavior actually delays rather than speeds up social change.

The third generalized expectancy I have listed is one of trust of leaders of the civil rights movements. It is a more specific generalized expectancy than trust of other people in general, which might have been substituted in the figure for trust of leaders. Some individuals, although genuinely desiring social change and accepting the principle of civil disobedience, may expect that the leaders in the movement in general are dominated by Communists, are self-seeking, have ulterior motives, or cannot be relied upon to carry through, and all such generalized expectancies will be partial determinants of the response of "yes."

The third formula, dealing with loss of other satisfactions, might well be placed second, depending again upon the specific issue and place. Perhaps far more important than in the answers to attitude questionnaires, this behavior potential will play a significant role in the determination of social action. Even the relatively mild behavior of signing a petition may involve specific and generalized expectancies for loss of business, physical harm, persecution via the telephone, and other significant reinforcements. It may, in fact, involve only an interruption of one's other activities, but in any case there are undoubtedly thousands of individuals who would join various protest activities were it not for the loss of other satisfactions.

The fourth formula deals with the values involved in consistency with other public statements. Obviously, the specific situation will play a role, particularly in regard to whether the individuals present have also been present when the other public statements have been made. While the total effect of this variable may not be as great as the three already discussed, I have shifted its position from that in Figure 5-1 to give it more importance here than consistency with private beliefs. Consistency between two public statements may not be of as great importance to some people as consistency between public statement and public action. Inconsistency here is not an intellectual matter but a matter of being a "four-flusher" or of not having "the courage of one's convictions." It could play an important role for many individuals who would have relatively little concern about consistency with private beliefs. The generalized expectancies in this formula would involve expectancies that lack of consistency would lead others to perceive the individual as a "four-flusher." What one has said on an attitude questionnaire might in fact play some role here, but far more important are public statements made under other circumstances.

Finally we come to consistency with private beliefs. Does the action involved represent what we truly believe in as right or proper? Our simple beliefs or cognitions regarding Negroes and the issues involved play a more direct role here in affecting E's and generalized expectancies. The reinforcement value of such consistency will vary greatly within our culture. It may, in fact, be the strongest motive of any we have described in Figure 5-2 for a few individuals. With the great majority of people in our society, my guess is that it plays a lesser role in determining social action behavior than the motives or reinforcement values we have previously discussed. If we use Benedict's (1946) distinction between shame and guilt, we can say consistency with public beliefs avoids shame and consistency with private beliefs avoids guilt. For the majority in our culture, I believe that, in this situation at least, the avoidance of shame is probably the stronger motive.

One implication of this analysis is that, while social psychologists are generally aware of the many sources of variance, they appear in their research emphases to exaggerate grossly the significance of simple beliefs about specific social groups in determining answers to questionnaires. To an even greater degree, they have exaggerated the significance both of beliefs about social objects and of responses to attitude questionnaires in determining the behavior of a person when faced with alternatives regarding social action.

I have not discussed in this model how change is effected in behavior. Previous publications (Rotter, 1965; Rotter, 7–8) have dealt with principles of changing expectancies and reinforcement values. By changing any of the variables in Figures 5-1 or 5-2 sufficiently, we can achieve behavior changes. The model in fact broadens considerably the conventional approach to behavior change in providing many more variables that can be manipulated in order to achieve such change.[1]

There are many possible additional variables and reinforcements which have not been included in this illustration. What the model does illustrate is a method of analysis of the problem and a crude attempt to indicate the relationship of simple cognitions, expectancies for behavior-reinforcement sequences, and expressed attitudes in the prediction of a significant social behavior.

The question naturally arises, "Can these variables be measured?" We have been measuring E', generalized expectancies, overall expectancies, and reinforcement values for many years. While difficulties and unexplained variance may be encountered in measuring any of the specific variables described in the two figures shown earlier, there do not seem to be any logical or insurmountable problems—providing a variety of methods are used. The more difficult question is "If they can be measured, how can they be combined mathematically to make a prediction?" Here I can provide no satisfactory answer. The *direction* of influence of each variable is specified and, with adequate controls, the potential effect of each variable can be tested by group comparisons. In more elaborate predictions, a few other things can be said. Previous attempts to assess the combined significance of expectancies and reinforcement values indicate that the relationship is probably a multiplicative one. We have also in several studies found support for the general hypothesis that the *relative* significance of E' and G.E. is a function of the amount of experience with the specific situation. The more novel the situation, the more weight the generalized expectancies will play. Perhaps when sufficient data are collected, analyzing as exhaustively as possible a large number of variables affecting a single behavior and repeating this for many different behaviors and situations, then we may be able to make some tentative mathematical formulations.

[1] Such an analysis has significant similarities to other formulations of the nature of social attitudes and attitude change, such as those of Katz and Stotland (1959) and Rosenberg (1960). In the present formulations, the expectancy concept has some rough equation to the "cognitive components" of these theories. The reinforcement value term is less clearly related to their use of an "affective component," since it includes not only the evaluation aspect that these writers posit but also designates the nature of the reinforcement involved. In this latter respect, this formulation appears to be somewhat closer to that of Katz and Stotland.

I have tried to indicate that simple beliefs limited to the nature of the objects which are the focus of some social attitude are only a partial and sometimes minor determinant of expressed attitudes and social action. Merely supplying new information is therefore clearly not a sufficient approach to attitude change. Generalized beliefs or expectancies involving broad classes of situations appear to hold much promise for the understanding and change of social action behavior. Sufficient data have now accumulated on one such variable—internal versus external control of reinforcement—to illustrate the potential utility of this kind of variable in studying the relationship between beliefs and observable behaviors.*

This group of studies [internal versus external control of reinforcement] lends strong and consistent support to the hypothesis that a generalized expectancy that one can affect the environment through one's own behavior is present in at least two different cultures, can be reliably measured, and is related to social action behavior. While significant correlations have been referred to throughout this section, it should be made clear that they are low, for the most part, and leave much variance unaccounted for. Such additional variance may be explained by specific expectancies in the particular area of behavior that were investigated and by other important variables.

I have assumed in these studies that the reinforcement value for the desired change is approximately equal for the groups designated as internals and those designated as externals. Even if this assumption is in error, it is not of great significance here since the purpose of presenting these studies is to indicate one of many variables which is apparently independent of social attitudes but which nevertheless significantly affects social action.

APPLICATION OF THE MODEL TO CLINICAL PSYCHOLOGY

What is the relevance of this analysis of the relationship between belief and behavior for clinical psychology? I have chosen to illustrate the relationship between beliefs and behavior with an example drawn from the field of social attitudes toward Negroes since there is available a great deal of published fact and public information in this area. The same analysis would apply to the relationship of a patient's beliefs about his mother, or his more generalized beliefs about women or people in general, to behavioral choice. It would apply also to beliefs about himself and perhaps provide a more general basis for testing the adequacy of hypotheses generated by self-theories.

An obvious application of this analysis would be to the prediction of behavior from self-report measures. While the relevant reinforcements for a particular behavior choice would vary with the nature of the belief being studied, the same *kinds* of variables and relationships would be involved.

---

* A section titled "Internal versus External Control of Reinforcement as a Generalized Expectancy" has been deleted, since its contents are covered by other articles in this and the preceding section of the book.

At a more specific level, the focus on broad generalized expectancies such as internal-external control may have very direct application to understanding why some people who are aware they need help seek therapy and others do not. It may also be an important variable in understanding why some people benefit more from therapy. Some recent data suggesting that improvement in therapy is associated with increased internality of attitudes have been obtained by Gillis and Jessor (1961).

SUMMARY

In summary, this paper represents an attempt to accomplish three things.

1. A general model has been described which attempts to show the systematic relationships between simple cognitions or beliefs and expectancies for behavior-reinforcement sequences and behavioral choice. The model has been illustrated with examples drawn from the area of social attitudes but would apply equally well to many significant problems in clinical psychology. While the model is a complicated one, perhaps recognition of the complexity of the problem is a first step toward enhancing prediction and allowing for the testing of hypotheses.

2. A model has been presented which can include many sources of variance in systematic relationship. This is in contrast with models which deal with only a few variables while treating others only as sources of error, thereby limiting prediction. At the same time the model suggests the large number of variables which can be manipulated to change behavior, many of which have been ignored since they were treated as unsystematic error. Further, the model indicates many of the variables that need to be controlled if theoretical tests of the significance or role of other variables are to be made.

3. Finally, we have reviewed some data involving a generalized expectancy for internal versus external control of reinforcement which is illustrative of many possible variables which may play a significant role in the determination of behavioral choice in a variety of important life situations.

5-2 | Interpersonal Trust, Internal-External Control, and the Warren Commission Report[1]

J. HERBERT HAMSHER, JESSE D. GELLER, and
JULIAN B. ROTTER

Acceptance of the Warren Commission Report among college students was predicted from 2 measures of personality presumably independent of political attitudes. Interpersonal trust and belief in internal vs. external control of reinforcement were the 2 measures. Both are conceptualized in social learning theory as broad generalized expectancies. Each personality test and the Warren Commission Questionnaire were given to students at widely spaced times by different examiners. Ss with consistent attitudes of disbelief of the Warren Report were significantly less trusting and more external. Within sexes, trust is a predictor for males and females, but internal-external control only for males. The study adds to the literature on the contribution of personality variables to understand public reactions to sociopolitical events.

In their initial statement of purpose, the President's Commission on the Assassination of President John F. Kennedy (referred to subsequently in this discussion as the Warren Commission Report) reflected that, "This commission was created . . . in recognition of the right of people everywhere to full and truthful knowledge . . ." (Warren Commission, 1964, p. 1). Mounting evidence suggests that a large portion of the American people consider the Warren Commission's report decidedly less complete, objective, and forthright than is implied by that statement. Both Gallup and Harris polls have reported surprisingly negative and disbelieving reactions to the Report. Among the four special programs devoted to the assassination, CBS television devoted one entirely to the disbelief with which the Warren Report has been received. Henry Steele Commager and Eric Severeid were among those interviewed who expressed the view that the public loss of faith in the Warren Commission represented a cultural phenomenon which Mr. Commager labeled "the conspiracy mentality" and Mr. Severeid called the "devil theory of politics."

Sheatsley and Feldman (1965), commenting on the widespread belief in a conspiracy interpretation of the assassination, emphasized people's need for explaining important events in some way which does not rely on fatalistic capriciousness or irrationality. They supported this "mundane"

[1] This investigation was supported by a grant from the National Institute of Mental Health (MH11455), J. B. Rotter, principal investigator.

basis for the phenomenon, rather than mass paranoia. A similar point was made by Greenstein (1965) who also explained belief in an assassination plot by the pervasive need to believe "that events are controlled (and therefore controllable) . . . [p. 529]." While these explanations may partially account for the general belief in a conspiracy, they do not deal with individual differences or with the influence of personality variables in the widespread disbelief of the Warren Commission's interpretation of the assassination.

The present research sought to investigate the role of personality variables in the public reaction to the Warren Report. It also sought to utilize a sociopolitical reality in an attempt to extend the application of psychological instruments to broader social research. The response to the Warren Commission and its report is singularly well-suited to this kind of investigation. The ambiguity of the controversy presents to the individual a situation in which he may be expected to impose those perceptions and convictions most consistent with his own personality functioning. It is clear that some criteria other than informational or factual ones must be utilized to settle the question for the individual. The expectation that the resolution of the dilemma would be related to individual differences in personality seems to be a reasonable one.

The present investigation has two goals. The first is to develop some understanding of why a large segment of the population finds criticism of the Warren Commission's report so persuasive and compelling. The second goal is to study further the construct validity of two theoretically derived personality measures which were developed and validated principally in controlled settings.

Both of the personality variables included in the present study were developed within the framework of a social learning theory (Rotter, 1954). Choice behavior is conceptualized in this approach as being determined by the preference value associated by the individual with a reinforcement eventuating from the behavior, and the expectancy that the reinforcement will occur. The central concept of expectancy is itself considered a function of specific and generalized expectancies. As a result of repeated experiences in the same and similar situations, the individual builds up a generalized expectancy of a relationship between behavior and consequent reinforcements which extends across situations. Experimental confirmation has been obtained for Rotter's (1954) formulation that expectancy in a given instance is a combination of situational expectancy and generalized expectancy which varies inversely with the number of experiences with the same or similar situations. This means that a new situation unique to the individual will involve a greater component of generalized expectancy than one that is familiar. It is in these novel situations that the person can be expected to behave in a way most reflective of generalized modes of reacting.

Since the assassination of a President of the United States is a dramatically unique event, it would be expected that generalized expectancies would contribute greatly to the reaction of an individual. The two predictor variables utilized in this investigation represent such generalized expectancies: *internal versus external locus of control (I-E) and interpersonal trust.*

The I-E dimension pertains to the degree to which an individual perceives reinforcements as resulting from his own actions or sees them as stemming from such forces as luck, chance, fate, or other powerful figures in his life. Considerable research has demonstrated the utility of this construct and the predictive efficiency of a measure of this generalized expectancy (Lefcourt, 1966; Rotter, 1966). Internals (I's) are individuals who see their own behavior determining their lives and what happens to them; they have been discovered to be more attentive to aspects of their environment which are personally relevant and potentially useful (Seeman, 1963a; Seeman & Evans, 1962), more oriented toward social action-taking behavior (Gore & Rotter, 1963), more involved in situations they see as depending on their own skill rather than on chance factors (Rotter & Mulry, 1965), and to evidence more resistance to subtle attempts to influence them (Getter, 1966; Gore, 1962; Strickland, 1962). Externals (E's) are characterized by opposite patterns of behavior.

In the sociopolitical realm Seeman (1959) has related I-E control to alienation in the sense of powerlessness. Both Rotter (1966) and Hersch and Scheibe (1967) have commented on the greater range of variability among external subjects, particularly in male populations. It was hypothesized that externals (particularly those who believe in powerful others controlling their world) would be more likely to assume a conspiracy covered up by the Warren Report.

The Interpersonal Trust Scale was developed by Rotter (1967b) as a measure of a generalized expectancy for one dimension of interpersonal functioning. Rotter defined interpersonal trust as "an expectancy held by an individual or a group that the word, promise, verbal or written statement of another individual or group can be relied upon [p. 651]." While the literature on this newer scale is less extensive than that on the I-E dimension, it has been found to be predictive of sociometric ratings of trust (Rotter, 1967b) and of behavior in an experimental laboratory situation (Geller, 1966). It was hypothesized that individuals obtaining high scores on the trust scale would respond with greater belief to the assertion of the Warren Commission that their report contains "full and truthful knowledge" of the facts of the assassination.

METHOD

All three measures used in the study were administered in groups during introductory psychology class time. The Interpersonal Trust Scale was completed by all students present during a session approximately 1 month before the experimental questionnaire was administered. The I-E Scale was given to members of only one section, a month and a half prior to the experimental questionnaire. *It is important to note that no connection was established among the three questionnaires and that different personnel were used for all three administrations.* The Warren Commission Questionnaire, Table 1, a specially constructed seven-item instrument, was presented to the students as an opinion survey. The totals for each of the instruments were as follows: Warren Commission Questionnaire, 657 (288 males, 369 females); Interpersonal Trust Scale, 577 (248 males, 329 females); and I-E Scale, 173 (60 males, 113 females).

RESULTS

Data for the total sample are summarized in Table 1. It is clear that this group of college students feel they have followed the controversy and that a majority of them are unwilling to accept the conclusions of the Warren Commission. While only one-fourth are prepared to characterize the report as an accurate account, nearly one-third endorse the most extreme position offered them, expressing a belief about a conspiracy which has been actively suppressed. Although a sizeable majority do not want the matter dropped, fewer than one-half report a willingness to sign a petition supporting a new investigation. Comparison of the sentiments of these college students with the selected samples of the Gallup and Harris Polls, obtained about the same time, suggests considerable

Table 1   Warren Commission Report Questionnaire and Summary of Responses

	% Responding[a]		
Item	Yes	No	Don't Know
1. I haven't followed the controversy and know very little about it.	14.9	84.5	—
2. I have read and heard some things about the controversy but have no real opinions myself.	22.5	73.0	—
3. I believe the Warren Commission Report provides an accurate account of what happened.	24.5	56.8	19.0
4. I believe the real facts about the assassination are not known by the public because of the way the Warren Commission conducted its investigation.	49.5	32.0	18.3
5. I believe there was in fact a conspiracy and information about it has been kept from the public.	28.0	52.0	18.6
6. I feel that the whole matter of President Kennedy's assassination should be dropped.	31.5	68.0	—
7. I feel that a new investigation should be held and would be willing to sign a petition to that effect.	44.5	54.0	—

[a] Totals less than 100% reflect failures to respond to the item.

similarity.[2] Attitudinal convergence among disparate groups is not only noteworthy sociopsychologically but should also accentuate the significance of relationships obtained with external criteria.

Means and standard deviations for the two personality measures are presented in Table 2. These values are consistent with those obtained in previous studies (Rotter, 1966; Rotter, 1967b). Scores on the two scales correlated −.14 for the females, −.53 for males, and −.28 for the groups combined. While the correlation for females is not statistically significant, the other two values are significant beyond the .01 level of confidence. Although the relationship between I-E and trust is typically higher for males than females, the value obtained for this male sample is unusually high.

The major analyses utilized a weighted score for the three opinion items. Responses were weighted in the direction of trust in the Warren Commission Report, and included a value of 3 for belief, 1 for disbelief, and 2 for a "don't know" or blank. Scores could range, then, from consistent disbelief, 3, to consistent belief, 9. A correlation of .16 (males, .18 and females, .14), significant at less than the .01 level, was obtained between the weighted total and Interpersonal Trust Scale Scores. Since the correlation between I-E and trust was significant, partial correlations were computed holding I-E scores constant. A partial r of .14 (males, .00, and females, .15) was obtained.

A second analysis was made using only those subjects who were consistent responders, that is, only subjects obtaining scores of 3 or 9. Trust scores for the high and low belief groups were compared by t tests. The obtained t values of 2.577 ($df = 97$) for males and 1.976 ($df = 107$) for

[2] The Gallup Poll referred to was published on January 11, 1967, and the Harris Poll on March 6, 1967. All three investigations antedated the announcements of the District Attorney of New Orleans that he possessed concrete evidence disproving the Warren Commission Report findings and verifying the existence of a conspiracy. The three polls, of course, did not word all items similarly. Where there were equivalent items regarding belief in the Warren Commission Report, the results were quite similar with the exception that considerably more of the general public thought the matter should *not* be reopened than did the college students.

Table 2   I-E and Trust Scale Means and Standard Deviations

	MALE		FEMALE		COMBINED	
	M	SD	M	SD	M	SD
Interpersonal Trust						
Scale	70.2	9.40	70.5	8.92	70.3	9.12
N	(248)		(329)		(577)	
Internal-External						
Locus of Control	10.1	3.95	11.0	3.96	10.7	3.97
N	(60)		(113)		(173)	

females were significant at the .01 and .05 confidence levels, respectively. Those subjects who consistently expressed belief and trust in the Warren Commission also scored higher on the Interpersonal Trust Scale than those consistently suspicious of the Report.

As with the Trust Scale, partial correlations were computed for the I-E Scale with the weighted Warren Questionnaire total. Uncorrected the r's were $-.10$ combined, $-.34$ for males, and .05 for females; partial correlation values with trust held constant were $-.05$ combined, $-.27$ for males, and .07 for females. Only the value for males ($p < .04$) was significant. Again using only the consistent responders to the questionnaire a 2×2 (two levels of belief and sex) analysis of variance was performed on I-E scores. Sex was included in this analysis because of the clear-cut sex differences in the overall correlations. While neither the sex of the subject nor the amount of belief manifested in the Warren Report was significantly related to differences in internality, the interaction of the two was significant beyond the .01 level ($F = 7.32$, $df = 1.49$). Table 3 shows that male subjects who disbelieved the Warren Commission Report were more external on the I-E Scale.

The two items concerned with following the controversy and the items tapping opinions about dropping the issue and signing a petition in favor of initiating a new investigation were all included because of an expected relationship between these reactions and internality. I-E scores for subjects responding "yes" and "no" to these items were examined by t tests. In no case was there obtained a t ratio significant beyond the .05 level.

Table 3   Trust Scale and I-E Scale Means for Subjects Scoring 3 and 9 on the Warren Commission Questionnaire

	M			
	Male		Female	
	9	3	9	3
Trust	75.0	69.1	72.1	68.9
N	(42)	(57)	(53)	(56)
I-E	8.1	13.0	12.5	11.6
N	(8)	(14)	(13)	(18)

DISCUSSION

The correlation between the I-E and Trust Scales casts the results of the Warren Commission Questionnaire in a somewhat different light for males and females. For females the Trust Scale, but not the I-E Scale, is related to responses on the three critical items concerning the Commission. It would seem that for females the predictive variance accounted for by the two personality dimensions is different. Males, on the other hand, evidence a strong relationship between internality and high trust scores.

External males in this sample distinguish themselves not only by obtaining low scores on the Trust Scale but by expressing distrust in the findings of the Warren Commission. Table 3 presents the mean I-E and Trust scores for consistent responses by sex. By comparing the I-E Scale scores with the means for the total male ($\overline{X} = 10.1$) and female ($\overline{X} = 11.0$) samples (Table 2) and with means obtained with other samples (Rotter, 1966), it can be established that the most distinctive group in comparison with the normative samples is the males who responded with consistent distrust of the Warren Commission and who obtained a highly external score on the I-E Scale.

These subjects admit their feelings of being manipulated by others, being at the mercy of chance factors and "powerful others," and respond with a marked suspiciousness toward a variety of authorities. This attitudinal pattern is consistent with that of the "defensive external" previously described by Rotter (1966). More common among males who are actually highly competitive and achievement oriented, this reaction has been understood as a projection of responsibility for failure. As conceptualized in previous research, these would be males who develop the somewhat suspicious conviction that authority figures are bent on using their positions to thwart attempts at self-control of the environment and to undermine efforts toward mastery. Those imputing incompetence and/or malevolent motives to the Warren Commission are, in essence, confirming the defensive strategy these individuals have come to rely on in explaining their own personal inadequacies and failures. Such theories as the conspiracy one in which Lee Harvey Oswald is considered only an unfortunate pawn would be expected to find credence among this group. The fact that this appears to be the case within our sample not only helps to explain some of the distrust of the Warren Commission but also provides support for the hypothesis that externality among male subjects more often has a defensive character than does externality among female subjects.

The failure of the I-E Scale to predict responses to the two items dealing with attention to the controversy over the Warren Commission Report and the items concerned with dropping the matter and with signing a petition in favor of a new investigation is not altogether clear. Previous investigators (e.g., Seeman, 1963a) established a relationship between I-E scores and acquisition of information directly related to an individual's own life, while memory for general information was not different for groups equal in general intellectual ability. It may be that Is do not tend to acquire more information than Es unless there is a greater personal immediacy. In this case Es could become highly involved since the events tend to support the belief that powerful others could interefere with the achievement of anyone's goals. The surprisingly high percentage of subjects who deny that they haven't followed the controversy (84.5%) may suggest that both internals and externals are highly involved. Definitive explanation would require a measure for assessing personal involvement as well as a measure of information actually acquired. The results on the question of dropping the matter perhaps can best be explained in the same way. Is do not see themselves as in any more direct control over future investigation, even through the device of petition signing, and do not, as a group, show a greater inclination toward promoting its continuation. Other motives or personal characteristics appear to be cutting across the I-E dimension and accounting for these reactions. This finding repeats those of earlier studies (Rotter, 1966) which also concluded that willingness to sign a petition is not predictable from I-E scores. While at this point quite conjectural, one possible explanation rests in some internals' conviction that petitions are not only ineffective instruments of social change but may be realistically dangerous in that signatures can be retained and used against one subsequently in a different context.

In all, however, the present study lends support to previous work such as that with the F Scale (Titus & Hollander, 1957) and Dogmatism Scale (Rokeach, 1960) in relating personality variables to the study of social phenomena. The variance accounted for by personality measures in the Warren Commission Report survey is admittedly small. Yet it is also apparent that these data argue cogently for the existence of predispositions to believe or disbelieve which have no direct relationship to this particular social issue but which clearly contribute to determining reactions to it.[3]

The present study also has implications for the instruments employed and the constructs for which they were developed. The data are seen as extending the validity of the Interpersonal Trust Scale in a situation markedly different from the relatively limited complexity of the laboratory. While some of the hypotheses with regard to the I-E Scale were not supported, strong support for the hypothesis of more defensive externality among males was obtained and is of major import to the I-E construct.

[3] Twenty hospital employees (aides, nurses, and secretaries) were administered the I-E Scale, Interpersonal Trust Scale, and the Warren Commission Report Questionnaire. Although conditions of administration were both less controlled and more variable, the replication of results within this sample, strikingly different from our college one, is of interest. Of these 20, 7 had a weighted Questionnaire score of 3 and 5 had a weighted score of 9. Trust scales for the two groups were significantly different in the same direction as the larger sample at the < .05 level (two-tailed test) by the Mann-Whitney U Test. For the I-E Scale the difference was also in the same direction, but the Mann-Whitney U Test was at the .11 (two-tailed test) level of significance.

5-3

Internal-External Control as a Determinant of Amount of Social Influence Exerted[1]

E. JERRY PHARES

Internally vs. externally controlled Es were used in the attempt to change female S's expressed attitudes on various issues. Prior to the experiment, Ss had filled out an attitude questionnaire. Es read from standard instructions in their attempt to influence Ss. As hypothesized, internally controlled Es were able to induce significantly greater changes in expressed attitudes than were externally controlled Es. Control Ss who merely filled out the questionnaire the 2nd time without any attempted influence showed changes equal to those Ss run by externally controlled Es.

The induction of attitude change has historically been a crucial area of study in psychology and currently still represents a major psychological research effort. Both the nature of the individual to be influenced and the characteristics of the forces which apply the influence have been studied. One factor which may affect the amount of influence that one person exerts upon another in changing the latter's attitudes is the concept of internal versus external control of reinforcement. This is a concept which has developed out of social learning theory (Rotter, 1954) and refers to the extent to which an individual feels that he has control over the reinforcements that occur relative to his behavior. Externals feel that forces beyond their control are the essential factors in determining the occurrence of reinforcements (such forces might include fate, chance, powerful others, the complexity of the world or its unpredictability, etc.). Internals, however, tend to feel that they control their own destiny and are the effective agent in determining the occurrence of reinforcements. All of this represents a continuum of individual differences that cuts across specific need areas. It is, in short, a generalized expectancy relating behavior to reinforcement in a wide variety of learning situations. Seeman (1959) has discussed this variable in terms of "powerlessness" and its relationship to the sociological concept of "alienation." The related notion of "mastery" has also been treated by Strodtbeck (1958).

A number of studies have shown that expectancies are differentially affected when tasks are perceived as dependent upon skill as opposed to chance or luck (James, 1957; James & Rotter, 1958; Phares, 1957, 1962; Rotter, Liverant, & Crowne, 1961). Concurrent with this research, however, has been the development of a scale that would measure individual differ-

[1] This study was supported by Grant NSF GS-112 from the National Science Foundation.

Reprinted from *The Journal of Personality and Social Psychology*, 1965, **2**, 642–647. Copyright 1965 by the American Psychological Association and reprinted by permission of the author and the publisher.

ences in the generalized expectancy for internal-external control of events. Starting with Phares (1957), the scale was revised by James (1957) and subsequently developed into a forced-choice scale (Rotter, Seeman & Liverant, 1962). The test now being used is composed of 23 items and 6 filler items (Internal-External—I-E—Control Scale). Illustrative items are presented elsewhere (Gore & Rotter, 1963). In general, the I-E concept has shown relationships to a variety of behaviors including those in some learning situations (Bialer, 1961; James, 1957; Phares, 1957), conformity situations (Crowne & Liverant, 1963), and risk taking (Liverant & Scodel, 1960). It relates to specific, logically selected tests (Holden, 1958; Simmons, 1959) and also to differences among known groups (Battle & Rotter, 1963; Cromwell, Rosenthal, Shakow, & Zahn, 1961).

Perhaps more directly related to the present research are studies involving I-E and attitudes, social action behaviors, and experimenter influence. For example, Seeman and Evans (1962) demonstrated that patients in a tuberculosis hospital who scored toward the internal end of the continuum knew more about their physical condition, were better informed about the nature of tuberculosis, and were seen by hospital personnel as being more informed, better patients than were externals. Gore and Rotter (1963) have shown that scores on the I-E scale relate directly to social action-taking behavior. That is, the I-E scale predicted the type and degree of commitment behavior manifested by Negro college students to effect social change. Another study by Gore (1962) relates to experimenter influence. She used three groups: one in which the hypothesis was revealed to the subject; one in which subtle attempts were made to influence the subject in the direction of the hypothesis; and a control group. She found no differences between internals and externals in her overt-influence and control conditions but in her subtle-influence condition the internals showed both less influence than the controls and also tended to respond more in the opposite direction of her subtle suggestion than controls.

Based upon the presumed construct properties of the I-E scale as well as the preceding research it was hypothesized that internal subjects are able to exert more influence upon others than are external subjects. Thus, in influencing the attitudes of others, internal subjects should be more effective than externals. Internals, having the generalized expectancy that they are in control of their own behavior-reinforcement sequences, should thus be more effective agents in the induction of change than individuals not having such an expectancy. In effect, this study may be construed as a study of experimenter influence where the *true* subjects are experimenters. The prediction is basically that internal experimenters will induce greater changes in attitude statements on the part of their subjects than will external experimenters.

METHOD

The I-E scale was administered to 179 males and 256 females in two large general psychology classes at Kansas State University. Scored in the internal direction, the means were 16.45 for males and 16.30 for females. At the same time a so-called College Opinion Survey (COS) was administered. This survey consisted of 12 items to which students responded each time on an 11-point scale from "strongly disagree" to "strongly agree." The survey dealt with topics of current campus interest as illustrated by the following items:

1. Fraternities and sororities serve a *vital* and *necessary* part of college life.
3. College athletics have gotten out of hand and should, therefore, be put in their proper perspective.
11. Class attendance ought to be completely optional for all students.

Based upon the data from the foregoing two scales, two experimental groups were formed. The first was composed of 27 males (internals) with scores on the I-E scale ranging from 19 to 23 and the second group consisted of 27 males who received I-E scores from 0 to 14 (externals). Both groups were matched as closely as possible on the basis of COS scores. Since the COS consisted of diverse items, there was no possibility of deriving a single score that would meaningfully describe a student. Therefore, in matching groups, care was taken to insure that both members of each internal-external pair had the same number of COS items that fell into each of five designated intervals along the 11-point COS scale. This matching procedure accounts for the fact that only 50% of students from either I-E extreme was utilized. These two groups, representing the extremes on the internal-external control variable and matched as regards COS scores, served as experimenters for this study. They were the ones who attempted to induce attitudinal changes on the part of the subjects to be described below.

The subjects for this study were two groups of females with scores on the I-E scale near the mean (16 or 17). Females with such scores were used exclusively since Gore (1962) reports data indicating that internal subjects are more resistant to social influence than are externals. The two groups were matched on the basis of their responses to the COS in the manner described previously for the experimenters. In general, both groups tended toward the moderate ranges of opinion. Thus, in summary, there were two groups of female subjects with scores of either 16 or 17 on the I-E scale and matched on the basis of COS responses. One group of females served as subjects for the internal males, while the other matched group of females served as subjects for the external males. There were 27 subject-experimenter pairs in each group.

In addition, 30 females, drawn on a volunteer basis from the remainder of the classes, served as a quasi-control group. These subjects were simply readministered the COS approximately 10 weeks after the initial classroom administration. This procedure was designed to provide a rough index of the amount of attitude change that might be expected as a function of the passage of time. This is only a quasi-control group inasmuch as the conditions of readministration of the COS were not entirely comparable. Indeed, these control subjects were also slightly different from the experimental subjects inasmuch as they were subjects with scores on the I-E scale other than 16 or 17 and were thus more heterogeneous. However, the major purpose of this study was to demonstrate differences between two experimental groups; not whether attitude changes could be effected.

Upon appearance, each subject-experimenter pair was checked to insure that they were not acquainted. Following this, a research assistant led the experimenter to a small room where the following instructions were read:

This is a study of social influence. The subjects that you will be running have previously taken an attitude test and we have their scores on this test. In this experiment, you will read a series of arguments to the subject to see whether or not it is possible to alter her attitudes from what they were when she took the test. We do not know whether it is possible for experimenters like yourself to influence subjects in their stated attitudes about these issues. In effect, we want to know whether it is or is not possible. Okay?

Just read the instructions to the subjects. Say *nothing* else to them. If, for any reason, you should have to depart from this procedure, make a note of it and tell me afterwards. Please do not discuss this project with anyone until you are told it is alright.

At this point, the research assistant showed the experimenter the instructions he was to read to the subject and went over them with him, answering any questions that arose. Following this, the experimenter went back to the first room and brought the subject with him. The research assistant then left and the experimenter was on his own. The instructions which the experimenter read to the subject are as follows:

I am going to read you a series of statements that reflect positions on various attitudes that students have. It is possible that you may have filled out this questionnaire earlier in your General Psychology class—I believe it was used in some of them.

Before you indicate whether you agree or disagree with the statement, however, I will read you some of the arguments that have been used regarding the statement. In short, then, I will read you a statement and then give you some of the arguments that support a particular point of view. You will then rate your degree of agreement or disagreement with that statement using this scale as a guide. Okay? (No further explanation may be given.)

The scale mentioned was an 11-point scale ranging from "strongly agree" (+5) to "strongly disagree" (−5). The attitude statements read were the same 12 items that appeared on the COS, 3 of which were illustrated earlier. Following each statement, the experimenter read the arguments, whereupon the subject indicated her degree of agreement-disagreement. An illustration is as follows:

1. Fraternities and sororities serve a *vital* and *necessary* part of college life.

The arguments are:

a. Fraternities and sororities interfere with educational goals.
b. They too often foster discrimination and snobbishness.
c. They emphasize superficial values.
d. They often psychologically damage those persons who aren't selected as members.

What scale number indicates your degree of agreement or disagreement with the statement, "Fraternities and sororities serve a vital and necessary part of college life"?

This general format was followed for each of the 12 items.

RESULTS AND DISCUSSION

The essential data for this experiment are the differences between the scale values assigned to the 12 items prior to the exertion of social influence and those assigned subsequent to that influence. It was hypothesized that internally controlled experimenters would exert greater influence than externally controlled experimenters. In testing this hypothesis, each subject was given a score which consisted of the sum of magnitudes of scale change for all items which were in the direction of the influence (arguments) presented by the experimenter. From this value was subtracted the sum of the magnitudes of change which were in the direction opposite to that of the influence. These data are presented in Table 1. The data indicate that internal experimenters were able to induce significantly more attitudinal change than were their external counterparts. Indeed, the amount of influence exerted by externals was essentially no different than the amount of change which occurred simply as a function of taking the COS for the second time (control group). Thus, the amount of change showed by the control group may be considered in part a reflection of the unreliability of the COS and may serve also as a base line against which to compare changes which occurred in the two experimental groups. The variance in the three groups is rather high. The fact that it is high in all three groups may indicate that much of it is likely a function of the COS or the general procedure. In testing for homogeneity of variance between the internal and external control groups, an F value of borderline sig-

Table 1 Means and Sigmas for Subjects Run by Internal and External Experimenters and for Control Group

	M	σ	N	t
Internal experimenters	9.7	9.6	27	I versus E, 1.9*
External experimenters	3.1	15.3	27	E versus C, ns
Control group	2.8	10.2	30	C versus I, 2.6**

* $p < .03$, one-tailed.
** $p < .01$, one-tailed.

nificance was obtained. Accepting the variance as heterogeneous does not, however, significantly alter the confidence levels shown in Table 1. Leaving aside, for the moment, the COS or questions of its reliability, the fact that significant differences between externals and internals were obtained is quite striking when one considers that this variable was the only one considered in selecting experimenters or subjects. Thus, no attempt was made to control such variables as personal appearance, skill in reading orally, social skill, or other organismic variables. Lack of control of such factors may also account for some of the high variance.

Since data other than those of I-E and COS were not used in constituting the groups it may be argued that other variables might have accounted for the significant differences in experimenter influence. However, based on test scores available in the Kansas State University Counseling Center, it was found that such an obvious factor as intelligence was not seemingly operative. For example, the mean predicted grade-point average (based on ACT scores and high school rank) for high I-E experimenters was 1.74 and for low I-E experimenters, 1.79. Similar scores for subjects run by high experimenters and low experimenters were 2.27 and 2.22, respectively. Also available were scores on the Marlowe-Crowne Social Desirability (M-C SD) scale (Crowne & Marlowe, 1960). Such scores are presumably indicative of a need for social approval so that females who score high on this scale might be expected to be more susceptible to social influence than those scoring low. In our sample, subjects run by low I-E experimenters had mean M-C SD scores of 15.50 while subjects run by high I-E experimenters achieved mean M-C SD scores of 14.96. Analogous scores for high and low experimenters were 16.77 and 16.00, respectively. Thus, it is apparent that neither intelligence nor need for social approval, as measured by the above scales, contributed to the obtained differences in social influence.

As further evidence for the hypothesis, frequency counts were made of the number of times each subject changed the scale value of an item. Separate counts were made of the instances when the change was in the

Table 2   Frequency of Predicted and Unpredicted Changes in Attitude Statements for Three Groups

	PREDICTED CHANGES	UNPRE-DICTED CHANGES	TOTAL	PROPORTION OF PREDICTED CHANGES TO TOTAL CHANGES
Internal experimenters	158	86	244	.65
External experimenters	135	128	263	.51
Control group	131	119	250	.52

predicted direction (direction of the arguments) as opposed to change in the nonpredicted direction. These data are presented in Table 2. In testing for the significance of the difference (.14; SE of difference = .045) between the external and internal proportions a z of 3.1 was obtained which is significant beyond the .01 level. The same difference between internals and controls (.13; SE of difference = .045) yielded a z of 2.9, significant at better than the .01 level.

Thus, regardless of whether the measure of influence is based upon the magnitude of change or upon the frequency of change, the indications are the same—internally controlled experimenters exert greater influence than do externally controlled experimenters. In fact, the influence exerted by externals (regardless of the measure) is no greater than those changes exhibited by subjects who merely retake the COS without any attempt at influencing them.

The major hypothesis of this study was thus confirmed. These results strongly suggest that a major variable in the study of social influence situations is the internal-external control dimension. A previous study has demonstrated that susceptibility to social influence is mediated by I-E dimension (Gore, 1962). The present study complements this finding by indicating that the I-E dimension likewise operates with those who would exert the influence. Indeed, the present findings were demonstrated under rather restrictive conditions. That is, the experimenters read rather routine, nonexpansive types of arguments and were not permitted to add anything to the printed statements. Also, subject and experimenter selection was based solely upon I-E scores and COS responses; other organismic characteristics were not considered.

These results seem striking. However, in essence, they serve to outline a future course of study. Several questions are left unanswered by this research. For example, the specific techniques by which internals are better able to exert influence remains for further research to elucidate. What are the specific mechanics (tone, gesture, facial expression, etc.) by which the influence is better exerted? Some of the experimenter bias research by Rosenthal and Fode (1963) suggests the importance of visual cues. Furthermore, should such differences be identified, what are the previous conditions which have led to the superior development or use of such skills on the part of internals as compared to externals? Also left unanswered is the question of the interaction between internal-external control and the strength of attitudes held. Thus, would the same results obtain when the subject held very strong attitudes about various issues?

An alternative hypothesis to account for the obtained results revolves around the demand characteristics of the situation. In view of the work of Orne (1959) and Rosenthal (1963), it could be argued that internal experimenters were subtly influenced by the research assistant to perform in a manner differently from that of external experimenters. Such an eventuality is possible although it was reduced by the fact that the research assistant worked from lists of subjects and experimenters and did not usually know which people belonged to which groups. At any rate, systematic studies involving all the preceding points are either planned or underway and should shed even further light on the construct validity of the I-E scale.

5-4 A Personality Correlate of Social Action[1]

PEARL MAYO GORE and JULIAN B. ROTTER

Social scientists have long been interested in the conditions under which the initiation of social change will take place. It has fallen to the social psychologist in particular to attempt predictions of individual differences in behavior directed toward a changing of the social structure. Usually, the problem has been approached through the measurement of the intensity or strength of attitudes. However, it is now widely recognized that the apparent desirability of some social outcome is a poor predictor of the degree to which an individual will commit himself toward action to obtain the desired goal. This is particularly true when the social action runs counter to majority opinion and entails risk of rejection, failure, or other punishment.

The concept of internal vs. external control of reinforcement may be of value in predicting social action behavior. This dimension distributes individuals according to the degree to which they attribute what happens to themselves to their own behaviors or characteristics vs. the degree to which they attribute what happens to themselves to forces outside their own control. Such forces would be represented by ideas of fate, chance, powerful others, or a general inability to understand the world. In social learning theory (Rotter, 1954), this variable is viewed as a generalized expectancy relating behavior to reinforcement in a large number of learning situations, cutting across specific need areas. In other words, it involves a higher-level learning skill affecting behavior in a wide variety of problem-solving situations.

Previous research by Phares (1957, 1962), James and Rotter (1958), James (1957), Rotter, Liverant, and Crowne (1961) and others has shown unequivocally that the growth and extinction of expectancies for reward vary considerably in different laboratory tasks if the tasks are perceived by S as chance, luck, or controlled by E vs. those which are seen as skill tasks with reinforcement dependent upon the individual's ability.

In addition to the findings from studies of expectancy changes, it has been hypothesized that individuals differ in a stable personality characteristic of whether they expect reward in a large variety of situations to be the function of external forces or their own behavior or attributes. The first attempt to measure such a generalized characteristic was made by Phares (1957). His test was revised by James (1957) into a longer Likert

[1] This research was supported in part by the United States Air Force under Contract No. AF 49 (638)-741 monitored by the Air Force Office of Scientific Research, Office of Aerospace Research. This paper was read at the Midwestern Psychological Association Meeting, 1962.

type scale, and Liverant, Rotter, Crowne, and Seeman have developed successive forms of a forced choice scale starting from the James-Phares test (Rotter, Seeman, & Liverant, 1962). The test now being used at Ohio State for research with adults consists of twenty-three items with six filler items (I-E Scale). Illustrative items are as follows.

I more strongly believe that:

6. a. Without the right breaks one cannot be an effective leader.
   b. Capable people who fail to become leaders have not taken advantage of their opportunities.
9. a. I have often found that what is going to happen will happen.
   b. Trusting to fate has never turned out as well for me as making a decision to take a definite course of action.
17. a. As far as world affairs are concerned, most of us are the victims of forces we can neither understand, nor control.
    b. By taking an active part in political and social affairs the people can control world events.
23. a. Sometimes I can't understand how teachers arrive at the grades they give.
    b. There is a direct connection between how hard I study and the grades I get.

Approaches to the assessment of individual differences along these lines with children have been developed by Bialer (1961), Crandall, Katkovsky, and Preston (1962), and Battle and Rotter (1963). Previous studies with adult and child scales have shown predictiveness in some learning situations (Phares, 1957; James, 1957; Bialer, 1961), an achievement situation (Crandall & Katkovsky, in press), a conformity situation (Crowne & Liverant, 1963), risk taking tasks (Liverant & Scodel, 1960), logical relationships to other tests (Holden, 1958; Simmons, 1959), and mean differences among known groups, (Battle and Rotter, 1963; Cromwell, Rosenthal, Shakow, & Zahn, 1961).

The most closely related research to the present study, however, was conducted by Seeman and Evans (1962) who related the concept and measure of internal vs. external control to the sociological concept of alienation, in the sense of powerlessness. Using one revision of the current test, Seeman and Evans studied patients in a tuberculosis hospital. They found statistical support for their general hypothesis that those patients who scored toward the internal control end of the dimension would know more about their own condition, would be better informed about the disease of tuberculosis in general, and would be regarded by the ward personnel as being better patients and better informed about their own condition. These predictions held in spite of the fact that none of the items in the questionnaire dealt with tuberculosis specifically or any disease or attitude toward disease. If patients' efforts to find out about their own serious physical condition can be affected by such a generalized attitude, it seems likely that where people are highly involved in desire for certain social change, as Negroes are in desegregation, social action-taking behavior could be likewise predicted from a generalized attitude of internal vs. external control of the locus of reinforcement. This is the major hypothesis of the present study. It should be emphasized that no test items in the I-E Scale deal directly with political liberalness,[2] prejudice, attitudes toward Negro rights, or the Ss' own present or past social action behavior.

In addition, it was hypothesized that predictiveness of this behavior would be improved by a knowledge of the social desirability motives of the Ss. Hence, a secondary hypothesis was that Ss high in measured social desirability motive (high SD) would be less likely to participate in actions toward social change than Ss low in this trait.

Since it appeared likely that the assumed high reinforcement value of the social change might be differently affected by the individual's social class membership, a measure of social class was included in the investigation. The direction of the relationship between social class membership and social action taking behavior was not hypothesized.

METHOD

Ss of the present study were students at a Southern Negro college that has featured prominently in recent social protest movements. Three psychology classes, including 62 males and 54 females, were given the Internal-External Control of Reinforcements Scale (I-E), and the Marlowe-Crowne Social Desirability Scale (S-D) (Crowne & Marlowe, 1960). Socioeconomic status and religious preference data were also obtained.

Four weeks (including two weeks of vacation) after the questionnaires were given, a student confederate went into all three classes on the same day, five minutes prior to dismissal and made the following statements, "Thank you, Dr. ———, for allowing me this time. I would like to ask the cooperation of each of you in a Students for Freedom Movement. To that end, I will pass out slips for you to fill out and hand back to me as you leave." The questions on the slip are shown in Table 1. Class attendance was used to identify S who turned in slips without signing them.

Ss were divided into groups according to their category of social action-taking behavior. If a S checked more than one item, he was placed in the category of highest commitment, in the order A, B, C, D. The mean I-E, S-D, and Social Class (Warner) of each group was then determined. F and t tests were computed.

RESULTS

The means and sigmas for each category of social action-taking are given in Table 2. Using the "mean square ratio" for unequal N's (Lindquist, 1953), a significant F relationship between scores on the I-E scale and

[2] Data recently collected by Rotter show no significant difference in the I-E Scale scores of Ohio State University students who identify themselves as Republicans from those who identify themselves as Democrats.

Table 1 *Questionnaire To Determine Degree of Social Action-Taking Behavior*

Students for Freedom Rally

Please check any or all aspects of our program in which you would be willing to participate.

I would be interested in: Check here:

(A) Attending a rally for civil rights.   _____

(B) Signing a petition to go to local government and/or
      news media calling for full and immediate integration
      of all facilities throughout Florida.   _____

(C) Joining a silent march to the capitol to demonstrate
      our plea for full and immediate integration of all facili-
      ties throughout Florida.   _____

(D) Joining a Freedom Riders Group for a trip during the
      break.   _____

(E) I would not be interested in participating in any of
      the foregoing.   _____

                              Signature: _____

                              Address: _____

                              Tel. No.:   _____

social action-taking behavior was found. ($F = 2.89$, $df = 4$ and 111, $p = < .05$).

The following t tests were significant (all two-tailed): categories of high commitment B, C, and D vs. little commitment A ($p = < .05$); category of no commitment E vs. high commitment B, C, and D ($p = < .05$); category A vs. category C alone ($p = < .01$), and category C vs. category E ($p = < .01$). In general, it can be seen that the means on the I-E test follow closely the order of degree of social action-taking involved in the various alternatives shown in Table 1.[3] The order is C and D most; B in

[3] Shortly before the time of testing, a large number of Negroes were arrested and placed in jail for a similar march on the state house of a nearby state.

Table 2 *Mean Scores by Categories of Commitment*

	I-E		S-D		SOCIAL CLASS		
CATEGORY	Mean	Sigma	Mean	Sigma	Mean	Sigma	N
A	10.3	3.1	18.10	6.4	4.76	1.6	20
B	9.2	3.4	17.05	5.5	5.00	1.5	20
C	7.4	2.9	16.95	6.4	5.95	1.3	24
D	8.1	3.8	16.82	4.4	5.29	1.5	20
E[a]	10.0	3.9	18.74	4.9	5.50	1.4	32

[a] E category includes those who did not sign a slip but were present.

the middle; and A and E least. Those individuals who were more inclined to see themselves as the determiners of their own fate tended to commit themselves to more personal and decisive social action. There was a trend, not reaching statistical significance, for persons high in measured social desirability motive to commit themselves to less social action.

An analysis of these data by sex indicates that the same trend was present for males and females. The males provided slightly more differentiation of groups than females.

Little class difference in this essentially homogeneous population was present. Class V was the modal class position (Warner scale). A non-significant curvilinear trend was noted. Ss at both extremes of the social action-taking continuum obtained the lowest social class ratings.

SUMMARY

Students in a Southern Negro college very much involved in the current social protest movement against segregation were used as Ss of a study of prediction of social action-taking behavior. A forced choice test of a generalized attitude toward internal or external control of reinforcements, not specifically dealing with the issue studied, predicted the type and degree of commitment behavior manifested to effect social change. The social desirability motive and social class showed a weak trend in the predicted direction in the case of the former and a logically consistent one on an ad hoc basis in the case of the latter. These findings may serve as an impetus for much needed research in the important area of ongoing social action and social change.

5-5 | The Prediction of Social Action from a Dimension of Internal-External Control

BONNIE RUTH STRICKLAND[1]

A. INTRODUCTION

Of importance in a time of increased political and social upheaval is an adequate description of the persons initiating action in an attempt to change existing conditions. While it is interesting to speculate on the motivation of the people in the forefront of activity, little empirical evidence is available to support explanations. From a social-learning expectancy theory, one rather clear personality variable can be expected to delineate social action takers from nonaction takers. Rotter, Seeman, and Liverant (1962) have described a dimension of internal versus external control of reinforcement in which a person may be characterized according to the degree to which he attributes the events that happen to him as a function of his own control, skills, or behaviors as opposed to these events being the result of luck, chance, fate, or powers beyond his control.

Gore and Rotter (1963) have demonstrated that those individuals who are inclined to see themselves as determiners of their own fate tend to commit themselves to personal and decisive action. The foregoing experimenters had a student confederate go into classes at a Southern Negro college that had figured prominently in social-protest movements. The students were asked by the confederate to sign a questionnaire designed to elicit commitment to civil-rights movements. Students designated their willingness to participate in mass rallies, to sign petitions, to embark on freedom rides, and so on. Prior to and independent of the civil rights questionnaire the students had completed a scale designed to assess degree of internal versus external control of reinforcement as well as a social-desirability questionnaire assessing a dimension of need for approval. In general, the group means on the internal-external scale followed closely the order of degree of verbalized commitment to social action on the questionnaire, with the more-internal subjects being those stating the most commitment. The need-for-approval motive showed weak trends across the degrees of social action, with the higher-need-for-approval subjects being less likely to verbalize willingness to become involved in civil-rights action.

The purpose of the present study is to elaborate on Gore and Rotter's findings, with one essential refinement of their research. The persons de-

[1] The author gratefully acknowledges the valuable assistance and advice of William A. Coppedge, James H. Harris, and Wendy Richardson who served as examiners. The author is also indebted to Mrs. Charles Perkins, Jr., Dr. Dorothy Rowley, Dr. Ralph McC. Chinn, and the members of the Student Nonviolent Coordinating Committee.

scribed as action takers in the present experiment are those individuals actively engaged in civil-rights movements. Gore and Rotter have shown that verbalized commitment may be predicted by the internal-external dimension. It seems appropriate to extend Gore and Rotter's research to a prediction of behavioral commitment. It is hypothesized that persons engaged in social action are characterized as more internal than a comparable group of persons who are not involved.

B. METHOD

Subjects and Procedure

All of the subjects of the present study were Negroes, predominantly college students, who were in one of two groupings. One was an active or experimental group composed of individuals who were engaged in civil-rights movements throughout the Southern part of the United States in February and March of 1963. Approximately 33 subjects were active members of the Student Nonviolent Coordinating Committee (SNCC) predominantly engaged in voter registration. Civil-rights leaders suggested 20 other subjects known to be active in protest movements. Two independent samples were collected. The first sample consisted of the students designated by the leaders plus six SNCC members. These subjects were asked individually by three white college students (one female and two males), who served as examiners in the experiment, to complete two personality inventories and a questionnaire designed to assess the degree of activity in which they were engaged. The second sample of 27 subjects consisted of SNCC members who were attending a civil-rights rally in a large southern city during April of 1963. These persons came from many areas in the United States, with the majority being from the Northeast and South. Again the personality inventories and the activity questionnaire were administered by the white college students mentioned earlier. It should be noted that both samples consisted of subjects who in a sense volunteered to participate in the study. The subjects were told that they were being asked to complete the scales and questionnaire in conjunction with a large-scale research project. Cooperation ranged from fair to good. All subjects who indicated that they were willing to participate completed the inventories. Nineteen female subjects and 34 male subjects comprised the total active sample. Every active subject stated on the civil-rights questionnaire that he had participated in some phase of civil-rights protest, such as voter registration, sit-ins, and demonstrations. The mean number of arrests per person in conjunction with civil-rights activities was about five, with a range from zero to 62. Nineteen of the subjects answered that because of their involvement they had received threats of violence directed either at themselves or their families.

The control group of 105 subjects consisted of students at three Negro colleges in a large Southern city. These subjects were tested while enrolled in three different required classes within their colleges. The three white examiners who tested the active group distributed the inventories. Professors within the institutions active in civil-rights movements assured examiners that the classes tested would include few, if any, students active in protest movements. Thirty-three females and 72 males in the control group completed the personality inventories.

2. Measures

The Internal-External Scale[2] is a 29-item forced-choice scale assessing the degree to which a person attributes the events that happen to him as being within or beyond his personal control and understanding. An illustrative item is "I more strongly believe that: (a) I have often found that what is going to happen will happen. (b) Trusting to fate has never turned out well for me as making a decision to take a definite course of action."

The inventory used as a measure of the approval motive is the Marlowe-Crowne Social Desirability Scale. This scale is a 33-item true-false questionnaire containing descriptions of highly socially sanctioned behaviors that are improbable of occurrence. An illustrative item is "I am always courteous even to people who are disagreeable."

The activity questionnaire that was completed by the experimental group was a short-answer inventory asking subjects to indicate the kinds of civil-rights movements in which they had been active, the amount of activity in which they had engaged, the number of arrests in connection with civil rights, and any threats of violence that had been directed toward them or their families.

Each subject was asked to state his age and the number of school grades completed. These data served as control variables.

C. RESULTS

The data were first analyzed for sex differences across the personality inventories. No significant differences were found; so the data were subsequently analyzed without regard to sex. The two different samples of active subjects were examined for significant differences on the two personality inventories. No differences were found, and the two separate samples were combined into one active group for the overall analysis of the data.

Means and standard deviations of the experimental and control groups for the personality inventories, age, and education are presented in Table 1. In the control group, four subjects failed to state their age, and 12 subjects did not give the number of grades in school that they had completed. To simplify computations, these subjects were given the mean age or education of the group in which they were members. As expected, the great majority of the control subjects were of freshman or sophomore standing.

Comparison of the active and the nonactive groups on internal-external control scores produces a t of 3.58, significant beyond the .01 level. A biserial correlation between internal-external control scores and activity

[2] A scale developed but not published by S. Liverant, J. B. Rotter, M. Seeman, and D. P. Crowne, Spring, 1961.

Table 1 Means and Standard Deviations for Active and Nonactive Groups

	GROUP			
	Active (N = 53)		Nonactive (N = 105)	
VARIABLE	Mean	SD	Mean	SD
Internal-external scale	7.49	3.49	9.64	3.70
Marlowe-Crowne Scale	18.41	5.75	17.00	4.98
Age	21.47	4.19	19.17	1.56
Education	14.26	1.64	12.69	.70

status is .35 ($p < .01$). Active group members are significantly more likely to be assessed as internal than are the nonactive group members.

Active-group members appear to be higher in need for approval than do nonactive-group members; however the difference is not significant. Active-group members are significantly older and have completed more grades in school than the nonactive-group members ($t = 3.83$, $p < .01$; $t = 6.54$; $p < .01$). Pearsonian correlations were computed between internal-external scores and age and amount of education. No significant relationships were found. See Table 2.

Table 2 Correlations of the Internal-External Scores with Activity and the Control Variables
$$(N = 158)$$

VARIABLE	r
Activity status	.35*
Age	−.04
Education	−.14

* $p < .01$.

D. DISCUSSION

It was hypothesized that persons involved in social action would be assessed as more internal in their feelings of personal control and understanding of the events that happen to them than would a control group of persons not engaged in social action. Results confirm the hypothesis, with Negro students who were known to be active in civil-rights demonstrations being significantly more internal than Negro students who had had no experience in protest movements. The study validates a personality inventory assessing internal control versus external control of reinforcement, as well as adding to a description of the persons involved in social action.

Comparisons between active groups and nonactive groups were complicated by the fact that the active group was found to be older and to have completed more grades of school. While this finding may be due to the sampling procedures or to the fact that commitment to social action attracts an older or more educated person, it still poses a problem with respect to prediction from the personality variable alone. However, no significant relationships were found between the internal-external score and age and amount of education.

The dimension of need for approval, as measured by the Marlowe-Crowne Social Desirability Scale offers little to a prediction of social action. The trend within the present study for the more-active students to be assessed higher in the approval motive than were members of the control group is a reversal of the trend reported by Gore and Rotter (1963). However, in neither study does the relationship attain significance.

As an essential refinement of Gore and Rotter's study, it was necessary to test persons behaviorally active in social movements. The experimental group in the present study consisted of persons clearly and dramatically committed to direct action. Many of the students, some of whom were working only for subsistent pay for SNCC, were everyday in situations of danger and harassment to themselves and their families. A few were field secretaries for SNCC, spending long months in pressure areas engaged in voter registration. Many had participated in demonstrations in Albany, Georgia, and sit-ins throughout the South. It should be noted, also, that the data were collected in the spring of 1963 before a large general onset of protest demonstrations that gained strong support within Negro communities. The persons tested were pioneers in the movements and were members of an organization that came into being not only as a positive force toward integration but as a protest against early civil-rights organizations that were not moving in a sufficiently aggressive manner for the original SNCC members. Further research might be pointed toward testing other groups of varying commitment to social action, including the White Citizen's Councils.

Clearly, the internal-external scale appears to be a useful instrument for the prediction of social action. Of primary importance, however, are the implications of the research in regard to identifying variables, such as internality-externality, that underlie behavioral commitment.

E. SUMMARY

Two personality inventories, the Internal-External Scale and the Marlowe-Crowne Social Desirability Scale were given to a group of 53 Negroes actively engaged in civil-rights movements in the South and a control group of 105 Negroes who were not active. The Marlowe-Crowne Scale did not differentiate the active and the nonactive groups, but a significant relationship was found between internal-external scores and social action. The more internal the subject, the more likely was he to be a member of the active group. The study validates a dimension of internal-external control, as well as adding to a description of the persons involved in social action.

5-6 | The Effect of the Commitment Situation on the Generalization of Expectancies[1]

WALTER MISCHEL

Recent psychological research has been concerned increasingly with the isolation of specific variables determining resistance to change. It has already been demonstrated, for example, that modification of attitudes and opinions is more difficult when an individual is ego-involved (Sherif & Cantril, 1947), when social supports are strong (Festinger, 1953), and when stimuli are highly unambiguous (Asch, 1948; Coffin, 1941; Moos & Koslin, 1952). More recently, investigators have begun to isolate the effect of commitment, i.e., making a particular position known or public, on the ease with which that position can be influenced and changed (Argyle, 1957; Bennett, 1955; Deutsch & Gerard, 1955; Fisher, Rubenstein & Freeman, 1956; Hobart & Hovland, 1954; Kelley & Volkart, 1952) and have emerged with contradictory findings. In most of this research the commitment which the S makes involves perceptual judgments, opinions, or attitudes, and modifications of Asch's situation (Asch, 1952) are used. In the present study "expectancy statements" were the commitments made. Operationally, an expectancy statement is a quantitative goal statement (e.g., an expected score in a series of scores) elicited by level of aspiration instructions which emphasize accuracy in the selection of the goal. For example, S is asked to predict, as accurately as possible, what score from 0 to 100 he is most likely to get on a specified test. Expectancy statements are typically used to measure Rotter's expectancy construct (Rotter, 1954), and may be considered referents for that construct.

More specifically, this study investigated the relationship between the public-private nature of the situation in which expectancy statements are made and the amount of generalization of expectancy changes (Chance, 1951; Jessor, 1954) following negative reinforcement. Generalization of expectancy changes was defined as changes (lowering) in expectancy statements on a second task following obtained failure, or negative reinforcement, for performance on a related first task. Thus, change in a second related position, rather than in the original position around which reinforcement is manipulated, was studied. This is in contrast to most

[1] This paper is based in part upon portions of a doctoral dissertation done at the Ohio State University, supplemented by data collected in subsequent studies at the University of Colorado. Special thanks are due to Dr. Julian B. Rotter for his consistent encouragement and helpful assistance. A summary of this paper was read at the 1957 meetings of the American Psychological Association in New York City.

previous research on resistance to change which, generally, has dealt with change in the original task around which influence attempts are made. Negative reinforcement was used throughout, and was defined as a manipulated obtained score given to S for his performance on a first task, at a fixed interval (11 points) below the expectancy statement for that first task.

The major hypothesis, formulated in accord with social learning theory (Rotter, 1954), predicts less generalization of expectancy changes (as indicated by lowered expectancy statements for the second task) under conditions of public commitment (to another person, face-to-face) than under conditions of private commitment.[2] That is, it was predicted that Ss who made their expectancy statements in a public, face-to-face situation with another person directly present would show less lowering of expectancy statements for Task Two following negative reinforcement for Task One than Ss who made their expectancy statements privately. The rationale for this prediction was as follows. It was assumed that S's choice with respect to changing his expectancy statements is influenced, in part, by his expectancies concerning the reinforcement consequences of changing or not changing, of raising or lowering, his expectancies (e.g., satisfaction of conforming to what E might want from S). Following obtained failure (e.g., in the form of a score below his expectancy statement) for performance on a task, S can be considered as subject to two major influences with respect to readjusting his expectancy statements for related tasks. On the one hand, lowering related expectancies following evidence of failure is a sign of accuracy and realism, which he is apt to see as appropriate behavior, particularly when accuracy of behavior is stressed. On the other hand, lowering expectancy statements, in spite of evidence of obtained failure, can also be construed by S as a sign of "weakness," "loss of face," "confirmation of failure," etc., and the admission of this, in the form of lowering his statements, may be seen as leading to negative reinforcement from others as well as from himself. It was anticipated that admission of failure, by lowering expectancy statements, would be more difficult in the face-to-face situation than in the private situation, since in the former situation S is exposed to direct potential negative reactions for his admission of failure from another social agent (E) as well as from himself. It was further anticipated that these differential expectancies regarding the negatively reinforcing consequences of admission of failure would outweigh possible differences in expectancies concerning the positive reinforcement consequences of realism in the two situations.

---

[2] "Public and private" commitment has been used in various ways. In the present study, a position which S makes explicit to himself (in writing) but not in the direct, face-to-face presence for another person (E) is considered a private commitment; an explicit position made in the direct, face-to-face presence of E, i.e., witnessed by E, is considered a public commitment.

METHOD

Subjects

A total of 143 male and female Ss from introductory classes in psychology was used to test this hypothesis. The majority of the students were freshmen and sophomores. No Ss exceeding the age of 25 were used.

Tasks

Two experimental tasks, both word lists, were used with each S. The first task included a list of 20 stimulus words, each followed by four possible response words. S was to match each stimulus word with the response word which best fit. The second task consisted of a list of 20 stimulus words to each of which S was to write his first free-association. The lists were described as two "personality scales" of a word-association type which E was attempting to standardize. The first list was presented as the "Scale of Social Adjustment," and the second list as the "Scale of Leadership Adjustment." Test booklets and verbal instructions were aimed at giving face validity to these instruments as projective-type personality tests. The purpose of this procedure was to enhance S's interest and involvement and to make the situation personally important.

The first word list (Task One) was used as the original task for all Ss and is the task on which reinforcement was manipulated. The second word list (Task Two) served as the generalization task.

Procedure

A level of aspiration paradigm was used in this experiment. The two tasks were described in detail and Ss were told that possible scores on each scale ranged from 0 to 100, with 50 as the average score for college students. To test the hypothesis the following variations on the level of aspiration situation were employed:

1. *Public (Face-to-Face) Commitment* Forty-two Ss were tested individually in a face-to-face setting. The seating was so arranged that E could always clearly see all of S's written responses. E explained the procedure and distributed booklets describing the two tasks. E read the description and instructions for Task One while S followed in his booklet. Then E said that in addition to standardizing these tests he was also interested in how Ss predicted they would do before actually performing the tests. S was asked to predict as accurately as possible, in writing only, the score that "you are *most likely* to get" and to record this on a signed data sheet. The S's response to the request that he predict his score is the referent for the construct of expectancy. The description of Task Two was then read and the same procedure was used in asking S to record what he thought he was most likely to get (expectancy statement) for the second task. S performed on Task One and, upon completion, Task One was collected and "scored." The scoring procedure consisted of subtracting 11 points

from the expectancy statement for Task One. Face validity was given to this by the use of complex-looking tables of norms and an elaborate scoring method. The obtained score, formulated by this method for all Ss, defines the negative reinforcement or failure experience within this study. Following the scoring, S was handed a slip of paper containing his name and the score. The instructions for Task Two were reviewed briefly and S was told that, if he wished, he could re-estimate, by writing in the appropriate place on the data sheet, what score he now thought he was most likely to make on Task Two.

2. *Private Commitment* This situation was identical with the face-to-face situation with the following exceptions. One hundred and two Ss were tested in groups ranging in size from 5 to 15. The members of these groups were unfamiliar with each other and were not in communication throughout the course of the experiment, each S performing at a desk well separated from others and with his written responses clearly out of view from all others. Thus, Ss in this condition performed in an essentially private situation, each performing without having his performance exposed to the direct face-to-face observation of others, in contrast to the public situation in which Ss' responses were directly viewed by E.

RESULTS AND DISCUSSION

The primary data used in the analysis of the results are the changes (re-estimations) in expectancy statements for Task Two following failure on Task One. The measure of generalization is the difference score between the expectancy statements for Task Two before and after obtaining negative reinforcement on Task One. Due to a preponderance of "no change" scores the distribution of difference scores was not sufficiently normal to permit the use of parametric statistics. The chi-square test (McNemar, 1949) was therefore employed to test the relationship between amount of change (lowering) of expectancy statements for Task Two following obtained negative reinforcement for performance on Task One for Ss in the public, face-to-face situation as compared to Ss in the private situation. (All Ss either lowered or retained unchanged their Task Two expectancies following the reinforcement procedure, with the exception of one S in the private situation who raised his expectancy and was omitted from the analysis.) The difference scores were categorized in such a way that, as closely as possible, 25 per cent of the total Ss could be grouped into each of the categories (Table 1).

Exact quartiles could not be obtained due to the abundance of tied scores. Table 1 shows the number of Ss from the public and private groups who fall into each of these quartiles of difference scores. The chi-square test applied to this table yields a chi-square of 16.77 which, with three degrees of freedom, is significant beyond the .01 level of confidence. It should be noted that in the public situation no S lowered Task Two expectancies more than 10 points, whereas in the private situation 24 Ss lowered between 11 and 30 points.

Table 1   Task Two Expectancies in Public and Private Testing Situations

TASK TWO EXPECTANCIES	SITUATION			
Amount of Lowering	Public N	Private N	Chi-square	p
0	18	26		
1 to 9	14	18		
10	10	33		
11 to 30	0	24		
			16.77	<.01

A chi-square test comparing the frequency of Ss in the two conditions who lowered or retained expectancy statements for Task Two following negative reinforcement on Task One yields a chi-square of 4.09 which, with two degrees of freedom, is significant beyond the .05 level of confidence. The results of both comparisons were in the expected direction. Namely, Ss who made their expectancy statements in the public, face-to-face situation, in the direct presence of another person (E), showed less generalization (i.e., lowering) of expectancy changes than Ss who made their expectancy statements in the private situation, not in the direct, face-to-face presence of E.[3]

It may be suggested that differences as a function of the group vs. individual testing situations, rather than as a function of the direct presence or absence of another social agent (E), may account for the obtained differences. To explore this question a follow-up study was conducted in which 50 Ss were tested in a situation essentially similar to the one reported above, with the following major variations. All Ss were tested in an individual setting in a room with a one-way vision screen. E introduced S to the task, and left him to make his expectancy statements and perform in isolation. E returned to collect the expectancy statements and the completed first test, left to score it, returned the score on a slip of paper, and left S to re-estimate his score for Task Two, if he wished to do so, before performing on that task. Half the Ss were told that they

---

[3] It should be noted that, in addition to testing the major hypothesis, an attempt was also made to test the differential effect of making explicit (written) or implicit (unverbalized) expectancy statements in the private situation for the generalization task. Thus, in addition to the group which wrote its expectancy statements for both tasks before performing on either in the private situation, 75 Ss underwent the same experimental procedure but did not record or verbalize in any way their initial expectancy statements for task two before performing on Task One. Statistical comparisons between these groups on terminal means of the expectancy statements for Task Two following performance on Task One yielded results which, on the whole, indicated trends towards significant differences but which did not reach acceptable probability levels. The trends were consistently in the predicted direction, namely, lower terminal means for Ss who had not made explicit expectancy statements for Task Two before performing on Task One. A number of methodological problems complicated the interpretation of these data and they must be considered equivocal.

would be observed throughout by a student on the other side of the one-way screen; half the Ss were not given this information. Comparisons of the two groups on amount of change yielded p values less than .05 (one-tailed U test) in the same direction as reported above.

"Publicness" can also be considered in terms of the *potential* for a position to become known to others. That is, simply by giving his name, as all Ss did, S's positions become potentially public. Do differences in the potential publicness of a position through S's identification or non-identification of his position (e.g., by giving or not giving his name), yield effects on the generalization of expectancy changes? Since elicitation or nonelicitation of such identifying information is often used as the major operation for publicness of a situation, data relevant to this question were collected.

Sixty-two Ss were tested in small groups of approximately 10 to 20 Ss. The procedure used was essentially similar to that described under private commitment. Ss were randomly selected for experimental groups and in half the groups filled out a detailed personal data sheet including name, address, telephone, and college information immediately prior to performing on the experimental tasks, whereas in the other half no personal data sheet was required, anonymity was stressed, and Ss were identified only with seat numbers. Comparisons of these two conditions yielded no differences approaching statistical significance.

The over-all results indicate that public-private situations exert the predicted effects on the generalization of expectancy changes following negative reinforcement when direct contact with E, either in the face-to-face situation or in the situation with direct suggestion of E's presence (one-way screen behind which E is said to be), occurs in the public situation. However, these differences were not obtained when the public situation consisted of eliciting only name and background information from S thus making his behavior potentially public through indirect means.

In conclusion, the results obtained from the comparison of the public and private conditions strongly indicate that the situation in which expectancy statements are elicited, with respect to the public-private setting in which the individual makes his commitments, significantly affects the ease with which later, related expectancy statements can be influenced. The main implications of this appear to be as follows. First, it seems of methodological import that studies concerned with goal-setting take into account the commitment aspects of the situation in which S is making his goal statements. Further, and more broadly, the findings appear relevant to research on the relationship between E and S with respect to behavior change in public and private testing situations in a large variety of research and applied settings—e.g., diagnostic testing, poll-taking, or conformity investigations. The present results indicate that such situational aspects may significantly effect not only the task around which manipulations are being directly attempted (the original task) but also related positions (the generalization task) which are elicited in the same situation.

It should be noted that the confirmed hypothesis was predicted from assumptions concerning the reinforcement consequences of changing *vs.*

not changing one's expectancy as a function of the committing situation. The same differences might have been produced by quite different procedures and should not be exclusively dependent on characteristics of the public and private situation. It is suggested that further research aim at predicting differential change by *directly* measuring expectancies for negative (and positive) reinforcement consequences for changing or not changing a particular position as well as by inferring such expectancies indirectly through analysis of situational differences as was done in the present experiment.

SUMMARY

This study investigated the relationship between the public-private nature of the situation in which expectancy (goal) statements are elicited and the amount of change in related expectancy statements following negative reinforcements for performance on a first task. The hypothesis was that there would be less lowering of expectancy statements on a second related task following negative reinforcement for performance on a first task in a public, face-to-face situation as compared to a private situation. This hypothesis was confirmed. Supplementary data are presented and the over-all results are interpreted as lending evidence to the importance of the commitment variable in the study of resistance to change. The results indicate that the public–private nature of the situation in which expectancy statements are elicited can significantly affect the subsequent modifiability of such statements.

5-7	*Conformity Under Varying Conditions of Personal Commitment*[1]
	DOUGLAS P. CROWNE and SHEPHARD LIVERANT[2]

This study tested a central proposition, stemming from Rotter's Social Learning Theory, that conformity is related to low expectations of success in socially evaluative situations and is consequently accompanied by defensive processes. 2 variants of an

[1] This research was supported in whole by the United States Air Force under Contract No. AF 49 (638)-741, monitored by the Air Force Office of Scientific Research of the Air Research and Development Command.

[2] We would like to thank our colleagues Julian B. Rotter and Milton J. Rosenberg for their helpful suggestions and advice in the preparation of this report.

Asch situation representing increasing degrees of personal commitment were compared to a control condition. Situational measures of confidence included betting and statements of expectancy. Additional personality indices included level of aspiration, need for approval, and internal vs. external control of reinforcement. The Ss were 110 introductory psychology students. Results depict the conformer as one who has a low expectation of success in evaluative situations. His lesser confidence leads to avoidant behavior to resolve the ensuing conflict. Defensive processes of the conformer tend to become more marked as personal commitment increases.

The experimental conformity situation, in which a conflict is induced between an individual's belief, opinion, or judgment and an oppositional group norm, rests on the supposition of personal commitment to, or investment in, the contravened position. While considerable experimental analysis has been devoted to variations in group pressure (Asch, 1952; Crutchfield, 1955; Mouton, Blake, & Olmstead, 1956), the present study is addressed to the question of the effects of manipulating personal commitment by increasing the penalty for conforming behavior.

Punishing conformity, and correspondingly increasing the value of independence, was accomplished by providing subjects with an amount of money and requiring them to bet on the correctness of their judgments.[3] The underlying rationale was that the introduction of negative consequences for yielding should increase the subject's commitment to his judgment. A lesser degree of investment was envisioned in a second condition in which subjects had to make public estimates of confidence in their stated judgements.

These procedures were intended to make the choice of conformity or independence a more meaningful and crucial one and thereby to extend analysis of the spectrum of conforming behavior. On a more tentative level, however, conformity under these conditions might suggest an answer to the persistent question of the degree of awareness, or of defensive distortion, involved in conforming behavior. The defensive nature of the conformity of some subjects has been inferred from the postexperimental interviews employed in such prior studies as those of Asch (1956). The present study, by exacting a price for conformity, makes it more difficult for the subject to explain his yielding to himself; there is, thus, the suggestive implication that to the degree that conformity occurs under the conditions outlined above, it is accomplished with relatively little awareness and with *defensive* justification.

Besides delineating certain aspects of conforming behavior under

---

[3] Subsequent to the completion of this experiment, it was discovered that Siegel (1956) briefly described a procedure similar to this in his *Nonparametric Statistics*. No data relevant to the concerns of the present study were reported, however, and the experimental procedure was described only in connection with the illustration of a statistical technique.

conditions of increased conflict, the present design lends itself to the study of personality differences between conformers and independents. Most relevant is the question of the relation between conformity and betting or expectancy-stating. The major rationale for postulating differential expectations (betting is considered a measure of expectancy) regarding the probability of being correct is provided by Rotter's (1954) Social Learning Theory (SLT). Within SLT, the conformer can be characterized as one who has a low expectation of success in socially evaluative situations. In consequence, he is inclined to use avoidant or defensive behavior in anticipation of punishment and threats to self-esteem. In other words, conformity in such situations represents protective behavior designed to avert expected failure. It follows that conformers, as compared to independents, should bet or state expectancies in a manner indicative of less confidence in their judgments, particularly on nonconforming trials.

A further test of the adequacy of this theoretical formulation was made by administering the Rotter (1942) Level of Aspiration (LOA) Board. Rotter has described this goal setting technique as a problem solving situation which calls for self-evaluation on the part of the subject. Odell (1959) found a high relationship between extreme scores on the Independence of Judgment scale (Barron, 1953a), a questionnaire index of tendencies to conform, and overly cautious and defensive aspiration patterns on the LOA Board.

Two personality inventories were also utilized to extend the network of propositions concerning individual differences in the self-evaluative behaviors of conformers and independents. The first of these was a measure of the need for approval (Marlowe & Crowne, 1961), previously shown to be related to social conformity (Strickland & Crowne, 1962). A high score on this test demands that the subject depict himself in a culturally sanctioned but highly improbable light. Recent research, notably a study by Conn (1963), suggests that high scores manifest a need for approval based, at least in part, on defensive components. Dependence on the favorable evaluation of others may thus be taken to reflect low self-esteem, which would tend to result in irreal or self-protective behavior in important evaluative situations. On this basis, approval motivated subjects should be less able to resist group pressure and should display less confidence in their judgments.

The second personality inventory represents an attempt to measure an expectancy construct recently derived from SLT entitled Internal versus External Control of Reinforcement (Rotter, Seeman, & Liverant, 1962). Internal versus External Control (I-E) refers to the degree to which an individual tends to perceive the consequences of his actions as being within (internal) or beyond (external) his control. The externally controlled individual sees relatively little instrumentality in his own behavior and regards himself as the passive recipient of reinforcements dispensed by external forces (chance, fate, impersonal social forces, or powerful others). In the previously cited study by Odell, a significant relationship was found between the index of I-E and the Independence of Judgment scale, with externals showing greater tendencies to conform.

METHOD

Subjects

The subjects were 110 introductory psychology students, 40 males and 70 females, apportioned to the three experimental conditions as follows: The Control group contained 32 subjects (14 males, 18 females); the Expectancy group consisted of 35 subjects (14 males, 21 females); and in the Betting group were 43 subjects (12 males, 31 females).

Conformity Situations

The basic conformity situation utilized in the three conditions was an adaptation of the Asch perceptual discrimination procedure. The task set for the subjects required them to distinguish, on each of 20 trials, the larger of two groups of dots which were presented tachistoscopically for a 1-second interval by means of a 2 by 2 slide projector. Each slide differed in the geometric arrangement of the groups of dots. The identification of the larger cluster on each slide was quite unambiguous, as established by accuracy levels ranging between 90 and 100% for the 20 slides as rated by 12 judges.

In the Control condition, the confederates and the naïve subject were informed that the experiment was concerned with perceptual discrimination and speed. On each trial, they were required to publicly announce, in a given order, the letter (A or B) designating the larger cluster of dots.

Exactly the same procedure was followed, and the identical task instructions were given, in each of the other conditions. The Expectancy group, however, was told that, in addition to perception, discrimination and speed, their confidence in the accuracy of their perceptual judgments was being investigated. Subjects in the Expectancy group indicated their certainty of being right on a scale from 0 (little or no confidence) to 10 (very high confidence). In this group, then, the members were required to announce their confidence statements following each judgment. The confederates made confidence statements of a prearranged magnitude. They were assigned consistent roles in an attempt to give them credibility, although in actuality the total distribution of the confederates' expectancy statements was approximately normal, with the modal expectancy at the midpoint of the scale.

As in the case of the Expectancy group, the Betting group was informed that confidence was being evaluated. In this group each member was given $10.00 in quarters with which he could bet nothing, $.25, or $.50 on each of his judgments. As in the Expectancy group, the bets of the confederates were so prearranged as to prevent the naïve subject from forming his own betting pattern on the basis of consistent group behavior. The instructions indicated that at the end of the session the accuracy of each judgment would be determined and that subjects' bets would be matched for those trials on which they were correct. Subjects declared their bets by dropping $.25 or $.50 (or nothing) into small boxes in front of them. The subjects could keep a proportion of their winnings, and this was explained to them in the initial instructions. Each subject's take was determined by adding the amount he won to any remaining portion of the original $10.00. If this total was $10.00 or less, the subject kept 10%; if he ended up with more than $10.00, he kept $1.00 plus 20% of everything over $10.00. Thus, if a subject bet $.50 on every trial and was correct each time, he won $3.00.

Personality Measures

The need for approval was assessed by means of the Marlowe-Crowne Social Desirability (M-C SD) scale (Crowne & Marlowe, 1960), a 33-item, true-false questionnaire. An illustrative item is, "I would never think of letting someone else be punished for my wrongdoings."

The index of I-E was a 60-item, forced-choice inventory, the I-E scale (Liverant & Scodel, 1960), which pairs internal with external choices as in the following example:

I more strongly believe that

(a) I have usually found that what is going to happen will happen, regardless of my actions.

(b) trusting to fate has never turned out as well for me as making a decision to take a definite course of action.

The scores obtained on the LOA Board are the D score, an algebraic summation of the differences between past performance and estimates of subsequent success, and the number and appropriateness of shifts or changes in estimates. In addition, these indices may be combined to yield a series of nine patterns which describe the individual's overall approach to the setting of goals. Rotter (1954) has described the criteria for the assignment of these patterns and reported evidence on their reliability and validity.

The patterns constituted our measure of self-evaluation and were divided into two major groups. The first of these groups, consisting of Patterns 2, 4, and 7, indicates overcautiousness, self-protection, and defensive goal setting and reflects lack of self-confidence and avoidance of expected failure. The second group of patterns, 1 and 3, represents a greater degree of confidence and more appropriate expectations of goal attainment.

Procedure

The two personality inventories were administered to all introductory psychology students on the first day of classes. For each experimental appointment, the naïve subject and the confederates, two males and two females, were met in the waiting room and escorted to the room in which the experiment was conducted. The confederates were instructed to pre-empt the first four chairs, leaving the seat on the far right for the naïve subject. To forestall suspicion, the order of responding was rotated from trial to trial, beginning with the confederate at the far left. Thus, the naïve subject came first in the response order on every fifth trial. These were the noncritical trials. At the conclusion of the conformity procedure, each naïve subject was questioned in detail to determine his awareness of the nature of the experimental procedures, the purpose of the experiment, and his account of his own behavior.

Finally, the LOA Board was administered to all the subjects in the Control group. Twenty-eight of the 35 subjects in the Expectancy group were recalled for a second appointment and given this measure as were 17 of the 43 Betting group subjects.

RESULTS

As a preliminary step, the post-experimental interviewers were carefully examined for suspicion, and 13 subjects (10 from the Control group and 3 from the Expectancy group) who correctly surmised the contrived nature of the experimental procedures were eliminated.

For all of the major analyses to be reported below, except the basic comparison of the amount of conformity in the three conditions, standard scores were utilized in order to achieve comparability between conditions and sexes. A range of values with a mean of 50 and a standard deviation of 10 was chosen.

Conformity in the Three Conditions

The amount of conformity in the three conditions was separately compared for males and females as shown in Table 1. A simple analysis of variance of the number of conforming trials by males in the three conditions yielded a nonsignificant F. A similar analysis for females was highly significant ($F = 7.56$, $p < .005$, $df = 2/62$). For females, the Betting condition produced a significantly greater amount of conformity than either the Control ($t = 2.72$, $p < .01$) or Expectancy ($t = 3.55$, $p < .001$) conditions. The between-conditions effects for females were sufficiently

Table 1 Mean Number of Conforming Trials in the Three Conditions

CONDITION	N	M	SD
Control			
Males	9	4.78	4.05
Females	13	6.31	3.64
Combined	22	5.68	3.80
Expectancy			
Males	11	6.18	3.68
Females	21	5.90	4.35
Combined	32	6.00	4.07
Betting			
Males	12	4.92	4.54
Females	31	9.77	3.59
Combined	43	8.42	4.41

powerful to yield significant differences between the Betting and Control and Expectancy groups (t's, respectively, of 2.57 and 2.51, $p < .02$) with males and females combined. Thus, the effect of introducing negative sanctions for conformity did not decrease yielding among males and produced a striking *increase* in conforming behavior among females. Public declarations of confidence in the Expectancy group did not influence the amount of conformity.

Confidence of Conformers and Independents

For the purposes of this and subsequent analyses, conformers were separately defined for each condition as subjects who yielded on more than the mean number of conforming trials. Subjects denoted as independents conformed less than the mean number of conforming trials.

The confidence of conformers and independents was examined by comparing their expectancy statements and bets on three categories of trials: those on which subjects yielded, trials on which they remained independent, and the four noncritical trials on which subjects' confidence statements and judgments preceded those of the confederates. Tables 2 and 3 present, respectively, the expectancy statement and betting patterns on these three types of trials for conformers and independents.[4]

The analysis of variance of conformers' and independents' expectancy statements is presented in Table 4. Conformers tended to express a lesser degree of confidence in their judgments than independents, and this difference was significant on trials on which subjects remained independ-

---

[4] Certain differences were found between males and females in expectancies and bets, particularly in the overall amount bet ($M > F$, $t = 2.64$, $p < .02$). However, the patterns of expectancy statements and bets for males and females were very similar, and the analyses of confidence in each group were accordingly based on the combined results of males and females.

Table 2   Mean Expectancy Statements of Conformers and Independents on the Three Categories of Trials

| | | TRIAL CATEGORY | | | | | | AVERAGE EXPECTANCY | |
| | | Conforming | | Independent | | Noncritical | | | |
GROUP	N	M	SD	M	SD	M	SD	M	SD
Conformers									
Males	6	4.20	2.21	4.50	1.41	5.17	2.42	4.60	0.86
Females	8	4.90	1.26	5.29	1.45	7.47	1.48	5.54	1.25
Combined	14	4.62	1.10	4.95	1.30	6.55	2.17	5.17	1.17
Independents									
Males	5	6.20	0.84	6.98	0.72	7.75	1.76	7.07	0.99
Females	11	3.83	2.09	6.29	1.44	7.02	1.49	6.20	1.10
Combined	16	4.57	2.29	6.49	1.29	7.23	1.55	6.46	1.12

Table 3   Mean Amount Bet by Conformers and Independents on the
Three Categories of Trials

		Conforming		Independent		Noncritical		Average Bet	
Group	N	M	SD	M	SD	M	SD	M	SD
Conformers									
Males	5	.35	.11	.30	.13	.32	.14	.33	.11
Females	17	.27	.06	.17	.09	.24	.13	.23	.07
Combined	22	.29	.08	.20	.11	.26	.13	.25	.09
Independents									
Males	5	.31	.18	.37	.10	.39	.13	.36	.12
Females	13	.27	.09	.24	.11	.36	.11	.29	.09
Combined	18	.28	.12	.28	.12	.37	.12	.31	.10

Table 4   Analysis of Variance of the Expectancy Statements of
Conformers and Independents

Source	df	MS	F
Between groups	29		
Conformers versus Independents (A)	1	330.70	3.20*
Error (b)	28	103.33	
Within groups	60		
Trial category (B)	2	1,015.48	17.26**
A × B	2	92.24	ns
Error (w)	56	58.84	

* $p < .10$.
** $p < .001$.

ent ($t = 2.69$, $p < .02$). Conformers and independents did not differ in their declarations of confidence on conforming or noncritical trials. There was a highly significant trial category effect: Least confidence was expressed by both conformers and independents on conforming trials, and independent and noncritical trials followed in an increasing order of expressed confidence.

Although failure of the interaction term to attain significance renders internal comparisons somewhat tenuous, we compared the expectancies on the three trial categories for conformers and independents separately. The confidence estimates of conformers on conforming and independent trials did not differ significantly, while independents stated significantly higher expectancies on independent trials relative to conforming trials ($t = 3.27$, $p < .01$). Conformers were more confident on the noncritical trials than on either independent ($t = 2.66$, $p < .02$) or conforming ($t = 3.30$,

$p < .01$) trials. Independents were more confident on noncritical as compared to conforming trials ($t = 4.96$, $p < .001$), but their expectancies on noncritical trials were only slightly higher than on independent trials ($t = 1.69$, $p < .10$).

The summary of the analysis of variance of betting patterns is presented in Table 5. An analysis of the initial main effect indicates that conformers tended to bet less on independent trials than did independents ($t = 1.95$, $p < .07$) and were also less confident on noncritical trials than independents ($t = 2.48$, $p < .02$). Additionally, there were significant differences between trial categories. Of major importance in this analysis is the significant interaction, indicating differences in the betting patterns of conformers and independents.

Conformers were much less confident when resisting the influence of the group than on trials on which they reported wrong judgments in alignment with the confederates ($t = 3.73$, $p < .01$). In the case of independents, divergence from the group judgment did not result in reduced confidence. On the noncritical trials, independents bet considerably more than on either their conforming or independent trials (t's respectively, of 3.55 and 3.87, $p < .001$). Conformers, on the other hand, bet less on independent than on noncritical trials ($t = 2.73$, $p < .01$), but did not differ in the amount bet on conforming and noncritical trials.

Sequential Changes in Conformity and Confidence

To clarify the underlying processes mediating the unexpected effects of the Betting condition, the amount of conformity and the measures of confidence for the first half of the experimental situation were compared with conformity and confidence in the second half. Of interest in these comparisons were possible changes in yielding and any increments or decrements in confidence on conforming trials as the task progressed. If increased yielding and greater confidence on conforming trials in the last half were found among Betting group conformers as opposed to independ-

Table 5   Analysis of Variance of the Bets of Conformers and Independents

SOURCE	df	MS	F
Between groups	39		
Conformers versus Independents (A)	1	638.43	3.76*
Error (b)	38	169.95	
Within groups	80		
Trial category (B)	2	507.17	10.95***
A × B	2	268.98	5.81**
Error (w)	76	46.30	

* $p < .07$.
** $p < .005$.
*** $p < .001$.

ents and as compared to conformers in the Expectancy group, suggestive evidence for a process of inconsistency reduction would be afforded. The rationale for this hypothesis is that conforming under conditions of increased investment in the outcome of one's judgment is incongruous when the correct choice is unambiguous. Having made a commitment to alignment with the group, it is necessary to justify this behavior. Accordingly, the Betting group conformer would be expected to continue or even to increase his influenced judgements and to show greater confidence as the situation progressed in an attempt to rationalize a tenuous and objectively unsupportable decision. It is not as likely that this process of inconsistency reduction would hold under conditions of lesser personal involvement.

For the comparison of the number of conforming trials in the first versus the last half, subjects were divided into those conforming equally on both halves or more in the last half. Contrasting conformers in the Betting group with their counterparts in the Expectancy and Control groups, 19 of 22 Betting conformers yielded at least as often or more in the last half ($\chi^2 = 11.64$, $p < .001$), while the corresponding proportion for Expectancy and Control conformers was 13 of 23 ($\chi^2 = .39$, $p = ns$). The same comparison of independents revealed no difference in yielding initially versus later.

A similar analysis was carried out for confidence statements on conforming trials, contrasting Betting group conformers with yielders in the Expectancy group in the relative magnitude of expressed confidence initially versus later. Here, the number of subjects who were initially more confident was compared to the number whose confidence was greater in the last half. Of 22 conformers in the Betting group, 16 increased their confidence as the task progressed ($\chi^2 = 4.54$, $p < .05$), while 7 of 13 Expectancy group conformers showed increments in confidence, a proportion not beyond chance expectation. Independents in the Betting group were about as likely to express greater confidence initially as later, and this was similarly the case among the independents in the Expectancy group. These trends were not in evidence on either the independent or noncritical trials.

Personality Measures

LOA. As a first step, the yielding of the 27 subjects with Patterns 1 or 3 (high confidence) was compared to the conformity of the 31 subjects with Patterns 2, 4, and 7. Contrary to prediction, the 2, 4, 7 group did not show significantly greater conformity. Upon examination, it became clear that the Pattern 2 subjects were more similar to the 1 and 3 group than to the 4s and 7s.

Repeating the analysis after the elimination of the 10 subjects with Pattern 2 resulted in a significant difference ($t = 2.25$, $p < .05$), with the Pattern 4 and 7 group conforming more (standard score $M = 55.19$) than subjects with Patterns 1 or 3 ($M = 48.11$).[5] An even clearer differentiation was obtained when subjects with Patterns 3 and 4 were contrasted. These patterns represent the greatest contrast in terms of our personality analysis of independents and conformers. Pattern 3 is indicative of the most confident, achievement oriented LOA, while Pattern 4, denoted as the achievement follower pattern by Rotter, represents the kind of goal setting behavior most analogous to social conformity. The mean for the Pattern 3 group was 44.11 ($N = 9$) as compared to a mean of 56.18 ($N = 17$) for the Pattern 4 subjects, yielding a t of 2.54 significant beyond the .02 level.

The confidence of Pattern 1 and 3 subjects was compared to that of the 4 and 7 group by pooling the mean confidence estimates expressed in standard scores of the Expectancy and Betting conditions. There was a trend for the 4 and 7 group to be less confident than the 1 and 3 group (46.83 versus 51.31), but this difference was not statistically significant.

Need for Approval Scores on the M-C *SD* scale were separately dichotomized at the mean of each condition for males and females in order to yield the high and low need for approval groups. Only in the case of females in the Control and Expectancy groups was the predicted relationship found between amount of conformity and scores on the scale. Expressed in standard scores, the mean amount of conformity by high need for approval females was 55.21 as compared to 46.35 for low need for approval subjects ($t = 2.61$, $p < .02$). No significant differences in the confidence of the high and low need for approval subjects were found in either condition.

I-E Scores on the I-E scale were dichotomized at 15 − and 16 +, a split previously found to be effective in discriminating internals and externals. Preliminary analyses indicated comparable findings for males and females, and the following comparisons were carried out without regard to sex. In the Betting group, externals conformed more than internals (*M*s, respectively, of 53.04 versus 45.83), yielding a t of 2.35 significant beyond the .05 level. A slight but not significant trend in the predicted direction was found in the combined Control-Expectancy group.

While no differences in the confidence of internals and externals were found in the Expectancy group, patterns suggestive of differential confidence were obtained in the Betting group. Here, a tendency was found for externals to be less confident overall than internals ($F = 3.58$, $p < .10$), and there were, additionally, differences in the relative amounts bet on conforming and independent trials. Internals bet approximately the same on these two categories of trials; externals bet significantly less on independent trials than they did on trials on which they yielded ($t = 2.68$, $p < .02$), a result similar to that obtained for conformers in this condition. Also, the greatest differentiation between internals and externals in amount bet occurred on independent trials.

Combinations of Personality Measures The results to be presented in this section are based on the SLT analysis of conflict and maladjustment and are predicated on the general proposition underlying this study that social conformity represents an attempt to cope with conflicting

---

[5] Pattern 2 is a more commonly found pattern than either 4 or 7 and signifies a minimum of cautious, protective goal setting behavior.

demands by avoidant means. In SLT, conflict occurs and maladjusted behavior is probable when a goal is positively valued but the individual has a low expectancy of goal attainment. The M-C *SD* scale may be considered as an index of the relative value of, or preference for, approval and affectional reinforcements, and LOA may be regarded as a measure of expectancy. In terms of the foregoing analysis, high need for approval subjects with LOA Patterns 4 and 7 should constitute the conflict group and should display a much greater amount of conformity than low need for approval subjects with LOA Patterns 1 or 3. The mean amount of conformity in standard scores of the high need for approval-Pattern 4 and 7 group was 57.44 ($N = 9$), in contrast to a mean of 43.69 ($N = 13$) for the low need for approval-Pattern 1 and 3 group. The resulting t was 3.71 significant beyond the .01 level.

A similar procedure, predicated on the same rationale, was followed by combining the need for approval and I-E scales. High need for approval externals ($N = 19$), were compared with low need for approval internals ($N = 16$) in the amount of conformity. The resulting means were, respectively, 54.32 and 46.00, yielding a t of 2.57 significant beyond the .02 level.

DISCUSSION

Situational Effects on Conformity
In accounting for differential effects of the Betting condition on conformity, the common sense prediction would hold that rewarding independence, and concomitantly punishing conformity, would tend to reduce yielding to a minimum. Whatever the determinants of conformity in situations involving less personal commitment, directly rewarding reliance on the individual's own ability should tend to obviate the effects of social influence. Contrary to such a view, the Betting condition produced significantly more conformity for females and not appreciably less yielding for males.

To explain the effects of the Betting condition, it might be argued that the introduction of betting serves to increase the credibility of the group. That is, it is inconceivable to the naïve subject that the other group members would bet to lose money.

It would appear that a primary effect of greater credibility in this context is to render the individual less certain of his own abilities and the validity of his own judgments. As a consequence of decreased certainty, the conformer in the Betting group apparently finds himself yielding more and having a greater need to justify this behavior to himself and others. It was demonstrated that Betting group conformers yielded as much or more in the later stages of the task and displayed increasing confidence on their yielding trials as compared to independents and Expectancy group conformers. These findings suggest the operation of a process of inconsistency reduction.[6] This interpretation is necessarily

---

[6] There are apparent similarities between our analysis of inconsistency reduction and Festinger's (1957) theory of cognitive dissonance. However, our procedure cannot be considered as a formal test of the propositions of dissonance theory.

tentative, but it suggests, for Betting group conformers, a process of defensive rationalization by which the individual masks his inability to resist the erroneous influence of the group. In support of this interpretation, the explanations offered by these subjects in the post-experimental interviews revealed a striking lack of correspondence with their actual behavior. To be noted is the fact that the tendency to increase conformity and confidence as the task progressed operated alike for males and females.

Conformity and Confidence

In both the Expectancy and Betting conditions, conformers tended to be less confident than independents. The differences between conformers and independents were more pronounced in the Betting group, a finding consonant with the effects of this condition as reviewed above. The low expectancies of personal adequacy revealed by conformers in this situation were especially evident on those trials on which they resisted the influence of the group. These findings are generally supportive of an expectancy theory which predicates conformity on lack of self-confidence or low expectancies of success in situations of social evaluation and in which conformity is regarded as failure-avoidant, self-protective behavior.

Personality Measures

The results with each of the three personality measures indicate the degree to which self-evaluating behaviors are complicated by differences in sex and by situational influences. Nevertheless, our findings support the view that confidence in one's abilities is to a degree generalized and trans-situational. The disposition to subordinate one's abilities to the group is clearly related to failure-avoidant LOA patterns on a motor skills task. Further, those who conform under conditions of high personal involvement tend to believe that they have less personal control over their lives and regard the occurrence of reinforcements as outcomes of luck, fate, or powerful others.

Conformity and Conflict

The applicability of the SLT analysis of conflict to the problem of conformity is suggested by the marked differences in yielding which were obtained when the measure of the need for approval was, respectively, paired with the two expectancy measures, the LOA Board and the I-E scale. These results imply that the conformer can be conceptualized as an individual who has a high need for approval and affection from others, but relatively low expectancies that these much desired reinforcements can be obtained as a result of his own abilities and efforts. His low evaluation of himself and his fear of social rejection result in a strong disposition to conform. Although there is no direct evidence bearing on the point, it is by no means clear that these subjects can explain the nature of the conflict to themselves and account for their own behavior. Indeed, approval motivated individuals tend to represent themselves in a highly positive and stereotypically acceptable manner on personality inventories (Crowne & Marlowe, 1960). It is suggested, thus, that they engage in defensive personal enhancement. Indirectly supporting this line of reasoning are the findings of Barron (1953a) and Tuddenham (1959) that conformers tend to describe themselves in favorable terms on self-report devices. It must be said, however, that these results are more heuristic than definitive and will require cross-validation.

The same cautious attitude must be extended to additional findings as well. The effects of the Betting condition are not well delineated for males as a result of the small sample. A second case is afforded by the two personality inventories, which imperfectly conformed to prediction. Third, there is the issue of the generality or situational relevance of self-confidence and self-evaluative behavior.

Beyond these specific reservations, the general convergence of a set of methodologically independent indices of self-evaluation and expectancies of success on conforming behavior suggests the utility of the theoretical formulations underlying this study. The present findings imply a rather complex interaction of enduring dispositions to yield and influences specific to the situation in the determination of conforming behavior. It would appear that as personal involvement in the conformity situation increases, defensive processes are set in motion by which to maintain self-esteem and to protect the individual from expected failure.

5-8 | Social Learning Theory and the Theory of Mass Society[1]

MELVIN SEEMAN

Social psychology has been, and remains, a sharply divided discipline. Despite some recent congruences in small group research, the social psychology that is typically practiced among psychologists is quite different from the sociological brand: different in viewpoint, in problems addressed, and in research technique. It may be that no better representation of this difference can be found than in the psychologist's concentra-

[1] Paper read at the annual meeting of the American Sociological Association, Los Angeles, September 1963.

Published for the first time in this volume; we are grateful to the author for permitting its use.

tion upon learning theory and the sociological concern with the mass society. The former symbolizes the microscopic interests and style that predominate in the psychological journals, while the latter embodies the classical sociological effort to describe the course and impact of macroscopic trends in society.

The influence of that effort on sociology is best seen in the legacy of our great dichotomies and in the great names associated with them: Durkheim's mechanic-organic; Tonnies' gemeinschaft-gesellschaft; Weber's traditional-rational (Coser & Rosenberg, 1964). With due regard for what it simplifies, the designation "mass society theory" can be conveniently applied to this tradition in sociological thought. My thesis is that this mass society tradition is not so far removed from learning theory as it might seem, and that the effort to exploit what these viewpoints share is useful to both sides: it extends the perspective of the microscopic work, and provides greater system and controlled demonstration for the macroscopic side. The elaboration of my thesis calls for some comment first on the essentials of the two theories involved (without seeking to do either of them full justice), and then for a review of recent work that exemplifies the union of these seemingly divergent interests.

With regard to mass society theory, the critics (e.g., Bell, 1960; Gusfield, 1962) have been active of late, and one may well wonder whether any of it is salvageable. It has been charged with serious faults: with romanticizing the pre-industrial order, underestimating the emancipating features of the new order, falsifying the extent of contemporary social isolation, and disguising an *ideology* about society as a description of it. For myself, I confess that I have often found it difficult to establish the exact sense in which one might properly speak of the mass society perspective as a theory.

Despite all this, I think that the mass society viewpoint contains the ingredients of a useful theory. In a capsule, it becomes a theory by combining (a) a historically oriented account of contemporary social structure, (b) assertions about the psychological effects of that structure, and (c) predictions about the resulting individual behavior. Bramson (1961) captures the point nicely, in his work on the political context of sociology, when he speaks of "the persistent parable of alienation that is the theory of mass society" [p. 72], for in this theory, personal alienation is the crucial intervening variable: it is produced by the social structure, and in turn produces distinctive behavior.

Each of these three elements in mass society theory has been elaborately (and often enough, carelessly) described. The *social structural* features I have in mind that constitute the independent variables are the standard ones: for example, the decline of kinship as a criterion of place; the increase in social differentiation; and the rise of secularized, rational forms (bureaucracy, mechanization, etc.). The *alienation* that the theory predicates takes several forms, and I have elsewhere (Seeman, 1959) suggested that there are at least five distinguishable varieties of alienation that are regularly invoked (including, for example, powerlessness, normlessness, self-estrangement). The gamut of *behaviors* that constitute the dependent variables include, for example, conformity, political passivity, and volatile mass action.

Though one may wonder about the predominantly negative character of this portrait of contemporary life, three points can be made. First, one does not have to idealize the old days to make the theory, as depicted here, workable and interesting. Things may have been better or worse in those days, but the postulated connection between the structural facts and the alienative states can be made reasonably clear and testable. Second, mass society theory presents two main questions to be tested: whether the structural conditions have the alienative effects, and whether alienation has the specified behavioral consequences. Third, and most important for present purposes, given the emphasis upon alienation as an intervening variable, it is clear that some version of psychological theory is necessarily implicated in the propositions of mass society theory.

The version that I find most useful is Rotter's (1954) social learning theory—a theory which developed primarily out of an interest in clinical psychology, but which has been most extensively used thus far in experimental studies of learning. This theory uses both expectancy and reinforcement constructs. The simplest formulation of its main tenet is that behavior is a function of (a) the expectancy or probability held by the individual that a particular behavior will, in a given situation, have a successful outcome, and (b) the value of that outcome (i.e., the preference value—or RV, for reinforcement value—that the individual assigns to the reward or goal in question). Thus, the basic "formula" becomes: $BP = f(E \, \& RV)$; behavior potential is a function of expectancy and reinforcement value. From this groundwork, Rotter develops the ideas required for handling more complex behavior—for example, notions about the development and change of personal goals; the generalization of expectancies from particular experiences to classes of experience; the role of language, and the meaning of social attitudes.

It is neither possible nor necessary to present Rotter's theory in detail. The question for us here is: What is it like and what does it help us to do? Even the bare outlines I have given may serve to suggest some important features of social learning theory for sociological purposes. First, it is *not* a theory which rests upon physiological properties (like drive reduction in Hullian theory); hence, for the sociologist, it is a learning theory which neither diverts attention to physiological questions nor makes unnecessary assumptions about them. Second, it does not, like so much of personality theory, employ a relatively fixed and trait-like conception of the individual's functioning: the situation is an element of prime importance, and the need to conceptualize it is recognized in Rotter's scheme. This is a point, of course, on which sociologists have been adamant, both before and after Mead and Cooley. Third, the inclusion of the expectancy variable makes use of the elementary distinction between the *value* of a goal as against the *subjective probability* of attaining it. The theory thus becomes, in my judgment, both more flexible, and more applicable to common sociological interests, than the strict reinforcement theories. Specifically, for example, this means that it is easy to go from this psychological theory to propositions involving such expectancy-based sociological concepts as social roles and normative standards. Furthermore, the theory works constantly for clarity about the very great difference between behavior, values, and expectations—a clarity that has not been especially noteworthy in the literature on the mass society (nor, I might add, in the vast literature on attitudes and attitude-testing). Fourth, and finally, the theory is essentially process-centered: unlike Freudian theory, for example, it says very little about the content of human goals or needs, the priority among them, their fixity, or the like. Some may take this as a serious deficiency, but I should point out that this process emphasis helps to make the theory reasonably congruent with (and certainly not antithetical to) the favorite sociological brand of social psychology, namely, interactionism (Manis & Meltzer, 1967). There is no self-concept as such in Rotter's theory, but there is room within it to accommodate the subtleties of situational definition, self-identification, motive attribution, and interpersonal negotiation, which are the stock in trade of the interactionist.

I have said that these features (among others) make Rotter's theory easily applicable to sociological concerns. It is instructive to examine some well-known sociological work from the standpoint of social learning theory—for example, Merton's (1957) analysis of anomie and social structure, or Sutherland's (Sutherland & Cressey, 1960) theory of differential association. Despite the general tendency to think of these formulations by Sutherland and Merton as specifically sociological approaches (and, indeed, sometimes as alternatives to psychological views), it quickly becomes clear that social learning theory is quite congruent with both of them.

Sutherland's theory is, in fact, a rather direct social learning theory. Sutherland proposes, in effect, that the individual's differential association teaches him either or both (a) the value of criminal activity—for itself, or for what it gets him as a derivative (esteem from others, a sense of group belonging, etc.); and (b) expectancies concerning the likelihood of success in achieving these goals (e.g., the chances of being apprehended, or the specific procedures that "guarantee" success). Sutherland's propositions about criminal behavior can be seen as an instance of Rotter's general scheme applied to the learning of criminality.

In similar fashion, despite the sociological language employed (cultural structure, social structure, anomie, structural strain), Merton's classic paper is easily conceivable in social learning terms. Merton seeks to answer the following question: What alternative resolutions are open when (as some socio-cultural systems encourage) an individual has learned to place high value on a given goal though his expectancies for attaining that goal by approved means are very low? Merton answers the question by developing his famous types of behavioral adjustment: innovation, rebellion, etc. It takes nothing away from Merton's insight, and makes it no less sociologically interesting, to note two things. First, Merton's scheme is thoroughly consistent with Rotter's theory in that it is an analysis of one kind of situation involving high goal values and low expectancies for attainment. Second, Merton's sociological conception of strain—found in the inconsistency between the normative demands and the socially structured opportunities for achievement—is paralleled in Rotter's theory by the psychological conception of strain—the inconsistency between highly valued goals and low subjective probabilities of achievement.

By now, some of you will be thinking that this is all well and good, but that there is actually little to be gained by showing that a variety of sociological problems can be recast in the language of social learning theory. In one sense that is true, though I would personally not underestimate even that simple effort. There is a good deal of sociological imperialism that, figuratively speaking, takes Durkheim's antipsychological attitude too literally and leads to an unwillingness to examine the possibilities. Still, I would agree that merely recasting the sociological classics in the language of expectancy and reward value is no great achievement (as we have had occasion to note in the case of parallel recastings using Hullian learning theory). The real test of the utility of this theory, and of the way of thinking involved in it, comes not through post-facto interpretation but through a demonstration of what it can help the sociologist to do with the problems that commonly engage him. I would like to proceed by describing what I think are some modest achievements of this kind that are grounded in social learning theory.

This brings me back to the title of this paper: to mass society theory and to the problem of alienation embedded in it. I have already noted that alienation is the key intervening variable in the theory of mass society; and if one is to test the theory, it is important that we should be very clear about this variable that, so to speak, translates the structural conditions of mass society into social behavior. In a recent paper on the meaning of alienation, I sought to encourage such precision by isolating five common usages of alienation in the classical literature, and, more important for present purposes, by providing a viable research formulation of these five alternative brands of alienation. The significant point is that this sharpening of the alienation construct was guided by explicit attention to the main elements of social learning theory. The five variants of alienation (powerlessness, normlessness, meaninglessness, isolation, and self-estrangement) were defined either in terms of individual expectancies or in terms of reward values. Thus, to give one example, the idea of powerlessness—certainly one of the more common meanings of alienation—refers to the expectancy of probability held by the individual that he cannot control the occurrence of given outcomes or events. As several critics (e.g., Scott, 1963) have noted, and as I would agree, such conceptual clarification is not yet a theory of alienation: it does not in itself tell us what relation holds (or may hold) among the several kinds of alienation, nor provide the substantive propositions that need testing. But the formulation does help to encourage reasonably clear and strict tests of propositions involved in mass society theory, and at the same time it encourages us to see how these propositions are related to learning theory proper. Let me document and illustrate this by reference to research, bearing on the idea of powerlessness, that has been explicitly designed to demonstrate the point.

In the theory, which served as the basis for clarifying the meanings of alienation, we find an important corollary to powerlessness. This variable has been called "internal vs. external control of reinforcements"; and in Rotter's theory this distinction refers to a more or less generalized expectancy. It points to differences (among persons or situations) in the degree to which success or failure is attributed to external factors—to chance, luck, powerful others, etc.—as against rewards which are seen to be the outcome of one's personal skills or characteristics. The laboratory work employing this concept of internal vs. external control has two important features for sociologists: first, it challenges some of the basic features of contemporary studies in learning and does so in a way that is parallel to sociological criticisms of learning theory; and second, these laboratory studies of learning involve hypotheses that are not far removed from the mass society problem.

On the first of these counts, Rotter and his co-workers have argued that the paradigm employed in the usual study of animal and human learning has unwittingly been one which stresses *external* control: the tasks are simple; symbolic behavior is minimized; and the reinforcements are primarily contingent upon the control of the experimenter. Social learning theory would predict, however, that learning patterns would be quite different in situations where the individual holds the expectancy that his own behavior or skill is determinative. In a series of laboratory studies comparing learning in "skill" vs. "chance" situations, the predicted differences have been regularly demonstrated (cf. Rotter, 1966).

These differences are important for learning theory proper, since they show *directly* how limited these generalizations are which do not take account of the human capacity to make complex assessments of oneself and of the situation. But these studies also bear directly on the sociologist's substantive interests. Among the hypotheses tested, for example, is one which says in effect that an expectancy of low personal control goes with poor learning. For all its derivation from, and applicability to, learning theory *per se*, this proposition is similar to that which has engaged mass society theorists. In the famous Cincinnati experiment on the United Nations (Star & Hughes, 1950), the widespread turning away from political knowledge was attributed to "the apathetic conviction that there is nothing an ordinary individual can do"; and for Kornhauser (1959), the politics of mass society is best understood in terms of a structural defect —the unavailability of voluntary organizations—which amounts to a structured source of low expectancies for control. In Kornhauser's scheme, these low expectancies for control have the standard consequences: people are uninformed about national and international affairs, and they become readily available for highly irrational and extremist solutions.

Thus, at one central point, the theory of mass society involves constructs and propositions very similar to those employed in the learning studies on internal vs. external control. Mass theory proposes that given social structural conditions encourage the development of a sense of powerlessness; and that in turn such low expectancies for control lead to poor learning—to ignorance and disengagement. In my own studies, I have tried to devise relatively controlled tests of this important proposition in the theory of mass society—the proposition that alienation (i.e., powerlessness) leads to poor learning and low knowledge. I must insist, however, that in light of the foregoing, such tests are not only relevant to mass society theory, but are also relevant to the learning theory problems I have just described. These studies can be conceived as extensions of the laboratory investigations of internal and external control, for they explore the degree to which the laboratory findings hold in institutional settings and for workaday rather than simulated tasks.

The first of these studies (Seeman & Evans, 1962) compared highly alienated with less alienated tuberculosis patients, and found, as predicted, that the alienated patients scored relatively poorly on a test of objective knowledge about tuberculosis. Since the high and low alienation groups were matched on many socio-economic variables and on hospital history, the difference in knowledge seems most reasonably attributable to the difference in their expectancies for control: where there is a low expectancy for control, there is the predicted poor learning. And here the demonstration was made using subjects who are dealing with a critical circumstance in their life careers—namely, a prolonged hospitalization which in many ways is a replica in miniature of the mass society: there is low control over one's fate; heavy reliance upon specialized experts; bureaucratic authority; the loss of community ties.

But interesting as this may be, both as an extension of the learning studies and as a demonstration bearing on the credibility of the alienation theme in mass society theory, there are serious questions raised by the hospital study. Most important is the fact that the causal imputation (alienation *leads to* poor learning) is tenuous. The study may equally well be said to demonstrate the reverse: that a sense of powerlessness flows from inadequate knowledge. This difficulty is not academic when one is seeking to develop a systematic set of *learning* studies, and at the same time to test a theory which proposes that one of the critical *consequences* of alienation is withdrawal and ignorance.

A second defect of the hospital study is that it makes no distinction among kinds of knowledge, hence one is left wondering how generalized the tie between powerlessness and learning may be—wondering, for example, whether the poor health knowledge shown by the alienated patients might be paralleled in almost any domain of their knowledge one might tap, suggesting perhaps that the alienated are characterized by a highly generalized withdrawal of interest, or by fundamental differences in capacity or in willingness to learn.

With these problems in mind, a second study was designed (Seeman, 1963a), examining the relation between alienation and learning in a reformatory. The key feature of this study was that it involved the presentation of three kinds of *new knowledge*, and a subsequent testing of the inmates' learning of this material. The three kinds of information items differed essentially in their potential usefulness for controlling one's destiny. The first set of items implied no time perspective and no planning;

they were merely descriptive statements about the reformatory (example: It costs about $5 per day to keep an inmate at Chillicothe.). The second, and most critical, set of information items involved knowledge about parole—i.e., knowledge which predicated a world of manageable and plannable events (example: In 60% of the cases where parole is delayed beyond the date set by the parole board, difficulty in arranging employment is the reason for the delay.). The third set of information items concerned the long-range future—dealing with employment trends and projected programs that might be of interest to ex-convicts (example: A sizeable increase in federal funds for vocational training of young adults who have a prison record is predicted by 1965.).

These items were presented to the inmates (unlabeled as to type, and interspersed, of course), and the inmates were then tested on their retention of the information involved. The essential prediction was that the alienated and unalienated prisoners (meaning those high and low in their generalized expectancies for control) would *not* differ in the learning of the descriptive reformatory items, but that they *would* differ in their learning of the parole material. This prediction says, in effect, that differences in learning between the alienated and unalienated are not a matter of general ability, IQ, character type, test-taking skills, ability to learn, or the like: the learning difference reflects a relatively specific *powerlessness* phenomenon; and those who differ in their expectancies for control will show it in their learning of material which implies the possibility of planning and controlling one's destiny.

I will not try to detail the findings of this study here, but two main results are of interest here. First, the data fall generally as predicted. The alienated and unalienated inmates did not differ in their learning of the descriptive reformatory information; and of the three main correlations involved (level of alienation correlated with learning score for each of the three kinds of information), only the correlation between alienation and learning of the parole material was significant. But though significant, the r was not high: $-.23$ (high alienation goes with low parole learning).

Despite any gratification one might feel concerning the relative tightness of the design in showing the causal direction (through the presentation of new information to be learned) and in showing the specificity of that learning, one is left wondering why the correlation is not higher. I can return, with that wonderment, to my theme concerning social learning theory, for in that theory we may find a guide to further analysis that may clarify matters. We have been dealing thus far with the association between alienation and learning, and alienation is here conceived as an expectancy construct—the individual's expectancies for control. But Rotter's theory makes behavior (including learning behavior) contingent not only upon expectancies but upon values as well, and it suggests what needs to be done.

We need to recognize that the parole items not only imply that a high *expectancy* for control is valid (i.e., that one can plan careers) but also that the conventional *values* favoring parole are valid (that parole is a worthwhile objective). Parole, after all, is part of the prison's rehabilitation apparatus, and in the well-known argot of the prison, it may be something for the "Square Johns," not the "Real Cons." The latter are dedicated to the values of the criminal culture, while the Square Johns are oriented to the conventional norms of the authorities and the rehabilitation apparatus.

This line of thinking suggests that if we could take into account not only the inmates' expectancies for control but also the value they place on the events to which the learning is relevant, a sharper prediction might be made. Specifically, one might expect that for those who reject the conventional values (the Real Cons), differences in alienation would *not* be associated with differential learning of the parole material, for that material deals with the alien world of rehabilitation objectives. It is among the more conventional Square Johns that one might expect to find the clearest associations between alienation and learning. These predictions, derived through the social learning viewpoint, are nicely substantiated in the data. When the inmates are divided into "conventionals" and "unconventionals" (a division that was based upon information taken from the prison records), the correlation between alienation and parole learning was an insignificant $-.16$ for the unconventional Real Cons, but among the conventional inmates the obtained r was $-.40$. I trust that the research detail has not by now obscured my main point, which is that social learning theory here serves as a systematic guide to data analysis, and the result of that analysis is a sharper portrait of the conditions under which, and the groups for whom, the connection between alienation and poor learning holds.

I have dealt thus far, however, with only one portion of mass society theory—with that part of it which postulates that alienation has specifiable behavioral outcomes. As I have noted earlier, the theory also describes the structural sources of alienation: it tells where alienation *comes from* as well as what it *leads to.* On that part of the problem, too, the perspective of social learning theory has proved helpful.

Mass society theory makes much of the organizational ties that must mediate between the potentially isolated, powerless individual and the massive state. This theme has been persistent and prominent in the mass society literature: one can choose one's statement of it from Durkheim (1958) or from a number of recent works in the same tradition (for example, from Nisbet, 1953; Rose, 1954; or Kornhauser, 1954). If we restrict our attention for the moment to work-related organizations, the theory predicts that the individuals who are members of some type of work-based organization will exhibit less of a sense of powerlessness than those without an organization to speak for them on occupational matters.

This is, to be sure, a simple statement of the problem; and obviously things are rarely so simple. But what are the complications that ought to be entertained if one is to avoid merely testing the organized and the unorganized for their degree of powerlessness? One complication can be handled by taking into account the expectancy and reward value formulation in social learning theory. It so happens that at the same time one takes into account a favorite proposition among sociologists, the proposition that "much in American attitudes and behavior can be explained by the cultural emphasis on achievement, on getting ahead." The quote is from a recent paper by Lipset (1961), in which he seeks to show that American labor organizations differ from their West European counterparts largely because the American worker is less collectively oriented and more oriented to individual success. All this is relevant here because it suggests that if one is going to examine the mass society thesis concerning the effect of organization upon the individual's *expectancies* for control, it might be quite important to include a measure of the *value* placed upon individual success: that value (for Lipset and for others) is potentially a key one in determining the individual's response to work organizations (for example, his willingness to join, and the effect of membership or non-membership).

Preliminary analysis of data embodying this view suggests that this simultaneous eye to expectancies and values—the expectancy for control and the value of mobility—is very useful in testing the mediation hypothesis in mass society theory. Neal and Seeman (1964) found the predicted high powerlessness among the unorganized; but for both manual and white collar workers, it was among the *mobility-minded* (i.e., among those who place high value on occupational success) that the mass society prediction was most clearly borne out (cf. also Seeman, 1966). I will not try at this late juncture to present the details or to interpret them. The point of the illustration is that in this case the social learning viewpoint aids in sharpening research that bears on the *sources* of alienation rather than its *consequences.*

I have tried, with all these illustrations, to make only one central point. It is that a systematic psychological theory like social learning theory helps in many ways if one is concerned with the classical problems that have engaged sociological theorists (not only, but including, the theorists of the mass society). I have suggested a number of quite specific ways in which it helps. It helps in the statement and resolution of conceptual difficulties (as in my example regarding the meaning of alienation). It helps to guide data analysis in systematic ways (as in the example concerning conventional and unconventional inmates). It aids in the design of research by suggesing ways of managing the potentially endless, and sometimes aimless, complicating variables (as in the example dealing with the importance of mobility values in testing the mediation hypothesis in mass society theory). It helps one to discern the parallel features in propositions which emanate from seemingly unrelated, if not unreconcilable, interests (in the present illustration, the interests of learning theorists and mass society theorists—who are, it turns out, building quite related demonstrations about knowledge processes). And it can help as a counter balance to some of the unfortunate features of sociologism, by encouraging omnipresent attention to the conceptual similarities and formal parallels in sociology and psychology (as in the illustrations regarding Merton and Sutherland). Perhaps more simply, yet more grandiosely put, what is at stake here is some promise of integrating our disparate social psychologies—symbolically speaking, the social psychology of the laboratory and of institutional studies, of learning theory and the mass society.

5-9 Children's Feelings of Personal Control as Related to Social Class and Ethnic Group[1]

ESTHER S. BATTLE and JULIAN B. ROTTER

Social class and ethnic group membership are generally accepted as important determinants of personality. This study is devoted to an exploration of the interaction of class and ethnic group with one personality variable: "internal versus external" control of reinforcements.

This construct distributes individuals according to the degree to which they accept personal responsibility for what happens to them, in contrast to the attribution of responsibility to forces outside their control. The external forces might be those of chance, fate, an inability to understand the world, or the influence of other, powerful people. In social learning theory (Rotter, 1954), this construct is considered to describe a generalized expectancy, operating across a large number of situations, which relates to whether or not the individual possesses or lacks power (or personal determination) over what happens to him.

The sense of "powerlessness" has been discussed by Seeman (1959) as one meaning of the sociological variable of "alienation." It is thought to relate to the individual's social circumstances (class and ethnic group status) as well as affecting his social learning. An individual who is thus alienated would hold the expectation that his own behavior cannot determine the outcome he desires. There is some empirical evidence to support this interpretation. Seeman and Evans (1962) used a form of the forced-choice, adult scale of internal-external control (I-E Scale) developed by Liverant, Rotter, Crowne, and Seeman (Gore and Rotter, 1963), to study the behavior of patients in a tuberculosis hospital. Although the I-E scale makes no reference to disease, they found statistical support for their hypotheses that patients scoring as "internals" would know more about their own condition, would be better informed about T. B. in general, and would be regarded by ward personnel as "better" patients.

In another study, Seeman (1963a) studied the effect of such alienation on the learning of prison inmates. He found that the alienated inmate (externally controlled) learned significantly less material relevant to release than those less alienated. It was in the realm of long-range planning and control that the variable was predictive.

The related attitude of "mastery" was discussed by Strodtbeck (1958) as it is affected by religious, national, and social-class orientations perpetuated within the family. He found that Jewish middle- and upper-class

[1] This research was supported in part by the United States Air Force under contract No. AF 49(638)-741, monitored by the Air Force Office of Scientific Research, Office of Aerospace Research.

Ss were differentiated from lower-class Italians on the basis of this variable. Most of the variance was attributable to factors of social class. Graves and Jessor adapted the I-E Scale for high school students (Graves, 1961) and studied ethnic differences in an isolated tri-ethnic community. They found whites to be most internal, followed by Spanish Americans. Indians were most external in attitudes. These findings were consistent with their predictions. Although economic factors undoubtedly contributed to differences, Graves felt that "ethnicity" was an important source of variance after other factors were controlled.

The effect of this personality characteristic has been studied by Phares (1957) and James (1957), who were instrumental in the development of the first I-E scales. The latest form of the adult scale has recently been related to the prediction of the type and degree of commitment behavior manifested by Southern Negro students to effect social change in the cause of desegregation (Gore & Rotter, 1963). Crowne and Liverant (1963) showed a relationship between conformity under conditions of high personal involvement and scores on this same scale.

Other approaches to the assessment of this attitude with children have been developed by Crandall, Katkovsky, and Preston (1962), relative to achievement situations, and by Bialer (1961). Bialer's *Locus of Control* questionnaire was developed from the James-Phares (James, 1957) adult scale of internal-external control. Bialer was interested in the developmental aspects of this attitude as well as its relation to the conceptualization of success and failure. He found the more mature child to be more internally controlled and to show greater response to success and failure cues. The Bialer questionnaire was used in the present study.

James (1957) studied the effect of this variable on behavior in angle and line-matching tasks. He demonstrated that externals had more "unusual shifts" in their expectancy for success. That is, they were more likely to expect future success when they had just failed and more likely to expect failure after succeeding. He also found the internals to have a greater increment in expectation for success in a 75 per cent reinforced sequence, substantiating the hypothesis that when one believes he is in control of what happens, positive reinforcement leads to an increasing certainty for future success.

Phares (1957, 1962), James and Rotter (1958), James (1957), Rotter, Liverant, and Crowne (1961), Holden and Rotter (1962), and others have shown that the growth and extinction of expectancies for reward vary predictively under different experimental conditions if the tasks are perceived by S as chance, luck, or E-controlled, rather than as a matter of personal skill.

The present study involves the development of a projective test of the internal-external control attitude to be used with children; the establishment of the relationship between I-E and several sociological and demographic variables (age, sex, class, ethnic group, and IQ); and the replication of some previous findings with adult I-E scales in a performance task.

The behavioral task was an adaptation of James's line-matching task

(James, 1957), which allows E to control success and failure without S's knowledge. The child is required to match a series of lines which vary in length. Before each trial, he states his expectancy for success on an eleven-point scale. Following a ten-trial training sequence (with a 50 per cent reinforcement schedule), his responses to continuous failure are examined over the 30 extinction trials. This task yields three measures which reflect the effect of the experimental variables: (a) Ss mean expectancy for success over the ten training trials; (d) the number of "unusual shifts" in expectancy during training (raised expectation for success after failing or lowered expectancy after succeeding); and (c) the number of trials to extinction (two successive trials at zero or one expectancy on a scale of zero to ten.)

The projective task was a "Children's Picture Test of Internal-External Control" originated by Battle. On the six-item cartoon test, the child states "what he would say" in various "lifelike" situations which involve the attribution of responsibility. The reliability of the scoring procedure was established with an independently scored sample of 40 protocols.[2] The result was a Pearsonian $r = .93$ ($p < .001$).

In the development of the test, 29 cartoon items were eliminated because of strong "picture pull" toward one or the other end of the scale. Six items were selected from a remaining eleven on the basis of correlation with the total scores with that item removed. Thirty-eight school children were used as pretest Ss for this analysis. Table 1 gives the six final items (their correlations with total score given in parenthesis). The items are scored along a seven-point scale with three degrees of "internality," three of "externality," and a nondiscriminatory midpoint. The *higher* the score, the more external the orientation.

METHOD

Ss in this study were 80 sixth- and eighth-grade children selected on the basis of sex, social class, and ethnic group membership (Negro-white) from five metropolitan schools.[3] The California Mental Maturity total score was used as a crude measure of "intelligence."

Each child was given the three tasks individually in the same order: (a) line matching, (b) cartoons, and (c) Bialer scale.

The Bialer *Locus of Control* questionnaire was administered to the last 40 Ss primarily to determine its relationship to the projective test being studied. This is a 23-item "yes" or "no" questionnaire in which S attributes the locus of control to himself or others. A *low* score on

[2] Mr. Forest Ward's help in the development of the scoring manual and in rating responses is gratefully acknowledged.

[3] Half of the Ss came from two lower-class, ethnically integrated schools in Columbus, Ohio. The other 40 Ss were obtained from three Dayton, Ohio, schools. Of the latter Ss, most of the middle-class Negro children came from the same elementary school. Most middle-class white students came from a second school. Only seven Ss came from the last school which is situated in a lower-class, ethnically integrated, rooming-house district.

Table 1   Items from the Children's Picture Test of Internal-External Control

---

1. How come you didn't get what you wanted for Christmas? (.32)
2. Why is she always hurting herself? (.49)
3. When you grow up do you think you could be anything you wanted? (.25)
4. Whenever you're involved something goes wrong! (.22)
5. That's the third game we've lost this year. (.39)
6. Why does her mother always "holler" at her? (.32)

---

this scale indicates an external orientation. Since only 40 of the 80 Ss received the Bialer, some analyses made with the picture test were not repeated with the Bialer scale because of insufficient N.

Any child expressing doubt was reassured that there were no punishments or rewards associated with his performance. If the child asked the purpose of the line-matching technique, he was told it was a test to "see how well he could match the length of lines." No child persisted in his questions after this explanation. Each child was thanked and requested not to tell the other children about the tests before a specific day, at which time the testing would be completed. An attempt was made to test all the children in one class and school as rapidly as possible to prevent gossip from contaminating the results.

Demographic characteristics were obtained in the following manner: age, sex, and ethnic group were reported on the cumulative record for each child. IQ also was obtained from the cumulative record and was based, in most cases, on the full score of the California Mental Maturity Test most recently attained. Socioeconomic status was determined on the basis of the father or mother's occupation as given on the cumulative record. These occupations were categorized according to Lloyd Warner's classification (Warner, Meeker, & Eels, 1949). For purposes of analysis, classes one, two, three, and four were grouped together and called "middle class" in contrast to the "lower class" of five, six, and seven.

RESULTS

The means and sigmas of the Children's I-E scale scores for each combination of class and ethnic group are given in Table 2.

With an analysis of variance for unequal Ns (Walker & Lev, 1953), a significant F ratio was found between social classes ($F = 5.13$; $df = 1$ and 72; $p < .05$); for the interaction of ethnic group and social class ($F = 72.50$; $df = 1$ and 72; $p < .01$); and for the triple interaction of ethnic group, social class, and IQ ($F = 8.12$; $df = 1$ and 72; $p < .01$). The following two-tailed t tests isolate the source of variance for the interaction effects.

A contrast of the middle-class white with the lower-class Negro gives a t of 2.75, $p < .01$. The only other significant comparison was between the lower-class Negro and the middle-class Negro groups ($t = 2.10$, $p < .05$).

Table 2 Means and Sigmas of Children's I-E Scores by
Social Class and Ethnic Group

	MIDDLE CLASS			LOWER CLASS		
	Mean	Sigma	N	Mean	Sigma	N
White	15.0	4.4	20	16.4	3.5	21
Negro	15.8	3.5	16	18.3	3.4	23

It can be seen that the most significant comparison is between the middle-class white as most "internal" and the lower-class Negro as most "external." In addition, it is apparent that it is the lower-class Negro group which differs from all the others.

The means and sigmas of the children's I-E scale scores for each combination of social class, ethnic group, and IQ are given in Table 3.

The significant comparison is between the lower-class Negro with a high IQ (mean I-E score = 19.1) and the middle-class white with a low IQ (mean I-E = 13.8). For the combined N of 11 Ss the $t = 2.21$, $p < .06$. One interpretation is that it is the externally scoring lower-class Negro whose higher IQ scores reflect a greater need value for academic achievement. When such a person encounters deprivation, due to his class and ethnic group membership, he defends himself with an "external" attitude. The middle-class white with a low IQ may have incorporated his class values of personal responsibility and when faced with the fact of his low ability, he responds characteristically by blaming himself for the failure.

Of the three line-matching measures, only the mean expectancy for success during the ten training trials was found to relate significantly to the children's I-E test ($r = -.31$, $p < .01$). That is, "internals" were "more certain of success" than "externals."

The Bialer questionnaire (1961) was found to relate significantly to the Children's Picture Test ($r = -.42$, $p < .01$). A high score on the Bialer is similar to a low score on the children's I-E scale. Bialer scores were also found to relate to the "number of unusual shifts" in expectancy during the training trials ($r = -.47$, $p < .01$). That is, "external" Ss raised expect-

Table 3 Means and Sigmas of Children's I-E Scores by Social Class,
Ethnic Group, and IQ

	NEGRO						WHITE					
	Middle Class			Lower Class			Middle Class			Lower Class		
	Mean	Sigma	N	Mean	Sigma	N	Mean	Sigma	N	Mean	Sigma	N
IQ												
High	16.1	2.9	10	19.1	3.2	7	15.4	4.5	16	17.0	.8	4
Low	15.3	5.1	6	18.0	3.8	16	13.8	4.0	4	16.3	4.2	17

ancies after failure and lowered them after success more often than "internals." "Internal control" on the Bialer scale was found to relate significantly to higher social class (r pt. bis. $= .53$, $p < .01$). Since the Bialer scale is a questionnaire test and the children's I-E scale is a projective test, the correlation of these two instruments ($-.42$) lends support to the construct validity of the internal-external control dimension as applied to grade school children.

Neither age (sixth vs. eighth grade) nor sex were found to relate to either children's I-E scale or the Bialer questionnaire.

The most interesting finding in this study is the effect of the interaction of social class and ethnic group on I-E scores. Analysis of the means in Table 2 shows clearly that the combined influence of the two variables is to make the lower-class Negro more external than all other groups. The results suggest that the middle-class Negro in this community might be raised to accept the white cultural beliefs in responsibility and opportunity. These results suggest that one important antecedent of a generalized expectancy that one can control his own destiny is the perception of opportunity to obtain the material rewards offered in a culture. Direct teaching of attitudes of internal vs. external control may also be involved.

SUMMARY

A generalized expectancy for internal vs. external control of reinforcement was examined in 80 Negro and white school children. To assess this characteristic, a newly developed cartoon test was given to all children and a questionnaire scale developed earlier by Bialer was given to half the children. The relationship of test scores to sex, age, social class, ethnic group, and behavior on a line-matching task was investigated. The following findings were obtained.

1. The interaction of social class and ethnic group was highly related to internal-external control attitudes. Lower-class Negroes were significantly more external than middle-class Negroes or whites. Middle-class children, in general, were significantly more internal than lower-class children.

2. Lower-class Negroes with high IQ's were more external than middle-class whites with lower IQ's. Caution must be exercised in interpreting this triple interaction because of the small N involved. The findings suggest, however, that brighter lower-class Negroes may develop extreme attitudes as a defense reaction to perceived reduced choices for cultural or material rewards.

3. Sex was not a determiner of I-E scores in this study nor was age for the two-year difference investigated. California Mental Maturity Test scores did not relate to I-E scores when class and race were undifferentiated.

4. On a line-matching test, higher children's I-E scores were significantly associated with lower mean expectancy for success but not significantly associated with unusual shifts or trials to extinction.

5. The Bialer questionnaire of internal-external control expectancies correlated significantly ($-.42$) with the projective measure used in this study. The Bialer scale was also significantly related to social class.

6. For the 40 Ss who had taken the Bialer scale, a significant predicted relationship was found between test scores and number of unusual shifts on the line-matching task; but not with mean expectancy or trials to extinction.

7. The overall findings lend support to the construct validity of the internal-external control variable as a generalized personality dimension and suggest some of the developmental conditions involved in the acquisition of such generalized expectancies.

5-10 | Father-Absence and Delay of Gratification: Cross-Cultural Comparisons[1]

WALTER MISCHEL[2]

The dual purpose of this study is to investigate the effect of father-absence in the home on children's ability to delay gratification, as measured by their preference for immediate, smaller reinforcement (ImR) over delayed, larger reinforcement (DelR); and to test hypotheses based on ethnographic data concerning cross-cultural and intracultural differences in preferences for ImR or DelR. Opportunities to study systematically the effect of father-absence on the child's behavior, in this case on his delaying the immediately available but relatively trivial for the sake of later but larger outcomes, are rare. Either fathers are not absent for long periods or other conditions tend to be so deviant that generalizations to less extreme cases must be most tentative. The possible effect of prolonged absence of a parent is nevertheless of such import for any theory of identification and personality development that data are much needed. For example, Whiting (1959) is persistently concerned with developmental and

[1] This study was carried out under the partial support of a grant from the Laboratory of Social Relations, Harvard University, and Grant M-2557 (A) from the National Institute of Mental Health.

[2] Grateful acknowledgment is made to the Education Office of the Government of Trinidad and Tobago, and of the Government of Grenada, and to their officials for kind cooperation in testing within the school systems.

identification differences between children reared in mother-child and children reared in nuclear (father-present) households.

The present research, based on investigations in the southern Caribbean, presents data on a large number of father-present and father-absent boys and girls, sampled from a variety of settings, and differing sufficiently in age so that the role of the latter can be tested. Father-presence or absence is related in this study to the individual's choice preference for ImR or DelR. Such choice preferences are fairly easily elicited and provide lifelike behavior which is readily quantified and some of whose empirical correlates have been explored independently. Namely, preference for DelR (as opposed to ImR) has been related positively to accuracy in time statements and to social responsibility (Mischel, 1961c). The latter was measured by an independently validated scale (Harris, 1957) and found to correlate substantially with other measures of personal and social adjustment and maturity. Preference for DelR has also been negatively related to delinquency, positively to strength of n Achievement, and negatively to acquiescence or "yeasaying" (as opposed to "naysaying") tendencies (Mischel, 1961a). The preference for DelR-ImR distinction may thus be thought of as delineating two empirically-elaborated clusters, associated with significant differences in "maturity," responsibility, delay over time, long-term goal direction, and autonomy.

Singer and his associates (e.g., Singer, Wilensky, & McCraven, 1956) have investigated "delaying capacity," primarily as inferred from the frequency of human movement (M) in Rorschach responses, and have pointed to relevant correlates of delaying which overlap to some degree with those just indicated. Conceptually, the empirical correlates of preference for DelR and ImR are related to Freud's (1922) distinction between functioning on the pleasure principle as opposed to the reality principle and are relevant to Mowrer and Ullman's (1945) position. The latter maintain that the inability to delay gratification is an important factor in immature, neurotic, and criminal behavior.

The data on preference for DelR or ImR from the previous studies in this program all come from the same general culture area outside the United States and are based on West Indian children's responses, tested in comparable settings and with techniques similar to those used in the present study. Thus a network of correlates associated with the two reinforcement preference patterns with respect to delay has begun to be established. The findings of this study on choice behavior of father-absent and father-present children become meaningful in that context. In an earlier exploratory study (Mischel, 1958b), using a small sample of Trinidadian rural children aged 7-9, a significant relationship was found between father-absence and preference for ImR. Further, Negro subjects were found to show greater ImR preference when compared with East Indian subjects in the same cultural setting, the differences between the two groups seemingly being due to greater father-absence in the Negro sample. The present study is in part directed at replicating this relationship and testing its generality by sampling male and female children from a large variety of settings.

More important, however, is the attempt to test also the effect of father-absence on older children. Thus far investigations on the effects of father-absence (Bach, 1946; Lynn & Sawrey, 1959; Sears, Pintler, & Sears, 1946; Tiller, 1958) have all been based on samples of children under age 10. Lynn and Sawrey (1959) summarized these findings. Their own research included hypotheses of greater immaturity and poorer peer adjustment on the part of father-absent boys as compared to father-absent girls and a control group of father-present boys. These (and other) hypotheses were generally supported by data based on Norwegian boys and girls, ranging in age from 8 years to 9 years 6 months. The present study offers data for this age group (ages 8 and 9) as well as for a second, older group, aged 11-14. Lynn and Sawrey rightly point out that the findings of the earlier studies are limited by the fact that the father-absence with which they were concerned was a temporary state of affairs during wartime. In contrast, Lynn and Sawrey's subjects came from Norwegian sailor families where the father is often away from home for periods of 2 years or more with only infrequent visits. These authors recognized that "unknown cultural factors specific to the samples may be operating instead of or in addition to the variable of father-absence. Women who marry sailors may, for example, be such a select group that the variable 'sailor wife' may be the crucial one" (p. 259). The present data on father-absence from the Caribbean have the additional advantage of coming from a culture in which father-absence is a common and widely accepted pattern. Common-law marriage is extremely popular and according to some estimates a permanent father or father-figure is prolongedly absent in over one-third of all households.

The general hypothesis here expects an inverse relationship between father-absence and preference for DelR. Father-absent children should show relatively less preference for DelR and relatively more preference for ImR in choice situations, when compared with comparable father-present children. This relationship is expected to reflect the relatively greater immaturity and other correlates of preference for ImR which, it is anticipated, should characterize the father-absent group more than the father-present group.

The second aim of the study is to test experimentally an anthropological hypothesis concerning gross personality (or "national character") differences with respect to preference for DelR or ImR existing between the populations of two islands, Trinidad and Grenada, both in the southern Caribbean. The two islands may be thought of as subcultures within the same larger culture of the West Indies. The significance of this second aim lies in the application of quantitative, experimental techniques for testing a cross-cultural hypothesis, in this case a hypothesis dealing with an important psychological dimension that has been used frequently to make global but largely untested characterizations of groups and societies. This requires some explication of the cultural contexts within which the anthropological hypothesis was formulated.

On the basis of anthropological observation, a major personality difference between the Negro groups of the two islands was noted. This difference, as expressed by many informants with experience in both subcultures, is that the Trinidadian tends to be more impulsive, indulges himself, and settles for relatively little if he can get it right away. He is described as not working or waiting for larger rewards in the future, but tending instead to prefer immediately available relatively trivial gratifications. In contrast to this, the Grenadian, although on the whole poorer, is said to be more willing and able to postpone immediate gains and gratifications for the sake of larger rewards and returns in the future.[3] These observed personality or "national character" differences are supported by the further observations that the Trinidadian's savings (e.g., for the education of children) tend to be less than the Grenadian's of equally poor or even poorer circumstances.

Such differences between the islands may be related historically to the fact that the Grenadian, in contrast to the Trinidadian, has tended to hold on to his own land from generation to generation, and has been able to develop a much more autonomous role with respect to dependence on non-Negroes and colonials in government, in the professions, and in all forms of business.

The observed distinction between Trinidadians and Grenadians may be thought of as reflecting differences with respect to preference for ImR as opposed to DelR in choice situations, with the Trinidadian preferring the former more and the latter less than the Grenadian. This difference between individuals from the two islands may be conceptualized, at least in part, as related to differences in "trust" experiences with respect to the actual anticipated occurrence of delayed reward.

Indeed, in accord with Rotter's (1954) social learning theory we have conceptualized earlier (Mischel, 1958b) that the person's choice of an immediate, smaller or delayed, larger reward in a choice situation is, at least to some extent, a function of his expectation that the reward will actually occur and the reward value, or preference value, of the particular reinforcement. Mahrer (1956) has already shown that the person's expectancy that reinforcement would follow from the social agent making the promise, even after time delay, is an important variable in such choice behavior. In common sense terms, this kind of behavior may be thought of as "trust" or the belief that the agent promising delayed reinforcement will actually supply it.

The Grenadian may be thought of as having had a longer history of actual reward occurrence in delay situations (e.g., in the form of long-term gratifications accruing from land ownership) and as living in a cultural situation in which there is a good deal of trust with respect to promise-keeping and with respect to other means through which reward delay may be mediated, (i.e., long-term "payoff"). Certainly direct observation suggests the Grenadian to be far less suspicious and skeptical in his relations to strangers as well as to his own peers than is the Trinidadian. In sum,

---

[3] The distinction in this respect between Trinidadians and Grenadians has been made previously to differentiate the Negro and East Indian subgroups within Trinidad (Mischel, 1958), and will be referred to again, with replicating data, later in this paper.

the former may be thought of as having long experiences in a relatively stable "delayed reward culture" (at least in its economic aspects) within which he himself has had a relatively autonomous and "trusted" role; in contrast, the Trinidadian may be thought of as participating in a relatively "immediate reward culture" within which he has had a highly dependent and "untrusted" role. These differences should, in turn, be reflected in the expectations with respect to reward delay transmitted to the children within the two cultures. The prediction follows that there would be greater preference for ImR than DelR on the part of Trinidadian as compared to Grenadian children of comparable age and socioeconomic background.

Lastly, a hypothesis concerning differences between the Negro and East Indian populations of the same island, Trinidad, on the same dimension of preference for ImR or DelR is tested. Ethnographic observation suggested differences between these two intra-island groups similar to those noted between Trinidadians and Grenadians (where reference is made only to the Negro populations of both islands). Namely, when compared to Trinidadian Negroes, the East Indian group of Trinidad appears to show clearly greater preference for DelR in daily behavior. As previously indicated, this observation has been made and supported in earlier research (Mischel, 1958b). Here, an attempt is made to replicate these findings, taking into account any possible differences in extent of father-absence in the samples tested.[4] This also permits comparisons of intra-island differences between large groups on the dimension of concern.

METHOD

Subjects

A total of 68 Trinidadian Negro children (30 boys and 38 girls), and of 69 Grenadian Negro children (36 boys and 33 girls), all in the age. group 8 through 9 were tested. The Trinidadian subjects came from two schools, both on the outskirts of the capital city. The Grenadian subjects similarly came from two schools, both located on the outskirts of Grenada's capital city. Care was taken to select all schools so that subjects of roughly comparable socioeconomic backgrounds (all lower middle and lower class) would be obtained. This selection was guided by impressions formed on the basis of inspection of a variety of schools, participant observation in both cultures, and the counsel of local school officials. Inspection of the father's occupation reported by father-present subjects in all samples reveals no striking differences. Over 90% of the responses seemed classifiable as "unskilled workers."

[4] With respect to household structure in the three samples studied, the following tentative observations were made. Trinidad and Grenada are alike in the household structure of lower class and lower middle class Negro families. In both islands common-law marriage is extensive and accepted, fathers are frequently prolongedly or permanently absent, and the mother-child relationship is the family nucleus. The child usually knows who his natural father is or was, although the mother's partner may change at irregular intervals. In contrast, in East Indian Trinidadian families the father tends to be permanent and common-law marriage is rare.

Further data were collected on two samples of Trinidadian East Indian subjects aged 8 through 9 from the same Trinidadian schools. The first sample consisted of 22 boys and 15 girls; the second of 20 boys and 23 girls. In addition to these young subjects, similar data were collected from a total of 112 older Trinidadian Negro subjects (68 boys and 44 girls) aged 11 through 14 at one of the Trinidadian schools indicated above, and on 75 Negro subjects (40 boys and 35 girls) in the same age range, coming from the second Trinidadian school.[5]

Task and Measures

The reinforcements used with the younger group were selected through pretesting with a random sample of 20 boys and girls, aged 8 and 9, tested at another government school on the outskirts of the capital city in Trinidad. In these pre-experimental sessions subjects were seen in individual sessions and their preferences for specific reinforcements, all candy, were elicited. As a result, two candy reinforcements, varying markedly in price, size, and packaging (i.e., a $.02 and a $.10 candy bar) were selected. These met the desired requirements inasmuch as the larger reinforcement was uniformly preferred in a straight choice situation ("which *one* of these two would you like to take?"), but when the choice was "you can have this one (the smaller) today *or* this one (the larger) in one week," approximately 50% of the group chose the former and approximately 50% the latter. The purpose of this procedure was to select a reinforcement pair which would, as closely as possible, dichotomize the choices of subjects in one of the two ethnic groups being compared supplying an approximate 50-50 split in the Trinidadian sample which could be used as the criterion for comparison with the Grenadian data.

With the older subjects, a different reinforcement pair, namely, a $.10 and a $.25 candy bar were used on the basis of the procedure reported earlier (Mischel, 1961c). In addition, two verbal items, to which the subject was to respond with "yes" or "no," one inserted near the beginning of the total procedure and the other in the middle, were included with the older subjects. The items were:

1. I would rather get ten dollars right now than have to wait a whole month and get thirty dollars then.
2. I would rather wait to get a much larger gift much later than get a smaller one now.

The behavioral choice (candy) of preference for ImR as opposed to DelR was given as the last item of the total battery. Previous research (Mischel, 1961c) has shown that the use of these three measures in combination is more fruitful than the use of single items.

Although there are no formal data available on the comparative subjective value of the candy bars in the two cultures to be compared,

[5] The 112 older subjects were also administered other measures, the results of which have been previously reported (Mischel, 1961a).

direct observation, confirmed by those with intimate knowledge of both cultures, indicated that in both Grenada and Trinidad the particular candies used were of similar appeal and availability. In both cultures such candies are sold in virtually every corner store and are popular with, and commonly consumed by, middle and lower class children alike. Candy allowances in the two cultures appear to be essentially the same.

The measure of father-absence or presence consisted of the response ("yes" or "no") to the question: "Does your father live at home with you?" Twenty-eight out of 30 such responses, randomly selected, were in agreement with the child's mother's response to the question "Does his (specifying the child's name) father live at home with you?" asked in subsequent interviews with mothers of subjects in the older Trinidadian sample.

Procedure
The same experimenter was used in all testing. He was introduced as an American from a college in the United States interested in gathering information on the children in the various schools of the island. To help with this, subjects were asked to answer a number of simple questions, e.g., name, age. The details of this procedure have been described previously (Mischel, 1958b).

Upon completion of the questions, the experimenter expressed his wish to thank the group for their cooperation. He displayed the two kinds of reinforcement and said: "I would like to give each of you a piece of candy, but I don't have enough of these (indicating the larger, more preferred reinforcement) with me today. So you can either get this one (indicating the smaller, less preferred reinforcement) right now,

Table 1 Number of Father-Present (Fa+) and Father-Absent (Fa—) Subjects Choosing Immediate, Smaller or Delayed, Larger Reinforcement[a]

| Reinforcement Preference | GRENADA (NEGRO) | | | | | | TRINIDAD (NEGRO) | | | | | |
| | School 1 | | School 2 | | Total[b] | | School 3 | | School 4 | | Total[a] | |
	Fa+	Fa—	Fa+	Fa—	Fa+	Fa—	Fa+	Fa—	Fa+	Fa—	Fa+	Fa—
Immediate, smaller	5	4	4	4	9	8	11	10	8	7	19	17
Delayed, larger	16	6	26	4	42	10	16	6	10	0	26	6

Note.—Grenada versus Trinidad × Reinforcement Preference: $\chi^2 = 10.40$, $p < .01$ (corrected for continuity).
[a] Subjects are aged 8 and 9.
[b] $\chi^2 = 5.15$, $.05 > p > .02$; $\chi^2 = 3.80$, $.10 > p > .05$, if corrected for continuity.
[c] $\chi^2 = 4.93$, $.05 > p > .02$ (corrected for continuity).

today, or, if you want to, you can wait for this one (indicating) which I will bring back next Friday (one week delay interval)." These instructions were repeated in rephrased form to insure clarity and both reinforcements were carefully displayed. It was stressed that getting the (smaller) candy today precluded getting the (larger) one next week and vice versa. Subjects were asked to indicate their choice by writing T (today) or F (Friday, next week) on their questionnaires. The response made here was the measure of preference for ImR and DelR. Subjects were seated sufficiently far apart from each other to insure reasonably that their choices were made independently. All testing was done in group settings, and conducted on the same weekday (but in different weeks) and at similar times of day, within each of the schools in large classrooms.

RESULTS AND DISCUSSION

The data from the present study were analyzed in terms of differential preference for ImR as opposed to DelR in relationship to cultural group (Trinidad as compared to Grenada), and in relationship to presence or absence of the father within the home in each culture. In addition, the relationship between the experimental choice of preference for ImR as opposed to DelR and presence or absence of the father in the home was examined in data from the group of older Trinidadian subjects, for whom a Grenadian comparison group is not available. All statistical analyses were made with the chi square test.

Careful examination of possible sex differences with respect to either extent of father-absence or preference on the experimental choice, within each of the subsamples and in combination, revealed no differences approaching statistical significance. Indeed, no consistent sex trends were observed in examining all reported relationships separately for each sex. Consequently, the male and female data were combined for all subsequent statistical analyses. The similar choice preferences with respect to delay of father-absent boys and girls in this Caribbean sample is of interest in view of Lynn and Sawrey's (1959) Norwegian data, in which differential effects of father-absence on the sexes were found.

The data used for relating the experimental choice with cultural group are given in Table 1, which shows the number of Negro subjects (ages 8 through 9) within each of the schools, in Trinidad as compared to in Grenada, preferring ImR or DelR. Comparison of the number of subjects preferring ImR or DelR *within* each of the two cultures (i.e., comparing School 1 with School 2 in Grenada and School 3 with School 4 in Trinidad) results in no chi square which reaches significant probability levels, and consequently the data from the two schools within each culture can be combined for further comparisons. This combination, namely, a comparison of the total number of Negro Trinidadian subjects preferring ImR or DelR with the total number of Negro Grenadian subjects preferring ImR or DelR, results in a chi square (using Yates' correction for continuity) of 10.40, with $p < .01$. As predicted by the cultural hypothesis, a significantly larger proportion of the Trinidadian subjects, as compared to the Grenadian subjects, chose ImR rather than DelR.

The data used for relating father-absence and the experimental choice, in Trinidad and in Grenada, are also presented in Table 1. The chi square test applied to the relevant data yields uncorrected chi square values of 6.14 for Trinidad and of 5.15 for Grenada. These values are significant ($p < .02$ and $p < .05$, respectively) and indicate a greater proportion of father-absent subjects, as compared to father-present subjects choose ImR rather than DelR in each culture. If extreme caution is used and the Yates correction is employed on all fourfold contingency tables (in spite of the fact that all expected and marginal frequencies are relatively large) the chi square value for Trinidad becomes 4.93 ($p < .05$) and for Grenada 3.80. A value of 3.84 is required for $p < .05$ when $df = 1$.

In view of this support for the relationship between father-absence and preference for ImR, it becomes important to examine the differences between the two cultures with respect to degree of father-absence. Table 1 shows the number of father-absent and father-present subjects within each of the samples from the two cultures. Among the Grenadians, 18 of the 69 subjects reported father-absence; among the Trinidadians, 23 of the 68 subjects reported father-absence. Application of the chi square test to these data results in no p values approaching statistical significance, and suggests that the difference between the two cultures on the experimental choice cannot be attributed to differential father-absence, although within each culture father-absence is related to the choice behavior.

This finding is of special interest in view of the finding obtained earlier (Mischel, 1958b) in a comparison of Negro and East Indian subjects, both within the Trinidadian culture, on preference for delayed reinforcement. Although the two Trinidadian subgroups differed significantly in the choice behavior (the Negro subjects more frequently preferring the immediate, smaller reinforcement), the differences appeared attributable to differences in father-absence (the Indian subjects being characterized by more father-present households). The present data permit an attempt to replicate this relationship. The new data for Trinidadian East Indian subjects aged 8 through 9 were as follows. Among the Indians, 26 chose the ImR and 54 the DelR. Only 4 subjects in the Indian group were father-absent, 2 of these choosing ImR and 2 DelR. Comparing the Indians with the Trinidadian Negro subjects on preference for ImR as opposed to DelR results in a corrected chi square of 5.50 ($p < .02$). As was found earlier, the East Indian group again shows greater preference for DelR as opposed to ImR relative to the preferences of the Trinidadian Negro group. Note that there are no significant differences in reinforcement preference with respect to delay between the Trinidadian Indian group and the Grenadian group, although the latter shows significantly greater father-absence (chi square $= 11.47$, $df = 1$, $p < .001$). Comparison of the Trinidadian Indian group with the Trinidadian Negro group on extent of father-absence results in a corrected chi-square of 18.5 ($df = 1$, $p < .01$); clearly the latter show significantly greater father-absence than the former. If *only* father-present subjects from the two groups (Trinidadian Indian and Trinidadian Negro) are compared on preference for ImR or DelR, no significant relationship holds. In contrast, comparison of only father-present Trinidadian Negroes with Grenadian father-present subjects on reinforcement preference still yields a corrected chi square of 5.85 ($p < .02$), the Grenadians showing greater DelR preference. Thus the intra-island observed differences between the two Trinidadian groups appear to be largely related to differential father-absence between the two groups. However, the Trinidadian-Grenadian Negro differences with respect to reinforcement preference cannot be attributed to differential father-absence.

Summarizing the results thus far, the following relationships, condensed in Table 2, should be noted. Grenadian Negro children showed significantly greater preference for DelR as opposed to ImR when compared with Trinidadian Negro subjects. This difference cannot be attributed to differential father-absence since the two groups show no significant difference with respect to that variable, and since the difference in DelR-

Table 2   Summary of Relationships between Ethnic Group,[a] Subjects with Father-Present (Fa+) or Father-Absent (Fa—), and Preference for Delayed, Larger (DelR) as Opposed to Immediate, Smaller (ImR) Rewards

Comparison	Greater DelR Preference	p Value[b]
Trinidadian Negro vs. Grenadian Negro (Fa+ and Fa—)	Grenadian	<.01
Trinidadian Negro vs. Grenadian Negro (Fa+ only)	Grenadian	<.02
Trinidadian Negro vs. Grenadian Negro (Fa— only)	—	ns
Trinidadian Negro Fa+ vs. Fa—	Fa+	<.05
Grenadian Negro Fa+ vs. Fa—	Fa+	<.07
Trinidadian East Indian vs. Trinidadian Negro (Fa+ and Fa—)	East Indian	<.02
Trinidadian East Indian vs. Trinidadian Negro (Fa+ only)	—	ns
Trinidadian East Indian vs. Grenadian Negro (Fa+ and Fa—)	—	ns
Trinidadian East Indian vs. Grenadian Negro (Fa+ only)	—	ns

Note.—Comparisons with East Indian subjects on father-absence in relation to other variables cannot be made in view of the small N (4) of such father-absent subjects. Trinidadian Negro subjects as well as Grenadian Negroes, show significantly greater father-absence ($p < .01$) than Trinidadian East Indian subjects, but the difference between the two Negro groups in extent of father-absence is ns.

[a] Using Trinidadian Negro, Trinidadian East Indian, and Grenadian Negro subjects, all aged 8 and 9.

[b] Based on chi square comparisons, corrected for continuity: ns = p value > .10.

ImR preference holds even when only father-present subjects from the two islands are compared. In contrast, comparisons between Trinidadian Negro subjects and Trinidadian East Indian subjects reveal that the difference between these two, namely, the relatively greater DelR preference on the part of the East Indian group, does appear attributable to differential father-absence. This seems the case since the Trinidadian Negro subjects show significantly greater father-absence than do the East Indian subjects, and since the latter's relatively greater DelR preference does not hold when this differential father-absence is taken into account, i.e., when comparisons are based only on father-present subjects. Also note that Negro subjects from Trinidad and Grenada do not differ in their choice behavior *if* only father-*absent* Negro subjects from the two islands are compared (see data in Table 1). The small *N* of father-absent East Indian subjects prevents their being compared with other father-absent groups. Finally, the Trinidadian East Indian Group and the Grenadian Negro group are not significantly different in their reinforcement preferences, although the latter show significantly greater father-absence.

The present results thus suggest that the difference between the Trinidadian and Grenadian subjects on the experimental choice must be sought in sources other than family constellation with respect to father-absence or father-presence. This illustrates a situation commonly encountered in cross-cultural research. In spite of overlapping rearing conditions, not merely in terms of the father in the family constellation but also in terms of numerous patterns that link the two cultures and make them homogeneous in many ways, other unspecified sources of variance must account for gross observed differences, in this case differences in the delay of gratification patterns. The writer is inclined to focus on some of the cultural and economic differences, especially differences in autonomy and independence, as indicated earlier. The lack of a significant difference between father-*absent* Trinidadian and Grenadian Negro subjects in preference for DelR as opposed to ImR (Table 2) also suggests the possible argument that when fathers are absent differences in cultural values are less likely to be internalized by the children, since fathers may be needed to transmit such cultural values.

We turn next to the data on the relationship between father-absence and reinforcement preference obtained from the 112 older (ages 11 through 14) Trinidadian subjects. Here, as previously described, three measures of reinforcement preference with respect to delay were available. Application of the chi square test resulted in no *p* value less than .30. This lack of relationship was obtained in comparisons using the candy choice alone, as well as all possible combinations of preferences over the three measures. To inquire further into this failure of the anticipated relationship for older subjects, the same experimental procedure was repeated on another sample of 75 Trinidadian subjects of the same age range, tested in another but highly similar Government school, comparably located, and with subjects of similar socioeconomic and ethnic backgrounds. Again, no relationship between the experimental choices and presence or absence of the father in the home was obtained that reached or approached significant probability levels. Thus although the expected relationship was repeatedly obtained at the younger age levels, the null hypothesis cannot be rejected for seemingly similar subjects at older age levels.

The possibility exists that the instructions for the experimental choice, specifically the phrase "but I don't have enough of these (DelR) with me today," may have partially confounded the results by producing a conflict in older subjects, eager for the DelR yet reluctant to make the experimenter return. However, this seems extremely unlikely. First, during the administration, that phrase, used only as an introduction to make the choice plausible, was probably overshadowed by the frequent repetitions of the actual choice conflict and the implication that the experimenter would *definitely* return next week to hand out the DelR to those in the group who chose it. Second, and more definitive, in over 20 pre-experimental sessions with other comparable subjects from the same culture, used to select the particular reinforcements sets, postchoice inquiries into reasons for the choices yielded nothing remotely suggestive of such an "obliging response."

It is tempting to argue that for older subjects the measures of preference for ImR as opposed to DelR is meaningless or invalid, and consequently relations with father-absence should not be expected. It must be recalled, however, that the same measures used with Caribbean subjects of this age, and indeed including subjects from the present older sample, have yielded significant correlations with conceptually relevant variables (social responsibility, need for achievement, nonacquiescence), all of the above being positively correlated with preference for DelR (Mischel, 1961a, 1961c). In this context, it should also be noted that no relationships approaching statistical significance were obtained in attempts to relate father-absence with these correlates of preference for DelR. This suggests that father-absence at older age levels may not have some of the effects (e.g., "immaturity," poorer adjustment) apparently associated with it at the earlier age level (e.g., Lynn & Sawrey, 1959). The question cannot be answered at present in view of the lack of research on father-absence with older children. Of course, the present data are seriously hampered in the gross measure of father-absence or presence used, which gives no information on the extent or duration of the father's absence or presence. Nevertheless, the same gross measure did yield the expected results with the younger subjects, and excellent agreement between older subjects' reports of father-absence and mother's reports on the same question was obtained.

The *post hoc* interpretation being suggested for these findings is that as the individual develops and matures, he begins to participate in an environment that extends beyond the immediate family and consequently his expectations with respect to promise-keeping, his "trust," and his choice behavior with respect to delay of gratification become contingent upon numerous factors and experiences other than those within the household itself. Similarly, at least in southern Caribbean cultures, sources of influence outside the immediate family may become important determinants of other variables correlated with ImR-DelR preferences, such as "social responsibility" and need for achievement, at relatively early periods in the person's life.[6]

Although this interpretation is clearly tentative, pending further and more controlled research, the data illustrate the complexity of some of the conditions that may influence such choice behavior. In spite of these complexities, significant support was obtained for the anthropological hypothesis concerning cross-cultural differences between Trinidad and Grenada with respect to delay of gratification. Earlier findings of differences with respect to ethnic groups on the same variable were replicated. It is recognized, of course, that the findings are necessarily limited by sampling problems which make any generalizations tentative. Nevertheless, the findings are construed as illustrative of the possibilities of applying quantitative simple experimental techniques for testing cross-cultural differences on important psychological dimensions.

SUMMARY

This study tested an anthropological hypothesis concerning differences in preference for immediate, smaller (ImR) as opposed to delayed, larger reinforcement (DelR) between two subcultures (Trinidad and Grenada) within the West Indies. The data, in the form of choice preferences for Imr or DelR elicited from children in both islands, supported the cultural hypothesis. Further, a significant relationship between absence of the father within the home and greater preference for ImR as compared to DelR was found in both cultures, using subjects aged 8-9. However, this relationship was not found for older subjects (aged 11-14). These results were discussed in terms of increased sources of variance relevant to the formation of trust behavior and expectancies outside the household with increasing age. Data replicating previously obtained differences with respect to preference for ImR as opposed to DelR between two ethnic groups (Indian and Negro) within the island of Trinidad were also presented.

[6] It should be noted that in the cultures studied, the individual becomes independent of the family and autonomous, e.g., vocationally, relatively early in life. For example, official "student-teachers" in public schools are often 13 years old. In all three samples, the child from age 10 or 11 on, becomes increasingly free to move about, visiting with other relatives (e.g., uncles, grandparents, etc.) who may or may not be living in the immediate neighborhood, and whom he may visit for a day or longer periods.

5-11

The American Negro: A Problem in Expectancies[1]

HERBERT M. LEFCOURT and GORDON W. LADWIG

This study dealt with differences between Negro and white inmates in their expectancies that events are internally or externally controlled. 60 white and 60 Negro inmates from correctional institutions were compared on 3 scales pertinent to the internal-external control dimension, and on 3 performance variables from Rotter's Level of Aspiration Board task. On all measures Negroes revealed greater expectancy of control being external. The results have implications for interpreting the frequently observed differences between white and Negro intelligence test performance and achievement striving.

Recent reviews of research pertaining to Negro-white differences by Shuey (1958) and Dreger and Miller (1960) have noted the reliable finding that Negroes perform less adequately than whites on intelligence measures. This kind of data has resulted in such polemic arguments as that between Chein and Garret (1962) which debates hereditarian versus environmentalist interpretations and conclusions. Recently, a body of research findings has been developing which emphasizes the situational and personality variables operative in Negroes which produce the apparent intellectual inferiority noted in intelligence testing.

Roen (1960) found Negroes' intelligence scores correlated with certain personality measures. He concluded that Negroes

incorporate intellectually defeating personality traits that play a significant role in their ability to score on measures of intelligence [p. 150].

In a series of studies by Katz (Katz & Benjamin, 1960; Katz & Cohen, 1962; Katz & Greenbaum, 1963) Negro students were found to be anxious and unproductive in problem-solving situations especially when confronted with white partners.

The present research represents a further exploration of Negro-white differences on personality variables related to achievement behavior and its correlate, intelligence test performance. Rotter, Liverant, and Seeman

[1] This report is based partially on a doctoral dissertation submitted by the senior author to the Graduate School, Ohio State University, August 1963. The senior author wishes to express his appreciation to Alvin Scodel for his guidance in the course of the study. This research was supported in part by the United States Air Force, under Contract No. AF 49(638)-317 monitored by the Air Force Office of Scientific Research of the Air Research and Development Command.

(1962) have described an expectancy construct referred to as internal-external (I-E) control of reinforcements. Internal control refers to a generalized expectancy that reinforcements occur as a consequence of one's own actions and are thereby under personal control. External control refers to the belief that reinforcements are unrelated to one's own behaviors and therefore beyond personal control.

This variable may prove important in attempting to understand the problems of Negroes' intelligence test difficulty. Crandall, Katkovsky, and Preston (1962) have found that internal-control children show more intellectual interest and better intelligence test performance than external-control children. This suggests that a person perceiving his reinforcements as being externally controlled, is less likely to try and succeed. Rose (1956), in his condensation of Myrdal's *The American Dilemma*, noted that

> the ambition of Negro youth is cramped not only by . . . segregation and discrimination but also by the low expectation from both white and Negro society. . . . And if he is not extraordinary he will not expect it of himself and will not really put his shoulder to the wheel [p. 218].

The Negro may be characterized as a person who has a low expectancy that he can control his reinforcements. The first hypothesis in this study, then, is that Negroes will score higher on external control than a comparable group of whites, in tests designed to measure the I-E dimension. Second, in achievement tasks that demand self-evaluation Negroes will perform in a manner that can be described as reflecting a greater expectancy of external control.

METHOD

To test these hypotheses 60 Negro and 60 white inmates from two correctional institutions were used as subjects. There were no significant differences in social class, intelligence, age, or reason for incarceration between the two groups. For the most part the subjects were of lower class origin. Their intelligence levels were within the average range with beta IQs between 90 and 110 (Kellogg & Morton, 1935). The mean age was 21.6 years and the typical crime leading to incarceration was car theft.

Each subject was given the Rotter Level of Aspiration Board (LOA) using Rotter's (1942) standard instructions. In addition, the subject was instructed that he would earn a pack of cigarettes for each 50 points he had at the conclusion of the task. This was done to enlist cooperation and to encourage "realistic" goal setting.

Three indices of LOA performance which theoretically are related to the I-E dimension were employed: number of shifts, number of unusual shifts, and patterns. The number of shifts (changes in the subject's prediction of his next score) in the LOA relates to general stability and self-confidence. High frequencies of shifts characterize individuals who do not use previous experience to establish consistent estimates of their performance. Unusual shifts (up after failure, down after success) likewise suggest failure of the subject to establish reliable estimates of his skill. Unusual shifts tend to indicate dependence on luck or magical, externally controlled factors. Of the LOA patterns described by Rotter (1945) Patterns 1 and 3 indicate a stable, ambitious, confident approach while the other patterns generally indicate a failure-avoidant, defensive approach. In both patterns there are an average number of shifts and generally an absence of unusual shifts. In Pattern 1, D scores usually range from 0.0 to +3.0, while in Pattern 3, the range is from +3 to +6.0. Patterns 1 and 3 demonstrate the task involvement and realistic self-appraisal characteristic of internal controls. Previous research has demonstrated the relationship of these latter two indices (unusual shifts and patterns) with the I-E dimension (Simmons, 1959).

After the LOA task the subjects were given the I-E scale of Rotter et al. (1962) and Dean's (1961) Powerlessness and Normlessness scales. The former was developed in the framework of Social Learning Theory (Rotter, 1954) to assess the I-E control variable. The test consists of 23 forced-choice items with 6 filler items. Illustrative items are as follows:

I more strongly believe that:

6. a. Without the right breaks one cannot be an effective leader.
   b. Capable people who fail to become leaders have not taken advantage of their opportunities.
9. a. I have often found that what is going to happen will happen.
   b. Trusting to fate has never turned out as well for me as making a decision to take a definite course of action.
17. a. As far as world affairs are concerned, most of us are the victims of forces we can neither understand nor control.
    b. By taking an active part in political and social affairs the people can control world events.
23. a. Sometimes I can't understand how teachers arrive at the grades they give.
    b. There is a direct connection between how hard I study and the grades I get.

Dean's scales were constructed to measure two of the five variables that Seeman (1959) has defined as components of alienation. Powerlessness, like external control, refers to an individual's expectancy that he cannot control his fate. Normlessness refers to the high expectancy that socially unapproved behaviors are required in order to achieve given goals. The Powerlessness measure consists of nine Likert scale items. Illustrative items are as follows:

There is little or nothing I can do towards preventing a major "shooting" war.

We're so regimented today that there's not much more room for choice even in personal matters.

Typical of the six Likert scale items in the Normlessness measure were:

Everything is relative, and there just aren't any definite rules to live by.

The only thing one can be sure of today is that he can be sure of nothing.

The predictions are that Negroes will score higher on external control and claim greater powerlessness and normlessness than whites. In the LOA task it is predicted that Negroes will shift more, make more unusual shifts, and will produce fewer Patterns 1 and 3 than whites.

RESULTS

As indicated in Table 1, all predicted differences in Level of Aspiration Board performance were obtained. Negroes shifted more frequently and made more unusual shifts than whites. In a comparison of the overall patterns of performance, significantly fewer Negroes showed Patterns 1 and 3, the patterns indicative of internal control.

In the comparison of number of shifts Negroes were more variable than whites (t between standard deviations $= 2.57$, $p < .02$). However, since the Ns were equal a parametric test of differences between the means was justified (Boneau, 1960).

Subjects making no unusual shifts were compared with those making one or more unusual shifts. A second comparison of those making zero to one, versus those making two or more unusual shifts, was also made to minimize the possibility that subjects were included in the "unusual-shift" group who made an occasional unusual shift for justifiable reasons, i.e., when a previous failure was just short of the stated goal.

Table 2 indicates that Negroes scored significantly higher on the three attitude measures related to the I-E control dimension. Since the largest

Table 1 Level of Aspiration Board Results

	Negroes	Whites	t
Number of shifts			
M	9.08	7.00	
SD	5.02	3.57	2.60*
Proportion of subjects making one or more unusual shifts	.72	.48	2.68**
Proportion of subjects making two or more unusual shifts	.52	.22	3.41***
Proportions of subjects showing Patterns 1 and 3	.25	.53	3.14**

Note. All tests are two-tailed based on samples of 60 in each group.
   * $p = .02$.
  ** $p = .01$.
 *** $p = .001$.

Table 2   Comparisons on Scale Measures

MEASURE	NEGROES	WHITES	t
I-E			
M	8.97	7.87	2.00*
SD	2.97	3.03	
Powerlessness			
M	17.30	14.63	2.89**
SD	5.02	4.98	
Normlessness			
M	12.60	9.37	3.49***
SD	4.40	4.53	

Note. All tests are two-tailed based on samples of 60 in each group.
   * $p = .05$.
  ** $p = .01$.
 *** $p = .001$.

difference between Negroes and whites was obtained on the Normlessness scale it might be plausible to suggest that Negroes are even more dubious about the avenues open to them than about their own adequacy to achieve.

A third comparison was undertaken between the Negro and white inmate samples and norms reported by Dean which were based on a stratified sample of 384 male subjects drawn from the Columbus, Ohio, area. It was expected that reformatory inmates, in general, would score higher on powerlessness and normlessness than a noninstitutionalized population, and that Negroes, in particular, would be more markedly deviant from such norms.

As Table 3 indicates, Negro inmates' scores are considerably higher in an external-control direction than Dean's normative group. A similar comparison with white inmates showed no significant difference from the norm group in powerlessness ($t = .71$, ns) although on normlessness white inmates also scored higher than Dean's norm group ($t = 2.48$, $p < .05$).

Table 3   Comparison of Negro Inmates with Dean's Norms for the Powerlessness and Normlessness Scales

	DEAN'S SAMPLE (N = 384)	NEGRO INMATES (N = 60)	t
Powerlessness			
M	13.65	17.30	4.35*
SD	6.1	5.0	
Normlessness			
M	7.62	12.60	7.73*
SD	4.7	4.4	

   * $p = .001$.

In brief, reformatory inmates seem to have higher expectancies than the general population that socially unapproved behaviors are required to achieve valued goals. Negro inmates appear even more pessimistic about socially acceptable means than white inmates. However, only Negro inmates appear radically different from the general population in regard to the powerlessness variable which is more directly related to the I-E control dimension than is normlessness.

DISCUSSION

Literature concerning the American Negro has often focused on his feelings of low self-esteem and pessimism. This investigation has been directed toward a study of these problems making use of the I-E control variable. Negroes have been found to have low expectancies for internal control of reinforcements both in attitude and behavior measures. Although research is required to clarify the development of the expectancy of external control, it would seem likely that segregation and discrimination facilitate the growth of an external orientation. They deny positive reinforcements to Negroes despite individual achievements, thus providing the kind of experience necessary for the development and maintenance of generalized expectancies of external control. As Rose has suggested, such expectancies should result in a minimum of effort to achieve and a lack of interest in achievement-related pursuits. Crandall's findings, noted previously, tend to support this thesis. In view of the findings in this study it may be hypothesized that Negroes' poorer performance on intelligence tests reflects a withdrawal from middle-class achievement goals. The externally oriented Negro may well see these goals as being unobtainable through his own efforts. It is possible that in the current Negro mass movement for civil rights, there will be greater opportunity for Negroes to witness concrete changes deriving from their social action. If so, the differences between Negroes and whites obtained in this study may not be as extreme in the not too distant future.

PART 5: SUMMARY

The social sciences have a common core. Human learning, personality, social psychology, sociology, cultural anthropology, economics, and political science all have a great deal in common. They are concerned with the acquired, or partially acquired, goal-directed behavior of people. Where they differ is in the size and nature of the units they work with and the problems they seek to address. To the extent that they deal with different units and different problems and arise from different historical antecedents, they are organized around different constructs. Yet there is recognition of much overlap, and frequent attempts at interdisciplinary research and theorizing are made but often lead to failure because of communication and status difficulties. Nevertheless, there is much unsystematic borrowing and lending of constructs among the social sciences.

If one accepts a construct point of view, a social learning theory of personality, concerned as it is with socially learned behaviors, expectancies, and reinforcement values in different psychological situations, should have much utility for other social sciences. Not that other social sciences can be *reduced* to social learning theory terminology, but specific constructs regarding process and content in personality may be useful to social scientists operating in a variety of fields other than personality. Similarly, concepts from other social sciences can be useful to a psychologist adopting a social learning approach to the study of personality. Although differences in expectancies, reinforcement values, and goal-directed behavior can be found to describe social classes, they do not constitute all of the differences to be found among social classes. A clinical psychologist working with a set of personality descriptions can still know something *more* about an individual by knowing his social class, race, economic condition, or national origin. Each social science provides different ways of abstracting functional relations and can add predictive information to another.

The scientific abstractions or constructs of one approach can be useful to another in that they can provide for efficiency in measurement and suggest hypotheses for explanation or prediction about change. They are useful to one another to the degree that they overlap on the problems being investigated, the units they are studying, or the aspects of events they are focusing on. That such commonalities frequently appear in the social sciences is clearly evident from some familiar examples. The anthropologist has often used psychoanalytic developmental hypotheses to explain cultural differences. Sociologists rely on differential association or social learning to explain delinquency. Personality and social psychologists make considerable use of concepts such as social class or race to explain group differences. The economist frequently calls upon motivational constructs to explain economic behavior, and the political scientist is currently relying more and more on concepts such as rising expectations and national character to explain political behavior.

In addition to these commonalities, there are methodological commonalities shared by many of the social sciences, since data is often collected from individuals in the form of verbal responses. Veridicality for the sampling of social attitudes is a common problem for social psychologists, sociologists, anthropologists, economists, and political scientists, as is the problem of the relation of verbally expressed attitudes to other behavior.

Social learning theory has implications for the measurement of social attitudes; for the study of social behavior; for the learning of mores, customs, and roles; and so on. It is also true that the social learning theorist trying to make predictions can make great use of the more molar concepts developed by the other social sciences. In understanding situational differences, in making assumptions about the nature of objective reinforcements, and in presuming that certain behaviors have been acquired and have some potential for occurrence, we need to lean heavily on other social sciences which describe the subgroups of which the individual is a member. Although personality theory supposedly deals with individuals, it must assume some group similarities in order to carry out research with reasonable efficiency. For example, we are assuming something about the culture when we expect that a particular kind of insult will make one group angry, or that they will be positively reinforced if we say "good" following a task performance. Such assumptions may involve some error, and one reason the personality researcher requires additional constructs is that his studies involve relatively few individuals. Sociologists who wish to study sexual mores may be able to tolerate a greater error in individual cases if they want to study the hypothesis that the middle class is more prudish than the upper class.

While social class as a construct may not be sufficiently efficient to examine some theoretical questions involving the relations of specific past experience and present behavior as an *explanatory* construct, it may, nevertheless, still be useful as a *control* variable. The same could be said about the constructs of race or subcultural group. As control variables they serve the purpose of equating individuals on a series of variables which, though important, are not being examined in the problem being investigated.

Not only do the social sciences hold promise for one another in understanding methodology, providing control variables, and explanatory variables but they also can provide the scientist with the possibility of developing new hypotheses. This is particularly true when there has been some attempt to integrate or translate concepts from one social science to another, or to develop a common language for at least a portion of their constructs. For example, if internal-external control is seen as closely related to alienation in the sense of powerlessness (as Seeman perceives it) and also to cultural fatalism, then studies of individual antecedents for differences in internal-external control *may* provide important directions to the search for relevant social conditions which are historically related to social class differences or subculture differences in this dimension. It is equally true that the personality theorist looking for antecedents of individual differences may find important hypotheses in studying class and institutional differences in groups differing in alienation or from the study of cultures differing in fatalism.

It is clear, then, that if the social sciences had a partial common language, one could freely use data obtained by scientists of other social sciences both to question, support, or interpret one's own data and to suggest limits of generalization from one's own data.

It is in this context that we have brought together a selection of articles in this chapter in which personality variables have been used to explore problems often investigated by social psychologists, sociologists, and cultural anthropologists and in which the constructs of these fields are related to the constructs of social learning theory.

The first paper in this section (5-1) presents a social learning analysis of attitude measurement and social action behavior. It is not necessary to repeat this analysis here. Several of the following papers suggest the heuristic value of this analysis and support many of the hypotheses. The papers by Hamsher, Geller, and Rotter (5-2), Phares (5-3), Gore and Rotter (5-4), and Strickland (5-5) detail the significance of generalized expectancies for understanding and predicting social behavior. In the formulation of such generalized expectancies it seems likely that social learning theory can contribute something new to the investigations of other social scientists.

Mischel's (5-6) paper on the effect of public commitment on verbalized expectancies also supports the general analysis presented by Rotter (5-1). A similar study by Watt (1965), in general, replicates Mischel's work and reinforces the idea that public commitment is an important variable in determining some kinds of social behavior. Rotter (5-1) explains this effect as a need to maintain consistency among public statements.

The role of conformity is explored by Crowne and Liverant (5-7), who demonstrate the relation of freedom of movement and need value to the analysis of conforming behavior. In this study the predictable individual differences point the way to explaining the variables involved in the development and maintenance of conformity in groups and illustrate how individual and group variables are interrelated.

Other sociopsychological problems have been tackled from a social learning point of view, but space did not allow their inclusion here. A series of studies by Rettig et al. (Rettig & Rawson, 1963; Rettig & Singh, 1963; Rettig & Pasamanick, 1964) analyze ethical behavior from an expectancy-reinforcement point of view. That is, they conceive of ethical behavior as varying predominantly as a function of perceived risk (expectancy for being caught) and the differential values of punishment and gain for the unethical behavior. On this basis they have been able to successfully predict ethical behavior in a number of situations, including cheating in test-taking and two-person non-zero-sum game situations, both in our society and in a cross-cultural replication.

A fruitful combination of individual personality and broad social variables was studied by Crowne (1966). Crowne investigated the level of aspiration behavior and "prisoner's dilemma" behavior of the children of bureaucratic and entrepreneurial families. His findings, including an interesting interaction, could serve as a valuable source of hypotheses for a variety of social scientists interested in the effects of different economic orientations on the behavior of succeeding generations.

The remaining papers in this chapter deal more specifically with sociological and cultural anthropological variables. Battle and Rotter (5-9) and Lefcourt and Ladwig (5-11) contribute to the understanding of group differences in personality in the American Negro. The Battle and Rotter (5-9) paper, in addition, suggests an interesting interaction among the variables of social class, race, and externality and intelligence which might provide a valuable clue to the understanding of black militant leadership. Mischel's (5-10) cross-cultural analysis of delay of gratification also illustrates the value of studying both individual and group variables in combination.

Seeman's (5-8) paper details specifically how sociological and social learning constructs can be translated and how each can help illuminate the problems encountered in the other field of interest.

Jessor (1964) has described an application of SLT to excessive alcohol use, analysing both the personality system and the sociocultural system as predictors. More specifically, he states that deviance rates should be higher where value-access disjunctions (which can be translated into freedom of movement and need-value discrepancies) are greater in the social situation or in the individual's perceived opportunity structure, including the person's belief structure and his sense of internal control. In effect, Jessor relates sociological, cultural, and social learning variables and suggests the enhanced prediction possible when theoretically related constructs from different social sciences are applied to a specific problem of prediction. Jessor (1962) has also described this point of view in a more general statement. Graves and Van Arsdale (1966) have applied a similar analysis to the relocation problems of the Navajo migrant to Denver. In their classic interdisciplinary study of deviant behavior in a triethnic community, Jessor, Graves, Hanson, and Jessor (1968, pp. 335-363) show that a combination of predictors is better than personality variables or sociocultural variables alone; each set of variables accounted for some predictive variance not included in the other.

6 | *Applications to Psychopathology*

INTRODUCTION

The initial paper by Phares (6-1) in this section presents a fairly lengthy overview of an SLT construction of psychopathological behavior. It is intended to provide a way of looking at deviant phenomena that will have heuristic benefits. The four papers that follow are intended to demonstrate applications of SLT to specific problem areas.

The paper by Jessor, Carman, and Grossman (1968; 6-2) illustrates how the concept of discrepancy between expectancies and needs can be employed to predict the occurrence of deviant behavior—in this case, drinking behavior.

Jessor, Liverant, and Opochinsky (1963; 6-3) show how an overly strong need relative to an individual's other needs can lead to maladjusted behavior.

Dies (1968; 6-4) applies SLT to an analysis of the effects of electroconvulsive shock and suggests how expectancies for punishment can lead to a reduction in symptomatology.

Finally, the paper by Cromwell (1967b; 6-5) provides a brief introduction to a program of research which has utilized SLT to understand the reactions of mental retardates to success and failure.

Since the paper by Phares discusses many of the implications of SLT for psychopathology, the summary at the end of this section is devoted only to a brief discussion of the reprinted papers along with other SLT research which bears specifically on psychopathology.

6-1

A Social Learning Theory Approach to Psychopathology

E. JERRY PHARES

Social learning theory does not offer any special principles to cover the field of psychopathology apart from those that apply to social behavior generally. In effect, this statement implies the continuity of social behaviors across the domains of so-called normal and abnormal phenomena. However, before going into a more detailed presentation of the application of social learning theory to maladjustment or psychopathology, let us first provide some introductory comments from the standpoint of social learning theory. Another exposition of a number of these points may be found both in Phares (1967) and Katkovsky (1968).

Definitions of Psychopathology

Over the years, a variety of definitions of abnormality have been offered. Such variety is perhaps responsible for a great deal of conceptual confusion and is reflected ultimately in research difficulties (Scott, 1958). Many definitions are, in essence, *statistical* ones. For example, anyone who departs behaviorally from the mean or some area surrounding the mean is regarded as pathological. To have delusions is abnormal since most people do not. To engage in homosexual behaviors is abnormal since most people do not. To be terribly withdrawn is abnormal since most people are not. There are many difficulties with such a definition. First, how far from the mean must a behavior depart before it is to be considered deviant or abnormal? In short, what are the cutoff points and what are the rational justifications for putting them at any given place? Second, it is surely too much to ask that a given person conform to the mean with respect to all of his behavior. Therefore, how many behavioral departures from the mean are permitted? A third point concerns the temporary or chronic aspects of aberrant behavior. Do we infer pathology from a deviant behavior which occurs for two days or two years? Or does this make any difference?

Statistical definitions also pose very difficult problems because they would literally force us to conclude that an exceptionally sensitive or intelligent person is also abnormal. To exclude such behaviors or others like them from the realm of pathology is to implicitly establish a set of values—the very thing that, seemingly, many people wish to avoid. In short, we end up with "good" deviations and "bad" deviations.

Cultural relativism was once thought to provide a way out of many of these difficulties. That is, abnormality should be inferred only when a behavior violates the prevailing norms of the community or group. Thus, extreme violence is not abnormal if it is carried out by a person whose reference group condones or encourages such behavior. Basically, this approach is also a statistical one except that the departure from the mean is studied with reference to a specific group or culture. It is obvious that both cultural relativism and the statistical approach tend to place the

This paper is published for the first time in this volume.

436

reference group above reproach. Conformity becomes the crucial test for the determination of maladjustment.

Another approach to the definitional problem is to rely on *subjective report*. To feel anxious, unhappy, unfulfilled, and so on, is to be abnormal or maladjusted. Here, the important thing is not conformity but one's awareness of some unpleasant inner state. If one feels right and good, that is all that matters. Likewise, if one feels miserable, tense, depressed, and so on, he is maladjusted. Of course, many institutionalized patients report inner tranquility; surely there must be a reason for their hospitalization. Likewise, to be alive is to be anxious. It is almost impossible to imagine an environment that does not engender stress. If this is the case, then, how much stress is permitted? And we are right back where we started.

Other definitions often have recourse to what is called *symptom manifestation*. In this instance, one observes behavior and then refers to a psychiatric manual to determine whether the behavior in question is included. Such a procedure is largely an appeal to authority and incurs, of course, all the previous objections and problems.

Many theories of personality have offered or have been said to offer definitions of maladjustment. Although perhaps an oversimplification, the psychoanalytically oriented individual often seems to define abnormality as the presence of repressions. The quest for adjustment seems to coincide with the quest for insight. Indeed, the whole thrust of analysis is toward the breaking down of repressions and the acceptance of one's unconscious impulses. At any rate, the ultimate in adjustment seems to be the absence of repressions.

In summary, it would appear that there are at least three broad approaches to the definition of maladjustment. The first of these (emphasizing statistical deviation, conformity, and social norms) is what Rotter (1954) refers to as the *social-centered* approach, while the second, emphasizing internal states of unhappiness, depression, and so on, he refers to as the *self-centered* approach. The third approach represents an attempt to solve the definitional problem at a theoretical level of analysis. Although couched in theoretical terms, the latter kinds of definitions are more often than not simple restatements of the self-centered or social-centered approaches.

It appears, then, that usage of such terms as deviant, maladjusted, psychopathological, abnormal, and so on, is basically predicated on value considerations. When we label someone as abnormal what we really are saying is that his behavior deviates from some established set of norms. Furthermore, to define abnormality is to go outside one's theoretical system. Such labels are merely descriptive. They describe someone's view that the behavior in question deviates in some manner from a prescribed set of norms. It is usually true that when one is described as being abnormal it is also said that he needs treatment. In short, he ought to get help so that he will behave in a more acceptable fashion—more acceptable to society, to relatives, to a psychiatrist, or even to himself.

However, within social learning theory there is nothing that tells us when treatment or psychotherapy should be initiated. Both the decision to institute treatment and the decision as to "what kind of person the patient ought to be" are value judgments. Once these judgments are made, however, social learning theory can then offer specific principles relevant to the creation of the desired outcome. In this connection, it is interesting to make note of an experience that most clinical psychologists have had if they do much public speaking before parents' groups. Very often the psychologist is asked at the close of his presentation what to do if Johnny does such and such. Although not many of us are prone to do so, perhaps what we really should say is something like this. "If you want your child to become a _____ kind of person, then you should do X. On the other hand, if it is important that he turn into a _____ kind of person, then you should do Y." Such a response is not calculated to win you friends among those parents who want straight answers to straight questions. However, it does serve to illustrate the point that there are no right and wrong answers as regards childrearing practices. There are only different procedures which lead to different outcomes. The definition of what is a desirable outcome resides with the parent. Once that decision is arrived at, then social learning theory or perhaps some other approach can provide advice and principles on how best to implement it.

The Disease-Entity Approach

In view of the preceding discussion it becomes apparent that very nearly any behavior may be considered pathological depending upon the circumstances or situation. This point is made by Zigler and Phillips (1961), who reinforce the impossibility of ever compiling a definitive list of abnormal behaviors. Nonetheless, for a variety of reasons it is important to be able to utilize a classification scheme. As examples of the possibilities here, Katkovsky (1968) identifies several possible criteria for such classification. For example, the predominant feature of the behavior may be used. We can describe behavior as being anxious, depressed, paranoid, obsessive, and so on. This is not to deny that there may be problems of consensual validation and interjudge agreement involved. Another possibility relates to the major need involved in the behavior. There might be maladjusted recognition behavior, maladjusted dependency behavior, and so on. Or one could identify the particular life area involved; for example, vocational difficulties, marital problems. Still other approaches might involve the number of life areas involved, the degree of incapacitation, the acute-chronic nature, and so on. In every case there are the usual problems in developing a reliable basis on which to make such judgments, but these are, nonetheless, possibilities.

Perhaps the dominant classification scheme still in use is represented by the official nomenclature of the American Psychiatric Association (1952). This approach, of course, has its roots in the work of Kraepelin (1913). Such approaches whose major tenet seems to be the categorization of behaviors into disease entities are contrary to social learning theory. Whether such approaches deal with diseases, types, mental illness, or a variety of other psychiatric categories, the basic thesis seems the same. Since this so-called disease-entity approach is still widely used, although increasingly criticized, it may be useful to discuss it. By doing so we hope to partially explicate a social learning theory approach to psychopathology.

Such an approach generally tends to regard certain behaviors as symptoms of a more basic illness or disease. For example, a long list of behaviors or symptoms has been identified which presumably indicates the presence of the disease called schizophrenia. Such a procedure represents the attempt to apply a medical frame of reference to what should be regarded as social behaviors. As in the field of medicine, there is the attempt to regard behavior as being either healthy or diseased. All too often, then, deviant behavior tends to be equated with "mental illness." We would agree with Szasz (1960) that mental illness is largely a myth. For years, many very well-meaning individuals have been waging a campaign to reduce the public's fear, prejudice, or apathy toward people whose behavior is rather bizarre. To accomplish this, they have convinced many people that deviant behavior is just like physical illness and therefore is nothing to be ashamed of. The goal has been laudable, but the means have led to distortions which have created a great deal of confusion. What we really mean is that the individual is deviating in his behavior from norms that someone regards as valuable. In short, the individual has learned to solve his problems in living in ways which are quite deviant and unacceptable to many people. This is not to say, however, that he is "suffering" from some dread disease.

The limitations of disease-entity approaches to the field of psychopathology are many. However, only a few of the more salient points will be discussed here. First, the whole language system and structure of the approach seem to encourage a process of reification. The terms *symptoms* or *condition* or *disorders* all seem to lead to a view that considers behavior as an outgrowth of some insidious or malignant internal process. This, in turn, leads to a search for "cures"—very often chemical or biological in nature.

A related criticism is the fact that such approaches are basically typological in character. One is a schizophrenic, a manic, a psychopath, and so on. Leaving aside the consideration that too often such approaches seem to explain by categorizing, the fact remains that they almost always fail to incorporate a situational analysis in their attempts to account for behavior. Within social learning theory there is, of course, an emphasis on situational factors as prime determinants of behavior along with expectancies and need value. Thus, from a social learning theory point of view it does not appear useful to place extreme reliance upon the identification of internal characteristics or the assignment to class membership to the exclusion or de-emphasis of situational factors.

As Liverant (1963) pointed out several years ago, psychiatric models tend to invest the patient with the qualities of paranoia or some other disease, but then fail to provide any conceptual rules for predicting when paranoid behavior is likely to occur. That behavior is not static seems too obvious to mention; it has been documented repeatedly (Masling, 1960; Phares & Rotter, 1956; and many others).

Perhaps even more crucial, however, is the fact that disease-entity or psychiatric approaches have yet to demonstrate satisfactory reliability or validity. As summarized elsewhere (Phares, 1967), psychiatric categories suffer from at least three difficulties: (1) people within the same diagnostic category are notoriously dissimilar from one another; (2) psychiatrists have never been able to agree among themselves as to who belongs in which category; and (3) categorization of patients has very little to do with their ultimate treatment or case disposition.

To briefly summarize a social learning theory orientation in the light of the previous discussion we might say the following. We view abnormal or maladjusted behavior as learned techniques for achieving gratifications or minimizing punishments. It is not necessary to invoke notions of disease to account for such phenomena. Nor is it necessary to dissolve some internal pathology in order to effect more desirable behavioral outcomes. What others might regard as symptoms, we regard as learned attempts to solve problems in living, and these solutions or behaviors are subject to the same laws of acquisition, modification, and extinction as any other behavior. Long overdue is a *rapprochement* between the fields of psychopathology and learning so that we come to understand that what is relevant to human learning generally is also relevant to psychopathology.

Implicit in the foregoing is the relegation of such dichotomies as normal-abnormal or neurotic-psychotic to a status as low-level descriptive terms which have no explanatory power. Although many people accept this, as one uses the terms they very often become reified and assume more significant proportions than they otherwise should. From a social learning vantage point, there is no necessity for invoking different levels of explanation to account for so-called neurotic and psychotic reactions. Neurotic behaviors simply represent learned ways of behaving with respect to specific rewards and/or punishments. Although psychotic reactions are perhaps more difficult to analyze or understand because of their extremity, there appears little reason as yet to rule out social learning as an explanatory basis. Extremity of reaction should not compel one to seek out disease processes as an explanation. Naturally, there are a number of "organic" psychoses that do not lend themselves to a psychological conceptualization. All theories, however, be they medical, psychological, or otherwise, have a range of convenience. To accept the fact that learning theory cannot account for Huntington's chorea is not to regard that theory as meaningless in general.

Furthermore, acceptance of a social learning theory approach to psychotic behavior is not to assert that genetic, physiological, or biochemical studies of psychopathological behavior should be abandoned. We very much need studies to determine the genetic antecedents and physiological and biochemical correlates of behavior. It does not appear fruitful, however, to regard functional psychoses or neuroses as disease entities. This would seem to represent the reification of learning processes into disease entities and the acceptance of a classificatory scheme that has little demonstrated reliability or validity.

DEVIANT BEHAVIOR

At this point we should reiterate that deviant behaviors require no special principles apart from those relevant for social behavior generally. Basically, it is behavior that is considered undesirable from the standpoint of a given set of norms or values. Furthermore, it is behavior that has been learned and is thus maintained because the individual has a relatively high expectancy that such behavior will lead to a reinforcement of value (or avoid or reduce some potential punishment). Finally, the behaviors in question are essentially social behaviors in the sense that they have been learned in a social context with reference to goals that have acquired value because of their relation to people.

Avoidant Behavior, Need Value, and Freedom of Movement

When an individual places a high value on a particular need area and at the same time has low expectancies that more desirable behavior will lead to satisfactions in that area, he will typically engage in avoidant behaviors. In most of these instances, failure to be rewarded in a strong need area is perceived as punishing. Thus, whether we are talking about a simple expectation for punishment or the failure to receive rewards that one values highly, the outcome is the same—a very unpleasant affective state which the individual will attempt to avoid. Viewed in this manner, much of the behavior that is typically described in textbooks on abnormal psychology would be construed from a social learning theory point of view as avoidant behavior.

In short, when an individual expects punishment he will typically engage in avoidant behaviors. Likewise, when he does not expect to achieve important reinforcements, he will usually adopt defensive behaviors whose aim is to minimize the punishment associated with such a failure. Perhaps some examples of this general notion will be useful at this point.

If a college student places a high value on doing well in college (receiving A's and B's, being well regarded by his professors, being looked up to by his peers for his academic achievements) and yet has low expectancies (freedom of movement) that he will achieve these reinforcements, a state of affairs exists that encourages the utilization of avoidant behaviors. In other contexts they might be regarded as symptoms, neurotic reactions, and so on. Let us assume that for a variety of reasons this student has come to value academic reinforcements (perhaps because of the association of parental pleasure). At the same time, let us agree that because of mediocre grades in high school the student has come to expect failure in the academic area, or perhaps because of family interaction patterns he is convinced that he is not as bright as his brother. At any rate, he does not expect to succeed. However, to fail is to engender a very unpleasant feeling state. Therefore, he will do things calculated to avoid this feeling of failure and the ensuing negative affective state.

At this point it would seem logical to argue that he should study harder or otherwise attempt to improve his grades. The need potential relative to a variety of study behaviors is not very high, however, because he does not expect that they will lead to gratification (attainment of good grades). More probable, then, are a wide variety of potentially avoidant behaviors. He may miss examinations because of some hypothetical illness. He may feverishly engage in fraternity activities so that he will have an excuse for not doing well. He may come to regard his professors as incompetent and thus provide himself with a rationalization. The important element in all these behaviors is, however, that they are avoidant in character. Each of them enables him to avoid or minimize in some manner the unpleasantness that accompanies failure.

Another example might involve the love and affection or sexual need area. A girl who is convinced that she is not attractive or sexually acceptable is essentially stating a low freedom of movement in that need area. Her expectations are low that she can achieve gratifications in that area. Of course, if for some set of reasons she places a very low value on such gratifications, there is no particular problem. This illustrates the point that we are really talking about a discrepancy between need value and freedom of movement. This point will be elaborated later. The girl in question, however, will very likely adopt a variety of avoidant behaviors to counteract the negative feelings associated with failure to attain love and affection gratifications. She may simply avoid all situations where heterosexual reinforcements occur. Thus she avoids failure (but at the same time avoids potential success as well). She may learn to devote all her attention and energies to other goals. To the extent that such behavior is reinforced by its success in neutralizing the negative feelings, then such behaviors will occur again with greater frequency.

In short, the vast array of so-called neurotic behaviors so vividly described in most texts is basically a set of avoidant behaviors. These behaviors have been learned as a way of handling the discrepancy between need value and freedom of movement. Whether we are talking about obsessive behaviors, hysterical behaviors, phobic reactions, and so on, they all have in common the fact that they represent attempts to avoid punishment. The obsessive individual may have constant intrusions of aggressive thoughts, but such behavior does serve the function of keeping him away from potentially more threatening situations where he might actually harm someone. The mother who fears doing harm to her child may be extra scrupulous in her behavior relative to that child. The hysteric may develop a leg cramp before the annual office picnic so he won't have to play softball and thus humiliate himself before his peers. The phobic may keep a wide distance between himself and guns so as to avoid the possibility of satisfying an aggressive urge and thereby ultimately punishing himself. In every case, the behavior in question is utilized because the person has the expectancy that by so doing he will avoid reinforcements which he regards as punishing. To the extent that such behaviors work, they are self-perpetuating.

It is certainly true that many avoidant behaviors are directly observable. The individual physically avoids certain objects, people, places, or situations. In other cases, however, the avoidance is more cognitive in nature. For example, the individual may avoid certain thoughts, ideas, or images. In still other instances, people engage in fantasy or other "irreal" behaviors in an attempt to obtain satisfaction on a symbolic basis. Even here, however, such behavior may be construed as avoidant inasmuch as it attempts to substitute for more direct and thus more "dangerous" activities. In short, a host of behaviors qualify as avoidant. They range from the so-called defense mechanisms of reaction formation, projection, rationalization, repression, and so on, to phobic behaviors, neurasthenic reactions, fantasy, and so on.

The key to understanding the function of such behavior is to begin by determining what reinforcements the individual regards as important and valuable. In brief, what are the need areas which are valuable to him? This, of course, is no easy task and requires a great deal of what is commonly called clinical sensitivity. Indeed, we might digress for a moment here and point out that historically, perhaps one of the attractions of psychoanalytic theory has been that it seemed somehow to be more congenial to those who were clinically or sensitively inclined. The system, the language, and the emphasis on the dark, inaccessible aspects of the personality seemed to lend themselves to those who wished to make use of their sensitivity. It seems fair to point out, however, that approaches which place importance on the determination of needs and expectancies along with an analysis of the situational determinants of behavior require just as much clinical sensitivity. It is no easy task to sort out the verbalizations and behaviors of a patient to determine, for example, that what she desires is a career rather than a home and children; a nonchallenging job rather than one fraught with pressures; an illicit sexual relationship rather than spinsterhood. It would not appear that an acceptance of the importance of learning requires that one abdicates his clinical sensitivity.

Conflict

In many instances, a determination of the individual's needs will lead to the discovery that several of these high-value needs are incompatible. For example, the individual values sexual reinforcements but also places a high value on parental reinforcements. To achieve one is perceived by the person as negating the other. A further example is the male who places a great deal of value on dependency satisfactions but also has the need to be reinforced for his masculinity. To the extent that one need area is stronger than the other, the avoidant behavior will orient itself around the weaker need area. Thus, if the male who wishes both dependency and masculine reinforcements possesses a need for masculinity which is stronger than his dependency urges, then he will attempt to engage in behaviors to assert his masculinity (particularly since to pursue dependency rewards is to engender negative reinforcements such as loss of self-esteem). Obviously, the closer the needs are in their value, the greater the conflict. If there is a wide value disparity between the two need areas, then little avoidant behavior would be expected. As is noted elsewhere in this book, one of the goals of psychotherapy may then be construed either to demonstrate to the patient that, in fact, these goals are not incompatible or else attempt to increase the value-disparity between need areas.

On a cultural basis we would expect that reinforcements associated with certain areas would more frequently conflict with other needs. For example, although there has been a general relaxation in the culture in the degree to which individuals may seek sexual rewards, this is still an area that tends to bring the individual into conflict with other goals. These other goals are, of course, acceptance by parents, morality considerations, and so on. Aggression and hostility are other instances of a similar situation.

Failure to Develop Competency

In very nearly all the cases we have been discussing, the avoidant behavior ultimately results in the failure to develop competency. That is, such avoidance typically creates further deviant behavior because of its tendency to preclude more constructive activities. The result is a vicious cycle which often spirals the individual into more difficulty and interferes with adjustive techniques. As noted before, the person who fears rejection may increasingly turn to fantasy as a substitute solution. Here, his expectations for gratification are high and the reinforcements inevitable. To the extent, therefore, that such behavior is reinforced, it tends to occur again and again. As a result, the individual will make fewer and fewer attempts to achieve real-life gratifications through social interaction. Such a state of affairs increases the probability that any attempts he could make will be unsatisfactory. In short, effective learning is impossible. As he turns more and more to fantasy, the likelihood also increases that his thinking may become rather idiosyncratic—there is little possibility that his thought processes will be conditioned through interactions with others. Such a situation can quite obviously lead to extreme deviancy or what is often described as psychotic reactions. In this case, one can see that what began as avoidant behavior leads to the failure to develop a repertory of potentially adjustive behaviors that could be a way out of the individual's problems.

It appears clear that although the avoidant behavior may be temporarily successful in warding off negative reinforcement, it typically leads ultimately to negative reinforcements. For example, an individual may avoid going to a party because he has a low expectancy that he will behave in such a way as to achieve social rewards. Indeed, he may expect to make a fool of himself, to be rejected, or a number of other negative outcomes. To avoid such pain, he does not go to the party. Temporarily, this strategy may be successful—the avoidance of negative reinforcement is rewarding. However, later he may be asked why he did not come or else he notes that others tend to ignore him, and so on. Thus, the long-term consequences of his avoidant behaviors are self-defeating. In an essentially similar analysis Mowrer (1948) explicated the neurotic paradox (why do neurotics continually engage in self-defeating behavior when the outcomes are inevitably negative?) which had provided so many difficulties for Freud. Thus, it would seem that immediate rewards are often more effective than delayed punishments.

In his discussion of maladjustment and social learning theory, Katkovsky (1968) analyzes the role of failure to learn or the absence of adjusted behaviors. As he points out, not all maladjusted behavior may be thought of as simply avoidant or the product of a discrepancy between freedom of movement and need value. Or, put another way, it is often the absence of adjusted behaviors that leads us to describe someone as maladjusted. As noted elsewhere in the section dealing with psychotherapy, it is probably safe to assert that one of the difficulties that psychoanalysis has faced is its tendency to restrict analysis to the patient's maladaptive behaviors. As a result of the failure to deal with the absence of adjustive behavior, the patient has nothing with which to replace the maladaptive behavior and the process of psychotherapy is unduly prolonged in too many instances.

It should be apparent that deviant behavior considered as being avoidant or the consequence of distortion is not necessarily incompatible with maladjustment considered as the failure to respond in an adjusted fashion. There is very often an intimate relation. For example, as we indicated earlier, the individual who utilizes excessive avoidant behavior very often fails to learn the very adjustive behavior that society values highly. The school-phobic child is exhibiting avoidant behavior but is, at the same time, failing to learn arithmetic, reading, and so on. This will eventually lead to other failures. Likewise, the individual with an excessive achievement need may so distort reality or concentrate upon such a narrow range of activities that he fails to learn a whole host of social responses that the culture expects of the individual.

Beyond such preceding bases for the failure to learn adjustive techniques, it is sometimes the case that the individual belongs to a subculture that does not promote or encourage the learning of behaviors which the larger culture values or requires. To the extent that the individual subsequently comes into prolonged contact with the larger culture, he may run into severe difficulties with that culture. One is reminded of the instances that inevitably occur during the drafting of large numbers of men for the army. Very frequently many of these individuals have failed to learn skills or behaviors because they come from areas of the country or subgroups whose values are quite different from the culture at large. A number of such individuals experience severe difficulties in the service and are considered maladjusted or at least unfit for service.

In other cases, physical barriers in the life space of the individual may block appropriate learning. For example, someone with severe physical illnesses as a child may have never been able to learn the multitude of things required for success in our society. Failure of parents to permit adequate exploratory or independence behaviors may have much the same effect. To the extent that much of learning may be based on imitation or modeling (Bandura & Walters, 1963), absence from the home of suitable role models could also account for deficiencies in learning.

Unfortunately, such behavioral or learning voids do not remain such. Rather, the holes in the individual's learning-behavior repertory often become filled with behaviors that society does not sanction and thus the failure-to-learn problem is only compounded.

Minimal Goals

Any discussion of needs would be incomplete without reference to minimal goal level. As noted elsewhere in this book, minimal goal refers to the lowest goal in a reinforcement hierarchy that is perceived by the individual as reinforcing. Thus, for some an income of $5000 is reinforcing —for others, only a minimum of $10,000 per year is perceived as rewarding and satisfying. High minimal goals, naturally, tend to be associated with maladjustment and unhappiness. It generally follows that the higher a person's minimal goal, the less probable is the attainment of that goal. Therefore, parents who manage to inculcate excessively high goals in their children are increasing the likelihood that that child will encounter despair. Obviously, however, if the individual is an exceptionally capable person, he may be successful in achieving the goals and will not, therefore, run into difficulty.

On the other side of the coin, it is true that many people have what others in the culture might regard as very low minimal goals. This can lead to a lack of understanding and a tendency to view such people as showing deviant behavior. It may be deviant in the statistical sense of the term but does not necessarily arise out of need-value–expectancy disparities.

Distortion and the Failure To Discriminate

At this point it may be useful to emphasize another potential outcome of high need value. For a variety of reasons (which only a careful analysis of the learning history will reveal) an individual may come to place an uncommonly high value on a given set of goals or reinforcements. This may lead him to distort reality or fail to discriminate among social situations to such an extent that his behavior becomes patently inappropriate to the situation. For example, the individual who has exorbitant needs for love and affection may construe a whole variety of situations as being occasions for the attainment of such goals. He will then behave in a manner that many other people find quite unusual or unsatisfactory. He may, for example, give expensive gifts to casual acquaintances; he may misinterpret the behavior of others and repel them, in turn, by his own love and affection overtures. Or, someone with excessive achievement needs may become incensed when he loses in an unimportant bridge game. Every occasion becomes an arena for the attainment of achievement reinforcements. In short, very strong needs may tend to prevent the individual from discriminating among situations. Thus, he fails to judge accurately the impact of his behavior on others and may be quite shocked or puzzled by the negative reinforcements he receives from others. It is a situation where one need preempts the field and the consequent distortions of reality ultimately lead to a wide variety of negative consequences. It should be noted, of course, that very often such inappropriate behavior leads to negative reactions from others which, in turn, tends to lower the individual's expectancies that he will be able to achieve the rewards he seeks. This situation then becomes related to the condition of a discrepancy between need value and freedom of movement.

Anxiety

One of the most frequently encountered terms in the psychological literature is *anxiety*. It has become such an integral part of the psychological language that when the term is omitted in a theoretical discussion it almost appears as if a piece of reality has been left out. Sarbin (1968), in a recent paper, has provided a brief historical recapitulation of the term and concludes with a description of anxiety as the "reification of a metaphor." Certainly anxiety has been a highly ubiquitous term. In many cases it is regarded as a response or set of responses (often physiological in character). In other cases it may be referred to as a stimulus or perhaps an affective state. Or it may assume the general status of an intervening variable and be utilized as an explanatory concept. Although a great lack of precision seems to characterize the use of the term, anxiety has come to occupy a place of centrality in both personality theory and clinical practice.

What is often forgotten, however, is that systems of personality (and the individual conceptualizations or terms that go to make up those systems) are simply convenient methods of abstracting reality for the purposes of prediction and understanding. Specifically, anxiety has no particular reality. It is just a way of characterizing reality. Therefore, no theory, personality or otherwise, is under any obligation to include such a concept. If one theory utilizes the term and does a good job of handling behavior while another theory which is otherwise rather similar does not utilize the concept and does a poor job of predicting behavior, one might conclude that the latter theory would have been better off with the concept. Nonetheless, it is important to recognize the difference between reality and terms which are constructed to predict behavior.

Social learning theory is one such theory which eschews the use of an anxiety construct. This is not to say, however, that social learning theory does not attempt to account for behaviors described by others as anxious or motivated by anxiety. Any personality theory would have to deal with such behaviors or be accused of excessive narrowness. Dealing with such behavior does not, however, require that one use the term *anxiety*. Social learning theory is a psychological theory while the typical anxiety conceptualization generally implies a physiological level of analysis. In place of anxiety, the theory substitutes either low expectancy for success or high expectancy for failure. Rotter (1954) discusses this substitution, while recent papers by Rychlak and Lerner (1965) and Phares (1968b) also empirically illustrate this usage. On the other hand, the reaction of the individual to body cues following positive and negative reinforcement is an area in which current work is proceeding.

To briefly illustrate the point, to say that someone is anxious is to suggest that he has a high expectancy for punishment or else a low expectancy for success relative to a reinforcement of value. Thus, if I expect to be attacked while walking through a park at night I will be anxious. If I am anxious about passing an examination, then my expectancy for success is not as high as it might be. In effect, the higher the expectancy for punishment, the greater the emission of what are usually designated as anxiety behaviors. Likewise, if a person shows a marked inability to concentrate, worries a great deal, or trembles while speaking before a group, he would be said to be manifesting a low expectancy for success (or contrariwise, a high expectancy for punishment). These behaviors would be accounted for by expectancy constructs. Similarly, should we wish to measure expectancy for punishment, we might well inquire about the frequency with which such behaviors occur and use them as referents for such expectancies.

For relatively restricted predictive situations or those involving a specific reinforcement, the construct of expectancy would be used. In broader predictive situations the freedom of movement construct would be employed. In such a case, it would be said that the individual's mean expectancy (freedom of movement) for success in achieving a group of functionally related reinforcements is low. In the latter instance, one committed to a drive-reduction point of view might say that the individual carries with him a chronic state of high drive (manifest anxiety, for example). Again, from a social learning theory point of view, we would assert that the individual's freedom of movement across a variety of need areas is low. Where others would describe a person as having chronic test anxiety, we would describe him as being one whose mean expectancy for attaining success in the valued need area of academic achievement is low.

Several studies have pursued the implications of this point of view. Rychlak and Eacker (1962) have suggested that manifestly anxious Ss show less stable generalized expectancies than low-anxious Ss. Rychlak and Lerner (1965) report data to support their contention that so-called anxious Ss are particularly influenced by the effects of recent successes and failures. Phares (1966) demonstrated that prior to performance on the first trial of a task, anxious Ss state significantly lower expectancies for task success than do nonanxious Ss. This finding was replicated in a further study (Phares, 1968b). The latter two studies, of course, suggest the point that the conceptualizations of low expectancy for success and of anxiety (manifest anxiety or test anxiety) are probably correlated descriptions of the same event.

This view which equates so-called anxiety with expectancies is assumed to play an important role in maladjusted behavior. The point was noted before that much of maladjusted behavior involves avoidance. The function of avoidance is to handle those situations that involve a high expectancy for punishment or a low expectancy for success. In short, most of the usually described syndromes of neurosis may be characterized as being composed of avoidance behaviors which have been adopted to meet expected punishment. Of course, as noted earlier, not all forms of maladjusted or deviant behavior may be construed in avoidance terms. Thus, in some instances deviant behavior comes about because the individual has not learned the more socially approved means of attaining goal satisfaction. In such instances, the anxiety-expectancy point of view would not apply. Rather, the individual's behavioral repertoire simply does not contain the appropriate behaviors. In still other cases the strength of one's need may be such that situations are distorted and the resultant behavior cannot be characterized in avoidance terms.

In effect, then, it is not necessary to assume that low expectancies for success or high expectancies for punishment underlie every case of deviant or pathological behavior. They may do so with great frequency, but to lump all such behaviors into the avoidance category is to frequently ignore the crucial role that lack of learning plays in many maladjusted reactions.

Many theories that rely heavily on drive level (anxiety) seem to imply that once the individual's anxiety is reduced, then his difficulties will be solved. Put in expectancy terms, this means that when the individual no longer expects to receive punishment in certain situations, then his problem is finished. These views seem to assume that the "correct" responses are in the person's repertory and will pop out once the inhibitory restrictions of high anxiety or expectancies for punishment are removed. Such a view is very often suggested in highly verbal or analytical forms of psychotherapy. Whether we are talking about the delinquent who may clearly have learned socially undesirable ways of responding or a typical neurotic who shows a variety of avoidance techniques, it is still true that lack of learning plays an important role. Although it is certainly true that "anxiety-reduction" or lowered expectancy for punishment can pave the way for new learning, many brands of therapy do not appear to systematically attempt to instigate new learning in patients.

Repression
Since the advent of Freud the concept of repression has played a key role in nearly every theory or exposition of psychopathological behavior. Unquestionably, this concept has enabled us to understand such phenomena in a way that was not possible before. As with many concepts, however, there are limitations and heavy reliance leads to difficulties. Therefore, we shall attempt to retain the baby and not the bath; or put another way, the insights that have come about as a function of the concept are important and should be used in any attempt to provide a viable alternative. Most clearly, however, the concept of the unconscious as a mind entity or the reified storehouse of instinctual urges and banished impulses must be rejected.

In the final analysis, evidence that an individual is repressing comes down to the point that he cannot verbalize the determinants of his behavior in the way that an observer or psychologist can. For example, if a patient repeatedly describes his mother as beautiful, the object of many men's attentions, and the patient also has a penchant for picking up women in bars who resemble his mother, we may say that the patient is motivated by sexual urges toward his mother. The fact that the patient denies this or else cannot, even under fairly direct prodding by the therapist, verbalize the relation between his behavior and his sexual feelings toward his mother leads the therapist to assert that the patient is exhibiting repression. As Maher (1966) points out, the validity of the observer's hypotheses about behavior is determined by the accuracy with which they predict behavior. Just because the patient attributes his behavior to a stressful job while the psychologist attributes it to repressed oedipal strivings does not automatically confer more validity upon the latter hypothesis than the former one. Indeed, even if the patient finally agrees with the therapist this may only mean that the therapist is very persuasive.

It seems clear, then, that operationally the definition of repression involves a disagreement between the individual and an expert observer as regards the determinants of that individual's behavior. When this happens, the observer tends to look to the unconscious and, indeed, usually sets about getting the material conscious again. It would seem, however, that such failure to verbalize can come about for several reasons, none of which has much to do with an entitized unconscious.

Maher (1966) cites three possible antecedent learning conditions which could lead to this inability to verbalize. First, considerable evidence suggests that learning can occur in infants before they are able to verbalize or be particularly aware of much of anything. It is probable that when learning occurs before language it will remain inaccessible to verbalization. Second, there are many instances cited in the experimental literature wherein learning occurs in adults without their being able to verbalize it. Ss can be "conditioned" to emit a higher rate of pronouns, for example, without being able to verbalize the relation between their behavior and the concomitant rewards. Third, a variety of responses, such as pupillary or GSR, can be conditioned to appropriate stimuli without Ss' being aware that the response is occurring. Briefly, when people exhibit behaviors and yet cannot verbalize the conditions under which they were learned or are not aware of a variety of aspects of their behavior, there does not appear to be any requirement that we automatically ascribe this to the process of repression or assert that the person was once aware of these things.

If we discard the classical notions of repression, then what do we substitute in their place? The concepts of repression and the unconscious have so permeated our language that lack of such concepts seems to create an intolerable void. There seem to be several possibilities that can effectively account for phenomena without recourse to concepts of repression or the unconscious.

Dollard and Miller (1950) a number of years ago discussed "stopping thinking" as a response. Thus, one might argue that when certain thoughts or verbalizations lead to an expectancy for punishment, then such thoughts or verbalizations will occur with lessened frequency. For example, if the child has been repeatedly taught that verbalizing hatred is bad (and has been punished for saying such things), it is not unusual to expect that the child will eventually cease such verbalizations. Also, through generalization, possibly, thoughts will come to function in pretty much the same fashion as overt verbalizations. That is, when the expectancy develops that thoughts or verbalizations will lead to punishment (either direct or engendered by self), then appropriate behavior will develop to avoid such thoughts and/or verbalizations. Also, to the extent that thoughts have replaced verbalizations prior to action, as is the case with most adults, it is not unreasonable to conclude that such thoughts can serve as conditioned stimuli to fear in much the same manner as external stimuli.

At any rate, in such situations the most probable behavior that will occur is either behavior calculated to stop the thought (so-called stopping thinking) or behaviors likely to interfere with the thoughts (substitution of other thoughts or activities). In the latter event, the possibilities are enormous—ranging from projection, rationalization, and so on, to obsessions, compulsions, hypochondriacal behaviors, and so on.

An interesting analysis of the role of the unconscious and repression is presented by Phillips (1956). He begins by providing an example of the accident-prone individual. If an individual is known to be accident prone (repeatedly has accidents) and on a given day falls down a stairway and breaks an arm, the classical interpretation is that he had an unconscious need to punish himself. Is such an explanation necessary, however? If, for example, the individual has an excessively strong achievement need, it could be that he was so taken with thoughts of how to impress his employer or to make his peers think highly of him that he simply did not notice the short step. In brief, we might analyze this behavior by stating that the value of the need preempted the field so that his attention was focused on the wrong set of cues. Phillip's argument is that perceptually present events can be utilized to account for the behavior rather than dark, inaccessible forces of the unconscious.

The use of this latter example along with the previous discussion of stopping thinking or the substitution of thoughts and actions that will avoid unpleasant thoughts is consistent with the previous analysis of maladjusted behavior. That is, just as much maladjusted behavior may be thought of as avoidant or as being a function of an overly strong need (or both), so too can a similar framework be applied to what is more commonly called repression. Furthermore, the absence of learned adjustive behaviors can also be shown to correspond to those cases of "repression" where the inability to verbalize relations seems less a matter of forgetting than of the failure of the individual's environment to teach him to think or describe his environment in ways that most of us accept.

To be more specific, many people are described as maladjusted because they engage in avoidant behaviors (fantasy, obsessions, denial, hysteria, and so on). Falling into this category would be those instances of repression explained in social learning theory terms as stopping thinking or the substitution of behaviors or thoughts likely to avoid the unpleasantness associated with particular thoughts or ideas. A second aspect of maladjustment involved behaviors that were perhaps less avoidant than they were a function of an overly strong need. Thus, the individual with excessive sexual needs may behave in a sexual manner in situations that the culture generally does not consider to be sexual in nature. The result is that people regard the individual as behaving quite peculiarly. In a similar category would be those instances of so-called repression when the individual's thoughts and verbalizations are less avoidant than they are assertive in the light of a particularly strong need. Thus, the individual with excessive achievement needs cannot accept the therapist's interpretation of his behavior in terms of dependency needs because of what he is asserting about himself relative to his achievement needs. In other cases, perhaps there is a mixture of the two categories. In still other instances, however, the failure of the individual to behave acceptably may not be a function of avoidance or strength of need but essentially due to the fact that he has never learned the appropriate responses. Likewise, most therapists have encountered patients whose mode of thought and verbalization turned out to have little of an avoidant character and did not reflect a particularly strong need. Rather, the patient's environment simply did not teach him to think or verbalize in ways common to most people in our culture.

In the case of many types of functionally described amnesias we have a situation that seems to cry out for the utilization of a repression concept or an appeal to the unconscious. However, such instances seem related both to what we have called avoidant and assertive. That the avoidance and/or assertion is rather more massive or pervasive in nature should not automatically require that we give up our explanation couched in learning terms. Although amnesias may be extreme, they can be understood in terms both of what the individual is attempting to avoid and what he is accomplishing in the light of a very strong need.

Perhaps we might conclude this discussion with a quotation which seems highly congruent with many of the things we have been saying.

> From our discussion of forgetting, of learning without awareness, and of the avoidance of thinking about feared topics, we can see that much human behavior is carried out under conditions in which the person is not able to verbalize readily about the determinants of his own actions. He may never have known what they are because he acquired them under conditions in which verbalization was at a minimum. He may at one time have been able to verbalize them, but both the verbalization and the covert thinking about them have become an occasion for avoidance behavior. When the determinants seem clear to an observer, it is tempting to conclude that the subject "really knows" what they are but has actively "buried" his knowledge of them in some remote recess of his being. Metaphorical thinking of this kind is valuable for dramatic or literary purposes but has no place in science. Responses which a person is unable to make do not have a covert existence somewhere else. When a memory is "repressed," what we mean is that the stimuli which we are presenting in an attempt to elicit recall have failed to do so; it also implies that we believe that some configurations of stimuli could elicit it. When we find the effective conditions for recall, it is unnecessary for us to conclude triumphantly that the memory was there all the time. . . . (Maher, 1966, p. 59).

Neurosis versus Psychosis

There is little place in social learning theory for this dichotomy. To use it implies acceptance of a classification scheme which has essentially been demonstrated to be unreliable and of little validity. The two terms are very difficult to define. In general, they are differentially applied on the basis of severity of behavior (degree of departure from culturally valued behavior norms), number of areas of the personality affected, and the extent of personal and social danger. Although extremely deviant or bizarre behavior is readily agreed upon as psychotic, what constitutes neurotic behavior is seriously open to disagreement and the differences between psychotic and neurotic behavior are difficult to chart. Furthermore, in the absence of a great deal of additional information about the individual, such terms have very few implications for treatment except in the most general sense. As a dichotomy, then, it shows little more functionality than such terms as tall versus short or thin versus fat. Although containing some information, the classification does not have important implications as regards treatment, antecedents, and so on.

Alternative classifications that would be much more functional might include such things as the following: (1) ease with which psychotherapists may establish contact with the patient or develop reinforcement value for him; (2) degree of the dependency relation likely to develop between clinician and patient; (3) duration of the undesirable behavior (behavior with a longer reinforcement history would presumably be more difficult to modify than behaviors of a more reactive nature). As noted earlier, classifications could also be oriented around needs as they relate to deviant behavior. As Rotter (1954) points out, the most desirable classification scheme is something that will have to be determined empirically. It will also have to be determined on the basis of one's purposes. Certainly it is improbable that a single scheme, such as the Kraepelinian one, will turn out to be useful for every purpose. Just as there is no omnibus test in clinical psychology, there is no omnibus classification scheme either.

Another issue we should comment upon involves the continuity-discontinuity controversy. Continuity implies that there is a continuum of severity of deviant behavior from normal to neurotic to psychotic. Discontinuity implies that neurosis and psychosis are not continuous but, rather, are qualitatively different from each other. The basic issues have been discussed in more detail elsewhere (Buss, 1966; Maher, 1966) and will not be repeated here. However, it does appear that there is no definitive answer to the question as yet. Indeed, the whole question may be phrased in too general terms to permit a reasonable answer. For example, continuity-discontinuity could refer to the learning process, in which case we could say that neurosis and psychosis are continuous if the learning processes involved in each follow the same principles. Likewise, we might think of the continuity-discontinuity dichotomy in terms of treatment. In this case, continuity would exist if the principles of learning can be applied to both neurotics and psychotics with success. Finally, if biological differences are found to exist between those with a neurotic diagnosis as opposed to those with a psychotic one, then discontinuity would seem to apply. In short, the continuity-discontinuity question may be applied to a series of questions.

In general, the continuity position would be more consistent with social learning theory inasmuch as it assumes that both mildly and extensively deviant individuals behave on the basis of similar learning principles. Just as the obsessive patient has learned to use his thought processes as a way of avoiding greater punishment, so too has the seriously deviant person learned to stand mute in order to avoid human contact which he regards as punishing. In short, the extremity of certain behaviors should not blind us to the possibility that such behaviors may be accounted for on the basis of expectancies and need values, just as in the case of less deviant behaviors. Similarly, from a social learning theory standpoint, it appears possible to modify such extreme behavior by the application of learning principles that are equally relevant for the modification of mildly deviant behavior. It should be made clear, however, that such statements are offered solely as working hypotheses, since there is a lack of impressive evidence of this sort within social learning theory. It would appear, however, with the increased popularity of operant techniques and behavior therapy approaches it is becoming clear that there are ways to modify extremely deviant behavior other than the exclusive application of biological or chemical remedies. Likewise, just because it is possible to modify behavior chemically does not imply that this is the only way or even, in the long run, the most efficient way. At the present time it would appear that the greatest value that chemical and biological techniques have had is their ability to make patients amenable to the operation of new learning. Thus, nothing has been "cured," but the individual has been enabled to be reached so that learning theory can be applied.

In the final analysis it must be asserted that biological, chemical, or learning approaches to deviant behavior are simply alternative ways of approaching the same phenomenon. It may well be the case that ultimately one approach will have a range of convenience more appropriate to one area of deviant behavior than will another. Or, perhaps, ultimately a super theory will develop that will subsume both learning and biology.

As regards the question of genetics, a similar position would be adopted. Social learning theory does not incorporate genetic principles into its system. This leaves the theory with obvious difficulties in accounting for individual differences in very young children or infants, for example. It has serious difficulty in trying to account for certain behavioral clusters which are known to follow genetic lines. For example, certain forms of organic psychosis and mental retardation are known to occur only in those individuals who have had a close relative similarly affected. It should be pointed out, however, that specific behavior within such categories cannot be accounted for solely on the basis of inheritance. That is, even though the onset of the over-all behavioral pattern could be predicted from a genetic position, the specific behavior occurring within the pattern would have to be accounted for on the basis of learning-experiential factors.

Perhaps a quotation discussing both intelligence and schizophrenia would be useful here inasmuch as it seems to summarize our stance toward psychosis generally.

However, such notions have recently been undergoing considerable revision (Hunt, 1961; Liverant, 1960). Both Hunt and Liverant have marshaled evidence to show that ideas of fixed intelligence and predetermined development are outmoded ones. No characteristic occurs as a sole function of either heredity or environment. There is an interaction between the two. The occurrence of any specific characteristic is a function of genetic factors operating within a specific environmental milieu. Within any environment there are perhaps fixed potentials, but the net result is that in practice genetic potential becomes a function of all possible environmental variation, just as the limits of environmental influences are moderated by genetic potentials or limits. (Phares, 1967, p. 506).

Our earlier points concerning the re-examination of intelligence apply equally as well here. Just as intelligence is a function of genetics *and* one's encounters with an environment, so too may be the so-called schizophrenic syndromes. Genes may set limits, but the limits vary with every conceivable environmental eventuality. Thus, the most profitable course would seem to be the investigation of the various situational conditions which produce schizophrenic behavior. Unless the notion of an innate potential can also specify the conditions under which schizophrenia occurs (which it cannot now do), the genetic hypothesis does not appear very promising.

Also, like intelligence, schizophrenia is not a unitary phenomenon. Perhaps the major difficulty in pursuing the genetic hypothesis of schizophrenia is the tacit assumption that it is a unitary thing. Actually, as noted in our ,previous discussions, the category of schizophrenia subsumes a very heterogeneous group of people, so that it seems unlikely that one could reasonably talk about the inheritance of schizophrenia. (Phares, 1967, p. 507).

Another aspect of many analyses of psychotic behavior involves again the concept of anxiety. For example, Mednick (1958) argues that the peculiarities of schizophrenic thought may be handled as an instance of anxiety-drive reduction. The acutely schizophrenic individual is presumably in a state of heightened drive. This raises the generalization gradient so that more and more stimuli are now capable of engendering anxiety. More anxiety is then generated, and the next effect is a disruption of reality thinking through the intrusion of many irrelevant thoughts. We have, then, the patient's tendency to fixate on remote associations which are reinforced through anxiety reduction.

Besides the implications of the term *anxiety*, a major difficulty with this view from a social learning standpoint is its exclusive emphasis on drive level. Ignored is the point that people learn differing ways of handling their anxiety or high expectancies for punishment. Both a preschizophrenic and a preneurotic may experience a severe trauma. However, their mode of reaction (neurosis or psychosis) is predictable not so much from the standpoint of drive level but from their previous history of reinforcement and their modes of protecting themselves from punishment. The psychotic's reaction may be less a matter of drive level than the fact that his history of social isolation and lack of peer group monitoring of thought processes have disposed him toward highly idiosyncratic modes of thought. These peculiarities, in turn, lead to highly aberrant behaviors.

In short, prediction of adjustment behavior solely in terms of drive level ignores the importance of learning history. Even accepting the notion of drive level, it would appear that behavior occurs not only as a function of that drive level but also as a function of the expectancy that such a behavior will reduce the anxiety. These expectancies, of course, have been developed out of previous failures and successes in coping with threatening situations.

A recently emphasized classification in the realm of psychopathology is the process-reactive dichotomy (Herron, 1962). Process refers to the fact that some psychotics seem to develop their behavior patterns gradually over a long period of time—a relatively insidious process. On the other hand, others (the reactives) seem to develop their psychotic behavior rather suddenly and in the absence of any particularly malignant history. Although these two types of individuals do not differ particularly in terms of presenting behavior, they do show differences in their lives prior to the onset of the behavior. As Zigler and Phillips (1962) describe it, the process schizophrenic tends to display poor premorbid social adequacy, an insidious onset, no clear precipitating event, and poor prognosis. Reactives tend to show a relatively good premorbid level of adjustment, a sudden onset, a specific precipitating event, and a more favorable prognosis.

Such a system of classification is more congenial to a social learning theory approach for a variety of reasons. It removes classification from the realm of major reliance on present behavior and considers learned history of expectations for adjustive behavior. The built-in notion of social competency implies a closer examination of learning history. Also, such notions tend to de-emphasize the exclusive role of drive level by emphasizing notions of prior learning history.

Throughout the previous discussion the emphasis has been on behavior. Indeed, we have used a variety of adjectives, such as *deviant*, *maladjusted*, *avoidant*, and so on, preceding the word *behavior*. This procedure was adopted quite consciously. In short, the emphasis has been on behaviors rather than people. To operate differently is often to subtly adopt a categorical or psychiatric classification approach. Thus, although the following two sentences do not appear much different, they are actually quite disparate in terms of their implication:

1. He is engaging in paranoid behaviors.
2. He is suffering from paranoia (or paranoid state).

The first sentence, by implication, sets the stage for an inquiry into the conditions that led to the display or learning of the behaviors; the conditions in the environment that serve as cues for the behavior; the conditions that will moderate or extinguish the responses, and others. The second statement seems to imply that one should shift the search to internal states and characteristics with relative de-emphasis of situational factors. In the latter event, the net result is that much of the psychology of learning, perception, and so on, becomes somehow irrelevant to psychopathology. This we regard as unfortunate.

Indeed, the two previous sentences illustrate how much of an effect language can have in directing our thinking and ultimately our research investigations. Certainly such an analysis is consistent with some of the notions of Whorf (1956). In fact, it sounds almost ludicrous to say that an individual is suffering from avoidant behavior or even deviancy or maladjustment. To say that he is suffering from schizophrenia or paranoia, however, rolls easily off the tongue.

SOME EXAMPLES

The preceding sections have provided a general framework by which to approach psychopathological phenomena from a social learning point of view. In the pages that follow, an attempt will be made to describe some selected instances of deviant behavior. No pretense is made of being comprehensive. Rather, the hope is that by selecting a few examples of deviant behavior and describing them from a social learning viewpoint, some of the previous discussions can be highlighted. First, however, a few general comments should be made.

In many cases the learning history of the individual is clear enough so that both the function of avoidant behaviors and their origin is quite clear. In many other cases, however, the origins are very obscure, and only with a great deal of painstaking investigation is the connection between avoidant behavior and the basic need apparent. In this connection, one is reminded of the example cited by Dollard and Miller (1950). They point out that someone observing the rather bizarre behavior of a rat in what is obviously a nonthreatening test chamber would be greatly puzzled. The rat's behavior makes no sense and is utterly inappropriate to the situation. However, had the same person been present during the rat's earlier learning history he would have observed that the rat was shocked whenever he was placed in a black test chamber. Naturally, the rat learned a variety of avoidance behaviors and also typically emitted many anxietylike behaviors. Subsequently, when placed in the test chamber without the shock, the rat behaved in the light of his expectations which were derived from past experience. He generalized, albeit erroneously, from the past. Indeed, viewed from the rat's vantage point, the behavior was quite appropriate. It seems that the parallel between this example and that of many instances of human avoidant behavior is not too difficult to accept.

It is very nearly impossible to chronicle all the possible reasons that might account for deviant or avoidant behavior. Granted, there are commonalities among people, but the similarity among several avoidant behaviors does not necessarily imply the same degree of similarity in learning history. This would appear to account in part for the fact that psychiatric classification schemes have been rather unsuccessful. That is, there has been a tendency to classify people into disease categories on the basis of the similarities in their overt behavior. Unfortunately, their so-called dynamics or histories do not show the same degree of similarity, and the beginning student is dismayed, for example, when two catatonics show such different backgrounds. In short, categorization of the patient on the basis of presenting behavior does not allow one to predict with any degree of confidence his learning history.

Although some now argue that knowledge of past learnings are unimportant in altering deviant behaviors, we would assert that such knowledge is invaluable. That is, to change expectancies or reinforcement values (or both), it is often necessary to know how these expectancies developed and what the connections are among reinforcements. We would not, however, go to the lengths embodied in psychoanalytic approaches that require enormous and tedious reconstruction of vast arrays of the individual's past. Our position would lie somewhere between the extremes of psychoanalysis on the one hand and ultrabehavioristic approaches on the other.

Furthermore, it is likely that the beginnings of many maladjustive behaviors are quite "accidental" or occur simply because human organisms have a potentially enormous repertory of behaviors. Once the behavior occurs, however, and is reinforced, it tends to occur again. Many times, of course, the individual's environment unwittingly or subtly encourages the avoidant behavior. Such encouragement is often very difficult to ferret out. Thus, parents often have no idea of the effects of their own behavior on the child. Indeed, it has only been too well documented that there is usually very little relation between parents' scores on a variety of personality indexes and the scores of their children. Briefly, the crucial thing is probably not what parents think or what scores they get on personality inventories. The crucial thing is how they *behave* in relation to their children.

Freud discussed the concept of "secondary gain" many years ago. It is certainly true that many forms of avoidant behavior bring the concern, attention, and sympathy of others. These can be powerful reinforcements that exert a strong influence on the maintenance of what may have simply started out as avoidant behaviors. Their ability to achieve reinforcements for the individual raises further the expectancy that such behaviors will work in the future.

Anxiety Reactions: *Example 1*

A 35-year-old insurance executive reports that for the past 2 months he has been experiencing intermittent panic reactions, nausea, insomnia, and a variety of other rather vague physical complaints. A complete medical work-up fails to reveal any somatic basis for these complaints. The patient himself is quite alarmed and despite the negative medical report feels that he has some dread and yet subtle disease. He can provide no psychological explanation and reports that everything in his life is going quite well. With a great deal of reluctance, he finally accepts his physician's recommendation and visits a psychiatrist. With the material elicited during his therapy contacts it was possible to construe his problem in the following terms.

For many years the patient had been motivated by strong needs for achievement and recognition. His father had been quite prominent in the community and his mother had made it clear in abundant ways during his childhood that great things were expected of the patient.

Nonetheless, the patient always harbored strong doubts about his capabilities. In short, his expectancies for the achievement of success and recognition were not commensurate with the strength of these needs. In most instances, however, during childhood, high school, and college he operated in fairly structured situations and was able to perform quite well. Prior to examinations in both high school and college he would become quite anxious. In other words, the cues in the examination situations were so overwhelming that the discrepancy between expectancy for success and the strength of his recognition needs generated a great deal of subjectively felt distress. By virtue of diligent preparation, however, he was able to do well. Indeed, at the time this anxiety did not alarm him, since he "explained" it to himself as purely situationally determined and something that everybody experienced.

After college he joined the insurance firm and through hard work, following orders, and just doing his job, he was steadily promoted. During this period he acquired a wife and two children and all the usual responsibities inherent in middle-class America.

It was only after his promotion to the executive position that massive anxiety reactions occurred. Suddenly he was placed in an unstructured position—he was no longer following orders; he had to establish policy, develop original ideas, and so on. His expectancies were quite low that he could achieve success in such a situation. Through generalization, he construed the present situation where both his employers and family expected great things from him as being very similar to those situations early in life where his parents expected him to achieve in the image of his father. Now he was expected to achieve in the image of an executive.

Placed in this situation he clearly expected to encounter failure. Added to this situation was the fact that failure would now disrupt the lives of his wife and children also. Such, then, was the onset of his anxiety attacks.

Example 2

An 18-year-old college freshman reports to the Student Health Service shortly after the beginning of his first semester on campus. He is in an acute panic and requires strong sedatives to put him to sleep. The following day he is still quite upset, paces the floor, and cannot eat. After several days he calms down and is able to return to his classes. Continuing sessions at the Health Service reveal the following.

The source of his anxiety behaviors resided in strong homosexual feelings toward his roommate. Since all of his learning experiences had taught him to strongly reject such feelings, his panic was quite understandable. He was motivated by two highly conflicting needs: the need to achieve homosexual gratifications on the one hand and the need to maintain a heterosexual view of himself as his culture and family had taught.

During adolescence the student was not aware of any homosexual inclinations and thus did not seek such gratifications. Once, however, during a Boy Scout camping venture his tentmate made some overtures and they engaged in mutual masturbation. This experience was both pleasurable and also the occasion for considerable guilt. The latter was so strong, in fact, that he learned to stop thinking about the episode completely. That, in conjunction with participating in a variety of masculine activities with great gusto, enabled him to completely "forget" the event.

As he entered college, however, he was placed in a dormitory room with another student who bore a striking physical resemblance to his Boy Scout friend of some years before. Both this and the fact that they occupied a small room (similar to the intimacy of the tent) combined to create a situation highly reminiscent of the previous one. Not only was the expectancy strong that illicit behaviors would occur and thus lead to negative reinforcement through guilt, but through generalization it was almost as if he were reliving the previous experience with the accompanying anxiety.

Again, the student was unable to verbalize his homosexual urges and thus could provide no explanation for his panic.

So-called anxiety responses are highly pervasive throughout the field of psychopathology. Most individuals, whether showing predominantly hysterical, phobic, or compulsive features also display frequent instances of marked anxiety. In other cases, anxiety appears to be the major clinical feature. The two previous examples are instances of the latter and highlight a number of points relevant to a social learning analysis of anxiety reactions.

First, as White (1956) has commented, anxiety reactions often occur before the individual has developed an effective defense or avoidance technique to handle this anxiety. Thus it might be expected that the insurance executive in Example 1 would have eventually learned a technique for controlling his anxiety and distress. For example, he might have rejected psychotherapy and instead insisted on a somatic basis for his complaints. In all likelihood, by visiting enough physicians he would have been reinforced to the extent that hypochondriacal concerns would diminish the anxiety somewhat and thus begin to serve a defensive function.

Likewise, the college student in Example 2 might have developed phobic responses to small dormitory rooms. Such a feeling would then take him out of the dormitory and away from the cues which engendered the initial panic. Although phobic responses are hardly a panacea, they might be better than panic and thus lead to reinforcement.

Also, anxiety experiences are likely to result from either of two situations. First, whenever the individual encounters a cue (or system of cues) which leads to the expectancy that he will be punished or encounter pain, subjective distress is the likely outcome. Second, whenever the individual is faced with the failure to achieve certain reinforcements which are extremely valuable to him, he will experience anxiety. By extremely valuable is meant such reinforcements as those of recognition, achievement, dependency. These are crucial reinforcements which occupy a central place in the individual's life. It may be that this second case is merely a more specific instance of the first.

In neither of these cases is it necessary that the cues involved signify a real and impending danger. The important consideration is that the person so perceives the cues. This is illustrated, of course, by Mowrer's (1948) analysis of the neurotic paradox. In Example 2 it is possible that neither the small room nor the roommate *actually* posed any threat. It was sufficient that these were cues associated with previous distress— thus the panic reaction. In brief, something in the individual's experience leads him to associate the cue with eventual punishment or failure, and under such conditions he, of course, experiences marked distress.

These latter points also suggest the reasons why it is difficult to extinguish such expectancies. Once the individual has learned to expect punishment or failure on the basis of a given stimulus, he develops behaviors calculated to avoid that punishment. Very often, such avoidance precludes the possibility of remaining in the threatening situation long enough to relearn. Thus, his "faulty" expectancies never extinguish and he continues to behave in an avoidant fashion.

Another matter of importance concerns generalization. Through the process of generalization we would anticipate that the anxiety response would occur in conjunction with a range of cues that resemble those initially associated with the painful situation or outcome. Again, in Example 2, the physical similarity between present roommate and previous Boy Scout chum was a basis for alarm. However, even contiguity can serve as a basis for such generalization. That is, even cues which "just happened" to be present when the initial anxiety responses occurred may be sufficient to arouse anxiety later.

Quite beyond generalization on the basis of physical similarity are those instances that involve the generalization of expectancies. To illustrate, in Example 1 the individual became quite anxious following a promotion. Although this situation bore little physical resemblance to others encountered earlier, the situations were *need related.* Thus, as discussed by Rotter (1954) and demonstrated empirically by Chance (1959), expectancies will generalize along a common sense gradient of similarity of goals or reinforcements.

One of the vicious cycle aspects of maladjusted behavior is the tendency during periods of intense anxiety to fail to discriminate among situations in which individuals have very strong needs. Likewise, when the individual is intensely anxious he may fail to discriminate and thus behave in such a way as to increase the likelihood of being negatively reinforced by others. For example, the patient in Example 1 became even less likely to behave in a creative, original fashion on the job (behaviors that would have resulted in strong positive reinforcements from others). Rather, he probably utilized behaviors that had served him in the past—behaviors that were likely to fail and thus raise the anxiety level even further.

Intense anxiety reactions are not too difficult to understand when the individual can clearly identify the stimuli involved and verbalize these to an observer. The anxiety-ridden soldier in combat or the very apprehensive woman alone in a house when she hears sounds that suggest a prowler are both readily understandable instances. Even the relatively chronic situation of a harried executive who is anxious over the demands of his job is comprehensible, particularly when the executive himself knows the problem.

More difficult, however, are those situations where the individual is unable to identify the cues that lead him to expect punishment or to fail to achieve highly valued goals. Indeed, under such circumstances the awareness of one's bodily changes (rapid breathing and heart rate, muscular tension, "strange sensations," and so on) enhances an already high anxiety level. People have strong learned needs to be able to account not only for their behavior but also for their body sensations. The expectancy that one cannot achieve this goal is indeed quite frightening. Such is the reason why so many patients desperately search their environment for a plausible explanation and so often, initially at least, postulate some somatic basis, as we saw in Example 1.

To understand why the individual cannot identify the threat that is responsible for these subjective feelings of distress we must go back to our earlier discussions. In Example 2, the student had been busy asserting his masculinity for a number of years. Such pre-emptive thinking in connection with strong needs to consider himself masculine left little opportunity to contemplate homosexual possibilities. Second, he learned to stop thinking as a way of reducing the distress that occurred whenever such thoughts began to arise. Indeed, it is likely that in the past such techniques of stopping thinking and the assertion of masculinity essentially controlled any marked anxiety. However, in the dormitory situation the student was continually confronted with stimuli that evoked anxiety responses. This situation made both stopping thinking and the physical avoidance of such situations extremely difficult and probably contributed greatly to his final panic reaction. In essence, previous adjustive techniques were considerably strained in this situation.

Furthermore, in Example 2 we can see that the patient began to fixate on a somatic basis for his anxiety. Such an hypothesis probably has a strong potential for occurrence with most people. Coupled with the learned tendency to stop thinking whenever thoughts of strong inadequacy began to occur and a marked potential to regard himself as successful, one can understand how the patient might have difficulty identifying the painful cues leading to his anxiety. While his previous position with the firm did not, perhaps, threaten his adjustive techniques, his promotion did. For example, avoiding other executives who might serve as a reminder of his inadequacies could no longer be carried out without his appearing rather strange. Likewise, stopping thinking as a response would have to occur with tremendous frequency now that everything was conspiring to remind him of inadequacies. Thus, such avoidance would only compound his problems by forcing him to become rigid and thus preventing him from performing as was expected of an executive.

Avoidant Responses

We have repeatedly talked about the relation between expectancy for punishment and subsequent avoidance. Thus, when the individual expects to be punished he learns to make responses that will avoid, diminish, or delay that punishment.

As examples of avoidance we shall consider phobic, obsessive-compulsive, and hypochondriacal behaviors. These should be representative of the general realm, although other behaviors such as amnesias, denial patterns, hysteria, and so on, could be included just as readily.

Phobic behaviors are defined as the avoidance of certain objects, places, or events due to a strong fear that, on a consensual basis, is considered unrealistic and inappropriate. For example, a given individual may be phobic in relation to guns. Whenever he comes into contact with such objects, marked distress occurs. Through avoidance of such objects, the expectancy that such behaviors will be reinforced is strengthened by the decline in distress that occurs following that avoidance. It is true in many instances, perhaps, that the object or event is feared because it is associated with an earlier situation which was extremely punishing. Thus, the man who inadvertently drops his gun while hunting and severely injures a companion may develop a phobia of guns. It is apparent that high expectancies for punishment will generalize along a dimension of physical similarity. Thus, the above hunter may become quite fearful when in the presence of rifles, less so in the presence of hand guns, and perhaps very little in the presence of knives.

In many other instances, however, phobias are more complex and may develop in connection with certain "forbidden" needs. For example, an individual may develop strong fears while sitting in church and yet show no distress while in the midst of just as many people in a theatre. If we assume the existence of strong aggressive needs in relation to authority and at the same time a high expectancy for punishment should such needs gain expression, then the differential fear arousal makes sense. In effect, there is generalization here along lines of need relatedness more than on the basis of physical similarity. That is, situations that for the individual are aggressive lead to expectancies for punishment and thus fear. The situations may be physically quite different, but if they are categorized as aggressive or sexual, for example, then similar expectancies may occur. As in other instances, once the individual learns to avoid such situations the expectancy for punishment lessens and he may be said to have become phobic (especially when others, including the individual, can see no realistic basis for the avoidance).

In many cases of phobias the person is unable to verbalize the basis for his avoidance reaction. As noted earlier, this can be explained on the basis of (1) attention to the "wrong" set of cues, (2) stopping thinking, or (3) pre-emption of thought by other stronger needs (perhaps a special case of 1).

It is certainly true that a variety of childhood experiences could easily dispose one to subsequently develop phobic responses. The hunter who developed a gun phobia may have been frequently punished through disapproval by parents for aggression. He may also have been taught vehemently to take responsibility for his own acts. Such a combination of earlier reinforcements could easily predispose him toward a phobic reaction following a traumatic hunting accident later in life.

Likewise, the individual who becomes phobic in response to situations that engage sexual needs and thus lead to expectancies for punishment may exhibit a learning history that suggests a predisposition to react phobically. To be repeatedly negatively reinforced by parents for sexual-like behavior or verbalizations leads to an expectancy for punishment whenever the individual is in a situation that he categorizes as sexual. The anticipation of punishment may stem from internalized goals or standards, but this makes it no less real. For awhile cultural goals or exhortations that he marry and have a family may be so strong as to override the negative reinforcements anticipated from sex that was learned during childhood (although they may make him a less than ardent sexual partner). However, once the cultural standards or reinforcements have been achieved, the childish expectations once more become dominant and may lead to avoidance which culminates in near phobic responses to sex within the marriage.

Obsessive thoughts clearly serve an avoidance function when they are used in such a way as to avoid thinking about potentially threatening events. Instead of merely stopping thinking, the individual substitutes thoughts that pre-empt the field and are thus reinforced by a reduction in distress.

Many *compulsive behaviors* fulfill a similar function. Often, however, compulsive behaviors seem to serve the additional function of guilt reduction. Thus, when an individual has a high expectancy for self-punishment through the intrusion of hostile thoughts, he may begin to engage in compulsive behaviors to reduce the guilt or self-punishment. For example, he may utilize frequent hand washing or he may compulsively utter a prayer 20 times. Such behavior may be particularly prevalent in an individual who has been repeatedly reinforced as a child for making explicit amends for behaviors regarded by the parents as transgressions. In short, as a child the individual develops the expectancy that such behavior will be reinforced. Later, when the "forbidden" thoughts or impulses arise, such atonement responses will have a high potential for occurrence.

In other cases, obsessive thoughts seem to increase discomfort rather than avoid or reduce it. For example, the individual may be tortured by frequent intrusions of thoughts of aggression, incest, murder, and so on. Indeed, such thoughts are usually quite disturbing and, in the initial stages at least, quite foreign to the person. Thus, constant punishment during childhood for aggressive or sexual behavior would obviously lead to the avoidance of such behavior. Even thoughts would be avoided in such areas. However, events may conspire later to bombard the individual with sexual or aggressive cues. His avoidance techniques of stopping thinking, attending to other cues, or physically avoiding potentially threatening situations may be reinforced for a long period of time. Indeed, the avoidance may be so effective that later when obsessive thoughts occur they appear quite foreign to the individual and "not a part of him." The reasons for the occurrence of obsessive thoughts at any point in the individual's life are dependent upon several factors. Most important would be the increase in reinforcement value associated with forbidden thoughts and the relatively low expectancy that such thoughts will actually culminate in overt behavior. When the latter expectancy begins to increase, it would be expected that obsessive thoughts would begin to arouse so much discomfort that other defensive measures would be taken (physical avoidance of the cues that lead to the obsessive thoughts, thinking of other things, and so on).

An example of this analysis might be a woman who is obsessed with thoughts about doing violence to her child. Such a woman was very likely punished for acts of hostility while herself a child. Thus, her freedom of movement in the aggressive area was quite low. Concomitantly, she probably developed a strong expectancy that "good" people do not think or behave in an aggressive, hostile manner. As a result, the whole area of aggression and hostility became, over the years, quite foreign to her. Let us also assume that her needs for being considered beautiful, attractive, desirable, and so on, grew through the years. After her marriage to a successful young executive she became pregnant and subsequently gave birth to a child. During the pregnancy, but especially afterward, her obsessions concerning the child began.

The obsession arose because the infant required time and effort that detracted from her need to appear beautiful and desirable. Therefore, her expectancy for achieving gratification in this area became quite low and led to hostility toward the infant. The situational cues became so strong as to force the thoughts upon her. However, such thoughts were very alarming and engendered strong anticipations of self-punishment, since they ran counter to her needs to be a good wife, mother, person, and so on. Also, her aggressive thoughts appeared quite foreign to her inasmuch as for many years she had simply avoided contemplating such things. Their intrusion, of course, aroused expectancies regarding sanity, and this only increased her problems. If the discrepancy between her needs to be regarded as attractive and her expectancies of achieving this goal had continued or become greater, the obsessions would have likely continued or grown stronger, at which point she would probably have invoked additional defensive behaviors such as physical avoidance of her child. Should the discrepancy have become less, the obsessions would have likely decreased.

Hypochondriacal behavior serves to further illustrate the avoidant character of many so-called psychopathological reactions. Extreme attention to one's bodily functions and health (in the absence of any apparent basis for the concern) serves to divert the individual from more effective coping behaviors that would deal with his problems. Obviously, the child who is allowed to get away with feigning illness in order to escape a school examination is also developing expectancies for the success of such behaviors that will generalize to future similar situations. A mother who is frequently "ill" is inadvertently providing the child with a set of expectancies that problems can be dealt with by becoming ill. Such a child may also learn that illness brings a great deal of concern and affection from others. Later, when such a person fails to gain the affection he desires, he may utilize hypochondriacal techniques to gain that affection. Obviously, he will have the generalized expectancy that such behaviors will lead to affectional responses from others. Therefore, with the appropriate situational cues, the behavior in question will arise.

It frequently happens also that such a person's bodily concerns are reinforced by the usual physiological accompaniments of a high expectation for punishment. For example, the person who expects to fail an examination may develop a number of bodily reactions in connection with that expectancy (particularly when the need to pass the examination is high). He may become dizzy, flushed, and so on. Such reactions may only solidify his concerns about his body.

Depressive Behavior

Such behaviors occur when the individual's freedom of movement in an important need area is low. On the face of it, this appears little different from other instances that have previously been discussed. There are, however, some other conditions that appear to interact with low freedom of movement and high need value and thus lead to depression.

First, there is an element of permanency in the situation. The individual who has a date cancelled by his girlfriend may become angry over this frustration. However, if the girl becomes engaged to another, he may well become depressed because there is the element of finality in the situation.

The second condition frequently involves the concept of minimal goal level. That is, in an important need area, failure on the part of the individual to achieve up to the level of his minimal goal often leads to depression—particularly when the condition of finality is operative and leads to an expectancy that he will never reach the desired minimal level of achievement.

Third, it is hypothesized that depressions tend to be associated with people who possess a strong generalized expectancy that outcomes are their own responsibility. This, of course, is suggestive of the internal versus external control of reinforcement variable (Rotter, 1966).

In addition, clinical experience suggests that depressions are frequently observed where the individual has been rejected or abandoned by a loved one. This, perhaps, represents a specific application of several of the preceding points. It also appears that depressive responses often follow from a situation wherein the individual has concentrated his attempts at need satisfaction within a very narrow range. Thus, when that source is no longer possible, the individual has few if any alternative behavior pathways available for satisfaction.

As illustrations of the preceding considerations, the following examples may be useful. The first involves a woman who was married for many years to a man who was very effective in life and, in essence, pretty well ran his wife's life for her. He made all the important decisions, gave her an allowance, comforted her, and so on. Following thirty-five years of marriage, the husband died. Shortly after the funeral, the woman lapsed into a severe depression and showed no signs of improving.

Here we have a woman who placed a tremendous amount of her need satisfaction in the hands of one person. His removal created a precipitous drop in freedom of movement while need value remained high.

Furthermore, the finality of death served as a cue for low expectancies for any substantial improvement in the state of her need satisfaction. Over the years, she had failed to establish expectancies that others, including herself, could satisfy her needs. No alternate need satisfaction pathways were created, with the result that her need potentials were uniformly low. Such a massive history of dependency coupled with a sudden drop in freedom of movement led to behaviors of severe depression and withdrawal. Had her husband merely decided to take a week's business trip, her reaction might well have been anger—the recognition of a temporary inability to satisfy her dependency needs. At the most her reaction would probably have been moderate sadness. Likewise, had she previously established some minimal behavior potentials for need satisfaction she would probably have undergone a period of marked grief which eventually would have lessened as she began to recontact the environment. Such contact would have been possible because of the existence of some low-level expectancies for the success of a few independent behaviors.

Another example might be that of a middle-aged male with strong recognition-achievement needs who, following the failure to receive a promotion, became markedly depressed. The essential ingredients in this case were (1) a childhood that reinforced beliefs or generalized expectancies for self-determination of events, thus leading him to take responsibility for his failures; (2) a relatively high set of minimal goals brought about through selective reinforcement of achievements by the parents during his formative years; (3) a progressive focalization of need area (that is, a tendency to regard achievements in a narrow area as the only route toward success); (4) a tendency to regard his failure to achieve a promotion as signifying the end of the road (put otherwise, this last failure established a very low expectancy that any future possibilities remained for reaching his minimal goal level).

The question, of course, arises as to why the depressive reaction took place when it did rather than sooner or later. The easiest general answer is that a given situation involving loss or failure is composed of cues which lead to the expectancy that future satisfaction of needs is highly improbable inasmuch as the individual does not possess (or at least thinks he does not possess) alternative behaviors to satisfy the needs in question. Likewise, the severity and length of the depression will be determined by the individual's behavioral repertoire. That is, if his learning history has not provided him with alternative behaviors, it is likely that depression will be relatively long and perhaps severe. This is especially true when there is no possibility of reducing the value of the need involved. Perhaps the adequacy of prior learning history is the real difference between so-called neurotic, reactive depressions and psychotic depressions.

Failures in Learning

On the one hand it seems rather contradictory to describe failures in learning in social learning terms. At the same time, perhaps all psychopathology represents a failure in learning to some degree or other. More specifically, there is not so much a failure to learn as there is a failure to learn the right things in terms of society's standards.

Criminal behavior is, of course, defined by the courts and not by psychology. This means that many people engage in the same behavior, but by virtue of not being detected are not labeled criminals. For this and other reasons it is particularly absurd to talk about criminal behavior as if (1) it were a distinct diagnostic entity, and (2) it somehow required a special set of explanatory principles.

Many instances of criminal behavior simply reflect a situation wherein the individual has learned to value goals or reinforcements that, while bringing the disapproval of the larger culture, lead to approval and acceptance from those in the criminal's reference group. Thus, quite simply, he engages in such activity because of the expectancy that it will lead to the rewards of approval and recognition from those people who are particularly reinforcing for him. In short, the principles by which he becomes a criminal are the same as those that turn someone else into a social conformist. He is not deviant in terms of his own subculture.

Other potential influences leading to crime range from a variety of parental relations, frustration, and lack of responsiveness from others to quirks of fate. Even within this narrow range we have such examples as (1) the juvenile gang member who seeks reinforcements from his peers, (2) the child whose parents are punitive and rejecting, with the result that he generalizes his hostility responses to all authority figures and perhaps provokes a fight with a policeman, and (3) the careless driver who hits a pedestrian and is charged with manslaughter. Such heterogeneity defies any single analysis. It is evident that in some cases a discrepancy between freedom of movement and need value could lead to criminal acts. In many other cases, no such discrepancy exists and a failure to learn sanctioned behaviors is more important.

Psychopathic behavior seems to be an instance where an adult is apparently unable to learn to avoid punishment by eliminating his antisocial acts. Even though he may be jailed or penalized repeatedly it does not lead him to substitute socially acceptable behaviors.

Such behavior has been described many times (Buss, 1966; Cleckley, 1964). There is not always agreement regarding the descriptive features of such behavior and even less when it comes to explanations. However, several aspects seem prominent. The behavior generally occurs in a bright and socially adept male who shows a real gift for being charming and persuasive when he wishes to be. He tends to be particularly effective with women and often exhibits rather amoral sexual behavior. He also shows a marked capacity for repeatedly destroying himself through impulsive antisocial or criminal acts—often when he is on the brink of establishing himself as a success in a job, marriage, or some other socially desirable venture. Other characteristics involve his inability to establish sincere emotional relations with others and a kind of narcissistic preoccupation with himself. Little anxiety or guilt seem apparent except when it suits his purposes.

One plausible explanation for the above patterns involves the notion of pampering. The psychopathic individual is one who has been indulged as a child and allowed to escape punishment for his transgressions by saying he is sorry or promising not to do it again. The child learns to be very skillful in manipulating others by suitable verbalizations and the appearance of being "cute." Such a child is learning a set of expectancies that escape from punishment is thus possible. In brief, the parents are reinforcing the wrong behaviors. The parents may be reinforcing the cuteness or verbalizations of contrition rather than increasing his expectancy for punishment should the antisocial behavior occur again.

Similarly, it is likely that such a child rarely has to endure frustration or delay in gratification. His parents cater to his every whim. Perhaps his parents protect him so much from distress that he is unable to understand such a feeling in others. Thus, he does not refrain from producing such a state in others because he does not really understand the emotion and what it feels like.

Schizophrenic Behaviors

This group of behaviors is so diverse as to defy inclusion under a single heading. Indeed, in some instances the term has become so expansive as to be almost synonymous with psychosis. Until a wider array of distinctions is made (for example, process-reactive, acute-chronic), it is unlikely that any single approach will provide a satisfactory account of so-called schizophrenic phenomena. Thus far, social learning theory has made few direct contributions to this area. Great potential exists, however, for the application of social learning theory to such areas as development, motivation, performance, attention, and language and thought in what is commonly referred to as schizophrenia. For example, work by Efran (1968) and Efran and Broughton (1966; 4–5) suggests the importance of both expectancy for approval and the reinforcing qualities of that approval in mediating looking behavior. This could easily relate, for example, to attentional deficits in schizophrenia. Likewise, Lefcourt and Steffy (1966) have combined the process-reactive category with expectancy for reinforcement in the prediction of social interactive behavior in schizophrenics.

SUMMARY

The foregoing has been intended as a rather molar discussion of the relation between social learning theory and pathology. The approach has been one of suggesting how pathological behaviors may be conceptualized within an SLT framework. Thus, a variety of SLT concepts were discussed and their relevance to pathology suggested. A number of examples were presented in the service of this goal. As noted earlier, SLT has not been systematically applied as yet to the field of abnormal psychology (in particular, its relevance to psychotic or extreme forms of deviance has yet to be fully exploited). As was stated in Part 1 of this volume, it is important to emphasize that the goal of SLT is less that of providing the "facts" of personality and more that of providing a vehicle for the conceptualization of facts.

6-2	*Expectations of Need Satisfaction and Drinking Patterns of College Students*[1]

RICHARD JESSOR, RODERICK S. CARMAN, and
PETER H. GROSSMAN

The variety of social and psychological functions served by drinking seems to be limited only by the social definitions and the personal learnings with which alcohol use has been associated. The use of alcohol to solve personal problems and to cope with frustration, failure and the anticipation of failure has long been recognized. The aim of the present study was to investigate this particular function of drinking in the adaptation of college students to the demands and opportunities of the college environment.

Research and observation in different cultures and social structures have shown that drinking behavior is usually institutionalized and regulated by tradition, by its relation to religious ceremonies, by its contribution to diet and by its definition as a symbol of group solidarity. Much of the variation in drinking can be understood by reference to such sociocultural concepts. In addition, the properties of alcohol and the nature of individual experience with it are such as to make possible personal variation in its use, and an account of this type of variation would seem to require concepts at the level of personality. Such an account draws attention to the processes which mediate between society and behavior and can help to explain individual variation where the sociocultural context remains generally the same.

The present study was conducted within the framework of a social learning theory of personality (Rotter, 1954, 1955) in which behavior is construed as the outcome of the tendency to maximize expectations of attaining valued goals in any given situation or over time. Most crucial to our research was the following general formulation which is central in Rotter's social learning theory of personality: when experience has shown that certain behavior has a relatively low expectation of leading

---

[1] Prepared during R. Jessor's tenure as a National Institute of Mental Health Special Research Fellow at the Harvard-Florence Research Project, Florence, Italy. Concepts and measures employed in the present research were developed within the Tri-Ethnic Research Project which was supported by grant No. 3M-9156 from the National Institute of Mental Health. Analysis of a portion of the present data was facilitated by a grant-in-aid to R. Jessor from the University of Colorado Council on Research and Creative Work. The bulk of the data reported in this paper is drawn from R. S. Carman's master's thesis (1965). The remaining data derive from P. H. Grossman's doctoral dissertation (1965). This paper is Publication No. 101 of the Institute of Behavioral Science, University of Colorado.

From *The Quarterly Journal of Studies in Alcohol*, 1968, 29, 101–116. Copyright 1968 by Publications Division of the Rutgers Center of Alcohol Studies, New Brunswick, N.J., and reprinted by permission of the authors and the publisher.

to goals which are valued by the person, alternative behavior which has a relatively higher expectation of leading to these goals, or of coping with the failure to attain them, will be adopted.

Within the college environment a large variety of needs or motivations are involved in the goals toward which students strive. Two goals, however, seem to be of pervasive importance: the goal of academic achievement or recognition, and the goal of social affection or interpersonal liking. Failure to attain these goals should have major consequences for the student: it should lower his expectations of future attainment in these areas and result, theoretically, in recourse to other activities learned in the past to be ways of achieving the same or similar goals. These are likely to include such instrumental activities as redoubling one's efforts, spending more time at studying, doing extra work, preparing further in advance for exams, seeking out new groups to join, being more friendly and warm in social contacts and going out of one's way to help others. It was our basic thesis that one of the learned activities available to college students for dealing with low expectations of attaining valued goals is the drinking of alcoholic beverages.

The young person has many opportunities for learning that drinking can be a technically effective alternative to unsuccessful behavior. For example, he can learn that certain goals are more easily attained in drinking than in nondrinking situations: thus, dating accompanied by drinking may more readily yield communication and expression of affection and intimacy than dates in which no drinking occurs. In this example the original goal was attained through drinking. But it is also possible to learn that drinking situations provide other, new or different goals than the original ones toward which striving has been unsuccessful. Thus the student who has been denied academic success may learn that drinking situations provide other satisfying goals—affection, dominance, independence—which may substitute or compensate for the failure to attain the original ones.

The present interpretation of drinking also depends at least in part on the physiological effects of alcohol. Alcohol, especially in large quantities, can affect internal cognitive processes, such as memory and recall, and thereby enable the drinker to avoid or repress thinking about his failures and inadequacies. This narcotizing use of alcohol can also be seen to be a learned way of coping with expectations of adversity. Since narcotization depends upon frequent drinking of relatively large amounts of alcohol, it tends to be a pattern of use associated with drunkenness and complications. Because frequent drunkenness results in social disapproval, such use is likely to occur only when expectations of attaining satisfactions in most other ways are very low. This function of alcohol, then, serves to facilitate retreat from instrumentally oriented goal-striving behavior, and represents a way of coping with failure, or its anticipation, by withdrawal.

Drinking behavior can be seen, in short, as essentially adaptive. The socialization of alcohol use shows how drinking can be used to attain goals otherwise felt to be unattainable, to attain substitute goals for those for which the expectation of attainment is low, and to cope with failure or its anticipation through forgetting or through inhibiting or interfering with the relevant thought processes. Given the sharp competition in the academic and social spheres of campus life, low expectations of attaining academic success and peer affection are inevitable among some students. Given also the general availability of alcohol to persons of college age, some degree of relationship should exist between expectations of goal attainment or need satisfaction and pattern of drinking.

We tested this general hypothesis in two phases. In the first, we assessed the relation between expectations of need satisfaction and certain aspects of the pattern of drinking behavior. The assumption was that students with low expectations of need satisfaction would show greater recourse to alcohol; therefore they would drink more, be drunk more often and have more drinking-related social complications. If this relation can be shown to hold, there would be an initial basis for inferring that drinking may serve as an alternative way of gaining goals, solving problems or coping with failure.

But such an inference, even if strongly supported by the data, would remain relatively indirect. A more direct assessment of the meaning of alcohol or of its actual psychological function for students would need to be made. This was the concern of the second phase, in which we investigated the relation between expectations of need satisfaction and the functions of alcohol which the subject describes as applying to his own use. The assumption was that subjects with low expectations of need satisfaction would more frequently describe or define alcohol as providing them with alternatives for goal attainment or with a way of coping with frustration and failure.

PART I: METHODS

The subjects were 300 students selected from the introductory psychology classes at the University of Colorado. The personality questionnaire for the measurement of expectations was administered during regular class hour. About 2 weeks later we administered a drinking questionnaire, outside of class, to groups of 20 students from the original group who had voluteered to participate in "a drinking study." The administrator was a different person on the second occasion in order to avoid connection between the 2 measures. The voluntary nature of the second session reduced the size of the group on which both personality and drinking data were available to 110. Further reduction to 88 (50 female) occurred when married students and nondrinkers were excluded from the sample. Their mean age was 19.2 years, with no difference between the sexes. The subjects had attended college for an average of just under 2 years.

Expectations of Need Satisfaction

We assessed expectations of need satisfaction in academic achievement (ACH) and peer affection (AFF) by means of a 30-item questionnaire.[2] The 15 ACH items and the 15 AFF items were interspersed in order of appearance in the questionnaire. Each item involved the presentation of a verbal referent for each goal area and a linear rating scale along which the subject marked the degree to which he expected to attain that referent or that specific goal: the linear scale measured from 0 ("sure it will not happen") to 100 ("sure it will happen"). The item scores assigned ranged from 1 to 10. Expectancy was scored by totalling across the 15 items in each need area. Thus the measure of expectation of need satisfaction yielded 2 scores, one for the ACH and one for the AFF need area.

The personality measure has been used successfully in a number of studies (Jessor, Graves, Hanson, & Jessor, 1968; Opochinsky, 1965) and has been shown to have adequate reliability and validity. This was confirmed in the present study: test-retest reliability of a sample of 16 of the students retested approximately 2 weeks after the first administration was very satisfactory: expectations of achievement, $r =$ .95; expectations of affection, $r =$ .92. That the two scores are actually measuring different need areas was shown by the relatively low correlation between the ACH and AFF expectancy measure (despite the method of measurement being common to both); the Pearson correlation of .36 shows the two scores to have less than 15% of their variance in common.

We also tested the validity of the expectation scores by their relations to relevant external criteria in the two need areas: grade-point average and membership in one of the Greek-letter organizations on campus. The ACH score correlated with grade-point average .55, while the AFF score correlated about zero ($-$.01). Not only is this difference in the correlations a source of validity for the ACH score, but

[2] The ACH referents were as follows: To be in the top half of the class at graduation; To be able to get my ideas across in class; To get on the Dean's list during the year; To be able to answer other students' questions about school work; To be thought most likely to amount to something by my instructors; To understand new material quickly in class; To be well-prepared for class discussion; To win a scholarship while in college; To get at least a B average this year; To be considered a bright student by my instructors; To have good enough grades to go on to graduate school if I want to; To be thought of as a good student by my classmates; To be encouraged by my instructors to go on to graduate school; To do well in some of the more difficult courses here; To come out near the top of the class on mid-term exams. The 15 AFF referents were: To be well-liked by most of the people around here; To be asked to take part in many social activities; To be thought of as a best friend by several persons around here; To have groups show real pleasure when I join them; To be one of the most popular undergraduates on campus; To go out of my way to help others; To have friends want to do things with me during vacations; To get along well with most of the students; To be in on the fun that goes on around here; To have other students enjoy having me around; To openly express my appreciation of others; To do things with the group just because I like being with them; To be known as one of the best-liked persons in my class; To have many friends in different groups; To know that the instructor actually likes me as a person.

it also adds further evidence that the two expectation scores are not measuring the same need area. With respect to the Greek-letter membership criterion, the pattern is similar although not as striking, and is reversed as expected. The AFF score is significantly related to the criterion $(r = .20)$, whereas the correlation of the ACH score is less $(r = .12)$ and falls short of significance.

Drinking Behavior

Three aspects of the pattern of drinking behavior were assessed— intake, reported frequency of drunkenness and reported frequency of drinking-related complications. We included a large number of additional questions, covering such aspects as the initial drinking experience, the usual context of drinking and definitions of heavy drinking, but the data will not be dealt with in this paper.

Measure of Intake The procedure for obtaining a measure of quantity-frequency (Q-F) of alcohol use has been described in detail elsewhere (Grossman, 1963; Jessor, Graves, Hanson, & Jessor, 1968, *ch. 7*). For each beverage type (wine, beer, spirits), we asked a frequency question ("How often do you usually drink beer?") and a quantity question ("When you drink beer, how much do you usually have at one time?"), and provided a series of response categories for each question. The quantity responses were converted to units of absolute alcohol and multiplied by a weighted frequency score to yield a Q-F index for each type. The Q-F indexes for the three together yielded a total Q-F index. The interpretation of the Q-F score is given as the average amount of absolute alcohol consumed per day. The index shows increases in either quantity or frequency of intake, or with greater use of beverages of higher alcohol content.

The Q-F scores show, as expected, that the men drank more on the average than the women. The mean Q-F scores of the men were, total Q-F .72, wine .04, beer .51 and spirits .19; women, total Q-F .36, wine .05, beer .15 and spirits .19. The sex difference in total alcohol intake is thus accounted for entirely by the difference in beer consumption.

Measure of Drunkenness The measure consisted of a single question: "How many times have you gotten drunk or pretty high in the last year? [Circle one only.] (a) 10 or more times, (b) 8 or 9 times, (c) 6 or 7 times, (d) 4 or 5 times, (e) 2 or 3 times, (f) 1 time, (g) never."

The item was scored from 0 to 6 with the higher score assigned to the higher reported frequency of drunkenness. The utility of this type of item as a measure of drunkenness had been demonstrated in previous research (Jessor, Graves, Hanson & Jessor, 1968, *ch. 7*). As expected, there was a sex difference in reported frequency of having been drunk or pretty high in the past year: the mean score of the men was 3.0, reflecting the response category of "4 or 5 times"; the mean score of the women was 2.2, reflecting the response category of "2 or 3 times."

Measure of Drinking-Related Complications Specific problems such as loss of status or position, accidents, or damage to social relationships associated with drinking were assessed, using Straus and Bacon's (1953) 4 categories of drinking-related problems: formal punishment or discipline, accidents or injuries, damage to friendships and failure to meet everday obligations. The format of the 16 questions, 4 for each category, was as follows: "How many times have you ever lost a job due to drinking? (a) several times, (b) once or twice, (c) never."

We tried to take into account the seriousness of the reported problem, the frequency of occurrence of each problem, and both seriousness and frequency combined, when scoring. Since the various scores correlated among themselves (.90+) the decision was made to use as the drinking-related complications score the simplest and most direct measure, namely, the number of items out of the 16 to which a response other than "never" was given.

The mean complications score was 2.09 out of a possible 16 (men 2.6, women 1.7). The 3 measures of drinking behavior showed a consistency when treated by sex groups. Men reported greater intake of alcohol (higher Q-F scores) and also reported more drunkenness and drinking-related complications than women. The three measures of the pattern of drinking behavior correlated significantly among themselves; the higher the reported intake, the higher the reported drunkenness and drinking-related complications: Drunkenness correlated with total Q-F, men .32, women .60; drinking-related complications with total Q-F, men .52, women .70; and with drunkenness, men .54, women .66 (Pearson correlations are all significant at the .05 level or beyond, one-tail test). The correlations for women were all higher than those for men, a fact of interest in relation to subsequent results. The consistency among the 3 scores, as well as the obtained sex differences in magnitude of each score, can be taken, in the absence of outside criteria, as providing a degree of validity for the drinking measures.

RESULTS

We analyzed the data in two ways to test the hypothesis that when expectations are low the measures of intake, drunkenness and complications would tend to be higher. First, we ran correlations between the two expectations scores and the three drinking measures. Second, we divided students into subgroups depending on the level of both of their expectation scores, and then compared the subgroups in terms of their mean scores on the drinking measures.

It can be seen in Table 1 that all but one of the correlations were in the expected, that is, the negative, direction. For the women, 5 out of the 6 predicted relationships were significant, providing strong support for the hypothesis. The data of the men, however, were considerably weaker: although 3 of the 6 correlations are over .20 in the predicted direction, they nevertheless fall short of significance ($r = .275$ is needed for significance of the .05 level, one-tail test, with an N of 38).

For the second analysis, four subgroups of subjects were constituted

Table 1   Correlations between Expectations of Need Satisfaction in Academic Achievement and Peer Affection and Measures of Drinking Behavior of Men (N = 38) and Women (N = 50)

	TOTAL Q–F		DRUNKENNESS		DRINKING-RELATED COMPLICATIONS	
	M	F	M	F	M	F
Achievement	.11	−.26*	−.25	−.33*	−.23	−.28*
Affection	−.10	−.26*	−.08	−.07	−.24	−.39*

* Pearson correlation significant at the .05 level or beyond, one-tail test.

within each sex group as follows. The two expectancy scores of each subject were examined to determine whether they were above or below the group mean for that score. Depending on their two scores, subjects were then assigned to one of four groups: (1) High ACH and High AFF; (2) High ACH and Low AFF; (3) Low ACH and High AFF; and (4) Low ACH and Low AFF. This analysis, unlike the correlational analysis, considers both need areas at the same time. Theoretically, the group which should show the highest scores on the drinking measures is Group 4, the group which is low on both expectation measures.

The data are presented in Table 2. Despite the small Ns which result when each sex group is partitioned into four subgroups, it can be seen that, in both sexes, Group 4 had the highest score on each of the three drinking measures. The finding is clearest on the measure of Drinking-Related Complications where the mean score of Group 4 is significantly higher than the mean score of each of the other three groups; and this finding holds for both sexes. The results of the women on the other two measures, Total Q-F and Drunkenness, are again more supportive than those of the men. The female Group 4 mean score on each of the two drinking measures is significantly higher than that of at least one other expectation subgroup; this is not true of the men.

The data provide initial evidence for the inference that drinking behavior may function, at least in part, as an alternative mode of striving for goals otherwise unlikely to be attained or as a mode of coping with the lack of their attainment. To make this inference more compelling, more direct knowledge about the way in which alcohol is perceived, described or defined by the students with low expectations of goal attainment actually attribute more problem-solving functions to their use of alcohol than do other students.

PART II: METHODS

Measurement of Drinking Functions

We measured the meanings which are attached by the subject to alcohol use or the functions which alcohol is subjectively perceived to

Table 2   Mean Scores on Drinking Measures of Subgroups Established on Level of Both Expectation of Achievement (ACH) and Affection (AFF) Scores

Group	Total Q–F	Drunken-ness	Drinking-Related Complications
1 (High ACH, High AFF)			
Men (13)	0.71	2.54	2.15
Women (16)	0.23	1.94	1.19
2 (High ACH, Low AFF)			
Men (6)	0.69	2.33	1.50
Women (9)	0.19	1.44	1.11
3 (Low ACH, High AFF)			
Men (6)	0.54	3.50	1.83
Women (9)	0.41	2.67	1.11
4 (Low ACH, Low AFF)			
Men (13)	0.83	3.54	4.0[a]
Women (16)	0.57[b]	2.75[c]	2.81[a]

[a] Significant mean difference between Group 4 and Groups 1, 2 and 3, at .05 level; *t* test, one-tail.
[b] Significant mean difference between Group 4 and Groups 1 and 2, at .05 level; *t* test, one-tail.
[c] Significant mean difference between Group 4 and Group 2, at .05 level; *t* test, one-tail.

serve for him. Earlier work by Mulford and Miller (1959, 1960a, 1960b) as well as the analysis of drinking functions provided by Fallding (1964) influenced our approach. The measurement technique, based on that used in the Tri-Ethnic Research Project (see Jessor, Graves, Hanson, & Jessor, 1968, *ch. 7),* presents the subject with a list of drinking functions to which he is asked to respond by checking all of those which characterize his own reasons for drinking. The list of functions was part of the larger drinking behavior questionnaire.

We defined four categories of drinking functions and made up items to represent each category.[3] The categories and their definitions were as follows:

Positive Social Functions (PS) Motivations and attitudes which link drinking to activities of a pleasant, festive, social nature. Drinking is engaged in largely for the convivial pleasure which surrounds it.

[3] Obviously there are other ways of categorizing the possible functions of alcohol, and these will likely vary in different cultures or groups. R. Jessor has recently completed a cross-cultural study of functions of alcohol use comparing youth in Palermo, Sicily, in Rome, and in Boston, the latter being of Italian-born grandparents, in which a category of dietary functions was also included, e.g., "it rounds out a good meal," "it's important for a good diet."

Conforming Social Functions (CS) Motivations and attitudes which link drinking to a sense of obligation for meeting group pressure or expectations with regard to what is seen as appropriate to or necessary for certain social situations.

Psychophysiological Functions (PH) Motivations and attitudes which link drinking to physical aches, pains, fatigue or other forms of physical discomfort. Drinking is seen as a learned remedy for or relief from such physical symptoms.

Personality Effects Functions (PE) Motivations and attitudes which link drinking to unresolved problems or inadequacies of a psychological nature. Drinking is used as an escape from or relief for such problems or shortcomings, or as a way of achieving goals not otherwise attainable.

Of the four, the PE category most directly bears upon our interpretation of alcohol use as a learned way of striving or of coping with failure. Our basic prediction was that a negative relationship should obtain between expectations of need satisfaction and the degree to which PE functions were attributed to drinking. The possibility of a negative relationship obtaining with CS and PH functions was also anticipated; CS functions suggest a learned reliance on alcohol in dealing with certain social situations, and PH functions, insofar as they represent psychosomatic difficulties, also suggest a possible problem-solving use of alcohol. Finally, PS functions were expected to have a positive relation with expectations of need satisfaction; the higher the expectations the greater the use of alcohol would tend to be for positive social (rather than problem-solving) reasons.

A pool of function items was collected from previous work and from inquiry with selected groups of students other than those used in the later study. Six research workers familiar with the theory of drinking functions being employed in the research sorted the items into one of the 4 categories of functions. Agreement was clearcut on 32 items which constituted the final list.[4]

---

[4] The items, their order in the list, and the category to which they were assigned were as follows: PS: (1) makes get-togethers fun; (7) it's a pleasant way to celebrate; (8) just to have a good time; (12) because it's a pleasant recreation; (14) just because it's fun; (18) adds a certain warmth to social occasions; (21) it's a nice way to celebrate special occasions; (23) makes dinner dates out seem more special; (29) because it's enjoyable to join in with people who are enjoying themselves; (32) it's often a pleasant part of a congenial, social activity. CS: (2) to be part of the group; (5) it's the accepted thing to do; (9) because everybody does it; (13) to be one of the crowd; (27) it's just a part of college life; (30) the places where I go to be with others serve drinks. PH: (3) helps you get to sleep at night; (10) feeling tired; (16) eases aches and pains; (19) to get over headaches; (24) when I have a cold; (31) it settles your stomach. PE: (4) feeling lonely; (6) makes you worry less about what others are thinking about you; (11) gives you more confidence in yourself; (15) helps you forget you're not the kind of person you'd like to be; (17) makes you feel less shy; (20) makes you more satisfied with yourself; (22) feeling under pressure; (25) feeling mad; (26) makes the future seem brighter; (28) to get my mind off failures in course work.

Internal analyses of the function items provide evidence that four different categories of functions were actually being measured. Correlations between the number of items checked in each category were all low, ranging from −.08 to .29, with an average correlation of .13. A Tryon cluster analysis (Tryon & Bailey, 1966) yielded four virtually uncorrelated cluster composites, which directly parallel our four function item categories, with five of the PS, all six of the CS, three of the PH and five of the PE items clustering. The domain validities of the four clusters ranged from .76 to .94, providing evidence that the items comprising each cluster represent a unidimensional subdomain of drinking motivation.

We examined two scores for each function category: (1) a number of functions score based on number of items checked within each category; (2) a proportion of functions score to reflect the differential importance to the subject of the four categories of functions while taking into account the fact that the number of items in the different categories is not the same.[5]

The drinking functions items showed no appreciable sex differences. The average number of items checked by the total group was close to 10, with the items in the PS category being chosen by far the most frequently. Relative frequency of category use, taking into account differential category size, is shown in the following scores: PS .63; CS .25; PE .15; and PH .08.

RESULTS

We analyzed the data as in Part I. Correlations between the two expectation scores and the eight functions scores (Table 3) lend support to the hypothesis. While none of the men's number of functions scores correlated significantly with their expectation scores, three significant relationships were found when the proportion of functions scores was considered: the higher the expectation of achievement, the larger the proportion of functions chosen attributable to PS functions ($r = .30$); the lower the expectation of affection, the higher the proportion of functions chosen which are attributable to the PH ($r = −.43$) or the PE function ($r = −.28$).

Findings in the women were more consistently supportive. The number of functions score that related significantly, in the direction predicted, to both the ACH and the AFF expectation scores is in the PE category, the one most clearly related to our principal hypothesis ($r = −.40$ with ACH and −.36 with AFF). When proportion scores are considered, five out of the eight expected relationships were significant, four of the five coming

---

[5] The latter score evaluates the proportion of a student's total number of checked functions attributable to each of the four categories. The score is the number of functions checked in a category divided by the number there are in that category, and the result is divided further by the total number of functions checked by the student from the entire list.

Table 3   Correlations between Expectation of Achievement (ACH) and Affection (AFF) Scores and Number and Proportion of Drinking Function Scores

	ACH		AFF	
	M	F	M	F
PS*				
Number	.06	.01	.08	.07
Proportion	.30†	.25†	.16	.34†
CS				
Number	−.03	−.17	.17	.02
Proportion	.10	−.25†	.25	−.08
PH				
Number	−.04	.05	−.26	−.23
Proportion	−.11	.17	−.43†	−.08
PE				
Number	−.16	−.40†	−.16	−.36†
Proportion	−.16	−.34†	−.28†	−.27†

* PS = positive social functions; CS = conforming social functions; PH = psychophysiological functions; PE = personality effects functions.
† Significant at .05 level or beyond; Pearson correlation, one-tail test.

from the PE and the PS categories. Taken together, these correlational results of both men and women provide additional support for our interpretation of drinking among college students.

The second mode of analysis, that involving groups high on both expectations, low on both, or high on one and low on the other, showed no significant differences in the men. Both the number of functions score and the proportion of functions score of the women in Group 4, the Low ACH and Low AFF group, were significantly higher on PE functions than any of the other expectation groups. Differences among these other expectation groups tend to be minimal. This mode of analysis is consistent with the findings from the preceding correlational analyses; low expectations in both need areas were associated with higher reports of PE use of alcohol among women.

The data we have presented thus far in Part II have been concerned with examining the link between expectations and drinking functions. To complete the bridge, we examined the further link between PE drinking functions and drinking behavior.

Intake of the men, as measured by total Q-F, shows no significant relation to the PE function scores (Table 4). With respect to frequency of drunkenness, however, the PE category was a significant predictor, and this is consistent on both number and proportion of functions scores. On the Drinking-Related Complications measure the correlations were short of significance. In the women, all three of the measures of drinking be-

Table 4   *Correlations between Number and Proportion of Personality Effects Function Scores and Drinking Behavior of Men (N = 38) and Women (N = 50)*

	NUMBER		PROPORTION	
	M	F	M	F
Total Q–F	.10	.32*	.13	.27*
Drunkenness	.52*	.50*	.40*	.39*
Drinking-related complications	.23	.41*	.20	.34*

* Pearson correlation significant at .05 level or beyond, one-tail test.

havior were significantly predicted by the PE functions category. Its relation to the drinking measures holds in all cases, whether the number or the proportion score is considered, and the level of relationship is substantial, the average *r* for the six Personality Effects correlations being .37.

DISCUSSION

The present study has identified as relevant to college drinking two major areas of striving for goal attainment or need satisfaction: achievement and affection. Low expectations here are related to the pattern of drinking behavior and, more directly, the meaning of alcohol for the user. These relationships support the inference that alcohol use may be a learned behavior for attaining goals otherwise unattainable or for coping with the failure to attain valued goals.

The inference must be tentative at this point. The cross-sectional research design employed is incapable of establishing the causal direction contained in the inference that low expectations of goal attainment may cause alcohol use as an alternative behavior. Further, we have focused on only one interpretation of alcohol use; the applicability of alternative interpretations was not investigated. One direction for possible investigation of alternatives would be to consider drinking as a satisfying and meaningful activity in its own right. Some support for this notion may be adduced from the data in Table 2 where there is a slight suggestion of curvilinearity; the students with high expectations in both need areas have somewhat greater recourse to drinking than those low in one need. Although the data are not clear, they suggest the need for consideration of multiple interpretations in order to exhaust the variance in drinking behavior.

The present research dealt with only two need areas. Given the large number of needs college students seek to gratify, stronger and more consistent support for our main hypothesis might be obtained if a larger set of needs were examined. Recourse to alternatives such as drinking may become more probable only when low expectations obtain in all need areas. The fact that Group 4, Low ACH and Low AFF, tended to differ from the other three groups supports the possibility. A more comprehensive sampling of need areas would provide an opportunity to locate groups with generalized low expectations, and to make a less ambiguous test of the low-expectation-high-drinking behavior hypothesis.

Next in importance to the support of the research hypothesis itself, was the finding that the results in the women were consistently more substantial than in the men, possibly because the two needs measured were of different importance to each sex, or because each sex responded to the inventories with a different degree of truthfulness. A further interpretation draws attention again to the limited nature of our hypothesis. Sex differences in alcohol use are ubiquitous among American youth (e.g., Maddix & McCall, 1964). What seems clear is that social norms regulate alcohol use distinctively for each sex, men not only being allowed greater freedom of use but in certain situations, such as college, being expected to use alcohol. It may well be that much more of the variance in male than in female drinking is to be accounted for by norms; i.e., that more of the variance in female drinking may be the result of personality factors since norms for women tend to emphasize abstinence or restraint. This interpretation is consistent with our findings, and suggests that explanatory systems more comprehensive than ours would need to consider simultaneously such social and personality determinants.

In the present study, the bridge between expectations of need satisfaction and the pattern of drinking behavior was shown to involve the subjectively defined functions of alcohol. The data support the position of Mulford and Miller (1959, 1960a, 1960b): definitions held about alcohol should influence its use. Focus upon the meaning of alcohol emphasizes individual idiosyncratic understanding rather than the general properties of alcohol or institutionalization of its use. Further work on variation in meanings clearly needs to be done, sampling diverse groups, sampling the different stages of the developmental trajectory to assess age-related changes, and sampling the variation in meanings attributed to alcohol when used in different situations.

The usefulness of the Personality Effects category of functions was strongly demonstrated in this study. It seems to be a worthwhile category of meaning to apply to college drinking. The Positive Social Functions category also proved useful. On the other hand, neither the Conforming Social nor the Psychophysiological Functions categories yielded consistent results. It is possible that neither of the latter categories is central to college-student use of alcohol or to this particular age level. Psychophysiological functions may, for example, increase in appropriateness in middle or late-middle age. Further research on drinking functions seems likely to prove fruitful.

Our study represents a start in the direction of relating personality factors to variations in the use of alcohol among youth of college age. Since previous research on personality and drinking behavior has not proved too successful, some degree of encouragement is to be taken from the support generated by the present findings.

ABSTRACT

The hypothesis that alcohol use may serve as an alternative behavior for the attainment of goals otherwise unattainable or for coping with the failure to attain valued goals was studied. The subjects were 38 men and 50 women (mean age 19.2 years) from sophomore-level psychology classes at the University of Colorado who volunteered to participate in a drinking study. Two areas of need satisfaction thought to be central for college students were investigated: achievement and affection. Expectations of attaining satisfaction in these areas were measured by means of a 30-item questionnaire. Test-retest reliability of the questionnaire was above .90, and significant correlations with external criteria of achievement and affection provided validity evidence. Drinking behavior was assessed by questionnaire in small groups of 20: men reported greater intake and more drunkenness and drinking-related complications.

Analyses of the relationship between expectations of need satisfaction and drinking behavior lent initial support to the hypothesis that the lower the expectations of need satisfaction, the greater the recourse to alcohol and alcohol-related consequences, especially among women. Subgroup analyses considering both need areas simultaneously provided additional support; the group with low expectations in both need areas had the highest drinking behavior scores; results were more consistent among women.

The functions attributed to alcohol use were then studied. A list of meanings or psychological functions of drinking was constructed comprising four separate categories: positive-social, conforming-social, psychophysiological and personality-effects functions. Significant negative relationships were obtained between expectations of need satisfaction and the degree to which personality-effects functions were attributed to the subjects' use of alcohol. Results were clearest in women. The degree to which personality-effects functions characterize alcohol use was shown to relate to amount of intake, drunkenness and complications, especially in women.

The study has provided evidence for linking low expectations of need satisfaction to patterns of drinking behavior among college youth. It has also shown that the link is mediated by the psychological functions attributed to alcohol use. The evidence supports the view that drinking may serve as an alternative means to goal attainment or as a way of coping with failure to attain valued goals.

6-3

Imbalance in Need Structure and Maladjustment[1]

RICHARD JESSOR, SHEPHARD LIVERANT, and SEYMOUR OPOCHINSKY

4 studies are reported which replicate the test of the hypothesis that extreme imbalance within a need structure is associated with poorer adjustment. The Rotter Incomplete Sentences Blank (ISB) was the adjustment-maladjustment measure. Imbalance in need structure was measured by Liverant's Goal Preference Inventory which assesses the relative strength of Affection and Recognition needs. Extremely imbalanced and extremely balanced need groups were compared on ISB scores in each of the 4 independent studies. All results were in the predicted direction, with 11 out of 16 comparisons statistically significant. Within the limitations of the measures, the studies provide support for the hypothesis that a structural characteristic of a personality need system—extreme imbalance—is associated with poorer adjustment.

The aim of the present researcn has been to coordinate adjustment-maladjustment to a characteristic of the need structure of an individual. Four separate and independent studies, modified replications of each other, will be reported. The general hypothesis has been that where the structure of needs is such that one need is prepotently stronger than other needs in that structure, the index of maladjustment will be higher than in the condition where there is relative balance among needs in the structure.

Although this hypothesis is compatible with several interpretations, the reasoning which led to its development and testing in the present context was that an overvalent or prepotent need would dominate the goal oriented behavior of an individual and lead him to seek goals relevant to the strong need in all or most situations, including situations in which such goals are not considered by others to be socially appropriate or even potentially available. The consequence of such a process over time would be: conflict, since prepotent goal seeking is at the expense of other needs; frustration, since goals are often sought in situations where

[1] Financial assistance from the University of Colorado Council on Research and Creative Work and Grant 3M-9156 from the National Institute of Mental Health, United States Public Health Service, is gratefully acknowledged. The following persons have provided invaluable assistance in scoring protocols or in the statistical analyses of the data from the various studies: Theodore Graves, Lee Jessor, Jaswant Khanna, Laurie MacTavish, Sandra Nugent, and Robert Titley.

From *Journal of Abnormal and Social Psychology*, 1963, 66, 271–275. Copyright 1963 by the American Psychological Association and reprinted by permission of the authors and the publisher.

they are unavailable or unlikely (e.g., seeking affection in a college class-room situation); and social rejection, since interpersonal reactions to inappropriate goal seeking (e.g., seeking recognition in social affection situations) would ultimately tend to be negative. This general reasoning follows from Rotter's (1954) Social Learning Theory, and the procedures employed to test the hypothesis were developed more or less system-atically within the framework of that theory.

METHOD

Four separate studies have been carried out over the past 5 years, each employing the same measuring instruments and general procedure, with minor modifications.

Maladjustment Measure

The Rotter Incomplete Sentences Blank (ISB), college or high school form where appropriate (Rotter & Rafferty, 1950; Rotter, Rafferty, & Lotsof, 1954), was the measure of adjustment-maladjustment in each study. The ISB is a well-standardized instrument with established reli-ability and validity for discriminating, among students, maladjustment leading to clinical referral or clinic self-presentation. It consists of 40 stems, completions to each of which are scored on a scale from 0 to 6 with higher scores being assigned where completions indicate con-flict, feelings of isolation, and low expectation of success. Interscorer reliability (above .90) is easily obtained even among undergraduate student scorers trained only by instructions and examples in the ISB manual (Churchill & Crandall, 1955). In the present research interscorer reliability was either directly assessed, or scoring was done by a psychologist whose interscorer reliability had been previously estab-lished. In all cases, Pearson product-moment r's between scorers, for total ISB score, were above .95.

Measure of Need Structure

The Goal Preference Inventory (GPI), a forced-choice procedure in which behavioral referents from different need areas are paired into items, was used in all four studies. The original version of this in-ventory consisted of 120 items made up into six sub-scales measuring *relative* strength of two major needs, Recognition and Love and Affec-tion. These two major needs were constituted from four lower-order needs: Academic Recognition (ACR) and Social Recognition (SOR) on the one hand, and Academic Love and Affection (ALA) and Social Love and Affection (SLA) on the other. Referents for each of these four needs, when paired against each other, yield the six subscales men-tioned above. The full development and construct validation of this inventory by Liverant (1958) is described in his monograph, and this form of the inventory was used in Studies I, II, and III. Subsequently, the GPI was revised to eliminate the Academic Love and Affection need, which resulted in a 60-item inventory comprised of only the three remaining lower-order needs (ACR, SOR, and SLA) which, when paired against each other, yielded three subscales. This revision was then modified further, primarily in wording of the items, to make it suit-able for students in a small town high school, the subjects in Study IV.

Need structure in these studies, then, refers to relations *among* those needs measured by the GPI. Clearly, the GPI measures only a small number of needs, and structural relations among these few needs may not represent characteristics of the overall need structure. Nevertheless, the needs dealt with by the GPI are central ones and are particularly pertinent to student life and to this age range. It was, there-fore, deemed satisfactory as a partial assessment of need structure for a student group.

The procedure of identifying subjects with a prepotent need was similar but not identical in the four studies. Generally the procedure involved administering the GPI to a large sample of subjects and then, from the distribution of scores, selecting three comparison groups—a group scoring extremely high on need for Academic Recognition (ACR group); a group scoring extremely high on need for Social Love and Affection (SLA group); and a group scoring relatively in the middle range, i.e., having ACR and SLA scores about equal (Balance group). It should be clear to the reader that scoring high on one need auto-matically lowers the scores on one or more of the other needs by virtue of the pairing which occurs in forced-choice measures. The cri-terion of extremeness of score was generally a score 1 standard deviation or more from the total sample's mean score on one or on several subscales. The criterion for balance of needs was generally a score, for each need, within + and − 1 standard deviation from the total sample's mean for that need. In all studies, efforts were made to maximize the separation between extremeness and balance by selecting the most extremely imbalanced subjects and the most extremely bal-anced subjects. The success in this effort varied, of course, with the size of the original sample to which the GPI was administered in each study.

When extreme-need groups and a balance-need group were estab-lished in each study, all subjects in these groups were administered the ISB. Scores on the ISB were then compared among the groups. The specific hypothesis in all studies was that ISB scores for all extreme-need groups (irrespective of the content of the extreme need) would be *higher* than ISB scores for the comparable balance-need group.

Subjects

In Study I, the GPI was administered to 283 students in an intro-ductory psychology class at the University of Colorado. In Study II, the GPI was given to 153 students in introductory psychology at Ohio State University. In Study III, the GPI was administered to 931 students in an introductory psychology class at the University of Colorado. In Study IV, the GPI was administered to 68 juniors and seniors in a small high school in southwestern Colorado. (This group was made up of

Anglo-Americans, Spanish-Americans, and Indians.) The size and sex breakdown of the extreme-need and balance-need groups established in each study will be shown in the next section.

RESULTS

Study I
The Academic Recognition (ACR) extreme group was composed of subjects scoring 1 standard deviation or more above the mean when Academic Recognition was paired with Social Recognition, Academic Love and Affection, and Social Love and Affection and, at the same time, scoring less than 1 standard deviation above the mean on each of the three remaining need areas, SOR, ALA, and SLA. Likewise, the Social Love and Affection (SLA) extreme group was composed of subjects scoring 1 standard deviation or more above the mean when Social Love and Affection was paired with Academic Recognition, Social Recognition, and Academic Love and Affection and less than 1 standard deviation above the mean on each of the three remaining need areas. The balance group is established when ACR = SLA (Subscale III) and when scores are between + and −1 standard deviation from each of the means on the other five subscales. The results of this analysis are shown in Table 1. The Mann-Whitney *U* test was used in assessing results in all four studies and all *p* levels reported are for one-tailed tests.

On this analysis, although all differences are in the predicted direction, only two of the four comparisons yield statistically significant support for the hypothesis.

Study II
A replication was carried out at Ohio State University as part of a larger project. Because of requirements stemming from the larger project, only male subjects were used. The criteria for group selection are identical to those used in Study I. The results are presented in Table 2. Again, only the comparison with the ACR group is significant.

Table 1   Comparison of Extreme Groups with Balance Groups on ISB Scores

	ACR		BALANCE		
SEX	M	N	M	N	U
Females	134.6	13	121.8	12	37.5*
Males	132.9	9	121.4	10	18.5*
	SLA		BALANCE		
Females	127.6	10	121.8	12	44.5
Males	128.1	8	121.4	10	30

* *p* < .025.

Table 2   Comparison of Extreme Groups with Balance Groups on ISB Scores

	ACR		BALANCE		
	M	N	M	N	U
	132.4	10	121.2	8	17*

	SLA		BALANCE		
	121.9	10	121.2	8	39.5

* $p = .025$.

Study III

The large population ($N = 931$) administered the GPI in this study permitted somewhat more stringent criteria of selection of the various groups. Here the procedure was to compose the ACR extreme groups from subjects scoring 1 standard deviation or more above the mean when ACR was paired with ALA and SLA and, at the same time, scoring close to the mean on the remaining subscales. Likewise, the SLA extreme group was established as scoring 1 standard deviation or more above the mean when SLA was paired with ACR and SOR and scoring close to the mean on the other subscales. The balance group is established when ACR = SLA and when scores are close to the mean on the other five subscales. The results of this analysis are shown in Table 3.

These data provide strong support for the hypothesis that the index of maladjustment will be higher where need structure involves an extremely prepotent need than where need structure is extremely balanced. All differences were statistically significant in the predicted direction. This

Table 3   Comparison of Extreme Groups with Balance Groups on ISB Scores

	ACR		BALANCE			
	M	N	M	N	U	z
Females	145.4	14	125.4	16	55***	—
Males	142.1	16	130.7	15	52***	—

	SLA		BALANCE			
Females	140.0	23	125.4	16	115.5**	1.96
Males	140.9	8	130.7	15	33*	—

* $p = .05$.
** $p = .025$.
*** $p < .01$.

study provides the strongest confirmation of the hypothesis of any of the studies reported in this paper.

Study IV

A final investigation of the hypothesis was made possible by the availability of the relevant measures as part of a larger community study. The GPI used in this investigation consisted of the revision described earlier, a form including only three subneeds—Academic Recognition, Social Love and Affection, and Social Recognition. Each is paired against both of the others: ACR versus SOR, ACR versus SLA, and SOR versus SLA. The score for any single subneed is based, then, upon 40 items. Since the total sample to which the GPI was administered was so small in this study ($N = 68$), the establishment of extreme and balance groups was handled in a less stringent way. All students obtaining a score 1 standard deviation or more above the mean on *any* of the three subneeds measured by this form of the GPI were considered to have an extreme need. All other students were considered to have balance among the three needs. Results of this analysis are shown in Table 4.

Again, all differences are as predicted and those for males alone and for the combined sexes are statistically significant. Further analysis was made by breaking down the combined extreme need group into the separate extreme needs and comparing each of these groups with a more refined balance group. The latter was constituted of those students whose scores on all three need areas were within .5 of a standard deviation, or less, of the respective mean for each need. These results are shown in Table 5.

DISCUSSION

The hypothesis which was independently examined in four separate studies reported in this paper was that a substantial departure from balance in a structure of needs or motives will be associated with a higher level of maladjustment (or a lower level of adjustment). Given the measures employed, the results are generally supportive of the hypothesis.

Table 4 Comparison of Extreme Groups with Balance Groups on ISB Scores

Sex	Extreme ACR, SLA, and SOR		Balance		U	z
	M	N	M	N		
Female	137.2	15	136.4	16	—	—
Male	131.8	14	124.0	23	97.5	1.82*
Combined	134.6	29	129.1	39	433.5	1.64*

*$p \leq .05$.

*Table 5   Comparison of Extreme Groups with Balance
Groups on ISB Scores*

| | EXTREME | | BALANCE | | |
MEASURE	M	N	M	N	U
ACR	131.1	11	126.0	14	52.5*
SLA	139.5	10	126.0	14	29.0***
SOR	133.3	8	126.0	14	31.5**

* $p = .10$, approximate.
** $p = .05$.
*** $p < .01$.

From this final analysis it is clear again that all differences are in the expected direction, and two out of the three are statistically significant. Although not all the predicted differences were statistically substantiated, all showed differences in the expected direction, and 11 out of 16 comparisons did reach an acceptable level of statistical significance.

A closer analysis of the data suggests, however, that the *content* of the need may not be entirely irrelevant to our findings. The significant relationships within Studies I and II are entirely accounted for by the extreme ACR groups. None of the SLA comparisons is significant. While this observation does not hold up at all in Studies III and IV, it is worth speculating upon for a moment.

The greater likelihood for ACR dominated college students to have higher maladjustment scores than SLA dominated students may be a function (at least in part) of the differential reinforcements provided by their respective college cultures. That is, the culture at large state universities is perhaps more accepting of the person who is strongly affection oriented, even in achievement-demand situations, and relatively less accepting of one who pursues academic recognition goals at the expense of social interaction. Another possible explanation for the higher maladjustment scores of academically oriented college students may lie in the ISB scoring system itself. A review of the sentence completions suggests that the SLA dominated students say, to a greater degree, that they like people and tend to give brief and socially conforming answers (responses which yield low scores), whereas the ACR dominated individuals tend to be more introspective and less socially conforming in their responses.

The overall conclusion to be reached from the data, despite the foregoing, is that there is a relationship between need *structure* and maladjustment within the limited assessment of need structure and maladjustment made in this research.

Even though small *N*s were used, it is supportive of the selection procedure employed to find that in most instances the mean ISB scores of the college balance groups are below the means of the normative sample established by Rotter and Rafferty (1950) (females = 127.4, males

$= 127.5$), whereas the means of the extreme groups tend to be above the norms. Also of interest is that in Study III, wherein the most stringent criteria were employed, all of the extreme-need groups had mean ISB scores higher than the maladjustment cutoff point of 135 suggested in the ISB manual for the most efficient discrimination of students in need of counseling.

The higher scores of all groups selected from the high school population relative to the normative high school sample (Rotter, Rafferty, & Lotsof, 1954) (females $= 116.9$, males $= 120.9$) may well reflect the unusual ethnic composition and lower socioeconomic level of this group compared to the middle-class suburban high school subjects used in establishing the norms.

A final caution should be offered perhaps. Our measures suggest a relation between a structural characteristic of a need system—imbalance—and a particular index of adjustment-maladjustment. The implications of such a relationship are, on the face of it, neither good nor bad, and one should be wary of applying value judgments. Need-imbalance may be as much a source of creative accomplishment, despite feelings of frustration and rejection, as it is of personality debilitating maladjustment as that term is used in common parlance.

6-4	*Electroconvulsive Therapy: A Social Learning Theory Interpretation*
	ROBERT R. DIES[1]

The literature concerned with the various aspects of electroconvulsive therapy (ECT) is as controversial as it is voluminous, with reports ranging from extreme skepticism to enthusiastic support. The contradictions are due largely to inadequately designed studies, notable for their independence of theory: they are seldom derived from any theoretical framework and only infrequently is there any attempt to integrate results into a

[1] The author is indebted to Julian B. Rotter, Ph.D., for his encouragement and helpful comments. Special thanks go to J. Herbert Hamsher for major suggestions with regard to content and for constructive criticisms throughout the preparation of the paper, and to his wife, Caroline, for valuable assistance during the later stages of writing.

meaningful and systematic model. This lack of theoretical orientation has forced the adoption of strictly empirical approaches to the selection of psychometric techniques and to the interpretation of results.

Difficulties in objective assessment of clinical status are partly responsible for the confusing state of the literature on ECT. Current nosological terminology lacks sufficient precision for purposes of comparing results of treatment, and diagnostic criteria vary considerably among psychiatrists. Moreover, evaluations of clinical change following treatment are lacking in standard and reliable methods of assessment. Until comparatively recently there has been insufficient attention devoted to the initial planning of investigations to allow for the application of appropriate statistical techniques and the avoidance of potential pitfalls (Roberts, 1959).

Many of the earlier experiments submitted as evidence for psychological changes after ECT fail to satisfy even minimal methodological standards; were only those with adequate experimental designs considered, the number included would be remarkably small. Ironically, concomitant with increased research sophistication in this area has been a dwindling interest in ECT as a method of treatment and as an area of psychological investigation. In consequence, no appreciable increase in well designed and controlled studies is evident in recent years.

Numerous rationales have been offered to explain the action of ECT, but with the paucity of directly relevant contributions from the basic sciences, theoretical speculations have been of meager assistance in understanding its fundamental operation (Gonda, 1964). Most explanations of ECT rely heavily upon psychoanalytic theory, focusing upon presumed intrapsychic phenomena and motivational processes usually regarded as lying outside the realm of awareness. Consequently, few attempts are made to integrate many of the findings on ECT into any systematic theoretical explanation. With the exception of diagnosis the many factors associated with effectiveness of treatment are not considered; nor is attention given to the various aspects of change occasioned by shock. In recent years, however, the emphasis upon motives in general psychology theory has decreased and an accent on cognitive variables has increased (Sanford, 1963). Accompanying this stress on cognition has been an accent on consciousness and contemporaneous environmental determinants of behavior as opposed to unconscious processes and to historical or developmental antecedents of action. Because of these recent changes, typical psychological accounts of the operation of ECT have become increasingly outmoded.

A SOCIAL LEARNING THEORY INTERPRETATION

It has become customary to single out one or another psychological phenomenon which is most conspicuous during treatment and to develop a rationale for ECT on this basis. The search for a single factor grossly oversimplifies the treatment process. That one or two features are more prominent cannot be denied, but this does not justify ignoring the totality of the treatment procedure. A social learning theory analysis emphasizes the complexity of behavior while isolating some of the numerous variables that need to be recognized in any attempt to account for change due to ECT.

Social learning theory (Rotter, 1954) focuses on the interaction of the individual with his meaningful environment and on the instrumental behaviors used by the person to attain satisfaction or to avoid frustrations. The theory utilizes three basic constructs to understand behavior. The first of these is *behavioral potential*, which is the potentiality of any behavior's occurring in any given situation as calculated in conjunction with the anticipation of reinforcements. *Expectancy*, the second construct, is defined as the probability held by the individual that any specific reinforcements, or set of reinforcements, will occur in a given situation, as the result of his behavior. Expectancy is presumed to be independent of the value or importance of the reinforcement. *Reinforcement value*, the third basic construct, is the degree of preference an individual maintains for any reinforcement, assuming the possibility of occurrence of this and other reinforcements to be equal. Rotter stated, ". . . the potentiality of a given behavior or set of behaviors to occur in some specific situation is dependent on the individual's expectancy that the behavior will lead to a particular goal or satisfaction, the value that satisfaction has for him, and the relative strength of other behavior potentials in the same situation [Rotter, 1954; p. 59]." The psychological situation is given a major role in the theory and is essential to all behavioral predictions.

In social learning theory terms, ECT can be characterized as having a decidedly negative reinforcement value. It is suggested that as treatment progresses, essentially two processes are operative. First, expectancy for the negative reinforcement (i.e., punishment) increases as a function of repeated exposure to shock. Secondly, expectancy for punishment becomes associated with those additional reinforcements resulting from shock, namely the profound but transient disorientation (Fetterman, Victoroff, & Horrocks, 1951; Huston & Strother, 1948; Kalinowsky & Hoch, 1952; Zubin, 1948) which leads to a variety of cognitive (Stone, 1947) and perceptual and motor disturbances (Campbell, 1961) as the patient's heightened perplexity limits his ability to understand and/or to attend to events that nontreated patients ordinarily comprehend. Not only do the confusion and painful feelings of helplessness initially carry a negative reinforcement value, but the effects of shock accumulate, thus increasing the total negativity associated with ECT. Therefore, while more and more negative reinforcement values become attached to the treatment complex, expectancy for punishment in the situation increases.

In various ways the patient learns that ECT has been recommended for him because of his pathological behavior; this is why he has been hospitalized and selected for treatment and why he is so closely observed by the hospital staff. It is communicated to him by the psychiatrist and other personnel, as well as by his general culture, including his fellow patients, that his symptoms are generally unacceptable and must therefore be eliminated. In many and often subtle ways he discovers that getting along in the hospital requires changes in his behavior; this is conveyed dramatically and forcefully by electric shock. The constant feedback concerning the pathological implications of his behavior leads to an increased expectancy that demonstration of symptoms will result in punishment. Kalinowsky and Hoch (1952) observed, for example, that fear increases during the series of electric shocks. As this expectancy for punishment increases, the relative behavior potential for alternative and more adjustive actions in the individual's response hierarchy likewise increases as a result of the greater expectancy that these alternative behaviors will lead to satisfaction or at least to avoidance of shock. Thus, the maladaptive behaviors eventually tend to diminish as the patient attempts to improve his conduct. Fear of treatment has often been considered an important motivation for the patient to eliminate pathological behavior (Crumpton, Brill, Eiduson, & Geller, 1963; Gallinek, 1956). Such symptom reduction will depend, of course, on the specific adjustive behaviors available to the patient, on the cues he picks up concerning the appropriateness of alternative actions, and on the expectancies he holds for subsequent reinforcements. One method available to avoid negative reinforcements is to conform with hospital routine and demands to cooperate, to refrain from complaining and to eliminate undesirable conduct. Conformity in this situation represents protective action designed to avert expected punishment. The degree to which the patient changes his behavior influences ratings of psychiatric improvement and thus accounts for some of the favorable findings due to ECT noted in the literature (Staudt & Zubin, 1957).

Prior to a series of electroconvulsive shocks, Janis (1950a) obtained from both experimental and control subjects a substantial sample of personal memories. His structured interview covered a wide variety of recent and remote experiences and required rather detailed descriptions. Approximately 4 weeks after termination of ECT, patients were given the same interview and asked to repeat their histories. Failure to recall earlier statements led to increasingly specific questions designed to elicit this material. Results demonstrated more clear cut instances of retroactive amnesias in the ECT group. Interviewing some of the subjects in the treatment group 4 months later, Janis discovered that most of the original failures of recall were maintained. While amnesias were found for experiences occurring at almost all periods of patients' lives, loss of memory appeared to be concentrated on events which had taken place during the 6 months immediately preceding treatment. Other investigators have also discovered that memories for recent experiences are more susceptible to the effects of ECT than are memories of more remote events (Abse, 1944; Campbell, 1961; Lowenbach & Stainbrook, 1942; Zubin & Barrera, 1941). Findings contradictory (Bogoch, 1954; Worchel & Narciso, 1950) to this observation may be explained by the use of very brief post-treatment test periods in these studies. Janis found that the more recent memories related primarily to the patients' symptoms, events associated with the onset of the disturbance and conditions leading to hospitalization. He concluded that recall failures were likely to involve experiences which tend to arouse anxiety, to stimulate guilt feelings and to lower self-esteem. One plausible interpretation of these selective, retroactive amnesias would consider the differential expectancies of the patients in the two interview sessions. It seems likely that in the first interview patients expected that admission of pathological behaviors would lead to therapeutic attention and were, therefore, more willing to be open. Also, the reinforcement value of disclosing symptoms was high compared to other strategies in the interview since such acknowledgement had presumably led to desirable results in the past or the individual would not have adopted these behaviors in the first place. In the second interview, however, a different set of expectancies was operative for the ECT patients. Revealing symptoms and conflicts was no longer a favorable mode of action since this had recently led to a strongly aversive stimulus. In contrast to the untreated controls, patients in the ECT group had learned to avoid disclosure of undesirable behavior and thus to prevent punishment.

Examination of the comments of some of Janis' treatment patients support this interpretation. In the second interview, statements like the following were often observed: "I already told you that," "I don't want to remember," and "A person likes to forget the past." Although these statements appear to reflect deliberate manipulation, Janis concluded that there was no general tendency of patients to guard their amnesias. That is, patients sometimes actively looked for cues to enhance recall of forgotten material. This may indeed be the case, for according to Rotter (1954) it can readily be demonstrated that the directionality of the goals of human behavior frequently cannot be verbalized and that people learn many behaviors to avoid recognition, awareness or verbalization of their own motivations. Associations and ideas may serve as cues for expected punishment and their occurrence will likewise lead to avoidant behaviors. Breger and McGaugh (1965) have stated that there is no reason to assume that people can give accurate descriptions of the cognitive processes mediating much of their behavior any more than a child can give a description of the grammatical rules which govern the understanding and production of his language. Social learning theory conceptualizes expectancies as lying along a continuum of awareness or of potential verbalization. Thus, in some instances the avoidant behavior of ECT patients may be beyond their awareness while, at other times, they may be fully conscious of their defensive tactics. Occasionally, the defensive nature of their behavior may be clearly apparent to others. A not uncommon observation in psychotherapy with former ECT patients, for example, is the readiness with which they attribute memory failure to the effects of shock treatment, particularly when they are faced with stressful material.

Janis and Astrachan (1951) further found that ECT patients, as opposed to controls, were unable to answer a significantly large number of questions about their life histories, and when they could give an answer, their responses contained fewer details. The authors reported a statistically significant increase in reaction time for the ECT group in initiating production of memories. This last observation coincides with Lotsof's (1958) findings that the higher the expectancy for negative reinforcement, the longer the decision time. Similarly, Barthel and Crowne (1962) presented taboo words tachistoscopically and found that approval-motivated subjects, perceiving the task as involving social disapproval, employed more defensive or avoidant maneuvers. Their subjects delayed responses until they had arrived at an interpretation of the purpose of the experiment and what the consequences would be for them.

When Janis (1950b) used a word association test in a pre- and post-shock design, the treatment group exhibited significant increase in remote or idiosyncratic associations, stimulus repetitions and multiword responses. He concluded that the specific types of disturbances noted seemed to imply difficulty in maintaining the "task set" and a failure to produce the type of association ordinarily given in response to the test instructions. His interpretation of this failure was primarily in terms of an involuntary evasiveness on the part of his subjects. However, in addition to the nonverbalizable aspects of these behaviors, they may also be partially explained in terms of deliberate attempts to avoid anticipated negative consequences. Finally, Janis (1950c) examined changes in responses on several self-rating scales. Relative to his controls, the ECT patients evidenced greater decrements in feelings of anxiety and inadequacy, greater reduction in distressing memories, and a larger decrement in the admission of current symptoms, particularly those affective disturbances constituting the "depressive" syndrome. These findings are fairly consistent with those of studies using pre- and postshock administration of projective tests to demonstrate effects of ECT. For instance, Pacella, Piotrowski and Lewis (1947) have generalized that ECT results in the patient's improved capacity to be on his guard in disclosing his pathology. They reported that patients who experience a series of shocks are usually more controlled in manifesting their symptomatology. Similarly, Henry and Rotter (1956), using the Rorschach, found that when normal subjects were instructed that the test measured "sanity" they produced more "cautious" or inhibited responses.

Particular attention has been given to the series of investigations conducted by Janis since they are representative of many other studies drawing similar conclusions and are among the more adequately designed experiments. In interpreting his accumulated findings, Janis theorized about the possible role of post-treatment amnesias in producing affective changes. He suggested that, by partially eliminating from a patient's consciousness a substantial block of affectively laden memories, the post-ECT amnesias may be equivalent to a new mode of defense which has an effect similar to repression in facilitating the avoidance of disturbing feelings. By providing a new defensive process for fending off painful subjective states and thereby reducing the frequency and intensity of depressive reactions, the post-treatment amnesias may contribute to the relinquishment of pathological symptoms which have formerly served as a defense against intense affective responses. In this manner Janis attempted to account for the selective, retroactive amnesias produced by electric shock. Janis' collective findings are also readily accommodated within a social learning point of view. Stated simply, the behavior of ECT patients is explicable in terms of an attempt to adopt more acceptable forms of conduct and thereby to avoid responses which they have come to expect will lead to the "punishing" ECT. Thus, a social learning theory analysis addresses itself directly to the issue of the circumscribed or selective nature of memory failure, beyond those profound disruptions of general cognitive efficiency subsequent to shock which result from the patient's temporary confusion and disorientation. This analysis has a major advantage over the one offered by Janis since it provides a more systematic and operationally based theoretical framework.

Although pathological behaviors often lead to negative consequences, these outcomes are less unfavorable than those which the patient expects will result from more acceptable and realistic actions. In addition, Mowrer (1948) and Dollard and Miller (1950) have described why maladjusted individuals do not learn adjustive behavior automatically. Since they are characterized by avoidant behaviors, the very nature of their withdrawal keeps them out of situations where they might learn more adaptive responses. They thus continue to repeat avoidant behavior as a means of coping with the particular type of problem and never have the opportunity to learn alternative ways of behaving. According to Mowrer, symptoms also persist because the punishments to which they lead are delayed, and the two are therefore not associated by the patient. Such is not the case for ECT recipients, however; suddenly and forcefully they are confronted by a punishment directly associated with their symptoms. Here the symptomatic means of responding no longer served to prevent immediate punishing consequences but, on the contrary, elicits them. ECT functions as a negative stimulus to reduce the patient's expectancies for satisfaction derived from unrealistic behavior and, therefore, to change behavior potentials. If he is able, he adjusts his behavior to meet with this new threat, shifting his strategy to denial and repression instead of an admission of pathological behavior. The consequence (ECT) of his pathological behaviors has now become more negatively valued than the reinforcements the actions were originally developed to avoid. The observation that subconvulsive stimulations are generally less effective than complete shocks (Alexander, 1953; Berkwitz, 1939; Kalinowsky, 1959; Ulett, Smith & Goldine, 1956) is probably because of their less dramatic effects; the typical post-treatment disturbances do not ordinarily result and those reactions that do occur are far less intense and do not accumulate. Hence, the total expectancies and reinforcement values in the situation are altered significantly less.

Reduction in expectancies which have been built out of past experience is likely to eventuate in changed behavior only if there are alternative behaviors which are objectively more likely to lead to satisfaction. When a symptom is eliminated, the next most dominant set of responses in the response hierarchy will tend to occur. These patterns may or may not be deviant. According to Bandura and Walters (1963), if these behavior patterns are not deviant, removal of the symptom effectively completes the treatment. However, if the patient has learned few prosocial means of obtaining gratification, another set of deviant responses will result.

One consideration to which this leads is an examination of which patients benefit from ECT. That depressed patients improve most with ECT is not surprising (Kalinowsky, 1959); this is reportedly true for most forms of therapy and is consistent with the greater proportion of spontaneous remissions noted among depressive patients. Several factors can be hypothesized to account for the greater advantage of the affective disorders over the schizophrenias, neuroses and psychosomatic disturbances. In the depressions identifiable precipitating factors are more likely, the onset of the depression is typically more acute, and the duration of the disturbance prior to hospitalization is less prolonged. These factors have all been shown to be related to improvement (Arieti, 1955; Baker, Game & Thorpe, 1960; Gottlieb & Huston, 1951; Hobson, 1953; Rickles & Polan, 1948). Furthermore, depressives are characteristically more socially responsive than are schizophrenic patients and are, therefore, more likely to respond favorably to therapeutic intervention; schizophrenics, on the other hand, will more probably withdraw from and/or actively avoid such attempts. Finally, when recommended for ECT, depressive patients will more probably recognize that treatment is designed to eliminate their dysphoric mood. For patients carrying other diagnoses, symptoms will probably be more heterogeneous, less pervasive than is depression, and less urgently experienced; thus, symptoms are less clearly linked to treatment. That is, these patients will not as readily understand which behaviors to eliminate in order for them to be regarded as clinically improved. In addition, it is general knowledge in our culture that ECT as a treatment procedure is almost specific to depression.

The less severe a patient's maladjusted behavior and the shorter the period of time that it has constituted his mode of interaction, the more likely it is that he will benefit from any form of treatment. The chronicity of the illness is clearly, then, a major variable in the influencing of behavior potentials. Rotter has said, "As our experiences become repetitive in a given situation, our expectancy becomes stabilized and a new occurrence (e.g., ECT) has less effect in changing our behavior [Rotter, 1954; p. 176]." The more a patient has experienced satisfactions in the past, the easier it will be to arouse anticipatory responses toward gaining satisfactions in the future.

Other factors associated with the efficacy of ECT, i.e., adequacy of the environmental situation (Gottlieb & Huston, 1951) and marital and occupational status (Herzberg, 1954), are also understandable from purely a common sense point of view. ECT has no "magical" or unique effects; most factors associated with improvement from ECT are similarly related to benefit from other forms of treatment.

It has been noted that long term treatment effects of ECT have not been established (Staudt & Zubin, 1957). This seems explicable in terms of the failure to provide the patient with alternative solutions to his problems. According to Rotter,

One major problem in therapy, then, may be said to be that of lowering the expectancy that a particular behavior or behaviors will lead to gratifications or increasing the expectancy that alternative or new behaviors would lead to greater gratification in the same or similar situations. In general learning terms we might say we have the choice of either weakening the inadequate response, strengthening the correct or adequate response, or doing both [*Rotter, 1954; p. 338*].

As a therapeutic agent ECT seems clearly to effect a weakening of the inadequate response; the focus in treatment is not on increasing the expectancies that new and adjustive forms of behavior will lead to satisfaction. The patient is punished for his pathology and the psychological rug is virtually pulled out from under him. Upon release from the hospital the patient usually encounters the same environment in which his pathology developed. Without alternative solutions it is to be expected that many patients will again develop the same symptomatic methods of responding. To the extent that other forms of treatment are carried on concurrently with ECT, however, the less likely will the focus be solely upon eliminating undesirable behaviors. Traditional psychotherapy, for instance, will generally serve a complementary function by emphasizing the acquisition of more adjustive and socially appropriate responses, which ECT has failed to provide. This broader conception of treatment should yield more positive results.

This analysis has incorporated the major findings in the literature on ECT into a single theoretical framework. The comprehensiveness and flexibility of a social learning theory approach represent its most important advantages over others in the area. It has in common with many theoretical accounts of the operation of ECT an interpretation of treatment as a series of negative reinforcements, but it provides a more thorough analysis of the treatment complex based upon a more elaborate and systematic theoretical model. In contrast to previous approaches, the orientation offered here gives greater weight to contemporaneous factors, both those directly associated with treatment and those environmental factors influencing the patient's conception of his psychological status. The social learning theory interpretation resorts not to vague, ambiguous and untestable concepts, but to common sense and to a consistent set of constructs which can be both defined and operationalized. Expectancies, reinforcement values, behavioral potentials, and psychological situations provide the variables for analyzing and understanding behavior. There is a greater emphasis upon consciousness as opposed to previous attempts to isolate unconscious processes and presumed intrapsychic phenomena to account for therapeutic change.

6-5 Success-Failure Reactions in Mentally Retarded Children

RUE L. CROMWELL[1]

This paper represents a brief review of a series of studies which apply Rotter's social learning theory constructs to mental retardation. The studies reported here are selected, because of theoretical significance, from a program of studies conducted at George Peabody College, Nashville, Tennessee. The research was initiated with one major assumption: that the mentally retarded child on the trainable and educable levels typically has a greater than usual amount of failure experience in his life situation. Following from this, one would expect from social learning theory that the retarded child would tend to have a lower generalized expectancy for success.

As may be seen in Figure 1, the assumption is one of overlapping,

[1] Based on a paper presented March 24, 1965, at the meetings of the Society for Research on Child Development, Minneapolis, Minnesota, and on a colloquium presentation in the Department of Psychology, University of California, Los Angeles, on April 1, 1965. Some of the material is summarized from Cromwell, 1963.

Most of the research and theoretical work reported here was carried out in the NIMH mental deficiency research training program at George Peabody College, Nashville, Tennessee.

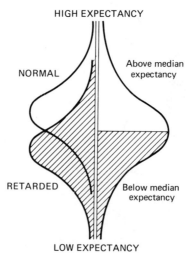

FIGURE 1. Illustration of expectancy levels in retarded and normal groups. (Cromwell, 1959)

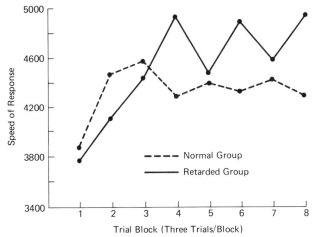

FIGURE 2. Mean (reciprocal) reaction-time performance under a series of predominantly success trials. *Note:* Speed of response measure is based on the reciprocal of the latency score. From Heber, 1957.

rather than discrete, differences between the mentally retarded and the normal child. Furthermore, since the research here is applied to mental retardation rather than being purely theoretical, groups are selected in terms of retarded-normal differences rather than generalized expectancy differences. This assumption led to three hypotheses upon which research was conducted. Each of these hypotheses received support from the investigations.

The first hypothesis, as depicted in the data graph of Figure 2, is as follows: When predominant success experience occurs, the retarded individual will tend to make greater initial gains in performance than the intellectually normal individual. In other words, the person with low generalized expectancy will increase his specific expectancy in that situation and show more gain than the person who already has a high expectancy for success when he enters the situation. It is worth noting here that this hypothesis had to be tested with a task which was maximally susceptible to motivational effects but not to practice effects. The reaction time task was chosen.

Another control measure concerned differences in level of initial performance. In order to control this variable adequately, a judge matched pairs of normal and retarded subjects on performance in the first trial block (three trials) without having access to their performance on subsequent trials. A few unmatched subjects from both groups were discarded. In this way, the normal and retarded subject groups began at an approximately equal level of performance and, as can be seen from Figure 2, diverged from each other in the predicted direction.

The other two hypotheses are illustrated in Figure 3. Each of these concerns the effect of failure in the mentally retarded. First, one would predict that the mentally retarded would have less change in magnitude

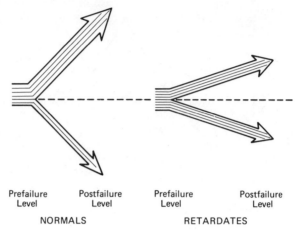

| Prefailure Level | Postfailure Level | Prefailure Level | Postfailure Level |

NORMALS   RETARDATES

FIGURE 3. Reactions to interpolated failure experience. An illustration of Gardner's hypotheses. (Gardner, 1958)

of response following failure. In common-sense language, this would result from the fact that he is expecting failure already. The other hypothesis is that the mentally-retarded will have less of a tendency than the normal to increase effort following failure. As it turns out (see Table 1), both the retarded and normal children frequently show a tendency to increased effort, but the normal children show it to a significantly greater degree.

To summarize briefly, initial experimental support for all three of these hypotheses was found during the early period of the research program.

Our initial research on expectancy level led us to take a closer look at the nature of symbolic reinforcement in mentally retarded and in normal preschool and kindergarten children. We wanted to understand more carefully what happened when the child was told "right" or "wrong" or was given a signal to indicate the correctness of his response. The reason for our questioning is as follows: Very often, when symbolic reinforcements were given, the child did not seem to see these reinforcements as relevant to the experimental task or to his own behavior on the task. Some children would just keep on playing or working with the task and were not concerned with the correctness or success of their activity.

Historically, theories such as those of Thorndike and Hull have raised

Table 1   Direction of Change in Performance Following Failure
           (Gardner, 1958)

	PERSONS INCREASING AFTER FAILURE	PERSONS DECREASING AFTER FAILURE
Normal Ss	37	3
Retarded Ss	25	15

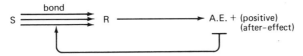

FIGURE 4. Illustration of Thorndike's reinforcement paradigm. (Cromwell, 1964)

the question of how words such as "right" and "wrong" assume reinforcing properties. As may be seen from Figure 4, these early explanations fall into the following format: An individual responds to a stimulus situation, and the reinforcement (referred to appropriately by Thorndike as the aftereffect) strengthens the bond between the stimulus situation and the subject's response. When neutral stimuli, such as spoken words, are associated with the positive aftereffect (drive satisfaction), they become reinforcers also.

The investigations reported here suggest that Thorndike, and later Hull, may have profited from giving more research attention to young children than to the mentally retarded. Their view, as I have indicated, tends to suggest that the aftereffect invariably strengthens the association between the stimulus situation and the subject's *own* response. As indicated in Figure 5, this may be viewed as only one of the alternatives, the path of which proceeds toward the lower right corner of the illustration. In actuality, what seems to happen very often with children on a lower developmental level is that the aftereffect (call it reinforcement or goal attainment, if you will) is often associated by the child with the behavior of other people or with other factors in the situation. In other words, the association of goal attainment with one's *own* behavioral effort is missing. Instead, as may be seen from the path moving to the upper right on the illustration, the aftereffect is often seen as a consequence of the actions of others.

With this framework of thinking, the conventional terms, "success" and "failure," appear to be ambiguous. In some situations, the child sees his own behavior as instrumental in the event. In other situations, he sees

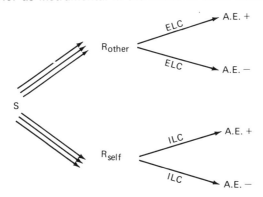

FIGURE 5. Illustration of a reinforcement paradigm wherein stimuli may be associated with responses of self or others. (Cromwell, 1964)

the teacher, the parent, other forces—even chance—as responsible for the outcome.

As it happens, there seem to be no words in our conventional language to distinguish between success from the reference point of the individual's behavioral effectiveness and success from the reference point of other factors, such as goal-attainment through the efforts of others. This led us to formulate a narrow formal definition of success and failure. *Success* was defined as an event of goal-attainment only when the individual viewed the event outcome as the consequence of his own control. *Failure* was defined as an event of goal-nonattainment as the consequence of his own ineffectiveness.

Schematically:

Success = f *(goal-attainment with internal locus of control)*
Failure = f *(goal-nonattainment with internal locus of control)*

The term "locus of control" (LC) was thus evolved along with these definitional revisions. Viewed in a developmental context, it was also thought of, and later proved to be, in close identity with the I-E (internal-external control of reinforcement) construct developed by Phares, James, James and Rotter, and Liverant.[1] Locus of control was formally defined as the degree to which an individual viewed the outcome of events as the consequence of his own control vs. the control of outside forces or chance.

Once it was assumed that the child conceptualizes some events in terms of success-failure and other events without regard to it, three major assumptions gave a basis for the next research study. *First,* it was assumed that the success-failure conceptualization of events would increase as the child grows older. Since success and failure concerns the child's conceptual system, one would expect this change to be more in relation to mental rather than chronological age. In other words, the child would see his own behavior as instrumental in the outcome of more and more events as he grows older in mental development.

Second, it is assumed that the success-failure conceptualization of the child takes on motivational aspects. That is, to the extent a child has developed success-failure conceptualization, he will strive for successful outcomes and avoid failure—regardless of the hedonistic (immediate) gratifications in the situation. Without the sufficient conceptualization of success and failure, the child will tend to choose the pleasant and avoid the unpleasant alternative, regardless of its success-failure connotations.

Third, it was assumed that the success-failure conceptual system could be operationally inferred simply through asking the subject whether he is in control of the outcome of various sample events. This is done with a brief questionnaire, called the Locus of Control Scale for Children.[2]

---

[1] Liverant's I-E scale, entitled Social Reaction Inventory, was obtained by personal communication and was never published in its original form because of his death.

[2] It should be acknowledged that both M. B. Miller and J. O. Miller did subsequent refinements and standardization work on the scale.

From this line of thinking, a number of hypotheses were deduced. First of all, there should be positive correlations among five variables relevant to success-failure conceptualization. These are: (1) mental age; (2) chronological age; (3) internal locus of control; (4) repetition choice of failure: the tendency to return to a previously failed rather than a previously succeeded task; and (5) delayed gratification pattern: the tendency to delay for a more attractive reward rather than accept an immediate less attractive reward. As may be seen in Table 2, these intercorrelations were borne out, except for the repetition choice variable.

Second, besides the positive intercorrelations (i.e., a general factor) for all five variables, there should also be a separate factor showing a positive relationship among the behavioral measures: (1) locus of control, (2) repetition choice, and (3) gratification pattern. This factor should occur if the three behavioral measures, independently of age, are related to success-failure conceptualization. As may be seen from column II in Table 3, this factor emerges, again with the exception of the repetition choice variable.

After some elaborate theoretical explanations were developed in order to explain why the repetition choice predictions were not borne out, two further studies (personal communications from E. C. Butterfield and T. M. McConnell) were done wherein the repetition choice variable was indeed significantly related to locus of control in the positive direction. This has led to suggestions that the mode of administration of the repetition choice task determines whether it is related to locus of control and other success-failure variables.

In general, the findings just mentioned gave some initial support to the theoretical formulations regarding the development of success-failure conceptualization in children.

Now that the developmental change had been examined, the next question was how internal locus of control (ILC) and external locus of control (ELC) children behave under positive, negative, and neutral learning climates. Concerning this question, the theoretical formulation would predict the following: (1) the ILC child, being more oriented toward

Table 2   Intercorrelation of the Developmental and Behavioral Measures Related to Success-Failure Conceptualization $(N = 89)$ (Bialer, 1961)

NUMBER	VARIABLE	1	2	3	4	5
1	MA	—	.63	.56	.31	.39
2	CA	.63	—	.37	.24	.20
3	LC	.56	.37	—	.06	.47
4	RC	.31	.24	.06	—	.02
5	GP	.39	.20	.47	.02	—

Mental age (MA); chronological age (CA); locus of control (LC); repetition choice (RC); and gratification pattern (GP).

success-failure than the hedonistic aspects of the situation, would be less influenced in general by the positive-negative nature of the learning climate. (2) The ELC child, on the other hand, being more influenced by the hedonistic aspects of the situation, would tend to be "up" with the positive climate and "down" with the negative climate.

As can be seen from Table 4, educable retardates were separated into ILC and ELC subjects. This was done by the Children's Locus of Control Scale (modified). The ILC and ELC subjects were divided into three groups. All groups were given a serial learning task, but they differed in the manner of reinforcement for correct and incorrect responses. The group with the positive climate received a chip for each correct response and nothing for incorrect responses. The group with the negative climate received nothing for correct responses but had one chip taken away for an incorrect response. Finally, in the neutral learning climate, the examiner did nothing for either correct or incorrect performance. As may be seen in Table 4, the ILC subjects were fairly uniform in performance, regardless of learning climate. On the other hand, the ELC subjects, while doing well under the positive climate, had a dramatic reduction in performance under the negative climate. Although not specifically predicted, the neutral climate, wherein the examiner was present but not giving feedback, brought a lowered performance in the ELC subjects.

When these same subjects were shifted in learning climate from positive to negative and from negative to positive, other theoretical hypotheses were examined. These are shown in Figure 6. Of particular note are the shifts from positive to negative climate for the two groups of subjects.

Table 3   A Rotated Factor Solution for the Variables Related to Success-Failure Conceptualization (Bialer, 1961)

Number	Variable	I′	II′
1	MA	.84	.10
2	CA	.74	−.10
3	LC	.57	.48
4	RC	.35	−.23
5	GP	.39	.54

Table 4   Serial Learning Performance (Mean Trials to Criterion) in Retardates as a Function of Locus of Control and Learning Climate (Miller, 1961)

Learning Climate	Internal LC	External LC
Positive (N = 18)	8.94	8.94
Negative (N = 18)	8.72	16.78
Neutral (N = 9)	9.22	15.89

These are shown in the first bar graph for the ILC and ELC subjects, respectively. As expected, the ILC subjects increased in performance. The ELC subjects, on the other hand, showed a nonsignificant decrease in performance. The two groups were significantly different from each other. Also of note is the response of the ELC subjects when shifting from a negative to a positive climate. Shifting into the hedonistically positive learning climate caused the ELC subject to increase greatly in learning performance.

Although other studies have tested other predictions—some with positive results, some with negative results—the studies described here have been the initial ones which had greatest theoretical significance.

One might now ask: What are the implications of these findings? Although extreme caution is needed in generalizing from laboratory findings, the following implications have at times been discussed:

In the area of personality, some tentative initial support has been obtained for the notion of a success-failure motivational system which develops with the increasing mental age of the individual. No evidence has been found that retarded children are qualitatively different in these personality factors than normal children. Evidence has been found, however, to suggest that qualitative differences occur in reaction to success-failure at different mental age levels—regardless of the intellectual status of the child.

In terms of psychodynamics, there is the suggestion that, since reaction to success-failure is acquired late in childhood, the critical period for the development of feelings of inadequacy or inferiority cannot come until this later period. On the other hand, phobias, compulsive reactions, and other phenomena not related to the success-failure motivational system could originate in this earlier period.

In terms of education, it is perhaps necessary to discuss the implications in terms of two current and opposing educational philosophies. One philosophy holds that the child should have continuously programmed success experience in order to obtain the optimal educational benefit from his classroom training. The other philosophy holds that high standards and high goals should be set for the child. The inevitable consequence is that the child will fail more often but, according to this philosophical position, will also achieve more. The theoretical formulation developed here would *reject both* of these philosophies, as stated in their simple forms. Instead,

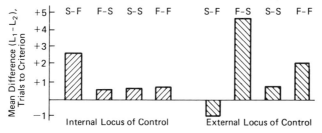

FIGURE 6. Shifts in serial learning performance (list 1 minus list 2) as a function of locus of control and shifts in learning climate.

the developmental level of the child would be emphasized as necessary information before deciding what to do with him. In particular, it would depend upon the development of his success-failure conceptual and motivational system. If the child is developmentally at a low level—that is, if he responds in the direction of external locus of control, etc.—then a program of continued success experience would be ideal for him. Indeed, according to the research evidence, his performance would be impaired if failure, or even the absence of feedback, was emphasized. One would expect this child to avoid such hedonistically negative situations.

On the other hand, if the child has progressed to a higher developmental level in his success-failure conceptual system—that is, if he has developed a greater feeling of internal control over his life situation—a moderate amount of failure (from the setting of high standards) would seem appropriate and even necessary. For one thing, the child with increasing ILC could learn to use failure as a cue to increase effort appropriately rather than to withdraw from the situation. Second, the failure could be used as a cue for flexible behavior modification. In this way, new and more successful responses may be acquired.

SUMMARY

A great number of retarded children, by virtue of their intellectual shortcomings, may be assumed to expect failure. Through making this assumption, support has been obtained for a number of theoretical hypotheses: (1) Continued success will bring greater initial performance gains in retardates than in normals. (2) Magnitude of reaction to failure will be less in retardates than in normals. (3) Increased effort following failure will occur more frequently in normals than in retardates.

During the research studies it was observed that children on a low developmental level did not always associate their own behavior with the reinforcement received. Through attempting to explain these findings, success and failure came to be defined only in terms of events where the individual sees his own behavior as crucial in determining the outcome.

With these new definitions of success and failure, it was then assumed, first, that success-failure conceptualization became evident in children only on more advanced developmental levels. Less developed children were viewed as being more prone to see the outcome of events along hedonistic dimensions. Second, it was assumed that success-failure conceptualization takes on motivational properties. Finally, it was assumed that success-failure conceptualization could be inferred operationally by asking the subject whether he is in control of various events. Thus the locus of control scale was developed and employed.

From these assumptions, certain successful predictions were made. Locus of control, repetition choice, and delay of gratification were predicted to be intercorrelated and to increase with age, especially with mental age. With these predictions, only the data in repetition choice was equivocal.

In a later study, internal locus of control children were shown to be fairly impervious to positive, negative, or neutral learning climates. External locus of control children, while doing as well as the internal group under the positive climate, performed much more poorly under the negative and neutral climates. This finding offered further support for the formulation that the "external" child is hedonistically oriented.

The implications from these studies emphasize that the level of development of success-failure conceptualization must be considered in understanding the personality dynamics and educative process of children.

PART 6: SUMMARY

The previous papers were intended to illustrate some of the possibilities for an SLT contribution to the study and understanding of psychopathological phenomena. There has not been a great deal of SLT research devoted primarily to issues within psychopathology. In a larger sense, of course, all SLT research is applicable to deviant behavior inasmuch as we do not postulate discontinuity between so-called normal and abnormal behavior. It is clear, however, that the SLT research that has been devoted to this area points to the feasibility of an SLT approach. It is hoped that this chapter will reinforce this feasibility.

Since the paper by Phares (6–1) provided a fairly lengthy overview of SLT conceptualizations of deviant behavior, this summary will be restricted to a discussion of the four papers reprinted earlier along with other SLT work which bears directly on psychopathology.

As noted earlier by Phares, a series of SLT investigations all provide evidence for the utility of the SLT view which equates anxiety with low expectancies for success in a valued need area or a high expectancy for punishment (Rotter, 1954; Rychlak & Eacker, 1962; Rychlak & Lerner, 1965; Phares, 1966; Phares, 1968b). Several studies, however, have carried this kind of analysis further.

For example, a recent book by Jessor, Graves, Hanson, and Jessor (1968) utilized SLT as a general personality framework with which to study deviant behavior in a triethnic community. Anglo-Americans, Spanish-Americans, and Indians in a single community were shown to have different rates of problem behavior. Applying the same theoretical concepts to three different ethnic groups in a single community, one finds a major implication to be that ethnicity has strong probabilistic implications. That is, although differences in values among the three groups were relatively minor, differences in expectations for the achievement of those values were quite important. Deviant behavior generally and drinking in particular seemed directly related to individuals' inability to achieve valued goals.

Again, we see the importance of the discrepancy between expectancies and reinforcement values in leading to deviant behavior.

Jessor, Carman, and Grossman (1968; 6–2) reached a similar conclusion with a college population. Drinking behavior is shown to be linked with the low expectation for achieving gratification in important need areas. This study also demonstrates that this linkage occurs in the light of both the availability of alcohol and the ability of alcohol to serve as a reinforcer.

A third study by Jessor and his colleagues, also reprinted earlier (Jessor, Liverant, & Opochinsky, 1963; 6–3), approaches maladjustment from a somewhat different point of view. Consistent with the point developed by Phares in his paper, these authors show that a very strong need is likely to lead to behaviors inappropriate to the situation, which in turn is likely to lead to rejection or other forms of negative reinforcement. Therefore, one can approach maladjustment not just in terms of a discrepancy between expectancy and reinforcement value but also in terms of an imbalance among needs. In either case, consequent behaviors are likely to lead to undesirable outcomes.

These studies, which are fairly molar and have provided very encouraging results, contrast sharply with one by Jessor and Hess (1958) which reports no relation between an incomplete-sentences measure of maladjustment and behavior on a level-of-aspiration task. The authors conclude that such a task may provide too restricted a sample of behavior (expectancy statements for the next trial). It also suggests that the more different the stimulus material is from the situations to which one is predicting, the less likely are we to show significant relations.

The paper by Dies (1968; 6–4) analyzes electroconvulsive therapy. Although this paper could just as easily be discussed in terms of SLT contributions to behavioral change, it does have particular implications for psychopathology as well. Dies not only shows that high expectancies for punishment through ECT can lead to a reduction in symptomatology. He also demonstrates how the acquired fear of ECT can also mediate inability to recall painful memories (memories that have become related to the punishment of ECT). In short, selective memory failures and improved adjustment following ECT may represent defensive reactions calculated to avoid responses that may lead to being shocked again. Thus, expectancies increase that such behavior will avoid the prospective punishment of ECT. As noted earlier by Phares, so-called symptoms are often a way of avoiding punishment. However, in this case, the symptoms themselves are directly and fairly immediately punished. This is perhaps why it is effective —it occurs immediately and is not delayed as is the punishment for symptoms in many situations.

Mosher (1968a) has discussed some similarities between the theories of Adler and Rotter. Parallels are drawn between such SLT concepts as freedom of movement and expectancies and Adlerian notions of feelings of inferiority and goals of superiority. Similarities between the concepts of distance and avoidance are also discussed along with the relation between high minimal goals and striving for unrealistic goals of superiority. Such an analysis provides us with insight into the continuity between a neoanalytic position like Adler's and the more behavioristic SLT formulations of Rotter.

Reactions both to frustration and threat have received recent attention. In the case of frustration, Ford (1963) hypothesized that the strength of reaction to goal-response blocking is an increasing function of expectancy for goal attainment. He found that failure produced an increase in the latency and a decrease in the force of response. Expectancy was non-monotonically related to increase in latency of response—Ss with intermediate expectancies showed the smallest increase. In two groups which differed in expectancy, the high group showed the greater increase in latency. In a study discussed earlier in Part 2, Mischel and Masters (1966; 2-7) showed that frustration of attainment of a goal increased the value of that goal. Both these studies indicate the utility of SLT by suggesting the importance of expectancies for goal attainment in mediating subsequent reactions to failure or goal blocking.

Several studies have utilized an SLT conceptualization of individual differences in attempting to understand responses to a threatening stimulus. For example, Barthel and Crowne (1962) showed that Ss with a strong need for approval differed in their responses to a tachistoscopic presentation of neutral and tabu words. Those Ss who perceived the task as one wherein social approval could be attained through rapid response tended to show a relatively low threshold for tabu words. Ss who categorized the task as one in which negative reinforcement could be averted by not reporting socially disapproved stimuli tended to show relatively high perceptual thresholds. Low need for approval Ss did not show any effects of task categorization.

The importance of such a study is twofold. First, it shows the interaction between needs and expectancies. Thus, avoidance behavior such as perceptual defense can be better understood by analyzing the effects of both expectancy and reinforcement value. Second, it provides an alternative to those views that, in one way or another, utilize an entitized or reified version of an unconscious. As emphasized by Phares earlier and demonstrated here, "repression" can be construed as a case where the individual has a high expectancy that an avoidance response will be rewarded. If he values approval and expects it to occur by giving socially desirable responses, he will fasten his attention on such cues in the situation. If he expects such approval to occur through speed of response, he will so respond and, in the process, report tabu words. Indeed, Barthel and Crowne report a high frequency of response-withholding on the part of Ss. This suggests that under proper conditions of interrogation (low expectancy for punishment), many Ss or patients may well give evidence of such blocking or response substitution.

In a similar vein, Efran (1963) found that Ss who felt reinforcement was not in their control (externals) tended to forget failures less frequently than Ss who felt responsible for attainment of reward (internals). In short, the latter tended to resort to forgetting as a defense against negative reinforcement. Lipp, Kolstoe, and Randall (1967) report a similar finding when using handicapped internals and externals on a tachistoscopic task. Likewise, Phares, Ritchie, and Davis (1968) noted that externals recalled significantly more threatening material than did internals. Recent work by Phares (1971) and by Phares, Wilson, and Klyver (1971) also indicates (1) that externals are more prone to use blaming behavior after failure and (2) that externals are more likely to lower the value they attach to a reinforcement following failure to attain that reinforcement.

It should be noted in this connection that the reported relations between internal-external control and anxiety are not clear. While relations are often significant (Watson, 1967; Rotter, 1966), they are also low. Further, as Rotter (1966) points out, studies of internal-external control and maladjustment have generally not found linear relations, and even the curvilinear relations appear to be highly complex. Indeed, Jessor *et al.* (1968) could find no relations between internal-external control and deviancy in their triethnic study.

Several studies have dealt with internal-external control in institutional populations. Wood, Wilson, Jessor, and Bogan (1966) report that designated trouble-makers in a correctional institution had higher external scores than did a control group. Cromwell, Rosenthal, Shakow, and Zahn (1961) suggest that schizophrenics answered questionnaires more in the direction of externality than did normals.

Kiehlbauch (1967), in a cross-sectional design, demonstrated that scores on the I-E scale (Rotter, 1966) follow an inverted U function over time in a population of reformatory inmates. That is, in the beginning of their sentences and near the end, inmates were relatively external. During the middle point of their sentences, their scores were relatively more internal. A special group, a work-release sample, which held jobs outside the reformatory prior to their release, did not show the rise in external scores as they neared the end of their sentences. These results were taken to show that the uncertainties of life both in the beginning and near the end of sentences are threatening and lead to an increase in externality. Such results need replication, however, in a longitudinal sample.

The foregoing studies suggest that further investigations of deviant behavior and internal-external control may be quite profitable. However, it is apparent that obtained relations will be quite complex and that it will be necessary to conceptualize deviancy in more specific terms.

Although relatively little work has been done with psychotic populations, a study by Lefcourt and Steffy (1966) bears mention. They found support for the hypothesis that process schizophrenics develop low expectancies for positive reinforcement in interaction with domineering mothers, while reactive schizophrenics develop low expectancies for positive reward with their overly dominant fathers. The particular merit of this study seems to reside in showing the efficacy of SLT terminology in the description of schizophrenic populations.

Cromwell's (1967b) paper reprinted earlier briefly describes a program of research that has applied SLT to a study of behavior in mentally retarded populations. Making particular use of the concept of generalized expectancies, Cromwell's research suggests that retardates have low generalized expectancies for success based on their history of negative reinforcement. This being the case, he is able to predict and verify hypotheses of greater initial performance gains in retardates than in normals following continued success, less reaction to failure in retardates, and greater increased effort in normals following failure. Also, he has utilized the concept of internal-external control to better understand the reactions of retardates following success and failure. Additional descriptions of this research program may be found elsewhere (Cromwell, 1959; 1963; and 1967a).

Such research is of great importance, since it takes mental retardation out of traditional constitutional or medical domains and demonstrates the importance of social learning in retardates. Specifically, it becomes apparent that the learning process is greatly affected (over and above questions of innate potentials) by reactions to success and failure. That is, level of performance in such children directly relates both to previous experiences and to the manner in which they construe such success-failure experiences.

7 | Applications to Psychotherapy and Complex Behavioral Change

INTRODUCTION

The organization of this section of the book departs slightly from that employed in the preceding sections. Six selections are presented; the sixth of these—Rotter's paper "Some Implications of a Social Learning Theory for the Practice of Psychotherapy"—serves as a summary of theory and research investigation in this area.

All the papers reprinted here emphasize the SLT point of view that personality change "in" and "out" of therapy is continuous and is not qualitatively different from change elsewhere. The mechanisms of change and the constructs describing the content of personality are the same across the entire range of human social interactions. "Therapy," "education," "attitude change" are only specialized instances of these interactions. Learning, as a mechanism, is not merely invoked to explain whatever changes may occur; rather, Rotter attempts to use the theory to suggest principles of therapeutic procedure (7-6). Although he suggests that the basic criteria of therapeutic practice should be its effectiveness and efficiency rather than purity of theoretical doctrine per se, in order to attain "effectiveness" and "efficiency" many practical questions must be answered. Whether these are questions concerning the processes or the outcomes of psychotherapy, and whether one attempts to answer the questions in a clinical context or in a laboratory analogue of the therapy situation, the SLT framework is a useful investigatory tool.

The first two papers in this section demonstrate the adaptability of SLT to a variety of procedures for looking at the processes of complex behavioral change. Marlowe (7–1) presents a case report formulated in SLT terms. Among other points, he illustrates the importance of conflict between a strong need and a low expectancy of obtaining satisfaction by means of constructive and socially mature behaviors, the role of the patient's excessively high goals for social approval, and the therapist's activity in encouraging and reinforcing more self-assertive behavior on the part of the patient.

In the second paper, Efran and Marcia (7–2) reinterpret Wolpe's desensitization procedure as both a means of preventing typical avoidant behavior and a means of changing S's expectancies about his own behavior toward the phobic object. Their strong experimental manipulation of subject expectancies does, indeed, produce as much reduction in phobic behavior as does a more standard desensitization procedure.

The next two papers deal with need for approval (Crowne & Marlowe, 1964) as a factor in verbal behavior which could influence the suitability of a chosen therapeutic procedure for a given patient. While Crowne and Strickland (1961) have found high-need-for-approval subjects to be more responsive to experimenter reinforcement than low-need-approval subjects, in a later study (7–3) they observe that high need for approval is also related to greater likelihood of premature termination from psychotherapy. Bates's (7–4) investigation clarifies the issue by controlling the social desirability of the verbal task the subject is required to perform. Responsive to reinforcement though the high-need-approval subject may be in other contexts, if the task involves making negative statements about himself, he manifests apparently resistant behavior.

The last paper, by Piper, Wogan, and Getter (7–5), is an attempt to explore the usefulness of the constructs of *expectancy* and *value* to conceptualize and to measure attitudes about therapy in order to predict whether patients will remain with the endeavor or terminate prematurely.

7-1

Social Learning Theory and Psychotherapy: A Case Study

DAVID MARLOWE

Rotter's SLT represents an attempt to formulate a systematic theory of human behavior. Consistent with the demands of modern theory building, Rotter has attempted to describe behavior with a single set of postulates and corollaries, thus avoiding, hopefully, the ambiguity and *ad hoc* creation of constructs characterizing earlier theory construction. This led Rotter to the belief that a psychological theory, to be meaningfully useful for valid prediction, should contain rigid formulations stated in a manner sufficiently general to explain and to predict all the diversities of psychological behavior: the infant's acquisition, for example, of the fear of hot stoves, and the changes that can occur in an adult in psychotherapy. For other than the physical and biological processes necessary for life, the theory holds that behavior may be viewed as the product of social learnings. Thus, a psychologist is interested in learned needs and learned methods of satisfying them; SLT is a theory of performance and acquisition of complex behavior.

The present paper will attempt to describe and to explain on the basis of SLT one type of behavior of interest to psychologists—the behavior of an adult in psychotherapy. It is intended to illustrate the techniques employed to "re-educate" a maladjusted man.

The patient was seen for 40 one-hour interviews, twice a week, in a VA Mental Hygiene Clinic. This was followed by 10 interviews on a once per week basis. Mr. R was a married, 32-year-old World War II veteran, with three children. He worked in his uncle's auto parts supply center. He was the fourth born of six children; the father died of septicemia when the patient was 14; his mother was still living.

Mr. R's initial complaint consisted of a remarkably generalized fear of making a fool of himself in social situations. He reported that he experienced considerable anxiety when he had to talk to customers or salesmen at work, when greeting friends on the street, when ordering from a waitress in a restaurant, and at social affairs (party, club meetings, etc.). In effect, his social life was close to nonexistent or else occurred at the expense of constant fear and anxiety, and perceptions of himself as being "stupid," "inadequate," and possibly heading for "insanity" and the mental hospital. Mr. R further stated during the first interviews that he wanted very much to have a "smiling, winning personality," that he wanted to be the confident, capable person who could do all the things they were trying to teach him at the Dale Carnegie course he was now attending (with no success).

Therapy based on SLT employs a historical approach insofar as it con-

This paper, written in 1957, is published for the first time in this volume. We are grateful for the author's permission to use it.

siders behavior the product of learned experiences or sequences of events. In addition, it holds that interpretation based on ivory tower speculation is less likely to have an effect on the patient's understanding and behavior than will interpretations based on concrete, actual events in the patient's life. Therefore, following the first few sessions where the patient elaborated the nature of his complaints and his present life situation, there was a series of interviews whose purpose was to discover the important conditions which led to learning of the present fears and maladaptive behavior. The therapist proceeded on the assumption that Mr. R's behavior was learned through interaction with the significant others in his life, particularly in regard to those acts which they rewarded or punished him for.

Mr. R's earliest memory was a situation occurring at the age of four. He was being visited by three cousins who "kidded" him. He describes these boys as "perfect, well groomed, nicely dressed, big and strong—I idolized them. I was weak and puny. It made me feel inadequate, not on a par with other children." One may abstract from this earliest memory, the already well-developed cross currents of Mr. R's style of life: the strong need (high reinforcement value) for social approval; the expectancy for rejection (low freedom of movement) because of physical and material shortcomings; and the high RV placed on belonging or love and acceptance. A major distinction between SLT and other theories should be restated at this point and brought into sharper focus. Psychoanalysis, for example, with its picture of *love* and *aggression* as derivatives of libido, would emphasize the instinctive basis for these needs. SLT, on the other hand, considers the need for love, the learned product of previous experience, and would seek to discover the specific incidents of reward and punishment which produced it and the techniques learned to obtain its satisfaction. More specifically, psychological needs may *first* arise as learned in relation to physiological drives. Very quickly, however, their strength and direction can be better predicted from their relationship to psychological goals rather than physiological drives. That is, needs are determined by external cues categorized by the person rather than by internal physiological conditions. The current situation of the person and his previous learning become the basis for predicting behavior. During this first "stage" of therapy then, the therapist (and the patient) seek to discover the significant situations, cues, expectancies and behaviors of the past.

R was highly motivated for therapy. He spoke freely and at length, was seldom resistive, and most eager to make progress. He described his mother as a punishing, rejecting person whose behavior was so nonloving that he often wondered "how could she be my mother". Only when he was sick does he recall his mother giving him love and attention. His father, in contrast, was described as "a great guy," who before his illness was always kind and attentive to R. His illness, however, led to frequent hospitalizations and considerable inroads on the amount of time he could spend with the children. When R was 10, a new child arrived who became the "family prize" and the "apple of his father's eye." The father was by now bedridden much of the time, and much taken up (so far as it was physically possible) with the new infant. R's uncertain feeling of being loved and accepted became even more intensified. Occasionally, he daydreamed of being somewhere else, and once stated in therapy that he had felt more secure at home when he was ill. An aunt, who was a favorite of his, once spontaneously commented to him, "You're always sick when I visit." Although he felt close to his next youngest brother, R was lonely and insecure at home. He came more and more to seek the love he thought he lost at home by becoming attached to adults in the neighborhood. A next door neighbor accompanied him to school on "open school day" as a substitute for his sick father. This man was described as "a great guy—like a father to me." He had a cousin who was bashful and whose social ineptness was discussed by the family. R became very self-conscious and wondered if the family discussed him in this way. Did people know, he wondered, that he also was shy and afraid of making a fool of himself with people? He began to worry about himself, about the things he could or could not do, and came more and more to feel isolated, unworthy of love and acceptance, and the subject of people's derisive talk.

In therapy, R made some remarks which suggested some hostility toward his father. He was, however, unable to admit *ever* feeling hostile toward his father. When he was 12, a family discussion about his father's illness led him to believe in a very vague, confused way that perhaps his father had syphilis. In junior high school a teacher commented that a certain football hero was in a mental institution because of syphilis. Later, the patient developed a syphilo-phobia which became extremely pronounced during his army service.

When R was 14, his father died. R was unable to describe his feelings at that time, although some of his remarks could be interpreted to indicate that in part his feeling was one of relief. Immediately following his discharge from the Army, the patient's fear of meeting people became so pronounced that he sought therapy at three different times. In each instance, the relationship was based on the patient's very marked dependency. He sought advice, "pep-talks," and closeness from his therapists. "They did not help me really"—but "they were great guys." R was unaware of the meaning of his behavior in therapy. He believed that a "sick man" was "entitled" to sympathy and attention from his doctor, wife, and friends. By now the patient was desperately trying to avoid social situations, especially those involving well-dressed persons whom he perceived as distant and authoritative. He understood that he brought the fears "on himself," that people were not evaluating him, but he was unable to prevent this anticipation and the resulting anxiety. He feared he would tremble or faint, that his voice would squeak and people would see him as weak, anxious, and a "schmo." At work, he feared his uncle, who had taken over his father's business. He felt his uncle was not warm or friendly, he feared he might be fired, he blamed himself for every business slump, and finally came to the VA for treatment.

During the 18 interviews while this material was being obtained, the therapist made occasional interpretations. These were usually in the form of asking direct questions which served to focus the patient on certain topics as important. Less frequently, mildly direct interpretations were made as to, for example, his use of illness to obtain love and acceptance, and his strong dependency needs. Two problems were left relatively untouched: his fear of syphilis, which he claimed had completely left him, and the indications that ambivalence might best describe his feelings toward his father. It is not inconceivable that R's fear of people and belief that they were always evaluating him involved the projected fear that people couldn't accept him because he had wished for his father's death. How those two "problems" were handled may further illustrate the SLT approach to psychotherapy. The therapeutic handling of these two topics reduces essentially to the questions: How detailed and in how much depth should the areas be discussed, and how direct should interpretations be? Other therapies, notably psychoanalysis, emphasize the cathartic basis of therapeutic progress, with a parallel importance placed on insight. Because man is held to be essentially irrational, it becomes necessary for the therapist to discover the "truth" for the patient and to help him accept these basic insights. Because neurotic behavior is seen as a derivative of repressed needs it becomes necessary to get things out in the open by "cleaning out the unconscious." SLT, on the other hand, emphasizes behavior, rather than the unconscious; it particularly emphasizes present-day alternatives available for more satisfactory living. The past serves only to provide illustrative material necessary to demonstrate to the patient the unreasonable basis for his present behavior. It is true that one can say analysis seeks to do the same. However, there is a fundamental difference; namely, how much and how long are what topics discussed, and toward what end? SLT has no preference for any particular "needs," be they sex, aggression, acceptance, or what not. In fact, SLT recognizes the wide latitude a therapist has in categorizing a patient's behavior. The theory makes explicit its awareness that different constructs can be used to describe the same behavior. The decision as to what is important involves a consideration of which particular expectancies in regard to anticipated outcomes the patient utilizes to "plan" his behavior in particular situations. This statement does not imply that the patient is always consciously aware of the determinants of his behavior; SLT accepts the existence of a continuum along which motivations exist which varies from nonverbalizable to readily discussed. For the most part, SLT considers as relevant material those problems whose discussion is likely to lead the patient to recategorize previous experiences so that his new understanding will lead to the increased expectancy that satisfaction can be obtained from behaviors other than the ones currently being used. Insights are "correct" if they are logically acceptable to the patient and they make a difference. That is, insight need not be "deep," incontrovertible, or all-explanatory; it need only make a difference in how the patient views his present situation and in leading to increased freedom for more mature behavior. How to interpret, like what is interpreted, involves similar considerations. Nothing is gained by convincing a patient that his motivations are aggressive or sexual if his common sense enables him to accept more easily an alternative explanation which in turn leads to changed expectancies. In fact, a law of least effort might apply here—that material is discussed and those interpretations made which lead to the maximum change while giving rise to the least amount of resistance.

Following this line of reasoning, the therapist elected not to explore further R's syphilo-phobia or his possible ambivalence toward his father. The fear of syphilis was no longer considered a problem by the patient in that he got "over it just before leaving the Army." R's possible ambivalence toward his father was the therapist's hypothesis based on rather minimal cues. The very vagueness and tentativeness of R's statements here suggested that considerable time would be necessary to overcome his "resistance" and that interpretations would not likely be consistent with his common sense. It was decided then that these areas would be rediscussed only should alternative procedures not lead to behavioral change.

Following this period when background material was obtained, the therapist's role became considerably more active. The 19th and 20th interviews could be said to have initiated the "second phase" of treatment; a detailed explanation was presented to R, pointing out the "reasons" for his current difficulties. In summary, R was told that his present difficulties were based on his failure to differentiate between his present life situation and his previous experiences. Believing himself to have lost the love of his parents as a child, and considering himself unworthy of people's acceptance as an adult, he engaged in behaviors calculated to make up for these defects. He avoided social situations to avoid being rejected and likened every contemporary event to some imagined rebuff he suffered in the past. He became overly sensitive to everything he did and believed others were similarly critical and evaluative. To get others to like him became a fixed idea, but anxiety and "anticipation" led to inevitable "failure." He was pursuing an impossible goal—"everyone ought to like me." It was pointed out that he had misinterpreted the meaning of many social situations—that waitresses in restaurants, for example, were not interested in whether he was a "nice guy" and that he was asking the impossible in hoping to get *everyone* to like him. He had countered these imagined rebuffs by capitalizing on what seemed to work in the past. R pretended to be ill when he wasn't, he exaggerated his supposed shortcomings and thus hoped to solicit the attention, sympathy, and acceptance he otherwise felt he could not get. Therapy became a safe refuge where an understanding "doctor" listened to his problems. It was further emphasized that he attended to the wrong "signs"—that people would not accept or reject him on the basis of whether he was a "good public speaker" or a "clever conversationalist" and that his fears were not only exaggerated but literally groundless.

R's immediate reactions to all this was to accept it with alacrity, pointing out that he "had to hand it to the therapist for his skill in figuring him out." Within two meetings, however, he began to raise some doubts as to the accuracy of the "explanations." He denied that he used his illness to gain sympathy and affection, he doubted that "as a child I really felt insecure," he wasn't sure he actually was a "dependent person who wanted to lean on people" or that he got satisfactions out of coming for treatment.

During the next ten interviews this was all rediscussed in the light of his present behavior with the goal of "concretizing" the interpretations. The manner in which R raised these doubts was also interesting, and has some significance for clarifying the SLT approach to dependency in therapy, i.e., the positive transference relationship. R was never able to deny vigorously that any interpretation was incorrect; he raised questions in a feeble, tentative manner, and almost always admitted in the long run that the therapist was correct. SLT sees in this behavior an expression of the patient's expectancy that the therapist is, and will continue to be, a source of positive reinforcement. To disagree too strongly would involve the risk of the therapist ceasing to be an interested, understanding person; for R always to agree is to convince the therapist that he is a reasonable person who is deserving of the therapist's attentions. This behavior was pointed out and interpreted to R, who in time did become less solicitous of the therapist. He was able to cancel appointments or to come late without being overly apologetic.

The final stage of therapy (which overlapped in time with the previous stage) involved the attempt to deal with R's question, "What do I do now that I understand and accept the reasons for my difficulties?" This stage involved essentially teaching the patient that greater satisfactions could be obtained from behaviors other than those currently used. Present and future situations were discussed, not only in terms of what he had been doing but in the light of new things he might do. Wherever possible R himself suggested these alternatives. For example, he was extremely anxious about the possibility of being asked to read the minutes at a veterans' meeting. Discussion considered how one reads minutes, why they are read, how the members were likely to react to a "good" or "bad" reading, and how this concern tied in with his previous fears and behavior. In like manner, other situations were discussed, and the patient's fears were always tied in with the "old, distorted way of looking at things." Considerable import was attached to de-emphasizing the significance R attributed to "success or failure" in social situations. Slowly but consistently R reported rather dramatic changes in the things he was able to do. He was now regularly attending services at the synagogue; he attended and spoke up at a veterans' organization meeting; he went to the bowling league and enjoyed himself; and he was no longer fearful of his uncle. He had gone so far as to discuss his future with his uncle and "laid it on the line to him." His uncle and he had agreed that he was to receive 50% of the business profits.

However, other statements that he was still anxious in some innocuous situations, that he still feared he would never change, were made as regularly as were the statements of improvement. The therapist's reaction to these was twofold: Questions were raised and discussed whether he was trying to hold on to therapy because the therapist provided some satisfactions for him and whether he was afraid to give up completely old behavior because he feared being left with only new behaviors on which he was not willing to rely exclusively. It was pointed out that it was his decision to make, whether to keep his "worries" and therapy or to try new behaviors. Subsequently, R stated that he did see how it all depended on him, that he could stop worrying and enjoy life.

Interviews were then reduced to one per week and continued on that basis. R's fears, though by no means completely gone, now had the flavor of isolated outcroppings in an otherwise fairly stabilized, better-adjusted pattern. The avoidance of what were previously upsetting situations and the exaggerated use of illness were almost nonexistent. His expectancy for satisfaction rather than negative reactions had greatly increased in routine social situations. Still voicing an occasional strong fear about some specific future situation, R seemed well on the way to realistic acceptance of the fact that there were certain things he could not do well and that it was inevitable that everyone would not be impressed with him.

There remained then necessity for further consolidation of the gains already made and additional discussion of his relationship with the therapist—the latter preparatory to conclusion of treatment. More and more emphasis was placed on R's working things out for himself. As a result, he began to feel embarrassment about bringing into therapy for discussion rather minor, isolated incidents. He was not, however, at this point willing to accept the therapist's interpretation that he was trying to hold on to treatment. However, as was expected, as R continued to derive increased satisfactions outside therapy, the relative reinforcement value of the therapist did lessen.

Postscript: A postscript is necessary to bring this case up to date. R was seen for only one additional interview during an interval of two months. During that last meeting he stated that "things are fine, all in all." He rarely experienced any of the old fears. However, he did not feel like a "completely new man" with absolutely no problems. The therapist again pointed out that he would probably always have some problems like almost everyone, and the important thing was to learn how to handle them without therapy. R. elaborated the many ways in which he had changed. He saw no reason to make any further appointments with the clinic, and the case was therefore closed.

Several months after the last meeting the patient dropped into the clinic to say hello. He reported that things were fine and made no reference to further therapy.

7-2 | Systematic Desensitization and Social Learning

JAY S. EFRAN and JAMES E. MARCIA

In 1958, Wolpe described a number of psychotherapeutic techniques based on principles of learning. Some of these have since become important parts of the behavior therapist's armamentarium, and one in particular—systematic desensitization—has been the subject of considerable research. The popularity of systematic desensitization as a clinical method and object of research is partly due to its apparent simplicity: it is highly structured, easy to describe, said to depend little upon the vicissitudes of the patient-therapist relationship, and is applicable to circumscribed (and thus more readily measurable) problems. But not everyone is satisfied with Wolpe's straightforward description of the method nor his stimulus-response explanations of its effects. Rotter (1969; **7–6**), for example, considers the derivation of the technique from principles of learning extremely loose and analogical, and Breger and McGaugh (1965, 1966) go further by insisting that the principles Wolpe cites are inadequate to explain the results he reports. A number of authors (Weitzman, 1967; Wolpin & Raines, 1966) call attention to the fact that the imagery clients experience seems to be more intricate and changeable than Wolpe's model implies, and others are bothered by the lack of correspondence between Wolpe's model and their observations of what therapists actually do in typical sessions. While some reports (e.g., Davison, 1968; Lomont & Edwards, 1967; Rachman, 1965, 1966) lend weight to Wolpe's contention that the essence of the treatment involves the pairing of graded hierarchies and muscle relaxation, other studies (e.g., Cooke, 1968; Folkins, Lawson, Opton & Lazarus, 1968; Wolpin & Raines, 1966; Zeisset, 1968) have demonstrated good results despite violations in these aspects of the procedure. Some authors (e.g., Rachman, 1968) now suggest that a subjective experience of calm or well-being is more important than actual muscle relaxation, but even this interpretation is open to question: Stampfl and his students, for example, report success using a procedure which aims at arousing fear rather than producing calm (Hogan & Kirchner, 1968; Stampfl & Levis, 1967). This method (also said to be based on principles of learning theory) seems to contradict Wolpe's notion that "exposure, and prolonged exposure in particular, to a very disturbing scene can seriously increase phobic sensitivity [Wolpe & Lazarus, 1966, p. 82]." Another reason for skepticism concerning Wolpe's conditioning model is that only a small amount of time is actually spent during therapy sessions pairing relaxation responses with graded anxiety stimuli. Taking into account opportunities clients have outside of therapy to think anxious thoughts

This paper was specially prepared for and is published for the first time in this volume. We are grateful for the authors' permission to use it.

or have anxiety-provoking experiences, it seems difficult to account for the effectiveness of the treatment in conditioning terms.

Because Wolpe's model does not seem adequate to us, we have undertaken to describe and analyze the systematic desensitization procedure from an alternative, social learning theory, point of view. For purposes of this analysis, we will assume that the method is at least as effective as traditional psychotherapeutic approaches—perhaps more effective—and is therefore deserving of careful examination from a variety of theoretical positions.

Systematic Desensitization

Before proceeding, it is necessary to describe briefly Wolpe's procedure. From his point of view, it can be thought of as a three-stage process. It consists first of training a patient in deep muscle relaxation and visualization. Then the patient and therapist construct an "anxiety hierarchy" of situations which are fear provoking, from the most innocuous to the most threatening. Finally, anxiety reactions to these items are "counterconditioned" by having the patient imagine the scenes one at a time while remaining relaxed. More frightening scenes are presented when less frightening ones no longer elicit anxiety. This continues until the entire list has been desensitized. Although the stimuli normally consist of mental images rather than real objects, the procedure is presumably effective in enabling the patient to face previously disturbing situations with equanimity. Wolpe offers the following principle to explain the operation of his method: "If a response antagonistic to anxiety can be made to occur in the presence of anxiety-provoking stimuli so that it is accompanied by a complete or partial suppression of the anxiety responses, the bond between the stimuli and the anxiety responses will be weakened [Wolpe, Salter, & Reyna, 1964, p. 10]."

A Social Learning Approach

As the reader of this volume has learned, Rotter's social learning theory states that an individual's behavior in a given situation is a function of both the subjective importance or reinforcement value of events and the subjective probability or expectancy that particular behaviors will lead to these events. Expectations and reinforcement values can change with experience, but the behavior patterns of many people who seek help, such as phobic desensitization clients, often preclude their gaining corrective experience. They usually try to avoid situations which would bring them into contact with the phobic stimulus, and, when they cannot, their dire anticipations result in avoidant responses which inhibit useful learning and confirm expectations of unpleasantness and lack of control. If a phobic individual could be induced to seek new experience with the phobic stimulus, while being prevented from making premature, biasing, avoidant, or protective responses, then the resulting experience would presumably produce favorable behavior change. In some cases, ideational rather than direct experience might be a sufficient initial step, although in the final analysis, an individual cannot be wholly confident about his reactions to a phobic stimulus unless he tests himself directly. The systematic desensitization procedure seems in many ways an excellent method for enabling clients to test themselves, using ideational preliminary steps. As we shall try to show, it succeeds less because of the method's properties as a conditioning procedure than because the method (1) helps a client fractionate a goal into manageable bits, (2) provides continuous reassuring feedback about his level of success, (3) teaches him useful (although perhaps inaccurate) beliefs, (4) increases the reinforcement value of taking certain risks while decreasing both the probability and value of potential setbacks, and (5) provides opportunities for conceptual refinement and reappraisal. These "nonconditioning" aspects of systematic desensitization will be more fully discussed in succeeding paragraphs.

Fractionation

While the client begins therapy with a relatively fixed attitude toward the difficulty of accomplishing his goal (for example, equanimity in the face of the phobic stimulus), he has not yet formed a firm, negative anticipation concerning his ability to succeed at various subgoals, particularly those which logically seem to require minimal fortitude. This makes the technique of fractionation a highly effective approach. The client is asked to relax while imagining, for example, a snake in a room at the other end of the city. He hasn't ever tried this before, may find that he can do it, and is encouraged by his successful performance. It is then suggested that he try to relax while imagining the snake in a room only halfway across the city. The subjective probability of being able to do this has been raised by the successful completion of the previous, related task, and in this way, each experience modifies slightly the expectation of performing the remaining tasks. If some of these tasks had been suggested at the outset, the client would have been prone to disbelieve his ability to accomplish them, and these failure anticipations would have become self-fulfilling prophecies. From this point of view a major advantage of the use of the anxiety hierarchy is the fact that low "minimal goal levels" (Rotter, 1954) are established and lead to success experiences in a domain which has been characterized by feelings of failure and impotence. The strong form of the view we are expressing is that the pairing of relaxation and anxiety images is important only because the experience raises the subject's expectations of being able to perform competently in situations he *construes* as relevant or related to his problem.

Feedback

The fractionation technique just described has another built-in advantage. It provides the individual with almost constant assurance that he is progressing, changing, becoming more competent. A frightened individual likes to know he has succeeded with one small part of a task before he commits himself to the next step—in real life it is rarely possible to have such helpful, immediate indication that one is on the right track. In this case, it is especially helpful that some of the feedback during the relaxation procedure is visceral and personal, and thus a particularly impressive testimonial to the client. Valins and Ray (1967) have demonstrated the effectiveness in modifying fears of providing even *false* physiological feedback. In order to change, clients need more than realistic information about the phobic object; they need to know not only what the snake will do but what *they* will do in the presence of the snake. Thus feedback about internal reactions is of prime value.

A Belief System

From the start of therapy, the client is indoctrinated in a number of beliefs, some of which may be inaccurate, but which are nevertheless useful in facilitating progress (Klein, Dittman, Parloff & Gill, 1969). He is told, for example, that his ability to imagine certain things while relaxing in the office indicates his ability to face certain situations in reality. This belief in the "transfer" of the desensitization procedure to real life enables the client to begin changing his expectations regarding his abilities before having to risk experimentation in the actual situation. By enabling him to take his first confidence-building steps in a relatively safe setting, it also helps to insure that his actual experience with the phobic stimulus will not be jeopardized prematurely by avoidance responses. Therapists usually inform clients that they should not deliberately test themselves in the phobic situation, but rather should wait until opportunities arise more naturally. They are also warned that there may be a "lag" in the transfer from office procedure to "real life." Again, these instructions protect the client from negative interpretations of premature encounters with the phobic situation. During the relaxation-training phase, belief in the correctness of the therapist's pronouncements is strengthened, since the client is usually impressed by his responsiveness to the therapist's relaxation suggestions. Most of the rest of the treatment program goes basically according to the structured plan of the therapist, and thus reinforces the client's notion that the therapist knows what he is doing and that a prescribed, scientific methodology is being used.

The Relationship

The fact of being in treatment, and having thus established a variety of formal and informal "contractual arrangements" with at least the therapist and perhaps friends and relatives, probably plays some role in the success or failure of the procedure. There is impetus to please or to displease the therapist and others by agreeing to take certain steps or by resisting them. The therapist usually reinforces the completion of "homework" and the taking of various limited experimental risks. By the same token, he agrees to provide support should experimentation prove unpleasant. Thus he increases the reinforcement value of certain goals and lessens the negative valence of some potential outcomes. Many patients, both those treated by desensitization and those treated by other methods, appear to try things first to please their therapist and then to continue those behaviors because they discover that they can obtain results which are reinforcing. Had they been on their own, it is doubtful that they would have been motivated to "take the plunge."

Cognitive Appraisal

During both the construction of the anxiety hierarchy and the imagining scenes, there are extensive opportunities to think about and evaluate the phobic situation. Reports of subjects make it clear that it is very difficult, if not impossible, to imagine exactly the same scene more than once. An active cognitive process seems to take place almost continually during this time period, during which various refinements and differentiations occur. A subject who initially visualizes a boa constrictor may begin to imagine many species of snake, some much smaller and meeker. Wolpin and Raines (1966) describe a subject who first pictured a snake as a "huge dragon" but later thought of it as "an interesting small snake." A subject who initially reacts with horror to the notion of handling a snake may begin to think about the difference between touching one gingerly with one finger and having one thrust into his hands, or the difference between being with the snake in a closed room versus a room which has several open doors. In short, the entire phobic experience may be differently conceived by the end of treatment. Rather than new reactions to identical ideational stimuli, the observed differences in approach behavior may be due to changes in the situation the client is picturing.

If our view of the procedure is at all accurate, then it should be possible to accomplish results similar to those obtained with desensitization by using procedures which facilitate changes in expectancies and reinforcement values without allowing opportunities for counterconditioning. This hypothesis formed the basis for the experiment reported below. A fuller description has appeared elsewhere (Marcia, Rubin, & Efran, 1968).

"T-Scope Therapy" Versus Desensitization

Forty-four introductory psychology students, preselected as snake- or spider-phobic by means of a questionnaire, interview, and runway avoidance test, served as subjects. One experimental group (2 males, 14 females) received a form of systematic desensitization treatment. A second (4 males, 6 females) received a treatment embodying many of the features thought to affect subject expectations, but not including opportunities for the pairing of relaxation and anxiety images. A third group (3 males, 4 females) also exposed to this expectancy treatment was told that they were "controls" and were therefore receiving an incomplete form of the treatment which would probably have little effect. A fourth group (3 males, 9 females) received no treatment, but was evaluated at the same time as the other groups. The therapists were fourteen graduate students and a faculty member in clinical and counseling psychology.

Details of the systematic desensitization treatment were as follows: Each subject constructed a hierarchy from a deck of fourteen cards, choosing the seven which were most personally relevant and which approximated an equal-interval scale. After two 45-minute practice sessions, during which hierarchy construction was completed, and the subject received training in deep-muscle relaxation and visualization, each subject began visualizing scenes and relaxing in the usual manner (Paul, 1966). To control the time factor, all subjects spent a full session on each hierarchy item. This aspect of the procedure deviates from traditional desensitization, where clients are allowed to proceed at their own pace. It was assumed on the basis of other studies (Davison, 1968; Lang, Lazovik, & Reynolds, 1965) that subjects could normally complete two or three items per session, and that a full session per item would allow more than sufficient time for desensitization. This assumption turned out to be incorrect, since many subjects did not desensitize completely (to a criterion of 15 seconds) to all of the scenes in the required time. Because this situation meant that some subjects were exposed to scenes before they would be considered "ready" by traditional criteria, it was important to assess whether this factor affected the power of the desensitization procedure. A number of analyses (see Marcia, Rubin, & Efran, 1968) indicated that there was no relationship between "premature" scene exposures and measures of success or level of final hierarchy item completed. Moreover, the over-all level of success obtained was similar to that obtained in other experimental studies of animal phobics using desensitization and comparable measures.

The expectancy procedure ("T-scope therapy") was conducted as follows: Subjects were met by their therapist and a white-coated GSR technician who manned a polygraph console during the treatment sessions. During the first of the eight twenty-minute treatment sessions, the therapist explained that two "well-established" principles formed the rationale for the treatment: the irrational, and, hence, unconscious nature of phobias, and the suppressibility of a response by means of a mildly unpleasant stimulus. The subject was told that phobic stimuli would be presented in a tachistoscope at a speed "too fast for the conscious mind to perceive, yet perceptible to the unconscious." These "subliminal stimuli" would evoke unconscious phobic responses which would be followed by a mildly painful electrical shock. For each session, the subject—with dummy GSR and EKG electrodes, as well as real stimulation electrodes, attached—sat on the edge of a chair in a sound-proof chamber and looked into a tachistoscope. Although he believed he was watching subliminal stimuli, some of which were pictures of the phobic object, he was actually looking at blank cards. Each session consisted of 100 presentations, 16 of which were shocked. At the end of each session, the GSR technician showed the subject a dummied polygraph printout to illustrate his "rate of improvement." An attempt was made to convince the subject that he was "getting better," although unlike actual desensitization treatment, subjects were not trained to focus on feeling states.

As indicated, subjects in one of the two groups receiving T-scope therapy were given low expectations concerning the usefulness of the procedure. They were told that a "crucial element"—the phobic stimulus on the T-scope—would be missing. This group was warned not to expect much change, so that subjects in this group were presumably less motivated to consider changes in their attitudes toward snakes or spiders, or to attempt better performance during the post-test.

Improvement was assessed by comparing subject's reactions during pre- and post-treatment runway tests, and by securing their opinions concerning change during a post-session interview. Evaluation procedures were administered by individuals who did not know in which group subjects had been. The runway measure was patterned after the one used by Lang and Lazovik (1963) and required subjects to approach, as closely as possible, a preserved specimen of a snake or spider which was located at the end of a 15-foot runway. Subjects who could get up to the object were required to see if they could touch or hold it.

A series of analyses generally indicated significant improvement for subjects treated by either desensitization or T-scope therapy presented under high expectancy conditions, but not for subjects in the control group or T-scope therapy presented under low expectancy conditions. In no comparison was the desensitization treatment significantly more effective than high expectancy T-scope therapy, although both were superior to the control group, and in some analyses, to the low expectancy T-scope group. Table 1 presents the results in terms of the major measure, runway change scores.

The results of this study suggest that (1) an expectancy-based procedure, which does not provide an opportunity for counterconditioning to take place, can cause significant improvement in snake- or spider-phobic subjects, (2) that this procedure is not less effective than a desensitization procedure, and (3) that the identical procedure administered under a different (low expectancy) set loses its effectiveness.

In T-scope therapy, as administered in this study, subjects *may* have imagined or thought about snakes or spiders while looking into the tachistoscope. If so, it is noteworthy that no subject in the high expectancy T-scope group, and only one subject in the low expectancy T-scope group, became more phobic, since, construed in counterconditioning theory terms, an aversive and tension-producing stimulus (shock) was being paired with phobic ideation.

A limitation of this study is related to the difference between the desensitization procedure used here and that used in clinical practice. However, results indicated that the modification in procedure was not reflected in outcome measures.

A fact which seems infrequently noted in the literature is that experimental studies of systematic desensitization with animal-phobic subjects have produced quite modest degrees of improvement in subjects, especially in comparison with clinical reports. The highest percentage of subjects in any group who actually touched the snake or spider during the final runway test in this study was 30, and only 12 percent were willing to pick the phobic object up. To describe even these subjects as "cured" would be inaccurate, since most were not yet entirely comfortable in the presence of the specimen. Thus, while significant differences in "improvement" were demonstrated in this study and others, the level of

Table 1   *Comparisons among Groups on Amount of Improvement on Runway Measure*

Groups Compared[a]	Mean Change[b]	Mean Rank of Change	p[c]
DS	.39	13.75	NS
Hi T	.33	11.44	
DS	.39	14.56	<.01
Lo T	−.01	6.14	
DS	.39	17.72	<.01
C	−.01	10.21	
Hi T	.33	10.50	<.05
Lo T	−.01	5.93	
Hi T	.33	14.83	<.01
C	−.01	8.38	
Lo T	−.01	11.42	NS
C	−.01	9.17	

[a] DS = Systematic desensitization, N=16
Hi T = High expectancy T-scope therapy, N=9
Lo T = Low expectancy T-scope therapy, N=7
C   = No treatment control, N=12
[b] Following Lang & Lazovik (1963), ratio scores were used, based on the formula:

$$\frac{(\text{Pre-treatment score}) - (\text{Post-treatment score})}{(\text{Pre-treatment score})}$$

[c] One-tailed, based on Mann-Whitney U tests.

success and the particular accomplishments of these subjects are not as impressive as one is sometimes led to believe in reading literature reviews (e.g., Rachman, 1967). Our initial concern about level of success motivated us to compare the results of our desensitization procedures with those obtained by other investigators. As indicated, these comparisons reveal that our results were equal to or superior to those reported elsewhere (Davison, 1968; Lang, 1964; Lang, Lazovik, & Reynolds, 1965). Perhaps the laboratory studies have resulted in more modest levels of "cure" because of the brief time periods usually employed, or differences in motivation between clinical and experimental subjects, resulting in different degrees of willingness to take risks, rehearse on their own, etc.

Conclusions

The original account of systematic desensitization as a counterconditioning process seems inadequate. In a recent review, Murray and Jacobson (1971) conclude that "The critical change required appears to be that the person comes to believe that he can cope with the situation. Once this belief is attained, anxiety declines. Such cognitive changes can come about through a variety of methods. . . ." According to Murray and Jacobson, available evidence indicates that "neither muscular relaxation, nor a progressive hierarchy, nor imaginal rehearsal are essential" and that "systematic desensitization may be viewed most adequately as a method of modifying beliefs and attitudes by the use of social influence." Our research and the social learning analysis which prompted it is, of course, consonant with this interpretation. The therapist and client who work together using systematic desensitization are participants in a social contract, and their behavior toward each other influences the values of various goals. Moreover, the client's view of his abilities is influenced by the interpretations offered by the therapist and the view of self he gains while engaging in the novel task suggested by the therapist.

The term "placebo effect" has been used to cover any improvement related to an expectation that one is being treated and should get better. However, the term has sometimes been used more broadly to mean any improvement produced by changes in expectation, attitude, or belief. These two uses must be clearly differentiated to avoid confusion, and we prefer to use the term in its more specific sense. Used in that way, we would hesitate to describe the effects of systematic desensitization as "placebo effects." Merely telling a client that he will improve, especially when he is gathering data to the contrary, is a relatively weak therapeutic manipulation. Systematic desensitization is a stronger manipulation in that the quality of "evidence" made available to the client concerning his abilities is much more compelling, specific, and, in some cases, has internal or visceral components which are hard for a subject to treat lightly.

In summary, the analysis of systematic desensitization in social learning terms, if valid, suggests the usefulness of turning our attention to the design of more varied and efficient means of modifying cognitions, rather than continuing to focus primarily on the *conditioning* parameters of behavior therapy techniques like systematic desensitization.

7-3	*Need for Approval and the Premature Termination of Psychotherapy*[1]

BONNIE R. STRICKLAND and DOUGLAS P. CROWNE[2]

This study tested the hypotheses that approval-dependent individuals (a) tend prematurely to terminate psychotherapy, and (b) are rated by therapists as more defensive and less improved than patients less approval-dependent. 85 psychiatric outpatients completed the Marlowe and Crowne Social Desirability scale (the measure of need for approval) and rated their improvement in psychotherapy. Therapists rated 30 of these patients on defensiveness, attitude towards patient, patient's attitude towards therapist, improvement and satisfaction with therapy. Additional measures included diagnosis, social class, and ordinal position. Results confirmed the hypotheses. The high need for approval group terminated significantly (p < .005) earlier. Approval-motivated patients were generally given more negative ratings by therapists. Approval-motivated females rated themselves as more improved. Ordinal position and social class failed to predict stay in therapy. The implications of these findings were discussed.

In a series of recommendations on the conduct of psychoanalysis, Freud (1949) observed that the premature termination of treatment could be attributed to the initial unsuitability of the patient for psychoanalysis (e.g., inadequate intelligence, low social class, psychosis) or to an early and dramatic manifestation of resistance. He advocated a period of trial analysis in order to permit the analyst to assess the patient's motivation for therapy and whether or not he met the (then extant) criteria for treatment.

Contemporary research on early termination has, in the main, taken a straight empirical approach to the problem. A not inconsiderable body of studies in the last decade has established, with certain inconsistencies and contradictions, two major predictors of abrupt termination. The first class of these variables roughly corresponds to Freud's criteria of unsuitability: education (Sullivan, Miller, & Smelser, 1958), social class

[1] Portions of this study were presented at the Midwestern Psychological Association meetings, Chicago, May 1962.

[2] We would like to express our gratitude to the therapists and patients who graciously and uncomplainingly completed the various measures required of them. Our thanks are also extended to Shephard Liverant, David Marlowe, and Julian Rotter, whose suggestions contributed both to the analysis and interpretation of the data of this study.

(Auld & Myers, 1954; Hollingshead & Redlich, 1958; Rosenthal & Frank, 1958), and intelligence (Affleck & Mednick, 1959; Auld & Eron, 1953). The second set of predictors is probably best conceptualized under the heading of defensiveness. Indices such as the Rorschach, MMPI, semiprojective sentence completions, and therapists' ratings have shown differences between patients who prematurely terminate and those who continue in psychotherapy. Unproductive Rorschach records (Affleck & Mednick, 1959; Gallagher, 1953; Gibby, Stotsky, Hiler, & Miller, 1954; Taulbee, 1958), more limited acknowledgment of symptoms and of personal dissatisfaction on the MMPI (Taulbee, 1958), sentence completions indicative of evasion and unwillingness to reveal oneself (Hiler, 1959), and a more limited prognosis as rated by therapists (Garfield & Affleck, 1961) appear to be characteristic of the abrupt terminator. These findings are further consonant with the essential meaning of Freud's early clinical observations.

The present study was undertaken to test a theoretically derived prediction concerning the phenomenon of defensive early termination of psychotherapy. The major hypothesis was that patients characterized by a high need for approval are more likely to terminate psychotherapy early. As a consequence of their need to maintain and defend a vulnerable self-image, these individuals are more likely to avoid the threats associated with personal disclosure (and, possibly, anticipated social censure for seeking this form of help with personal problems) by breaking off therapeutic contact. Previous research on the need for approval has found approval-motivated individuals to be more compliant, persuasible, eager to please, and conforming in a variety of situations: opinion conformity (Marlowe & Crowne, 1961), social conformity (Crowne & Liverant, 1963; Strickland & Crowne, 1962), verbal conditioning (Crowne & Strickland, 1961; Marlowe, 1962), perceptual defense (Barthel & Crowne, 1962), and attitude change (Salman & Crowne, 1962). The present hypothesis is based on an extension of the meaning of the construct of need for approval from an earlier conceptualization emphasizing compliance and influencibility (cf. Crowne & Strickland, 1961). Recent work by Conn (1962) and Crowne and Liverant (1963) suggests that individuals with a high need for approval are more defensive and are concerned with avoiding threats to self-esteem. This proposition receives further support from the initial finding of greater test taking defensiveness by persons with high scores on the Marlowe-Crowne Social Desirability (*M-C SD*) scale, the index of the need for approval.

METHOD

The data for the present study were collected as part of a large-scale research project at Columbus Psychiatric Clinic assessing both patient and therapist variables. The therapists were not apprised of the nature of the research, and none of them had any knowledge of the patients' standing on the independent variables.

Subjects

Eighty-five patients, in treatment during 1960 and 1961, served as subjects in this study. Throughout the interval spanned by the research, almost every patient seeking help was admitted to psychotherapy which, with only rare exceptions, consisted of weekly therapeutic hours. A majority of the patients were given neurotic or character disorder diagnoses, although a considerable number of them were classified as psychotic or prepsychotic. These diagnoses were made in staff meetings by resident psychiatrists on the basis of intake interviews and, occasionally, psychological test data. The age range of the patient sample was from 20 to 54, with a mean of 33.7 years. The therapists included psychiatrists and psychiatric residents, psychologists, and social workers.

The final sample was comprised of two groups of patients. In Group I were 23 patients, 13 males and 10 females, who terminated psychotherapy during the months of October and November 1960. Group II consisted of 62 patients, 26 males and 36 females. This was a replication sample. terminating sometime during May, June, or July 1961.

Measures

The index of the need for approval, the major independent variable, was the *M-C SD* scale (Crowne & Marlowe, 1960). The *M-C SD* scale is a 33-item, true-false questionnaire assessing the degree to which individuals avoid self-criticism and depict themselves in improbably favorable terms. An illustrative item is, "I'm always willing to admit it when I make a mistake."

The patients rated their own improvement in therapy on a nine-point scale ranging from improved (1) to unimproved (9). Within the compass of the larger project, therapists were required to rate each of their patients on a slightly modified version of the Seeman (1954) Case Rating scale. Of interest in this study were five items on the Case Rating scale: Number 5, the therapist's estimate of the patient's attitude towards him during therapy; Number 6, the therapist's attitude towards his patient; Number 7, the degree of personal integration versus defensiveness of the patient; Number 9, the therapist's estimate of the patient's satisfaction with the outcome of therapy; and Number 10, the therapist's rating of therapeutic outcome. In contrast to the original, which used nine-point scales, the range of values for the modified version was from 1 to 16.

The closing summaries of treatment in the patients' folders were rated on a five-point scale ranging from optimal improvement and mutual agreement on termination (1) to termination without the therapist's agreement and no improvement (5). Additional variables included education and occupational level, which were combined in a fashion similar to the procedure followed in the Hollingshead Index of Social Position (Hollingshead & Redlich, 1958), and ordinal position. Birth order was included in an attempt to replicate Schachter's (1959) findings that first- as opposed to later-born patients continue longer in psychotherapy. The number of hours of therapy at termination constituted the major dependent variable.

Procedure

The *M-C SD* scale was mailed to the patients in Group I within a 3-month interval from the date of termination. In Group II, 33 of the 62 patients were given the *SD* scale at the Clinic. The remaining 29 patients in this group completed the inventory at the conclusion of therapy as in Group I. As shown in Table 1, the *M-C* scale means and standard deviations of the patients in Groups I and II who completed the measure after terminating therapy are closely comparable to the mean and standard deviation of the Group II patients tested at the Clinic.

The rate of return on questionnaires mailed to the patients in Groups I and II was approximately 70%; in fact, most of the uncompleted questionnaires were undelivered due to incorrect addresses. A Mann-Whitney *U* test revealed no difference in the terminal number of therapy hours of the patients who returned the *SD* scale and those who did not ($U = 1366.5$, $z = .40$, ns). Thus, it appears unlikely that bias affecting either the independent or dependent variables was introduced into the study by the posttherapy administration of the *SD* scale. Neither does the sample appear to have been biased by selective returns nor were differences observed in *SD* scale scores between patients tested in therapy at the Clinic and patients tested after termination.

Ratings of our improvement in therapy were mailed to the patients within 3 months of termination. Sixty-three of the 85 patients completed their own improvement scale.

The therapists completed the Case Rating scale at varying times, depending on the date each patient began treatment, between November 1960 and May 1961. The therapists' ratings were uniformly made while the patients were in treatment. At the time the ratings were made, the therapists could have had no reliable knowledge of the patients' ultimate dates of termination. Thus, these ratings were not contaminated by the possibility of negative attitudes towards early terminating patients.

RESULTS

Preliminary to the major analyses, the data were examined for sex and age differences. None, except for the sex difference in patients' ratings of their own improvement reported below, were found, and the analyses were accordingly carried out without regard to sex and age.

To accomplish the test of the central hypothesis, patients' scores on the *M-C* scale were dichotomized at the overall mean (11.87) to yield the high and low need for approval groups. The distribution of the number of hours of therapy of these groups is shown in Table 2. By a Mann-Whitney *U* test, high and low need for approval patients differ significantly in the numbers of hours of therapy ($z = 2.84$, $p < .005$[3]). Looking at the distribution of therapy hours in Table 2, it is clear that above the median hours of therapy, highs are sharply underrepresented, while the reverse is true below the median hours of therapy. Patients low in the need for approval

[3] Two-tailed test.

Table 1 Mean M-C SD Scores of Patients Tested at the Clinic and
at the Conclusion of Therapy

Group	N	M	SD
I (Posttermination)	23	13.35	6.95
II_a (At clinic)	34	11.53	6.02
II_b (Posttermination)	28	11.08	6.76

Note: t (I versus II_a) $= 1.02$; t (II_a versus II_b) $= 0.27$; t (I versus II_b) $= 1.16$.

Table 2 Distribution of the Number of Hours of Psychotherapy for
High and Low Need for Approval Patients

Hours of Therapy	High Need for Approval ($N = 43$)	Low Need for Approval ($N = 42$)
71+ (to 284)	5	11
61–70	1	1
51–60	1	5
41–50	0	5
31–40	7	2
21–30	10	9
11–20	11	5
1–10	8	4

tend to be more equally split above and below the median. At the extremes of the distribution, however, low need for approval patients, in contrast to the highs, are overrepresented in the highest number of therapy hours and underrepresented among the very early terminators. It should be noted that differences of approximately the same magnitude were found in the two samples (Groups I and II); thus, at least within the same clinic, some evidence for the replicability of this finding is afforded.

For the 30 patients in the second group on whom the therapists completed the Seeman scale, correlations were computed between these ratings and the M-C scale, the number of hours of therapy, and the index of social class. These correlations, and the intercorrelations of the five Case Rating scale items, are presented in Table 3. Approval-dependent patients tended to receive more negative ratings on each of the five scales. The most striking of these correlations is that between the need for approval scale and therapists' ratings of personal integration versus defensiveness or disorganization ($r = -.67$). The remainder of the need for approval-therapists' ratings correlations are consistent but fail to reach a conventional level of significance.

Each of the Seeman scales correlated moderately and positively with

Table 3   *Intercorrelations of Hours of Therapy, Need for Approval, and Therapists' Ratings*

	Variable						
Variable	1	2	3	4	5	6	7
1. Need approval	.68[a]						
2. Hours of therapy	−.28[b]						
3. Patient's liking/respect for therapist	−.18	.23					
4. Therapist's liking/respect for patient	−.35	.40*	.66**				
5. Personal integration versus defensiveness of patient	−.67**	.57**	.27*	.38**			
6. Patient's satisfaction with therapy	−.32	.22	.60**	.46**	.55**		
7. Amount of improvement in therapy	−.34	.45*	.46**	.50**	.63**	.79**	
					N = 83		
8. Social class	−.07	.19	.27	.00	.28	.36*	.07
	N = 30				*N = 30*		

[a] Test-retest reliability, 5–6 month interval during which patients were in therapy $(N = 24)$.
[b] $N = 85$.
* $p < .05$.
** $p < .01$.

the number of hours the patient remained in therapy. The index of social class was found to be unrelated to the M-C scale $(r = -.07)$ and negligibly correlated with length of stay in therapy $(r = .19)$. Moderate positive correlations were obtained between social class and therapists' ratings of the patients' liking and respect for the therapist $(r = .27)$, satisfaction with therapy $(r = .36)$, and the defensiveness scale $(r = .28)$. Only the correlation with satisfaction with therapy attains significance $(p < .05)$.

Since the patients had been in therapy for varying lengths of time when the therapists' ratings were made (that is, it was not possible to obtain the therapists' ratings after a standard interval in therapy for all patients), it is conceivable that the approval-motivated group was rated lower simply as a function of their tendency to remain less long in therapy. Thus, the negative ratings may simply reflect the fact that their therapists knew them less well. As a test of this possibility, partial correlations were computed between the M-C scale and the therapists' ratings with the number of hours the patient had been in therapy at the time of rating partialed out. Table 4 shows these correlations. It is clear that the relationships between

Table 4 Partial Correlations between Need for Approval and Therapists' Ratings

THERAPISTS' RATINGS	PARTIAL CORRELATIONS WITH NEED FOR APPROVAL
Patient's liking/respect for therapist	−.11
Therapist's liking/respect for patient	−.29
Personal integration versus defensiveness of patient	−.63**
Patient's satisfaction with therapy	−.25
Amount of improvement in therapy	−.24

Note: N = 30.
** $p < .01$.

the need for approval and the therapists' ratings maintain approximately the same magnitude irrespective of the amount of time the patient had been in therapy at the time he was rated.

Examining the diagnoses of high and low need for approval patients, no differences were found. Psychiatric diagnosis was further unrelated to the other variables of the study.

As a further assessment of progress in, and the outcome of, therapy, the ratings of the closing summaries were compared with certain of the major variables of the study. The interrater reliability of these ratings was .68 (N = 25). The terminal ratings correlated .14 with the M-C scale, −.34 with hours of therapy, −.31 with the therapists' prior ratings of improvement, and −.29 with therapists' ratings of defensiveness.[4]

At termination, 63 patients completed ratings of their own improvement on a scale ranging from 1 (improved) to 9 (unimproved). For males, there was no relationship between ratings of own improvement and the M-C scale (r = .01). A significant correlation was obtained for females (r = −.39), with approval-dependent females tending to rate themselves as more improved. Ratings of own improvement correlated −.16 for males and −.26 for females with the number of hours of therapy.

To assess the stability of the index of need for approval during the course of therapy and as a further check on the legitimacy of administering the independent variables after termination to a sizeable proportion of the sample, the M-C scale was readministered to 24 patients who had been tested 5 months earlier and then remained in treatment. In this interval, patients completed between 20 and 25 hours of therapy. A test-retest correlation of .68 was obtained. The initial mean of the test-retest group was 10.92; at the second testing, the obtained mean was 10.42 (t = 0.57, ns). Moreover, in this subsample, the mean M-C scores are comparable to the mean of the remaining 61 patients (10.92 versus 12.25, t = 0.57;

[4] The negative sign of the last two correlations is due to the reversed scoring of the scales.

10.42 versus 12.25, $t = 1.42$ *ns*). It remains to note that the correlation between the measure of need for approval and number of hours of therapy among the 34 patients in Group II_a who took the scale at the Clinic was $-.34$. Partialing out the number of hours of therapy at the time the scale was given, the correlation was $-.29$. This, of course, is almost identical to the $-.28$ correlation reported in Table 3.

In an attempt to replicate the finding reported by Schachter (1959) that first-born and only-child patients remain longer in therapy than later borns, these two groups of patients were compared in length of stay in therapy. For 49 patients on whom ordinal position was recorded, a Mann-Whitney *U* test revealed no difference in hours of therapy ($z = 0.22$, *ns*).

DISCUSSION

High and low need for approval patients differ strikingly in the length of time they remain in psychotherapy. Approval-dependent patients terminate much earlier than those less approval-motivated. To accept the hypothesis that the earlier termination of high need for approval patients represents a means of avoiding anticipated threats to self-esteem, it is first necessary to exclude the possibility that they are simply less disturbed and less in need of help than those less dependent on approval. As established by therapists' ratings, approval-dependent patients appear to be more defensive or disorganized. Moreover, they tend to be judged by their therapists as less personally liked, less satisfied with the progress of therapy, and less improved in treatment. Finally, no systematic differences were found between high and low need for approval groups in type or severity of diagnosis. It would appear that the approval-motivated group did not terminate earlier as a result of progress and improvement, and their early termination thus takes on the character of resistance and defensiveness.

These findings are consonant with recent studies on the approval motive (Conn, 1962; Crowne & Liverant, 1963) and support the conceptualization of the approval-dependent person as one who is concerned with protecting and maintaining a vulnerable self-image. Thus, it seems likely that, faced with the prospect of self-revelation and the threats this poses to his defensive image of himself, the approval-dependent patient convinces himself that psychotherapy is really not worth while or that, in a very few hours, he has attained sufficient improvement. For the approval-dependent patient, the dilemma is one of giving up a defensive self-conception or defying the therapist. The outcome of such an avoidance-avoidance conflict is leaving the field. Additionally, it is possible that these patients fail to obtain highly valued affectional and dependency gratifications from their therapists which might alter the balance of the conflict. A corollary, but not incompatible interpretation, is that the approval-motivated individual is apprehensive about possible social criticism for seeking therapy and the (to him) implicit admission that he is "crazy." It is worth observing that the defensive test-taking behavior of high need for approval persons is consistent with this general interpretation of our major finding.

In this study, both time pressures and another large scale research project being conducted at the same time necessitated administering the SD scale to a large number of patients after the conclusion of psychotherapy. This raises a crucial methodological issue: whether, perhaps, scores on the scale were affected by participation in psychotherapy, thus rendering the findings more parsimoniously interpretable in terms of the influence of therapy on the questionnaire. As detailed above, an attempt was made to check on the possible effect of therapy on the scale by conducting a long term, test-retest analysis of the index of need for approval while patients were in treatment. No evidence for systematic changes was found. Also, the relationship with number of hours of therapy was maintained in the group given the M-C scale at the Clinic.

In fact, the test-retest data strongly suggest that the approval motive is very resistant to change. If any procedures could systematically alter dependence on the approval of others, it would certainly be expected that psychotherapy would be high on the list. Whether premature termination can be lessened among approval-dependent individuals is yet an open question, although it may be that, in the early hours of psychotherapy, before an enduring and trusting relationship with the therapist has been established, minimizing the demand for frank personal revelation and providing reassurance and support would tend to reduce this form of resistance.

Ratings of own improvement showed only a very slight relationship with hours of therapy: patients rating themselves as more improved tended to remain longer in therapy. While no relationship was found between the index of need for approval and own improvement ratings for males, approval-motivated females tended to rate themselves as more improved despite the earlier termination of the high need for approval group. The latter result lends further support to the defensiveness hypothesis.

The finding that therapists are able to make meaningful predictions and characterizations of their patients independent of the length of time the patient has been in therapy above a certain minimum, tends to support Meehl's (1960) demonstration that therapists arrive quite early at stable interpretations of their patients.

The discrepancies that were found between the therapists' ratings on the Case Rating scale and the ratings of the closing summaries raise some interesting issues. The Seeman scale ratings, in general, were the more predictively accurate; the terminal ratings, based on the therapists' impressions at the time of termination, did not correlate highly with hours of therapy, the index of need for approval, nor, surprisingly, the therapists' earlier ratings of improvement. Many therapists did not make closing summary statements on their patients; those who did gave accounts varying markedly in the amount of information conveyed. It seems clear that terminal statements of treatment are subject to vagaries that do not appear to affect in nearly the same degree structured ratings of patients.

In addition to their implications for the vulnerable self-esteem and defensiveness extension of the approval-motive construct, these results also have some suggestive value regarding the problem of a model for psychotherapy. The verbal conditioning paradigm has received considerable attention in the recent literature as an analogue of the process of psychotherapy (cf. Krasner, 1958). According to the verbal conditioning model, psychotherapy can be conceptualized as a process in which the therapist subtly reinforces changes in the patient's verbal behavior; these changes then generalize the verbal and behavioral changes in the patient's real life outside of therapy. If we can assume that what is measured by the *M-C* scale is comparable in patients and college students, then the greater amenability to verbal reinforcement of approval-motivated individuals in a verbal conditioning situation (Crowne & Strickland, 1961; Marlowe, 1962) and their tendency to terminate therapy early and with less improvement pose a real problem for the model. Whatever the other merits or demerits of the verbal conditioning analogue, it certainly fails to account for the effect of individual differences and the meaning of the situation as it is perceived by the individual. It is one thing for the approval-dependent person to be more influenced by the subtle reinforcers of an experimenter to produce more plural nouns; it is evidently quite another thing to ask him to surrender his defensive conception of himself.

In summary, the results of this study suggest that defensiveness and avoidance of self-criticism constitute a major determinant of abrupt termination of psychotherapy. In contrast to previous studies, both social class and ordinal position were unrelated to length of psychotherapeutic stay.

7-4 | The Effects of Dispositional and Contextual Social Desirability on Verbal Conditioning[1,2]

HENRY D. BATES

A Taffel task incorporating verbs scaled for social desirability (TSD) was administered by an IBM 1710 computer to Ss differing in Marlowe-Crowne need approval scores (DSD). Critical response frequencies were a function of verb class in the operant period, but showed the interaction of subject social desirability disposition and verb connotation during the reinforcement phase.

[1] Paper presented at the Eastern Psychological Association, April 6, 1967. Cited in *American Psychologist*, 1967, 22, 736.

[2] The paper is based upon a portion of a dissertation submitted in partial fulfillment of the requirements of the degree of Doctor of Philosophy in the Department of Psychology at the University of Missouri, Columbia. The author wishes to thank Dr. June Chance, his adviser, and the members of his doctoral committee for their guidance and support during this study.

This paper is published for the first time in this volume. We are grateful for the author's permission to use it.

There is ample evidence that interpersonal reinforcers can effectively alter the frequency with which subjects generally employ a specified verbal response class. However, while many investigators also report marked individual differences in responsivity to social reinforcement, the search for personality correlates of verbal conditionability has led to conflicting findings. Inconsistency among results may be partly attributable to relative lack of controls over the task-related stimuli presented to Ss.

This study investigates the effect on verbal conditioning of two aspects of social desirability, namely, that pertaining to subject characteristics (dispositional social desirability, DSD), and task-stimulus social desirability (TSD). It is proposed that the frequency with which Ss emit the reinforced response class in a sentence-construction verbal-conditioning experiment is jointly determined by DSD and TSD. Further, it is proposed that the pattern of the DSD × TSD interaction may be employed to test two current alternative interpretations of nontest behaviors reflected by high scorers on the Marlowe-Crowne Social Desirability (M-C) Scale (Crowne & Marlowe, 1960), which operationally defines DSD in terms of Ss' endorsements of culturally sanctioned behaviors which are unlikely to be true.

High M-C SD scale scores have been said to reflect: (a) greater discrimination of behaviors which lead to approval (Miller, Doob, Butler & Marlowe, 1965) or (b) more vulnerable self-esteem (Mosher, 1965a) than is reflected by low M-C scale scores. The present study employs task stimuli controlled for social desirability to determine whether high-DSD Ss seek approval when both favorable and unfavorable self-descriptions are positively reinforced (as predicted by the "situational discrimination" hypothesis) or whether reinforcement effects in this group are limited to favorable self-references (vulnerability hypothesis).

METHOD

Subjects

Of 66 female college freshmen, selected from a pool of 257 female undergraduates who took the M-C scale, 25 each were assigned to high-DSD and to low-DSD experimental groups. The remainder served as nonreinforced controls. All Ss had scored in the upper or lower 27% of the distribution of M-C SD scores.

Procedure

In order to reduce intraexperimenter variance, an IBM 1710 computer was programmed to administer a Taffel-type verbal-conditioning task (Taffel, 1955). The console typewriter was used for instruction, stimulus presentation, and the dispensing of reinforcement on the one hand, and as a responding device on the other in a manner similar to that described by Videbeck and Bates (1966). A postconditioning interview was conducted by E to determine whether S could state the response-reinforcement contingency. There were 81 trials: 27 nonreinforced, followed by 54 reinforced.

S was requested to type a sentence on each trial beginning with one of six pronouns (I, we, he, she, you, they) and a single verb. There were 81 verbs, scaled for impression value (TSD) by Dixon and Dixon (1964), who employed Osgood's methods (Osgood, Suci, & Tannenbaum, 1957). An equal number of Good-Impression verbs, Neutral-Impression verbs, and Bad-Impression verbs was presented, in a random order, within each block of 27 trials.

Base rates for use of the various pronouns were determined during the first block of trials. During the second and third blocks all sentences beginning with the self-reference pronouns "I" and "we" were reinforced by the computer's typing the words "Very Good" below S's sentence response. Sentences beginning with other pronouns were reinforced with "Not So Good." Control Ss received identical treatment, except that reinforcement was omitted.

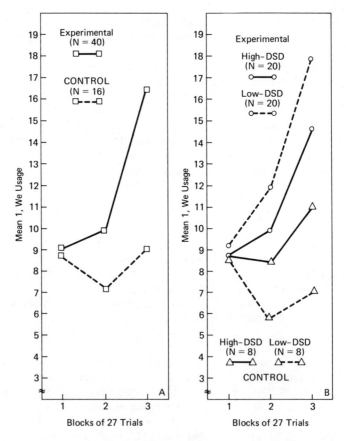

FIGURE 1. (A) Mean I-WE frequencies emitted by reinforced groups matched for verbal ability and non-reinforced control groups; (B) mean I-WE frequencies as a function of DSD and reinforcement.

RESULTS

The major unit of analysis was the frequency of sentences beginning with "I" and "we" (I-we sentences).[3] Three judges also rated response content for *mitigation* of "bad impressions" created when I-we pronouns were used in conjunction with Bad-Impression verbs [e.g., Ss could "soften" the effect variously—by using negative qualifiers ("I never cheated"), passive voice ("We were cheated"), etc.].

Operant Level Data

Since both reinforced and nonreinforced Ss received identical treatment during the initial trial block, their scores were combined for analysis of base rates. I-we frequencies prior to reinforcement were a function of TSD ($F = 34.82$, 2/128df, $p < .001$). Both DSD groups emitted significantly fewer I-we sentences in "bad impression" contexts than when the context was either "neutral" or "good."

Conditioning Data

Significant increments in the reinforced class of I-we pronouns were obtained under computer reinforcement (Blocks $F = 40.48$, 2/96df, p < .001) in contrast to the nonreinforced condition. Again, the TSD main effect was significant.

[3] Response latency and error are not reported here, but essentially yield the same picture of subject performance.

Table 1 Analysis of Variance of I-We Frequencies as a Function of TSD and Blocks of Trials for Reinforced DSD Groups Unmatched for Verbal Ability

Source	SS	df	MS	F
Between subjects	942.66	49		
DSD (A)	67.28	1	67.28	3.68*
error a	875.38	48	18.24	
Within subjects	2155.33	400		
Blocks (B)	529.52	2	264.76	40.48***
A × B	34.84	2	17.42	2.66*
error b	627.64	96	6.54	
TSD (C)	261.13	2	130.57	62.18***
A × C	16.78	2	8.39	3.99**
error c	201.42	96	2.10	
B × C	21.06	4	5.26	2.29*
A × B × C	21.54	4	5.38	2.34*
error bc	441.40	192	2.30	

* $p < .10$.
** $p < .05$.
*** $p < .001$.

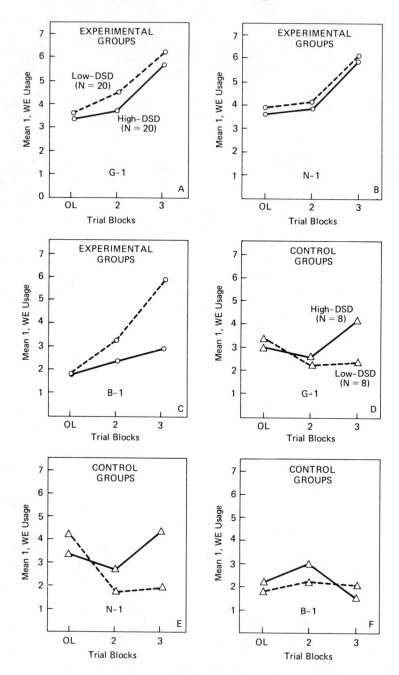

FIGURE 2. (A, B, C) Mean I-WE frequencies emitted by reinforced groups matched for verbal ability, as a function of TSD; (D, E, F) mean I-WE frequencies emitted by non-reinforced control groups, as a function of TSD.

While DSD groups did not differ significantly in rate of emission of I-we sentences using Good-Impression or Neutral-Impression verbs, the DSD × TSD interaction was significant, indicating that they did differ when using Bad-Impression verbs. Specifically, low-DSD Ss conditioned equally well in all three verbal contexts, while high-DSD Ss showed only minimal increments in critical responses made to Bad-Impression verbs from block to block.

Additional analyses showed that low-DSD Ss emitted significantly more critical responses to Bad-Impression verbs during the early reinforced block in comparison to the base rate, while high-DSD Ss did not do so until the later-reinforced block. Further, low-DSD Ss emitted significantly more I-we sentences under reinforcement than did high-DSD Ss.

These conditioning data support a "vulnerability" or "defensiveness" interpretation of the M-C SD scale rather than a "situational discrimination" interpretation. High-DSD Ss do not discriminate (and pursue) potentially rewarding aspects of their external environment to a greater extent than do low-DSD Ss. In fact, they forego rewards when such rewards seem contingent upon the emission of negative self-reference.

Additional support for the "vulnerability" interpretation of high M-C SD scores was obtained from the mitigation data. Emission of I-we sentences to Bad-Impression verbs did not increase for high-DSD Ss between the operant block and the early-reinforced block, and their percentage of mitigation remained essentially the same as in the operant block. However, when high-DSD Ss later showed a significant increase in use of self-reference pronouns in conjunction with Bad-Impression verbs in Block 3 (compared with Block 1), they also showed a significant increase in percentage of mitigation (40.7% vs. 28.6%, z = 1.96, $p < .05$). Low-DSD Ss showed a significant reduction in percentage of mitigation over their earlier performance.

Awareness and Interview Data

Statement of the correct response-reinforcement contingency was positively and significantly correlated with level of conditioning; low-DSD Ss verbalized the contingency more often than high-DSD Ss ($x^2 = 9.90$, 1 df, $p < .005$).

CONCLUSIONS

A constellation of findings (including response latency and error data not reported here) favors a "vulnerability" interpretation of the M-C SD scale; there is little evidence that high-DSD Ss are better able to discriminate situational cues than low-DSD Ss.

The finding that TSD diminishes in potency as a determinant of critical pronoun frequencies under reinforcement for low-DSD Ss, but not for high-DSD Ss, suggests that a complex model is required to explain the verbal conditioning process; simplistic models which fail to give systematic status to both dispositional and contextual factors are inadequate to account for the current data.

7-5 | Social Learning Theory Predictors of Termination in Psychotherapy

WILLIAM E. PIPER, MICHAEL WOGAN, and
HERBERT GETTER

This research was primarily concerned with a social learning theory approach to the prediction of termination in psychotherapy. Two main constructs from social learning theory (Rotter, 1954), *expectancy* and *reinforcement value*, served as predictor variables. It was predicted that the lower the expectancy that therapy would be helpful and the lower the reinforcement value of improvement for a patient, the more likely the patient would become a terminator.

Previous work has not considered the construct of reinforcement value in therapy research of this type, although some research has been conducted concerning the relation between expectancy of improvement and termination. Goldstein (1962) noted that indirect evidence provided by data from the Phipps Clinic (Frank, Gliedman, Imber, Nash & Stone, 1957; Imber, Frank, Nash, Stone, & Gliedman, 1957) suggested a relation between duration of therapy and patient prognostic expectancies; however, two other studies (Goldstein, 1960; Heine & Trosman, 1960) tested the relation between expectancy of improvement and termination directly and failed to find a significant relation. Prior to this present investigation, evidence for a significant relation between expectancy of improvement and termination was largely negative. However, social learning theory implies that a significant relation should be found between termination and some combination of expectancy and reinforcement value.

According to social learning theory, *behavior potential* (BP) is a function of expectancy (E) and reinforcement value (RV) in a specific situaiton (s1), $BP = f(E \& RV)$. Although the way in which E and RV combine is speculative at this point, Rotter suggests the relation may be a multiplicative one. Both terms of the right-hand member of the equation should be related positively to behavior potential. In his study, *behavior potential* was defined as the likelihood the patient would continue attending therapy. *Expectancy* was defined as the average rated expectancy of improvement for problems which the patient said concerned him. *Reinforcement value* was defined as the average rated importance of help with each of these problems. The first hypothesis was that patients who had low levels of expectancy *and* low reinforcement value were more likely to be *terminators*, while patients having high levels of expectancy and reinforcement value were more likely to be *remainers*.

The investigation also examined antecedents of expectancy of improvement. According to Rotter (1954), "expectancy (E_{s1}) is a function of probability of occurrence as based on past experience in situations per-

This paper is published for the first time in this volume. We are grateful for the authors' permission to use it.

ceived as the same (E'_{s1}) and the generalization of the expectancies for the same or similar reinforcements to occur in other situations for the same or functionally related behaviors (GE) [p. 166]." In the present study E'_{s1} was defined as the expectancy associated with previous problem-solving behavior with people who were not psychotherapists. Since no patient in the present study had previously been in psychotherapy, patients' expectancies should be solely a function of GE. Thus, the second hypothesis was stated that generalized expectancy (GE) would predict E_{s1} for patients with no previous experience with a psychotherapist. An empirical measure of GE was developed to test this hypothesis. It was hoped by this means to refine commonly used expectancy measures, which ordinarily ask the person if he expects to improve.

METHOD

Setting, Subjects, Therapists

The investigation was conducted at the Mental Health Clinic of the University of Connecticut Health Service. The potential patient-subjects were 52 female and 45 male undergraduates who came to the clinic seeking therapy. Patients coming to the clinic for other reasons, such as medication or one or two consulting sessions, were excluded from the study. Patients who had previous therapy were not included in the sample. Therapists were four psychiatrists, three social workers, three clinical psychology graduate students (postinternship), and one Ph.D. clinical psychologist. In almost all cases, therapy consists of individual, hour-long sessions at the rate of one per week. For a number of reasons (patients misread instructions, patients refused to complete parts of measures, patients failed to meet the definitions of terminators and remainders, etc.), Ns for different data analyses varied; N is specified with each analysis in presenting results.

Measures

The measures of the constructs, expectancy of improvement and reinforcement value, utilized a common set of items extracted from the Mooney Problem Checklist (Mooney, 1950). All items from the social-psychological relations and personal-psychological relations subscales were included. Some other items from the remaining nine subscales were included on the basis of diversity. The final set included 130 items.

Patients were instructed to go through the list of problems and to circle those which were of concern to them. They were encouraged to add any problems of concern to them which were not included in the list. Fifteen patients added problems. The patients were then asked to rate each of the items circled on a dimension of "expectancy regarding therapy" by choosing one of five responses which ranged from "I expect therapy to be of great help in solving this problem," to "I expect therapy to make this problem worse." The average of these ratings served as the operational measure of expectancy of improvement for each patient. Patients were then asked to rate each of the problems they had circled on a dimension of "importance" by choosing one of four responses ranging from "It is of great importance that I solve this problem," to "It is of no importance that I solve this problem." His average rating served as the operational measure of reinforcement value of improvement for each patient.

Generalized expectancy (GE) was measured by a short questionnaire asking the patient about his past attempts to obtain help by talking with others about his problems. The patient was asked to list those people to whom he had talked about his problems, and then asked to rate each of them on a dimension of "helpfulness" by choosing one of four responses. The responses ranged from "very helpful" to "made things worse."

Terminators were defined as patients who completed three or fewer sessions and left therapy prematurely. Prematurity of termination was judged by the therapist. This definition, rather than one based solely on an absolute number of sessions, was used as the criterion to avoid including short-term consultative cases in the termination sample. *Remainers* were defined as patients who remained in therapy for a minimum of eight sessions and were still engaged in therapy at the time of retesting.

Patients completed the measure of expectancy, RV and GE before their first therapy session. Therapists had no knowledge of the predictor measures. After eight weeks had elapsed, patients were classified as either terminators or remainers.

RESULTS

Termination
The first hypothesis predicted that terminators would have lower combined scores of expectancy and reinforcement value, as measured by the problem questionnaire, than remainers. To test this hypothesis, t tests were calculated between terminators (N = 19) and remainers (N = 21) on the basis of both an additive and a multiplicative combination of expectancy and reinforcement value. Table 1 shows that the additively combined scores of terminators were significantly lower than the combined scores of remainers ($t = 4.00$; $p < .001$). The multiplicative combination of scores also yields a difference between terminators and remainers ($t = 4.30$; $p < .001$). Table 1 also includes results of t tests calculated between terminators and remainers for expectancy scores alone ($t = 2.41$; $p < .05$) and for reinforcement value scores alone ($t = 3.33$; $p < .005$).

Data pertaining to the first hypothesis was also examined by means of chi-square analyses of the data. "High" and "low" scores for expectancy and for reinforcement value were defined by median splits. Table 2 describes the numbers and percents of remainers and terminators in each of the four resulting categories. The chi-square value obtained indicated a significant difference in the distribution of terminators and remainers among the four categories ($x^2 = 12.07$; $p < .01$, df 7). Examining the two extreme categories, 87% of patients who had both a high expect-

Table 1   Tests of Mean Differences between Remainers and
Terminators

SCORE	REMAINERS		TERMINATORS			
	$\overline{X}$	SD	$\overline{X}$	SD	df	t
Additive Combination of E + RV	.79	1.15	−.93	1.52	38	4.00***
Multiplicative Combination of E + RV	29.21	6.14	20.44	6.82	38	4.30***
E Independently	1.91	.42	1.50	.60	38	2.41*
RV Independently	3.43	.20	3.13	.37	41	3.33**

Note. Means and standard deviations for the two combinations of E and RV are expressed in standard score form. Three Ss provided data for RV but not for E.
* $p < .05$.
** $p < .005$.
*** $p < .001$.

Table 2   Number and Percent of Remainers and Terminators in Each of Four Categories Defined by E and RV

CATEGORY	TOTAL NUMBER OF PATIENTS	NUMBER AND PERCENT OF REMAINERS	NUMBER AND PERCENT OF TERMINATORS
High E and High RV	15	13(87%)	2(13%)
High E and Low RV	5	2(40%)	3(60%)
Low E and High RV	7	3(43%)	4(57%)
Low E and Low RV	13	3(23%)	10(77%)

ancy score and a high reinforcement value score were remainers, while only 23% of the patients who had both a low expectancy score and a low reinforcement value score were remainers. The first hypothesis is clearly supported by these data.

Generalized Expectancy

The second hypothesis predicted that overall, generalized expectancy (GE) measured by the antecedent questionnaire would be directly related to overall expectancy (E) as measured by the problem questionnaire for patients with no previous experience with a psychotherapist. The correlation coefficient between these two measures for $N = 97$ was nonsignificant ($r = .05$).

DISCUSSION

Termination

The results strongly supported the hypothesis that terminators have lower combined scores of expectancy and reinforcement value, as measured by the problem questionnaire, than remainers. This picture obtained whether expectancy scores and reinforcement value scores were combined additively or multiplicatively. These results suggest that whether a patient remains in psychotherapy or not depends on his expectancy of improvement and the urgency he feels for that improvement. In this situation both aspects (E and RV) are positively associated with each other for most Ss (28 of 40) when subjects are divided into high and low groups using a median split; however, in the 12 remaining cases E and RV for therapy-initiated improvement were disparate.

While it appears from Table 2 that E and RV are closely associated this is not actually the case. Within the High-High and Low-Low groups there is no relationship between E and RV. The overall correlation between E and RV for the 40 subjects was only $r = .18$, $p = > .20$. Partial correlation (point biserial) of E on terminator vs. remainers, with RV partialed out was $r = .33$, $p = < .025$. Partial correlation of RV on terminators vs. remainers with E partialed out was $r = .43$, $p = < .01$. In other words, both E and RV predict independently and significantly to the criterion. The overall point biserial correlation of E $\times$ RV with terminators vs. remainers was $r = .57$, $p = < .01$.

These results have practical implications for psychotherapy, in helping to identify potential terminators. The problem questionnaire takes little time to complete and score, and could be given easily at the beginning of therapy. Potential terminators could be identified, and were attention then directed to the patient's low expectancies and/or low reinforcement values early in therapy, perhaps changing them, it is possible that the patient would be less likely to become a terminator.

The measure of reinforcement value used in this experiment was an average score taken over the entire set of problems indicated by the patient. It could be argued that a measure of reinforcement value should take into account the number of problems endorsed, since a patient with many problems might have more to gain from attending therapy than a patient with few problems. This possibility could be tested by calculating a revised reinforcement value score, obtained by multiplying the average score by the number of problems circled. However, the terminators and remainers did not differ with respect to number of problems checked, making further analysis redundant.

Several variables not directly related to the first hypothesis were also investigated to see if they differentiated between terminators and remainers. The first variable was initial level of disturbance. Were terminators less disturbed initially than remainers, it would not be surprising if they left therapy before remainers. Four indices of initial disturbances were available. The first was the gross number of problems indicated by the patient on the problem questionnaire. The other three indices were affective state scores from the Multiple Affect Adjective Check List (Lubin

& Zuckerman, 1965), which each patient had completed approximately one week before his first therapy session. The check list is designed to measure states of anxiety, depression, and hostility. For each of these indices a t test was calculated between terminators and remainers. All four t's failed to reach significance. The second and third variables investigated were sex of patient and sex of therapist. Analysis by chi-square indicated no significant difference between terminators and remainers for either sex of patient or sex of therapist. The fourth variable investigated was the individual therapists. Analysis by chi-square indicated no significant differences in proportions of terminators and remainers contributed to the sample by each therapist.

Generalized Expectancy
The low correlation between overall expectancy of improvement as measured by the problem questionnaire and overall, generalized expectancy as measured by the antecedent questionnaire was surprising. The second hypothesis predicted that the two measures would be related; however, the results indicate that the patient's expectancy that therapy will lead to improvement was not related to his past attempts to get help from nontherapists. On second thought, the finding is not so surprising, if it is assumed that patients discriminate between therapists and nontherapists. In a study concerning the perceived similarity between psychotherapists and various other people in the patient's environment, Sechrest (1962) reported, "In general, therapists were described as being similar to those persons whom they did in fact resemble in age, sex, and occupational status, e.g., physicians, ministers. Therapist similarities to family members were not marked [p. 176]." Sechrest's findings suggest that therapists are perceived as similar to other professionals, but not to nonprofessionals.

With Sechrest's findings in mind, the data from the present experiment concerning GE were reanalyzed using only questionnaire responses which referred to professional people such as physicians, ministers, guidance counselors and professors. N was reduced to 31; however, correlation between the new measure of GE and expectancy of improvement was $+ .32 \ p > .05 < .10$).

These results suggest that expectancies of improvement do generalize to therapists from positive experience with other professionals. Generalization does not occur on a global basis, but depends on the perceived similarity between therapists and other professionals. The distinction between professionals and nonprofessionals whom the patient may consult about his personal problems should be considered in future investigations in this area.

In summary, the constructs of reinforcement value and expectancy of improvement as measured by the problem questionnaire proved to be useful predictors of terminators *versus* remainers after eight weeks of therapy. Although measures of E and RV as used here are highly related to each other, they are not identical with each other. Generalization of expectancy of improvement to therapists from experiences with other professionals was also demonstrated.

7-6 | Some Implications of a Social Learning Theory for the Practice of Psychotherapy[1]

JULIAN B. ROTTER

The problems of psychotherapy may be viewed as problems in how to effect changes in behavior through the interaction of one person with another. That is, they are problems in human learning in a social situation or context. In spite of this, there has been until recently relatively little application of formal learning theory and of laboratory research on human learning to the techniques of psychotherapy. Where learning theory has been used at all, it frequently has been applied in one of two ways. The first of these is as a justification for therapeutic procedures developed from other theoretical approaches rather than as a basis for deriving new methods and techniques. This approach frequently fails to make use of the implications of a considerable body of knowledge regarding human learning but rather selects particular principles to justify favorite therapeutic procedures. The second approach follows a restricted conditioning model that is limited to the kinds of problems to which it can be applied and which frequently fails to take into account much of what the individual has already learned when he comes to therapy. It fails to recognize that the complex attitudes, goals, skills and behaviors of the individual significantly affect what he will learn and under what conditions he will learn most efficiently. In such an approach the absence of functional content variables for stable human behavior, that is a personality theory, often reduces the efficiency of therapy because of failure to understand the gradients of generalization of behavior changes and to understand the nature of "hidden" reinforcements which strengthen an apparent maladaptive response.

This failure to fully apply learning theory can be explained in part because many individuals involved in studying complex *human* learning as a general area of investigation are not concerned with the application of their findings to psychotherapeutic practice. A more serious barrier to application, however, is that there is too great a disparity between the kind of laboratory situations in which human learning is typically studied and the complex social interactions which characterize psychotherapy.

The gap between theory and laboratory research, and the prediction of behavior in complex social interactions is a great one and cannot be closed by a single leap. The purpose of this paper, however, is to lessen that hiatus somewhat by illustrating some implications of one social learning theory for the practice of psychotherapy, as specifically as the present state of the theory and research allows. Since no special laws are assumed

[1] I am grateful to Miss Dorothy Hochreich for her helpful suggestions in the preparation of this manuscript.

From D. J. Levis (ed.), *Learning Approaches to Therapeutic Behavior Change* (Chicago: Aldine Publishing Company, 1970). Reprinted by permission of the author and the publisher.

that are peculiar to psychotherapeutic interactions many of the hypotheses generated here regarding psychotherapeutic change would apply equally to effecting social change.

In order to derive either implications or predictions from a behavior theory to the problem of psychotherapy, one must have available a theory suitable to the complex phenomena concerned and sufficiently developed that at least all of the major variables and their relationships are known and measurable, so that prediction can be made or control exercised. Second, one must know the dimensions along which behaviors may be categorized, generalizations predicted, etc. In other words, one must have integrated with such a learning theory, a content theory (sometimes called a personality theory) which presumes to have abstracted from such social interactions the relevant aspects of behavior into functional categories (i.e., needs, traits, habit families, etc.). There must be a useful descriptive terminology to characterize the generalized aspects of behavior as well as a theory which describes the process of change.

Behavior theories vary in the degree to which they fit this ideal. The degree to which they deviate may account for the apparent minimum connection between the theories of personality and/or learning and the psychotherapeutic methods which presumably derive from them. For example, both Kelly (1955) and Rogers (1951) have in common a phenomenological theory with many points of similarity. Yet the implications each sees from theory to psychotherapeutic practice are so different that in many instances they would have to be placed at opposite ends of a set of continua used to describe therapeutic techniques. A bewildering variety of practices have been advocated by therapists who justify them as stemming from something they all refer to as "psychoanalytic theory" (Rotter, 1960a). Similarly, Wolpe, among learning theorists, (1958) describes a learning and neurophysiological theory of behavior of Hullian origin and goes on to advocate therapeutic practices which have only a loose connection with his theory and appears opposed in many major ways to Dollard and Miller's (1950) application of presumably the same theory. Although awareness of this problem has led to an attempt to exercise caution in drawing implications from theory to practice in this paper, it should be stated at the outset that these implications are also loose and although they seem logical to the author, they may well not be so perceived by others.

There is a second difficulty in the drawing of specific implications from a personality theory for the problem of psychotherapeutic practice or of social change. An adequate theory of behavior may explain how changes take place or how to achieve the control of some behaviors, but a scientific theory does not specify what kinds of changes are good or bad from the point of view of social or ethical values. What constitute adequate goals for psychotherapy or social change and what constitute ethical means of achieving these goals is not a part of a scientific theory but of a value system. (That is, a set of judgments dealing with what is good and what is bad.) Different value systems utilizing the same theory might well lead to very different methods of practice. When one advocates a specific method of psychotherapy, one has explicitly or implicitly made a commitment to a specifiable set of values. For example, such a commitment might take the form that the therapist is ethically justified in helping the patient arrive at a better understanding of himself but should assiduously avoid affecting in any other way the kinds of changes that may take place in the patient's goals or behavior. Whether or not this is possible is a matter of controversy. However, it is clear that the methods that such a therapist would use would be quite different than those of another therapist, operating with the same theory, who explicitly states that the goal of psychotherapy is to increase the patient's capacity to love others. It is because of this latter point that it seems necessary to emphasize that the applications of social learning theory to follow have to be regarded as only one set of possible techniques.

Since social learning theory has not reached the stage where it is possible to make completely unambiguous deductions to specific complex social phenomena, it is not always possible to talk about implications at a highly specific level. The purpose of this paper is to illustrate at some middle level of generality one possible application of social learning theory to psychotherapy for a particular set of values. The intention is to apply a complex learning theory of personality as directly as possible to the problems of psychotherapy, rather than to use learning principles as post-hoc explanations of techniques derived from other points of view. The goal is to not only apply the abstract processes of learning to psychotherapy but also to take into account what the individual has already learned in order to determine what kinds of change will be most beneficial to him and under what circumstances he can learn most effectively. Before proceeding, it is necessary to indicate what value commitments are involved in the illustrative application that follows.

SOCIAL VALUES IN PSYCHOTHERAPY

Briefly stated, there are three implicit or explicit general positions that psychotherapists take in regard to the goals of treatment. Particular therapists may combine these goals in a variety of ways.

The first of these goals is one of conformity or normalcy as the ideal outcome of treatment. From this point of view the object of treatment is to help the person change so that he is more like other people, particularly in regard to any characteristics which are considered to be detrimental to himself or others. A special case of this orientation is the disease approach which considers that the patient's difficulty is characterized by certain symptoms. The descriptions of these illnesses are to be found in textbooks. As in medicine, the purpose of treatment is to eliminate the illness as evidenced by the reduction of symptoms.

The second general goal might be called one of subjective happiness. The purpose of treatment is to help the patient reach a state of greater happiness or comfort or pleasure. The emphasis is on internal feelings, resolution of internal conflict, acceptance of self, etc.

The third value orientation in psychotherapy might be called the socially constructive one. Here the goals of psychotherapy are seen as helping the patient to lead a more constructive life, to contribute to society, to maximize his potential for achievement, to maximize his feeling of affection or contribution to others.

It is a combination of the last two which forms the ethical or value background for the general suggestions regarding psychotherapy which follow. Briefly and more specifically, the following value commitments are made:

1. The therapist understands that his behavior has a definite effect on the patient, not only in regard to the patient's self-understanding, but also his behaviors, his specific goals, and his ethical judgments. The therapist is willing to accept *some* of the responsibility for these changes and to attempt to direct or control them.

2. The therapist seeks to provide the patient with a greater potential for satisfaction. That is, the therapist seeks to direct the patient's behavior to goals which the patient values or which provide him with satisfaction within the limitations expressed below.

3. The therapist seeks to eliminate, or to keep the patient from acquiring behaviors or goals which he feels are *clearly* detrimental to others in society.

4. The therapist believes that the patient should "carry his own weight" in society, at least to the extent that he makes some contribution to the welfare of others in return for the satisfaction he receives from others.

Applying such values to the particular patient is obviously not a cut and dried affair but will depend on the judgment of the therapist. It should be emphasized again that these are only the values of one person. They do not follow from social learning theory nor are they part of it, but it is necessary to have some explicit set of values before application of any theory to the practice of psychotherapy can be logically considered.

BASIC TERMS IN SOCIAL LEARNING THEORY

It is not possible to present all of the theoretical concepts relevant to the problem of psychotherapy. In one way social learning theory is a far more complex personality theory than most and requires the analysis of four variables in order to make a prediction, where many theories require only one or two. In some theories explanation and prediction is based on identifying a strongest trait or internal characteristic of the individual or the conflict between two traits. It is possible in a brief paper such as this to give only a rather disjointed account, hoping that this will provide at least the flavor of a more systematic and comprehensive exposition.

Social learning theory may be briefly characterized as an expectancy learning theory which utilizes an empirical law of effect. In this theory (Rotter, 1954) the basic formula for the prediction of goal directed behavior is as follows:

$$BP_{x,s_1,R_a} = f (E_{x,R_{a,s_1}} \& RV_{a,s_1}) \tag{1}$$

The formula may be read: The potential for behavior x to occur in situation 1 in relation to reinforcement a is a function of the expectancy of the occurrence of reinforcement a following behavior x in situation 1, and the value of reinforcement a in situation 1. It is assumed that expectancies can be measured along a continuum. Such a formula, however, is extremely limited in application for it deals only with the potential for a given behavior to occur in relationship to a single specific reinforcement. Practical clinical application requires a more generalized concept of behavior and the formula for these broader concepts is given below:

$$BP_{(x-n),s(1-n),R_{(a-n)}} = f\,[E_{(x-n),s(1-n),R_{(a-n)}} \,\&\, RV_{(a-n),s(1-n)}] \qquad (2)$$

This may be read: The potentiality of the functionally related behaviors x to n to occur in the specified situation 1 to n in relation to potential reinforcements a to n is a function of the expectancies of these behaviors leading to these reinforcements in these situations and the values of these reinforcements in these situations. For purposes of simplicity of communication, the three basic terms in this formula have been typically referred to as need potential, freedom of movement and need value as in the third formula below:

$$NP = f\,(FM \,\&\, NV) \qquad (3)$$

In this formula the fourth concept, that of the psychological situation, is implicit. Some of the content variables of this theory are empirically determined needs, arrived at by grouping behaviors which have some functional relationship on the basis of their leading to the same or similar reinforcements. The generality or breadth of such concepts depend on one's purpose. For example, at a very general level we may use terms such as need for recognition and status, need for love and affection, need for dependence, need for independence, need for dominance and need for physical comfort. At a more specific level typical concepts might be need for academic recognition, need for aggression towards authority figures, need for love and affection from same sex peers, etc. The basis for such groupings derives not from presumed instincts or drives but is empirically determined and follows from the learning experience of the individuals of a given culture.

The variables referred to above and operations for measurement have been defined and further explicated in previous publications (Rotter, 1954, 1955, 1967a, 1967b).

SOME MAJOR HYPOTHESES AND THEIR IMPLICATIONS

In psychotherapy we are usually concerned with classes of behaviors or more general characteristics. Consequently, this paper will deal primarily with the formula that *need potential* is a *function of freedom of movement* and *need value* for a particular class of situations. A crucial part of this theory for the problem of psychotherapy is that there are specific hypotheses regarding the behavior of an individual with low freedom of movement and high need value for a particular class of satisfactions. When such an individual has low freedom of movement and places high value on some class of reinforcements, he is likely to learn behaviors to avoid the failure or punishments that he anticipates in this area and may make attempts to achieve these goals on an irreal level. The person anticipating punishment or failure may avoid situations physically or by repression or may attempt to reach the goals through rationalization, fantasy or symbolic means. Most of the great variety of behaviors commonly regarded as defenses or psychopathological symptoms are here referred to as avoidance or irreal behaviors. Such avoidance and irreal behaviors themselves may frequently start a vicious cycle and lead to both immediate and delayed additional negative reinforcements. Expectancies for punishment may give rise to a number of implicit behaviors, thoughts or cognitions, that can be observed only indirectly. Such implicit behaviors might include awareness of disturbed body states, fixation on the punishment, narrowing the field of attention, rehearsal of obsessive thoughts, etc., which can seriously interfere with constructive behavior or problem solution. In other words, frequently at the bottom of a problem involving either lack of feeling of satisfaction, conflict, anticipation of punishment, irreal behavior, or lack of constructive activity, is a condition of low freedom of movement and high need value.

Low freedom of movement may result from the patient's lack of knowledge or ability to acquire adequate behaviors to reach his goals or may be a consequence of the nature of the goal itself (such as the desire to have others take all responsibility for one's actions) which frequently results in strong punishments in a specific society. Low freedom of movement may also result from "mistaken" evaluations of the present as a consequence of early experience. For a given person sometimes the behaviors, sometimes "erroneous" expectations, and sometimes the nature of the person's goals may be considered to be the primary source of difficulty.

An important aspect of the problem of low freedom of movement concerns the concept of minimal goal level in social learning theory. In any given situation the possible outcomes of behavior can be ordered from a very high positive reinforcement or goal to a very high negative reinforcement or goal. The theoretical point at which, in this ordering, the outcome changes from one which is positive or reinforcing to negative or punishing is called the minimal goal level. Such a concept can be applied either to a series of goals that are functionally related, e.g., all achievement goals, or to any combination of outcomes possible in a given situation or set of situations. An individual may have low freedom of movement although from the viewpoint of others he appears to succeed often, because his reinforcements usually are below his own minimal goal level. Such internalized high minimal goals are frequently involved in problems of low freedom of movement. It should be stressed at this point that the goals referred to can be of any kind: moral, ethical, achievement, sexual, affectional, dominating, dependent, etc. In social learning theory any functionally related set of reinforcements toward which the individual moves is considered the basis for assuming a need and for which a need potential, freedom of movement, and need value can be determined.

In order to increase the patient's freedom of movement for goals he values highly, one possible approach is to change the values of the goals themselves. This might be necessary under conditions in which the person has two or more goals of high value but of such nature that the satisfaction of one involves the frustration of the other, as in the case of individuals with strong desires for masculinity and dependency satisfactions in the same situations. Another instance would be one in which the goals of the patient, such as the desire to control and dominate others, lead to conflict with others' needs and eventuates in both immediate and delayed punishment. A third instance of changing the value of goals would involve the lowering of minimal goals when they are unrealistically high, such as in the case of an individual who regards any indication of fear in himself as proof that he is not sufficiently masculine.

To understand how minimal goal levels can be changed, one has to consider how reinforcement values, or the values attached to reinforcement, are acquired, maintained, or changed. In social learning theory, the value of reinforcement in a given situation is hypothesized to be a function of the expectancy that the reinforcement will lead to subsequent reinforcements, and the value of those subsequent reinforcements as in the formula below:

$$RV_{a,s_1} = f\,[E_{R_a \to R_{(b-n)},s_1} \,\&\, RV_{(b-n),s_1}] \tag{4}$$

If a child believes that when he gets an "A" in school it will lead to affection, then the value of the "A" is dependent upon the value of the affection and the expectancy that the affection will be forthcoming. If he feels that a "B" will lead to rejection, a similar analysis holds. For most goals each reinforcement is related to several consequent reinforcements rather than one.

The problem in changing minimal goals, then, or in changing the value of any goal or set of goals, is frequently one of changing expectancies for subsequent reinforcement. Adler (1939) has long emphasized the importance of discussing life goals with the patient in order to change immediate goals and behaviors. Many times the values of goals are maintained over a long period of time with the expectancy for subsequent reward relatively stable because the relationships have not been verbalized and the subject is not aware of them. In many instances delayed negative reinforcement follows from achieving an earlier reward but the subject fails to relate these to the prior goal. For example, a woman seeking to control her husband fails to recognize that the consequences of her behavior and her successful attempts at control, although bringing immediate gratification, also lead to subsequent negative reinforcements because of the hostility or rejection on the part of the husband. In other words, the value of goals can be changed sometimes by examining the early rewards with which they were associated but which may no longer be operating, and also by analysis of present and future consequences which the person has never associated directly with the goal.

One implication of such an analysis is that insight into the acquisition of particular goals may be helpful in changing their values if the subject sees that expectancies for subsequent reinforcements have changed since the time of acquisition or were mistaken in the first place. Such a conception is not different from any other insight type of therapy. However, a further implication is that it may be of equal importance to analyze also the consequences of present behaviors and goals which are frequently delayed but nevertheless result from the behaviors the individual uses or reinforcements which he seeks. It is frequently important not only to discover why it is, for example, that one seeks to demonstrate superiority over members of the opposite sex in terms of early experience but also important to discover what are the present and long term consequences of such goals and of the behaviors used to achieve them.

These comments deal with one method of changing freedom of movement or increasing freedom of movement by lowering minimal goals, or having the individual place greater value on alternative goals. There are other ways in which freedom of movement can be increased and presumably as a result both personal feelings of satisfaction as well as more constructive behavior will be increased. As Mowrer (1948) has pointed out in his discussion of the neurotic paradox, sometimes expectancy of punishment remains high because the individual fails to learn that what he fears is no longer realistic since he avoids the situation in which he can learn anything to the contrary. If his experience with competitive scholastic activity is such that it was negatively reinforcing as a child, he may never learn that he is capable of reaching satisfying goals in this area because he avoids involvement or competitive striving in situations involving academic or scholastic achievement. In this instance freedom of movement may be increased, sometimes by the therapist's own direct reinforcements, and by interpretation of how such an attitude came about and why it is no longer appropriate to present life situations. The emphasis here is on changing the expectancies directly and it may be possible not only to do this by the therapist's behavior and by interpretation but also by control, manipulation or use of other environmental influences. The studies on verbal conditioning (Krasner, 1958) suggest how important the role of the therapist may be as a direct reinforcer of behavior. Changes in the attitudes and behaviors of teachers, parents, spouses, supervisors, etc. may achieve the same effect as face to face therapy and in fact do so more effectively because they are not part of the temporary and artificial situation of the therapy room.

In some instances, although the patient's goals are realistic enough and appropriate enough for his social group and his expectancies are based accurately on present situations, the problem is one of having learned inadequate pathways to achieve these goals or perhaps of not having learned more effective methods of reaching his goals. Here the problem can be regarded as more pedagogical. The search for alternative ways of reaching goals must frequently be taught to the patient as a general technique of dealing with his problems and as a method of finding specific ways of achieving more satisfaction in current life situations.[2] The as-

[2] It can be seen here as in other discussions of implications that the value commitments described earlier are an implicit filter between theory and practice.

sumption that once the patient is free from some kind of internal disorganization, conflict, repression, etc. he will automatically be able to find adequate ways to reach his goals, does not appear useful to this writer. It is often precisely because the patient does not have alternate pathways that he frequently holds on to his less effective behavior in spite of insight into his situation. Frequently, the therapist then labels his failure to progress as due to "intellectual" but not "emotional" insight. Rather, the patient needs to know what the alternate pathways are and needs to have the experience of trying them out and finding them successful before he is willing to give up ineffective behaviors.

Although the warmth, understanding, interest and acceptance of the therapist are important in order to have the patient verbalize his problems and express himself freely, they also result in his becoming an important source of reinforcement for the patient in his present life circumstances. It should be noted that if the therapist is a powerful reinforcer for the patient, whether he is aware of it or not, then he should know a great deal about the life circumstances and the cultural milieu in which the patient lives. Only with such knowledge can he use his position as a reinforcer efficiently. To obtain this knowledge he must spend much time discussing these life situations. His independent knowledge of subcultures is an important aspect of his skill as a therapist.

Another pedagogical problem is frequently one of helping patients differentiate the nature of varied social situations. Low freedom of movement may not result so much from the use of ineffective behaviors in general as from the use of behaviors inappropriate for a given situation. The kind of behavior which may be admired and respected and reinforced in a situation calling for efficiency and the solution of a specific task (for example, a combat team or a committee seeking to make some change in the community) may lead to rejection at a party or in a bedroom. Sometimes because of the distortions of parents or the limited or protective environment of childhood, a particular person fails to learn or to make these discriminations among social situations which are necessary for obtaining satisfactions. When placed in these circumstances in later life he falls back on the techniques he has learned in other situations which may in fact be quite inappropriate. Analysis of what actually transpires in social situations, how other people feel and think, what are the purposes for which particular interactions take place in a variety of present day life situations, may help the patient make these discriminations which he has failed to make in the past. The low freedom of movement one may have in regard to a particular need, such as the desire to have others take care of one, may be a result of attempts to satisfy such needs at inappropriate times. If the individual seeks to satisfy his needs by recognizing that social situations are varied, that the needs of others change from situation to situation, and that the potential reinforcements in some conditions can be seriously limited, he may be far better able to deal satisfactorily with life problems.

This notion might give the impression of advocating the training of the patient to be a kind of chameleon who changes his personality for every situation, to be, in other words, a conformist or opportunist. This is not at all the intent. The therapeutic goal here is one in which the patient recognizes the real differences that exist in the purposes of people in different situations and the purposes which these situations are intended to serve. For example, it is important for some patients to discover that although competitive behavior may be admired and rewarded in academic and job conditions it is neither admired nor rewarded in many social situations. Behavior appropriate for one situation is not appropriate for another although one may maintain the same set of consistent goals in both. Although one may always choose to value achievement in any situation, there are some circumstances in which rewards for competitive achievement are not only not possible but attempts to gain such satisfactions are likely to lead to frustration of the patient's other goals. What the patient may wish to do in these different circumstances is his problem to work out, but that he realizes that there are differences and that he discovers what these differences actually are, is something with which the therapist can help. *It is usually believed that what the patient lacks most is insight into himself but it is likely that in general what characterizes patients even more consistently is lack of insight into the reactions and motives of others.*

Another implication of social learning theory deserves brief mention. Consistent research in human learning indicates that when the subject is set to attend to the relevant aspects of a complex problem, his problem solving is much more efficient (Johnson, 1955). It appears that there is an analogue to therapy here. Frequently much time is lost in treatment because the patient is attending to the wrong (less crucial) aspects of the situation. Uncovering unconscious repressions, dreaming more interesting dreams, achieving a less inhibited freedom of expression, which were all intended as a *means* of psychotherapy may become, for many, the *goals*. One implication of this is that therapy requires frequent and successive structuring. The therapist's as well as the patient's role in therapy needs to be discussed many times so that the patient is fully aware of why he is doing what he is doing in therapy, what his ultimate purpose is, and that there may be alternative ways of achieving the same ends. It is important that the patient does not get fixated on the means rather than the goals of psychotherapy. Too often ex-patients appear to leave therapy with behavior and characteristics which are learned to please the psychotherapist. However, their behavior continues to lead to a baffling kind of failure to obtain satisfactions from the significant people in their own life circumstances.

Finally, it is necessary to describe a last concept, that of broad generalized expectancies, which can be likened to the idea of higher level learning skills. These are very broad expectancies for behavior-reinforcement sequences which cut across need areas. Such expectancies are partial determinants of specific behaviors in many specific situations. Some examples of some of these, of particular significance to psychotherapy, are: (1) the now popular notion of internal versus external control or the belief that reinforcement is contingent upon one's own behavior or characteristics versus the notion that reinforcement is contingent upon chance, fate, or powerful others; (2) the expectancy that people cannot be believed or trusted to fulfill promises, which will affect the learning of delay of gratification and seriously affect the efficiency of almost any type of psychotherapy; (3) the expectancy that frustration can be overcome by seeking alternative ways of achieving goals; (4) an expectancy that reinforcement will follow from a better understanding of other people's motives; (5) an expectancy that directing attention to other people in a difficult situation will suppress distressing behaviors; and (6) a belief that many negative reinforcements can be avoided by better discrimination of situations previously regarded as the same. Clearly the learning of social skills may greatly enhance the patients' potentials to deal with difficult situations on their own without requiring the intervention of a therapist.

It can be seen from these illustrations of the implications of social learning theory for the practice of psychotherapy that the therapist's behavior must depend on the nature of the problem, the nature of the resources open to him outside of therapy as well as within therapy, and the kind of patient with whom he is dealing. For example, when the problem is one of reducing the patient's need for dependency and increasing the value he places on independence, the therapist's behavior would have to be considerably different from that in which the problem of the patient is one of seeking dominance satisfactions to the exclusion of almost all other needs. Similarly, a patient who seeks sympathy as an indication of social support for retreating from life's problems needs to be reacted to differently from one who is oppressed by his inability to meet successfully an unrealistic burden of responsibilities he has already accepted.

Just as highly dependent people will reject non-directive therapy—highly independent ones may reject direct reinforcement techniques. The broader needs of the patient may not be crucial in curing many cases of snake phobia, but they are in selecting a therapist and a method of treatment for a generally depressed young man who finds society a fraud, achievement meaningless, and feels that nothing is worth striving for.

It seems characteristic of this view that rather than leading to implications for a specific technique of therapist behavior, the theory itself implies that the therapist must exercise great flexibility in adjusting his own behavior to the specific needs of the patient. In fact, considering the limitations of flexibility of every therapist, there should be much more concern with matching patients and therapists and consideration of changing therapist or techniques early in therapy. Of course such a therapeutic attitude emphasizes the importance of understanding the basis for the patient's behavior as early as possible.

We have suggested five sets of content variables to provide such generalized descriptions from which gradients of generalization can be predicted: (1) behaviors leading to the same or similar reinforcements or need potentials; (2) expectancies for gratification for functionally related sets of reinforcements, or freedom of movement; (3) preference value of a group of reinforcements, or need values; (4) classes of situations functionally related on the basis of the predominant satisfaction usually obtained in them; and (5) broad generalized expectancies which cut across need areas and are related to a wide variety of behaviors and situations and have to deal with expectancies of how and under what conditions reinforcements are likely to occur. We have demonstrated in a great variety of studies that all of these variables are capable of reliable measurement.

In summary, in this view no mysterious process special to psychotherapy is assumed nor does every therapist have to discover the same special set of ideal behaviors which will maximally facilitate this mysterious process. Rather, it is assumed that psychotherapy is a social interaction which follows the same laws and principles as other social interactions, and from which many different effects can be obtained by a variety of different conditions. It is also possible that the same effects may be obtained by a variety of different methods. The effectiveness of the changes that take place and the efficiency in arriving at them are the criteria for adequacy of method rather than conformity to any doctrine.

IMPLICATIONS OF SOME RESEARCH FINDINGS

Thus far this paper discusses only some general implications of very broadly stated hypotheses regarding the nature of goal-directed behavior. One of the advantages of social learning theory is that it deals with constructs which are amenable to measurement and with hypotheses which are amenable to test. Under limited laboratory conditions exercising as much control as possible, a large number of studies testing some of the broader and some of the more specific hypotheses of the theory have been investigated. Many of these experiments deal with quite general propositions. A few of the studies, however, appear to have somewhat more direct analogical relationship to the type of social interaction involved in psychotherapy and to some of the specific problems encountered with particular kinds of patients. Primarily for purposes of illustration, it seems desirable to present briefly some of these and the implications they may have for more specific problems of psychotherapeutic practice.

In the course of psychotherapy the patient's own efforts need to be rewarded so that he maintains both involvement and expectation of success in this sometimes painful and slow process. If the patient experiences some positive change in himself this may frequently serve as a starting point for a benign cycle. Relevant to this are studies by Good (1952), Castaneda (1952), and Lasko (1952). In these studies the effects of success and failure on the expectancy for future success were studied as a function of amount of experience within a particular task. All three of these experiments demonstrate that expectancies built up on the basis of many previous trials will change least with new experience. On the other hand, expectancies based on only one or two events may change dramatically with new experience. One inference from these studies for the practice of psychotherapy is the suggestion that early in therapy the therapist might well deal with more recent and less "significant" problems which may be most amenable to change. This may have the effect of encouraging the patient and reducing his resistance to change, which is usually based on his fear that without his defenses he would have no alternate ways of dealing with his problems.

Efran and Marcia (1967) conducted a "pseudo" desensitization study of snake and spider phobias. They told subjects that their fears were based on unconscious learning. In order to eliminate them, subliminal stimuli had to be presented to the subject on a screen and the fear response had to be suppressed by an unpleasant stimulus while the subject was unconsciously reacting to the stimulus. Of course, nothing was presented on the screen, and following a signal occasional shocks were given. Fake G.S.R. improvement graphs were shown to subjects at the end of each session. Using less time than previous desensitization studies, their results compare favorably in cure and improvement measures.

What appears to have happened here is that the procedure succeeded in changing the patient's expectancies about whether or not he could be cured. Looking at fake improvement curves under convincing conditions, the subjects decided they were sufficiently cured to allow them to pick up or touch the spiders or snakes. Such an expectancy for cure may well be the basis for the start of a benign cycle allowing the patient to try, one after another, behaviors which previously have been strongly avoided. Whether conducted with relaxation or other behavior modification techniques such procedures, used as part of a more extensive psychotherapy, may serve to start a benign cycle.

A study of Rychlak (1958) pertains to the stability of freedom of movement as a function of the number of different kinds of experiences on which it is based. Varying the number of different tasks but controlling the number and kind of reinforcements, Rychlak demonstrated freedom of movement or generalized expectancies are more stable the greater the number of different but related kinds of events the expectancies were built upon. As an analogy, a male who has had several bad experiences with the same female would have his expectancies more likely to change after a new positive experience with another female than if he had had the same number of experiences of the same kind but with several different females. Like the studies of Good, Castaneda, and Lasko, Rychlak's experiment suggests another condition which may help identify the attitudes which can change most readily.

Phares (1964) and Schwartz (1966) have demonstrated that massed trials of success and failure experiences lead to quick changes in verbalized expectancies. Delay between trials, however, leads to a return to earlier levels of expectancy, presumably as previous experience is rehearsed by the subject during delay periods. There is a suggestion here that to achieve more stable changes spaced therapeutic interviews or training sessions would be more efficient for most cases.

The great quantity of work on verbal conditioning has shown both how a therapist may serve as a reinforcer unwittingly and in addition, the powerful potential the therapist has to change behavior by direct reinforcement. A study by Shaffer (1957) suggests in addition that various therapists would serve differentially as reinforcers for subjects who have identifiably different learning histories. Shaffer investigated one implication of social learning theory having to do with the potential reinforcement value of the therapist. From questionnaires given both to adjusted and maladjusted college students he determined the kind and amount of parental reinforcement during childhood. From these questionnaires he was able to predict to some extent the age and sex preferences for a therapist. Specifically, he found that female subjects who prefer a female therapist tend to have seen their mothers as more reinforcing than females who prefer a male therapist. Males almost universally state preferences for male therapists but those males who saw both parents as positively reinforcing tend to prefer an older therapist to a younger one. This study suggests that the utilization of such preferences significantly related to early learning experiences, by matching the patient to the therapist, may considerably increase the efficiency of psychotherapy.

Crandall, Good and Crandall (1964) have also studied the reinforcement effects of adults on children and found that children react to no reinforcement as either positive or negative depending on the previous history of reinforcement with these same adults in the same situation. These reactions may also be predicted from generalized expectancies for positive and negative reinforcement based on earlier childhood experiences.

A therapy investigation by Strickland and Crowne (1963) had similar implications for matching patients and techniques. They found that patients with a high need for social approval dropped out of insight type therapy prematurely. Possibly they did so because of the greater conflict engendered by the pressure to reveal their psychopathology. It is apparent that traditional insight therapy approaches would have to be modified with such patients or other techniques used.

Two other lines of research have important implications for the practice of psychotherapy. One of these deals with the specificity of behavior in various situations. Although recognizing the generality of some behaviors, one characteristic of social learning theory is the emphasis on interaction of the individual and his meaningful environment or life space (Rotter, 1955, 1960). Like the psychology of Lewin (1951) and of Brunswik (1947), emphasis is not on abstracted traits as the basic component of personality, but rather on potentials of given classes of responses in given classes of situations.

It would be impossible here to review the many studies indicating that there are strong and significant interactions between social situations and personal characteristics. A single example from the literature on Internal versus External Control will have to serve to illustrate the many implications these studies have for psychotherapy practice. On separate studies, one an experimenter bias study by Gore (1962) and a verbal conditioning study by Strickland (1962), it was found that Internals, if they are aware of subtle attempts to influence them, are much more resistant to the influence than Externals. However, if overt attempts at influence are made, Internals like Externals will respond positively. In general, these studies simply produce additional data to support the idea that therapist, method and patient have to be carefully matched in order to maximize the beneficial results from psychotherapy.

Another line of related research has to do with the generalization of changes in expectancies from one task to another. Studies by Crandall (1955), Jessor (1954), and Chance (1959) have all shown that a gradient of generalization is present which can be predicted on the basis of a common sense analysis of similarity along dimensions of psychological needs, goals, or reinforcements. In these studies expectancies for reinforcement were sampled in more than one situation or task, changes in expectancies in one task were then effected by experimental manipulations and changes in the other task or tasks were measured.

The implication from both of these kinds of studies is that in many instances the therapist is counting on *more* generalization of changes in behavior from the therapist in the therapeutic situation to other people in other situations than is warranted by the experimental evidence. It follows that if the therapist wishes to change attitudes and behaviors in situations outside of therapy most efficiently, then he would need to deal with these other situations, at least on a verbal basis, as much as possible in therapy. The working through an analysis of the relationship with the therapist has its value. However, these studies suggest that such behavior on the part of the therapist has its limitations in affecting changes in life situations outside of therapy or with individuals other than the therapist. When one considers how different the therapist's behavior toward the patient is from other people's and the therapeutic situation is from other life situations, this limitation takes on special significance.

Perhaps the most significant research relating to psychotherapy is the work on generalized expectancies which refer to how and under what conditions reinforcements may be expected. Investigation of generalized expectancies for internal-external control, looking for alternatives, delay of gratification, and interpersonal trust have clear implications for psychotherapy procedures.

The extensive work in internal-external control has been reviewed by Rotter (1966) and by Lefcourt (1966). It is clear that such broad generalized expectancies exist and that patients who feel that their own behavior and characteristics have little or no influence on what happens to them can learn only inefficiently from therapy. It seems evident that if significant improvement is to take place, the patient must become more internal as therapy progresses. Gillis and Jessor (1961) have shown such changes in improved versus unimproved delinquent therapy patients. In some cases this attitude itself must be dealt with prior to working on other more specific problems. One suggested technique is to have the patient, early in therapy, practice different ways of behaving in some specific situation, not merely to indicate to him that he can respond a different way, but also to show him that his behavior can, in fact, change the behavior of others toward him.

Delay of reinforcement is another more specific area in which there are investigations completed. The work of Mahrer (1956) and Mischel (1958, 1961a, 1961b) indicates that the preference for immediate over delayed gratification is directly related to the degree of expectation that the delayed rewards will actually occur. In these experiments children are offered the choice of obtaining a pre-established reward of lesser value (candy or a toy) immediately, or waiting a week or more for one of clearly greater value. To some extent such tendencies to delay or not to delay gratification are attached to specific social agents and to some extent they are generalized. Since the problem of therapy in many cases may be conceived of as one in which the patient must learn to give up some immediate gratification for delayed benefits, these studies have some possible implications for psychotherapy. One such implication is that the therapist himself is a social agent who must be careful not to make promises or unconsciously suggest to the patient that he is capable of "delivering the goods" in an effort to sell psychotherapy to the patient or encourage him to continue. Once he becomes an agent who does not keep his promises, his implicit or explicit attempts to get the patient to give up immediate gratifications for future benefits are not likely to be effective. Another inference from these studies is that in some cases the patient's generalization from specific figures in his past to others has led him to be overly distrustful, or to have low expectancies for reinforcements which are presumably likely to occur if he gives up his present defenses. Consequently, with such patients great emphasis must be placed on this overgeneralization and its negative consequences.

Recent work (Rotter, 1966) has supported the construct validity of a generalized expectancy for interpersonal trust defined as belief in the truthfulness of communications from others. Preliminary analysis of a study with Getter strongly suggests that attitudes of distrust impair therapeutic relationship and outcome.

Two investigations are related to the problem of teaching patients a general skill of looking for alternative solutions in problem situations. In one such study, Schroder and Rotter (1952) trained subjects on different sequences of simple concept formation problems by varying the number of *times* they were forced to find a new type of solution but keeping constant the number and type of solutions involved. They were able to demonstrate that the behavior of looking for alternatives could be rather easily learned and generalized to new problems, resulting in what is typically called flexible or nonrigid behavior. In a more direct study of therapy, Morton (1955) trained clients in a counseling center to look for alternative solutions in TAT stories they had told. Using this procedure as the primary basis for very brief psychotherapy, he was able to demonstrate a significant improvement in adjustment in comparison to matched control cases.

The generalized expectancies discussed above are only some of the important variables which describe how a person learns from experience. To find others is a task of considerable importance so that the therapist can make maximum use of what the subject has already learned in planning a therapeutic program. It is on the learning of such skills and their application to present and future life problems that the social learning therapist places reliance rather than the automatic generalization of changes in attitude toward the therapist.

SUMMARY OF IMPLICATIONS FOR THERAPEUTIC PRACTICE

The preceding discussion provides only a sketchy picture of the possible implications of social learning theory for psychotherapy. To summarize these comments it seems useful to point up some of the major differences between social learning theory and other points of view in the kinds of techniques the therapist might use were he to accept the same set of value commitments described earlier. It should be understood that these are frequently differences of degree, rather than of kind, or differences in relative emphasis.

1. The problem of psychotherapy is seen as a learning situation in which the function of the therapist is to help the patient accomplish planned changes in his observable behavior and thinking. Since patients come into therapy with many different motives, different values placed upon particular kinds of reinforcements, different expectancies for possible sources of gratification, different limits on skill, and different higher level learning skills, conditions for optimal learning will likewise vary considerably from patient to patient. One characteristic of therapy derived from a social learning theory point of view is that the technique must be suited to the patient. Flexibility, experimentation, marked variations in method from patient to patient might be considered characteristic of this approach. Consequently, there is no special technique which can be applied to all cases and differences in therapists must eventually be systematically related to patient differences to obtain maximally efficient results.

2. The patient's difficulties are frequently seen from a problem solving point of view. As a result, there tends to be a greater emphasis on the development of higher level problem solving skills, such as those of looking for alternative ways of reaching goals, thinking through the consequences of behavior, looking for differences or discriminations in life situations, and turning attention in social situations to the needs and attitudes of others and recognizing that one can exercise some control over one's fate by one's own efforts.

3. In most cases the therapist perceives his role partly as guiding a learning process in which there are not only inadequate behaviors and attitudes to be weakened but more satisfying and constructive alternatives to be learned. Consequently, the tendency is for a more active role in interpretation, suggestion and direct reinforcement for the therapist that would be typical of traditional analytic or Rogerian therapy. In this regard there is more awareness on the part of the therapist of his role as a direct reinforcer of behavior and presumably a more deliberate use of such direct reinforcement. While the more specific behavior modification (Ullmann & Krasner, 1965) techniques are happily included in this approach, for many kinds of problems they would be used as *part* of a more comprehensive attack on the patient's problems. The therapist, however, does not consider himself merely a mechanical verbal conditioner, but rather a person whose special reinforcement value for the particular patient can be used to help the patient try out new behaviors and ways of thinking. The patient

ultimately determines for himself the value of new conceptualizations and alternate ways of behaving in his experiences outside of therapy.

4. In changing unrealistic expectancies it is important to understand how particular behaviors and expectancies arose and how past experience has been misapplied or overgeneralized to present situations. Similarly, when there are conflicting goals in a situation, it is important to know how they arose and what they are. However, such insights are considered helpful but not a necessary part of change. The use of insight as a technique varies with the patient, depending on the patient's own need and ability to use rational explanations of his current problems. Another kind of insight is of equal importance and possibly tends to differentiate a social learning approach from other methods to a greater extent, that is, insight into the long term consequences of particular behaviors and of the values placed on particular goals. This includes not only an understanding of what consequences of behavior there are in present life situations, but also of probable consequences of current modes of behavior for the future. An individual may mold his behavior for many years in the expectancy of achieving some positive gratification (e.g., a college degree) which, in fact, he has never received. He may likewise mold his behavior considerably in expectation of a negative reinforcement (e.g., being left alone in one's old age) which he has not directly experienced.

5. Related to this latter point is a concern for the expectations, feelings, motives, or needs of others. Long term psychotherapy, as Otto Rank has observed, frequently encourages a patient to remain or sink deeper into his egocentric predicament through continuous emphasis on the patient's subjective reactions, past and present. However, many of the patient's problems arise from frustrations that are a result of misinterpretation of the behavior, reactions and motives of others. From a social learning point of view the patient's problem frequently requires considerable emphasis and discussion focused on understanding the behavior and motives of others, both past and present. In this regard learning through observation, modeling or imitation as Bandura and Walters (1963) have pointed out, can be a source of change in expectancies for behavior-reinforcement sequences. The use of movies, examples, books, and special groups have probably not been sufficiently exploited in psychotherapy.

In fact one of the chief values of some sensitivity, encounter, or marathon groups, now popular, is that they may provide persons with more accurate knowledge of how other people regard them as well as directly reinforcing more open and spontaneous behavior.

6. In place of the belief that experience changes people but little once they pass infancy and that only therapy can make major changes, a major implication of social learning theory is that new experiences or different kinds of experiences in life situations can be far more effective in many cases than those new experiences that occur only in the special therapy situation. While it is true that an analysis of the patient's interaction with the therapist can be an important source of learning, it is unsafe to overemphasize this as the main vehicle of treatment. Many times

improvements seen by the therapist are improvements or changes which take place in relationship to the therapist or in the therapy situation but the patient discriminates this situation from others and generalizes little to other life situations.

It is in the life situation, rather than in the psychotherapy room, that the important insights and new experiences occur. There are two implications of this view. One implication is that there should be considerable stress in treatment discussions of what is happening in the patient's present life circumstances. Questions such as "What are the motives of others?", "What are the motives of the patient?", "How does the situation differ from other situations past and present?" and "How may the patient deal with the same situation in a way which is more satisfying and constructive?" need to be discussed in detail.

The second implication is that, wherever it is possible and judicious to control the patient's experience outside of therapy by the use of what is usually called environmental manipulation, such opportunities be used maximally. Although the principal of environmental manipulation has long been accepted in the treatment of children, it is sometimes felt that this is only because the child lacks the ability to deal with his problems on a verbal or conceptual level. Environmental therapy is frequently seen only as second best treatment. However, no such hierarchy of importance seems logical. Changes in the behavior of parents, teachers, wives or husbands and other members of a family may frequently result in far greater changes in the patient than his direct experience with the therapist. The current trend toward behavior modification of parents fits in very well with this emphasis.

Likewise the opportunity for the patient making environmental changes himself, such as changes in jobs, living circumstances, social groups, etc., should not be overlooked or discarded in favor of a belief that all his problems lie inside of himself rather than in his interactions with the meaningful environment.

Hospitalizing a patient, whether psychotic or not, thereby removing him from a destructive environment to which he must eventually return, will reinforce his avoidance symptoms. Treating him in the absence of the situations which produce his symptoms, does not make much sense. It makes much better sense to keep him in his natural environment whenever possible, but to make concerted efforts to make it a more satisfying one by changing attitudes of relatives, bosses, encouraging job changes, utilizing public agencies for relief, etc., while at the same time directly treating the patient on an out-patient basis. Similar comments can be made about the problems of delinquency.

7. At the most general level, the implications of this theory are that psychotherapy should be viewed as a social interaction. The therapist helps the patient achieve a more satisfying and constructive interrelationship with his social environment. The laws and principles which govern behavior in other interpersonal learning situations apply as well to the therapy situation. There is no process special to psychotherapy and there is no need, even if it were possible, for the therapist to be a shadowy

figure or "catalyst." Rather, he is an active partner who utilizes learning principles, applied to a particular individual in a particular set of circumstances, to help that person achieve a better way of dealing with the problems of life.

References

Abse, W. Theory of the rationale of convulsive therapy. *British Journal of Medical Psychology*, 1944, **20**, 33–50.

Adams, D. K. Deviance, conformity, and expected consequences of aggression. Unpublished doctoral dissertation, University of Colorado, 1969.

Adams-Webber, J. Perceived locus of control of moral sanctions. Unpublished master's thesis, Ohio State University, 1963.

Adams-Webber, J. Generalized expectancies concerning the locus of control of reinforcements and the perception of moral sanctions. *British Journal of Social and Clinical Psychology*, 1969, 8, 340–343.

Adler, A. *Social interest: A challenge to mankind.* New York: Harper and Brothers, 1939.

Affleck, D. C., and Mednick, S. A. The use of the Rorschach test in the prediction of the abrupt terminator in individual psychotherapy. *Journal of Consulting Psychology*, 1959, **23**, 125–128.

Alexander, G. H. Electroconvulsive therapy: A five year study of results. *Journal of Nervous and Mental Disease*, 1953, **117**, 244–250.

Allport, G. W. *Personality: A Psychological interpretation.* New York: Henry Holt and Company, 1937.

Allport, G. W. What units shall we employ? In G. Lindzey (Ed.), *The assessment of human motives.* New York: Holt, Rinehart and Winston, 1958.

American Psychiatric Association, Mental Hospital Service, Committee on Nomenclature and Statistics of the American Psychiatric Association. *Diagnostic and statistical manual: Mental disorders.* Washington, D.C.: American Psychiatric Association, 1952.

Amsel, A. The role of frustrative nonreward in noncontinuous reward situations. *Psychological Bulletin*, 1958, **55**, 102–119.

Angyal, A. *Foundations for a science of personality*. New York: Commonwealth Fund, 1941.

Argyle, M. Social pressure in public and private situations. *Journal of Abnormal and Social Psychology*, 1957, **54**, 172–175.

Arieti, S. *Interpretations of schizophrenia*. New York: Brunner, 1955.

Aronson, E., and Carlsmith, J. M. Effect of severity of threat on the devaluation of forbidden behavior. *Journal of Abnormal and Social Psychology*, 1963, **66**, 584–588.

Arrington, R. E. Time sampling studies of social behavior: A critical review of technique and results with research suggestions. *Psychological Bulletin*, 1943, **40**, 81–124.

Asch, S. E. The doctrine of suggestion, prestige, and imitation in social psychology. *Psychological Review*, 1948, **55**, 250–276.

Asch, S. E. *Social psychology*. New York: Prentice-Hall, 1952.

Asch, S. E. Studies of independence and conformity: I. A minority of one against a unanimous majority. *Psychological Monographs*, 1956, **70**, (Whole No. 416).

Atkinson, J. W. Motivational determinants of risk-taking behavior. *Psychological Review*, 1957, **64**, 359–372.

Atkinson, J. W. (Ed.). *Motives in fantasy, action, and society*. Princeton, N.J.: Van Nostrand, 1958.

Atkinson, J. W. *An introduction to motivation*. Princeton, N.J.: Van Nostrand, 1964.

Atkinson, J. W., and Raphelson, A. C. Individual differences in motivation and behavior in particular situations. *Journal of Personality*, 1956, **24**, 349–363.

Atkinson, J. W., and Reitman, W. R. Performance as a function of motive strength and expectancy of goal attainment. *Journal of Abnormal and Social Psychology*, 1956, **53**, 361–366.

Auld, F., and Eron, L. D. Use of Rorschach scores to predict whether patients will continue psychotherapy. *Journal of Consulting Psychology*, 1953, **17**, 104–109.

Auld, F., and Myers, J. K. Contributions to a theory for selecting psychotherapy patients. *Journal of Clinical Psychology*, 1954, **10**, 56–60.

Austrin, H. The attractiveness of activities as determined by different patterns of negative and positive reinforcement. Unpublished doctoral dissertation, Ohio State University, 1950.

Bach, G. R. Father-fantasies and father-typing in father-separated children. *Child Development*, 1946, **17**, 63–80.

Baker, A. A., Game, J. A., and Thorpe, J. G. Some research into the treatment of schizophrenia in the mental hospital. *Journal of Mental Science*, 1960, **106**, 203–213.

Bandura, A. Influences of model's reinforcement contingencies on the acquisition of imitative responses. *Journal of Personality and Social Psychology*, 1965, **1**, 589–595.

Bandura, A., and Huston, A. C. Identification as a process of incidental learning. *Journal of Abnormal and Social Psychology*, 1961, **63**, 311–318.

Bandura, A., and McDonald, F. J. The influence of social reinforcement and the behavior of models in shaping children's moral judgments. *Journal of Abnormal and Social Psychology*, 1963, 67, 274–281.

Bandura, A., and Mischel, W. Modification of self-imposed delay of reward through exposure to live and symbolic models. *Journal of Personality and Social Psychology*, 1965, 2, 698–705.

Bandura, A., and Walters, R. H. *Social learning and personality development.* New York: Holt, Rinehart and Winston, 1963.

Barker, R. An experimental study of the resolution of conflict by children. In Q. McNemar and M. Merrill (Eds.), *Studies in personality.* New York: McGraw-Hill, 1942. Pp. 13–34.

Barron, F. An ego-strength scale which predicts response to psychotherapy. *Journal of Consulting Psychology*, 1953, 17, 327–333. (a)

Barron, F. Some personality correlates of independence of judgment. *Journal of Personality*, 1953, 21, 287–297. (b)

Barthel, C. E., and Crowne, D. P. The need for approval, task categorization, and perceptual defense. *Journal of Consulting Psychology*, 1962, 26, 547–555.

Battle, E. S. Motivational determinants of academic task persistence. *Journal of Personality and Social Psychology*, 1965, 2, 209–218.

Battle, E. S. Motivational determinants of academic competence. *Journal of Personality and Social Psychology*, 1966, 4, 634–642.

Battle, E. S., and Rotter, J. B. Children's feelings of personal control as related to social class and ethnic group. *Journal of Personality*, 1963, 31, 482–490.

Bayton, J. A. Interrelations between levels of aspiration, performance, and estimates of past performance. *Journal of Experimental Psychology*, 1943, 33, 1–21.

Becker, W. C. Consequences of different kinds of parental discipline. In M. L. Hoffman and L. W. Hoffman (Eds.), *Review of child development research: I.* New York: Russell Sage Foundation, 1964. Pp. 169–208.

Bell, D. America as a mass society: A critique. In D. Bell (Ed.), *The end of ideology.* Glencoe, Ill.: Free Press, 1960.

Benedict, R. F. *The chrysanthemum and the sword.* Boston: Houghton Mifflin, 1946.

Bennett, E. B. Discussion, decision, commitment and consensus in group decision. *Human Relations*, 1955, 8, 251–273.

Bennion, R. C. Task, trial by trial score variability of internal versus external control of reinforcement. Unpublished doctoral dissertation, Ohio State University, 1961.

Berkwitz, N. J. Faradic shock treatment of the functional psychoses. *Lancet*, 1939, 59, 351.

Bialer, I. Conceptualization of success and failure in mentally retarded and normal children. *Journal of Personality*, 1961, 29, 303–320.

Birney, R. C., Burdick, H., and Teevan, R. C. *Fear of failure motivation.* New York: Wiley, 1969.

Blackman, S. Some factors affecting the perception of events as chance determined. *Journal of Psychology*, 1962, 54, 197–202.

Block, J., and Martin, B. Prediction of behavior of children under frustration. *Journal of Abnormal and Social Psychology*, 1955, **51**, 281–285.

Blyth, D. D. Dependency, independency, and other factors related to veterans' reactions to an offer of psychotherapy. Unpublished doctoral dissertation, Ohio State University, 1953.

Bogoch, S. A. Preliminary study of post-shock amnesia by Amytal interview. *American Journal of Psychiatry*, 1954, **111**, 108–111.

Boneau, C. A. The effects of violations of assumptions underlying the t test. *Psychological Bulletin*, 1960, **57**, 49–64.

Borislow, B. The Edwards Personal Preference Schedule and fakability. *Journal of Applied Psychology*, 1958, **42**, 22–27.

Bott, H. *Method in social studies of young children.* Toronto: University of Toronto Press, 1933.

Bramson, L. *The political context of sociology.* Princeton, N.J.: University Press, 1961.

Breger, L., and McGaugh, J. L. Critique and reformulation of "learning-theory" approaches to psychotherapy and neurosis. *Psychological Bulletin*, 1965, **63**, 338–358.

Breger, L., and McGaugh, J. L. Learning theory and behavior therapy: A reply to Rachman and Eysenck. *Psychological Bulletin*, 1966, **65**, 170–173.

Brehm, J. W., and Cohen, A. R. *Explorations in cognitive dissonance.* New York: Wiley, 1962.

Brenner, B. Effect of immediate and delayed praise and blame upon learning and recall. *Teachers College Contributions to Education*, 1934, No. 620.

Brown, J. S. The generalization of approach responses as a function of stimulus intensity and strength of motivation. *Journal of Comparative and Physiological Psychology*, 1942, **33**, 209–215.

Brunswik, E. Organismic achievement and environmental probability. *Psychological Review*, 1943, **50**, 255–272.

Brunswik, E. *Systematic and representative design of psychological experiments.* Berkeley, Calif.: University of California Press, 1947.

Brunswik, E. The probability point of view. In M. H. Marx, (Ed.), *Psychological theory.* New York: Macmillan, 1951.

Buchwald, A. Experimental alterations in the effectiveness of verbal reinforcement combinations. *Journal of Experimental Psychology*, 1959, **57**, 351–361. (a)

Buchwald, A. Extinction after acquisition under different verbal reinforcement combinations. *Journal of Experimental Psychology*, 1959, **57**, 43–48. (b)

Buss, A. H. *Psychopathology.* New York: Wiley, 1966.

Buss, A., Braden, W., Orgel, A., and Buss, E. Acquisition and extinction with different verbal reinforcement combinations. *Journal of Experimental Psychology*, 1956, **52**, 283–287.

Butler, J. M. The use of a psychological model in personality testing. *Educational and Psychological Measurement*, 1954, **14**, 77–89.

Campbell, D. The psychological effects of cerebral electroshock. In H. J. Eysenck (Ed.), *Handbook of abnormal psychology.* New York: Basic Books, 1961. Pp. 611–633.

Campbell, D. T., and Fiske, D. W. Convergent and discriminant validation by the multitrait-multimethod matrix. *Psychological Bulletin,* 1959, **56,** 81–105.

Cantor, G. N., and Cromwell, R. L. The principle of reductionism and mental deficiency. *American Journal of Mental Deficiency,* 1957, **61,** 461–466.

Cardi, M. An examination of internal versus external control in relation to academic failures. Unpublished master's thesis, Ohio State University, 1962.

Carlsmith, J. M. Strength of expectancy: Its determinants and effects. Unpublished doctoral dissertation, Harvard University, 1962.

Carman, R. S. Personality and drinking behavior among college students. Unpublished master's thesis, University of Colorado, 1965.

Cartwright, D. A quantitative theory of decision. *Psychological Review,* 1943, **50,** 595–602.

Castaneda, A. A method for measuring expectancy as conceived within Rotter's social learning theory of personality. Unpublished master's thesis, Ohio State University, 1951.

Castaneda, A. A systematic investigation of the concept expectancy as conceived within Rotter's social learning theory of personality. Unpublished doctoral dissertation, Ohio State University, 1952.

Cattell, R. B. *Personality and motivation structure and measurement.* New York: Harcourt, Brace, & World, 1957.

Chance, J. E. Generalization of expectancies as a function of need-relatedness. Unpublished doctoral dissertation, Ohio State University, 1952.

Chance, J. E. Generalization of expectancies among functionally related behaviors. *Journal of Personality,* 1959, **27,** 228–238.

Chance, J. E. Independence training and first graders' achievement. *Journal of Consulting Psychology,* 1961, **25,** 149–154.

Chance, J. E. Internal control of reinforcements and the school learning process. Paper presented at meetings of Society for Research in Child Development, Minneapolis, March 1965.

Chance, J. E. Mother-child relations and children's achievement. Terminal Report on USPH Research Grant MH05268, 1968.

Chance, J. E., and Goldstein, A. G. Internal-external control of reinforcement and embedded-figures performance. *Perception and Psychophysics,* 1971, **9,** 33–34.

Chein, I., and Garrett, H. Rejoinder and surrejoinder. *Society for Psychological Study of Social Issues Newsletter,* May 1962.

Christie, R., and Merton, R. K. Procedures for the sociological study of the values climate of medical schools. *Journal of Medical Education,* 1958, **33,** 125–133.

Churchill, R., and Crandall, V. J. The reliability and validity of the Rotter Incomplete Sentences Test. *Journal of Consulting Psychology,* 1955, **19,** 345–350.

Cleckley, H. *The mask of sanity.* St. Louis: Mosby, 1964.

Cloward, R. A., and Ohlin, L. E. *Delinquency and opportunity: A theory of delinquent gangs.* Glencoe, Ill.: Free Press, 1960.

Coffin, T. E. Some conditions of suggestion and suggestibility. *Psychological Monographs,* 1941, **48,** (Whole No. 241).

Cohen, J. *Chance, skill and luck.* Baltimore: Penguin, 1960.

Coleman, J. S., Campbell, E. Q., Hobson, C. J., McPartland, J., Mood, A. M., Weinfeld, F. D., and York, R. L. Equality of educational opportunity. Superintendent of Documents Catalog No. FS 5.238:38001, U.S. Government Printing Office, Washington, D.C., 1966.

Conn, L. Instigation to aggression, emotional arousal, and defensive emulation. Unpublished master's thesis, Ohio State University, 1963.

Conn, L. The effects of the approval motive, generalized expectancy, and the threat to self-esteem upon the identification of emotional communications. (Doctoral dissertation, Ohio State University) Ann Arbor, Mich., University Microfilms, 1965, No. 65-7375.

Cooke, G. Evaluation of the efficacy of the components of reciprocal inhibition psychotherapy. *Journal of Abnormal Psychology,* 1968, **73,** 464–467.

Coser, L. A., and Rosenberg, B. *Sociological theory.* New York: Macmillan, 1964.

Coutu, W. *Emergent human nature.* New York: Knopf, 1949.

Cowen, E. L., and Beier, E. G. The influence of threat-expectancy on perception. *Journal of Personality,* 1950, **19,** 85–94.

Crandall, V. C. The effects of an adult's positive and negative reactions and nonreactions on children's expectancies of success. Unpublished master's thesis, Ohio State University, 1961.

Crandall, V. C. Reinforcement effects of adult reactions and nonreactions on children's achievement expectations. *Child Development,* 1963, **34,** 335–354.

Crandall, V. C., and Battle, E. S. The antecedents and adult correlates of academic and intellectual achievement efforts. In J. P. Hill (Ed.), *Minnesota Symposia on Child Psychology,* Vol. 4. University of Minnesota Press, Minneapolis, Minn., 1970.

Crandall, V. C., Crandall, V. J., and Katkovsky, W. A children's social desirability questionnaire. *Journal of Consulting Psychology,* 1965, **29,** 27–36.

Crandall, V. C., Good, S., and Crandall, V. J. Reinforcement effects of adult reactions and nonreactions on children's achievement expectations: A replication study. *Child Development,* 1964, **35,** 485–497.

Crandall, V. C., Katkovsky, W., and Crandall, V. J. Children's beliefs in their own control of reinforcements in intellectual-academic achievement situations. *Child Development,* 1965, **36,** 91–109.

Crandall, V. C., and McGhee, P. E. Expectancy of reinforcement and academic competence. *Journal of Personality,* 1968, **36,** 635–648.

Crandall, V. J. Induced frustration and punishment-reward expectancy in thematic apperception stories. *Journal of Consulting Psychology,* 1951, **15,** 400–404.

Crandall, V. J. An investigation of the specificity of reinforcement of induced frustration. *Journal of Social Psychology,* 1955, **41,** 311–318.

Crandall, V. J. Some problems of personality development research. *Child Development,* 1956, **27,** 197–203.

Crandall, V. J. Achievement. In H. W. Stevenson, J. Kagan, and C. Spiker, (Eds.), *Child psychology.* The 62nd yearbook of the National Society for the study of Education, University of Chicago Press, Chicago, 1963.

Crandall, V. J., Dewey, R., Katkovsky, W., and Preston, A. Parents' attitudes and behaviors and grade-school children's academic achievement. *Journal of Genetic Psychology*, 1964, **104**, 53–66.

Crandall, V. J., Katkovsky, W., and Preston, A. A conceptual formulation for some research on children's achievement development. *Child Development*, 1960, **31**, 787–799. (a)

Crandall, V. J., Katkovsky, W., and Preston, A. Parent behavior and children's achievement development. Paper read at American Psychological Association, Chicago, 1960. (b)

Crandall, V. J., Katkovsky, W., and Preston, A. Motivational and ability determinants of children's intellectual achievement behaviors. *Child Development*, 1962, **33**, 643–661.

Crandall, V. J., Orleans, S., Preston, A., and Rabson, A. The development of social compliance in young children. *Child Development*, 1958, **29**, 429–443.

Crandall, V. J., and Preston, A. Verbally expressed needs and overt maternal behaviors. *Child Development*, 1961, **32**, 261–270.

Crandall, V. J., Preston, A., and Rabson, A. Maternal reactions and the development of independence and achievement behavior in young children. *Child Development*, 1960, **31**, 243–251.

Crandall, V. J., and Rabson, A. Children's repetition choices in an intellectual achievement situation following success and failure. *Journal of Genetic Psychology*, 1960, **97**, 161–168.

Crandall, V. J., Solomon, D., and Kellaway, R. Expectancy statements and decision times as functions of objective probabilities and reinforcement values. *Journal of Personality*, 1955, **24**, 192–203.

Crandall, V. J., Solomon, D., and Kellaway, R. The value of anticipated events as a determinant of probability learning and extinction. *Journal of Genetic Psychology*, 1958, **58**, 3–10.

Cromwell, R. L. A methodological approach to personality research in mental retardation. *American Journal of Mental Deficiency*, 1959, **64**, 333–340.

Cromwell, R. L. A social learning approach to mental retardation. In N. R. Ellis (Ed.), *Handbook of mental deficiency*. New York: McGraw-Hill, 1963. Pp. 41–91.

Cromwell, R. L. Locus of control and symbolic reinforcements in the mentally retarded. Cincinnati, O.: Sound Seminars, 1963; also, *Acta Psychologica*, 1964, **23**, 336–337.

Cromwell, R. L. Personality evaluation. In A. A. Baumeister (Ed.), *Mental retardation*. Chicago: Aldine, 1967. (a)

Cromwell, R. L. Success-failure reactions in mentally retarded children. In J. Zubin and G. Jervis (Eds.), *Psychopathology of mental development*. New York: Grune & Stratton, 1967. (b)

Cromwell, R. L., Moss, J. W., and Duke, R. B. The Taylor Scale as a measure of avoidant behavior. *Abstracts of Peabody studies in mental retardation*, 1960, **1**, No. 33.

Cromwell, R. L., Rosenthal, D., Shakow, D., and Zahn, T. P. Reaction time, locus of control, choice behavior, and descriptions of parental behavior in schizophrenic and normal subjects. *Journal of Personality*, 1961, **29**, 363–380.

Cronbach, L. J. Response set and test validity. *Educational and Psychological Measurement*, 1946, 6, 474–494.

Cronbach, L. J. Further evidence on response sets and test design. *Educational and Psychological Measurement*, 1950, 10, 3–31.

Cronbach, L. J. Assessment of individual differences. In P. R. Farnsworth and Q. McNemar (Eds.), *Annual Review of Psychology*, Stanford, Calif.: Annual Reviews, 1956. Pp. 173–196.

Cronbach, L. J. The two disciplines of scientific psychology. *American Psychologist*, 1957, 12, 671–684.

Crowne, D. P. Family orientation, level of aspiration, and interpersonal bargaining. *Journal of Personality and Social Psychology*, 1966, 3, 641–645.

Crowne, D. P., and Conn, L. K. The hypnotic enhancement of self-esteem and persuasibility. Paper read at Midwestern Psychological Association, St. Louis, May 1964.

Crowne, D. P., and Liverant, S. Conformity under varying conditions of personal commitment. *Journal of Abnormal and Social Psychology*, 1963, 66, 547–555.

Crowne, D. P., and Marlowe, D. A. A new scale of social desirability independent of psychopathology. *Journal of Consulting Psychology*, 1960, 24, 349–354.

Crowne, D. P., and Marlowe, D. A. *The approval motive*. New York: Wiley, 1964.

Crowne, D. P., and Strickland, B. R. The conditioning of verbal behavior as a function of the need for social approval. *Journal of Abnormal and Social Psychology*, 1961, 63, 395–401.

Crumpton, E., Brill, N. Q., Eiduson, S., and Geller, E. The role of fear in electroconvulsive treatment. *Journal of Nervous and Mental Disease*, 1963, 136, 29–33.

Crutchfield, R. S. Conformity and character. *American Psychologist*, 1955, 10, 191–198.

Daily, J. Verbal conditioning without awareness. *Dissertation Abstracts*, 1953, 13, 1247–1248.

Darwin, C. A biographical sketch of an infant. *Mind*, 1877, 2, 285–294.

Davis, W. L., and Phares, E. J. Internal-external control as a determinant of information-seeking in a social influence situation. *Journal of Personality*, 1967, 35, 547–561.

Davis, W. L., and Phares, E. J. Parental antecedents of internal-external control of reinforcement. *Psychological Reports*, 1969, 24, 427–436.

Davison, G. C. Systematic desensitization as a counterconditioning process. *Journal of Abnormal Psychology*, 1968, 73, 91–99.

Dean, D. G. Alienation: Its meaning and measurement. *American Sociological Review*, 1961, 26, 753–758.

Dean, S. J. Sources of variance in individual statements of expectancy. Unpublished doctoral dissertation, Ohio State University, 1953.

Dean, S. J. The generality of expectancy statements as a function of situational definition. *Journal of Consulting Psychology*, 1960, 24, 558.

Deutsch, M. Trust and suspicion. *Journal of Conflict Resolution*, 1958, 2, 265–279.

Deutsch, M. Trust, trustworthiness, and the F scale. *Journal of Abnormal and Social Psychology*, 1960, **61**, 138–140.

Deutsch, M., and Gerard, H. B. A study of normative and informational social influences upon individual judgements. *Journal of Abnormal and Social Psychology*, 1955, **51**, 629–636.

Dies, R. R. Electroconvulsive therapy: A social learning theory interpretation. *Journal of Nervous and Mental Disease*, 1968, **146**, 334–342.

Dixon, T. R., and Dixon, J. F. The impression value of verbs. *Journal of Verbal Learning and Verbal Behavior*, 1964, **3**, 161–165.

Dollard, J., and Miller, N. E. *Personality and psychotherapy.* New York: McGraw-Hill, 1950.

Dreger, R. M., and Miller, K. S. Comparative psychological studies of Negroes and Whites in the United States. *Psychological Bulletin*, 1960, **57**, 361–402.

Dunlap, R. L. A study of the relationship of dependency to the seeking of psychological counseling in college freshmen. Unpublished master's thesis, Ohio State University, 1951.

Dunlap, R. L. Changes in children's preferences for goal objects as a function of differences in expected social reinforcement. Unpublished doctoral dissertation, Ohio State University, 1953.

Durkheim, E. *Professional ethics and civil morals.* Glencoe, Ill.: Free Press, 1958.

Edwards, A. L. *Manual of the Edwards Personal Preference Schedule.* New York: Psychological Corporation, 1953.

Edwards, A. L. *The social desirability variable in personality assessment and research.* New York: Dryden, 1957.

Edwards, W. The theory of decision making. *Psychological Bulletin*, 1954, **51**, 380–417.

Efran, J. S. Some personality determinants of memory for success and failure. Unpublished doctoral dissertation, Ohio State University, 1963.

Efran, J. S. Looking for approval: Effects on visual behavior of approbation from persons differing in importance. *Journal of Personality and Social Psychology*, 1968, **10**, 21–25.

Efran, J. S., and Broughton, A. Effect of expectancies for social approval on visual behavior. *Journal of Personality and Social Psychology*, 1966, **4**, 103–107.

Efran, J. S., and Korn, P. R. Measurement of social caution: Self-appraisal, role playing, and discussion behavior. *Journal of Consulting and Clinical Psychology*, 1969, **33**, 78–83.

Efran, J. S., and Marcia, J. E. Treatment of fears by expectancy manipulation: An exploratory investigation. *Proceedings*, 75th Annual Convention, American Psychological Association, 1967, 239.

Eriksen, C. W. Unconscious processes. In M. R. Jones (Ed.), *Nebraska Symposium on Motivation:* 1958. Lincoln: University of Nebraska Press, 1958. Pp. 169–227.

Eriksen, C. W. Discrimination and learning without awareness: A methodological survey and evaluation. *Psychological Review*, 1960, **67**, 279–300.

Eriksen, C. W., and Browne, C. T. An experimental and theoretical analysis of perceptual defense. *Journal of Abnormal and Social Psychology*, 1956, **52**, 224–230.

Erikson, E. H. Growth and crises of the "healthy personality." In C. Kluckhohn and H. Murray (Eds.), *Personality in nature, society, and culture.* (2nd ed.). New York: Knopf, 1953.

Eron, L. D. A normative study of the Thematic Apperception Test. *Psychological Monographs*, 1950, **64** (Whole No. 315).

Exline, R. V. Explorations in the process of person perception: Visual interaction in relation to competition, sex, and need for affiliation. *Journal of Personality*, 1963, **31**, 1–20.

Exline, R., Gray, D., and Schuette, D. Visual behavior in a dyad as affected by interview contact and sex of respondent. *Journal of Personality and Social Psychology*, 1965, **1**, 201–209.

Exline, R., Thibaut, J., Brannon, C., and Gumpert, P. Visual interaction in relation to Machiavellianism and an unethical act. *American Psychologist*, 1961, **16**, 396.

Exline, R., and Winters, L. Affective relations and mutual glances in dyads. In S. S. Tomkins and C. E. Izard (Eds.), *Affect, cognition, and personality.* New York: Springer, 1965. Pp. 319–350. (a)

Exline, R., and Winters, L. The effects of cognitive difficulty and cognitive style upon eye-to-eye contact in interviews. Paper read at Eastern Psychological Association, Atlantic City, N.J., April 1965 (b)

Fallding, H. The source and burden of civilization illustrated in the use of alcohol. *Quarterly Journal of Studies in Alcohol*, 1964, **25**, 714–724.

Feather, N. T. Subjective probability and decision under uncertainty. *Psychological Review*, 1959, **66**, 150–164. (a)

Feather, N. T. Success probability and choice behavior. *Journal of Experimental Psychology*, 1959, **58**, 257–266. (b)

Feather, N. T. The relationship of persistence at a task to expectation of success and achievement related motives. *Journal of Abnormal and Social Psychology*, 1961, **63**, 552–561.

Feather, N. T. The study of persistence. *Psychological Bulletin*, 1962, **59**, 94–115.

Feather, N. T. Mowrer's revised two-factor theory and the motive-expectancy-value model. *Psychological Review*, 1963, **70**, 500–515. (a)

Feather, N. T. Persistence at a difficult task with an alternative task of intermediate difficulty. *Journal of Abnormal and Social Psychology*, 1963, **66**, 604–609. (b)

Feather, N. T. Valence of success and failure in relation to task difficulty: Past research and recent progress. *Australian Journal of Psychology*, 1968, **20**, 111–122.

Ferguson, E., and Buss, A. A supplementary report: Acquisition, extinction, and counter-conditioning with different verbal reinforcement conditions. *Journal of Experimental Psychology*, 1959, **58**, 94–95.

Ferster, C. B. Control of behavior in chimpanzees and pigeons by time out from positive reinforcements. *Psychological Monographs*, 1958, **72**, (Whole No. 461).

Festinger, L. Studies in decision: An empirical test of a quantitative theory of decisions. *Journal of Experimental Psychology*, 1943, **32**, 411–417.

Festinger, L. An analysis of compliant behavior. In M. Sherif and M. O. Wilson (Eds.), *Group relations at the crossroads*. New York: Harper & Row, 1953. Pp. 232–256.

Festinger, L. A theory of cognitive dissonance. New York: Harper & Row, 1957.

Fetterman, J. L., Victoroff, V. M., and Horrocks, J. A. A ten-year follow-up study of electrocoma therapy. *American Journal of Psychiatry*, 1951, **108**, 264–270.

Fisher, S., Rubenstein, I., and Freeman, R. W. Inter-trial effects of immediate self-committal in a continuous social influence situation. *Journal of Abnormal and Social Psychology*, 1956, **52**, 200–207.

Fitzgerald, B. J. Some relationships among projective test, interview, and sociometric measures of dependent behavior. *Journal of Abnormal and Social Psychology*, 1958, **56**, 199–204.

Folkins, C. H., Lawson, K. D., Opton, E. M., Jr., and Lazarus, R. S. Desensitization and experimental reduction of threat. *Journal of Abnormal Psychology*, 1969, **73**, 100–113.

Ford, L. H., Jr. Reaction to failure as a function of expectancy for success. *Journal of Abnormal and Social Psychology*, 1963, **67**, 340–348.

Fordyce, W. E. Social desirability in the MMPI. *Journal of Consulting Psychology*, 1956, **20**, 171–175.

Frank, J. D. Individual differences in certain aspects of the level of aspiration. *American Journal of Psychology*, 1935, **47**, 119–128. (a)

Frank, J. D. Some psychological determinants of the level of aspiration. *American Journal of Psychology*, 1935, **47**, 285–293. (b)

Frank, J. D., Gliedman, L. H., Imber, S. D., Nash, E. H., Jr., and Stone, A. R. Why patients leave psychotherapy. *Archives of Neurology and Psychiatry*, 1957, **77**, 283–299.

Franklin, R. D. Youth's expectancies about internal versus external control of reinforcement related to N variables. Unpublished doctoral dissertation, Purdue University, 1963.

Freud, S. Formulations regarding the two principles of mental functioning. (Original Publication, 1911). In *Collected Papers*, Vol. 4. New York: Basic Books, 1959. Pp. 13–21.

Freud, S. *Beyond the pleasure principle*. New York: Boni and Liveright, 1922.

Freud, S. *The basic writings of Sigmund Freud*. New York: Random House, 1938. (First German edition, 1904).

Freud, S. Further recommendations in the technique of psychoanalysis. On beginning the treatment. The question of the first communications. The dynamics of the cure. In *Collected Papers*, Vol. 2. London: Hogarth Press, 1949.

Gallagher, J. J. The problem of escaping clients in nondirective counseling. In W. U. Snyder (Ed.), *Group report of a program of research in psychotherapy*. University Park, Pa.: Pennsylvania State University Press, 1953.

Gallinek, A. Fear and anxiety in the course of electroshock therapy. *American Journal of Psychiatry*, 1956, **113**, 428–434.

Gardner, W. I. Reactions of intellectually normal and retarded boys after experimentally induced failure—A social learning theory interpretation. Ann Arbor, Mich.: University Microfilms, 1958.

Garfield, S. L., and Affleck, D. C. Therapists' judgments concerning patients considered for psychotherapy. *Journal of Consulting Psychology*, 1961, **25**, 505–509.

Geller, J. D. Some personal and situational determinants of interpersonal trust. Unpublished doctoral dissertation, University of Connecticut, 1966.

Gellert, E. Systematic observation: A method of child study. *Harvard Educational Review*, 1955, **25**, 179–195.

Getter, H. A. Variables affecting the value of the reinforcement in verbal conditioning. Unpublished doctoral dissertation, Ohio State University, 1962.

Getter, H. A. A personality determinant of verbal conditioning. *Journal of Personality*, 1966, **34**, 397–405.

Gibby, R. G., Miller, N. R., and Walker, E. L. The examiner's influence on the Rorschach protocol. *Journal of Consulting Psychology*, 1953, **17**, 425–428.

Gibby, R. G., Stotsky, B. A., Hiler, E. W., and Miller, D. R. Validation of Rorschach criteria for predicting duration of therapy. *Journal of Consulting Psychology*, 1954, **18**, 185–191.

Gillis, J., and Jessor, R. The effects of psychotherapy on internal-external control. Unpublished manuscript, 1961.

Gladwin, T., and Sturtevant, W. C. *Anthropology and human behavior*. Washington, D.C.: The Anthropological Society of Washington, 1962. Pp. 96–114.

Goldstein, A. P. Therapist and client expectation of personality change in psychotherapy. *Journal of Counseling Psychology*, 1960, 7, 180–184.

Goldstein, A. P. *Therapist-patient expectancies in psychotherapy*. New York: Pergamon Press, 1962.

Gonda, T. A. Prediction of short-term outcome of electroconvulsive therapy. *Journal of Nervous and Mental Disease*, 1964, **138**, 586–594.

Good, R. A. The potentiality for changes of an expectancy as a function of the amount of experience. Unpublished doctoral dissertation, Ohio State University, 1952.

Goodenough, F. Measuring behavior traits by means of repeated short samples. *Journal of Juvenile Research*, 1928, **12**, 230–235.

Goodnow, J. J., and Pettigrew, T. F. Effect of prior patterns of experience upon strategies and learning situations. *Journal of Experimental Psychology*, 1955, 49, 381–389.

Goodnow, J. J., and Postman, L. Probability learning in a problem-solving situation. *Journal of Experimental Psychology*, 1955, 49, 16–22.

Gore, P. M. Individual differences in the prediction of subject compliance to experimenter bias. Unpublished doctoral dissertation, Ohio State University, 1962.

Gore, P. M., and Rotter, J. B. A personality correlate of social action. *Journal of Personality*, 1963, **31**, 58–64.

Gottlieb, J. S., and Huston, P. E. Treatment of schizophrenia; A comparison of three methods: Brief psychotherapy, insulin coma, and electric shock. *Journal of Nervous and Mental Disease*, 1951, **113**, 237–246.

Gough, H. G. A new dimension of status: I. Development of a personality scale. *American Sociological Review*, 1948, **13**, 401–409.

Gough, H. G. Studies of social intolerance: II. A personality scale for anti-semitism. *Journal of Social Psychology*, 1951, **33**, 247–255.

Gould, R. An experimental analysis of "Level of Aspiration." *Genetic Psychology Monographs*, 1939, **21**, 3–115.

Graves, T. D. Time perspective and the deferred gratification pattern in a tri-ethnic community. Unpublished doctoral dissertation, University of Pennsylvania, 1961. Also see: Research Report No. 5, Tri-Ethnic Research Project, University of Colorado, Institute of Behavioral Science, 1961.

Graves, T. D., and Van Arsdale, M. Values, expectations and relocations: The Navaho migrant to Denver. *Human Organization*, 1966, **25**, 295–307.

Green, R. F. Does a selection situation induce testees to bias their answers on interest and temperament tests? *Educational and Psychological Measurement*, 1951, **11**, 503–515.

Greenstein, F. I. Popular images of the president. *American Journal of Psychiatry*, 1965, **122**, 523–529.

Gross, L. R. Effects of verbal and nonverbal reinforcement in the Rorschach. *Journal of Consulting Psychology*, 1959, **23**, 66–68.

Grossman, P. H. The establishment of alcohol consumption criterion groups: Rationale and associated characteristics. Tri-Ethnic Research Project, Research Report No. 18, University of Colorado, Institute of Behavioral Science, 1963.

Grossman, P. H. Drinking motivation: A cluster analytic study of three samples. Unpublished doctoral dissertation, University of Colorado, 1965.

Grossman, S. P. *A textbook of physiological psychology*. New York: Wiley, 1967.

Gusfield, J. R. Mass society and extremist politics. *American Sociological Review*, 1962, **27**, 19–30.

Halpin, A. W., and Winer, B. J. Studies in aircrew composition: The leadership behavior of the airplane commander. Technical Report No. 3, Columbus, O.: Personnel Research Board, Ohio State University, 1952.

Hamsher, J. H., Geller, J. D., and Rotter, J. B. Interpersonal trust, internal-external control, and the Warren Commission Report. *Journal of Personality and Social Psychology*, 1968, **9**, 210–215.

Haner, C. F., and Brown, P. A. Clarification of the instigation to action concept in the frustration-aggression hypothesis. *Journal of Abnormal and Social Psychology*, 1955, **51**, 204–206.

Hanfmann, E. William Stern on "Projective Techniques." *Journal of Personality*, 1952, **21**, 1–21.

Harlow, H. F. The formation of learning sets. *Psychological Review*, 1949, **56**, 51–65.

Harris, D. B. A scale for measuring attitudes of social responsibility in children. *Journal of Abnormal and Social Psychology*, 1957, **55**, 322–326.

Heathers, L. B. Factors producing generality in the level of aspiration. *Journal of Experimental Psychology*, 1942, **30**, 392–406.

Heber, R. F. Expectancy and expectancy changes in normal and mentally retarded boys. Unpublished doctoral dissertation, George Peabody College for Teachers, 1957.

Heine, R. W., and Trosman, H. Initial expectations of the doctor-patient interaction as a factor in continuance in psychotherapy. *Psychiatry*, 1960, **23**, 275–278.

Helson, H. Adaptation level as a basis for a quantitative theory of frames of reference. *Psychological Review*, 1948, **55**, 297–313.

Helson, H., Blake, R. R., Mouton, J. S., and Olmstead, J. A. Attitudes as adjustments to stimulus, background, and residual factors. *Journal of Abnormal and Social Psychology*, 1956, **52**, 314–322.

Henker, B., and Rotter, J. B. Effect of model characteristics on children's play and task imitation. *The Proceedings*, 76th Annual Convention, American Psychological Association, 1968, **3**, 341–342.

Henry, E. M., and Rotter, J. B. Situational influences on Rorschach responses. *Journal of Consulting Psychology*, 1956, **20**, 457–462.

Herron, W. G. The process-reactive classification of schizophrenia. *Psychological Bulletin*, 1962, **59**, 329–343.

Hersch, P. D., and Scheibe, K. E. On the reliability and validity of internal-external control as a personality dimension. *Journal of Consulting Psychology*, 1967, **31**, 609–614.

Herzberg, F. Prognostic variables for electroshock therapy. *Journal of General Psychology*, 1954, **50**, 79–86.

Hess, H., and Jessor, R. The influence of reinforcement value on the rate of learning and asymptotic level of expectancies. *Journal of General Psychology*, 1960, **63**, 89–102.

Heyns, R., and Lippitt, R. Systematic observation techniques. In G. Lindzey (Ed.), *Handbook of social psychology*. Cambridge: Addison-Wesley, 1954. Pp. 370–404.

Hiler, E. W. The sentence completion test as a predictor of continuation in psychotherapy. *Journal of Consulting Psychology*, 1959, **23**, 544–549.

Hilgard, E. R., and Marquis, D. G. *Conditioning and learning*. New York: Appleton-Century-Crofts, 1940.

Hobart, E. M., and Hovland, C. I. The effect of "commitment" on opinion change following communication. *American Psychologist*, 1954, **9**, 394.

Hobson, R. F. Prognostic factors in electric convulsive therapy. *Journal of Neurological and Neurosurgical Psychiatry*, 1953, **16**, 275–281.

Hochreich, D. J. A children's scale for measuring interpersonal trust. Unpublished master's thesis, University of Connecticut, 1966.

Hoffman, H., Schiff, D., Adams, J., and Searle, J. Enhanced distress vocalization through selective reinforcement. *Science*, 1966, **151**, 352–354.

Hogan, R. A., and Kirchner, J. H. Implosive, eclectic verbal and bibliotherapy in the treatment of fears of snakes. *Behavior Research and Therapy*, 1968, **6**, 167–171.

Holden, K. B. Attitude toward external vs. internal control of reinforcement and learning of reinforcement sequences. Unpublished master's thesis, Ohio State University, 1958.

Holden, K. B. A non-verbal measure of differences in extinction in skill and chance interactions. Unpublished doctoral dissertation, Ohio State University, 1960.

Holden, K. B., and Rotter, J. B. A nonverbal measure of extinction in skill and chance situations. *Journal of Experimental Psychology*, 1962, **63**, 519–520.

Hollingshead, A., and Redlich, F. Social stratification and psychiatric disorders. *American Sociological Review*, 1953, **18**, 163–169.

Hollingshead, A. B., and Redlich, F. C. *Social class and mental illness*. New York: Wiley, 1958.

Holt, R. R. The effects of ego-involvement on levels of aspiration. *Psychiatry*, 1945, **8**, 299–317.

Hovland, C., Janis, I., and Kelley, H. *Communication and persuasion*. New Haven, Conn.: Yale University Press, 1953.

Hull, C. L. *Principles of behavior*. New York: Appleton-Century-Crofts, 1943.

Humphreys, L. G., Miller, J., and Ellson, D. G. The effects of intertrial interval on the acquisition, extinction, and recovery of verbal expectations. *Journal of Experimental Psychology*, 1940, **27**, 195–202.

Hunt, D. E. Changes in goal-object preference as a function of expectancy for social reinforcement. *Journal of Abnormal and Social Psychology*, 1955, **50**, 372–377.

Hunt, D. E., and Schroder, H. M. Assimilation, failure-avoidance, anxiety. *Journal of Consulting Psychology*, 1958, **22**, 39–44.

Hunt, J. McV. *Intelligence and experience*. New York: Ronald, 1961.

Huston, P. E., and Strother, C. R. The effect of electric shock on mental efficiency. *American Journal of Psychiatry*, 1948, **104**, 707–712.

Imber, S. D., Frank, J. D., Nash, E. H., Jr., Stone, R. S., and Gliedman, L. H. Improvement and amount of therapeutic contact: An alternative to the use of no-treatment controls in psychotherapy. *Journal of Consulting Psychology*, 1957, **21**, 309–315.

Irwin, F. W. Stated expectations as functions of probability and desirability of outcomes. *Journal of Personality*, 1953, **21**, 329–335.

Irwin, F. W., Armitt, F. M., and Simon, C. Studies in object preferences: I. The effect of temporal proximity. *Journal of Experimental Psychology*, 1943, **33**, 64–72.

Irwin, F. W., and Mintzer, M. G. Effect of differences in instructions and motivation upon measures of the verbal level of aspiration. *American Journal of Psychology*, 1942, **55**, 400–406.

Irwin, F. W., Orchinik, C. W., and Weiss, J. Studies in object preferences: The effect of temporal proximity upon adults' preferences. *American Journal of Psychology*, 1950, **63**, 237–243.

James, P. B., and Mosher, D. L. Thematic aggression, hostility-guilt, and aggressive behavior. *Journal of Projective Techniques and Personality Assessment*, 1967, **31**, 61–67.

James, W. H. Internal versus external control of reinforcement as a basic variable in learning theory. Unpublished doctoral dissertation, Ohio State University, 1957. Also, Ann Arbor, Mich.: University Microfilms, 1957.

James, W. H., and Rotter, J. B. Partial and 100 per cent reinforcement under chance and skill conditions. *Journal of Experimental Psychology*, 1958, **55**, 397–403.

James, W. H., Woodruff, A. B., and Werner, W. Effect of internal and external control upon changes in smoking behavior. *Journal of Consulting Psychology*, 1965, **29**, 184–186.

Janis, I. L. Psychologic effects of electric convulsive treatments: I. Post-treatment amnesias. *Journal of Nervous and Mental Disease*, 1950, **111**, 359–382. (a)

Janis, I. L. Psychologic effects of electric convulsive treatments: II. Changes in word association reactions. *Journal of Nervous and Mental Disease*, 1950, **111**, 383–397. (b)

Janis, I. L. Psychologic effects of electric convulsive treatments: III. Changes in affective disturbances. *Journal of Nervous and Mental Disease*, 1950, **111**, 469–489. (c)

Janis, I. L., and Astrachan, M. The effects of electroconvulsive treatments on memory efficiency. *Journal of Abnormal and Social Psychology*, 1951, **46**, 501–511.

Jersild, A., and Meigs, M. Direct observations as a research method. *Review of Educational Research*, 1939, **9**, 472–482.

Jessor, R. The generalization of expectancies. *Journal of Abnormal and Social Psychology*, 1954, **49**, 196–200.

Jessor, R. Phenomenological personality theories and the data language of psychology. *Psychological Review*, 1956, **63**, 173–180.

Jessor, R. The problem of reductionism in psychology. *Psychological Review*, 1958, **65**, 170–178.

Jessor, R. A social learning approach to culture and behavior. In T. Gladwin and W. C. Sturtevant (Eds.), *Anthropology and human behavior*. Washington, D.C.: The Anthropological Society of Washington, 1962.

Jessor, R. Toward a social psychology of excessive alcohol-use: A preliminary report from the Tri-Ethnic Project. In C. R. Snyder and D. R. Schweitzer (Eds.), *Proceedings of Research Sociologists' Conference on Alcohol Problems*. Southern Illinois University, 1964. Pp. 59–79.

Jessor, R., Carman, R. S., and Grossman, P. H. Expectations of need satisfaction and drinking patterns of college students. *Quarterly Journal of Studies on Alcohol*, 1968, **29**, 101–116.

Jessor, R., Graves, T. D., Hanson, R. C., and Jessor, S. L. *Society, personality, and deviant behavior: A study of a tri-ethnic community*. New York: Holt, Rinehart and Winston, 1968.

Jessor, R., and Hammond, K. R. Construct validity and the Taylor anxiety scale. *Psychological Bulletin*, 1957, **54**, 161–170.

Jessor, R., and Hess, H. F. Level of aspiration behavior and general adjustment: An appraisal of some negative findings. *Psychological Reports*, 1958, **4**, 335–339.

Jessor, R., Liverant, S., and Opochinsky, S. Imbalance in need structure and maladjustment. *Journal of Abnormal and Social Psychology*, 1963, **66**, 271–275.

Jessor, R., and Readio, J. The influence of value of an event upon the expectancy of its occurrence. *Journal of General Psychology*, 1957, **56**, 219–228.

Jessor, S. The effects of reinforcement and of distribution of practice on psychological satiation. Unpublished doctoral dissertation, Ohio State University, 1951.

Johnson, D. M. *The psychology of thought and judgment.* New York: Harper & Row, 1955.

Johnson, F. Y. Political attitudes as related to internal and external control. Unpublished master's thesis, Ohio State University, 1961.

Kagan, J. The measurement of overt aggression from fantasy. *Journal of Abnormal and Social Psychology,* 1956, **52,** 390–393.

Kalinwosky, L. B. Convulsive shock treatments. In S. Arieti (Ed.), *American handbook of psychiatry.* Vol. 2. Basic Books: New York, 1959. Pp. 1499–1520.

Kalinwosky, L. B., and Hoch, P. H. *Shock treatments, psychosurgery and other somatic treatments in psychiatry.* New York: Grune & Stratton, 1952.

Kantor, J. R. *Principles of psychology.* Vols. 1, 2. New York: Knopf, 1924.

Kantor, J. R. *Problems of physiological psychology.* Bloomington, Ind.: Principia Press, 1947.

Katkovsky, W. Social-learning theory and maladjustment. In L. Gorlow and W. Katkovsky (Eds.), *Readings in the psychology of adjustment.* New York: McGraw-Hill, 1968. Pp. 213–232.

Katkovsky, W., Crandall, V. C., and Good, S. Parental antecedents of children's beliefs in internal-external control of reinforcement in intellectual achievement situations. *Child Development,* 1967, **38,** 765–776.

Katkovsky, W., Preston, A., and Crandall, V. J. Parents' attitudes toward their personal achievements and toward the achievement behaviors of their children. *Journal of Genetic Psychology,* 1964, **104,** 67–82. (a)

Katkovsky, W., Preston, A., and Crandall, V. J. Parents' achievement attitudes and their behavior with their children in achievement situations. *Journal of Genetic Psychology,* 1964, **104,** 105–121. (b)

Katz, D., and Stotland, E. A preliminary statement to a theory of attitude structure and change. In S. Koch (Ed.), *Psychology: A study of a science.* Vol. 3. New York: McGraw-Hill, 1959.

Katz, H. A., and Rotter, J. B. Interpersonal trust scores of college students and their parents. *Child Development,* 1969, **40,** 657–661.

Katz, I., and Benjamin, L. Effects of white authoritarianism in biracial work groups. *Journal of Abnormal and Social Psychology,* 1960, **61,** 448–456.

Katz, I., and Cohen, M. The effects of training Negroes upon cooperative problem solving in biracial teams. *Journal of Abnormal and Social Psychology,* 1962, **64,** 319–325.

Katz, I., and Greenbaum, C. Effects of anxiety, threat, and racial environment on task performance of Negro college students. *Journal of Abnormal and Social Psychology,* 1963, **66,** 562–567.

Kelley, H., and Ring, K. Some effects of "suspiciousness" versus "trusting" training schedules. *Journal of Abnormal and Social Psychology,* 1961, **63,** 294–301.

Kelley, H. H., and Volkart, E. H. The resistance to change of group-anchored attitudes. *American Sociological Review,* 1952, **17,** 453–465.

Kellogg, C. E., and Morton, N. W. *Revised Beta Examination.* New York: Psychological Corporation, 1935.

Kelly, G. A. *The psychology of personal constructs.* Vols. 1, 2. New York: Norton, 1955.

Kiehlbauch, J. B. Selected changes over time in internal-external control expectancies in a reformatory population. Unpublished doctoral dissertation, Kansas State University, 1967.

Kimble, G. A. *Hilgard and Marquis' conditioning and learning.* New York: Appleton-Century-Crofts, 1961.

Klein, M. H., Dittman, A. T., Parloff, M. B., and Gill, M. M. Behavior therapy: Observations and reflections. *Journal of Consulting Psychology,* 1969, **33,** 259–266.

Korner, A. F. Theoretical considerations concerning the scope and limitations of projective techniques. *Journal of Abnormal and Social Psychology,* 1950, **45,** 619–627.

Kornhauser, W. *The politics of mass society.* New York: The Free Press, 1959.

Kraepelin, E. *Lectures on clinical psychiatry.* London: Bailliere, Tindall, and Cox, 1913.

Krasner, L. Studies of the conditioning of verbal behavior. *Psychological Bulletin,* 1958, **55,** 148–170.

Lacey, J. I. Psychophysiological approaches to the evaluation of psychotherapeutic process and outcome. In E. A. Rubinstein and M. B. Parloff (Eds.), *Research in psychotherapy,* 1959. Washington, D.C.: American Psychological Association. Pp. 160–208.

Ladwig, G. W. Personal, situational and social determinants of preference for delayed reinforcement. Unpublished doctoral dissertation, Ohio State University, 1963.

Lang, P. J. Experimental studies of desensitization psychotherapy. In J. Wolpe, A. Salter, and L. Reyna (Eds.), *The conditioning therapies.* New York: Holt, Rinehart and Winston, 1964.

Lang, P. J., Lazovik, A. D., and Reynolds, D. J. Desensitization, suggestibility and pseudotherapy. *Journal of Abnormal and Social Psychology,* 1965, **70,** 395–402.

Lasko, A. A. The development of expectancies under conditions of patterning and differential reinforcement. Unpublished doctoral dissertation, Ohio State University, 1952.

Lazarus, R. S. Emotions and adaptation: Conceptual and empirical relations. In W. J. Arnold (Ed.), *Nebraska symposium on motivation.* Lincoln, Neb.: University of Nebraska Press, 1968. Pp. 175–270.

Lazarus, R. S., Baker, R. W., Broverman, D. M., and Mayer, J. Personality and psychological stress. *Journal of Personality,* 1957, **25,** 559–577.

Lefcourt, H. M. Risk taking in Negro and white adults. *Journal of Personality and Social Psychology,* 1965, **2,** 765–770.

Lefcourt, H. M. Internal vs. external control of reinforcement: A review. *Psychological Bulletin,* 1966, **65,** 206–220.

Lefcourt, H. M., and Ladwig, G. W. The American Negro: A problem in expectancies. *Journal of Personality and Social Psychology,* 1965, **1,** 377–380.

Lefcourt, H. M., and Steffy, R. A. Sex-linked censure expectancies in process and reactive schizophrenics. *Journal of Personality*, 1966, **34**, 366–380.

Lesser, G. S. The relationship between overt and fantasy aggression as a function of maternal response to aggression. *Journal of Abnormal and Social Psychology*, 1957, **55**, 218–222.

Lesser, G. S. Population differences in construct validity. *Journal of Consulting Psychology*, 1959, **23**, 60–65.

Levis, D. J., and Carrera, R. Effects of ten hours of implosive therapy in the treatment of outpatients: A preliminary report. *Journal of Abnormal Psychology*, 1967, **72**, 504–508.

Lewin, K. *A dynamic theory of personality*. New York: McGraw-Hill, 1935.

Lewin, K. The conceptual representation and the measurement of psychological forces. *Contributions to Psychological Theory*, 1, No. 4, 1938.

Lewin, K. The nature of field theory. In M. H. Marx (Ed.), *Psychological theory*. New York: Macmillan, 1951.

Lewin, K. Behavior and development as a function of the total situation. In L. Carmichael (Ed.), *Manual of child psychology*. (2nd Ed.) New York: Wiley, 1954. Pp. 918–970.

Lewin, K., Dembo, T., Festinger, L., and Sears, P. S. Level of aspiration. In J. McV. Hunt (Ed.), *Personality and the behavior disorders*. New York: Ronald, 1944. Pp. 333–378.

Lewis, D. J. Partial reinforcement: A selective review of the literature since 1950. *Psychological Bulletin*, 1960, **57**, 1–28.

Lewis, M., and Goldberg, S. A generalized expectancy model as a function of mother-child interaction. *Merrill-Palmer Quarterly*, 1969, **15**, 81–100.

Lindquist, E. F. *Design and analysis of experiments in psychology and education*. Boston: Houghton Mifflin, 1953.

Lindzey, G. Thematic Apperception Test: Interpretative assumptions and related empirical evidence. *Psychological Bulletin*, 1952, **49**, 1–25.

Linton, H. R. Dependence on external influence: Correlations in perceptions, attitudes and judgement. *Journal of Abnormal and Social Psychology*, 1955, **51**, 502–507.

Lipp, L., Kolstoe, R., and Randall, H. Denial of disability and internal control of reinforcement: A study utilizing a perceptual defense paradigm. Paper presented at Midwestern Psychological Association, Chicago, 1967.

Lipset, S. M. Trade unions and social structure. *Industrial Relations*, 1961, **1**, 75–89.

Little, K. B., and Shneidman, E. S. Congruencies among interpretations of psychological test and anamnestic data. *Psychological Monographs*, 1959, **73** (Whole No. 476).

Liverant, S. The use of Rotter's social learning theory in developing a personality inventory. *Psychological Monographs*, 1958, **72** (Whole No. 455).

Liverant, S. Intelligence: A concept in need of re-examination. *Journal of Consulting Psychology*, 1960, **24**, 101–110.

Liverant, S. Learning theory and clinical psychology. In L. E. Abt and B. F. Reiss (Eds.), *Progress in clinical psychology*. Vol. 5. New York: Grune & Stratton, 1963.

Liverant, S., and Scodel, A. Internal and external control as determinants of decision making under conditions of risk. *Psychological Reports*, 1960, 7, 59–67.

Livson, N., and Mussen, P. H. The relation of ego control to overt aggression and dependency. *Journal of Abnormal and Social Psychology*, 1957, 55, 66–71.

Loevinger, J. Theory and techniques of assessment. In P. R. Farnsworth (Ed.), *Annual Review of Psychology*, Palo Alto, Calif.: Annual Reviews, 1959. Pp. 287–316.

Lomont, J. F., and Edwards, J. E .The role of relaxation in systematic desensitization. *Behavior Research and Therapy*, 1967, 5, 11–25.

Loomis, A. M. A technique for observing the social behavior of nursery school children. *Child Development Monographs*, No. 5, 1931.

Loomis, J. L. Communication, the development of trust, and cooperative behavior. *Human Relations*, 1959, 12, 305–315.

Lord, E. E. Experimentally induced variations in Rorschach performance. *Psychological Monographs*, 1950, 64, (Whole No. 316).

Lotsof, A. B. A study of the effect of need value on substitution. Unpublished doctoral dissertation, Ohio State University, 1953.

Lotsof, E. J. A methodological study of reinforcement value as related to decision time. Unpublished doctoral dissertation, Ohio State University, 1951.

Lotsof, E. J. Reinforcement value as related to decision time. *Journal of Psychology*, 1956, 41, 427–435.

Lotsof, E. J. Expectancy for success and decision-time. *American Journal of Psychology*, 1958, 71, 416–419.

Lotsof, E. J. Expectancy for success and certainty of response. *American Journal of Psychology*, 1959, 72, 600–602.

Lowenbach, H., and Stainbrook, E. J. Observations on mental patients after electroshock. *American Journal of Psychiatry*, 1942, 98, 828–833.

Lubin, B., and Zuckerman, M. *Manual for the multiple affect adjective check list*. San Diego, Calif.: Educational and Industrial Testing Service, 1965.

Lynn, D. B., and Sawrey, W. L. The effects of father-absence on Norwegian boys and girls. *Journal of Abnormal and Social Psychology*, 1959, 59, 258–262.

MacKinnon, D. W. Violation of prohibitions. In H. A. Murray (Ed.), *Explorations in personality*. New York: Oxford, 1938. Pp. 491–501.

Maddox, G. L., and McCall, B. C. Drinking among teen-agers: A sociological interpretation of alcohol use by high-school students. New Brunswick, N.J.: Publications Division, Rutgers Center of Alcohol Studies, 1964.

Maher, B. A. *Principles of psychopathology*. New York: McGraw-Hill, 1966.

Mahrer, A. R. The role of expectancy in delayed reinforcement. *Journal of Experimental Psychology*, 1956, 52, 101–105.

Mandell, E. E. Construct validation of a psychometric measure of expectancy. Unpublished master's thesis, University of Colorado, 1959.

Mandler, G., and Sarason, S. B. A study of anxiety and learning. *Journal of Abnormal and Social Psychology*, 1952, 47, 166–173.

Manis, J. G., and Meltzer, B. N. *Symbolic interactions: A reader in social psychology*. Boston: Allyn and Bacon, 1967.

Marcia, J. E., Rubin, B. M., and Efran, J. S. Systematic desensitization: Expectancy change or counterconditioning? Unpublished manuscript, 1968.

Marks, R. W. The effect of probability, desirability and "privilege" on the stated expectations of children. *Journal of Personality*, 1951, **19**, 332–351.

Marlowe, D. Need for social approval and the operant conditioning of meaningful verbal behavior. *Journal of Consulting Psychology*, 1962, **26**, 79–83.

Marlowe, D., and Crowne, D. P. Social desirability and response to perceived situational demands. *Journal of Consulting Psychology*, 1961, **25**, 109–115.

Masling, J. The influence of situational and interpersonal variables in projective testing. *Psychological Bulletin*, 1960, **57**, 65–85.

McCandless, B. R., and Castaneda, A. Anxiety in children, school achievement, and intelligence. *Child Development*, 1956, **27**, 379–382.

McClelland, D. C. The importance of early learning in the formation of motives. In J. W. Atkinson (Ed.), *Motives in fantasy, action, and society*. Princeton, N.J.: Van Nostrand, 1958.

McClelland, D. C., Atkinson, J. W., Clark, R. A., and Lowell, E. L. *The achievement motive*. New York: Appleton-Century-Crofts, 1953.

McGhee, P. E., and Crandall, V. C. Beliefs in internal-external control of reinforcements and academic performance. *Child Development*, 1968, **39**, 91–102.

McNemar, Q. *Psychological statistics.* (2nd ed.) New York: Wiley, 1955.

Mednick, S. A. A learning theory approach to research in schizophrenia. *Psychological Bulletin*, 1958, **55**, 316–327.

Meehl, P. E. On the circularity of the law of effect. *Psychological Bulletin*, 1950, **47**, 52–75.

Meehl, P. E. The cognitive activity of the clinician. *American Psychologist*, 1960, **15**, 19–27.

Meehl, P. E., and Hathaway, S. R. The K factor as a suppressor variable in the MMPI. *Journal of Applied Psychology*, 1946, **30**, 525–564.

Mellinger, G. D. Interpersonal trust as a factor in communication. *Journal of Abnormal and Social Psychology*, 1956, **52**, 304–309.

Melton, A. W. Learning. In C. Stone (Ed.), *Annual review of psychology*. Palo Alto, Calif.: Annual Reviews, 1950.

Merton, R. *Mass persuasion*. New York: Harper, 1946.

Merton, R. *Social theory and social structure*. Glencoe, Ill.: Free Press, 1949.

Merton, R. Social structure and anomie. In R. Merton (Ed.), *Social theory and social structure*. (Rev. ed.) Glencoe, Ill.: Free Press, 1957.

Meyer, W., and Seidman, S. Age differences in the effectiveness of different reinforcement combinations on the acquisition and extinction of a simple concept learning problem. *Child Development*, 1960, **31**, 419–429.

Meyer, W., and Seidman, S. Relative effectiveness of different reinforcement combinations on concept learning of children at two developmental levels. *Child Development*, 1961, **32**, 117–127.

Miller, M. B. Locus of control, learning climate, and climate shift in serial learning with mental retardates. Ann Arbor, Mich.: University Microfilms, 1961.

Miller, N. E. Experimental studies on conflict. In J. McV. Hunt (Ed.), *Per-*

sonality and the behavior disorders. Vol. 1. New York: Ronald, 1944. Pp. 431–465.

Miller, N. E. Liberalization of basic S-R concepts: Extensions to conflict behavior, motivation, and social learning. In S. Koch (Ed.), *Psychology: A study of a science.* Vol. 2. New York: McGraw-Hill, 1959. Pp. 198–290.

Miller, N. E., and Dollard, J. *Social learning and imitation.* New Haven, Conn.: Yale University Press, 1941.

Miller, N., Doob, N. A., Butler, D. C., and Marlowe, D. The tendency to agree: Situational determinants and social desirability. *Journal of Experimental Research in Personality,* 1965, **1,** 78–93.

Mischel, H. Trust and delay of gratification. Unpublished doctoral dissertation, Harvard University, 1963.

Mischel, W. Variables influencing the generalization of expectancy statements. Unpublished doctoral dissertation, Ohio State University, 1956.

Mischel, W. The effect of the commitment situation on the generalization of expectancies. *Journal of Personality,* 1958, **26,** 508–516. (a)

Mischel, W. Preference for delayed reinforcement: An experimental study of a cultural observation. *Journal of Abnormal and Social Psychology,* 1958, **56,** 57–61. (b)

Mischel, W. Delay of gratification, need for achievement, and acquiescence in another culture. *Journal of Abnormal and Social Psychology,* 1961, **62,** 543–552. (a)

Mischel, W. Father absence and delay of gratification: Cross-cultural comparisons. *Journal of Abnormal and Social Psychology,* 1961, **63,** 116–124. (b)

Mischel, W. Preference for delayed reinforcement and social responsibility. *Journal of Abnormal and Social Psychology,* 1961, **62,** 1–7. (c)

Mischel, W. Predicting the success of Peace Corps volunteers in Nigeria. *Journal of Personality and Social Psychology,* 1965, **1,** 510–517.

Mischel, W. Theory and research on the antecedents of self-imposed delay of reward. In B. A. Maher (Ed.), *Progress in experimental personality research.* Vol. 3. New York: Academic Press, 1966.

Mischel, W. *Personality and assessment.* New York: Wiley, 1968.

Mischel, W., and Gilligan, C. Delay of gratification, motivation for the prohibited gratification, and responses to temptation. *Journal of Abnormal and Social Psychology,* 1964, **69,** 411–417.

Mischel, W., and Grusec, J. Determinants of the rehearsal and transmission of neutral and aversive behaviors. *Journal of Personality and Social Psychology,* 1966, **3,** 197–205.

Mischel, W., and Liebert, R. Effects of discrepancies between observed and imposed reward criteria on their acquisition and transmission. *Journal of Personality and Social Psychology,* 1966, **3,** 45–53.

Mischel, W., and Masters, J. C. Effects of probability of reward attainment on responses to frustration. *Journal of Personality and Social Psychology,* 1966, **3,** 390–396.

Mischel, W., and Metzner, R. Preference for delayed reward as a function of age, intelligence, and length of delay interval. *Journal of Abnormal and Social Psychology,* 1962, **64,** 425–431.

Mischel, W., and Staub, E. Effects of expectancy on working and waiting for larger rewards. *Journal of Personality and Social Psychology*, 1965, **2**, 625–633.

Mooney, R. L. *Mooney problem check list*. New York: Psychological Corporation, 1950.

Moos, M., and Koslin, B. Prestige suggestion and political leadership. *Public Opinion Quarterly*, 1952, **16**, 77–93.

Morton, R. B. An experiment in brief psychotherapy. *Psychological Monographs*, 1955, **69**, (Whole No. 1).

Mosher, D. L. The development and validation of a sentence completion measure of guilt. Unpublished doctoral dissertation, Ohio State University, 1961.

Mosher, D. L. Approval motive and acceptance of "fake" personality test interpretations which differ in favorability. *Psychological Reports*, 1965, **17**, 395–402. (a)

Mosher, D. L. A social learning theory analysis of aggressive behavior. Unpublished manuscript, Ohio State University, 1965. (b)

Mosher, D. L. The development and multitrait-multimethod matrix analysis of three measures of three aspects of guilt. *Journal of Consulting Psychology*, 1966, **30**, 25–29.

Mosher, D. L. The influence of Adler on Rotter's social learning theory of personality. *Journal of Individual Psychology*, 1968, **24**, 33–45. (a)

Mosher, D. L. Measurement of guilt in females by self-report inventories. *Journal of Consulting and Clinical Psychology*, 1968, **32**, 690–695. (b)

Mosher, D. L., Mortimer, R. L., and Grebel, M. Verbal aggressive behavior in delinquent boys. *Journal of Abnormal Psychology*, 1968, **73**, 454–460.

Moss, H. The generality of cautiousness as a defense behavior. Unpublished doctoral dissertation, Ohio State University, 1958.

Moss, H. A. The influence of personality and situational cautiousness on conceptual behavior. *Journal of Abnormal and Social Psychology*, 1961, **63**, 629–635.

Moss, H. A. Sex, age and state as determinants of mother-infant interaction. *Merrill-Palmer Quarterly*, 1967, **13**, 20–35.

Moss, H. A., Robson, K. S., and Pedersen, F. Determinants of maternal stimulation of infants and consequences of treatment for later reactions to strangers. *Developmental Psychology*, 1969, **1**, 239–246.

Mouton, J. S., Blake, R. R., and Olmstead, J. A. The relationship between frequency of yielding and the disclosure of personal identity. *Journal of Personality*, 1956, **24**, 339–347.

Mowrer, O. H. Learning theory and the neurotic paradox. *American Journal of Orthopsychiatry*, 1948, **18**, 571–610.

Mowrer, O. H. *Learning theory and behavior*. New York: Wiley, 1960.

Mowrer, O. H., and Kluckhohn, C. Dynamic theory of personality. In J. McV. Hunt (Ed.), *Personality and the behavior disorders*. New York: Ronald, 1944. Pp. 69–135.

Mowrer, O. H., and Ullman, A. D. Time as a determinant in integrative learning. *Psychological Review*, 1945, **52**, 61–90.

Mulford, H. A., and Miller, D. E. Drinking behavior related to definitions of alcohol: A report of research in progress. *American Sociological Review,* 1959, **24**, 385–389.

Mulford, H. A., and Miller, D. E. Drinking in Iowa. III. A scale of definitions of alcohol related to drinking behavior. *Quarterly Journal of Studies on Alcohol,* 1960, **21**, 267–278. (a)

Mulford, H. A., and Miller, D. E. Drinking in Iowa. IV. Preoccupation with alcohol and definitions of alcohol, heavy drinking and trouble due to drinking. *Quarterly Journal of Studies on Alcohol,* 1960, **21**, 279–291. (b)

Mulry, R. C. Personality and test taking behavior. Unpublished doctoral dissertation, University of Connecticut, 1966.

Murray, E. J., and Jacobson, L. I. The nature of learning in traditional and behavioral psychotherapy. In A. E. Bergen and S. L. Garfield (Eds.), *Handbook of psychotherapy and behavior change.* New York: Wiley, 1971.

Murray, H. A. Toward a classification of interaction. In T. Parsons and E. A. Shils (Eds.), *Toward a general theory of action.* Cambridge, Mass.: Harvard University Press, 1952.

Murstein, B. I. A conceptual model of projective techniques applied to stimulus variations with thematic techniques. *Journal of Consulting Psychology,* 1959, **23**, 3–14.

Mussen, P. H., and Naylor, H. K. Relationship between overt and fantasy aggression. *Journal of Abnormal and Social Psychology,* 1954, **49**, 235–239.

Mussen, P. H., and Scodel, A. The effect of sexual stimulation under varying conditions on TAT sexual responsiveness. *Journal of Consulting Psychology,* 1955, **19**, 90.

Myers, J. L. *Fundamentals of experimental design.* Boston: Allyn & Bacon, 1966.

Nagge, J. W. *Psychology of the child.* New York: Ronald, 1942.

Naylor, H. K. The relationship of dependency behavior to intellectual problem solving. Unpublished doctoral dissertation, Ohio State University, 1955.

Neal, A. G., and Seeman, M. Organizations and powerlessness: A test of the mediation hypothesis. *American Sociological Review,* 1964, **29**, 216–226.

Neems, R., and Scodel, A. Authoritarianism and levels of aspiration scores. *Journal of Social Psychology,* 1956, **43**, 209–215.

Neff, J. Individual differences in resistance to extinction as a function of generalized expectancy. Unpublished doctoral dissertation, Ohio State University, 1956.

Nettler, G. A measure of alienation. *American Sociological Review,* 1957, **22**, 670–677.

Newcomb, T. M. *Personality and social change.* New York: Dryden, 1943.

Nisbet, R. A. *The quest for community.* New York: Oxford, 1953.

Odell, M. Personality correlates of independence and conformity. Unpublished master's thesis, Ohio State University, 1959.

Okel, E., and Mosher, D. L. Changes in affective states as a function of guilt over aggressive behavior. *Journal of Consulting and Clinical Psychology,* 1968, **32**, 265–270.

Olds, J., and Olds, M. Drives, rewards and the brain. In *New directions in psychology, II.* New York: Holt, Rinehart and Winston, Inc., 1965.

Olson, W. C. The incidence of nervous habits in children. *Journal of Abnormal and Social Psychology*, 1930–31, **25**, 75–92.

Opochinsky, S. Values, expectations, and the formation of impressions. Unpublished doctoral dissertation, University of Colorado, 1965.

Orne, M. T. The nature of hypnosis: Artifact and essence. *Journal of Abnormal and Social Psychology*, 1959, **58**, 277–299.

Orne, M. T. On the social psychology of the psychological experiment: With particular reference to demand characteristics and their implications. *American Psychologist*, 1962, **17**, 776–783.

Osgood, C. E., Suci, G. J., and Tannenbaum, P. A. *The measurement of meaning*. Urbana: University of Illinois Press, 1957.

Pacella, B. L., Piotrowski, Z., and Lewis, N. D. C. The effects of electric convulsive therapy on certain personality traits in certain psychiatric patients. *American Journal of Psychiatry*, 1947, **104**, 83–91.

Parten, M. B. Social participation among preschool children. *Journal of Abnormal and Social Psychology*, 1932, **27**, 243–270.

Paul, G. L. *Insight versus desensitization in psychotherapy*. Stanford, Calif.: Stanford University Press, 1966.

Peak, H. Problems of objective observation. In L. Festinger and D. Katz (Eds.), *Research methods in the behavioral sciences*. New York: Dryden, 1953.

Pepitone, A. Attributions of causality, social attitudes and cognitive matching processes. In R. Taguiri and L. Petrullo (Eds.), *Person perception and interpersonal behavior*. Stanford, Calif.: Stanford University Press, 1958. Pp. 258–276.

Peters, C. C., and Van Voorhis, W. R. *Statistical procedures and their mathematical bases*. New York: McGraw-Hill, 1940.

Pettigrew, T. F. The measurement of correlates of category width as a cognitive variable. *Journal of Personality*, 1958, **26**, 532–544.

Phares, E. J. Changes in expectancy in skill and chance situations. Unpublished doctoral dissertation, Ohio State University, 1955. Also, Ann Arbor, Mich.: University Microfilms, 1955.

Phares, E. J. Expectancy changes in skill and chance situations. *Journal of Abnormal and Social Psychology*, 1957, **54**, 339–342.

Phares, E. J. The relationship between TAT responses and leaving-the-field behavior. *Journal of Clinical Psychology*, 1959, **15**, 328–330.

Phares, E. J. Expectancy changes under conditions of relative massing and spacing. *Psychological Reports*, 1961, 8, 199–206.

Phares, E. J. Perceptual threshold decrements as a function of skill and chance expectancies. *Journal of Psychology*, 1962, **53**, 399–407.

Phares, E. J. Additional effects of massing and spacing on expectancies. *Journal of General Psychology*, 1964, **70**, 215–223. (a)

Phares, E. J. Delay as a variable in expectancy changes. *Journal of Psychology*, 1964, 57, 391–402. (b)

Phares, E. J. Effects of reinforcement value on expectancy statements in skill and chance situations. *Perceptual and Motor Skills*, 1965, **20**, 845–852. (a)

Phares, E. J. Internal-external control as a determinant of amount of social influence exerted. *Journal of Personality and Social Psychology*, 1965, **2**, 642–647. (b)

Phares, E. J. Delay, anxiety, and expectancy changes. *Psychological Reports,* 1966, **18,** 679–682.

Phares, E. J. The deviant personality. In H. Helson and W. Bevan (Eds.), *Contemporary approaches to psychology.* Princeton, N.J.: Van Nostrand, 1967.

Phares, E. J. Differential utilization of information as a function of internal-external control. *Journal of Personality,* 1968, **36,** 649–662. (a)

Phares, E. J. Test anxiety, expectancies and expectancy changes. *Psychological Reports,* 1968, **22,** 259–265. (b)

Phares, E. J. Internal-external control and the reduction of reinforcement value after failure. *Journal of Consulting and Clinical Psychology,* in press.

Phares, E. J., and Davis, W. L. Breadth of categorization and the generalization of expectancies. *Journal of Personality and Social Psychology,* 1966, **4,** 461–464.

Phares, E. J., Ritchie, D. E., and Davis, W. L. Internal-external control and reaction to threat. *Journal of Personality and Social Psychology,* 1968, **10,** 402–405.

Phares, E. J., and Rotter, J. B. An effect of the situation on psychological testing. *Journal of Consulting Psychology,* 1967, **20,** 291–293.

Phares, E. J., Wilson, K. G., and Klyver, N. W. Internal-external control and the attribution of blame under neutral and distractive conditions. *Journal of Personality and Social Psychology,* 1971, **18,** 285–288.

Phillips, E. L. *Psychotherapy: A modern theory and practice.* Englewood Cliffs, N.J.: Prentice-Hall, 1956.

Piaget, J. *The child's conception of physical causality.* New York: Harcourt, Brace, 1930.

Postman, L. Toward a general theory of cognition. In J. H. Rohrer and M. Sherif (Eds.), *Social psychology at the crossroads.* New York: Harper, 1951. Pp. 242–272.

Pribram, K. Emotion: Steps towards a neurophysiological theory. In D. C. Glass (Ed.), *Neurophysiology and emotion.* New York: The Rockefeller University Press and Russell Sage Foundation, 1967.

Rachman, S. Studies in desensitization—I: The separate effects of relaxation and desensitization. *Behavior Research and Therapy,* 1965, **3,** 245–251.

Rachman, S. Studies in desensitization—II: Flooding. *Behavior Research and Therapy,* 1966, **4,** 1–6.

Rachman, S. Systematic desensitization. *Psychological Bulletin,* 1967, **2,** 93–103.

Rachman, S. The role of muscular relaxation in desensitization therapy. *Behavior Research and Therapy,* 1968, **6,** 149–166.

Rafferty, J. E. Use of two interpretive projective techniques for prediction within a Social Learning Theory of Personality. Unpublished doctoral dissertation, Ohio State University, 1952.

Rafferty, J. E., Tyler, B. B., and Tyler, F. B. Observations of free play situations as a method of personality assessment. *Child Development,* 1960, **31,** 691–702.

Rapaport, A., and Orwant, C. Experimental games: A review. *Behavioral Science,* 1962, 7, 1–37.

Redl, F., and Wineman, A. *Children who hate.* Glencoe, Ill.: Free Press, 1951.

Rettig, S. An exploratory study of altruism. Unpublished doctoral dissertation, Ohio State University, 1956.

Rettig, S., and Pasamanick, B. Differential judgment of ethical risk by cheaters and noncheaters. *Journal of Abnormal and Social Psychology*, 1964, **69**, 109–113.

Rettig, S., and Rawson, H. E. The risk hypothesis in predictive judgments of unethical behavior. *Journal of Abnormal and Social Psychology*, 1963, **66**, 243–248.

Rettig, S., and Singh, P. N. The risk hypothesis in predictive judgments of unethical behavior: A cross-cultural replication. *Israel Annual of Psychiatry and Related Disciplines*, 1963, **1**, 225–234.

Rickles, N. K., and Polan, C. G. Causes of failure in treatment with electroshock: Analysis of thirty-eight cases. *American Medical Association Archives of Neurology and Psychiatry*, 1948, **59**, 337–346.

Riesman, D. *Individualism reconsidered*. Glencoe, Ill.: Free Press, 1954.

Ritchie, E., and Phares, E. J. Attitude change as a function of internal-external control and communicator status. *Journal of Personality*, 1969, **37**, 429–443.

Roberts, J. M. Prognostic factors in electroshock treatment of depressive states: The application of specific tests. *Journal of Mental Science*, 1959, **105**, 703–713.

Rockwell, A. F. The evaluation of six social learning need constructs. Unpublished doctoral dissertation, Ohio State University, 1951.

Rodnick, E. Clinical psychology and psychopathology. In S. Koch (Ed.), *Psychology: A study of a science*. Vol. 5. New York: McGraw-Hill, 1963. Pp. 738–779.

Roen, S. R. Personality and Negro-white intelligence. *Journal of Abnormal and Social Psychology*, 1960, **61**, 148–150.

Rogers, C. R. *Client centered therapy*. Boston: Houghton Mifflin, 1951.

Rokeach, M. *The open and closed mind: Investigations into the nature of belief systems and personality systems*. New York: Basic Books, 1960.

Rorschach, H. *Psychodiagnostics*. New York: Grune & Stratton, 1942.

Rose, A. *The Negro in America*. Boston: Beacon Press, 1956.

Rose, A. M. *Theory and method in the social sciences*. Minneapolis: University of Minnesota Press, 1954.

Rosen, B. C. Family structure and value transmission. *Merrill-Palmer Quarterly of Behavior and Development*, 1964, **10**, 59–76.

Rosenberg, M. J. A structural theory of attitude dynamics. *Public Opinion Quarterly*, 1960, **24**, 319–340.

Rosenberg, M. J. When dissonance fails: On eliminating evaluation apprehension from attitude measurement. *Journal of Personality and Social Psychology*, 1965, **1**, 28–42.

Rosenthal, D., and Frank, J. D. The fate of psychiatric clinic outpatients assigned to psychotherapy. *Journal of Nervous and Mental Disease*, 1958, **127**, 330–343.

Rosenthal, R. On the social psychology of the psychological experiment: The experimenter's hypothesis as unintended determinant of experimental results. *American Scientist*, 1963, **51**, 268–283.

Rosenthal, R., and Fode, K. L. Psychology of the scientist: V. Three experiments in experimenter bias. *Psychological Reports*, 1963, **12**, (Monograph Supplement No. 3-v12), 491–511.

Rosenzweig, S., and Fleming, E. E. Apperception norms for the Thematic Apperception Test. *Journal of Personality*, 1949, **17**, 475–503.

Rotter, J. B. Level of aspiration as a method of studying personality: II. Development and evaluation of a controlled method. *Journal of Experimental Psychology*, 1942, **31**, 410–422.

Rotter, J. B. Level of aspiration as a method of studying personality. III. Group validity studies. *Character and Personality*, 1943, **11**, 254–274.

Rotter, J. B. Level of aspiration as a method of studying personality. IV. The analysis of patterns of response. *Journal of Social Psychology*, 1945, **21**, 159–177.

Rotter, J. B. *Social learning and clinical psychology.* Englewood Cliffs, N.J.: Prentice-Hall, 1954.

Rotter, J. B. The role of the psychological situation in determining the direction of human behavior. In M. R. Jones (Ed.), *Nebraska symposium on motivation.* Lincoln: University of Nebraska Press, 1955. Pp. 245–269.

Rotter, J. B. Psychotherapy. In P. R. Farnsworth (Ed.), *Annual review of psychology.* Palo Alto, Calif.: Annual Reviews, Inc., 1960. (a)

Rotter, J. B. Some implications of a social learning theory for the prediction of goal directed behavior from testing procedures. *Psychological Review*, 1960, **67**, 301–316. (b)

Rotter, J. B. *Clinical psychology.* Englewood Cliffs, N.J.: Prentice-Hall, 1964.

Rotter, J. B. Generalized expectancies for internal versus external control of reinforcement. *Psychological Monographs*, 1966, **80**, (Whole No. 609).

Rotter, J. B. Beliefs, attitudes and behavior: A social learning analysis. In R. Jessor and S. Feshbach (Eds.), *Cognition, personality and clinical psychology.* San Francisco, Calif.: Jossey-Bass, 1967. (a)

Rotter, J. B. A new scale for the measurement of interpersonal trust. *Journal of Personality*, 1967, **35**, 651–665. (b)

Rotter, J. B. Personality theory. In H. Helson and W. Bevan (Eds.), *Contemporary approaches to psychology.* Princeton, N.J.: Van Nostrand, 1967. (c)

Rotter, J. B. Some implications of a social learning theory for the practice of psychotherapy. In D. J. Levis (Ed.), *Learning approaches to therapeutic behavior change.* Chicago: Aldine, 1970.

Rotter, J. B., Fitzgerald, B. J., and Joyce, J. A comparison of some objective measures of expectancy. *Journal of Abnormal and Social Psychology*, 1954, **49**, 111–114.

Rotter, J. B., Liverant, S., and Crowne, D. P. The growth and extinction of expectancies in chance controlled and skilled tasks. *Journal of Psychology*, 1961, **52**, 161–177.

Rotter, J. B., and Mulry, R. C. Internal versus external control of reinforcement and decision time. *Journal of Personality and Social Psychology*, 1965, **2**, 598–604.

Rotter, J. B., and Rafferty, J. E. The Rotter Incomplete Sentences Blank Manual: College Form. New York: Psychological Corporation, 1950.

Rotter, J. B., Rafferty, J. E., and Lotsof, A. B. The validity of the Rotter Incomplete Sentences Blank: High School Form. *Journal of Consulting Psychology*, 1954, **18**, 105–111.

Rotter, J. B., Seeman, M., and Liverant, S. Internal versus external control of reinforcement: A major variable in behavior theory. In N. F. Washburne (Ed.), *Decisions, values and groups*. Vol. 2. London: Pergamon Press, 1962, Pp. 473–516.

Rychlak, J. F. Task influence and the stability of generalized expectancies. *Journal of Experimental Psychology*, 1958, **55**, 459–462.

Rychlak, J. F., and Eacker, J. N. The effects of anxiety, delay, and reinforcement on generalized expectancies. *Journal of Personality*, 1962, **30**, 123–134.

Rychlak, J. F., and Lerner, J. J. An expectancy interpretation of manifest anxiety. *Journal of Personality and Social Psychology*, 1965, **2**, 677–684.

Salman, A. R. The development and validation of a projective measure of need for approval. Unpublished doctoral dissertation, Ohio State University, 1965.

Salman, A. R., and Crowne, D. P. The need for approval, improvisation, and attitude change. Paper read at Midwestern Psychological Association, Chicago, May 1962.

Saltzman, I. J. Delay of reward and human verbal learning. *Journal of Experimental Psychology*, 1951, **41**, 437–439.

Sanford, N. Personality: Its place in psychology. In S. Koch (Ed.), *Psychology: A study of a science*. Vol. 5. New York: McGraw-Hill, 1963. Pp. 488–592.

Sarason, I. G. Relationships of measures of anxiety and experimental instructions to word association test performance. *Journal of Abnormal and Social Psychology*, 1959, **59**, 37–42.

Sarason, S. The test situation and the problem of prediction. *Journal of Clinical Psychology*, 1950, **6**, 387–392.

Sarason, S., Davidson, K., Lighthall, F., Waite, R., and Ruebush, B. *Anxiety in elementary school children*. New York: Wiley, 1960.

Sarbin, T. R. Ontology recapitulates philology: The mythic nature of anxiety. *American Psychologist*, 1968, **23**, 411–418.

Schachter, S. *The psychology of affiliation*. Stanford, Calif.: Stanford University Press, 1959.

Schachter, S. The interaction of cognitive and physiological determinants of emotional state. In C. D. Spielberger (Ed.), *Anxiety and behavior*. New York: Academic Press, 1966. Pp. 193–224.

Schaefer, E. S., and Bell, R. Q. Development of a parental attitude research instrument. *Child Development*, 1958, **29**, 339–361.

Schroder, H. M. Development and maintenance of the preference value for an object. *Journal of Experimental Psychology*, 1956, **51**, 139–141.

Schroder, H. M., and Rotter, J. B. Rigidity as learned behavior. *Journal of Experimental Psychology*, 1952, **44**, 141–150.

Schroder, H. M., and Rotter, J. B. Generalization of expectancy changes as a function of the nature of reinforcement. *Journal of Experimental Psychology*, 1954, **48**, 343–348.

Schwarz, J. C. Factors influencing expectancy change during delay in a series of trials on a controlled skill task. Unpublished doctoral dissertation, Ohio State University, 1963.

Schwarz, J. C. Influences upon expectancy during delay. *Journal of Experimental Research in Personality*, 1966, **1**, 211–220.

Schwarz, J. C. Contribution of generalized expectancy to stated expectancy under conditions of success and failure. *Journal of Personality and Social Psychology*, 1969, **11**, 157–164.

Scodel, A. Induced collaboration in some non-zero-sum games. *Journal of Conflict Resolution*, 1962, **6**, 335–340.

Scott, M. The social sources of alienation. *Inquiry*, 1963, **6**, 57–69.

Scott, W. A. Research definitions of mental health and mental illness. *Psychological Bulletin*, 1958, **55**, 29–45.

Sears, R., Maccoby, E., and Levin, H. *Patterns of child rearing*. New York: Harper & Row, 1957.

Sears, R. R., Pintler, M. H., and Sears, P. S. Effect of father separation on preschool children's doll play aggression. *Child Development*, 1946, **17**, 219–243.

Sechrest, L. Stimulus equivalents of the psychotherapist. *Journal of Individual Psychology*, 1962, **18**, 172–176.

Seeman, J. Counselor judgments of therapeutic process and outcome. In C. R. Rogers and R. F. Dymond (Eds.), *Psychotherapy and personality change*. Chicago: University of Chicago Press, 1954.

Seeman, M. On the meaning of alienation. *American Sociological Review*, 1959, **24**, 783–791.

Seeman, M. Alienation and social learning in a reformatory. *American Journal of Sociology*, 1963, **69**, 270–284. (a)

Seeman, M. Social learning theory and the theory of mass society. Paper read at the annual meeting of the American Sociological Association, Los Angeles, 1963. (b)

Seeman, M. Alienation, membership and political knowledge: A comparative study. *Public Opinion Quarterly*, 1966, **30**, 353–367.

Seeman, M. Powerlessness and knowledge: A comparative study of alienation and learning. *Sociometry*, 1967, **30**, 105–123.

Seeman, M., and Evans, J. W. Alienation and learning in a hospital setting. *American Sociological Review*, 1962, **27**, 772–783.

Seligman, E. P., Maier, S. F., and Solomon, R. L. Unpredictable and uncontrollable aversive events. In F. R. Brush (Ed.), *Aversive conditioning and learning*. New York: Academic Press, 1969.

Shaffer, J. A. Parental reinforcement, parental dominance and therapist preference. Unpublished doctoral dissertation, Ohio State University, 1957.

Shaw, F. J. Some postulates concerning psychotherapy. *Journal of Consulting Psychology*, 1948, **12**, 426–431.

Sheatsley, P. B., and Feldman, J. J. A national survey of public relations and behavior. In B. S. Greenberg and E. B. Parker (Eds.), *The Kennedy assassination and the American public*. Stanford, Calif.: Stanford University Press, 1965.

Sheldon, W. H. *The varieties of temperament: A psychology of constitutional differences*. New York: Harper, 1942.

Sherif, M., and Cantril, H. *The psychology of ego-involvements*. New York: Wiley, 1947.

Shinn, M. W. *Biography of a baby*. Boston: Houghton Mifflin, 1900.

Shneidman, E. S. Manual for the Make-A-Picture-Story method. *Projective Techniques Monographs*, 1952, No. 2, 1–92.

Shuey, A. M. *The testing of Negro intelligence*. Lynchburg, Va.: J. P. Bell, 1958.

Siegel, S. *Nonparametric statistics*. New York: McGraw-Hill, 1956.

Simmons, W. L. Personality correlates of the James-Phares scale. Unpublished master's thesis, Ohio State University, 1959.

Singer, J. L., Wilensky, H., and McCraven, V. G. Delaying capacity, fantasy, and planning ability: A factorial study of some basic ego functions. *Journal of Consulting Psychology*, 1956, **20**, 375–383.

Smith, M. Concerning the magnitude of the behavior sample for the study of behavior traits in children. *Journal of Applied Psychology*, 1931, **15**, 480–485.

Soskin, W. F. Bias in postdiction from projective tests. *Journal of Abnormal and Social Psychology*, 1954, **49**, 69–74.

Srole, L. Social integration and certain corollaries: An exploratory study. *American Sociological Review*, 1956, **21**, 709–716.

Stack, J. J. Individual differences in the reduction of cognitive dissonance: An exploratory study. Unpublished doctoral dissertation, Ohio State University, 1963.

Stampfl, T. G., and Levis, D. J. Essentials of implosive therapy: A learning-theory-based psychodynamic behavioral therapy. *Journal of Abnormal Psychology*, 1967, **72**, 496–503.

Star, S. A., and Hughes, H. M. Report on an educational campaign: The Cincinnati plan for the United Nations. *American Journal of Sociology*, 1950, **55**, 389–400.

Staudt, V. M., and Zubin, J. A. A biometric evaluation of the somatotherapies in schizophrenia. *Psychological Bulletin*, 1957, **54**, 171–196.

Stone, C. P. Losses and gains in cognitive functions as related to electroconvulsive shocks. *Journal of Abnormal and Social Psychology*, 1947, **42**, 206–214.

Stone, L. J., and Church, J. *Childhood and adolescence*. New York: Random House, 1957.

Straits, B., and Sechrest, L. Further support of some findings about the characteristics of smokers and non-smokers. *Journal of Consulting Psychology*, 1963, **27**, 282.

Straus, R., and Bacon, S. D. *Drinking in college*. New Haven, Conn.: Yale University Press, 1953.

Strickland, B. R. The relationship of awareness to verbal conditioning and extinction. Unpublished doctoral dissertation, Ohio State University, 1962.

Strickland, B. R. The prediction of social action from a dimension of internal-external control. *Journal of Social Psychology*, 1965, **66**, 353–358.

Strickland, B. R., and Crowne, D. P. Conformity under conditions of simulated group pressure as a function of the need for social approval. *Journal of Social Psychology*, 1962, **58**, 171–181.

Strickland, B. R., and Crowne, D. P. Need for approval and the premature termination of psychotherapy. *Journal of Consulting Psychology*, 1963, **27**, 95–101.

Strodtbeck, F. L. Family interaction values and achievement. In D. C. Mc-Clelland, A. L. Baldwin, U. Bronfenbrenner, and F. L. Strodtbeck (Eds.), *Talent and society*. Princeton, N.J.: Van Nostrand, 1958. Pp. 138–195.

Sullivan, P. L., Miller, C., and Smelser, W. Factors of length of stay and progress in psychotherapy. *Journal of Consulting Psychology*, 1958, **22**, 1–9.

Sutherland, E. H. *Principles of criminology* (4th ed.). Philadelphia: Lippincott, 1947.

Sutherland, E. H., and Cressey, D. R. *Principles of criminology* (6th ed.). Philadelphia: Lippincott, 1960.

Szasz, T. S. The myth of mental illness. *American Psychologist*, 1960, **15**, 113–118.

Taffel, C. Anxiety and the conditioning of verbal behavior. *Journal of Abnormal and Social Psychology*, 1955, **51**, 496–501.

Taulbee, E. S. Relationship between certain personality variables and continuation in psychotherapy. *Journal of Consulting Psychology*, 1958, **22**, 83–89.

Taylor, J. A. A personality scale of manifest anxiety. *Journal of Abnormal and Social Psychology*, 1953, **48**, 285–290.

Thomas, W. I. (Collected Writings). In E. H. Volkart (Ed.), *Social behavior and personality: Contributions of W. I. Thomas to theory and social research*. New York: Social Science Research Council, 1951.

Tiller, P. O. Father absence and personality development of children in sailor families. *Nord. Psykol. Monographs*, 1958, Ser. No. 9.

Titus, H. E., and Hollander, E. P. The California F scale in psychological research. *Psychological Bulletin*, 1957, **54**, 47–64.

Todd, F. J., Terrell, G., and Frank, C. E. Differences between normal and under-achievers of superior ability. *Journal of Applied Psychology*, 1962, **46**, 183–190.

Tolman, E. C. Theories of learning. In F. A. Moss (Ed.), *Comparative psychology*. Englewood Cliffs, N.J.: Prentice-Hall, 1934.

Tolman, E. C. *Purposive behavior in animals and men*. Berkeley: University of California Press, 1949.

Tolman, E. C. Principles of performance. *Psychological Review*, 1955, **62**, 315–326.

Tolman, E. C., and Brunswik, E. The organism and the causal texture of the environment. *Psychological Review*, 1935, **42**, 43–77.

Tryon, R. C., and Bailey, D. E. The BC TRY computer system of cluster and factor analysis. *Multivariate Behavioral Research*, 1966, **1**, 95–111.

Tuddenham, R. D. Correlates of yielding to a distorted group norm. *Journal of Personality*, 1959, **27**, 272–284.

Turner, E. A., and Wright, J. C. Effects of severity of threat and perceived availability on the attractiveness of objects. *Journal of Personality and Social Psychology*, 1965, **2**, 128–132.

Tyler, B. B. Expectancy for eventual success as a factor in problem solving behavior. *Journal of Educational Psychology*, 1958, **49**, 166–172.

Tyler, B., Tyler, F. B., and Rafferty, J. E. A systematic approach to interviewing as a method of personality assessment. *American Psychologist*, 1959, **14**, 374.

Tyler, F. B. A conceptual model for assessing parent-child motivations. *Child Development*, 1960, **31**, 807–815.

Tyler, F. B., Rafferty, J. E., and Tyler, B. B. Relationships among motivations of parents and their children. *Journal of Genetic Psychology*, 1962, **101**, 69–81.

Tyler, F. B., Tyler, B. B., and Rafferty, J. E. Need value and expectancy inter-relations as assessed from motivational patterns of parents and their children. *Journal of Consulting Psychology*, 1961, **25**, 304–311.

Tyler, F. B., Tyler, B. B., and Rafferty, J. E. A threshold conception of need value. *Psychological Monographs*, 1962, **76** (Whole No. 530).

Uhlinger, C. A., and Stephens, M. W. Relation of achievement motivation to academic achievement in students of superior ability. *Journal of Educational Psychology*, 1960, **51**, 259–266.

Ulett, G. A., Smith, K., and Goldine, C. G. Evaluation of convulsive and sub-convulsive shock therapies utilizing a control group. *American Journal of Psychiatry*, 1956, **112**, 795–802.

Ullmann, L. P., and Krasner, L. *Case studies in behavior modification.* New York: Holt, Rinehart and Winston, 1965.

Valins, S., and Ray, A. A. Effects of cognitive desensitization on avoidance behavior. *Journal of Personality and Social Psychology*, 1967, **7**, 345–350.

Veblen, T. *The theory of the leisure class.* New York: Macmillan, 1899 (Modern Library edition, 1934).

Veroff, J., Atkinson, J., Feld, S., and Gurin, G. The use of thematic apperception to assess motivation in a nationwide interview study. *Psychological Monographs*, 1960, **74** (Whole No. 499).

Videbeck, R., and Bates, H. D. Verbal conditioning by a simulated experimenter. *Psychological Record*, 1966, **16**, 145–162.

Walker, H. M., and Lev, J. *Statistical inference.* New York: Holt, Rinehart and Winston, 1953.

Walters, R. H., Leat, M., and Mezei, L. Response inhibition and disinhibition through empathic learning. *Canadian Journal of Psychology*, 1963, **17**, 235–243.

Warner, W. L., Meeker, M., and Eels, K. *Social class in America.* Science Research Associates, Chicago, 1949.

Warren Commission. Report of the President's commission on the assassination of President John F. Kennedy. Washington, D.C.: U.S. Government Printing Office, 1964.

Watson, D. Relationship between locus of control and anxiety. *Journal of Personality and Social Psychology*, 1967, **6**, 91–92.

Watt, N. F. The relation of public commitment, delay after commitment, and some individual differences in changes in verbalized expectancies. Unpublished doctoral dissertation, Ohio State University, 1962.

Watt, N. F. Public commitment, delay after commitment, and change in verbalized expectancies. *Journal of Personality*, 1955, **33**, 284–299.

Webb, E. J., Campbell, D. T., Schwartz, R. D., and Sechrest, L. B. *Unobtrusive measures: Nonreactive research in the social sciences.* Chicago: Rand McNally, 1966.

Weisskopf, E. A. A transcendence index as a proposed measure of projection in the Thematic Apperception Test. *Journal of Psychology,* 1950, **29,** 379–390.

Weitzman, B. Behavior therapy and psychotherapy. *Psychological Review,* 1967, **74,** 300–317.

Welsh, G. S. Factor dimensions A and R. In G. S. Welsh and W. G. Dahlstrom (Eds.), *Basic readings on the MMPI in psychology and medicine.* Minneapolis: University of Minnesota Press, 1956.

White, R. N. *The abnormal personality.* New York: Ronald, 1956.

White, R. W. Motivation reconsidered: The concept of competence. *Psychological Review,* 1959, **66,** 297–323.

Whiting, J. W. Sorcery, sin, and the superego. In M. R. Jones (Ed.), Nebraska symposium on motivation. Lincoln: University of Nebraska Press, 1959. Pp. 174–195.

Whorf, B. L. Language, mind and reality. In J. B. Carroll (Ed.), *Language, thought and reality.* New York: Wiley, 1956.

Wiggins, J. S., and Rumrill, G. Social desirability in the MMPI and Welsh's factor scales A and R. *Journal of Consulting Psychology,* 1959, **23,** 100–106.

Wilcoxon, F. *Some rapid approximate statistical procedures.* American Cyanimid, 1949.

Williamson, E. G., and Darley, J. G. *The Minnesota Inventory of Social Behavior.* New York: Psychological Corporation, 1937.

Winer, B. *Statistical principles in experimental design.* New York: McGraw-Hill, 1962.

Winterbottom, M. The relation of need for achievement in learning experiences in independence and mastery. In J. W. Atkinson (Ed.), *Motives in fantasy, action, and society.* Princeton, N.J.: Van Nostrand, 1958. Pp. 453–478.

Witkin, H. A., Lewis, H. B., Hertzman, M., Machover, K., Meissner, P. B., and Wapner, S. *Personality through perception.* New York: Harper, 1954.

Wolpe, J. *Psychotherapy by reciprocal inhibition.* Stanford, Calif.: Stanford University Press, 1958.

Wolpe, J., and Lazarus, A. A. *Behavior therapy techniques.* New York: Pergamon Press, 1966.

Wolpe, J., Salter, A., and Reyna, L. J. (Eds.), *The conditioning therapies.* New York: Holt, Rinehart and Winston, 1964.

Wolpin, M., and Raines, J. Visual imagery, expected roles and extinction as possible factors in reducing fear and avoidance behavior. *Behavior Research and Therapy,* 1966, **4,** 25–37.

Wood, B. S., Wilson, G. G., Jessor, R., and Bogan, J. B. Troublemaking behavior in a correctional institution: Relationship to inmates' definition of their situation. *American Journal of Orthopsychiatry,* 1966, **36,** 795–802.

Worchel, P., and Narciso, J. C. Electroshock convulsions and memory: The interval between learning and shock. *Journal of Abnormal and Social Psychology,* 1950, **45,** 85–98.

Worell, L. The effect of goal value upon expectancy. *Journal of Abnormal and Social Psychology*, 1956, **53**, 48–53.

Wyckoff, L. B., and Sidowski, J. G. Probability discrimination in a motor task. *Journal of Experimental Psychology*, 1955, **50**, 225–231.

Zeisset, R. M. Desensitization and relaxation in the modification of psychiatric patients' interview behavior. *Journal of Abnormal Psychology*, 1968, **73**, 18–24.

Zigler, E., and Phillips, L. Psychiatric diagnosis and symptomatology. *Journal of Abnormal and Social Psychology*, 1961, **63**, 69–75.

Zigler, E., and Phillips, L. Social competence and the process-reactive distinction in psychopathology. *Journal of Abnormal and Social Psychology*, 1962, **65**, 215–222.

Zubin, J. Memory functioning in patients treated with electric shock therapy. *Journal of Personality*, 1948, **17**, 33–41.

Zubin, J., and Barrera, S. E. Effect of electroconvulsive therapy on memory. *Proceedings of the Society of Experimental Biology*, 1941, **48**, 596–597.

Zuckerman, M., Ribback, B. B., Monashkin, I., and Norton, J. A. Normative data and factor analysis on the parental attitude research instrument. *Journal of Consulting Psychology*, 1958, **22**, 165–171.

Zytkoskee, A., Strickland, B. R., and Watson, J. Delay of gratification and internal versus external locus of control among adolescents of low socioeconomic status. *Developmental Psychology*, 1971, **4**, 93–98.

Index*

Abse, W., 494
Academic recognition, 31
Achievement
  grade-school children's, parents' attitudes and, *143–154*
  motivational determinants of, *155–168*
  reinforcement effects of adult reactions on children's expectations of, *180–191*
Adams, D. K., 330
Adams-Webber, J., 283, 331
Adler, Alfred, 1, *510–511*, 560
Adult reactions, reinforcement effects of, on child's achievement expectations, *180–191*
Affection, need for, 32
Affleck, D. C., 534
Aggression, 30
  need for, 33
Alexander, G. H., 497
Alienation, 263
Allport, G. W., 2, 223
Amsel, A., 106

Angyal, A., 263
Anticipatory responses, 11
Anxiety, *446–449*, 455
  freedom of movement and, 35
  reactions, examples of, *458–462*
Approval, need for, and premature termination of psychotherapy, *533–542*
Argyle, M., 376
Arieti, S., 498
Armitt, F. M., 98
Aronson, E., 107
Arrington, R. E., 133
Asch, S. E., 376, 383
Astrachan, M., 495
Atkinson, J. W., 11, 107, 123, 124, 143, 155, 219, 222, 223, 263
Attitudes
  concept of, 2–3
  expressed, beliefs and, 340–344
  maternal, reinforcements and, *168–179*
  parents', relationship to child's academic achievement, *143–154*

* Page numbers given in italics refer to articles included in this volume.

Bell, D., 396
Bell, R. Q., 172
Benedict, R. F., 347
Benjamin, L., 424
Bennett, E. B., 376
Bennion, R. C., 123, 268, 269
Berkwitz, N. J., 497
Bialer, I., 200, 202, 205, 284, 285, 292, 330, 360, 367, 406, 407, 410, 411
Birney, R. C., 321
Blackman, S., 123, 268, 269, 270, 283
Blake, R. R., 227, 383
Block, J., 70
Blyth, D. D., 243, 329
Bogan, J. B., 512
Bogoch, S. A., 494
Borislow, B., 221
Bott, H., 133
Braden, W., 190
Bramson, L., 396
Brannon, C., 253
Breger, L., 495, 524
Brehm, J. W., 341
Brenner, B., 98
Brill, N. O., 494
Broughton, A., 128, 212, 253–260, 327, 330, 469
Broverman, D. M., 237
Brown, J. S., 91, 98, 106
Browne, C. T., 314
Brunswik, E., 11, 12, 48, 222, 567
Buchwald, A., 190
Burdick, H., 321
Buss, A. H., 190, 453, 468
Buss, E., 190
Butler, D. C., 543
Butler, J. M., 214
Butterfield, E. C., 505

California Achievement Test, 144, 171
Campbell, D., 493, 494
Campbell, D. T., 283, 327
Cantor, G. N., 5
Cantril, H., 376
Cardi, M., 277, 283, 331

Carlsmith, J. M., 107, 116
Carman, R. S., 435, 470–483, 510
Cartwright, D., 91
Castaneda, A., 29, 48, 58, 143, 565
Cattell, R. B., 8
Causes, 8
Cautiousness, situational, influence on conceptual behavior, 228–238
Cellura, 289, 292
Chance, June E., 47–56, 168–179
Chein, I., 424
Children's Intellectual Achievement Responsibility Questionnaire, 153–172
Children's Manifest Anxiety Scale, 172, 173
Children's Social Desirability Scale, 159
Christie, R., 297
Church, J., 133
Churchill, R., 485
Clark, R. A., 143, 222, 263
Classes, functional, 21
Cleckley, H., 468
Cloward, R. A., 202
Coffin, T. E., 376
Cohen, A. R., 341
Cohen, J., 262
Cohen, M., 424
Coleman, J. S., 168, 204
College Opinion Survey, 361
Comfort, physical, need for, 32
Commager, Henry Steele, 351
Commitment, personal, conformity and, 382–395
Commitment situation, effect of, on generalization of expectancies, 376–382
Competency, failure to develop, avoidant behavior and, 444–445
Compulsive behavior, 464–465
Conceptual terms, 2–3
    reliability of, 3
    utility of, 3, 6
Conditioning, verbal, effects of social desirability on, 542–547